ROMANTIC POETRY BY WOMEN

Romantic Poetry by Women

A BIBLIOGRAPHY, 1770–1835

J. R. de J. Jackson

CLARENDON PRESS · OXFORD

1993

Oxford University Press, Walton Street, Oxford OX2 6DP
Oxford New York Toronto
Delhi Bombay Calcutta Madras Karachi
Petaling Jaya Singapore Hong Kong Tokyo
Nairobi Dar es Salaam Cape Town
Melbourne Auckland
and associated companies in
Berlin Ibadan

Oxford is a trade mark of Oxford University Press

Published in the United States
by Oxford University Press Inc., New York

British Library Cataloguing in Publication Data
Data available

Library of Congress Cataloging in Publication Data
Jackson, J. R. de J. (James Robert de Jager)
Romantic poetry by women : a bibliography, 1770–1835 / J.R. de J. Jackson.
Includes indexes.
1. English poetry—Women authors—Bibliography.   2. Women and
literature—English-speaking countries—Bibliography.   3. American
poetry—Women authors—Bibliography.   4. English poetry—19th
century—Bibliography.   5. English poetry—18th century-
Bibliography.   6. Women—Poetry—Bibliography.   7. Romanticism-
Bibliography.   I. Title.
Z2013.5.W6J33 1993
[PR508.W6]
016.821 60809287—dc20   92–35190
ISBN 0–19–811239–4

Typeset by Hope Services (Abingdon), Ltd
Printed in Great Britain
on acid-free paper by
Bookcraft (Bath) Ltd
Midsomer Norton, Avon

FOR KATE AND BESS

Preface and Acknowledgements

This bibliography is founded on an earlier one, *Annals of English Verse 1770–1835: A Preliminary Survey of the Volumes Published* (1985), and it was undertaken as a way of testing the adequacy of *Annals* by examining copies of a definable segment of the whole field. I continue to be indebted to those whose assistance I acknowledged in *Annals*.

Among those who have helped me since, my greatest debt is to Stuart Curran. When *Annals* was published, I invited readers of it to send me corrections and additions. He had been concentrating on Romantic poetry by women and, without knowing that I too had turned my attention to this topic, he generously sent me a long list of authors and works that I had overlooked. At the time my new list of women who had written at least one volume of verse in the Romantic period consisted of about 450 names. Curran's list added at least fifty more. There was the momentary embarrassment, mutual I think, of finding that we were working so close to one another unawares, but we exchanged our information immediately and I have continued to benefit from his advice, his corrections, and his further additions ever since. Quite apart from his essential help, I should like to express my gratitude for his effective and friendly encouragement of the project.

I owe a debt of a different kind to Rea Wilmshurst, who for many years has entered my bibliographical materials into a word-processor, has kept track of them, has retrieved them when they appeared to be hopelessly lost, and has greatly helped me with her skills at organization and her resolute concern for accuracy.

My search for authors has been furthered by J. Harrison, Jane Millgate, and Andrew Ashfield, and I have received timely support from Jerome McGann. Catherine Gajarszky and Katherine Acheson helped me by checking references and cross-references in the typescript. Throughout I have been fortunate in having H. J. Jackson by my side, ready to share my satisfaction over unexpected discoveries and to commiserate with me over the inevitable setbacks.

A bibliography of this kind makes unusually heavy demands on the patience of librarians and their assistants. The bibliographer arrives, unfamiliar with the library, and typically wants to see large numbers of books for brief periods of time at short notice. In the course of my visits to many libraries I have frequently encountered initial dismay, but once what I was doing was explained I have always been looked after with exemplary concern and have often had useful aspects of collections and their catalogues that I had not been aware of drawn to my attention. Listing the names of the libraries concerned scarcely seems to be an adequate return for so much help.

Five of them deserve special mention. First and foremost is the British Library, where the core of my work has been carried out in annual visits over many years. I have also carried out systematic searches for all my authors at Bodley in Oxford and at the Widener (and Houghton) at Harvard, for all my American authors at the Huntington Library in San Marino, and for all my authors of children's books at the Osborne Collection in Toronto. In Toronto, the Robarts Library of the University of Toronto and the E. J. Pratt Library of Victoria College have been my chief resources for reference materials, and I have been able to augment these at crucial points by visiting the Library of St Michael's College and the Metro Library of Toronto.

I have paid briefer visits, these the most trying of all for librarians, to the following libraries, and have benefited from subsequent correspondence with several of them: the American Antiquarian Society in Worcester, Mass., the Andover Divinity Library at Harvard, the Boston Public Library, the Library of the Boston Athenaeum, the Brotherton Library in Leeds, the Harris and Rockefeller Libraries at Brown University, the Cambridge University Library, the Chapin Library at Williams College, the Clark Library in Los Angeles, Columbia University Library, the Library of the University of California in Davis, the Edinburgh University Library, the Folger Library in Washington, the Free Library of Philadelphia, the Hilles Library at Harvard, the Harry Ransom Humanities Research Center at the University of Texas in Austin, the Library Company of Philadelphia, the Library of Congress in Washington, the National Library of Ireland, the National Library of Scotland, the New England Book Depository in Boston, the New York Public Library (including its Annex, its

Rare Books Department, the Schomburg Collection, and the Berg Collection), the Library of the University of Pennsylvania, the Princeton University Library, the Pusey Library at Harvard, the Schlesinger Library at Harvard, the Library of Trinity College, Dublin, the Library of the University of California, Los Angeles, the Library of Union Theological Seminary, New York, the Library of Wellesley College, and the Libraries of Yale University (the Beinecke, the Mudd, and the Sterling). To all of these, at a time when all libraries are suffering from underfunding, I should like to express my thanks.

I have obligations too to the following libraries that responded to letters and sometimes were also able to provide me with essential photocopies: the Library of Albion College, the Library of the University of California, Berkeley, Birmingham Central Library, the Library of the University of British Columbia, the Library of the University of Chicago, the Library of Cornell University, the Library of Duke University in Durham, NC, the Enoch Pratt Free Library in Baltimore, the Library of Florida State University in Tallahassee, the Library of the University of Illinois in Urbana-Champaign, the Library of the University of Michigan in Ann Arbor, the Library of the University of Minnesota in Minneapolis, the Library of the University of Indiana, the Massachusetts Historical Society Library in Boston, the Newberry Library in Chicago, the Library of the University of North Carolina, the New York State Library in Albany, the Providence Public Library in Providence, RI, the Library of Rutgers University, the Library of Stanford University, and the Wagner Free Institute of Science Library in Philadelphia.

A bibliography of this kind obviously depends on the published catalogues, bibliographies, and reference works that precede it, and the ones that I have used will be found recorded in the list of Abbreviations. A number of new works have become available in the course of my preparation, however, and I should like to pay particular tribute to them as one who has been keenly aware of the various ways in which they have transformed the field. Of the catalogues I wish to acknowledge *The National Union Catalog of the Library of Congress: Pre-1956 Imprints* completed in 1980, *The Eighteenth-Century Short Title Catalogue: The British Library Collection* (1983) on microfiches, *Eighteenth-Century British Books: An Author Union Catalogue* (1981), and the *Nineteenth-Century Short*

Title Catalogue, Series 1 and 2, which began to appear in 1985. Of the recent reference works I wish to mention particularly *A Dictionary of British and American Women Writers, 1660–1800* (1985) and *Dictionary of British Women Writers* (1989), both edited by Janet Todd, and *The Feminist Companion to English Literature*, edited by Virginia Blain, Patricia Clements, and Isobel Grundy (1990).

Finally, I wish to acknowledge the indispensable support provided over the years by the Social Sciences and Humanities Research Council of Canada.

Contents

Brief Guide to the User

WORKS are grouped by author and, within each author group, in order of publication. Each first edition is numbered, and subsequent editions of a work (even if its title changes) are given the same number with the addition of a letter in parentheses. All editions of any title are listed before the first edition of the next title published. Anonymous and pseudonymous works are grouped with other works by the author in question if her identity is known, and a cross-reference is provided in the Index of Names of Authors to alert the reader to their locations. The Index of Titles provides another means of access to them. Pseudonyms that have not been identified are treated like ordinary names and there is a section of anonymous works. In the case of authors who used different names during their careers, works are grouped under the name used most often during the period with which this bibliography is concerned; again cross-reference is available in the Index of Authors' Names.

Individual entries consist of the following parts:

1. The number of the entry (to which the indexes are keyed).
2. The title.
3. The name of the editor or translator.
4. (*a*) The place of publication; (*b*) the name of the publisher; (*c*) the date of publication. In the case of books published in more than one place, the names of the places are separated by slash marks (/) and so are the names of the publishers in each place, both groups being listed in corresponding order.
5. Any indication of the edition if it is not the first.
6. The dimensions of the title-page.
7. The number of volumes if there are more than one.
8. The number of pages (not included if there is more than one volume).
9. The price.
10. The name of the author or authors.
11. Reference to the location of the copy examined or reference to other evidence for the existence of the book.

Other information is sometimes inserted in square brackets. The different parts of the entries are separated from one another by full stops. Not all entries contain all the parts. The arrangement of the bibliography is discussed in greater detail in the Introduction (below).

Introduction

The Scope

This book attempts to provide a record of all the volumes of verse published by women during the years 1770 to 1835. It has taken into consideration works written in languages other than English, with the exception of Welsh, Erse, Gaelic, and oriental languages, if they were written by women whose native language was English, and it includes translations by women from other languages if the translations are written in verse. It systematically excludes works that were first published before 1770, unless they had been substantially altered or added to; it excludes works intended for musical performance, and it defines the term volume as meaning a book of no fewer than eight pages. Following the practice of the British Library, it excludes annuals on the ground that they are a form of periodical. Authors whose only publications in verse were of fewer than eight pages are excluded; works of fewer than eight pages by authors who are admitted on account of their longer works are presented briefly in endnotes; they are not assigned numbers and they are not included in the statistics, but they are indexed and their titles are distinguished by quotation marks rather than italics.

The Search

The search for authors began in the preparation of *Annals of English Verse, 1770–1835: A Preliminary Survey of the Volumes Published* (1985). *Annals* was prepared rather unsystematically (it was the by-product of another book). The reviews and notices of new publications of two journals were read for each of the sixty-five years. All poetry entries in *The Cambridge Bibliography of English Literature* and in *The New Cambridge Bibliography of English Literature* were then read. Indexes were made of the authors and of the anonymous works found. The author index was checked against *The British Museum General Catalogue of Printed Books*, with occasional reference to *The National Union Catalog* (which was still incomplete). The index of anonymous titles was checked against *The National Union Catalog* as soon it was completed. The available single-author bibliographies for the period were also read. A few entries were arrived at by other means, often quite by chance, but unsystematically. This foundation bibliography was based on information derived from catalogues, books being examined only in order to clear up anomalies.

When the decision was made to develop a second bibliography devoted to poetry by women, the smaller scale of the undertaking made examination of single copies possible for a single investigator. That important difference aside, however, it turned out that a considerable amount of work remained to be done in the gathering of authors' names. *Annals* provided the names of about 450 women who wrote at least one volume of verse between 1770 and 1835; *Romantic Poetry by Women* doubles that number.

The new search for authors was carried out as follows. Volume i of *The English Catalogue* and the seven volumes of Halkett and Laing were read and so were the entries from 1770 to 1800 of the microfiche *Eighteenth-Century Short Title Catalogue*, the four volumes of the *Eighteenth-Century Short Title Catalogue*, the five volumes of the *Nineteenth-Century Short Title Catalogue, 1801–1815*, and as many volumes as had appeared of the *Nineteenth-Century Short Title Catalogue, 1816–1870* (the new volumes being read as they appeared—at the time of going to press up to the end of the letter 'i'). These catalogues were read *in toto*.

New indexes of authors and of female pseudonyms were prepared and the entries for both were read in the *National Union Catalog*, in the *British Library General Catalogue*, and in the unpublished catalogues of the Widener Library at Harvard and of the Bodley Library at Oxford. All American authors' names or pseudonyms were checked against the unpublished catalogues of the Huntington Library, and the entire catalogue, published and 'uncatalogued', of the Osborne Collection of Children's Books in Toronto was read. The results of this survey provided a wants list of books not found hitherto, and as I travelled from library to library examining copies of books the existence of which was already known to me I checked each catalogue in turn against the wants list.

When I began to examine copies of the books my procedure was a practical compromise between the locations of the libraries and the time at my disposal. The British Library was made the base library. I looked for copies elsewhere only when the books were not held there or, as sometimes happened, when they were temporarily unavailable or mislaid, or lost. My next bases were the Widener, Bodley, and the Huntington. Thereafter I tried to visit complexes of promising libraries that were in reasonable proximity to one another. In the United Kingdom I was able to visit Cambridge, Leeds, Edinburgh, and Glasgow; in Ireland, Dublin; in the United States, libraries in the vicinity of Boston, of New York (reaching as far as Yale and Brown to the north and Philadelphia in the south), and of Los Angeles. Special collections drew me to Davis, Calif., and to Williamstown in Massachusetts. Inevitably some books eluded me. Some are known to me only by inference, some that the *National Union Catalog* had led me to believe I should find at one of the libraries I was visiting turned out not to be there. Some copies were damaged, some were merely the results of catalogue errors. On the other hand, I often stumbled on books that I had no reason to expect. In a few cases, in spite of all my efforts to see copies, I have been obliged to provide descriptions from photocopies; in each case the fact is duly recorded to warn the reader.

Biographical Headnotes

My original intention was to provide only dates of birth and death (when I could) to accompany authors' names at the beginning of each group of entries. This procedure, I thought, would be a sufficient precaution against confusion of authors whose names were alike or identical. But I came to feel that many of the authors whose works I was recording were utterly unknown and that the provision of basic information about their lives would not only satisfy one legitimate kind of curiosity in the reader but might also be helpful to those who wanted to follow up a particular author, either by providing basic guidance or by demonstrating that it was still necessary to start at the beginning.

The headnotes have presented great difficulties. Anyone who has tried to pursue the lives of women through standard reference works will be familiar with them. Excluded as they were throughout the period in question from all public offices, from universities, from the armed services, and from the professions, one is deprived of the usual hooks and eyes of biographical history (matriculation, commission, promotion, graduation, ordination, etc.). This exclusion they shared with many men who did not belong to the social or political establishment. But to it is added a further complication that they did not share with the men, the change of surname on marriage, sometimes more than once in a lifetime. The many missing headnotes in this bibliography are a mute testimony to the resulting damage; it is my hope that they may also contribute in a small way to the beginning of repairs.

It will be apparent that while the description of copies of the books recorded in the bibliography is based on first-hand examination by the compiler, the facts in the headnotes are not in any sense first hand. Apart from those instances where it has been possible to supplement what was known in reference sources with evidence drawn from the books themselves, I have relied on the information gathered before me by others. In a few cases the biographical information has been so ample that reducing it to a paragraph for the sake of uniformity has seemed rather futile, but generally the information has been scanty and inconsistent. I have tried to provide birth and death dates, names of father (with occupation) and mother, record of marriage, evidence of children, and some indication of non-poetical activities, but frequently even this sparse record is unavailable. And the scantier the facts are the more likely the authorities are to disagree about them. Differing dates, differing spelling of names, confusions of one person with another, are the commonest discrepancies. Faced with these I have often wished that my sources had always followed the good example of *The Dictionary of National Biography* and cited their sources; I have tried to follow it myself and readers will be able to check for themselves the reliability of my evidence.

The Arrangement of the Entries

The bibliographical entries are arranged alphabetically by author, works by each author following the biographical headnote. The author's name appears surname first, the surname chosen being the one most often used by the author from 1770 to 1835. Cross-references to the chosen surname from other surnames is to be found in the Index of Authors' Names. When an author uses her married name and her own given name, or her unmarried name on some occasions and her married one on others, both names are given along with the husband's given name. Because the authorship of some books is unknown or, although known, because some have several authors, some groups of entries appear under special headings such as ANONYMOUS, COLLECTIONS (multiple authorship), A LADY, A YOUNG LADY, etc.

The entries consist potentially of eleven parts, each of which is separated from the rest by a full stop. Not all entries contain all the parts and in one case, the record of pagination, the part is routinely omitted from works of more than one volume.

1. Works are recorded in the order of publication of their first editions, subsequent editions following immediately upon the first edition, to be followed in turn by the first edition of the next published work. Each entry is numbered, the first title being numbered '1', the second '2', and so on; in the case of titles of which there is more than one edition, the first edition is numbered '1(*a*)', the second '1(*b*)'. In cases where the subsequent editions are sufficiently numerous to warrant it, the parenthesized letters are doubled and in one instance tripled: '1(*aa*)', '1(*aaa*)'.

2. Titles are given in full without any attempt to record either lineation or typographical peculiarities. When the name of the author appears as part of the title it is generally replaced by points of ellipsis; in some cases, if the name is arguably part of the title (for example, *Letters in Rhyme from a Mother at Home*) it is retained. Capitalization of titles has been normalized, substantives (with the exception of possessive pronouns), adjectives, non-copula verbs, and adverbs being routinely capitalized while articles, conjunctions, possessive pronouns, prepositions, and copula verbs are not unless they occur at the beginning of a sentence. Words appearing after a colon have been capitalized. When a work has an engraved title-page as well as a printed one, information is derived from the printed one.

3. If the work has an editor or translator, the name appears

immediately after the title. The term 'editor' is used here to include anyone, the writer of a preface or introduction, or the author of a preliminary memoir, who presided over the publication. The term 'translator' includes translations into languages other than English as well as translations from foreign languages.

4. The place of publication, the name of the publisher, and the date of publication constitute a single part, the elements being separated by a colon and then a comma (for example, London: Darton and Harvey, 1823). If there is more than one place of publication and, consequently, more than one publisher, the names of the places are separated from one another by a slash mark and the names of the publishers in each place are separated from one another by a slash mark also, the order of the names or groups of names so separated corresponding to the order of the places to which they belong (for example: Edinburgh/London: Constable/Murray, 1821). When no publisher's name is given but only the printer's, the printer's name is provided accompanied by the formula 'printed by'. Printers' names have not otherwise been recorded.

5. In the case of subsequent editions, the edition is described as it is described on the title-page, but in a normalized and abbreviated form (such as '2nd edn.' or 'new edn.'). In some cases more than one edition claims to be, say, a third edition. Usually this situation arises because the publisher did not take into account editions by other publishers, especially by publishers in other countries. There are instances in the Romantic period of the fictitious numbering of editions, usually to avoid prosecution for sedition or libel, but none have been identified in this bibliography.

6. Page size is recorded in centimetres, the top edge of the title-page being given first and then the right-hand edge. The measurement is rounded up to the nearest half centimetre to allow for the difficulty of making an exact measurement of the top edge. Where the top edge or the right-hand edge of the title-page is damaged, measurement has been made of the nearest undamaged part. In a few cases the title-page has been missing altogether and measurement has been made from a subsequent page, from the cover, or from the title-page of the

next volume, but a note in square brackets is provided to explain what has been done.

7. When there is more than one volume, the number is recorded and no pagination is given. In some instances where volumes have been published in different years or have some other measure of independence of one another they have been enumerated as if they were different one-volume books.

8. Pagination is given as it appears in the book in question without being normalized. Unnumbered pages are included in the enumeration without comment (for example, if the preliminaries are numbered from i to xii and are followed by three more blank pages and then a sequence of pages numbered in arabic numerals, say 194, the pagination will be rendered as 'Pp. xv + 194'. When, as is often the case with American books of the period, the roman numbers of the preliminary pages are part of the same numerical sequence as the arabic numbers of the main text (rendered in some bibliographies as, for example, 'Pp. xv + 16–194'), the pagination is simply combined in arabic numerals ('194 pp.'). When an edition is a subscription edition, because the presence of a list of subscribers usually bears directly on pagination, the fact is mentioned at this point, in square brackets. When a book contains a mixture of prose and verse, a statement is also provided at this point, in square brackets; if the verse constitutes only a minor part of the book, the number of pages of verse is given.

9. When the price is given in the book itself (usually on the title-page or the half-title, but occasionally on the cover) it is recorded without further comment. When it has been learned from another source (a review, a catalogue, etc.) the source is given as part of the reference for the entry (for which, see below).

10. The name of the author is given as it appears on the title-page. If the name of the author does not appear on the title-page it is sometimes supplied in square brackets, but only if there is some doubt about the attribution or if more than one author has contributed to the book. Otherwise the name of the author that appears at the beginning of the biographical headnote serves.

11. Following the name of the author, the final part of the entry is the reference on which the entry is based. It consists potentially of two or more elements that are separated from one another by semi-colons. The most important of these is the name of the library in which the copy of the book was seen; the name of the library is given in abbreviated form followed by a colon followed by the shelf-mark or catalogue number. In some cases a reference source has been used for further information that is not derived from the book itself (information about authorship, price, etc.); these reference sources are cited in abbreviated form preceding the name of the library and separated from it by a semi-colon. It may be taken for granted that information derived from the catalogue of the library in question may also have been used in the entry.

Appendix of Pseudonymous Works by Men

A number of books of verse by men were published with female pseudonyms. The motives seem generally to have been satirical or humorous, although not always. Where the pseudonyms have been identified, they appear in normal alphabetical order in the text accompanied by the author's real name, but the work or works are not recorded. In the case of pseudonymous works that are attributed only on the basis of internal evidence, they are grouped in the appendix but recorded in abbreviated form; their titles are included in the Index of Titles and the pseudonyms are included in the Index of Authors' Names.

Note on the Annual Rate of Publication

Because the bibliography aims to be an exhaustive account of the materials it attempts to describe, it has seemed worthwhile to consider it statistically. Although its exhaustiveness is certainly imperfect, the bibliography shares exhaustiveness as an aim with the short-title catalogues that have been appearing for the eighteenth and nineteenth centuries. It is hoped that bibliographies with a larger scope will also begin to provide statistics for analysis and afford a basis for comparing the publication of poetry by women with the norms of publication of poetry and of publication of all kinds of books. Two series of statistics are provided. The first lists the number of first editions published year by year, and the second lists the number of books, first and subsequent editions added together. One note of caution should be offered in the interpretation of these figures. Because the bibliography deliberately omits subsequent editions of works published before 1770, the figures for subsequent editions in the early years of the period are artificially lowered. The rate of publication of first editions, however, appears to be a reliable guide throughout.

To those with an interest in the literary environment, whether it is considered from a social, a political, or an aesthetic point of view, the bare statistics are likely to be tantalizing. Is it significant, for instance, that while in 1770 only four new books of poetry by women were published, in 1835 there were forty-five? A gradual increase over the years was to be expected, but that out of sixty-five years there should be only four in which more than forty new books appeared (1808, 1818, 1820, and 1835) is curious. Altogether 2,584 volumes of verse by women are recorded in the bibliography as having been published during the period. 258 of these have been excluded from the statistics because their dates are uncertain. Of the 2,325 that are included, 1,402 are first editions, not too many, perhaps, for an individual to consider reading.

Index of Authors' Names

This index attempts to list the various forms in which the authors' names appeared during the period and, in some cases, before or after it. Cross-reference is provided to the name used for the group of entries in the bibliography.

Index of Titles

Titles are listed in alphabetical order in this index. The titles are keyed to the names of authors and their appropriate entry numbers.

Index of Publishers

The index of publishers is arranged by place of publication, the places being presented in alphabetical order. Within each place the names of publishers are presented in alphabetical order. Because this practice is only helpful for finding the first name in a conger of publishers, each individual member of each conger is also listed alphabetically with a cross-reference to the name of the conger or congers of which he or she was a member. As with the Index of Titles, the publishers' names are keyed to the names of authors and their appropriate entry numbers. It is hoped that this index will provide a usable precedent for other bibliographies and that in the meantime it may make it easier to learn which publishers were active in the promotion of poetry, especially of poetry by women.

Index of the Location of Individual Publishers outside London

The Index of Publishers assumes that the reader already knows the location of the publishers sought. Because readers will not always know this, the index of locations is provided. The omission of London seemed the simplest way to identify the London publishers; if a publisher is not to be found in this index, it may be assumed that the reader should look at the London section of the preceding index.

Abbreviations

The abbreviations are for sources of bibliographical and biographical information and for archival locations of copies examined; other abbreviations appearing in parentheses following the
name of an author refer to works that are listed in the main
entry of the author in question.

AAS	American Antiquarian Society, Worcester, Mass.
Allibone	Samuel Austin Allibone, *A Critical Dictionary of English Literature and British and American Authors* . . . (Philadelphia, Pa., 1908), 3 vols.
Alumni Oxonienses	*Alumni Oxonienses: The Members of the University of Oxford, 1715–1886* . . ., ed. J. Foster (London, 1887–8), 4 vols.
Andover-Harvard	Andover-Harvard Theological Library, Cambridge, Mass.
Athenae Cantabrigienses	*Athenae Cantabrigienses*, ed. Charles Henry Cooper (Cambridge, 1858–1913), 3 vols.
Avero	*Nineteenth-Century Short Title Catalogue, Series I, Phase I, 1801–1815* (Cambridge, 1984–6), 6 vols.
BC	*The British Critic*
Berkeley	Library of the University of California, Berkeley, Calif.
Biographies of Good Women	*Biographies of Good Women, Chiefly by Contributors to 'The Monthly Packet'*, ed. [Charlotte M. Yonge] (London, 1862–5), 2 vols.
Birmingham	Birmingham Central Library, Birmingham
BL	British Library, London
Blain	*The Feminist Companion to Literature in English*, ed. Virginia Blain, Patricia Clements, and Isobel Grundy (London, 1990)
BLC	*The British Library General Catalogue of Printed Books* (London, Munich, New York, Paris, 1979–87), 360 vols.
Blue Guide	*England*, ed. L. Russell Muirhead (6th edn., London, 1957)

BM	*British Museum General Catalogue of Printed Books: Photolithographic Edition to 1955* (London, 1965–6), 263 vols.
Boase	Frederick Boase, *Modern English Biography* . . . (Truro, 1892–1921), 6 vols.
Boase and Courtney	George Clement Boase and William Prideaux Courtney, *Bibliotheca Cornubiensis* (London, 1874–82), 2 vols.
Bodley	Bodley Library, Oxford
Bodley LC	Catalogue (unpublished) of Bodley Library, Oxford
Boston Athenaeum	Boston Athenaeum, Boston, Mass.
Boston Public	Boston Public Library, Boston, Mass.
Boyle	Andrew Boyle, *An Index to the Annuals 1820–50,* i: *Authors* (repr. Worcester, 1967)
Brown (Harris)	Harris Library, Brown University, Providence, RI
Brown (Rockefeller)	Rockefeller Library, Brown University, Providence, RI
Burney	*The Journals and Letters of Fanny Burney,* ed. Joyce Hemlow *et al.* (Oxford, 1972–84), 12 vols.
CB	*The Cambridge Bibliography of English Literature,* ed. F. W. Bateson (Cambridge, 1940–57), 5 vols.
Chapin	Chapin Library, Williams College, Williamstown, Mass.
Chicago	University of Chicago Library, Chicago, Ill.
Clark	William Andrews Clark Memorial Library, Los Angeles, Calif.
Columbia	Butler Library, Columbia University, New York
Complete Peerage	*Complete Peerage of England, Scotland, Ireland and the United Kingdom* . . . (London, 1887–8), 8 vols.
Cornell	Cornell University Library, Ithaca, NY
Corson	James C. Corson, *Notes and Index to Sir Herbert Grierson's Edition of the Letters of Sir Walter Scott* (Oxford, 1979)
CR	*The Critical Review*
CUL	Cambridge University Library
DAB	*Dictionary of American Biography,* ed. Allen Johnson *et al.* (New York, 1928–36), 20 vols.
Davis	Library of the University of California at Davis, Calif.

DCB	*Dictionary of Canadian Biography*, ed. George W. Brown *et al.* (Toronto, 1979–), vols. iv–vi
DNB	*Dictionary of National Biography . . .*, ed. Sir Leslie Stephen and Sir Sidney Lee (Oxford, 1921), 22 vols.
Duke	William R. Perkins Library, Duke University, Durham, NC
EC	*The English Catalogue of Books . . . 1801–1836*, ed. Robert Alexander Peddie and Quintin Waddington (repr. New York, 1963)
Edin. Univ.	Library of Edinburgh University, Edinburgh
ESTC	*The Eighteenth-Century Short Title Catalogue: The British Library Collection*, ed. R. C. Alston and M. J. Crump (London, 1983) [microfiches]
F	H. Buxton Forman, 'The Shelley Library: An Essay in Bibliography', in *The Shelley Society's Publications*, 4th series, Miscellaneous No. 1 (London, 1886)
Florida	Robert Manning Strozier Library, Florida State University, Tallahassee, Fla.
Free Library of Philadelphia	Free Library of Philadelphia, Logan Square, Philadelphia, Pa.
Friends' Books	Joseph Smith, *A Descriptive Catalogue of Friends' Books . . .* (London, 1867 and 1893; repr. 1970), 2 vols. and Supplement
Folger	Folger Shakespeare Library, Washington, DC
Genest	John Genest, *Some Account of the English Stage, from the Restoration in 1600 to 1830* (Bath, 1832), 10 vols.
GM	*Gentleman's Magazine*
Griswold	Rufus Wilmot Griswold, *The Female Poets of America* (Philadelphia, 1849)
Hale	Sarah Josepha Hale, *Woman's Record; or, Sketches of All Distinguished Women . . .* (2nd edn., New York, 1855)
HEHL	Henry E. Huntington Library, San Marino, Calif.
HEHL LC	Catalogue (unpublished) of the Henry E. Huntington Library, San Marino, Calif.
Highfill	*A Biographical Dictionary of Actors, Actresses, Musicians . . . 1660–1800*, ed. Philip H. Highfill, Jr., Kalman A. Burnim, and Edward A. Langhans (Carbondale and Edwardsville, Ill., 1973–)

Hilles	Hilles Library, Cambridge, Mass.
HL	Samuel Halkett and John Laing, *Dictionary of Anonymous and Pseudonymous Literature*, ed. James Kennedy (Edinburgh and London, 1926–34), 7 vols.
Houghton	Houghton Library, Harvard University, Cambridge, Mass.
HRC Texas	Harry Ransom Humanities Research Center, University of Texas, Austin, Tex.
KL	John Keats, *Letters*, ed. Hyder Edward Rollins (Cambridge, Mass., 1958), 2 vols.
Kunitz 1	S. J. Kunitz and H. Haycraft (eds.), *British Authors of the Nineteenth Century* (New York, 1936)
Kunitz 2	S. J. Kunitz and H. Haycraft (eds.), *American Authors, 1600–1900: A Biographical Dictionary of American Literature* (New York, 1938)
Landry	Donna Landry, *The Muses of Resistance: Laboring-Class Women's Poetry in Britain, 1739–1796* (Cambridge, 1990)
LC	Library of Congress, Washington, DC
L. Cat.	Library Catalogue
Leeds	Brotherton Library, Leeds University, Leeds
Library Co. of Philadelphia	Library Company of Philadelphia, Pa.
Lonsdale	*Eighteenth Century Women Poets: An Oxford Anthology*, ed. Roger Lonsdale (Oxford, 1989)
Macm	*The Macmillan Dictionary of Canadian Biography*, ed. W. Stewart Wallace (3rd edn., Toronto, 1963)
Mainiero	L. A. Mainiero, *American Women Writers: A Critical Reference Guide from Colonial Times to the Present* (New York, 1979–82), 4 vols.
May	*The American Female Poets*, ed. Caroline May (Philadelphia, Pa., 1849)
Memoir	Henry Forster Burder, *Memoir of the Rev. George Burder* . . . (London, 1833)
Michigan	University Library, University of Michigan, Ann Arbor, Mich.
MR	*Monthly Review*
NCB	*The New Cambridge Bibliography of English Literature*, ed. George Watson and Ian Willison (Cambridge, 1974–7), 5 vols.

NEDL	New England Deposit Library, Cambridge, Mass.
Newberry	The Newberry Library, Chicago, Ill.
NLS	The National Library of Scotland, Edinburgh
North Carolina	The Library, University of North Carolina, Chapel Hill, NC
NUC	*The National Union Catalog: Pre-1956 Imprints* . . . (London and Chicago, 1968–80), 685 vols.
NY State	New York State Library, Albany, NY
NYPL	The New York Public Library, New York
NYPL (Schomburg)	Schomburg Center for Research in Black Culture (Harlem), New York
OCCL	*The Oxford Companion to Children's Literature*, ed. Humphrey Carpenter (Oxford, 1984)
OCFL	*The Oxford Companion to French Literature*, ed. Sir Paul Harvey and J. E. Heseltine (Oxford, 1959)
O'D	D. J. O'Donoghue, *The Poets of Ireland* . . . (Dublin, 1912)
Osborne	Osborne Collection of Early Children's Books, Toronto
Osborne L. Cat.	*The Osborne Collection of Early Children's Books* . . ., ed. Judith St. John (Toronto, 1958–75), 2 vols.
Princeton	Firestone Library, Princeton University, Princeton, NJ
Providence	Providence Public Library, Providence, RI
Pusey	The Pusey Library, Harvard University, Cambridge, Mass.
RLIN	Research Libraries Information Network Data Base
Rosenbach	A. S. W. Rosenbach, *Early American Children's Books* . . ., ed. A. Edward Newton (Portland, 1933)
Rowton	F. Rowton (ed.), *The Female Poets of Great Britain* . . . (London, 1848)
Russell	Norma Russell, *A Bibliography of William Cowper to 1837* (Oxford, 1963)
Rutgers	Rutgers University Libraries, New Brunswick, NJ
Sabin	J. Sabin *et al.* (ed.), *A Dictionary of Books Relating to America* . . . (New York, 1868–1936), 29 vols.

Schlueter	Paul Schlueter, *Encyclopedia of British Women Writers* (New York, 1988)
Shelley Circle	*Shelley and his Circle, 1773–1822*, ed. Kenneth Neill Cameron and Donald H. Reiman (Cambridge, Mass., 1970–), 8 vols.
Shoberl	*A Biographical Dictionary of the Living Authors of Great Britain and Ireland* . . . [ed. John Watkins and Frederic Shoberl] (London, 1816)
SL	*The Letters of Percy Bysshe Shelley*, ed. Frederick L. Jones (Oxford, 1964), 2 vols.
Stainforth	*Catalogue of the Extraordinary Library . . . Formed by . . . F. J. Stainforth . . .* (London, 1867) [Auction Catalogue of Sotheby, Wilkinson & Hodge]
Stainforth Album	'A Collection of . . . Portraits of English Poetesses . . .', ed. F. J. Stainforth, BL: 1876. f. 22
Stewart	C. D. Stewart, *The Taylors of Ongar: An Analytical Bio-Bibliography* (New York, 1975), 2 vols.
Todd 1	*A Dictionary of British and American Women Writers 1660–1800*, ed. Janet Todd (Totowa, 1985)
Todd 2	*Dictionary of British Women Writers*, ed. Janet Todd (London, 1989)
Trinity	Trinity College, Dublin
U. of Pennsylvania	Van Pelt Library, University of Pennsylvania, Philadelphia, Pa.
UBC	University of British Columbia Library, Vancouver
UCLA	University of California Los Angeles Library, Los Angeles, Calif.
Union	Union Theological Seminary Library, New York
USC	Edward L. Doheny Memorial Library, University of Southern California, Los Angeles, Calif.
Watt	*Bibliotheca Britannica; or a General Index to British and Foreign Literature*, ed. R. Watt (Edinburgh, 1824), 4 vols.
Watters	*A Check List of Canadian Literature and Background Materials, 1628–1950* . . ., ed. Reginald Eyre Watters (Toronto, 1959)
Wellesley	Margaret Clapp Library, Wellesley College, Wellesley, Mass.

Widener   Widener   Library,   Harvard   University,
                           Cambridge, Mass.
Widener LC   Catalogue (unpublished) of the Widener
                           Library, Harvard University, Cambridge, Mass.
WL   *The   Yale   Edition   of   Horace   Walpole's
                           Correspondence*, ed. W. S. Lewis (New Haven,
                           Conn., 1937–83), 48 vols.
Yale (Beinecke)   Beinecke   Library,   Yale   University,   New
                           Haven, Conn.
Yale (Mudd)   Seeley G. Mudd Library, Yale University, New
                           Haven, Conn.
Yale (Sterling)   Sterling   Memorial   Library,   Yale   University,
                           New Haven, Conn.

THE BIBLIOGRAPHY

ABDY, Maria, Mrs John (*c.*1797–1867), *see also* Collections 47, 48

Born in London. Her father, Richard Smith, was a solicitor, and her mother was a sister of the satirical poets Horace and James Smith. She married the Revd John Channing Abdy, Rector of St John's, Southwark. She was a contributor to the *New Monthly Magazine*, the *Metropolitan Magazine*, and to various annuals. Between 1830 and 1862 eight collections of her poems were printed for private circulation. (*BLC*, Boase, Burney, *DNB*)

1   *Poetry . . . The Greater Part of These Verses Have Appeared at Various Times, in Different Magazines and Annuals. (For Private Circulation)*. London: printed by J. Robins and Sons, 1834. 11 × 18 cm. Pp. iv + 139. By Mrs Abdy. NYPL: NCM Ford Collection.

ACTON, Eliza (1799–1859)

Born in Battle, Kent. She was the eldest daughter of John Acton, a Hastings brewer. As a young woman she spent some time on the continent for her health and she was briefly engaged to an officer in the French army. Both her volumes of verse were published in 500 copies. After 1835 she contributed verse, mostly occasional, to various annuals. She is best known, however, for her *Modern Cookery for Private Families* (1845), a popular forerunner of Mrs Beeton's *Household Management*, and for *The English Bread Book* (1857). (Boase, *DNB*, Todd 2)

1 *(a)*   *Poems*. Ipswich/London/Bury/Woodbridge/Hadleigh/Stow-market/Norwich: R. Deck, Cowell, Piper, and Shalders/Longman and Co./Deck/Loder/Hardacre/Stacy, 1826. 10.5 × 16.5 cm. Pp. xxii + 140. By Eliza Acton. BL: 994. f. 1.

1 *(b)*   *Poems*. Ipswich/London/Bury/Woodbridge/Hadleigh/Stow-market/Norwich: R. Deck, Cowell, Piper, and Shalders/Longman and Co./Deck/Loder/Hardacre/ Woolby/Stacy, 1827. 2nd edn. 10 × 16.5 cm. Pp. xxiv + 140. By Eliza Acton. BL: 11644. b. 10.

ADCOCK, Anna

According to *Cottage Poems* she was born 'among the wild and most sequestered scenes of nature', she was denied a 'liberal education', but she read voraciously. She published in order to pay her creditors. She seems to have lived in Leicestershire but the cottage of her title was in Wales.

1   *Cottage Poems*. London/Leicester and Melton/Stamford and Birmingham/Somerby: printed for the author by S. Couchman/Mrs Cockshaw's Libraries/the book-sellers/the author, 1808. 9.5 × 15.5 cm. Pp. xii + 164 [subscription edition]. By Anna Adcock, Late of Street-Hill. BL: 1607/1869.

ADELAIDE, *see* O'KEEFFE, Adelaide

AGUILAR, Grace (1816–47)

Born in Hackney, London, to Emanuel Aguilar and Sarah Diaz Fernandes. She was educated at home by her parents and helped her mother run a small private school for boys. She is best known for the novels her mother published for her post-humously, such as *Home Influence* (1847) and *The Mother's Recompense* (1862). Her *Spirit of Judaism* (1842) and *The Women of Israel* (1845) were unusual for the time in their presentation of a Jewish point of view. Although the early accounts of her life agree that *The Magic Wreath* was published in 1835 and Hale even quotes from it, no copy has been located. (*DNB*, *GM*, Hale, HL, Schlueter)

1   *The Magic Wreath*. 1835. 12mo. HL; *DNB*. Not located.

AIKIN, Anna Laetitia, *see* BARBAULD, Anna Laetitia

AIKIN, Lucy (1781–1864), *see also* Collections 15(*a–o*), 20

Born in Warrington, Lancs. She was the only daughter of John Aikin, MD, and Martha Jennings, and a niece of Mrs Barbauld (q.v.). Her family moved to Yarmouth when she was 3 years old. From 1792 to 1797 she lived in London and she then moved to Stoke Newington with her father. She contributed to periodicals from the age of 17, particularly to the *Annual Register*, and wrote biography, popular history, and books for children. Collections of her correspondence with the American clergyman William Ellery Channing were published in 1864 and 1874. (Lucy Aikin, *Memoirs, Miscellanies and Letters* [1865], Boase, *CB*, *DNB*)

1(*a*)   *Epistles on Women, Exemplifying their Character and Condition in Various Ages and Nations. With Miscellaneous Poems*. London: J. Johnson and Co., 1810. 18.5 × 23 cm. Pp. viii + 143. 12/- boards. By Lucy Aikin. *MR* 67: 380–90; BL: 1346. i. 10.

1(*b*)   *Epistles on Women, Exemplifying their Character and Condition in Various Ages and Nations. With Miscellaneous Poems.* Boston[, Mass.]: W. Wells and T. B. Wait and Co., 1810. 11 × 17 cm. 154 pp. By Lucy Aikin. LC: HQ 1206, A 3 copy 3.

AIR-BRAIN, Harriet, *see* APPENDIX 1

ALCOCK, Mary, Mrs (*c.*1741–98)

The youngest daughter of Denison Cumberland, Vicar of Stanwick (later Bishop of Clonfert and Kilmore), and Joanna Bentley, daughter of Richard Bentley, the classicist. She was a sister of the poet Richard Cumberland. She married Archdeacon Alcock and after his death moved to Bath where she was a member of the Batheaston circle of Lady Anna Miller (q.v.). She was an active philanthropist, but was hampered by a weak constitution. (*GM, Poems,* Todd 1)

1   *The Air Balloon; or, Flying Mortal. A Poem.* [Translated from French.] London: E. Macklew, 1784. 16.5 × 20.5 cm. Pp. [ii] + 7. 1/-. BL: 11630. b. 1(5).

2   *Poems, &c. &c.* Ed. [Joanna Hughes]. London: C. Dilly, 1799. 12.5 × 22 cm. Pp. xxxiii + 183 [subscription edition]. By the Late Mrs Mary Alcock. BL: 994. i. 1.

ALLEN, Brasseya, Mrs

An American whose maiden name was Johnson.

1   *Pastorals, Elegies, Odes, Epistles, and Other Poems.* Abingdon, Maryland: printed by Daniel P. Ruff, 1806. 10.5 × 16.5 cm. 163 pp. By Mrs Allen. BL: 11686. a. 39.

ALLEN, Elizabeth (1796–1849)

Born in Craftsbury, Vt., her parents having emigrated there from Brookfield, Mass., when northern Vermont was still a wilderness. Her father was Elijah Allen. She was fond of music when young but became totally deaf at the age of 15. She contributed to the local newspaper using the pseudonym 'Ada', and income from her book enabled her to tour the middle west in 1833. ([Elizabeth Allen,] *Sketches of Green Mountain Life; with an Autobiography of the Author* (1846), Walter John Coates, *A Bibliography of Vermont Poetry* (Montpelier, Vt., 1942))

1(*a*)   *The Silent Harp; or, Fugitive Poems.* Burlington[, Vt.]: Edward Smith, 1832. 11 × 18.5 cm. 120 pp. By Miss Elizabeth Allen. BL: 11687. c. 20.

1(*b*)   *The Silent Harp; or Fugitive Poems.* Lyons: printed by Wm. F. Ashley and Co., 1835. 2nd edn. 10.5 × 17.5 cm. 118 pp. By Elizabeth Allen. Brown (Harris): 76/A4258s/1835.

ALLEN, Lucy, Mrs David
An American Baptist who could neither read nor write. She was married to David Allen and they had at least one child, a daughter who died in 1784. (*Hymns, on Various Subjects*)

1   *Hymns, on Various Subjects.* Windsor (Vermont): printed by Alden Spooner, 1795. 10.5 × 16 cm. 38 pp. By Lucy Allen. Chapin Library: Am. Lit. 17—.

AMELIA, Princess, *see* COLLECTIONS 52

ANDREWS, Hannah

1   *Miscellaneous Pieces in Verse.* London: printed by T. Jones, 1805. 10.5 × 17 cm. Pp. vi + 93. By Hannah Andrews. BL: 11645. aaa. 13.

ANNA MARIA, *see* JONES, Anna Maria

ANNA MATILDA, *see* COWLEY, Hannah

ANNE (of Swansea), *see* CURTIS, Ann

ANONYMOUS

1   *Every Lady's Own Valentine Writer; in Prose and Verse. (For 1798.) Containing Humorous Dialogues; Witty Valentines, with Answers; Pleasant Sonnets, on Love, Courtship, Marriage, Beauty, &c. &c. being Entirely Original.* London: J. Roach, [1798]. 10 × 17 cm. 60 pp. 6*d.* BL: 11621. b. 23(3).

2   *Lady Byron's Responsive 'Fare Thee Well'.* London: Richard Edwards, 1816. 22 × 27.5 cm. 11 pp. BL: 1560/2704.

3   *The Trance. A Poem. Founded on Fact. In Which the Author*

Had a Vision of Heaven and Hell; with a Most Interesting Interview with the Redeemer. To Which is Added an Interesting Account of her Adventures Both by Sea and Land. London: for the author by H. and I. Gibbon, 1826. 10.5 × 17.5 cm. 36 pp. BL: T. 855(9).

4   *Poems for Youth, on Sacred Subjects.* London: for the author by G. Watkins, J. Douglass, and G. Cowie, [1831?]. 9.5 × 14.5 cm. Pp. iv + 56. By the Author of *Verses for Children, Botanical Multiplication Table*, &c., &c. BL: T. 1330(6).

5   *The Child's Daily Monitor.* London/Reading: Whittaker and Co./G. H. Lamb, 1832. 7 × 6.5 cm. Pp. iv + 186 [prose and verse]. BL: T. 1368(12).

APPLETON, Elizabeth

A governess in the family of the Earl of Leven and Melville. She also wrote fiction and books on education. Three editions were published of her *Private Education; or, a Practical Plan for the Studies of Young Ladies* (1815) and two each of her *Early Education; or the Management of Children* (1820) and *The Poor Girl's Help to a Knowledge . . . of the Christian Religion* (1819). By 1829 she was publishing as Mrs Lachlan. (Allibone, *BLC, NUC*)

1   *The Spring Bud, or Rural Scenery in Verse. With Descriptive Notes. For the Instruction and Amusement of Young Persons.* London: J. Harris, 1818. 10 × 16.5 cm. 31 pp. By Elizabeth Appleton, Author of *Private Education*, &c., &c. BL: 11645. aa. 42.

ARTHUR, Grace

1   *The Temple of Health, a Poetic Vision. Occasioned by the Universal Joy Expressed on His Majesty's Most Happy Recovery.* London: for the author by W. Chalklen and by E. and T. Williams, 1789. 22 × 27 cm. Pp. [ii] + 12. 1/6. By a Lady [Grace Arthur?]. HL; HEHL: 316013.

ATTERSOLL, Mrs

1   *Peter the Cruel King of Castile and Leon, an Historical Play in Five Acts.* [Angers: L. Pavie, 1818]. 9.5 × 16 cm. Pp. viii + 88. By Mrs Attersoll. BL: 11777. a. 16.

AUBER, Harriet (1773–1862)

Born in London, daughter of James Auber. The hymns are mainly her work and many of them have found a lasting place in hymnals. (Boase [Supplement])

1   *The Spirit of the Psalms, or, a Compressed Version of Select Portions of the Psalms of David, Adapted to Christian Worship.* Ed. [a Clergyman of the Church of England—Mr Harvey and Henry Auber Harvey]. London: T. Cadell, and C. and J. Rivington, 1829. 12 × 19 cm. Pp. xvii + 160. HL; *NUC*; BL: 692. b. 3.

AUTHOR OF *Cato*

1(*a*)   *Little Rhymes for Little Folks; or a Present for Fanny's Library.* London: J. Harris and Son, 1823. 10 × 17 cm. 17 pp. By a Lady, Author of *Cato, Infant's Friend,* etc. Osborne: uncatalogued.

1(*b*)   *Little Rhymes for Little Folks; or a Present for Fanny's Library.* London: J. Harris, 1825. 2nd edn. 11 × 17.5 cm. 17 pp. [printed on one side of the page only]. By a Lady, Author of *The Infant's Friend, Easy Rhymes, or Poetry for Children from Five to Ten Years of Age, Adventures of the Dog Cato,* etc., etc. Osborne: ii. 650.

2(*a*)   *Easy Rhymes for Children from Five to Ten Years of Age.* London: John Harris, 1825. 10 × 13 cm. Pp. iv + 92. By a Lady, Author of *Cato, or the Adventures of a Dog, The Infant's Friend, Little Rhymes for Little Folks,* etc., etc., etc. Osborne: ii. 634.

2(*b*)   *Easy Rhymes for Children from Five to Ten Years of Age.* London: John Harris, 1831. 9 × 14 cm. Pp. iv + 104. By a Lady, Author of *Cato; or, the Adventures of a Dog.* BL: 11641. a. 69.

AUTHORESS OF *Duke and No Duke*

1   *The Rights of Monarchy, a Poem; on the Late Unanimous Celebration of His Majesty's Birth Day, on the Fourth of June, 1792, at the Hotel, in Birmingham.* [Birmingham?]: all the booksellers, 1792. 12.5 × 21 cm. 16 pp. 4*d.* By the Authoress of *Duke and No Duke.* BL: 8135. b. 29(3).

AUTHORESS OF *The Observant Pedestrian*

All the other titles mentioned on the title-page are novels, ranging in date from 1795 to 1810.

1   *Blossoms of Fancy. Original Poems, and Pieces in Blank Verse.*
     London: printed for the author by T. Bayley, 1811. 10.5 ×
     17 cm. Pp. xii + 149 [subscription edition]. By the
     Authoress of the *Observant Pedestrian*, *Mystic Cottager*,
     Montrose, *Human Frailties*, *Splendid Follies*, etc., etc. BL:
     11643. b. 15.

AVELINE, E. L.

The Mother's Fables was evidently revised before publication by Ann and
Jane Taylor (q.v.). It remained anonymous until in 1845 the title-page
claimed it for the authors of *Original Poems* (the Taylors); in 1861 it was
credited to Aveline. (Stewart)

1   *Simple Ballads; Intended for the Amusement and Instruction of
        Children.* London: W. and T. Darton, 1810. 8.5 × 13 cm.
        Pp. [vi] + 104. BL: 11645. df. 31.

2(*a*) *The Mother's Fables, in Verse. Designed, through the Medium of
        Amusement, to Correct Some of the Faults and Follies of Children.*
        London: Darton, Harvey, and Darton, 1812. 8.5 × 14 cm.
        Pp. [x] + 96. 1/6 boards. *MR* 73: 210; BL: 12304. aaa. 2.

2(*b*) *The Mother's Fables, in Verse. Designed, through the Medium of
        Amusement, to Convey to the Minds of Children Some Useful
        Precepts of Virtue and Benevolence.* London: Darton, Harvey,
        and Darton, 1814. 9 × 13.5 cm. Pp. [x] + 96. BL: 012807.
        df. 36.

2(*c*) *The Mother's Fables, in Verse. Designed, through the Medium of
        Amusement, to Convey to the Minds of Children Some Useful
        Precepts of Virtue and Benevolence.* London: Darton, Harvey,
        and Darton, 1818. 8.5 × 13.5 cm. Pp. v + 96. BL: 012305.
        de. 3.

2(*d*) *The Mother's Fables, in Verse. Designed, through the Medium of
        Amusement, to Convey to the Minds of Children Some Useful
        Precepts of Virtue and Benevolence.* London: Harvey and
        Darton, 1824. 4th edn. 8.5 × 14.5 cm. Pp. viii + 96. BL:
        12304. aaa. 38.

2(*e*)   *The Mother's Fables, in Verse. Designed, through the Medium of Amusement, to Convey to the Minds of Children Some Useful Precepts of Virtue and Benevolence.* London: Harvey and Darton, [1835]. New edn. 9 × 15 cm. Pp. viii + 96. BL: 12305. aaa. 13.

AVERY, Sarah

Of Lyme Regis, Dorset. (*Divine Hymns*)

1   *Divine Hymns, Composed on Several Occasions.* Bridport: printed by R. Hallett, 1795. 9.5 × 15.5 cm. 32 pp. By Sarah Avery, of Lyme Regis, Dorset. BL: 3434. b. 49.

B., Mrs

1   *Poems on Various Subjects.* London: J. Thompson, 1826. 9.5 × 15 cm. 35 pp. By Mrs B. BL: 11644. aa. 54.

B., E., *see* BENTLEY, Elizabeth

B., F. H.

1(*a*)   *An Address to the Right Hon. Lord Byron, with an Opinion on Some of his Writings.* London: Wetton and Jarvis, 1817. 12.5 × 20 cm. 16 pp. 1/-. By F. H. B. BL: 992. i. 15(7).

1(*b*)   *An Address to the Right Hon. Lord Byron: With an Opinion of Some of his Writings . . . Sonnets and Odes, Elegies, Ballads, and Sketches, on Various Subjects, Chiefly Descriptive.* London: Wetton and Jarvis, 1819. 10 × 16.5 cm. Pp. 24 + 199 [F. H. B.'s verse occupies pp. 11–24 only]. By F. H. B., William Linley and Charles Leftley. Bodley: 280. o. 418.

B., L. M.

1   *Poems.* London: printed by Samuel Manning and Co., 1830. 10 × 15.5 cm. Pp. viii + 102. By a Young Lady [L. M. B.]. BL: 11642. b. 21.

BAILEY, Mary, Mrs

Her maiden name was Walker. Her *Reflections upon the Litany of the Church of England* (1833) was issued in three numbers. *Musae Sacrae*, a collection of hymns, was published to assist the missions of the Moravian Brethren. (*BLC*)

1(*a*)   *The Months; and Other Poems*. London/Ballingdon: for the author by Baldwin, Cradock, and Joy/W. Hill, 1822. 14 × 22.5 cm. 48 pp. BL: 1600/618.

1(*b*)   *The Months; and Other Poems*. London/Sudbury/Edinburgh/Dublin/Belfast: C. J. G. and F. Rivington, Seeleys, Hatchard, Nisbet/G. W. Fulcher/W. Oliphant, Oliver and Boyd/W. Curry, Jr. and Co., R. M. Tims/G. Philips and W. M'Comb, 1833. 2nd edn. 13.5 × 21 cm. 48 pp. By Mrs Bailey. BL: 11645. cc. 24.

2(*a*)   *Palmyra*. Inference.

2(*b*)   *Palmyra: A Poem*. 1833. 2nd edn. *EC*.

3   *Musae Sacrae. Collection of Hymns and Sacred Poetry*. London/Ballingdon: for the author by Hatchard and Son and Seeley and Son/Hill, [1835]. 8.5 × 14 cm. Pp. xiv + 168. By the Author of *The Months* and *Palmyra*. BL: 11606. a. 24.

BAILLIE, Joanna (1762–1851), *see also* COLLECTIONS 18, 32, 41

Born at Bothwell, Lanarks. She was the daughter of James Baillie, Professor of Divinity at Glasgow, and Dorothea Hunter. On her father's death in 1778 the family moved to London (where Anne Hunter [q.v.], an aunt by marriage, lived). *De Monfort* was performed at Drury Lane by Siddons and Kemble. Subsequent plays proved difficult to place, but *The Family Legend* was produced in Edinburgh and *The Beacon* (1812), a musical drama, was well received. A German translation of *A Series of Plays* (*Die Leidenschaften*) appeared in 1806. Many of her songs and ballads were set to music. (M. S. Carhart, *The Life and Work of Joanna Baillie* (1923), *DNB*, *NCB*, *NUC*, Todd 2)

1(*a*)   *A Series of Plays: In Which It is Attempted to Delineate the Stronger Passions of the Mind. Each Passion being the Subject of a Tragedy and a Comedy*. London: T. Cadell, Jr., and W. Davies, 1798. 13 × 21 cm. Pp. [iv] + 411 [prose and verse]. 6/- boards. *MR* 27: 66–9; *CR* 24: 13–22; BL: 642. i. 11.

1(*b*)   *A Series of Plays: In Which It is Attempted to Delineate the Stronger Passions of the Mind. Each Passion being the Subject of a Tragedy and a Comedy*. London: T. Cadell, Jr., and

W. Davies, 1799. 2nd edn. 13 × 21 cm. Pp. [iv] + 411 [prose and verse]. BL: 642. i. 15.

1(*c*)   *A Series of Plays: In Which It is Attempted to Delineate the Stronger Passions of the Mind. Each Passion being the Subject of a Tragedy and a Comedy.* London: T. Cadell, Jr., and W. Davies, 1800. 3rd edn. 13 × 20.5 cm. Pp. [iv] + 411 [prose and verse]. By Joanna Baillie. BL: 1509/887.

1(*d*)   *A Series of Plays: In Which It is Attempted to Delineate the Stronger Passions of the Mind: Each Passion being the Subject of a Tragedy and a Comedy.* Vol. i [of 3]. London: T. Cadell, Jr., and W. Davies, 1802. 4th edn. 13 × 21 cm. Pp. [iv] + 410 [prose and verse]. By Joanna Baillie. BL: 81. d. 24.

1(*e*)   *A Series of Plays: In Which It is Attempted to Delineate the Stronger Passions of the Mind: Each Passion being the Subject of a Tragedy and a Comedy.* Vol. i [of 3]. London: Longman, Hurst, Rees, Orme, and Brown, 1821. New edn. 14 × 22 cm. Pp. [iv] + 410 [prose and verse]. By Joanna Baillie. BL: 11771. ee. 5.

2(*a*)   *A Series of Plays: In Which It is Attempted to Delineate the Stronger Passions of the Mind Each Passion being the Subject of a Tragedy and a Comedy.* Vol. ii [of 3]. London: T. Cadell, Jr., and W. Davies, 1802. 13 × 21 cm. Pp. xii + 480 [prose and verse]. 8/- or 8/- boards. By Joanna Baillie. *MR* 43: 31–9; BL: 81. d. 25.

2(*b*)   *A Series of Plays: In Which It is Attempted to Delineate the Stronger Passions of the Mind. Each Passion being the Subject of a Tragedy and a Comedy.* Vol. ii [of 3]. London: T. Cadell, Jr., and W. Davies, 1802. 2nd edn. 13.5 × 22 cm. Pp. xii + 478 [prose and verse]. By Joanna Baillie. Bodley: M. Adds. 109 d. 74.

2(*c*)   *A Series of Plays: In Which It is Attempted to Delineate the Stronger Passions of the Mind. Each Passion being the Subject of a Tragedy and a Comedy.* Vol. ii [of 3]. London: Longman, Hurst, Rees, and Orme, 1806. 3rd edn. 12.5 × 21 cm. Pp. xii + 478 [prose and verse]. By Joanna Baillie. Bodley: Douce B. 695.

2(*d*)   *A Series of Plays: In Which It is Attempted to Delineate the Stronger Passions of the Mind: Each Passion being the Subject of a*

Tragedy and a Comedy. Vol. ii [of 3]. London: Longman, Hurst, Rees, Orme, and Brown, 1821. New edn. 14 × 22 cm. Pp. xii + 478 [prose and verse]. By Joanna Baillie. BL: 11771. ee. 5.

3(*a*)   *Miscellaneous Plays*. London/Edinburgh: Longman, Hurst, Rees, and Orme/A. Constable and Co., 1804. 13 × 21.5 cm. Pp. xx + 438 [prose and verse]. 9/- boards. By Joanna Baillie. *CR* 6: 238–54; *MR* 49: 303–10; BL: 642. i. 19.

3(*b*)   *Miscellaneous Plays*. London/Edinburgh: Longman, Hurst, Rees, and Orme/A. Constable and Co., 1805. 2nd edn. 13.5 × 22 cm. Pp. xxiv + 438 [prose and verse]. By Joanna Baillie. BL: 11771. ee. 4.

4(*a*)   *De Monfort; a Tragedy, in Five Acts . . . as Performed at the Theatre Royal, Drury Lane. Printed under the Authority of the Managers from the Promptbook with Remarks by Mrs Inchbald.* London: Longman, Hurst, Rees, and Orme, [1807]. 10.5 × 16.5 cm. Pp. [ii] + 95. By Joanna Baillie. BL: 1507/315(7).

4(*b*)   *De Monfort: A Tragedy, in Five Acts . . . As Performed at the Drury-Lane and New-York Theatres. With Remarks by Mrs Inchbald.* New York: David Longworth, 1809. 12mo. 9 × 15 cm. 84 pp. By Joanna Baillie. BL: 1506/352.

4(*c*)   *De Monfort; a Tragedy, in Five Acts . . . as Performed at the Theatre Royal Drury Lane. Printed under the Authority of the Managers from the Prompt Book. With Remarks by Mrs Inchbald.* London: Longman, Hurst, Rees, Orme, and Brown, [1816?—frontispiece dated 1816]. 10 × 15.5 cm. 95 pp. By Joanna Baillie. [Bound with other plays as vol. xxiv of *The British Theatre* (London, 1808).] BL: 1345. a. 24.

5(*a*)   *The Family Legend: A Tragedy.* Edinburgh/London: John Ballantyne and Co./Longman, Hurst, Rees, and Orme, 1810. 12.5 × 20 cm. Pp. xiv + 152. 3/6. By Joanna Baillie. *MR* 69: 382–93; BL: 643. g. 5(5).

5(*b*)   *The Family Legend: A Tragedy, in Five Acts.* New York: D. Longworth, 1810. 8.5 × 14 cm. 82 pp. By Joanna Baillie, Author of *De Monfort*, etc. LC: PR 2704. N3 1810.

5(*c*)   *The Family Legend: A Tragedy.* Edinburgh/London: John Ballantyne and Co./Longman, Hurst, Rees, Orme, and

Brown, 1810. 2nd edn. 13.5 × 21.5 cm. Pp. xii + 96. By Joanna Baillie. BL: 11779. f. 10.

6(*a*)   *A Series of Plays: In Which It is Attempted to Delineate the Stronger Passions of the Mind.* Vol. iii [of 3]. London: Longman, Hurst, Rees, Orme, and Brown, 1812. 12.5 × 20.5 cm. Pp. xxxii + 314 [prose and verse]. 9/- boards. By Joanna Baillie. *MR* 69: 382–93; BL: 81. d. 26.

6(*b*)   *A Series of Plays: In Which It is Attempted to Delineate the Stronger Passions of the Mind.* Vol. iii [of 3]. London: Longman, Hurst, Rees, Orme, and Brown, 1821. New edn. 14 × 22 cm. Pp. xxxii + 314 [prose and verse]. By Joanna Baillie. BL: 11771. ee. 5.

7   *Orra: A Tragedy, in Five Acts.* New York: the Longworths, 1812. 9.5 × 15.5 cm. 71 pp. By Joanna Baillie. Houghton: *EC8. B1582. D8120.

8(*a*)   *Metrical Legends of Exalted Characters.* London: Longman, Hurst, Rees, Orme, and Brown, 1821. 13 × 21.5 cm. Pp. xxxvi + 373. 12/- boards. By Joanna Baillie, Author of *Plays on the Passions*, &c. &c. *MR* 96: 72–81; BL: 994. i. 4.

8(*b*)   *Metrical Legends of Exalted Characters.* London: Longman, Hurst, Rees, Orme, and Brown, 1821. 2nd edn. 13 × 21 cm. Pp. xxxvi + 373. By Joanna Baillie, Author of *Plays on the Passions*, etc., etc. NYPL: NCM Baillie copy 2.

9   *A Series of Plays: In Which It is Attempted to Delineate the Stronger Passions of the Mind: Each Passion being the Subject of a Tragedy and a Comedy.* London: Longman, Hurst, Rees, Orme, and Brown, 1821. New edn. 14 × 22 cm. 3 vols. By Joanna Baillie. BL: 11771. ee. 5.

10   *The Martyr: A Drama, in Three Acts.* London: Longman, Rees, Orme, Brown, and Green, 1826. 13 × 21 cm. Pp. xviii + 78. By Joanna Baillie. BL: 11779. f. 11.

11(*a*)   *The Bride; a Drama. In Three Acts.* London: Henry Colburn, 1828. 13 × 21 cm. Pp. x + 112. By Joanna Baillie. BL: 11779. f. 12.

11(*b*)   *The Bride; a Drama, in Three Acts.* Philadelphia: C. Neal, 1828. 8.5 × 13.5 cm. 74 pp. By Joanna Baillie. Widener: 17476. 17(3).

11(*c*)   *The Bride; a Drama. In Three Acts.* London: Henry Colburn,
1828. 2nd edn. 13 × 21 cm. Pp. x + 112. By Joanna Baillie.
BL: T. 1249(4).

12   *The Complete Poetical Works.* Philadelphia: Carey and Lea,
1832. 13.5 × 22.5 cm. 574 pp. By Joanna Baillie. HEHL:
437359.

[*See also*: 'Epilogue to the Theatrical Representation at
Strawberry-Hill' ([1800], broadsheet); 'Lines on the Death of Sir
Walter Scott' ([1832], 4 pp.).]

BAILLIE, Marianne, Mrs Alexander (1795?–1831), *see also*
COLLECTIONS 41

Her maiden name was Wathen. She married Alexander Baillie and trav-
elled extensively. She also wrote *First Impressions of a Tour upon the
Continent . . .* (1819) and *Lisbon in the Years 1821, 1822, and 1823* (1824).
(*DNB*)

1(*a*)   *Guy of Warwick: A Legende. And Other Poems.* Kingsbury:
printed by A. Baillie, 1817. 11 × 18.5 cm. Pp. [iv] + 74. By
Marianne Baillie. BL: 11645. bb. 36.

1(*b*)   *Guy of Warwick: A Legende. And Other Poems.* Kingsbury:
printed by A. Baillie, 1818. 11 × 18 cm. Pp. [iv] + 74. By
Marianne Baillie. BL: 11643. b. 48.

2   *Trifles in Verse.* Ed. [Alexander Baillie]. London: [issued
privately], 1825. 11 × 19 cm. 48 pp. By Marianne Baillie.
BL: 11642. c. 17.

BAKER, Caroline, Mrs, *see* HORWOOD, Caroline

BALFOUR, Mary (1775?–1820)

She was born in Derry, Co. Londonderry, the daughter of a clergyman.
She kept a school with her sisters in Newtown Limavady. By
1813 she had moved to Belfast where she opened another school. She
published *Kathleen O'Neil. A Grand National Melodrame* anonymously in
1814. (*BLC*, O'D)

1   *Hope, a Poetical Essay; with Various Other Poems.* Belfast:
printed by Smith and Lyons, 1810. 11 × 18 cm. 192 pp.
By Miss Balfour. BL: 11641. bb. 1.

BALLANTYNE, Hermione, Mrs John (died 1854)

If, as seems likely, she was the wife of Scott's friend John Ballantyne, her name was Hermione. Her father was Charles Parker and her step-father the Revd William Rutherford. She came from Kelso like her husband, and she married in 1797. Her husband's death in 1821 left her in reduced circumstances, and Scott interested himself in literary projects to help her support herself. In 1828 she married John Glover of Kendal, but in 1829 she was reported to be living in 'great poverty' on an income of £44 a year, which she supplemented by teaching French and music. She wrote reminiscences of Scott for *Chambers's Edinburgh Journal.* (Corson, *DNB* (under John Ballantyne))

1   *The Kelso Souvenir: Or, Selections from her Scrap-book. (Entirely Original.)* Edinburgh/Kelso: W. Blackwood/Walter Grieve, 1832. 10.5 × 17 cm. Pp. iv + 99 [subscription edition]. By a Lady. BL: 11645. aaa. 21.

BALMANNO, Mary, Mrs Robert

Born in Derbyshire. She married Robert Balmanno and emigrated with him to New York. She was an accomplished artist and composer and her husband was the Secretary of the Artists' Benevolent Fund; she corresponded with Lawrence, Stothard, Fuseli, etc. She contributed to such annuals as *The Gem* and *The Forget-me-not* and in 1858 published her *Pen and Pencil* which combined prose, verse, and her own illustrations. (Allibone, Boyle)

1   *Poems.* London: [no publisher named], 1830. 13 × 21.5 cm. 19 pp. [pagination irregular, amounting to 10 pp.]. By Mrs Balmanno. BL: 11642. bbb. 27.

BANNERMAN, Anne (1765–1829), *see also* COLLECTIONS 41, 43

Born in Edinburgh. She was the daughter of William Bannerman and Isobel Dick. At the end of the 1790s she was left destitute by the death s of her mother and brother. She contributed to *The Poetical Register* and she became a governess to the Beresford family in Exeter. She was a friend of the ballad collector Robert Anderson. (Blain, *DNB, NUC,* Todd 1)

1(*a*) *Poems.* Edinburgh/London: Mundell and Son/Longman and Rees, and J. Wright, 1800. 11.5 × 19 cm. Pp. vi + 111. 5/- boards. By Anne Bannerman. *CR* 31: 435–8; BL: 992. i. 2(3).

1(*b*)   *Poems*. Edinburgh: printed by Mundell, Doig, and Stevenson, 1807. New edn. 22.5 × 28.5. Pp. [iv] + 227. By Anne Bannerman. BL: 1346. m. 1.

2   *Tales of Superstition and Chivalry*. London: Vernor and Hood, 1802. 10.5 × 17 cm. Pp. [iv] + 144. 4/- boards. *CR* 38: 110–13; HL; BL: 1066. f. 37.

BARBAULD, Anna Laetitia, Mrs (1743–1825), *see also* COLLECTIONS 12(*a–k*), 15(*a–o*), 16(*a–b*), 19, 21, 23(*a–b*), 25(*a–c*), 30(*a–g*), 32, 36, 38(*a–b*), 39, 40(*a–d*), 50(*a–c*), 52, 53, 56, and end-note

Born at Kibworth, Leics. She was the only daughter and eldest child of John Aikin, DD, and Jane Jennings. Her father was a tutor in the dissenting academy at Warrington, Lancs. She was carefully educated. She married the Revd Rochemont Barbauld in 1774, and together they ran a successful boys' school in Palgrave, Suffolk. After her husband's death in 1808 she undertook an edition of English novels in 50 volumes. She had a wide literary acquaintance, particularly in dissenting circles. (*DNB*, *NCB*, R. Rodgers, *Georgian Chronicle: Mrs Barbauld and Her Family* (1958), Todd 1)

1(*a*)   *Poems*. London: Joseph Johnson, 1773. 21 × 26 cm. Pp. vi + 138. 6/- sewed. *MR* 48: 54–9; BL: 643. k. 9(9).

1(*b*)   *Poems*. London: Joseph Johnson, 1773. 20 × 25.5 cm. Pp. vi + 138 [p. 2 misnumbered as p. 4; errata from the list in 1(*a*), above, have been corrected]. BL: 11656. e. 77.

1(*c*)   *Poems*. London: Joseph Johnson, 1773. 3rd edn. 11 × 18 cm. Pp. vi + 138. BL: 11633. bb. 3.

1(*d*)   *Poems*. London: Joseph Johnson, 1774. 4th edn. 11 × 17.5 cm. Pp. vi + 138. BL: 11631. bb. 1.

1(*e*)   *Poems*. London: Joseph Johnson, 1777. 5th edn. 11 × 18.5 cm. Pp. vi + 138. BL: 1164. e. 29.

1(*f*)   *Poems . . . a New Edition, Corrected. To Which is Added, an Epistle to William Wilberforce, Esq.* London: Joseph Johnson, 1792. 12 × 20 cm. Pp. iv + 152. By Anna Laetitia Barbauld. BL: 994. h. 4.

1(*g*)   *Poems . . . To Which is Added, an Epistle to William Wilberforce, Esq.* Boston[, Mass.]: Wells and Lilly, 1820. 9 × 14.5 cm. Pp. [ii] + 120. By Anna Laetitia Barbauld. Houghton: *EC75. B2323. 773 pi.

2(*a*)   *Epistle to William Wilberforce, Esq. On the Rejection of the Bill for Abolishing the Slave Trade.* London: J. Johnson, 1791. 20 × 25.5 cm. 14 pp. 1/-. By Anna Letitia Barbauld. BL: 644. k. 23(7).

2(*b*)   *Epistle to William Wilberforce, Esq. On the Rejection of the Bill for Abolishing the Slave Trade.* London: J. Johnson, 1791. 2nd edn. 19.5 × 25.5 cm. 14 pp. By Anna Letitia Barbauld. BL: 11631. g. 33(7).

3(*a*)   *Eighteen Hundred and Eleven, a Poem.* London: J. Johnson, 1812. 21.5 × 27 cm. Pp. [ii] + 25. 2/6. By Anna Laetitia Barbauld. *MR* 67: 428–32; BL: 78. g. 3.

3(*b*)   *Eighteen Hundred and Eleven, a Poem.* Boston[, Mass.]/ Philadelphia: Bradford and Read/Anthony Finley, 1812. First American from the London edn. 10.5 × 17 cm. 40 pp. By Anna Laetitia Barbauld. Houghton: Lowell *AC8. B8418. 821p.

3(*c*)   *Eighteen Hundred and Eleven, a Poem.* Philadelphia/New York/Baltimore/Pittsburg/Frankfort [NY]: Anthony Finley/ Farrand, Hopkins and Co./A. Miltenberger, George Hill, and Joseph Cushing/Cramer, Spear, and Eichbaum/Alexander Montgomery, 1812. 11.5 × 18 cm. Pp. [viii] + 40. By Anna Laetitia Barbauld. BL: 11633. de. 32.

4(*a*)   *The Works . . . With a Memoir.* Ed. Lucy Aikin. London: Longman, Hurst, Rees, Orme, Brown, and Green, 1825. 12 × 21 cm. 2 vols. [the poetry being in vol. i]. £1/4/- boards. By Anna Laetitia Barbauld. BL: 994. h. 2.

4(*b*)   *The Works . . . with a Memoir.* Ed. Lucy Aikin. Boston[, Mass.]: David Reed, 1826. 11 × 17.5 cm. 3 vols. [the poetry being in vol. i]. By Anna Laetitia Barbauld. Houghton: 17482. 32*.

4(*c*)   *The Works . . . With a Memoir.* Ed. Lucy Aikin. New York: G. and C. Carvill, E. Bliss and E. White, Collins and Hannay, S. C. Schenck, Collins and Co., H. I. Megary, G. Long, W. B. Gilley, S. B. Collins, R. Lockwood, J. F. Sibell, G. C. Morgan, and J. A. Burtus, 1826. 11 × 18.5 cm. 2 vols. [most of the poetry in vol. i]. By Anna Laetitia Barbauld and Lucy Aikin. Widener: 17482. 30.

5(*a*)   *A Legacy for Young Ladies, Consisting of Miscellaneous Pieces, in Prose and Verse.* Ed. Lucy Aikin. London: Longman, Hurst, Rees, Orme, Brown, and Green, 1826. 10 × 16.5 cm. Pp. viii + 265 [about 19 pp. of verse]. By the Late Mrs Barbauld. BL: 1030. e. 24.

5(*b*)   *A Legacy for Young Ladies, Consisting of Miscellaneous Pieces, in Prose and Verse.* Ed. [Lucy Aikin]. London: Longman, Rees, Orme, Brown, and Green, 1826. 2nd edn. 10.5 × 17.5 cm. Pp. viii + 263. By the Late Mrs Barbauld. Boston Athenaeum: VE. B23.

5(*c*)   *A Legacy for Young Ladies, Consisting of Miscellaneous Pieces, in Prose and Verse.* Ed. [Lucy Aikin]. New York: G. and C. Carvill, W. B. Gilley, Collins and Co., S. C. Schenck, Collins and Hannay, E. Bliss, H. I. Megary, G. Long, R. Lockwood, G. C. Morgan, and J. A. Burtus, 1826. 10 × 15.5 cm. 252 pp. By the Late Mrs A. L. Barbauld. Yale (Beinecke): 1974/2997.

5(*d*)   *Legacy for Young Ladies, Consisting of Miscellaneous Pieces, in Prose and Verse.* Boston[, Mass.]: David Reed, 1826. 11 × 17.5 cm. Pp. viii + 151. By the Late Mrs Barbauld. Boston Athenaeum: VE. B23. 2.

6   *Little Charles.* [Cover serves as title-page.] New York/Providence: C. Shepard/Shepard, Tingley and Co., [n.d.]. 10.5 × 18 cm. [8 pp. printed on one side only.] By Mrs Barbauld. NYPL: *KVD Barbauld.

Barclay, Rachel, Mrs David (1743–92)
She was the daughter of Sampson and Rachel Lloyd and a Quaker. She married David Barclay of Youngsbury, Herts. She was an editor of poetical miscellanies. Her obituary notice in *GM* stresses her philanthropy, calling her 'a most zealous friend to the widow, and a fostering parent to the rising generation'. (*CB, Friends' Books, GM,* Osborne L. Cat.)

1(*a*)   *Select Pieces of Poetry, Intended to Promote Piety and Virtue in the Minds of Young People.* London: James Phillips, 1795. 9.5 × 15.5 cm. Pp. viii + 168. Collected by Rachel Barclay. BL: 11602. aaa. 3.

1(*b*)   *Poems Intended to Promote Piety and Virtue in the Minds of Young People.* Ed. Rachel Barclay. London: James Phillips and Son, 1797. 2nd edn. 10 × 17 cm. Pp. xii + 170. By Rachel Barclay. BL: 11631. b. 7.

BARING, Ann

Probably the landscape painter. If so, she was the daughter of John Baring, a Devonshire businessman. She was active in 1791 and painted in Devon and in Ireland. (H. L. Mallalien, *The Dictionary of British Watercolour Artists up to 1920* (1976))

1 (*a*)   *Painting: A Poem, in Four Cantos. With Biographical Notes.* London: T. Dangerfield, 1792. 12.5 × 21 cm. Pp. viii + 74. Yale: In: P17. 792 [photocopy seen only].

1 (*b*)   *Painting, a Poem, in Four Cantos. With Biographical Anecdotes.* London: T. Dangerfield, 1794. 2nd edn. 18.5 × 23 cm. Pp. viii + 70. Bodley: Vet. A5 d 129.

BARKER, Jemima

1   *Poems, on Miscellaneous Subjects.* London: Lupton Relfe, 1822. 9.5×16 cm. Pp. 146 + x [subscription edition]. BL: 994. f.2.

BARKER, Mary (died 1850)

1   *Lines Addressed to a Noble Lord; (His Lordship will Know Why,).* London: printed by W. Pople, 1815. 12.5 × 20.5 cm. 23 pp. By One of the Small Fry of the Lakes. BL: 11645. bbb. 46.

BARNARD, Lady Anne (1750–1825), *see also* COLLECTIONS 37

The eldest child of James Lindsay, 5th Earl of Balcarres, and of Anne Dalrymple. She was a friend of the Southeys and Words-worths. With her sister Margaret (q.v.) she maintained a house in London that was much visited by literary and political celebrities. In 1793 she married Andrew Barnard and went with him to the Cape of Good Hope where he had been appointed as colonial secretary. She wrote 'journals and notes' on her experiences there. After her husband's death in 1807 she rejoined her sister in London and they revived their salon. 'Auld Robin Gray', written in 1771, was publicly attributed to her in Scott's *The Pirate* in 1823 and privately acknowledged. (*DNB*, Lonsdale, Madelaine Masson, *Lady Anne Barnard* (1948), *New Letters of Robert Southey* (1965))

1   *Auld Robin Gray; a Ballad.* Ed. [Walter Scott]. Edinburgh: printed [for the Bannatyne Club] by James Ballantyne

and Co., 1825. 19.5 × 25.5 cm. Pp. [vi] + 16. By the Right Honourable Lady Anne Barnard, born Lady Anne Lindsay of Balcarres. BL: G. 269(4).

BARNES, Esther

As her title-page reveals, from the Boarding School, Shepton-Mallett, Som. An acrostic to a 10-year-old nephew reveals that his name was Robert Morrant.

1   *The Disengaged Fair. Written the Tenth of September, 1796.* Bristol: S. Bonner, [1796]. 12 × 19.5 cm. 32 pp. By Esther Barnes, Boarding School, Shepton-Mallett, Somersetshire. BL: 11641. bb. 2.

BARON WILSON, Margaret, Mrs Cornwell (1797–1846), *see also* COLLECTIONS 39

Born in Shropshire. She was the only child of Roger Harries, of Islington, and of Sophia Arbouin. She wrote romantic dramas, novels, and biographies as well as poetry. In 1819 she married Cornwell Baron Wilson, a solicitor; they had 'several' children. She was editor of *La Belle Assemblée* from 1833, contributed to the annuals, and wrote the words for vol. iii of Parry's *Welsh Melodies*. In 1834 she won the prize for a poem on Princess Victoria at the Cardiff bardic festival, defeating 200 other contestants. Her comic interlude, *Venus in Arms*, was performed in London in 1836. (Boyle, *DNB*)

1   *Melancholy Hours. A Collection of Miscellaneous Poems.* London: John Richardson, 1816. 10 × 16.5 cm. Pp. xii + 186. 6/- boards. *MR* 82: 100–1; BL: 11641. aaa. 30.

2(*a*)   *Astarte . . . Inference.*

2(*b*)   *Astarte, a Sicilian Tale; with Other Poems.* London/Edinburgh: C. Chapple/Fairbairn and Anderson, 1818. 2nd edn. 10 × 17 cm. Pp. xvi + 236. By Miss Harries. BL: 11641. b. 16.

2(*c*)   *Astarte . . . 3rd edn. Inference.*

2(*d*)   *Astarte, a Sicilian Tale: With Other Poems.* London: C. Chapple, Fricker, Simpkin and Marshall, 1827. 4th edn. 9 × 15.5 cm. Pp. xii + 236. By Mrs Cornwell Baron Wilson. BL: 11644. bbb. 36.

3(*a*)   *Hours at Home. A Collection of Miscellaneous Poems.* London: Fricker, Simpkin and Marshall, 1826. 8 × 13.5 cm. Pp.

xxviii + 203. By Mrs Cornwell Baron Wilson. BL: 11644. aa. 60.

3(*b*)   *Hours at Home*. London: C. Chapple, Fricker, Simpkin and Marshall, 1827. 2nd edn. 8 × 13 cm. Pp. xxviii + 203. By Mrs Cornwell Baron Wilson. BL: 11644. aa. 31.

4   *The Cypress Wreath*. London: Smith, Elder, and Co., 1828. 10 × 16.5 cm. Pp. xii + 159. By Mrs Cornwell Baron Wilson. BL: T. 1218(2).

5   *Poems*. London: W. Wright, 1831. 12.5 × 21.5 cm. Pp. ii + ii + 95. By Mrs Cornwell Baron Wilson. BL: 994. i. 29.

BARRELL, Maria

Her maiden name was Weylar and she lived in London. She was probably the wife and then the widow of a soldier who fought in America and she was subsequently imprisoned for debt. She had two children. She wrote for periodicals as 'Maria'. (Blain, Stainforth, Todd 1)

1   *Reveries du Cœur: Or, Feelings of the Heart. Attempted in Verse*. London: for the author by Dodsley, Walter, Owen, and Yeats, 1770. 12 × 18.5 cm. Pp. xvi + 87 [subscription edition]. 2/6. By Maria Weylar. *MR* 43: 326; BL: 11631. bb. 90.

2   *British Liberty Vindicated; or, a Delineation of the King's Bench*. London: printed for the author, 1788. 19 × 25 cm. 22 pp. By Maria Barrell. BL: 643. k. 16(5).

BARRELL, P. (died by 1811)

Author of two novels, *Julia and the Illuminated Baron* (1800–1) and *Riches and Poverty: A Tale* (1808). (Blain, *BLC*, *NUC*)

1   *The Test of Virtue, and Other Poems*. London: C. Chapple and T. Boosey, 1811. 10 × 16 cm. 154 pp. 7/- boards. By the Late Miss P. Barrell. *MR* 69: 330; BL: 11645. aa. 8.

BARRETT, Elizabeth (1806–61)

Eldest daughter of Edward Moulton (who later took the surname Barrett) and Mary Graham. She was born at Coxhoe Hall, Durham Co., and grew up in a country house near Ledbury. She was a precocious child but became an invalid after a riding accident at the age of 15. In 1835 the family moved to London. Her first great critical success, *Seraphim and Other Poems* (1838), was followed up with *Poems* (1844) and *Sonnets from the Portuguese* (first published in a collected edition of her poems in 1850). In 1846 she married the poet Robert Browning. (*DNB*)

1   *The Battle of Marathon. A Poem.* London: W. Lindsell, 1820. 13 × 21.5 cm. Pp. xvi + 72. BL: Ashley 2512.

2   *An Essay on Mind, with Other Poems.* London: James Duncan, 1826. 10.5 × 17.5 cm. Pp. xvi + 152. BL: 994. f. 42.

3   *Prometheus Bound. Translated from the Greek . . . And Miscellaneous Poems.* Trans. [Elizabeth Barrett]. London: A. J. Valpy, 1833. 10.5 × 18 cm. Pp. xxvi + 163. By Aeschylus and the Translator, Author of *An Essay on Mind.* BL: 997. e. 18.

BATH, Elizabeth, Mrs Henry (1772–1856)
A Quaker. Married to Henry Bath of Mumbles near Swansea, Glamorganshire. (Bodley L. Cat., *Friends' Books*)

1   *Poems, on Various Occasions.* Bristol: printed by J. Desmond, 1806. 10 × 16 cm. 187 pp. [subscription edition]. By Elizabeth Bath. BL: 11641. aaa. 3.

BATTIER, Henrietta (1751?–1813)
Daughter of John Fleming of Staholmock, Co. Meath. In 1768 she married Major John Gaspard Battier, who died in 1794 leaving her ill provided for with two daughters. She acted as an amateur at Drury Lane in 1783–4. She lived in Dublin and was a bluestocking and an ardent patriot. She contributed verse to the *Anthologia Hibernica,* and to the *Sentimental Magazine* and the *Masonic Magazine* in 1792–5. *The Bitter Orange* appeared first in *The Press,* the newspaper of the United Irishmen. Her satire was read by Johnson and Reynolds. (Blain, O'D, Todd 1)

1   *The Protected Fugitives. A Collection of Miscellaneous Poems, the Genuine Productions of a Lady. Never before Published.* Dublin: printed for the author by James Porter, 1791. 13.5 × 22 cm. Pp. x + [10] + xi–xviii + 233 [subscription edition]. CUL: Hib. 5. 791. 40.

2   *The Kirwanade: Or Poetical Epistle. Humbly Addressed to the Modern Apostle! In Consequence of his Very Spirited Behaviour at the Chapter, Held Lately at St. Patrick's.* Number I [of 2]. Dublin: printed for the author by James Porter, 1791. 12 × 19.5 cm. 23 pp. By [Patt. Pindar]. HEHL: 281467(1).

3   *The Kirwanade: Or Poetical Epistle. Humbly Addressed to the Modern Apostle!* Number II [of 2]. Dublin: printed for the author by James Porter, 1791. 13 × 23 cm. 26 pp. 1/1. By [Patt. Pindar]. HEHL: 281467(2).

4   [*Gibbonade . . .* First Number (of 3?)] [Lacks title-page in this copy.] [Dublin: printed for the author, 1793?] 12 × 20.5 cm. 28 pp. By [Patt. Pindar]. BL: 11632. e. 64(1).

5   *The Gibbonade: Or, Political Reviewer.* Second Number [of 3?]. Dublin: printed for the author, 1793. 12 × 20.5 cm. 32 pp. 1/-. By [Patt. Pindar]. BL: 11632. e. 64(1).

6   *The Gibbonade: Or, Political Reviewer.* Third Number [of 3?]. Dublin: printed for the author, 1794. 12 × 20.5 cm. 44 pp. 1/-. By [Patt. Pindar]. BL: 11632. e. 64(1).

7   *Marriage Ode Royal, after the Manner of Dryden.* [The word 'Royal' in the title is printed upside down, deliberately.] [Dublin?], 1795. 12 × 20.5 cm. 16 pp. 1/1. By [Pat. T. Pindar]. BL: 11632. e. 64(3).

8   *The Lemon, a Poem . . . in Answer to a Scandalous Libel, Entitled, the Orange; Written (tho' Anonymous) by the Reverend Dr Bobadil.* Dublin: No. 60, Stephen Street, 1797. 12.5 × 21 cm. Pp. [ii] + 20. 1/- ['a British Shilling']. By [Mrs Battier?]. CUL: Hib. 5. 797. 31.

9   *An Address to the Subject of the Projected Union, to the Illustrious Stephen III, King of Dalkey, Emperor of the Mugglins, Elector and Archtreasurer of Lambay, Lord Protector of the Holy Island of Magee, Grand Duke of Bullock, Grand Master of the Noble, Illustrious, and Ancient Orders of the Lobster, Crab, Scollop, &c. &c.* Dublin: for the author at 60 Stephen-St[r]eet, 1799. 12.5 × 21 cm. 20 pp. 'Price a British Shilling'. By Patt. Pindar. Trinity: Crofton 160. No. 10.

BAYFIELD, Mrs E. G.

1   *Fugitive Poems.* London: for the author by Warde and Betham, Lindsell, Longman and Co., Vernor and Hood, 1805. 10.5 × 18 cm. 192 pp. [subscription edition]. By Mrs Bayfield. BL: 11641. c. 5.

A Beautiful Young Lady, *pseudonym of* Whalley, Thomas Sedgwick

Beeman, Anna, Mrs Park (born 1739?)

Hymn writer and Baptist polemicist. She was married to Park Beeman of Warren, Conn., and they had nine children. Her *Three Letters to a Lady in Opposition to the Baptist Plan* (1794) argues against the baptism of infants. (Todd 1)

1 *Hymn[s] on Different Spiritual Subjects. In Two Parts. Part I. Containing XXVI Hymns, on Various Subjects, Suitable for Christian Worship . . . Part II. Containing XXXII Hymns . . . And XXIV Hymns . . . To Which is Added a Number of Hymns by Different Authors. Particularly Adapted to the Baptist Worship.* [Title-page damaged.] Norwich[, Conn.]: printed by John Trumbull, 1792. 4th edn. [of Cleavland's book]. 9.5 × 16 cm. 120 pp. [of which pp. 33–76 are by Anna Beeman]. By Benjamin Cleavland, Anna Beeman, and Amos Wells. Brown (Harris): h Coll/C6232/1792.

Bell, Mrs A. S.

Fanny is offered as a 'religious novel' and its author seems, like its editor, to have lived in Whitby; the subscribers came mostly from the north of England. Many of the poems were previously published in periodicals.

1 *Fanny, or True Benevolence: To Which are Added Miscellaneous Poems.* Ed. [George Young]. Whitby/Hull/Leeds: R. Rodgers, and G. Clark, and B. Bean/Allen, Turner, and Topping and Dawson/Spink, 1821. 10.5 × 16.5 cm. Pp. viii + 168 [subscription edition; verse occupies pp. 145–60]. By Mrs A. S. Bell. BL: 1362. e. 28.

Belson, Mary, *see* Elliott, Mary

Benger, Elizabeth Ogilvy (1778–1827), *see also* Collections 32, 43

She was born in or near Wells, Som., and was an only child. Her father, John Benger, was a purser in the navy; her mother was Mary Long. Most of her formative years were spent in Chatham and Rochester. She lacked literary surroundings and later claimed to have been obliged to read the open books in shop windows, returning each day when the page had been turned. In 1797 she moved to Devizes where a well-stocked library was available. She moved to London in 1808 and found herself in congenial company among literary dissenters. She wrote novels and biographies. Mme de Staël said that she was the most interesting woman she had seen in England. (Lucy Aikin, *Memoirs, Miscellanies and Letters* (1864), Blain, Boyle, *DNB*, *GM*, Todd 1)

1   *The Female Geniad; a Poem. Inscribed to Mrs Crespigny.* London: T. Hookham and J. Carpenter, C. and G. Kearsley, 1791. 21 × 26.5 cm. Pp. [vi] + 55. 3/-. By Elizabeth Ogilvy Benger, at the Age of Thirteen. *MR* 8: 229; BL: 11611. k. 8(7).

2   *Poems on the Abolition of the Slave Trade* . . . London: R. Bowyer, 1809. 23 × 29.5 cm. Pp. [14] + ii + 141. £3/3/- or, large paper, £5/5/- boards. By James Montgomery, James Grahame and E. Benger [Benger's 'A Poem, Occasioned by the Abolition of the Slave Trade, in 1806' occupies pp. 101–41]. *MR* 64: 144–52; BL: 83. k. 10.

BENTLEY, Elizabeth (1767–1839), *see also* COLLECTIONS 10(*c*), 11(*a*), 12(*a–k*)

The only child of Daniel Bentley, a well-educated cordwainer in Norwich, who gave her an elementary education. Many of her poems were first published in the *Norfolk Chronicle*. She was the proprietor of a school in Norwich. The Revd John Walker sponsored an edition for her that gained 1,935 subscribers. (Landry, Todd 1)

1(*a*)   *Genuine Poetical Compositions, on Various Subjects.* Norwich: for the authoress and W. Stevenson, 1791. 10 × 15.5 cm. Pp. xxxiv + 69 [subscription edition]. 2/- sewed. By E. Bentley. *MR* 6: 284–6; *CR* 3: 94–5; BL: 993. c. 43(4).

1(*b*)   *Poems: Being the Genuine Compositions.* Norwich/London/ Cambridge: for the author, and Stevenson, Matchett and Stevenson/Taylor and Hessey/Deightons, 1821. 10.5 × 18 cm. Pp. xxviii + 168 [subscription edition]. By Elizabeth Bentley. BL: 11642. bb. 43.

2   *Miscellaneous Poems; being the Genuine Compositions. . . . Third Volume.* Norwich: Matchett, Stevenson, and Matchett, 1835. 11 × 18.5 cm. Pp. viii + 95 [subscription edition]. By Elizabeth Bentley, of Norwich. Princeton: 3626. 553. 1835.

[*See also*: 'An Ode on the Glorious Victory over the . . . Fleets' (1805, 4 pp.).]

BETHAM, Mary Matilda (1776–1852)

Eldest daughter of the Revd William Betham, the antiquary, and of Mary Damant. She had access to her father's genealogical library, learned sewing at school and was a competent painter of miniature portraits. She was a popular conversationalist, and had a wide literary acquaintance. She gave Shakespearean readings in London in 1803 and was the author of a biographical dictionary of women in 1804. (Boase, *DNB*, *GM*, Todd 1)

1   *Elegies, and Other Smaller Poems.* Ipswich/London: Jermyn and Forster/Longman, [1797]. 10 × 17 cm. Pp. xiv + 128. 3/6. By Matilda Betham. BL: 11642. aa. 31.

2   *Poems.* London: J. Hatchard, 1808. 9.5 × 16 cm. Pp. [iv] + 116. 4/- boards. By Matilda Betham. *MR* 56: 426–7; BL: 11642. aa. 41.

3   *The Lay of Marie: A Poem.* London: Rowland Hunter, 1816. 13 × 21 cm. Pp. viii + 276. By Matilda Betham. BL: 992. k. 29(1).

4   *Vignettes: In Verse.* London: Rowland Hunter, 1818. 15 × 23.5 cm. and 12 × 20 cm. 80 pp. By Matilda Betham. BL: 11642. bbb. 36 and 11642. dd. 7.

BEVERLEY, Charlotte, Mrs

1   *Poems on Miscellaneous Subjects, Composed and Selected.* Hull/London/York: E. Foster/C. Dilly, J. Todd/Wilson, Spence and Mawman, 1792. 10.5 × 17 cm. 261 pp. [subscription edition]. 4/6. By Charlotte Beverley. *CR* 12: 238; BL: 11633. aaa. 3.

BEVERLEY, Elizabeth, Mrs R.

An actress.

1   *A Poetical Olio.* London: for the author, 1819. 10 × 16 cm. 24 pp. 1/-. By Mrs R. Beverly, Comedian, Author of the *Mirror, Modern Times*, etc. BL: 992. g. 30(5).

2(*a*)   *Entertaining Moral Poems* . . . Inference.

2(*b*)   *Entertaining Moral Poems, on a Variety of Subjects.* London: for the authoress, 1826. 2nd edn. 10 × 17.5 cm. 13 pp. By Mrs Elizabeth Beverley, Comedian, Professor of Elocution, and Authoress of the Popular *Coronation Sermon*, etc. Widener: Q 496(3).

2(*c*)   *Entertaining Moral Poems* . . . 3rd edn. Inference.

2(*d*)   *Entertaining and Moral Poems, on Various Subjects, Expressly Designed for the Use of the Rising Generation.* London: for the authoress, [1820?]. 4th edn. 8.5 × 14.5 cm. 18 pp. By Elizabeth Beverley. BL: T. 892(5).

3(*a*)   *The Actress's Ways and Means, to Industriously Raise the Wind! Containing the Moral and Entertaining Poetical Effusions.* London: printed for the author by Macdonald and Son, [1820?]. 13.5 × 21 cm. 32 pp. 1/-. By Mrs R. Beverley, Comedian. BL: 11649. f. 15(2).

3(*b*)   *The Actress's Ways and Means.* 2nd edn. Inference.

3(*c*)   *The Actress's Ways and Means.* 3rd edn. Inference.

3(*d*)   *The Actress's Ways and Means, to Industriously Raise the Wind! Containing the Moral and Entertaining Poetical Effusions.* London: printed for the author by W. Glendinning, 1822. 4th edn. 13 × 21.5 cm. 32 pp. 1/-. By Mrs R. Beverley, Comedian. BL: 11642. bbb. 49.

3(*e*)   *The Actress's Ways and Means.* 5th edn. Inference.

3(*f*)   *The Actress's Ways and Means, to Industriously Raise the Wind! Containing the Moral and Entertaining Poetical Effusions* . . . London: printed for the author by John Stokes, 1822. 6th edn. 13 × 21 cm. 32 pp. 1/-. By Mrs R. Beverley, Comedian, Professor of Elocution, and Author of the popular *Coronation Sermon, Modern Times,* etc. BL: 1509/62.

3(*g*)   *The Actress's Ways and Means.* 7th edn. Inference.

3(*h*)   *The Actress's Ways and Means.* 8th edn. Inference.

3(*i*)   *The Actress's Ways and Means.* 9th edn. Inference.

3(*j*)   *The Actress's Ways and Means to Industriously Raise the Wind: Containing the Moral and Entertaining Poetical Effusions.* London: printed for the author by T. Dolby, [1823?]. 10th edn. 29 pp. 1/-. By Mrs R. Beverley, Comedian. BL: 11642. bbb. 22.

3(*k*)   *The Actress's Ways and Means.* 11th edn. Inference.

3(*l*)   *The Actress's Ways and Means to Industriously Raise the Wind: Containing Moral and Entertaining Poems, on a Variety of Subjects.* London: printed for the author by T. Dolby, 1823. 12th edn. 13.5 × 21.5 cm. 30 pp. 1/-. By Mrs

Elizabeth Beverley, Comedian, Professor of Elocution, and Author of the popular *Coronation Sermon, Modern Times, Cap, Mirror*, etc. Pusey: Thr 472. 29. 7.

4(*a*)   *Useful Subjects in Prose and Verse*. Inference.

4(*b*)   *Useful Subjects in Prose and Verse*. 2nd edn. Inference.

4(*c*)   *Useful Subjects in Prose and Verse*. 3rd edn. Inference.

4(*d*)   *Useful Subjects in Prose and Verse*. London: for the authoress, 1828. 4th edn. 11 × 19.5 cm. 27 pp. By Mrs Elizabeth Beverley, Comedian. BL: 1458. g. 9(2).

[*See also*: 'The Book of Variety . . . Poetry . . .' (1823 and 1824, 4 pp. of verse).]

BIGSBY, Sophia Mary

1   *Imilda de' Lambertazzi: And Other Poems*. London: Hurst, Chance and Co., 1830. 10 × 16.5 cm. Pp. viii + 200. By Sophia Mary Bigsby. BL: 994. f. 4.

BINGHAM, Margaret, *see* LUCAN, Lady

BIRCH, Eliza

Daughter of Thomas Birch of Warwick, War., and a Quaker. (*Friends' Books*)

1   *Poems on Various Subjects: To Which is Added a Selection of Hymns, &c.* Manchester: printed by C. Wheeler and Son, 1800. 12.5 × 21 cm. 69 pp. By Eliza Birch, daughter of Thos. Birch, late of Warwick, the Elder Branch of the Staffordshire Family. BL: 11633. bb. 5.

BIRKETT, Mary

A Dublin Quaker. (*Friends' Books*, Stainforth)

1   *A Poem on the African Slave Trade. Addressed to her Own Sex.* [Part I, of 2.] Dublin: J. Jones, 1792. 12 × 20 cm. Pp. [ii] + 19. By M. Birkett. BL: 11633. bb. 6.

2   *A Poem on the African Slave Trade. Addressed to her Own Sex.* Part II [of 2]. Dublin: J. Jones, 1792. 12 × 20 cm. Pp. [ii] + 25. By M. Birkett. BL: 11633. bb. 6.

BISHOP, Mary

Daughter of H. Bishop of Liverpool. (Shoberl)

1(*a*)   *Poetic Tales and Miscellanies.* Liverpool/London: William Robinson/Longman, Hurst, Rees, Orme, and Brown, 1812. 13 × 20.5 cm. 151 pp. BL: T. 1551(2).

1(*b*)   *St. Oswald, and Other Poetic Tales and Miscellanies.* London/Dublin: James Ilbery/John Cumming, 1813. 2nd edn. 12 × 19 cm. 151 pp. BL: 11650. cc. 19(11).

BLACKALL, Elizabeth

1   *Psalms and Hymns and Spiritual Songs.* Dublin: William Curry, Jr., 1835. 9 × 14.5 cm. Pp. xxii + 137. By Elizabeth Blackall. BL: 3434. aaa. 7.

BLACKETT, Mary, Mrs

A widow who lived in London, her husband having died young. Her maiden name was Dawes. She had a daughter in a French convent. She was acquainted with Chatterton. One of her poems is included in H. and M. Falconar's *Poetic Laurels* (q.v.). (Blain, Todd 1)

1   *Suicide; a Poem. Inscribed, by Permission, to Richard Cosway, Esq. R.A. Principal Painter to His Royal Highness the Prince of Wales.* London/Newcastle upon Tyne: for the author by Robinson, Debrett, Edwards, Sewell/Hodgson, 1789. 18 × 24.5 cm. Pp. vi + 14. 1/6. By Mary Dawes Blackett. BL: T. 20(7).

BLANCHARD, Anne

1(*a*)   *Midnight Reflections, and Other Poems.* London: John Arliss, 1822. 9.5 × 16 cm. Pp. xvi + 111 [subscription edition]. By Anne Blanchard. BL: 11642. aa. 9.

1(*b*)   *Midnight Reflections; and Other Poems.* London: John Arliss, 1823. 2nd edn. 10 × 16 cm. Pp. xvi + 116 [subscription edition]. By Anne Blanchard. BL: 11642. aa. 39.

BLEASE, Elizabeth Bower, Mrs

Her book mentions a daughter who died at the age of 17 and an uncle named Thomas Blake who lived in Croydon. She writes nostalgically of Wansbeck as a place 'to be beheld no more'.

I   *Poems, on Various Subjects.* London: for the author by
    Darton, Harvey, and Darton, 1817. 10 × 17 cm. Pp. xii +
    108 [subscription edition]. 4/- boards. By Miss Elizabeth
    Bower Blease. BL: 994. g. 4.

BLEECKER, Ann Eliza (1752–83)
Daughter of Brandt Schuyler and Margareta Van Wyck of Tomhanick,
near Albany, NY. In 1769 she married John Bleecker of
New Rochelle. She was the mother of Margaretta Faugeres (q.v.), who
edited her book. (Allibone, Blain, *DAB*, Mainiero, May)

I   *The Posthumous Works . . . in Prose and Verse. To Which is
    Added, a Collection of Essays, Prose and Poetical . . .* New
    York: printed by T. and J. Swords, 1793. 11 × 17.5 cm.
    Pp. [10] + 375. By Ann Eliza Bleecker and Margaretta V.
    Faugeres. HEHL: 105423.

BLENNERHASSETT, Margaret, Mrs (1788?–1842)
Her maiden name was Agnew. (Watters)

I   *The Widow of the Rock, and Other Poems.* Montreal: printed
    by E. V. Sparhawk, 1824. 9.5 × 16.5 cm. 192 pp. By a
    Lady. BL: 11688. bb. 17.

BLESSINGTON, Countess of, *see* POWER, Marguerite

B——N, Mrs
Identified on her title-page as living in Carnock, near Dunfermline. Her
poems are religious and she seems to have been orphaned at an early
age.

I   *A Collection of Miscellaneous Poems.* Edinburgh: printed by
    Caw and Elder, 1819. 10.5 × 17 cm. Pp. iv + 288. By Mrs
    B——n, in the Parish of Carnock, near Dunfermline. BL:
    11645. aaa. 19.

BOLDERO, Chris., Mrs George
The dedication to her only child, a daughter, is signed Chris. Boldero.

I   *Sacred Dramas, for the Improvement and Amusement of Young
    Persons, and as an Enticement to Them to Study the Holy
    Scriptures.* Holt: printed for the author by James Shalders,

1823. 10 × 17 cm. Pp. xx + 215 [subscription edition; prose and verse, the verse occupying pp. 5–31]. By Mrs Boldero, Widow of the Late Reverend George Boldero, Vicar of South Rainham in Norfolk. Osborne: uncatalogued.

BONHOTE, Elizabeth, Mrs Daniel (1744–1818)

She grew up in Bungay, Suffolk. Her father was James Mapes, a baker. She married Daniel Bonhote, a solicitor, who died in 1804. They had several children. She was a successful writer of prose, publishing six novels between 1773 and 1796 and a collection of moral essays entitled *The Parental Monitor*, which appeared in several editions. (*CB*, *DNB*, *GM*, Todd 1)

1   *An Ode on the Expected Arrival of Marquis Cornwallis in England.* Norwich: printed by Yarington and Bacon, [1793]. 10.5 × 17.5 cm. 8 pp. Bodley: G. A. Norf 8° 70(8).

2   *Feeling, or, Sketches from Life; a Desultory Poem. With Other Pieces.* Edinburgh/London: Manners and Miller, A. Constable and Co., Brown and Crombie/Longman, Hurst, Rees, and Orme, 1810. 10 × 15.5 cm. 5/- boards. By a Lady. HL; *MR* 64: 213–14; BL: 11643. aa. 18.

BOTSFORD, Margaret

She came from Philadelphia but lived in various parts of the Middle West. She was a novelist as well as a poet. (Blain)

1(*a*)   *Viola or the Heiress of St. Valverde, an Original Poem, in Five Cantos. To Which is Annexed, Patriotic Songs, Sonnets, &c.* Louisville[, Ky.]: printed by S. Penn, Jr., 1820. 8.5 × 14.5 cm. 96 pp. By a Lady of Philadelphia, Author of *Adelaide*. LC: PS 1110. B82 V5 1820 Office.

1(*b*)   *Viola; Heiress of St. Valverde. An Original Romance. To Which is Annexed a Variety of Original Poetical Pieces.* Philadelphia: R. Desilver, 1829. 2nd edn. 8.5 × 14.5 cm. 198 pp. By Mrs Botsford, Authoress of *Adelaide, Western Elysium* and *Modern Piety*. BL: 11644. c. 52.

BOURKE, Hannah Maria

1   *O'Donoghue, Prince of Killarney; a Poem: In Seven Cantos.* Dublin/London: William Curry, Jr., and Co./Hurst,

Chance and Co., 1830. 10.5 × 17.5 cm. Pp. [ii] + 284. By Hannah Maria Bourke. CUL: Q. 22. 8.

BOURNE, Jane, Mrs (born *c.*1794), *see also* COLLECTIONS 45, 47, 48

Born in Moresby, near Whitehaven, Cumb. She returned from abroad after an absence of about twenty years and visited the north with her children. She describes her husband as having 'professional avocations'. In 1829 and 1830 she contributed to *The Juvenile Keepsake*. (Boyle, *Northern Reminiscences*)

1   *Northern Reminiscences.* Whitehaven: J. Robinson, 1832. 9 × 15 cm. Pp. [ii] + 146 [prose and about 65 pp. of verse distributed through the volume]. By Mrs Bourne, Authoress of *Tales of Instruction and Amusement*, etc., etc. CUL: 1830 5 9.

2   *A Companion to the Noah's Ark, being Conversations between a Mother and her Children, on the Animals Contained in the Ark, Interspersed with Pieces of Poetry and Remarks on Heathen Mythology, Particularly That of the Egyptians.* Swaffham: F. Skill, 1833. 165 pp. By Jane Bourne. *NUC*: Florida. Not seen.

BOUSFIELD, Mrs W. C.

She contributed to *The Iris* in 1830. (Boyle)

1   *Poems on Scriptural Subjects.* 1823. (Stainforth).

BOWDLER, Harriet, Mrs, *see* BOWDLER, Henrietta Maria

BOWDLER, Henrietta Maria, *commonly called* BOWDLER, Mrs Harriet (1754–1830)

A daughter of Thomas Bowdler and Elizabeth Stuart Cotton. She lived with her parents near Bath. Her anonymous *Sermons on the Doctrines and Duties of Christianity* (1801) had its 44th edition in 1836; her novel *Pen Tamar, or the History of an Old Maid* appeared in 1831. *BLC* attributes *Creation* to her. She died of smallpox. (*BLC*, Burney, *DNB*)

1   *Creation, and Other Poems: To Which are Added, the Bowers of Happiness, a Vision, and an Essay on Sacred Poetry.* London/ Chichester: Cadell and Davies, Hatchard/printed by William Mason, 1818. 12 × 19.5 cm. 155 pp. By [H. M. Bowdler?]. BL: 11643. bb. 7.

BOWDLER, Jane (1743–84)

Eldest child of Thomas Bowdler and Elizabeth Stuart Cotton and sister of Henrietta Maria Bowdler (q.v.). She suffered a severe attack of small pox in 1759 and never fully recovered. She was bedridden from 1771 on and in her last years was unable to speak. She lived with her parents near Bath. (*DNB*, Todd 1)

1(*a*)   *Poems and Essays.* Bath: printed by R. Cruttwell [vol. ii also London: C. Dilly], 1786. 11.5 × 18.5 cm. 2 vols. 7/6 sewed. By a Lady Lately Deceased. *MR* 76: 408–10; BL: 12268. b. 17.

1(*b*)   *Poems and Essays.* Bath/London: printed by R. Cruttwell/C. Dilly, 1786. 2nd edn. 11 × 18 cm. 2 vols. 7/- sewed. By a Lady, Lately Deceased. *CR* 63: 204–7; BL: 722. f. 13.

1(*c*)   *Poems and Essays.* Dublin: printed by William M'Kenzie, 1787. 10.5 × 17 cm. Pp. vi + 233. By Miss Boudler [*sic*], Lately Deceased. BL: 1340. c. 9.

1(*d*)   *Poems and Essays.* Bath/London/New Edinburgh: printed by R. Cruttwell/C. Dilley, J. Robson and T. Hookham/ N. R. Cheyne, 1787. 3rd edn. 11 × 18 cm. 2 vols. By the Late Miss Bowdler. BL: 12270. bbb. 12.

1(*e*)   *Poems and Essays.* Bath/London/New Edinburgh: printed by R. Cruttwell/C. Dilly, J. Robson and T. Hookham/ N. R. Cheyne, 1787. 4th edn. 11 × 18 cm. 2 vols. By the Late Miss Bowdler. Edin. Univ.: V* 29. 46–7.

1(*f*)   *Poems and Essays.* Bath/London/New Edinburgh: printed by R. Cruttwell/C. Dilly, J. Robson and T. Hookham/ N. R. Cheyne, 1788. 5th edn. 11 × 17 cm. 2 vols. By the Late Miss Bowdler. BL: 12270. bbb. 13.

1(*g*)   *Poems and Essays.* Bath/London/New Edinburgh: printed by R. Cruttwell/C. Dilly, J. Robson and T. Hookham/ N. R. Cheyne, 1788. 6th edn. 11 × 17.5 cm. 2 vols. By the Late Miss Bowdler. BL: 11631. aaa. 4, 5.

1(*h*)   *Poems and Essays.* Bath/London/Edinburgh: R. Cruttwell/ C. Dilly, J. Robson and T. Hookham/N. R. Cheyne, 1793. 7th edn. 11.5 × 18 cm. Pp. viii + 289. By the Late Miss Bowdler. BL: 1508/951.

1(*i*)   *Poems and Essays.* Bath/Edinburgh: printed by R. Cruttwell/C. Dilly, J. Robson and T. Hookham/N. R.

Cheyne, 1793. 8th edn. 11.5 × 17.5 cm. Pp. [viii] + 289. By the Late Miss Bowdler. BL: 11644. c. 29.

1(*j*)   *Poems and Essays.* Bath/London/Edinburgh: printed by R. Cruttwell/C. Dilly, J. Robson and Hookham/N. R. Cheyne, 1797. 9th edn. 13 × 20.5 cm. Pp. viii + 274. By the Late Miss Bowdler. BL: 12269. d. 5.

1(*k*)   *Poems and Essays . . . Published for the Benefit of the General Hospital at Bath.* Bath/London/Edinburgh: printed by R. Cruttwell/C. Dilly, J. Robson and T. Hookham/N. R. Cheyne, 1798. 10th edn. 22.5 × 28.5 cm. Pp. xii + 232. By the Late Miss Bowdler. Princeton: (Ex) 3635. 722. 1798.

1(*l*)   *Poems and Essays.* Bath/London/Edinburgh: printed by R. Cruttwell/Wilkie and Robinson, and Hatchard/N. R. Cheyne, 1807. 11th edn. 11.5 × 18.5 cm. Pp. xii + 266. By the Late Miss Bowdler. Bodley: 2699 e. 256.

1(*m*)   *Poems and Essays.* Bath/London/Edinburgh: printed by R. Cruttwell/Wilkie and Robinson, and Hatchard/Cheyne, 1809. 12th edn. 11.5 × 19.5 cm. Pp. xiv + 266. By the Late Miss Bowdler. BL: 1560/321.

1(*n*)   *Poems and Essays.* Bath/London/Edinburgh: printed by Richard Cruttwell/Wilkie and Robinson, and Hatchard/Cheyne, 1811. 13th edn. 12 × 19.5 cm. Pp. xii + 273. By the Late Miss Bowdler. BL: 12269. d. 6.

1(*o*)   *Poems and Essays.* New York: printed at the Office of the Economical School, 1811. 1st American edn. from 11th English edn. 12 × 20 cm. Pp. xii + 269 [subscription edition]. By the Late Miss Bowdler. BL: 12273. cc. 7.

1(*p*)   *Poems and Essays.* Dublin: printed by Espy and Cross, 1815. 11th edn. 10 × 17.5 cm. Pp. xii + 228. By the Late Miss Bowdler. Trinity: 161. h. 155.

1(*q*)   *Poems and Essays.* Bath/London/Edinburgh: printed by Richard Cruttwell/John Robinson, and Hatchard/Cheyne, 1815. 14th edn. 12 × 20 cm. Pp. xii + 273. By the Late Miss Bowdler. BL: 12270. pp. 14.

1(*r*)   *Poems and Essays.* Bath/London/Edinburgh: printed by Richard Cruttwell/John Robinson, and Hatchard/Cheyne, 1815. 15th edn. 12.5 × 20.5 cm. Pp. xii + 273. By the Late Miss Bowdler. BL: 12275. f. 2.

1(*s*)   *Poems and Essays.* Bath/London: printed by Richard
         Cruttwell/John Robinson, and Hatchard, 1819. 16th edn.
         12 × 20 cm. Pp. xii + 273. By the Late Miss Bowdler. BL:
         12269. cc. 7.

1(*t*)   *Poems and Essays.* London/Edinburgh: William Baynes and
         Son/H. S. Baynes and Co., 1824. 8.5 × 13.5 cm. Pp. xii +
         176. By the Late Miss Bowdler. BL: 11644. aa. 20.

1(*u*)   *Poems and Essays.* Boston[, Mass.]: Wells and Lilly, 1827.
         From 16th English edn. 12 × 19 cm. 268 pp. By Miss
         Bowdler. Widener: 17412. 8. 7. A.

1(*v*)   *Poems and Essays.* Bath/London: printed by Frederick
         Collier Bakewell/Cadell, Longman and Co., Hatchard,
         1830. 17th edn. 13.5 × 21.5 cm. Pp. xii + 272. By the Late
         Miss Bowdler. BL: 11644. d. 39.

BOWEN, Melesina

The subscription list includes a Mr R. Bowen of Hope Square;
most of her subscribers are from the Bristol area. She is confused by
BLC and other catalogues with Mrs Lewis Bowen (q.v.).

1   *Original Poems, on Various Subjects.* Chepstow/London/
         Bristol/Abergavenny: S. Rogers/B. Crosby and Co./Barry,
         Brown, and Sheppard/Watkins, 1808. 9.5 × 16 cm. 98 pp.
         [subscription edition]. By Miss M. Bowen. BL: 11633.
         b. 7.

BOWEN, Mrs Lewis

Her book reveals that she had at least one son.

1   *Kenilworth Castle; and Other Poems.* Wellington, Salop./
         London: F. Houlston and Son/Scatcherd and Letterman,
         1818. 11.5 × 19 cm. Pp. viii + 111. By Mrs Lewis Bowen.
         BL: 11642. c. 54.

BOWES, Mary Eleanor, Countess of Strathmore (1749–1800)

The daughter of George Bowes, MP, of Durham Co. The family
lived in Gibside. She was an heiress, and her father, who had
taken an active interest in her education, died when she was still
young. In 1767 she married John Lyon, 9th Earl of Strathmore, who
died in 1776. They had five children. In 1777 she married Andrew
Robertson Stoney and they had two children before their divorce in

1789. Her *Confessions of the Countess of Strathmore* (1793) gives a lurid account of her domestic life. (*DNB*)

1   *The Siege of Jerusalem.* London: [privately printed], 1774. 12 × 20 cm. Pp. [ii] + 63. BL: 11633. bbb. 24.

BOWLES, Caroline Anne (1786–1854), *see also* COLLECTIONS 42, 43, 53, 55

Daughter of Captain Charles Bowles of the East India Company service, and of Anne Burrard. She was born at Lymington, Hants, and lived for most of her life at Buckland Cottage, her parents' house near Lymington. On her mother's death she was temporarily in financial distress and wrote to Southey, knowing that he had helped the poet Kirke White, but she was relieved by her foster brother. The correspondence with Southey continued, however, and on the death of his first wife she married him, a few months before the onset of his senility. From 1827 on she contributed to the annuals. (Boyle, *Correspondence of Robert Southey and Caroline Bowles* (1881), *DNB, NCB*)

1(*a*)   *Ellen Fitzarthur: A Metrical Tale, in Five Cantos.* London: Longman, Hurst, Rees, Orme, and Brown, 1820. 13 × 21.5 cm. Pp. viii + 134. 7/6 boards. *MR* 93: 430–3; BL: 992. i. 25(5).

1(*b*)   *Ellen Fitzarthur: A Metrical Tale, in Five Cantos.* London: Longman, Hurst, Rees, Orme, and Brown, 1822. 2nd edn. 9.5 × 16.5 cm. Pp. viii + 160. BL: 11647. ccc. 31.

2   *The Widow's Tale: And Other Poems.* London: Longman, Hurst, Rees, Orme, and Brown, 1822. 10 × 17.5 cm. Pp. [ii] + 222. 6/6 boards. By the Author of *Ellen Fitzarthur*. *MR* 98: 329–32; BL: 11644. f. 21.

3   *Solitary Hours.* Edinburgh/London: William Blackwood/ T. Cadell, 1826. 10 × 16.5 cm. Pp. viii + 236. [Verse and prose.] By the Authoress of *Ellen Fitzarthur* and *The Widow's Tale*. BL: 994. f. 41.

4   *The Cat's Tail: Being the History of Childe Merlin. A Tale.* Edinburgh/London: William Blackwood/T. Cadell, 1831. 10.5 × 17 cm. 31 pp. By the Baroness de Katzleben. BL: T. 1359(12).

5   *Tales of the Factories: Respectfully Inscribed to Mr Sadler.* Edinburgh/London: William Blackwood/T. Cadell, 1833. 11 × 16.5 cm. 85 pp. By the Authoress of *Ellen Fitzarthur*,

> *Widow's Tale, Solitary Hours, Chapters on Churchyards*, etc. BL: T. 1457(1).

BRAND, Barbarina, Lady Dacre, *see* WILMOT, Barbarina

BRAND, Hannah (*fl.* 1792–1821), *see also* COLLECTIONS 52

Born in Norwich, Norfolk, the daughter of John Brand, a tanner. She kept a school in Norwich with her sister Mary until 1792 when she decided to go on the stage. Her tragedy, *Huniades*, was performed at Drury Lane in 1792 with John Kemble as well as herself in the cast. Genest devotes a short chapter to this event. She also performed with Tate Wilkinson's Norwich-based company and he describes her in his *Wandering Patentee*, but her stage career was not in the end a success. She became a governess. (Blain, *DNB*, Genest, Highfill, *NCB*, Todd 1)

1   *Plays, and Poems.* Norwich/London: printed by Beatniffe and Payne/F. and C. Rivington, Elmsley and Bremner, 1798. 12 × 19 cm. Pp. xvi + 424 [subscription edition]. [Verse and prose.] 7/- boards. By Miss Hannah Brand. *CR* 24: 467–8; *MR* 32: 377–81; BL: 841. e. 3.

BRETTELL, Mrs (died *c.*1820)

The author of *Meriden; or Memoirs of Matilda* (1819) and, according to the title-page of *Susan Ashfield*, a former resident of Burslem, Staffs. (*BLC*)

1   *Susan Ashfield, and Other Poems.* London/Burslem: Richard Edwards, and Sherwood, Neely, and Jones/S. Brougham, 1820. 10 × 16 cm. Pp. viii + 101. By the Late Mrs Brettell, of Burslem, Staffordshire. BL: 11641. aa. 6.

BRISTOW, Amelia, Mrs

Her *Emma de Lissau* (1828) had six editions by 1847 and a French translation in 1855. Her *Sophia de Lissau* (2nd edn. 1829) had five editions by 1840. (*BLC*)

1   *The Maniac, a Tale; or, a View of Bethlem Hospital: And the Merits of Women, a Poem from the French: With Poetical Pieces on Various Subjects, Original and Translated.* London: J. Hatchard, 1810. 12 × 18.5 cm. Pp. xvi + 145 [subscription edition]. 10/6 boards. By A. Bristow and [G. M. J. B. Legouvé]. *MR* 63: 211–12; BL: 11646. cc. 38.

2   *The Scrap Book: Containing a Variety of Articles in Prose and Verse. Chiefly Original.* London: R. B. Seeley and

W. Burnside, and L. B. Seeley and Sons, 1833. 6.5 × 10.5 cm. Pp. viii + 115 [of which about 18 are in verse]. By the Author of *Emma and Sophia de Lissau, Elizabeth Allen, The Orphans of Lissau*, &c. HRC Texas: 828. B776s.

BRITTLE, Emilly, *pseudonym, see* APPENDIX 2

BRITTON, Frances

1   *Short and True Sketches on the Conflicts of Life, and Other Subjects*. [n.p.]: printed for the author, 1828. 9 × 16 cm. 16 pp. 6d. By Frances Britton. BL: 11646. aaa. 4.

BROOKE, Charlotte (1740–93)

Born in Rantavan, Co. Cavan, one of the youngest of the twenty-two children of Henry Brooke, the novelist and playwright, and of Catherine Meares. She looked after her father in his old age and was left poor at his death in 1783. She tried to make a living by writing, but in spite of some critical success she remained poor. Her novel, *Emma; or, the Foundling of the Wood* appeared in 1803. (*DNB*, memoir by Seymour in *Reliques* (1816), Todd 1)

1(*a*)   *Reliques of Irish Poetry: Consisting of Heroic Poems, Odes, Elegies, and Songs* . . . Trans. Miss Brooke [includes the original Irish texts]. Dublin: printed by George Bonham, 1789. 22 × 27 cm. Pp. xxviii + 369 [subscription edition]. 16/- boards. BL: 841. m. 27.

1(*b*)   *Reliques of Irish Poetry: Consisting of Heroic Poems, Odes, Elegies, and Songs, Translated into English Verse* . . . Ed. Aaron Crossly Seymour. Dublin: J. Christie, 1816. 12.5 × 21 cm. Pp. cxliv + 464 [subscription edition]. By Miss Brooke. BL: 11595. f. 15.

2   *Bolg an Tsohair: Or, Gaelic Magazine, Containing* . . . *the Famous Fenian Poem, Called the Chase; with a Collection of Choice Irish Songs*. Trans. Miss Brooke. Belfast: printed at the Northern Star Office, 1795. 10 × 15.5 cm. 120 pp. [Verse occupies pp. 73–120.] BL: P. P. 6180. cb.

BROOKE, Frances (1724–89)

Born in Claypole, Lincs. Her parents, the Revd William Moore and his second wife, a Miss Secker, died when she was still a child, and she was brought up with her sister by clerical relations in Lincolnshire. By 1756 she was married to the Revd John Brooke, Rector of Norfolk, and the mother of at least one child. In 1755–6 she edited a weekly, the *Old Maid*, and in 1756 she published her tragedy *Virginia*. Her first novel, *The History of Lady Julia Mandeville*, appeared in 1763. From 1763 to 1768 she lived in Quebec City, where her husband was military chaplain. *The History of Emily Montague* (1769) drew upon her Canadian experience. From 1773 to 1778 she and the actress Mary Ann Yates were co-managers of the Haymarket Opera House. *The Siege of Sinope* was performed at Covent Garden, as were her comic operas, *Rosina* (1783) and *Maria* (1788). (Blain, *DNB*, Todd 1)

1(*a*)   *The Siege of Sinope. A Tragedy. As It is Acted at the Theatre Royal in Covent-Garden.* London: T. Cadell, 1781. 13 × 20.5 cm. Pp. viii + 71. By Mrs Brooke. BL: 161. g. 63.

1(*b*)   *The Siege of Sinope. A Tragedy. As It is Acted at the Theatre-Royal, in Covent-Garden.* Dublin: Sam. Price, Wm. Watson, James Williams, Thom. Wilkinson, Wm. Gilbert, Rich. Moncrieffe, Tho. Walker, Caleb Jenkin, Jn. Beatty, Pat Higly, Robert Burton, and John Exshaw, 1781. 10 × 16.5 cm. Pp. x + 61. By Mrs Brooke. BL: 640. h. 38(7).

BROOKS, Mary Abigail, Mrs John (*c.*1794–1845)

Born in Medford, Mass. She was the daughter of William Gowen, a goldsmith, and of Eleanor Cutter. In 1810 she married John Brooks, the husband of her deceased sister. Her given name was Abigail but she changed it to Mary Abigail in 1819 and she wrote as Maria or Maria del Occidente. As a widow she travelled to Canada, to Cuba, and to Europe. She twice attempted to commit suicide because of an unhappy love affair. She made the acquaintance of Southey who admired *Zophiel* and wrote to Caroline Bowles, 'I do not know of any poet whose diction is so naturally good as Mrs Brooks's'. (Blain, *DAB*, *Correspondence of Robert Southey and Caroline Bowles* (1881))

1   *Judith, Esther, and Other Poems.* Boston[, Mass.]: Cummings and Hilliard, 1820. 8.5 × 14.5 cm. 112 pp. By a Lover of the Fine Arts [Maria]. BL: 11687. a. 36.

2(*a*)   *Zophiel, a Poem.* Boston[, Mass.]: Richardson and Lord, 1825. 8.5 × 14.5 cm. 72 pp. By Mrs Brooks. BL: 11687. a. 14.

2(*b*) *Zóphiël; or, the Bride of Seven*. London: R. J. Kennett, 1833. 10 × 16 cm. Pp. viii + 261. By Maria del Occidente. BL: 994. g. 26.

2(*c*) *Zóphiël; or, the Bride of Seven*. Boston[, Mass.]: Carter and Hendee, 1833. 10 × 15 cm. Pp. viii + 261. By Maria del Occidente. LC: PS 1123. B86Z4. 1833 Office.

2(*d*) *Zóphiël; or, the Bride of Seven*. Boston[, Mass.]: Hilliard, Gray, and Co., 1834. 2nd American edn. 11 × 17 cm. Pp. viii + 255. By Maria del Occidente. LC: PS 1123. B86Z4. 1834 Office.

BROOKS, Mary Elizabeth, Mrs James Gordon

Born in Poughkeepsie, NY, and educated at Troy, NY, at the school run by Miss Willard (q.v.). She married James Gordon Brooks in 1828. She contributed to periodicals under the name 'Norma'. (*DAB* (under J. G. Brooks), May)

1(*a*) *The Rivals of Este, and Other Poems*. New York: printed by J. and J. Harper, 1829. 11.5 × 20 cm. 260 pp. [the contribution of Mary Brooks occupies pp. 13–127]. By James G. Brooks, and Mary E. Brooks. HRC Texas: PS 1123. B85. 1829.

1(*b*) *The Rivals of Este, and Other Poems*. New York/Philadelphia: Collins and Hannay, Collins and Co., G. and C. and H. Carvill/Carey, Lea and Carey, Tower and Hogan, John Grigg, E. Littell, McCarty and Davis, and U. Hunt, 1829. 11 × 18.5 cm. 260 pp. By James G. Brooks and Mary E. Brooks [verse by the latter occupies pp. 11–127]. BL: 11686. c. 32.

BROUGHTON, Eliza

1 *Poems and Fugitive Pieces*. London/Edinburgh: Cadell and Davies/Bell and Bradfute, 1796. 9 × 15 cm. Pp. xii + 172. 6/- boards. By Eliza [Broughton]. *MR* 20: 224; BL: 11646. aaa. 55.

BROWN, Louisa

According to her dedication to *Historical Questions* she was a schoolteacher. It is dated from 9 Brighton Place, New Kent Road, London.

1   *The Heathen Mythology, in Easy and Pleasing Verse; (Divested of its Exceptionable Passages and Immoralities;) and Intended for the Instruction of Young Ladies.* London: printed for the author by J. Bailey, [n.d.]. 10 × 17 cm. 82 pp. 1/6 sewed. By Louisa Brown. BL: 11646. bb. 30.

2   *Historical Questions on the Kings of England, in Verse. Calculated to Fix on the Minds of Children, Some of the Most Striking Events of Each Reign.* London: Darton, Harvey, and Darton, 1813. 11.5 × 14 cm. 33 pp. 1/-. By Louisa Brown, Authoress of *The Mythology in Verse*. UCLA: CBC B812 h 1813.

BROWN, Margaret

1   *Lays of Affection.* Edinburgh/London: Waugh and Innes/ John Hatchard, 1819. 9.5 × 15.5 cm. Pp. vi + 224. 8/- boards. By Margaret Brown. *MR* 92: 438–9; BL: 11645. aa. 29.

BROWNE, Felicia Dorothea, *see* HEMANS, Felicia Dorothea

BROWNE, Mary Ann (1812–44), *see also* COLLECTIONS 42

Born in Maidenhead, Berks. She was a daughter of George Browne, a Liverpool merchant, and of Felicity Wagner, and a sister of Mrs Hemans (q.v.). She was taken to London as a child prodigy and then returned to her family circle in a provincial town in North Wales. She contributed to annuals from 1838 on and she married James Gray in 1842. Mary Russell Mitford says of her that 'Of all poetesses, George Sand herself not excepted, she seems to me to touch with the sweetest, the firmest, the most delicate hand, the difficult chords of female passion'. (Boyle, *DNB* (under Mrs Hemans), Mitford, *Recollections of a Literary Life* (1853))

1   *Mont Blanc, and Other Poems.* London: Hatchard and Son, Seeley, W. Benning, 1827. 13 × 22 cm. Pp. xii + 177. By Mary Ann Browne, in her fifteenth year. BL: 1164. l. 22.

2(a)   *Ada, and Other Poems.* London: Longman, Rees, Orme, Brown, and Green, Hatchard and Son, W. Benning, 1828. 11.5 × 18.5 cm. Pp. vi + ii + 277. By Mary Ann Browne, Authoress of *Mont Blanc*, &c. &c. HRC Texas: An. G7935 a. 1828.

2(*b*)   *Ada, and Other Poems*. London: Longman, Rees, Orme, Brown, and Green, Hatchard and Son, W. Benning, 1828. 2nd edn. 11.5 × 19.5 cm. Pp. viii + 277. By Mary Ann Browne. BL: 994. h. 5.

2(*c*)   *Ada, and Other Poems*. London: Longman, Rees, Orme, Brown, and Green, Hatchard and Son, W. Benning, 1828. 3rd edn. 11.5 × 19 cm. Pp. viii + 277. By Mary Ann Browne. BL: 11645. bb. 13.

3   *Repentance; and Other Poems*. London: Longman and Co., Hatchard and Son, Saunders and Benning, 1829. 12 × 19 cm. Pp. viii + 118. By Mary Ann Browne. BL: 994. h. 6.

4(*a*)   *The Coronal; Original Poems, Sacred and Miscellaneous*. London/Liverpool: Hamilton, Adams and Co./D. Marples, 1833. 8 × 12.5 cm. Pp. viii + 183. By Mary Ann Browne. BL: 1066. a. 2.

4(*b*)   *The Coronal; Original Poems, Sacred and Miscellaneous*. London/Liverpool: Hamilton, Adams and Co./D. Marples and Co., 1835. 2nd edn. 7.5 × 11 cm. Pp. viii + 199. By Mary Ann Browne. BL: 11644. aa. 28.

5   *The Birth-day Gift*. London/Liverpool: Hamilton, Adams and Co./D. Marples and Co., 1834. 8 × 12.5 cm. Pp. iv + 183. By Mary Ann Browne. BL: 1066. a. 3.

BROWNING, Elizabeth, *see* BARRETT, Elizabeth

BRYAN, Mary, Mrs Edward

She came from Sedgemoor, Som., and in 1815 was a widow with six children. Her husband had been a Bristol printer and bookseller. (Blain)

1   *Sonnets and Metrical Tales*. Bristol: City Printing Office, 1815. 13 × 21 cm. Pp. xviii + 141. By Mrs Bryan. BL: 992. i. 13(4).

BRYTON, Anne

1   *Richmond, a Pastoral*. London: printed for the author by W. Franklin, [1780?]. 16.5 × 20.5 cm. Pp. [ii] + 16. By Anne Bryton. BL: 840. h. 19.

BULLEN, Sarah

Apparently the daughter of an inn-keeper in Cambridge. (Cambridge L. Cat.)

1   *Mary de Rochford; or, the Banks of Cam. A Poem.* London: Richard Priestley, 1821. 14 × 22.5 cm. Pp. [ii] + 128. By [the Inn-keeper's Daughter]. CUL: Cam. c. 821. 20.

BULMER, Agnes, Mrs (1775–1836)

Born in London and a member of the Wesleyan community to which she was admitted by Wesley himself. Her surname, before she married, was Collinson. She also wrote *Memoirs of Mrs Elizabeth Mortimer* (1836). (*BLC, DNB*)

1   *Thoughts on a Future State, Occasione[d by the D]eath of Mrs Hester An[n] Rogers . . . Also, an Elegy on the Same Occasion . . .* [title-page damaged]. Birmingham: printed by J. Belcher, 1795. 11 × 18 cm. 12 pp. 1*d.* By a Young Lady, Who Met in her Class and Another Lady [Agnes Bulmer] Who Enjoyed the Same Privilege of her Maternal Instructions in the Way to Glory. BL: 10347. e. 32(5).

2(*a*)   *Messiah's Kingdom. A Poem. In Twelve Books.* London: J. G. and F. Rivington, 1833. 10.5 × 16.5 cm. Pp. xvi + 486. By Agnes Bulmer. BL: 994. b. 5.

2(*b*)   *Messiah's Kingdom. A Poem. In Twelve Books.* New York: for the Methodist Episcopal Church by B. Waugh and T. Mason, 1833. 9 × 14.5 cm. 364 pp. By Agnes Bulmer. LC: PS 1199. B4 M4 1833.

BULWER, Elizabeth Barbara, Mrs William Earle (*c.*1782–1843)

The only child of Richard Warburton Lytton, of Knebworth, Herts., and of a Miss Joddrell. Her parents separated shortly after she was born and she lived with her father, who was an eccentric but eminent classical scholar. She married Colonel (later General) William Earle Bulwer of the Norfolk Rangers in 1798. They had three sons, one of them the novelist Bulwer Lytton. She was widowed in 1807. (*DNB* (under Bulwer Lytton))

1   *The Abbey de la Trappe. A Poem.* London: 'not published', 1826. 16 × 21.5 cm. Pp. [ii] + 67. By [Eliz. B. B. L.]. CUL: Syn. 5. 82. 59.

BURDER, Sophia Maria (1796?–1823?: *Memoir* (1833))

1   *Poetical Efforts . . . Intended Chiefly for Private Circulation.* Ed.
     [G.B., i.e. George Burder]. London: Westley and Davis,
     1826. 10.5 × 17 cm. Pp. v + 67. By Sophia Maria Burder.
     BL: 11641. de. 14(2).

BURGESS, Miss, *see* COLLECTIONS 1(*a–c*), *and, perhaps,* BURGESS,
Elizabeth

BURGESS, Elizabeth
Probably from Canterbury.

1(*a*) *Life and History of Betty Bolaine, (Late of Canterbury,) a Well
       Known Character for Parsimony and Vice, Scarcely Equalled in
       the Annals of Avarice and Depravity. Interspersed with Original
       Poetry.* Canterbury/London: for the author by J. Saffery/
       Tipper and Richards, Lane, Newman, and Co., H. D.
       Symonds, 1805. 10.5 × 16 cm. 67 pp. [about 24 pp. of
       verse interspersed]. 1/6. BL: 615. b. 28(3).

1(*b*) *Life and History of Betty Bolaine, (Late of Canterbury,) a Well
       Known Character for Parsimony and Vice, Scarcely Equalled in
       the Annals of Avarice and Depravity; Interspersed with Original
       Poetry.* Canterbury: Henry Ward, 1832. 2nd edn. 14 × 22
       cm. 40 pp. BL: 1414. f. 43(3).

BURNEY, Frances (1776–1828)
Daughter of Charles Rousseau Burney, a music teacher in Bath, and of
Esther Burney, and the niece of Mme D'Arblay. She was employed as
a governess. (Burney, R. Brimley Johnson, *Fanny Burney and the Burneys*
(1826))

1   *Tragic Dramas; Chiefly Intended for Representation in Private
     Families: To Which is Added, Aristodemus, a Tragedy, from the
     Italian of Vincenzo Monti.* London: for the author by J.
     Murray, 1818. 12.5 × 20 cm. Pp. xviii + 191. 9/6 boards.
     By Frances Burney. *MR* 91: 99–100; BL: 841. h. 4.

BURRELL, Sophia, Lady (1750–1802), *see also* COLLECTIONS 12(*b–k*)
The elder daughter of Sir Charles Raymond, Bart., and of Sarah Webster.
She married William Burrell, an advocate and MP with antiquarian
interests, and they had seven children. She was independently wealthy.

A year after her husband's death in 1791 she married her son's tutor, the Revd William Clay. (Burney, Todd 1)

1   *Poems. Dedicated to the Right Honourable the Earl of Mansfield* [title-page of vol. ii omits dedication]. London: Leigh and Sotheby, T. Payne, and J. Robson, 1793. 12.5 × 21 cm. 2 vols. 12/- boards. By Lady Burrell [vol. i omits authorship]. *MR* 11: 445–9; *CR* 10: 46–9; BL: 11642. e. 23.

2   *Telemachus.* London: Leigh and Sotheby, T. Payne, and J. Robson, 1794. 13 × 20.5 cm. Pp. [ii] + 78. 4/- boards. By Lady Burrell, [after Fénelon]. *MR* 16: 37–8; BL: 11642. e. 36(2).

3   *The Thymbriad, (from Xenophon's Cyropoedia.)* London: Leigh and Sotheby, T. Payne, and J. Robson, 1794. 12.5 × 20.5 cm. Pp. [ii] + 154. 4/- or 6/- boards. By Lady Burrell. *CR* 18: 177–9; *MR* 16: 37–8; BL: 11632. f. 9.

4   *Maximian; a Tragedy: Taken from Corneille, and Dedicated to William Lock, Esq.* London: Leigh and Sotheby, 1800. 13.5 × 21.5 cm. Pp. [iv] + 98. 3/6 sewed. *MR* 33: 221–2; BL: 164. g. 53.

5(a)   *Theodora; or, the Spanish Daughter: A Tragedy. Dedicated (by Permission) to Her Grace Georgiana, Duchess of Devonshire.* London: Leigh and Sotheby, 1800. 13.5 × 22 cm. Pp. viii [iv] + 100. 3/6 sewed. *MR* 33: 220–1; BL: 164. i. 19.

5(b)   *The New British Theatre; a Selection of Original Dramas, Not Yet Acted; Some of Which have been Offered for Representation but Not Accepted* . . . Ed. [John Galt]. London/Edinburgh/Dublin: Henry Colburn/G. Goldie/J. Cumming, 1814. 13 × 21 cm. Vol. i ['Theodora; a Tragedy' occupies pp. 277–338]. *NUC*; BL: 642. i. 1.

6   *The New British Theatre* . . . London/Edinburgh/Dublin: Henry Colburn/G. Goldie/J. Cumming, 1814. 12 × 21 cm. Vol. ii ['Villario; a Play, in Five Acts' occupies pp. 137–90]. BL: 642. i. 2.

BURTON, Harriet Emma

She seems to have visited the West Indies as a child and she also writes nostalgically of home from France, mentioning Mapledurham woods and Caversham Church. Her dedication to Queen Adelaide and several poems to or about members of the royal family suggest that she had been a member of the court. Bodley L. Cat. attributes the anonymous *Lindah; or, the Festival* (1845) to her. (*The White-Rose Wreath*)

1   *The White-Rose Wreath. With Other Poems. Dedicated, by Permission, to the Queen.* London: J. Hatchard and Son, 1833. 10 × 16 cm. 126 pp. Davis: Kohler I 83–183.

BURTON, Margaret, Mrs (1785–1830)

Her maiden name was Dunn. (John Dungett, *Life and Correspondence* (1832))

1   *Poetical Effusions on Subjects Religious, Moral, and Rural.* London/York/Hull/Leeds/Newcastle upon Tyne/Darlington: for the author by Butterworth and Son, Gale and Fenner, and Blanchard/Wilson and Son, and R. Spence/J. Craggs/Baynes/Clarke and Son/by the author, 1816. 10 × 16.5 cm. Pp. xvi + 9–149. 5/-, in extra boards. By Margaret Burton of Darlington. BL: 11642. aaa. 6.

BURY, Catherine Maria, Countess of Charleville (1762–1851), *see also* COLLECTIONS 41

She was the daughter of Thomas Townley Dawson, of Kinsaley, Co. Dublin, and of Joanna Saunders. She was educated in a French convent and married James Tisdall, of Bawn, Co. Louth. After his death she married in 1798 Charles William Bury, Viscount Charleville (later Earl of Charleville). They had at least one child. Lady Sarah Lennox said of her, 'Her manners were Irish, and not exactly the sort that pleased me, but after many years' acquaintance, the excellence of her heart, her sense, her wit, and friendship, has completely attached me to her.' (*CB, Complete Peerage*)

1   *La Pucelle; or, the Maid of Orleans: A Poem, in XXI Cantos.* Trans. [C. M. Bury]. Vol. i [of 2]. [Private], 1796. 15 × 23 cm. [one of 12 large paper copies]. 227 pp. By Voltaire. BL: 11474. h. 32.

2   *La Pucelle; or, the Maid of Orleans: A Poem, in XXI Cantos.* Trans. [C. M. Bury]. Vol. ii [of 2]. [Private], 1797. 15 × 23 cm. 218 pp. By Voltaire. BL: 11474. h. 32.

3   *The Henriade, an Epic Poem, in Ten Cantos.* Trans. [C. M. Bury]. London: printed by Burton and Co., 1797. 22 × 28

cm. Pp. viii + 224 [subscription edition]. 10/6 sewed. By Voltaire. *MR* 23: 167–70; *CR* 22: 407–9; BL: 640. l. 5.

BURY, Charlotte, Mrs Edward John, *see* CAMPBELL, Lady Charlotte Susan Maria

BUTLER, Ann

She lived in Benson, Oxon.

1   *Fragments in Verse Chiefly on Religious Subjects.* Oxford: Bartlett and Hinton, 1826. 10.5 × 18 cm. Pp. [xii] + 155 [subscription edition]. By Ann Butler. BL: 1164. i. 11.

BUTLER, Harriette

1   *Lays of the Heart.* Manchester: J. Gleave, 1833. 12 × 18.5 cm. 104 pp. By Harriette Butler. BL: 11646. cc. 40.

BYRNE, Mary (born *c.*1771: O'D)

1   *The Blind Poet.* Dublin, 1789. 8vo. 24 pp. 3/3. O'D. Not located.

C——, Countess of, *see* COLLECTIONS 13

C——, Lady, *see* APPENDIX 3

C***, Miss, *see* COLLECTIONS 16(*a*)

C., E., *see* COCKLE, Mary

C., M. A., *see* CURSHAM, Mary Anne

CALCOTT, Berkeley (born *c.*1823)

1   *Stanzas.* Dublin: printed by George Folds, 1834. 11.5 × 18 cm. 16 pp. By Miss Berkeley Calcott, Eleven Years of Age. BL: 11641. c. 10.

CAMPBELL, Ann

1   *A Wreath of Poesy; or Effusions or the Heart.* London: printed for the author by R. Weston, 1828. 10.5 × 17.5 cm. Pp. vi + 88. By Ann Campbell. BL: 11646. bb. 39.

CAMPBELL, Lady Charlotte Susan Maria (1775–1861), *see also* COLLECTIONS 41

Born in London, the youngest child of John Campbell, 5th Duke of Argyll, and of Elizabeth Gunning. She spent her early life in France and Italy with her mother, who was an invalid. She was presented at court in 1790. She married her cousin, Colonel Jack Campbell, MP, in 1796 and they had nine children. After his death in 1809 she was appointed lady-in-waiting to Princess Caroline, whose service she left in 1815. In 1818 she married the Revd Edward John Bury, her eldest son's tutor. He died in 1832 leaving her with two more children. She wrote a number of romantic novels for which she is said to have been paid £200 each, but she is best known for her anonymous *Diary Illustrative of the Times of George IV* (1838). (Todd 1)

1   *Poems on Several Occasions.* Edinburgh, 1797. 12 × 19.5 cm. 48 pp. By a Lady. BL: 11633. e. 24.

2   *The Three Great Sanctuaries of Tuscany, Valombrosa, Camaldoli, Laverna: A Poem, with Historical and Legendary Notices.* London: John Murray, 1833. 36 × 26.5 cm. Pp. xiv + 139 [subscription edition]. By the Right Honourable Lady Charlotte Bury. BL: 1899. c. 73.

CAMPBELL, Dorothea Primrose (*c.*1794–1863)

She came from the Shetland Isles. Her father was Duncan Campbell and her mother Eliza (or Betty). The family was encumbered with a grandfather's debt. She set up a school for girls in Lerwick. She met Walter Scott on his journey to the northern islands and dedicated her book to him. Her novel, *Harley Radington*, appeared in 1821. She moved to London in 1842, and died in an asylum for aged governesses there. (Allibone, Blain, *NUC, Poems*)

1(*a*)   *Poems.* Inverness: for the authoress by J. Young, 1811. 9.5 × 16.5 cm. 198 pp. By D. P. Campbell. BL: 11641. aa. 9.

1(*b*)   *Poems.* London: for the authoress by Baldwin, Cradock and Joy, 1816. 12 × 20 cm. Pp. iv + 228 [subscription edition]. 10/6 boards. By Miss D. P. Campbell, of Zetland. *MR* 83: 95–6; BL: 11645. bbb. 41.

CANDLER, Ann, Mrs (1740–1814)

Born in Yoxford, Suffolk. Her father, William More, was a glover. Her mother, a Miss Holder, died when Ann was about 11. In 1762 she married and moved to Sproughton, near Ipswich. She was deserted by her

husband and reduced to the workhouse with four of their nine children. She spent twenty years there. She published poems in the *Ipswich
Journal.* (Blain, *DNB, Poetical Attempts,* Todd 1)

1   *Poetical Attempts, . . . with a Short Narrative of her Life.* Ed.
[anon.]. Ipswich/London: John Raw/T. Hurst, 1803. 9 ×
15 cm. Pp. xiv + 68 [subscription edition]. By Ann
Candler, a Suffolk Cottager. BL: 11632. aa. 11.

CANNON, M. Maria
She lived in Hungerford, Berks.

1(*a*)   *Maria and St. Flos, a Poem, in a Series of Letters: To Which
is Added, a Search after Happiness.* Newbury/Trowbridge/
Frome/Hungerford: M. P. Price/Sweet/Penny/ Lye, 1824.
13.5 × 22 cm. Pp. x + 64 [subscription edition]. By M.
Maria Cannon. Bodley: 280 d. 285.

1(*b*)   *Maria and St. Flos, a Poem, in a Series of Letters: To Which is
Added, a Search after Happiness.* London: Wm. Charlton
Wright and John Hatchard and Son, 1825. 13.5 × 22 cm.
Pp. viii + 64 [subscription edition]. By M. Maria Cannon.
BL: 1164. k. 4.

CAPP, Mary Elizabeth

1   *The African Princess, and Other Poems.* Yarmouth/London:
printed by J. Keymer/Longman, Hurst, Rees, Orme, and
Browne, 1813. 13.5 × 22 cm. Pp. [vi] + 188. By Mary
Elizabeth Capp. BL: 11642. f. 18.

CAPPER, Louisa
She wrote an abridgement of Locke's *Essay Concerning Human
Understanding.* (Allibone)

1(*a*)   *A Poetical History of England; Written for the Use of the Young
Ladies Educated at Rothbury-House School, and Dedicated to
Them by the Author.* London: for the author by C. Law,
1810. 13.5 × 21 cm. Pp. viii + 156. HL; BL: 11642. cc. 23.

1(*b*)   *A Poetical History of England; Written for the Use of the Young
Ladies Educated at Rothbury-House School and Dedicated to
Them by the Author.* London: for the author by Law and
Whittaker, 1815. 12.5 × 21.5 cm. Pp. viii + 156. Edin.
Univ.: 5. 20. 33/6.

CAREY, Elizabeth Sheridan, *see* COLLECTIONS 39

CARMICHAEL, Rebekah
She later married a Mr Hay.

1   *Poems.* Edinburgh: for the author by Peter Hill, 1790. 13.5
    × 21.5 cm. Pp. xii + 92. By Miss Carmichael. BL: 1466. g.
    61(2).

CARNES, Hannah

1   *The Widow's Cottage, and Other Pathetic Poems, Designed for the
    Improvement of Youth.* Gloucester: printed by William
    Verrinder, 1829. 11 × 18.5 cm. 36 pp. By Hannah Carnes.
    BL: 11646. cc. 34.

CARR, Jane

1   *Original Hymns for Sunday Schools.* Derby: printed by Henry
    Mozley, [1818]. 6.5 × 10 cm. [41 pp.]. 2*d*. By Jane Carr,
    Author of *Tasks for Sunday Scholars.* BL: 1111. a. 17.

2   *Tasks for Sunday Scholars, to be Committed to the Memory during
    the Week.* Derby: H. Mozley, [1820?]. 6.5 × 10 cm. 47 pp.
    [prose and verse]. 2*d*. By ['Composed and Selected'] Jane
    Carr, Author of *Original Hymns for Sunday Schools,* etc. etc.
    CUL: 1820 4 2.

CARROLL, Frances, *see* O'NEILL, Frances

CARSTAIRS, Christian
Daughter of James Bruce Carstairs of Kinross and said to have been a
governess. Her curious prose burlesque, *The Hubble-shue,* may be usefully
compared with Blake's *Island in the Moon.* The Bodley copy of *Original
Poems* is ascribed by the catalogue to Charlotte Carstairs, a name that
does appear in the subscription list. The book is dedicated to Margaret,
Countess of Moray, and is subscribed to by half a dozen countesses.
(Bodley L. Cat., information in Folger copy, Lonsdale)

1   *Original Poems. By a Lady, Dedicated to Miss Ann Henderson.
    A Tribute to Gratitude and Friendship.* Edinburgh, 1786. 15.5
    × 20 cm. 8 + 72 pp. [issued, apparently, as eight separate
    'numbers', the first five with half-titles that describe the

author as 'the Author of *The Hubble-shue*'; subscription edition]. By a Lady. Folger: PR 3339/C33/H8/Cage.

CARTER, Elizabeth (1717–1806), *see also* COLLECTIONS 10(*b*), 11(*b*), 12(*a–k*), 17, 19, 20, 23(*a–b*), 25(*a–c*), 31, 52 *and* FENN, Lady Eleanor

Born in Deal, Kent. She was the eldest daughter of the Revd Nicholas Carter, DD, and of Margaret Swayne. Her mother died when Elizabeth was about 11, but her father gave her a classical education. She became a notable linguist, began contributing to the *Gentleman's Magazine* in 1734, and was the most learned of the bluestockings. She was a friend of Samuel Johnson, contributed to the *Rambler*, translated Epictetus, and wrote on popular science. (*CB, DNB,* Todd 2)

1   *Twelve Poems Translated into French; Six in Prose and Six in Verse, Selected from the Works . . . Intitled Poems on Several Occasions.* Trans. Count de B****. London: Mrs Lowes, J. Reed, Dulau, 1796. 10.5 × 17.5 cm. Pp. viii + 65 [the French and English texts, including the title-page, on facing pages]. 4/- on fine paper, 2/6 common. By Eliza Carter. BL: 1164. e. 24.

2(*a*)   *Memoirs of the Life of Mrs Elizabeth Carter, with a New Edition of her Poems, Some of Which have never Appeared before; to Which are Added, Some Miscellaneous Essays in Prose, together with her Notes on the Bible, and Answers to Objections concerning the Christian Religion.* Ed. Montagu Pennington. London: F. C. and J. Rivington, 1807. 20.5 × 27 cm. Pp. [vi] + 643 [the poetry occupies pp. 341–643]. £2/2/- boards. By Montagu Pennington [and Elizabeth Carter]. *CR* 12: 138–46; *MR* 56: 225–40; CUL: 8720. b. 14.

2(*b*)   *Memoirs of the Life of Mrs Elizabeth Carter, with a New Edition of her Poems . . .* London: F. C. and J. Rivington, 1808. 2nd edn. 12.5 × 20.5 cm. 2 vols. [the poems occupy pp. 1–120 of vol. ii]. By Montagu Pennington [and Elizabeth Carter]. BL: 613. e. 19.

2(*c*)   *Memoirs of the Life of Mrs Elizabeth Carter, with a New Edition of her Poems; to Which are Added, Some Miscellaneous Essays in Prose, together with her Notes on the Bible . . .* Ed. Montagu Pennington. London: F. C. and J. Rivington, 1816. 3rd edn. 13 × 21.5 cm. 2 vols. [the poems occupy pp. 1–120 of vol. ii]. By Montagu Pennington [and Elizabeth Carter]. CUL: D. 30. 40.

2(*d*)   *Memoirs of the Life of Mrs Elizabeth Carter, with a New Edition of her Poems* . . . London, 1825. 4th edn. 8vo. 2 vols. *NUC.* Not seen.

[*See also*: 'The Evening Walk' [1802], 2 pp. in *Religions* (1802).]

CARTWRIGHT, Frances Dorothy (1780–1863)

Born in Goadby Marwood, Leics. She was the youngest daughter of Edmund Cartwright, DD, and of his first wife Alice. She was adopted in infancy by her uncle, Major John Cartwright, the political reformer, and his wife Anne Katharina Dashwood. She attended school in Richmond, Yorks., and became interested in Spanish literature through meeting the Spanish patriots who visited her uncle. Her *Life and Correspondence of Major Cartwright* appeared in 1826. (Boase, *DNB*)

1   *Poems, Chiefly Devotional.* London: printed by G. Woodfall, 1835. 10 × 16 cm. 55 pp. By [F. D. C.]. BL: 1164. e. 28.

CASELLI, Elizabeth, Mrs (died *c.*1830)

Lived in Plymouth, Devon, and later in Falmouth. An acrostic in her *Poems* reveals that her maiden name was Richards. (Boase and Courtney, *Poems*)

1   *Poems on Religious & Moral Subjects.* Falmouth: James Trathan, the author, and all the booksellers, 1818. 9.5 × 17 cm. 48 pp. By Elizabeth Caselli, Falmouth. BL: 11642. aa. 33.

CASSAN, Sarah, Mrs Stephen

Daughter of Charles Mears. As the title-page of her *Poems* reveals, she was the widow of Stephen Cassan, a barrister who seems to have practised in Bengal. They had at least one child.

1   *Poems.* London: printed by G. Sidney, 1806. 20 × 25.5 cm. Pp. vi + 96. By Mrs Cassan, Widow of Stephen Cassan, Esq. Barrister at Law, Late of Bengal. BL: 840. i. 23.

CAULFEILD, Frances Sally, Mrs Edwin Toby

Her *The Deluge, a Poem* appeared in 1837.

1   *The Innocents; a Sacred Drama. Ocean; and the Earthquake at Aleppo; Poems.* Bath/London: S. Simms/Hurst, Robinson

and Co., and Baldwin, Cradock, and Joy, 1824. 11 × 19 cm. 63 pp. BL: 11644. cc. 13.

CAVE, Jane, *see* WINSCOM, Jane

CAVENDISH, Georgiana, Duchess of Devonshire (1757–1806), *see also* COLLECTIONS 16(*a–b*), 35

Daughter of John Spencer, 1st Earl Spencer, and of Margaret Georgiana Poyntz. In 1774 she married the 5th Duke of Devonshire and they had one son. She was the most famous society woman of her time, noted for her intelligence, her cultural interests, and her political activity in the Foxite interest. She was acquainted with Samuel Johnson and Mme D'Arblay, both of whom left comments on her, and she was painted by Reynolds and Gainsborough. Her poem 'on the passage over Mount Gothard' prompted Coleridge's 'Ode to Georgiana, Duchess of Devonshire'. HEHL has the MSS of two plays and a novel by her. (*DNB*, HEHL L. Cat.)

1(*a*)   *The Passage of Mount St. Gothard . . . To Which are Added, The Chevalier's Lament . . .* Glasgow: Stewart and Meikle, [n.d.]. 9 × 15.5 cm. 16 pp. ['The Passage' occupies pp. 2–6 only]. By the Dutchess of Devonshire and others. NLS: 42/581.

1(*b*)   *Dithyrambe sur l'immortalité de l'âme, suivi du passage du St.-Gothard . . .* Trans. Jacques Delille. Paris/London: Giguet and Michaud/Prosper and Co., 1082 [1802]. 13.5 × 21 cm. 115 pp. By Jacques Delille and [the Duchess of Devonshire]. BL: 11484. bb. 20(1).

1(*c*)   *Dithyrambe sur l'immortalité de l'âme, suivi du passage du St.-Gothard . . .* Trans. Jacques Delille. Paris/London: Giguet and Michaud/Prosper and Co., 1082 [1802]. [2nd issue]. 14 × 21.5 cm. 115 pp. By Jacques Delille and [the Duchess of Devonshire]. BL: 11474. g. 7.

1(*d*)   *Dithyrambe sur l'immortalité de l'âme, suivi du passage du St.-Gothard . . .* Trans. Jacques Delille. Paris/London: Giguet and Michaud/Prosper and Co., 1802. 11 × 18.5 cm. 125 pp. [the 'passage' and its accompanying matter occupy pp. 58–125]. By Jacques Delille and [the Duchess of Devonshire]. BL: 1164. l. 6.

1(*e*)   *The Passage of the Mountain of Saint Gothard, a Poem.* [Trans. Abbé De Lille]. London: Prosper and Co., 1802. 21 × 26.5

cm. Pp. vii + 44 [English and French texts, title-pages included, on facing pages]. By Georgiana, Duchess of Devonshire. BL: 1346. i. 8.

1(*f*)   *The Passage of the Mountain of Saint Gothard, a Poem.* Trans. L'Abbé de Lille. London: Prosper and Co., 1802. 12 × 19 cm. Pp. vii + 52 [English and French texts, including title-pages, on facing pages]. By Georgiana, Duchess of Devonshire. BL: 1161. g. 40.

1(*g*)   *The Passage of the Saint Gothard.* Trans. [into Italian on facing pages] G. Polidori. London: Gameau and Co., 1803. 33 × 50 cm. Pp. viii + 43. By Georgiana Duchess of Devonshire. BL: C. 5. e. 7.

1(*h*)   *L'allegro . . . ed il tragitto di san gotardo . . .* Trans. Gaetano Polidori. London: Didier and Tebbet, 1805. 10 × 16.5 cm. 54 pp. By Milton and the Duchess of Devonshire. BL: 11626. b. 38.

1(*i*)   *The Passage of the Mountain of Saint Gothard.* Trans. [Abbé de Lille]. Paris, 1816. 22.5 × 30 cm. 74 pp. [of which pp. 35–74 are unnumbered and are occupied, on one side only, by illustrations. The entire text is engraved rather than type-set and the French and English versions are on facing pages]. By Elizabeth, Duchess of Devonshire. CUL: S. 721. b. 81. 2.

1(*j*)   *Scizze einer mahlerischen Reise durch die Schweiz . . .* Trans. Bern: J. J. Bürgdorfer, 1816. 13 × 21.5 cm. Pp. [vi] + 154 ['The Passage of the Saint Gothard', in German, occupies pp. 74–8]. By [Rowley Lascelles?], [the Duchess of Devonshire], and an unknown translator. BL: 10195. cc. 9.

1(*k*)   *Sketch of a Descriptive Journey through Switzerland to Which is Added the Passage of S. Gotthard a Poem.* Berne: J. J. Bürgdorfer, 1816. 13 × 20.5 cm. Pp. iv + 92 [the poem occupies pp. 79–85]. By [Rowley Lascelles?] and the Duchess of Devonshire. HEHL: 314995.

CAVENDISH, Margaret, Duchess of Newcastle (1623–73), *see also* COLLECTIONS 21

Born in Colchester, Essex. She was the daughter of Sir Thomas Lucas and Elizabeth Leighton. She was one of Queen Henrietta Maria's maids of honour at Oxford and she accompanied the queen into exile in Paris. In 1645 she married William Cavendish, Marquis (later Duke) of Newcastle. She was noted for her social eccentricity ('Mad Madge of Newcastle') and for her ambitious but unconventional learning. She wrote a biography of her husband (1667) and several scientific and philosophical books. Her *Playes* (1662) are less well regarded. Sir Egerton Brydges published her autobiography (*A True Relation*) in 1814. (*Complete Peerage, DNB*, Schlueter)

1   *Select Poems.* Ed. Sir Egerton Brydges. Lee Priory: private, 1813. 14 × 23 cm. Pp. [iv] + 20. By Margaret Cavendish, Duchess of Newcastle. BL: 1087. k. 13(1).

CELESIA, Dorothea, Mrs Pietro Paulo (1738–90)

Daughter of the poet and playwright David Mallet and of his first wife Susanna. She married Pietro Paulo Celesia, the Genoese ambassador, and in 1759 accompanied him to Genoa where she remained, apart from a brief visit to Spain in 1784. They had two children. *Almida* was successfully produced by Garrick at Drury Lane in 1771 with Mrs Barry in the title role. (*CB, DNB*)

1(*a*)   *Almida, a Tragedy, as It is Performed at the Theatre Royal in Drury-Lane.* London: T. Becket and Co., 1771. 12 × 19.5 cm. Pp. [viii] + 68. 1/6. By a Lady [after Voltaire]. BL: 11777. f. 8.

1(*b*)   *Almida, a Tragedy. As It is Performed at the Theatre Royal, in Drury-Lane.* Dublin: W. Wilson, J. Exshaw, H. Saunders, H. Bradley, W. Sleater, D. Chamberlaine, J. Potts, J. Williams, W. Colles, R. Moncriefe, and T. Walker, 1771. 9.5 × 17 cm. 59 pp. By a Lady [after Voltaire]. National Library of Ireland: J. 842.

1(*c*)   *Almida, a Tragedy, as It is Performed at the Theatre Royal in Drury-Lane.* London: T. Becket and Co., 1771. New edn. 12 × 20 cm. Pp. [iv] + 68. By a Lady [after Voltaire]. NLS: H. 28. c. 21(5).

2   *Indolence: A Poem.* London: T. Becket, 1772. 20.5 × 25 cm. 23 pp. 1/-. By the Author of *Almida*. MR 46: 454; BL: 840. l. 11(2).

CHADWICK, Frances, Mrs John

Her maiden name was Dromgoole and she came from Lowth. She married John Chadwick and they lived in Drogheda. They had three children, one of whom was Bishop James Chadwick. (Boase, *A Literary and Biographical History . . . of English Catholics*)

1   *Rural and Other Poems.* London/Ludlow: Longman, Rees, Orme, Brown and Green/Procter and Jones, 1828. 13 × 22 cm. Pp. [ii] + 178. By Mrs Chadwick. BL: 994. i. 8.

CHALMERS, Margaret (born 1758)

She was the daughter of William Chalmers, a customs officer and steward, and of Kitty Irvine. She lived in Lerwick in the Shetland Islands. The death of her brother at Trafalgar left the family destitute. (Blain)

1   *Poems.* Newcastle: printed by S. Hodgson, 1813. 13.5 × 21.5 cm. Pp. viii + 160 [subscription edition]. By Margaret Chalmers, Lerwick, Zetland. BL: 1346. g. 16.

CHAMPION DE CRESPIGNY, Lady Mary, *see* DE CRESPIGNY, Lady Mary Champion

CHANTRELL, Mary Ann

According to her title-page, she lived in Newington Butts, London.

1   *Poems, on Various Subjects.* London: for the author by Boucher and W. Simmons, 1798. 13.5 × 21.5 cm. Pp. viii + 116 [subscription edition]. 2/6 bound. By Mary Ann Chantrell, of Newington Butts. *MR* 27: 347–8; BL: 11632. e. 13.

CHAPMAN, Jane

The title-page of *Miscellaneous Poems* identifies her as daughter of the late Dr Kirkland. He was a well-known medical writer. They both lived in Ashby de la Zouch, Leics. (*DNB* (under Thomas Kirkland))

1   *Miscellaneous Poems . . . Dedicated (by Permission) to the Right Honorable Lady Charlotte Rawdon.* Derby: printed by G. Wilkins, 1802. 17 × 22.5 cm. 44 pp. [subscription edition]. By Jane Chapman, Daughter of the Late Doctor Kirkland. Bodley: 280 d. 800.

2   *Elegies on the Deaths of Several of her Valuable Friends, (Affectionately Inscribed to their Memory,) &c., &c.* Burton-upon-Trent: printed [for the author?] by T. Wayte, 1805. 16 × 19.5 cm. 30 pp. By Jane Chapman. BL: 11641. e. 5.

CHAPONE, Hester, Mrs John (1727–1801), *see also* COLLECTIONS 23(*a–b*)

Born in Twywell, Northants. Her father was Thomas Mulso and her mother a Miss Thomas. Her mother is said to have discouraged her early literary promise. In 1750 she contributed to Johnson's *Rambler*. She was acquainted with Samuel Richardson and Elizabeth Carter (q.v.). In 1760 she married John Chapone, an attorney, who died in 1761. She had a small income which she supplemented by writing. Her *Letters on the Improvement of the Mind* was published anonymously in 1773 and a third edition appeared in 1774. She also contributed to the *Gentleman's Magazine*. She was an excellent singer. (*DNB*)

1(*a*)   *Miscellanies in Prose and Verse* . . . London: E. and C. Dilly, and J. Walter, 1775. 10 × 16 cm. Pp. xii + 178. 3/- bound or 2/6 sewed. By Mrs Chapone. *MR* 53: 240–7; *CR* 39: 410–14; BL: 992. f. 41.

1(*b*)   *Miscellanies in Prose and Verse* . . . *To Which is Added, the Temple of Virtue, a Dream*. Dublin: J. Williams, W. Wilson, and R. Moncrieffe, 1775. 10 × 16 cm. Pp. viii + 143 + 105 [the verse occupies pp. 103–43]. By Mrs Chapone and James Fordyce. CUL: Hib. 7. 775. 37.

1(*c*)   *Miscellanies in Prose and Verse*. London: E. and C. Dilly, and J. Walter, 1775. 2nd edn. 9 × 15 cm. 190 pp. By Mrs Chapone. BL: 12271. aa. 5.

1(*d*)   *Miscellanies in Prose and Verse*. London: E. and C. Dilly and J. Walter, 1777. 3rd edn. 9 × 15.5 cm. 216 pp. By Mrs Chapone, Author of *Letters on the Improvement of the Human Mind*. Houghton: *EC75. C3678. 775mc.

1(*e*)   *Miscellanies in Prose and Verse*. London: C. Dilly and J. Walter, 1783. New edn. 9.5 × 15.5 cm. 216 pp. By Mrs Chapone, Author of *Letters on the Improvement of the Mind*. BL: 1568/5679.

1(*f*)   *Miscellanies in Prose and Verse*. London: C. Dilly and J. Walter, 1787. New edn. 9.5 × 16 cm. 216 pp. By Mrs Chapone. BL: 8404. aaa. 19.

1(*g*)   *Miscellanies in Prose and Verse*. London: C. Dilly and J. Walter, 1789. New edn. 9 × 15.5 cm. 216 pp. By Mrs Chapone. BL: 8404. b. 14.

2(*a*)   *The Works* . . ., *Containing Letters on the Improvement of the Mind, Addressed to a Young Lady. And Miscellanies in Prose and*

Verse. Dublin: J. Williams, 1775. 10 × 17 cm. 2 vols. [Verse occupies pp. 69–99 of vol. ii.] By Mrs Chapone. BL: 1507/1696.

2(*b*)   *The Works . . . Containing Letters on the Improvement of the Mind, Addressed to a Young Lady: And Miscellanies in Prose and Verse.* Dublin: W. Colles, 1786. 9 × 16.5 cm. 2 vols. [Verse occupies pp. 69–99 of vol. ii.] By Mrs Chapone. BL: 12268. aa. 7.

2(*c*)   *The Works . . . Addressed to a Young Lady.* London: J. Warlters, 1793. New edn. 9.5 × 15.5 cm. 2 vols. [the verse occupies pp. 73–103 of vol. ii]. By Mrs Chapone. North Carolina: BJ 1520. C 53 1793 [photocopies seen only].

2(*d*)   *The Works . . . Addressed to a Young Lady.* London: J. Warlters, 1796. New edn. 9 × 14.5 cm. 278 pp. [the verse occupying pp. 243–64]. By Mrs Chapone. Yale (Sterling): Im/C367/C786c.

2(*e*)   *The Works . . .* London/Edinburgh: John Murray/A. Constable and Co., 1807. 9.5 × 16.5 cm. 4 vols. [the verse being in vol. iv]. By Mrs Chapone. BL: 12270. aaa. 3.

2(*f*)   *The Works . . . Now First Collected . . . To Which is Prefixed, an Account of her Life and Character, Drawn up by her Own Family.* Boston: W. Wells and T. B. Wait and Co., 1809. 8.5 × 14.5 cm. 4 vols. [the verse being in vol. iv]. By Mrs Chapone. Houghton: *EC75. C3678. C809w.

2(*g*)   *The Works . . . Now First Collected . . .* New York: Evert Duyckink, 1818. 8.5 × 14 cm. 4 vols. [bound as 2; verse occupies pp. 98–144 of vol. iv]. By Mrs Chapone. Yale (Beinecke): Im/C367/B807D.

CHARLEVILLE, Countess of, *see* BURY, Catherine Maria

CHARLOTTE ELIZABETH, *see* PHELAN, Charlotte Elizabeth

CHARLOTTE MARY, *see* GIBSON, Charlotte Mary

CHARLTON, Mary (*fl.* 1794–1830)
She was a novelist. (Allibone, *CB*)

1(*a*)   *Pathetic Poetry for Youth; Calculated to Awaken the Sympathetic Affections.* London: Knevett, Arliss and Baker, 1811. 8.5 × 14 cm. 97 pp. By Mrs Charlton. Osborne: ii. 625.

1(*b*)   *Pathetic Poetry for Youth; Calculated to Awaken the Sympathetic Affections.* London: Whittingham and Arliss, 1815. 8 × 12.5 cm. 74 pp. By Mrs Charlton. BL: 12804. gg. 12(1).

CHASE, Elizabeth, *see* COLLECTIONS 20, 31

CHEEK, Elizabeth, *see* COLLECTIONS 14

CHETWYND, Mary Anne, Mrs H., *see* COLLECTIONS 39

CHILCOT, Harriet, Mrs MEZIERE (1754–84)
She came from Bath and was probably the daughter of Henry Chilcot, a jeweller, and of his wife Ann. (Blain)

1   *Elmar and Ethlinda; a Legendary Tale: Adalba and Ahmora, an Indian Tale: With Other Pieces.* London: J. Debrett, 1783. 12 × 18.5 cm. Pp. [xxii] + 88. 3/- bound. By Miss Harriet Chilcot, now Mrs Meziere. *MR* 69: 599; BL: 11633. bb. 9.

CHILD, Lydia Maria, Mrs David Lee (1802–80)
Born in Medford, Mass. She was the daughter of Convers Francis, a baker, and of Susanna Rand. She attended public schools and spent one year in a seminary. Her novels, *Hobomak* (1824) and *The Rebels* (1825), were popular. In 1825–8 she kept a private school in Watertown, NY, and in 1826 she started a magazine called the *Juvenile Miscellany.* She married the Boston lawyer and journalist David Lee Child in 1828. They were both active abolitionists and the sales of her books suffered for a while as a consequence. From 1841 to 1849 she edited the *National Anti-slavery Standard.* In 1860 a pamphlet of her correspondence with Mrs Mason of Virginia, a survey of slavery, was circulated in 300,000 copies. She continued writing novels and books of practical advice. (*DAB*)

1(*a*)   *The Coronal. A Collection of Miscellaneous Pieces, Written at Various Times.* Boston[, Mass.]: Carter and Hendee, 1832. 9 × 14.5 cm. Pp. vi + 285 [prose and about 14 pp. of verse].

By Mrs Child, Author of *Hobomok, The Rebels, The Mother's Book, The Girl's Own Book*, etc. Houghton: AL 1043. 10*(A).

1(*b*)   *The Western Coronal; a Collection of Pieces, Written at Various Times*. Glasgow/Edinburgh/London: John Reid and Co./Oliver and Boyd/Whittaker, Treacher, and Arnot, 1833. 2nd edn. 9 × 14.5 cm. Pp. iv + 207 [of which about 14 pp. are in verse]. By Mrs Child. BL: 12355. aa. 23.

2   *A Garland of Juvenile Poems. Written and Selected* . . . London: John Limberd, [1835?]. 8.5 × 13.5 cm. Pp. ii + 104. By Mrs D. L. Child [and others]. BL: 11687. aaa. 13.

CHRISTIANA, *see* RING, Mrs Thomas

CHUDLEIGH, Elizabeth, Lady (1720–88), *see* COLLECTIONS 21

The only child of Colonel Thomas Chudleigh and Harriet Chudleigh (cousins). She was appointed as maid of honour to the Princess of Wales in 1743. In 1744 she secretly married Lieutenant the Hon. Augustus John Hervey (later Earl of Bristol); they had one child. Her public behaviour in high society caused comment. In 1769, having sworn that she was not already married, she married the Duke of Kingston. After his death she was tried for bigamy in 1775 and satirized by Foote as Kitty Crocodile in his play *A Trip to Calais*. She left England after the trial and died abroad. (*DNB*)

CLARA, Cousin, *pseudonym*

1(*a*)   *The Infant's Daily Sacrifice. A Book of Short Hymns for Children*. London: J. Hatchard and Son, 1830. 10.5 × 13.5 cm. Pp. xx + 75. 5/- with plates. Bodley: 14722 f. 61.

1(*b*)   *The Infant's Daily Sacrifice. A Book of Short Hymns for Children*. London: J. Hatchard and Son, 1831. 10.5 × 13.5 cm. Pp. xx + 75. 5/- with plates. BL: 11647. a. 50.

CLARISSA, *see* COLLECTIONS 46, 48

CLARK, Emily

Her mother was the daughter of the Colonel Frederick mentioned on the title-page of her *Poems* and her father was a customs house officer in Dartmouth, Devon. She exhibited as a miniature painter at the Royal Academy in 1799. She was still alive in 1833. (Blain, *DNB* (under Col. Frederick))

1   *Poems: Consisting Principally of Ballads.* London: F., C., and
     J. Rivington, 1810. 9.5 × 16 cm. Pp. [x] + 144 [subscrip-
     tion edition]. By Miss Emily Clark, Grand-daughter of the
     Unfortunate Colonel Frederick, and Author of *The Banks
     of the Douro,* etc., etc. BL: 11641. aa. 10.

CLARK, Sylvia, Mrs Robert

According to her title-page her unmarried name was Lewis, she lived in
Tetbury, Glos., and came from Holt.

1   *Poems Moral and Entertaining, Written Long Since* . . . Bath/
     London/Bristol, Glo[u]cester and Tetbury: S. Hazard/
     G. G. J. and J. Robinson/the booksellers, 1789. 11.5 × 18
     cm. Pp. xii + 336. 4/- boards. By Miss Lewis, then of
     Holt, now, and for almost thirty years past, the Wife of
     Mr Robert Clark, of Tetbury. *CR* 67: 135–6; *MR* 81: 181;
     BL: 11632. aaa. 32.

CLARKE, Ann, Mrs

The second edition of her poems reveals that by 1825 she was a widow
with five daughters and one son. She seems to have been living in
Birmingham in 1820 and to have visited Dover. She was probably a
Baptist.

1(*a*) *Poems, Moral & Entertaining* . . . Northampton/London: for
        the author by W. Cooper/Nisbet, Westley, Offer, and
        Whittemore, 1824. 8 × 13 cm. 48 pp. 6*d.* BL: 11648. a. 92.

1(*b*) *Poems, Moral, Entertaining, and Religious.* London: Nisbet,
        Westley, 1825. 10.5 × 17.5 cm. 2 vols. By Mrs Clarke,
        Author of *The World an Inn, The Christian Life a Journey,* etc.
        BL: 11645. aaa. 11.

2   *The Saviour's Triumph, and Satan's Downfall; or Captivity Led
     Captive. A Tragical Poem, in Ten Parts.* Northampton/
     London: for the author by W. Cooper/Nisbet, Westley,
     Offer, and Whittemore, 1824. 8 × 13 cm. 48 pp. BL:
     11641. a. 30.

CLARKE, Anne

She seems to have lived in Shipston on Stour, War.

1(*a*) *Small Literary Patchwork* . . . Shipston, 1808. By a Country-
        woman. HL; not located.

1 (*b*)   *Small Literary Patchwork: Or, a Collection of Miscellaneous Pieces,*
in Prose and Verse, Written on Various Occasions, Chiefly on
Moral and Interesting Subjects. London/Shipston on Stour: for
the author by Nichols, Son, and Bentley, E.
Bentley/Bromley, 1814. 2nd edn. 10.5 × 18 cm. Pp. xii +
118 [subscription edition]. 7/6 boards or 7/6. By Anne
Clarke. *MR* 75: 222–3; *CR* 5: 548; BL: 11644. c. 24.

A Clergyman's Daughter, *see* Hitchener, Elizabeth

A Clergyman's Wife, *see* Fallows, Mrs T. M.

Clinckett, Mary Abel (born *c*.1798)
Early Attempts reveals that her father was Abel Clinckett (the editor),
that she was one of four children, and that her mother died when she
was 5 years old. The family seems to have lived in or near Bristol, but
she had visited the Barbados earlier. She returned there in 1814 and in
1816 she married Alfred Bartrum, who was attached to the commis-
sariat in Barbados.

1   *Early Attempts at Poetry, Written at Different Periods, from*
1811, to 1816. Ed. [Abel Clinckett]. Bristol: printed by Wm.
Major, 1817. 10.5 × 17.5 cm. 168 pp. By Mary Abel
Clinckett. Davis: Kohler I 83–229.

Clio, *pseudonym of* Williams, Joseph

Cobbold, Elizabeth, Mrs John (1767–1824), *see also* Collections
19, 35
Born in London. Her father was Robert Knipe and her mother a Miss
Waller. In 1790 she married William Clarke, a comptroller of customs
in Ipswich, who died in 1791. She then married John Cobbold, an
Ipswich brewer, and they had seven children. She contributed to annu-
als and to Ipswich publications and she was an active philanthropist.
(Boyle, *DNB*, *GM*)

1   *Poems on Various Subjects.* Manchester: printed by C.
Wheeler, 1783. 19 × 25 cm. 112 pp. By Eliza Knipe, of
Manchester. Bodley: 280 l. 124.

2   *Six Narrative Poems.* London: for the author by C. Dilly,
1787. 21 × 26 cm. Pp. xii + 74 [subscription edition]. 3/6.
By Eliza Knipe. *MR* 77: 282–3; BL: 643. k. 16(2).

3   *The Mince Pye; an Heroic Epistle: Humbly Addressed to the Sovereign Dainty of a British Feast.* London: printed by Thomas Bensley, 1800. 21 × 28.5 cm. Pp. vi + 33. 5/-. By Carolina Petty Pasty. *MR* 34: 421–3; BL: 11642. h. 9.

4   *Cliff Valentines, 1813.* Ipswich: private, [1813]. 8 × 13.5 cm. 26 pp. BL: 11641. a. 15.

5   *Cliff Valentines, 1814.* Ipswich: private, [1814]. 8 × 13 cm. 32 pp. By [Elizabeth Cobbold]. BL: 1163. a. 30.

6   *Ode on the Victory of Waterloo.* Ipswich/London/Bury St. Edmunds/Colchester: for the author by J. Raw/Longman, Hurst, Rees, Orme, and Brown/Deck/Keymer, 1815. 15 × 23 cm. 18 pp. By Elizabeth Cobbold. HEHL: 438778.

7(a) *Poems . . . with a Memoir of the Author.* Ed. [Laetitia Jermyn]. Ipswich: J. Raw, 1825. 14.5 × 23 cm. Pp. viii + 383. By Mrs Elizabeth Cobbold. BL: 11642. f. 33.

7(b) *Poems . . . with a Memoir of the Author.* Ed. [Laetitia Jermyn]. Ipswich/London: J. Raw/Longman, Hurst, Rees, Orme, Brown and Green, 1825. 10 × 16 cm. Pp. viii + 192 [subscription edition]. By Mrs Elizabeth Cobbold. BL: 11645. aaa. 12.

COCKLE, Mary, Mrs E., *see also* COLLECTIONS 48

She was governess to the Misses Fitzclarence. She contributed to annuals such as *The Iris* and *The Keepsake*. (Boyle, Shoberl)

1   *The Fishes Grand Gala. A Companion to the 'Peacock at Home'* . . . Part I [of 2]. London: C. Chapple, B. Tabart, J. Harris, Darton and Harvey, 1808. 9.5 × 11.5 cm. 16 pp. By Mrs Cockle, Author of *The Juvenile Journal*, etc. BL: C. 40. a. 57(11).

2(a) *The Fishes Grand Gala. A Companion to the 'Peacock at Home'* . . . Part II [of 2]. London: C. Chapple, B. Tabart, J. Harris, Darton and Harvey, 1808. 9.5 × 11.5 cm. 16 pp. By Mrs Cockle, Author of *The Juvenile Journal*, etc. BL: C. 40. a. 57(11).

2(b) *The Fishes Grand Gala. A Companion to the 'Peacock at Home,'* &c. &c. Part II [of 2]. Philadelphia: Benjamin C. Buzby, 1809. 9.5 × 12 cm. 16 pp. By Mrs Cockle, Author of *The Juvenile Journal*, etc. Boston Public: XH. 99B. 138.

3 *Lines on the Lamented Death of Sir John Moore, Suggested by Reading 'Moore's Narrative of the Campaign in Spain'.* London: printed by D. N. Shury, 1810. 18.5 × 22 cm. 11 pp. By E. C. BL: 11632. g. 60(13).

4 *Simple Minstrelsy.* London: C. Chapple, 1812. 11 × 18.5 cm. Pp. viii + 237. 10/-. By Mrs Cockle. *CR* 2: 108; BL: 11641. bb. 20.

5 *National Triumphs.* London: C. Chapple, 1814. 11.5 × 18.5 cm. 31 pp. 2/6. By Mrs Cockle, Author of *Simple Minstrelsy*, a Collection of Poems; an *Elegy on Sir John Moore*; *Important Studies for the Female Sex*; *Moral Truths, or Studies from Natural History*, etc. etc. *MR* 74: 433–4; Bodley: Harding C 767.

6(*a*) *An Elegy on the Death of His Late Majesty George the Third.* London/Edinburgh: Baldwin, Cradock, and Joy and C. Chappell/A. Constable and Co., 1820. 19 × 23.5 cm. 8 pp. By Mrs Cockle. BL: 11632. g. 60(9).

6(*b*) *An Elegy on the Death of His Late Majesty George the Third.* Newcastle: Emerson Charnley, 1820. 18.5 × 24 cm. 8 pp. By Mrs Cockle. BL: 11632. g. 60(8).

6(*c*) *Elegy on the Death of His Late Majesty George the Third.* Newcastle upon Tyne: printed by S. Hodgson, 1820. 11.5 × 19.5 cm. 8 pp. By Mrs Cockle. BL: 11632. g. 60(7).

[*See also*: 'Elegy to the Memory of Her Royal Highness the Princess Charlotte of Wales' (1817, 7 pp.); 2nd edn. (1817, 7 pp.); 3rd edn. (1817, 7 pp.); new edn. (1817, 7 pp.); 'Reply to Lord Byron's "Fare Thee Well"' (1817, 7 pp., anonymous, but signed 'C.'); 'Verses Written at the House of Mr Henderson, at Longleeford, near Cheviot, Northumberland, during the Winter of 1817' (1823, 4 pp.); 'Lines to a Boy Pursuing a Butterfly' (1826, 4 pp.), by a Lady.]

COCKS, Mrs S.

1 *Original Hymns for the Family and the Closet.* London/Birmingham/Bristol: Hamilton, Adams and Co., Simpkin and Marshall, Suter, Nisbet/J. S. Showell, Beilby, Knott and Beilby, Hudson, Broughall, Deritend/Brown, 1831.

9 × 14.5 cm. Pp. xvi + 201 [subscription edition]. By Mrs S. Cocks. BL: 3434. aaa. 10.

COLCHESTER, Lady, *see* LAW, Elizabeth Susan

COLE, Adeline, *see* COLE, M.

Her given name is found in M. and A. Cole's *Days Gone By* (below). Her brother's death is recorded in *GM*; he was at the time aide-de-camp to the Governor of Mauritius. Their uncle, probably on their mother's side, was Lieutenant-General Sir W. Cockburn. The family seems to have lived in Bath. (*Days Gone By, GM*)

COLE, M., *see* COLE, Adeline

1   *Days Gone By. Written on the Anniversary Birth-day of a Beloved Brother, Who Died on the 31st July, 1827.* Dublin: printed by R. Carrick, [1829]. 10.5 × 18.5 cm. 135 pp. [verse on pp. 3–17 and 132–5 only]. By [M. and Adeline Cole]. BL: 10826. aa. 27.

COLERIDGE, Sara (1802–52)

Daughter of Samuel Taylor Coleridge and Sara Fricker. She was born in Keswick, Cumb., and brought up there by her mother in the household of Robert Southey. She early revealed a talent for languages and her three-volume translation of Dobrizhoffer's Latin *Account of the Abipones* appeared in 1822. In 1829 she married her first cousin, Henry Nelson Coleridge, a barrister, with whom she edited her father's literary remains, continuing very ably after her husband's death in 1843. They had three children. She suffered from ill health and from opium addiction. (*DNB*, Bradford Keyes Mudge, *Sara Coleridge, a Victorian Daughter* (1989))

1(*a*)   *Pretty Lessons in Verse for Good Children.* London: John W. Parker, 1834. 9.5 × 13.5 cm. 128 pp. HRC Texas: PZ. 8.3 C65. Pr. 1834.

1(*b*)   *Pretty Lessons in Verse, for Good Children; with Some Lessons in Latin, in Easy Rhyme.* London: John W. Parker, 1835. 2nd edn. 9 × 13.5 cm. 128 pp. NLS: Mas. 86.

COLLECTIONS

1(*a*)   *Poetical Amusements at a Villa near Bath.* Ed. [Anne Miller]. Bath/London: L. Bull/Hawes, Clarke, and Collins, 1775.

11 × 18.5 cm. 150 pp. 2/6. By [Miss Burgess, Miss D——s, Miss El–k–r, Mrs M–ll–r, Miss M—n–ll, Mrs R—s, and others]. BL: 992. b. 37(1).

1(*b*)   *Poetical Amusements at a Villa near Bath.* Ed. [Anne Miller]. Vol. i [of 2]. London/Bath: Edward and Charles Dilly/W. Frederick, 1776. 2nd edn. 11 × 17.5 cm. By [Miss Burgess, aged 10, Miss D——s, Miss El–k–r, Mrs G–v–l, Laura [Mrs Miller], Mrs L–r–che, Mrs M–ll–r, Mrs R—s, and others]. BL: 11602. cc. 2.

1(*c*)   *Poetical Amusements at a Villa near Bath.* Ed. [Lady A. Miller]. London/Bath: Edward and Charles Dilley/W. Frederick, 1776. 3rd edn. 11.5 × 18.5 cm. Pp. viii + 150. By [Miss Burgess, Miss D——s, Miss El–k–r, Mrs G–v–l, Laura [Mrs Miller], Mrs L–r–che, Mrs M–ll–r, Miss M–n–ll, Her Gr–ce the D—ss of N—m—r—d, Mrs R—s, and others]. HRC Texas: PR. 1171. P65. 1776c.

2   *Poetical Amusements at a Villa near Bath.* Ed. [Anne Miller]. Vol. ii [of 4]. London/Bath: Edward and Charles Dilly/W. Frederick, 1776. 11 × 17.5 cm. By [Miss Davis and others]. BL: 11602. cc. 2.

3   *Poetical Amusements at a Villa near Bath. Printed for the Benefit of the Pauper-Charity in That City.* Vol. iii [of 4]. London/Bath: Edward and Charles Dilly/W. Frederick, 1777. 11 × 17.5 cm. By [Miss D–v–s, the Hon. Mrs G—v–lle, and others]. BL: 11602. cc. 3.

4   *Poetical Amusements at a Villa near Bath. Printed for the Benefit of the Pauper-Charity in That City.* Vol. iv [of 4]. Bath/London: Pratt and Clinch/R. Baldwin, 1781. 11 × 17.5 cm. By [Mrs Prideaux, Miss Rogers of Staffordshire, Miss Seward, Miss Winford, and others]. BL: 11602. cc. 3.

5(*a*)   *The Poetry of the World.* Ed. [Edward Topham]. London: printed by John Bell, 1788. 9.5 × 16 cm. 2 vols. By Anna Matilda [Hannah Cowley], and others. BL: 11602. b. 40, 41.

5(*b*)   *The British Album. Containing the Poems . . .* London: J. Bell, 1790. 2nd edn. 9.5 × 16 cm. 2 vols. By Anna Matilda [Hannah Cowley] and others. BL: 1162. e. 31, 32.

5(*c*)   *The British Album. Containing the Poems* . . . Dublin: printed by Bernard Dornin, 1790. 3rd edn. 9.5 × 16.5 cm. Pp. [viii] + 290. By Della Crusca [Robert Merry], Anna Matilda [Hannah Cowley], and others. BL: 11603. bbb. 6.

5(*d*)   *The British Album. Containing the Poems* . . . London: J. Bell, 1790. 3rd edn. 9.5 × 15.5 cm. 2 vols. By Della Crusca [Robert Merry], Anna Matilda [Hannah Cowley], Laura [Mary Robinson?], and others. BL: 11603. b. 10.

5(*e*)   *The British Album. Containing the Poems* . . . London: J. Bell, 1792. 4th edn. 9.5 × 15 cm. 2 vols. By Anna Matilda [Hannah Cowley] and others. BL: 1162. e. 29, 30.

5(*f*)   *The British Album. Containing the Poems* . . . London: J. Bell, 1792–3. 4th edn. 9.5 × 15.5 cm. 2 vols. By Anna Matilda [Hannah Cowley] and others. BL: 11603. b. 12, 13.

5(*g*)   *The British Album. Containing the Poems* . . . Boston[, Mass.]: Belknap and Hall, 1793. First American edn. 10 × 16.5 cm. Pp. [iv] + 326. By Anna Matilda [Hannah Cowley] and others. BL: 1162. d. 39.

5(*h*)   *The Poetry of the World.* London: James Ridgway, 1795. 5th edn. 9.5 × 15.5 cm. 2 vols. By [Hannah Cowley and others]. Yale (Sterling): Ib55/td795/1–2.

6   *The Arno Miscellany being a Collection of Fugitive Pieces* . . . Florence: printed in the Bonducciana press, 1784. 12 × 18.5 cm. 43 pp. By the Members of a Society Called the Oziosi at Florence [Mrs Piozzi and others]. BL: 11641. aaa. 1.

7   *The New English Valentine Writer, or the High Road to Love; for Both Sexes. Containing a Complete Set of Valentines, Proper for Almost Every Trade in Town and Country, with their Answers* . . . London: T. Sabine, [1784]. 10.5 × 17.5 cm. 84 pp. 6*d*. By Miss Rose, of the City of Canterbury, Miss Lovejoy, of the City of York, Miss Gray, of the City of Bristol, and others. BL: 1078. d. 13(1).

8   *The Florence Miscellany.* Florence: G. Cam, [1785]. 13.5 × 20.5 cm. 224 pp. By [Mrs Piozzi and others]. HEHL: 227302.

9   *The Young Men and Maids Delight; or, the New English Valentine Writer; Containing a Variety of Verses Calculated to*

Crown with Mirth and Good Humour, the Happy Day Which is Called St. Valentine . . . London: T. Sabine, [1785]. 10.5 × 17.5 cm. 82 pp. 6*d*. By A. Rose and another. BL: 1078. d. 13(2).

10(*a*) *Miscellany in Prose and Verse, for Young Persons. Designed Particularly for the Amusement of Sunday Scholars.* London: John Marshall, [1790?]. 9.5 × 16.5 cm. Pp. [iv] + 70. By [Mrs Lovechild, *i.e.* Eleanor Fenn]. BL: 1210. l. 3.

10(*b*) *The Family Miscellany, in Prose and Verse; Designed to Supply Lessons for Children of Various Ages.* Ed. Mrs Lovechild [Eleanor Fenn]. London: J. Harris, Darton and Harvey, 1805. 9 × 13.5 cm. Pp. [vi] + 164. [prose and verse]. By [Mrs Carter, a Lady, Miss More, Charlotte Smith, Mrs Steele, Jane Taylor, and others]. Osborne: ii. 1044.

10(*c*) *A Miscellany, in Prose and Verse, for Young Persons, on Sunday.* Ed. Mrs Lovechild [Eleanor Fenn]. London: J. Harris, 1807. 8 × 13 cm. Pp. vi + 82. By [Mrs Bentley, Mrs Lovechild(?), and others]. BL: 11642. aa. 54.

11(*a*) *A Miscellany in Prose and Verse, for Young Persons, on a Sunday.* Ed. [Mrs . Lovechild (Eleanor Fenn)]. Norwich/London: Bacon/Mrs Newbery, [1798?]. 10 × 16.5 cm. Pp. [ii] + 74. By [Mrs Bentley, Mrs Lovechild, and others]. BL: Ch 790/151(1).

11(*b*) *The Family Miscellany, in Prose and Verse; Designed to Supply Lessons for Children of Various Ages.* Ed. Mrs Lovechild [Eleanor Fenn]. London: J. Harris, and Darton and Harvey, 1809. 2nd edn. 8 × 14 cm. Pp. [iv] + 167. By [Mrs Carter, H. More, Charlotte Smith, Mrs Steele, Ann and Jane Taylor, R. Wilkinson, and others]. BL: 012806. i. 10.

12(*a*) *The Poetical Monitor: Consisting of Pieces Select and Original, for the Improvement of the Young in Virtue and Piety: Intended to Succeed Dr Watts' Divine and Moral Songs.* Ed. [Elizabeth Hill]. London: for the Shakespear's-Walk Female Charity-school by T. N. Longman, J. Johnson, C. Dilly and A. Cleugh, 1796. 9.5 × 15 cm. Pp. [vi] + 160. 2/- bound, or 3/6 on fine wove paper, hot-pressed, bound in calf. By [Mrs Barbauld, Eliz. Bentley, Mrs Carter, E. Hill, Mrs Masters, Miss H. More, Mrs Steele, and others]. BL: 11644. ee. 12.

12(*b*)   *The Poetical Monitor: Consisting of Pieces Select and Original, for the Improvement of the Young in Virtue and Piety; Intended to Succeed Dr Watts's Divine and Moral Songs.* Ed. [Elizabeth Hill]. London: T. N. Longman, J. Johnson, C. Dilly, A. Cleugh, 1798. 2nd edn. 9 × 15.5 cm. Pp. [x] + 160. 2/- bound. By [Mrs Barbauld, E. Bentley, Lady Burrell, Mrs Carter, E. Hill, Mrs Masters, Mrs H. More, Mrs Spurrell, Mrs Steele, and others]. BL: 3437. cc. 3.

12(*c*)   *The Poetical Monitor: Consisting of Pieces Select and Original, for the Improvement of the Young in Virtue and Piety; Intended to Succeed Dr Watts' Divine and Moral Songs.* Ed. [Elizabeth Hill]. London: for the Shakespear's Walk Female Charity School by Longman and Rees, Johnson, Mawman, Cleugh, 1803. 3rd edn. 9.5 × 15.5 cm. Pp. [x] + 160. 2/6 bound. BL: 11602. bb. 19.

12(*d*)   *The Poetical Monitor . . .* 4th edn. Inference.

12(*e*)   *The Poetical Monitor . . .* 5th edn. Inference.

12(*f*)   *The Poetical Monitor: Consisting of Pieces Select and Original, for the Improvement of the Young in Virtue and Piety; Intended to Succeed Dr Watts's Divine and Moral Songs.* Ed. [Elizabeth Hill]. London: Longman and Co., Law, Darton and Co., and Cleugh, 1812. 6th edn. 9 × 15.5 cm. Pp. viii + 160. 2/6 bound. HRC Texas: PR. 1173. P587. 1812.

12(*g*)   *The Poetical Monitor: Consisting of Pieces Select and Original, for the Improvement of the Young in Virtue and Piety; Intended to Succeed Dr Watts' Divine and Moral Songs.* Ed. [Elizabeth Hill]. London: Longman and Co., Law and Co., Darton and Co., Cleugh, 1815. 7th edn. 9 × 15.5 cm. Pp. viii + 160. 3/- bound. BL: 11643. aa. 1.

12(*h*)   *The Poetical Monitor: Consisting of Pieces Select and Original, for the Improvement of the Young in Virtue and Piety; Intended to Succeed Dr Watts' Divine and Moral Songs.* Ed. [Elizabeth Hill]. London: Longman and Co., Law and Co., and Darton and Co., 1819. 8th edn. 9.5 × 16 cm. Pp. viii + 160. 3/- bound. Bodley: 1477 f. 93.

12(*i*)   *The Poetical Monitor: Consisting of Pieces Select and Original, for the Improvement of the Young in Virtue and Piety; Intended to Succeed Dr Watts' Divine and Moral Songs.* Ed. [Elizabeth

Hill]. London: Longman and Co., Whitaker, Darton and Co., 1822. 9th edn. 10 × 17.5 cm. Pp. viii + 160. 3/- bound. BL: 11602. cc. 24.

12(*j*) *The Poetical Monitor* . . . 10th edn. Inference.

12(*k*) *The Poetical Monitor: Consisting of Pieces Select and Original, for the Improvement of the Young in Virtue and Piety; Intended to Succeed Dr Watts's Divine and Moral Songs.* Ed. [Elizabeth Hill]. London: Longman, Rees, Orme, Brown, and Green, 1831. 11th edn. 9.5 × 15.5 cm. Pp. xii + 166. BL: 11602. aaa. 23.

13 *Amatory Pieces. The Invitation* . . . *Edwyn and Eltruda* . . . *&c. &c.* Ludlow/London: George Nicholson/T. Knott and Champante and Whitrow, 1799. 8 × 14 cm. 28 pp. By Miss Williams, [the Countess of C——, Mrs Greville, Ann Yearsley, and others]. BL: 1506/285(2).

14 *Miscellaneous Poems.* Ed. [Elizabeth Cheek]. Manchester: printed by W. Shelmerdine and Co., [1801]. 9.5 × 17 cm. 144 pp. [subscription edition]. By [Elizabeth Cheek, Delia, a Lady, and others]. BL: 994. c. 21.

15(*a*) *Poetry for Children. Consisting of Short Pieces, to be Committed to Memory.* Ed. Lucy Aikin. London: R. Phillips and B. Tabart, 1801. 8.5 × 13.5 cm. Pp. xii + 158. 2/6. By [Lucy Aikin, Mrs Barbauld, Lady Luxborough, and Hannah More]. Library Co. of Philadelphia: O Eng Aiki.

15(*b*) *Poetry for Children. Consisting of Short Pieces, to be Committed to Memory.* Selected by Lucy Aikin. London: R. Phillips and B. Tabart, 1803. 2nd edn. 8.5 × 13.5 cm. Pp. xii + 168. 2/6. BL: 11644. aa. 15.

15(*c*) *Poetry for Children. Consisting of Short Pieces to be Committed to Memory.* Ed. Lucy Aikin. London: Richard Phillips, Tabart and Co., 1804. New edn. 8.5 × 13.5 cm. 168 pp. 2/-. Florida: Shaw PN 6110. C4 P53 1804. [Photocopy seen only.]

15(*d*) *Poetry for Children. Consisting of Short Pieces, to be Committed to Memory.* Selected by Lucy Aikin. London: R. Phillips and B. Tabart, 1805. 3rd edn. 8.5 × 13.5 cm. Pp. xii + 168. 2/-. BL: 1490. pp. 28.

15(*e*)   *Poetry for Children: Consisting of Short Pieces to be Committed to Memory.* Ed. Lucy Aikin. London: R. Phillips and Tabart and Co., 1806. 4th edn. 8.5 × 13 cm. Pp. xii + 161. 2/-. Bodley: 2805 f. 593.

15(*f*)   *Poetry for Children: Consisting of Short Pieces to be Committed to Memory.* Ed. Lucy Aikin. London: R. Phillips and B. Tabart, 1808. 5th edn. 2/-. Bodley: 2805 f. 594.

15(*g*)   *Poetry for Children. Consisting of Short Pieces to be Committed to Memory.* Selected by Lucy Aikin. London: Longman, Hurst, Rees, Orme, and Brown, 1815. 6th edn. 8.5 × 13.5 cm. Pp. xii + 168. 2/-. BL: 12835. aa. 124.

15(*h*)   *Poetry for Children: Consisting of Short Pieces to be Committed to Memory.* Selected by Lucy Aikin. London: Longman, Hurst, Rees, Orme, and Brown, 1818. 7th edn. 8.5 × 13.5 cm. Pp. xii + 168. 2/-. BL: 12835. aa. 125.

15(*i*)   *Poetry for Children: Consisting of Short Pieces to be Committed to Memory.* Selected by Lucy Aikin. London: Longman, Hurst, Rees, Orme, and Brown, 1820. New edn. 8.5 × 14 cm. Pp. x + 168 [BL copy lacks pp. xi–xii of 'Contents']. 2/-. BL: 11604. a. 67.

15(*j*)   *Poetry for Children: Consisting of Short Pieces to be Committed to Memory.* Ed. Lucy Aikin. London: Longman, Hurst, Rees, Orme, and Brown, 1822. New edn. 8.5 × 13.5 cm. Pp. xii + 168. 2/-. Wellesley: Juvenile Collection X.

15(*k*)   *Poetry for Children: Consisting of Short Pieces to be Committed to Memory.* Selected by Lucy Aikin. London: Longman, Hurst, Rees, Orme, Brown, and Green, 1825. New edn. 9 × 14 cm. Pp. xii + 168. 2/-. BL: 11601. bb. 6.

15(*l*)   *Poetry for Children, Consisting of Short Pieces to be Committed to Memory.* Selected by Lucy Aikin. London: Longman, Rees, Orme, Brown, and Green, 1826. New edn. 9 × 14.5 cm. Pp. xii + 180. 2/-. By [Lucy Aikin, Joanna Baillie, Mrs Barbauld, Lady Luxborough, Hannah More, and Charlotte Smith]. BL: 992. f. 1.

15(*m*)   *Poetry for Children, Consisting of Short Pieces to be Committed to Memory.* Ed. Lucy Aikin. London, 1828. New edn. *NUC.* Not found.

15(*n*) *Poetry for Children; Consisting of Short Pieces, to be Committed to Memory.* Ed. Lucy Aikin. Dublin: John Cumming, 1828. 9.5 × 14 cm. Pp. vii + 160. Duke. [Photocopy seen only.]

15(*o*) *Poetry for Children, Consisting of Short Pieces to be Committed to Memory.* Ed. Lucy Aikin. London: Longman, Rees, Orme, Brown, Green, and Longman, 1834. New edn. 8.5 × 14 cm. Pp. xii + 179. 2/-. Columbia: Hist. Col. Children's Lit.

16(*a*) *The Metrical Miscellany: Consisting Chiefly of Poems Hitherto Unpublished.* Ed. [Maria Riddell]. London: T. Cadell, Jun. and W. Davies, 1802. 13.5 × 21 cm. Pp. xii + 224. By [A. L. Barbauld, Miss C***, the Duchess of Devonshire, a Lady, Mrs O'Neil, Mrs R****, and Maria Riddell]. BL: 11644. d. 43.

16(*b*) *The Metrical Miscellany: Consisting Chiefly of Poems Hitherto Unpublished.* Ed. [Maria Riddell]. London: T. Cadell and W. Davies, 1803. 2nd edn. 13 × 21 cm. Pp. xiv + 257. By [A. L. Barbauld, the Duchess of Devonshire, a Lady, Mrs O'Neil, Mrs R****, Maria Riddell, and Mrs D. S.]. BL: 1164. k. 33.

17 *A Selection, in Prose and Verse; with Some Original Pieces.* Cranbrook: printed by S. Waters, 1803. 13.5 × 22 cm. Pp. [vi] + 5–123 [subscription edition]. By Mrs A. G. [Gibbs] of Lamberhurst, Kent [and Mrs Carter, H. More, A. Seward, P. Wheatley, Mrs Yearsley, and others]. BL: 1162. h. 30.

18 *The Wild Wreath. Dedicated (by Permission) to H.R.H. the Duchess of York.* Ed. M. E. Robinson. [London]: Richard Phillips, 1804. 11 × 18 cm. Pp. viii + 228. 7/- boards. By [Joanna Baillie, M. E. Robinson, Miss Seward, Susan, and others]. *MR* 45: 318–19; BL: 11642. bbb. 55.

19 *The Chaplet, a Collection of Poems; Partly Original and Partly Selected from the Most Approved Authors.* Ipswich/London: J. Raw/Longman, Hurst, Rees and Orme, and Vernor and Hood, 1805. 8 × 13 cm. Pp. vi + vi + 204. By [Mrs Barbauld, Miss Carter, Mrs J. Cobbold, Mrs J. Hunter, Mrs Opie, Miss A. M. Porter, Mrs Robinson and others]. Houghton: *EC8. A100. 805c.

20   *Extracts in Prose and Verse . . . together with a Collection of Original Poetry, never before Published . . .* Ed. [Elizabeth Chase]. Annapolis[, Md.]: printed by Frederick Green, 1808. 10.5 × 18.5 cm. 2 vols. [subscription edition]. By a Lady of Maryland and by Citizens of Maryland [Miss Aikin, Miss Carter, Elizabeth Chase, Mrs H. of Anne-Arundel County, Mrs Hole of Sheffield, Miss Lee of Maryland, a Mother, Mrs Pilkington, Charlotte Smith, Lady Winchilsea, and others]. NYPL: NBF 1808.

21   *Macauley's Literary Amusements; Consisting of a Variety of Original and Fugitive Pieces, Scarce Productions, and a Chaste Selection of the Best Compositions of our Most Esteemed Writers, Both in Prose and Verse.* Ed. [E. W. Macauley]. Newcastle upon Tyne: for the author by Preston and Heaton, and K. Anderson, 1809. 11 × 18.5 cm. 348 pp. [subscription edition]. By [Mrs Barbauld, Lady Chudleigh, Queen Elizabeth I, Mrs Hunter, E. W. Macauley, Duchess of Newcastle, Miss Remington, Mrs Robinson]. BL: 12354. i. 7.

22(*a*) *The Associate Minstrels.* London/Bucklersbury: printed by George Ellerton/Thomas Conder, 1810. 10.5 × 18.5 cm. Pp. vi + 216 + 14. By [Mrs Conder, Jane Taylor, and another]. HL; BL: 1465. g. 11.

22(*b*) *The Associate Minstrels.* London/Bucklersby/Edinburgh: Gale, Curtis and Fenner/Josiah Conder/John Ballantyne and Co., 1813. 2nd edn. 9.5 × 16.5 cm. Pp. xii + 222. HL; BL: 11641. c. 38.

23(*a*) *A Sequel to the Poetical Monitor . . .* London: Longman, 1811. 12mo. 3/- bound. By Elizabeth Hill. *CR* 24: 216–17; *MR* 65: 434. Not located.

23(*b*) *A Sequel to the Poetical Monitor, Consisting of Pieces Select and Original, Adapted to Improve the Minds and Manners of Young Persons.* Ed. Eliz. Hill. London: Longman, Hurst, Rees, Orme, and Brown, Law and Whittaker, Darton and Co., and Cleugh, 1815. 2nd edn. 9 × 16 cm. Pp. iv + 163. 3/6 bound. By [Mrs Barbauld, Mrs Carter, Mrs Chapone, Miss S. Evance, E. Hill, Mrs A. S. Hunter, Mrs Moody, Mrs More, Mrs Opie, Mrs C. Smith, Miss Eliz. Smith, Mrs Temple, and others]. BL: 992. f. 7.

24   *Miscellaneous Poems.* Windsor: printed by E. Harding, 1812.
        16 × 20 cm. Pp. vi + 90. By [Ellis Cornelia Knight and
        others]. BL: 11602. f. 9.

25(*a*) *The Parent's Poetical Anthology: Being a Selection of English
        Poems, Primarily Designed to Assist in Forming the Taste and the
        Sentiments of Young Readers.* Ed. [Mrs Elizabeth Mant].
        London: F. C. and J. Rivington, J. Richardson, C. Law, J.
        Mawman, R. Baldwin, Cradock and Joy, and Sherwood,
        Neely, and Jones, 1814. 10.5 × 18.5 cm. Pp. xvi + 444. 6/-.
        By [Mrs Barbauld, Mrs Carter, Mrs H. More, Miss
        Pearson, Mrs Sheridan, Mrs C. Smith, Mrs Thrale, the
        editor, and others]. *CR* 5: 101; BL: 11602. cc. 13.

25(*b*) *The Parent's Poetical Anthology: Being a Selection of English
        Poems Primarily Designed to Assist in Forming the Taste and the
        Sentiments of Young Readers.* Ed. [Mrs Elizabeth Mant].
        London: F. C. and J. Rivington, J. Richardson, J.
        Mawman, Baldwin, Cradock and Joy, Sherwood, Neely,
        and Jones, G. and W. B. Whittaker, 1821. 2nd edn. 10 ×
        18 cm. Pp. xii + 444. BL: 1608/3524.

25(*c*) *The Parent's Poetical Anthology: Being a Selection of English
        Poems Primarily Designed to Assist in Forming the Taste and the
        Sentiments of Young Readers.* Ed. [Mrs Elizabeth Mant].
        London: Longman, Rees, Orme, Brown, and Green, John
        Richardson, Baldwin and Cradock, J. G. and F. Rivington,
        Whittaker, Treacher, and Arnot, Simpkin and Marshall,
        and J. Souter, 1832. 3rd edn. 10.5 × 18 cm. Pp. xvi + 472.
        LC: PR 1175. P357.

26(*a*) *Tracts Published by the New England Tract Society.* Andover
        [, Mass.]: printed by Flagg and Gould, 1814. 10.5 × 17 cm.
        2 vols. [A collection of previously circulated tracts, pagi-
        nated as individual tracts and also consecutively as parts
        of the collection and individually dated. Vol. ii contains
        [Ann and Jane Taylor] *Hymns for Infant Minds.* Andover,
        1814. 1st edn. and [Rebecca Wilkinson] *Sermons to Children.*
        Andover, 1814. 1st edn.] AAS: DATED BOOKS.

26(*b*) *Tracts Published by the New England Tract Society.* Andover
        [, Mass.]: printed by Flagg and Gould, 1815. 10.5 × 17 cm.
        2 vols. [Vol. ii contains [Ann and Jane Taylor] *Hymns for
        Infant Minds.* Andover, 1814. 1st edn. and [Rebecca

Wilkinson] *Sermons to Children.* Andover, 1814. 1st edn.].
AAS: DATED BOOKS.

26(*c*)   *The Publications of the New England Tract Society.* Andover
[, Mass.]: printed by Flagg and Gould, 1820. 10.5 × 17 cm.
6 vols. [Vol. ii contains [Ann and Jane Taylor] *Hymns for
Infant Minds.* Andover, 1820. 3rd edn. and [Rebecca
Wilkinson] *Sermons to Children.* Andover, 1819. 4th edn.].
AAS: DATED BOOKS.

26(*d*)   *The Publications of the American Tract Society.* [Andover,
Mass.]: printed for the Society by Flagg and Gould, 1824.
10.5 × 17 cm. 6 vols. [Vol. ii contains [Ann and Jane
Taylor] *Hymns for Infant Minds.* Andover, 1823, and
[Rebecca Wilkinson] *Sermons to Children.* Andover, 1815.
2nd edn.]. AAS: IUS. Amer. T. Amer. T. P824. Ed. B.

27   *Original Poems, on a Variety of Subjects, Descriptive, Moral, and
Entertaining.* Ed. [the Misses Hutchinson]. Durham:
printed by L. Pennington, 1815. 13 × 21 cm. Pp. xxviii +
164. By Different Hands [several of them identified as
ladies or young ladies]. BL: 11644. d. 23.

28(*a*)   *The Infant Minstrel: Or, Poetry for Young Minds.* London:
Darton, Harvey, and Darton, 1816. 8.5 × 13.5 cm. 106 pp.
By Various Female Writers. Osborne: ii. 645.

28(*b*)   *The Infant Minstrel: Or, Poetry for Young Minds.* Philadelphia:
Edward Parker, 1820. 8.5 × 13.5 cm. 108 pp. By Various
Female Writers. Brown (Harris): Coll/IN57.

29(*a*)   *Tributary Tears.* Inference.

29(*b*)   *Tributary Tears, Sacred to the Memory of the Illustrious and
Amiable Princess Charlotte of Wales, and Saxe-Coburg; Who
Died November 6, 1817, in the Twenty-second Year of her Age.
Being a Collection of the Best Poems that Have Appeared on the
Occasion. To Which is Prefixed, a Brief Memoir of her Life.* Ed.
[Alice Tribe]. London: R. Edwards, 1818. 2nd edn. 9 × 14
cm. Pp. xxviii + 224. By [a Lady, Mrs McMullan, Mrs
M. A. Reid, Mrs W. Serres, Mrs Eliza Smith, Miss S. E.
Tattershall, and others]. BL: 11644. aa. 36.

30(*a*)   *Hymns Selected from Various Authors, and Chiefly Intended for
the Instruction of Young Persons.* Ed. [Priscilla Gurney].
London/Norwich: Darton, Harvey, and Darton/Wilkin

and Youngman, 1818. 9.5 × 16 cm. Pp. iv + 260. By [Mrs Barbauld, A. Opie, and others]. BL: 3437. d. 38.

30(*b*)   *Hymns Selected from Various Authors, for the Use of Young Persons.* Ed. Priscilla Gurney. London/Norwich: Harvey and Darton/S. Wilkin, 1821. 2nd edn. 10 × 16.5 cm. Pp. xii + 272. BL: 3437. ff. 31.

30(*c*)   *Hymns Selected from Various Authors, for the Use of Young Persons.* Ed. Priscilla Gurney. London/Norwich: Harvey and Darton/S. Wilkin, 1822. 3rd edn. 8.5 × 14 cm. Pp. xiv + 189. BL: 3435. gg. 72.

30(*d*)   *Hymns Selected from Various Authors, for the Use of Young Persons.* Ed. Priscilla Gurney. London/Norwich: Harvey and Darton/S. Wilkin, 1822. 4th edn. 9 × 16 cm. Pp. xiv + 278. BL: 3434. cc. 34.

30(*e*)   *Hymns Selected from Various Authors, for the Use of Young Persons.* Ed. Priscilla Gurney. London/Norwich: Harvey and Darton/S. Wilkin, 1825. 5th edn. 10 × 16.5 cm. Pp. xiv + 286. BL: 3434. cc. 29.

30(*f*)   *Hymns Selected from Various Authors, for the Use of Young Persons.* Ed. Priscilla Gurney. London/Norwich: Harvey and Darton/S. Wilkin, 1825. 6th edn. 9 × 14 cm. Pp. xii + 202. BL: 3437. bbb. 1.

30(*g*)   *Hymns Selected from Various Authors, for the Use of Young Persons.* Ed. Priscilla Gurney. Philadelphia: Benjamin and Thomas Kite, 1826. 1st American edn. 8.5 × 14 cm. Pp. x + 188. LC: BV 459. G8 1826.

31   *Miscellaneous Selections and Original Pieces, in Prose and Verse Consisting Principally of Pieces of Moral Instruction, Descriptions of Fine Scenery, Delineations of Distinguished Characters, etc.* Ed. Elizabeth Chase. [N.p.]: for the editor by E. J. Coale, 1821. 11.5 × 18.5 cm. 228 pp. [about 32 pp. of verse]. By [Mrs Eliza Carter, Mrs L——, Mrs C—— L——, a Lady of Baltimore, Miss Lee, a Young Lady of Baltimore, the editor, and others]. Union: VS64/1821C.

32   *A Collection of Poems, Chiefly Manuscript, and from Living Authors.* Ed. Joanna Baillie. London: Longman, Hurst, Rees, Orme, and Brown, 1823. 13 × 22 cm. Pp. xliv + 330 [subscription edition]. £1/1/- boards. By [Joanna Baillie,

Mrs Barbauld, Miss Benger, Lady Dacre, Mrs Dixon, Mrs Grant of Laggan, Mrs Hemans, Miss Holford, Mrs John Hunter, Anna Maria Porter, and others]. *MR* 103: 410–17; BL: 992. l. 1.

33   *The Selector, Comprizing a Selection from the Most Celebrated British Poets, with Several Original Pieces.* Ed. [Susannah Watts?]. Royston/London: J. Warren/Hodgson and Co., 1823. 11 × 18 cm. Pp. [vi] + 208. By [Susannah Watts? and others]. BL: 11601. ccc. 19.

34(*a*)   *The Sorrows of Yamba, or the Negro Woman's Lamentation . . . the Negro's Complaint . . . Etc.* Newcastle: for the Newcastle Religious Tract Society, 1823. 10 × 17 cm. 12 pp. By Hannah More, William Cowper and [James Montgomery]. BL: 1480. aaa. 6(4).

34(*b*)   *The Anti-Slavery Album: Selections in Verse.* London: printed by Howlett and Brimmer, 1828. 12 × 15.5 cm. 12 pp. [printed on rectos only]. By Cowper, Hannah More, Montgomery, Pringle, and others. BL: T. 1218(6).

35   *Specimens of British Poetry: Chiefly Selected from Authors of High Celebrity, and Interspersed with Original Writings.* Ed. [Elizabeth Scott]. Edinburgh/Liverpool/Ipswich/Manchester/Lancaster/Penrith/Carlisle/Branthwaite/Kendal/Kirkby Lonsdale/Appleby/Ulverston: John Richardson, Oliver and Boyd/T. Kaye/Raw/Clarkes/Leeming/Shaw/Jollie/Dowson/Richardson/Foster/Chapelhow/Soulby, 1823. 13 × 21.5 cm. Pp. [ii] + 395. By [Mrs Cobbold, the Duchess of Devonshire, Miss Holcroft, Mrs John Hunter, Miss Inman, Miss Lickbarrow, Mrs Opie, Mrs Radcliffe, Mrs Robinson, Eliza Ryves, Mrs Savell, Elizabeth Scott, Mrs Tighe, Charlotte T. S. V., Mrs West, and others]. BL: 11604. f. 22.

36   *The Gleaner, a Selection of Poems for Youth.* Ed. [Anne Knight and another?]. Woodbridge: B. Smith, 1824. 9.5 × 15 cm. Pp. viii + 136. By [Mrs Barbauld, Miss Browne, Mrs Flowerdew, Mrs Radcliffe, Mrs Steele, and others]. Bodley: 2805 f. 720.

37   *Lays of the Lindsays; being Poems by the Ladies of the House of Balcarras.* Edinburgh: printed by James Ballantyne and Co.,

1824. 21 × 26.5 cm. Pp. ii + 123. By [Lady Anne Barnard, Lady Elizabeth Scott Lindsay, Countess of Hardwicke, and Lady Margaret Lindsay]. NLS: H. 30. a. 6.

38(*a*) *Poetic Gleanings, from Modern Writers; with Some Original Pieces.* Ed. a Governess [A. K. (Ann Knight)]. London: Harvey and Darton, 1827. 8.5 × 14 cm. Pp. viii + 160. By [A. K., L. Barbauld, F. Hemans, Mrs Opie, Anne Taylor, Mrs Tighe, and others]. BL: 11602. aa. 39.

38(*b*) *Poetic Gleanings, from Modern Writers; with Some Original Pieces.* Ed. a Governess [A. K. (Ann Knight)]. London: Darton and Harvey, 1834. 2nd edn. 8.5 × 14 cm. Pp. viii + 169. BL: 11646. bb. 66.

39 *Choice Selections, and Original Effusions; or, Pen and Ink Well Employed.* Ed. the Daughter of a Clergyman [Mrs H. Chetwynd]. Royston/London: John Warren/Thomas Hurst, Edward Chance and Co., 1828. 10.5 × 18 cm. Pp. xii + 300. By [Mrs Barbauld, Miss Elizabeth Sheridan Carey, Mrs H. Chetwynd, Mrs Emmerson, Mrs Hemans, L. E. L., Mary Queen of Scots, Mrs H. Rolls, Mrs C. B. Wilson, and others]. BL: 11644. ccc. 14.

40(*a*) *Sabbath Recreations.* 1829. Inference.

40(*b*) *Sabbath Recreations: Or, Select Poetry, of a Religious Kind, Chiefly Taken from the Works of Modern Poets; with Original Pieces never before Published.* Ed. Emily Taylor. London/Wellington, Salop.: Houlston and Son/, 1829. 2nd edn. 8.5 × 14 cm. Pp. xii + 393. By [Mrs Barbauld, Caroline Fry, Mrs Hemans, Mrs Opie, Emily Taylor, J. Taylor, Mrs H. Tighe, and others]. BL: 11645. df. 6.

40(*c*) *Sabbath Recreations; or, Select Poetry of a Religious Kind, Chiefly Taken from the Works of Modern Poets; with Original Pieces never before Published.* Boston[, Mass.]: Bowles and Dearborn, 1829. Ed. Miss Emily Taylor and John Pierpont. 1st American edn. 8 × 14 cm. Pp. x + 278. By [Mrs Barbauld, Caroline Fry, Mrs Hemans, L. E. Landon, Mrs Sigourney, Emily Taylor, Jane Taylor, Mrs H. Tighe, H. M. Williams, and others]. LC: PN 6110. R4T3 1829.

40(*d*) *Sabbath Recreations: Or, Select Poetry, of a Religious Kind, Chiefly Taken from the Works of Modern Poets; with Original Pieces never before Published.* Ed. Emily Taylor. London: Houlston and Son, 1835. 3rd edn. 9 × 14 cm. Pp. xii + 393. By [Mrs Barbauld, Caroline Fry, Mrs Hemans, Mrs Opie, Emily Taylor, Jane Taylor, Mrs H. Tighe, and others]. BL: 3441. ee. 6.

41   *The Casket, a Miscellany, Consisting of Unpublished Poems.* Ed. [Mrs Blencowe]. London: John Murray, 1829. 14 × 22.5 cm. Pp. xxiv + 451. By [Mrs Alexander Baillie, Joanna Baillie, Miss Bannerman, Lady Charlotte Bury, Countess of Charleville, Mrs Grant of Laggan, Miss L. M. Hawkins, Mrs Hemans, L. E. L., Mrs Marley, Miss Mitford, Countess of Morley, Mrs Opie, Anna Maria Porter, Mrs West]. BL: 11602. g. 4.

42   *The Lady's Poetical Album.* Glasgow: Richard Griffin and Co., 1830. 8 × 13.5 cm. 384 pp. By [Caroline Bowles, Mary Ann Browne, Mrs Embury, Mrs C. Gore, F. Hemans, Mary Howitt, Miss Jewsbury, E. Landon, Miss Mitford, Hon. Mrs Norton, Eliza Rennie, Miss Sheridan, and others]. NLS: T. 13. i.

43   *The Laurel. Fugitive Poetry of the XIXth Century.* Ed. [Sarah Lawrence]. London: John Sharpe, 1830. 8.5 × 13 cm. Pp. xii + 368. By [Miss Bannerman, Miss Benger, Miss Bowles, Mrs Embury, Mrs Hemans, Mary Howitt, Miss Landon, Miss Mitford, Mrs Opie, Hon. Miss Stewart, Jane Taylor, Mrs H. Tighe, and others]. BL: 11602. aa. 13.

44   *The Moral Muse. A Present for Young Ladies.* Ed. Emma Price. London: Holdsworth and Ball, 1830. 11 × 19 cm. Pp. xx + 205. By [Mrs Fry, Mrs Hemans, Mrs H. More, Mrs Phillips, Miss E. Smith, Mrs Steele, Miss Jane Taylor]. BL: 993. d. 36.

45   *The Poetic Garland: A Collection of Pleasing Pieces, for the Instruction and Amusement of Youth.* Ed. Clara Hall. London: Edward Lacey, [1830?]. 8.5 × 14 cm. Pp. iv + 72. By [Jane Bourne, Mrs Hemans, Anna Maria Porter, J. E. Roscoe, Emily Taylor, the editor, and others]. BL: 11646. aa. 60.

46   *The Poetic Primer: A Circlet of Little Rhymes for Little Readers.* Ed. Clara Hall. London: Edward Lacey, [1830?]. 8.5 × 14 cm. Pp. iv + 72. By [Clarissa, Mrs S. C. Hall, Mrs

Hemans, Mary Howitt, Miss Roberts, Anna Seward, Miss Webb, the editor, and others]. BL: 11647. aa. 48.

47   *Rhymes, & Reason: Or, Mirth & Morality for the Young: A Selection of Poetic Pieces, Chiefly Humourous.* Ed. Clara Hall. London: Edward Lacey, [1830?]. 8.5 × 14 cm. Pp. iv + ii + 72 + 72 [2 vols. bound together with the table of contents to vol. ii (pp. iii–iv) appearing between pp. iv and 1 of vol. i]. By [Mrs Abdy, Jane Bourne, Mrs Cockle, Mrs Hemans, Anna Maria Porter, J. E. Roscoe, Susanna Strickland, Emily Taylor, Mrs Washbourn, the editor, and others]. BL: 11601. aa. 7(1–2).

48   *The Poetic Present; a Collection of Superior Pieces from the Best Authors. Calculated to Interest and Improve the Minds of Young People.* Ed. Clara Hall. London: Edward Lacey, [1830?]. 9 × 14 cm. Pp. [ii] + 72 + 72 + 72 + 72 [incorporating *The Poetic Primer, Rhymes, and Reason, New Original Poems,* and *The Poetic Garland*]. By [Mrs Abdy, Jane Bourne, Charlotte Elizabeth, Clarissa, Mrs Cockle, Mrs Hemans, Mary Howitt, L. E. L., a Mother, Mrs Opie, Anna Maria Porter, Miss Roberts, J. E. Roscoe, Anna Seward, Susanna Strickland, Emily Taylor, Mrs Washbourn, Miss Webb, a Young Lady of Thirteen, the editor, and others]. BL: 11644. d. 45.

49(*a*)   *The Sisters' Budget; a Collection of Original Tales in Prose and Verse.* Ed. the Authors of *The Odd Volume,* etc. [the Misses Corbett]. London: Whittaker, Treacher, and Co., 1831. 11.5 × 19 cm. 2 vols. [About 16 pp. of verse.] By Mrs Hemans, Miss Mitford, Miss Jewsbury [no contribution included], Mrs Hodson, Mrs Kennedy, and others. BL: N. 848.

49(*b*)   *The Sisters' Budget; a Collection of Original Tales in Prose and Verse.* Baltimore: W. and J. Neal, 1832. 17 cm. 2 vols. By the Authors of *The Odd Volume,* etc. with contributions from Mrs Hemans, Miss Mitford, Miss Jewsbury, Mrs Hodson, Mrs Kennedy, Mr Macfarlane, Mr Kennedy, Mr H. G. Bell, Mr Malcolm, etc. *NUC.* Not found.

50(*a*)   *A Bridal Gift.* Inference.

50(*b*)   *A Bridal Gift.* 2nd edn. Inference.

50(c)   *A Bridal Gift.* Ed. the Editor of *A Parting Gift to a Christian Friend* [E. Maurice?]. Liverpool/London: D. Marples/ Hamilton, Adams, and Co., 1832. 3rd edn. 7.5 × 12 cm. Pp. x + 180. By [Mrs Barbauld, H., Mrs Hemans, Mrs Norton, Mrs Opie, Mrs Tighe, and Z. (H. More?)]. Davis: Kohler I 83–153.

51   *The Christian Bouquet; a Selection of Religious Poetry, from the Pens of Various Admired Authors; with an Original Introductory Essay.* Ed. Frances Blair. London: Richard Baynes, 1832. 9.5 × 15.5 cm. Pp. 204. By ['an esteemed female friend,' Miss Taylor, and others]. BL: 11645. aa. 7.

52   *Flowers of Poetry, for Young Persons: Arranged from Various Authors, as a Companion or Sequel to Miss Taylor's Original Poems.* London: Hamilton, Adams, and Co., 1834. 8 × 14 cm. 2 vols. By [Princess Amelia, Mrs Barbauld, H. Brand, Mrs Carter, Mary M. Colling, Mrs Hemans, Mrs Howitt, M. A. J[evons?], Mrs Leicester, H. More, Mrs Norton, Mrs Opie, Charlotte Smith, Emily Taylor, Mrs Tighe, Miss Williams, and others]. Bodley: 35. 134, 135.

53   *Flora and Thalia; or Gems of Flowers and Poetry; being an Alphabetical Arrangement of Flowers, with Appropriate Poetical Illustrations, Embellished with Coloured Plates.* Ed. a Lady. London: Henry Washbourne, 1835. 9 × 14 cm. Pp. xii + 200. By [the editor, Mrs Barbauld, Caroline Bowles, Mrs Hemans, M. J. Jewsbury, Miss Landon, Mary Robinson, Mrs Brinsley Sheridan, Caroline Symonds [Symmons?], Jane Taylor, Mrs Tighe, Louisa Anne Twamley, Mrs T. Welsh, and others]. BL: 969. a. 26.

54   *The New Original Poems, for the Instruction of the Young.* Ed. Clara Hall. London: Edward Lacy, [1835?]. 9 × 14 cm. Pp. iv + 72. By [Clara Hall, Mrs Hemans, Mary Howitt, Mrs Opie, Emily Taylor, a Young Lady of Thirteen, a Mother, and others]. Osborne: ii. 642.

55   *Sacred Melodies: A Christian and Literary Remembrancer.* Ed. Mrs Charles Cecil. London/Liverpool: Edward Lacey/ Henry Lacey, [1835?]. 8.5 × 13.5 cm. Pp. viii + 136. By [Caroline Bowles, Maria Griffith, Mrs Hemans, Mrs Norton, and others]. BL: 11601. aa. 4.

56   *The Seraph: Or, Gems of Poetry, for the Serious and Contemplative
      Mind: And the Promotion of Genuine Religion.* Ed. Mrs Charles
      Cecil. London/Liverpool: Edward Lacey/Henry Lacey,
      [1835?]. 8.5 × 13.5 cm. Pp. v + 140. By [Mrs Barbauld,
      Mrs Josiah Conder, Felicia Hemans, Miss Mitford, Mrs
      Norton, Anna Maria Porter, and others]. BL: 11601. aa. 5.

[*See also*: 'The Female Speaker; or, Miscellaneous Pieces, in Prose
and Verse . . .' ed. Anna Laetitia Barbauld (1811 and 1816, about
4 pp. of verse).]

COLLING, Mary Maria (born 1805), *see also* COLLECTIONS 52

Born in Tavistock, Devon. She was the daughter of Edmund Colling, a
husbandman, and his wife Anne. She was sent to a dame school to
learn to sew and to knit but taught herself to read. She was patronized by Anna Bray. (Blain, *Fables*)

1   *Fables and Other Pieces in Verse.* Ed. Mrs [Anna Eliza] Bray.
      London: Longman, Rees, Orme, Brown, and Green, 1831.
      12.5 × 20 cm. Pp. xx + 178 [subscription edition; verse
      occupies pp. 87–178]. By Mary Maria Colling. BL: 994.
      h. 8.

COLLINS, Miss

1   *Poems.* London: T. Hookham, 1816. 11 × 19 cm. Pp. [ii] +
      66 [subscription edition]. By Miss Collins. CUL: XIV. 6.
      68(1).

COLTHURST, E.

She seems to have lived in Cork. In 1840 she published *The Storm*
anonymously. (*BLC*)

1   *Emmanuel.* Ed. Henry H. Beamish. London: James Nisbet,
      1833. 10.5 × 17 cm. 54 pp. BL: T. 1457(12).

2   *Life: A Poem.* Cork: John Bolster, 1835. 12 × 18.5 cm. 79
      pp. By the Author of *Emmanuel.* BL: 11644. cc. 60(2).

COMPTON, Margaret Maclean, Marchioness of Northampton
(died 1830)

Eldest daughter of Major-general Douglas Maclean Clephane and his
wife Marianne. She grew up in Mull, Argyllshire. When she was a teen-
ager her stoical reaction to a dislocated arm impressed Walter Scott and

they corresponded thereafter. In 1815 she married Spencer Joshua Alwyne Compton, 2nd Marquess of Northampton, and they had at least one child. They moved to Italy in 1820 after he lost his seat in parliament. She died in childbirth in Rome. (*Complete Peerage*, Edgar Johnson, *Sir Walter Scott: The Great Unknown* (1970))

1   *Irene, a Poem, in Six Cantos. Miscellaneous Poems.* London: printed by Mills, Jowett, and Mills, 1833 [not published]. 14 × 22 cm. Pp. [ii] + 206. By [Margaret Compton, Marchioness of Northampton]. BL: 1466. g. 39.

CONDER, Joan Elizabeth, Mrs Josiah, *see* COLLECTIONS 22(*a–b*), 56

The second daughter of Roger Thomas, of Southgate, Middlesex, and granddaughter, on her mother's side, of the sculptor Roubilliac. She married the bookseller and writer Josiah Conder in 1815. She contributed to such annuals as *Friendship's Offering, The Literary Souvenir*, and *The Amulet.* (Boyle, *DNB* (under Josiah Conder))

CONKEY, Mrs M.

1   *Cottage Musings; or, Select Pieces, in Prose and Verse.* New York: printed by H. R. Piercy, 1835. 11 × 18 cm. 184 pp. [the verse occupies pp. 1–146]. By Mrs M. Conkey, an American Lady. Widener: AL1075. 8. 55.

CONYNGHAM, Elizabeth Emmet Lenox, *see* LENOX-CONYNGHAM, Elizabeth Emmet, Mrs George William

COOK, Eliza (1818–89)

She was the youngest of the eleven children of Joseph Cook, a Southwark brewer. When she was 9 her father retired to a small farm near Horsham, Sussex. She was encouraged by her mother but was largely self-taught. She attracted notice with a series of anonymous verses, mainly in the *Weekly Dispatch*. Her *Melaia and Other Poems* (1836) went through several editions; she also produced *Eliza Cook's Journal* from 1849 to 1854. She received a civil list pension of £100 in 1863. (Boase, *DNB*, Todd 2)

1   *Lays of a Wild Harp: A Collection of Metrical Pieces.* London: John Bennett and E. Spettigue, 1835. 7 × 11.5 cm. 167 pp. By Eliza Cook. BL: 11644. a. 49.

COOKSON, Mary Ann

1(*a*) *Poems on Various Subjects, never before Published.* Leith: printed by William Heriot, 1829. 10.5 × 18.5 cm. 86 pp. [subscription edition]. By M. A. Cookson. BL: 11645. bb. 16.

1(*b*) *Poems on Various Subjects, never before Published.* Leith: printed by William Heriot, 1829. 2nd edn. 10.5 × 17 cm. 88 pp. [subscription edition]. By M. A. Cookson. BL: 11646. bb. 18.

1(*c*) *Poems on Various Subjects, never before Published.* Leith: printed by William Heriot, 1829. 3rd edn. 10 × 17.5 cm. 88 pp. [subscription edition]. By M. A. Cookson. BL: 11646. bb. 19.

COOMBE, Sarah Matilda

She lived at Bath Cottage, Fareham, Hants. (*Aurestine*)

1 *Aurestine; a Tale of Fancy.* Portsea: Williams and Son, 1829. 13.5 × 21.5 cm. 45 pp. By Sarah Matilda Coombe. BL: 11645. bb. 44.

COOPER, Mrs

1 *An Address to the People of Wapping and its Environs.* London: for the author at 12 Russels Buildings, Bell Dock, Wapping, [1770?]. 12 × 19 cm. 23 pp. 1/-. By Mrs Cooper. BL: 11641. df. 38.

COOPER, Cecilia

1 *The Battle of Tewkesbury. A Poem. Written on a View of the Intrenchments near the Town* . . . Tewkesbury/London/ Cheltenham/Gloucester/Worcester/Kidderminster/ Stourbridge/Stourport: E. Reddell/Longman and Co./the Booksellers, 1820. 12 × 21 cm. [45 pp.]. By Cecilia Cooper. BL: 992. i. 24(13).

COOPER, Maria Susanna, Mrs Josiah

She was the daughter of James Bransby of Shottisham, Norfolk, and of Anna Maria Paston. Early in life she married Samuel Cooper, DD, of Great Yarmouth, and they had ten children, one of whom, Bransby, became an MP, while another, Astley, became the famous surgeon. She

86   *Cooper*

wrote books for children and epistolary novels. Beloe's *The Sexagenarian*, chapter 49, provides an account of her as 'Mrs C.' (Allibone, Blain, *CB*, *DNB* (under Sir Astley Cooper))

1   *Jane Shore to her Friend: A Poetical Epistle.* London: T. Becket and J. Fiske, 1776. 16 × 21 cm. Pp. viii + 16. 1/-. By the Authoress of *The Exemplary Mother*, etc. BL: 162. l. 41.

COPE, Harriet

1(*a*)   *The Triumphs of Religion; a Sacred Poem, in Four Parts.* London: F. C. and J. Rivington, 1811. 9.5 × 15.5 cm. Pp. x + 121. 7/- or 7/- boards. *CR* 23: 215; *MR* 66: 320–1; BL: 11644. aaa. 46.

1(*b*)   *The Triumphs of Religion; a Sacred Poem. In Four Parts.* London: F. C. and J. Rivington, 1819. 2nd edn. 9.5 × 16.5 cm. Pp. xii + 169. By Miss Harriet Cope. BL: 11646. cc. 14.

2   *Suicide: A Poem. In Four Parts, Illustrated with Notes.* London: F. C. and J. Rivington, 1815. 14.5 × 24 cm. Pp. xvi + 198. By Harriet Cope. BL: 11645. h. 6.

3   *Waterloo, a Poem, in Two Parts: Inscribed by Permission, to His Grace the Duke of Wellington . . .* London: J. Hatchard and Son, [1822]. 12.5 × 20 cm. Pp. iv + 162. By the Author of *Triumphs of Religion, Suicide, a Poem*, etc. BL: 992. i. 21(1).

4   *A Monody to the Memory of Thomas Lord Erskine. Inscribed by Permission to His Royal Highness the Duke of York.* London: for the author by J. C. and F. Rivington, 1824. 11 × 18 cm. 35 pp. By Miss Harriet Cope. BL: T. 854(11).

5   *The Brazen Serpent. A Sacred Poem: In Two Parts. Respectfully Inscribed to His Royal Highness the Duke of York.* London: W. Morgan, 1827. 10.5 × 18.5 cm. Pp. xii + 60. By Harriet Cope, Author of *The Triumphs of Religion.* BL: T. 1312(1).

6   *The Death of Socrates, a Poem.* Trans. Harriett Cope. London: for the translator, 1829. 12.5 × 19.5 cm. Pp. xx + 64. By A. de Lamartine. BL: T. 1312 (3).

COSTELLO, Louisa Stuart (1799–1870)

Born in Ireland. She was the daughter of James Francis Costello, a captain in the 14th Regiment. On his death in 1814 she accompanied her mother to Paris and maintained them there, as well as a younger brother at Sandhurst, by painting miniatures. On her return to London she became acquainted with Sir Francis and Lady Burdett, Thomas Moore, and Sir Walter Scott. In 1852 she received a civil list pension of £75. She was a popular writer of memoirs and travel literature. (Blain, *CB*, *DNB*)

1(*a*)   *The Maid of the Cyprus Isle, and Other Poems.* London: Sherwood, Neely, and Jones, Sharpe, Walker, Harper and Co., R. Rees, and Lloyd, 1815. 9.5 × 16.5 cm. Pp. [iv] + 82 [subscription edition]. By Louisa S. Costello. BL: 11642. aa. 42.

1(*b*)   *The Maid of the Cyprus Isle, and Other Poems.* London: Sherwood, Neely, and Jones, Sharpe, Walker, Harper and Co., R. Rees, and Lloyd, 1815. 2nd edn. 9.5 × 15.5 cm. Pp. vi + 86 [subscription edition]. By Louisa S. Costello. BL: 11645. aa. 47.

2   *Redwald; a Tale of Mona: And Other Poems.* Brentford/[London]: P. Norbury/Baldwin, Cradock and Joy, 1819. 9.5 × 16 cm. 70 pp. By Louisa Stuart Costello. BL: 992. g. 29(3).

3   *Songs of a Stranger.* London: for the author by Taylor and Hessey, 1825. 13 × 21.5 cm. Pp. xii + 158. By Louisa Stuart Costello. BL: 994. h. 9.

4   *Specimens of the Early Poetry of France from the Time of the Troubadours and Trouveres to the Reign of Henri Quatre.* Trans. Louisa Stuart Costello. London: William Pickering, 1835. 10 × 18 cm. Pp. xlix + 298. BL: 1065. d. 40.

A COUNTRYWOMAN, *see* CLARKE, Anne

COUTIER, Louisa H. R.

1   *Hours of Reverie: Or, the Musings of a Solitaire.* London: Whittaker, Treacher and Arnt, 1832. 13 × 20.5 cm. Pp. xii + 103. By Louisa H. R. Coutier. BL: T. 1422(12).

COWLEY, Hannah, Mrs Thomas (1743–1809), *see also* COLLECTIONS 5(*a–h*)

Born in Tiverton, Devon. She was the daughter of Philip Parkhouse, a bookseller. In 1772 she married Thomas Cowley, a captain in the East

India Company service and moved to London. He died in India in 1797. They had children. She was a successful comic playwright in London from 1776 to 1794, best known for *Who's the Dupe?* (1779) and *The Belle's Stratagem* (1780). In 1801 she retired to Devon. Her Della Cruscan poetry was satirized by Gifford. (Blain, *CB, DNB,* Todd 2)

1(*a*)   *Albina, Countess Raimond; a Tragedy* . . . London: J. Dodsley, R. Faulder, L. Davis, T. Becket, W. Owen, T. Lowndes, G. Kearsly, W. Davis, S. Crowder, T. Evans, Richardson and Urquhart, 1779. 12.5 × 20 cm. Pp. xii + 84. By Mrs Cowley. BL: 161. h. 31.

1(*b*)   *Albina, Countess Raimond; a Tragedy* . . . *as It is Performed at the Theatre-Royal in the Hay-market.* London: J. Dodsley, R. Faulder, L. Davis, T. Davies, T. Becket, W. Owen, T. Lowndes, G. Kearsly, W. Davis, S. Crowder, T. Evans, Richardson and Urquhart, 1779. 2nd edn. 12 × 19 cm. Pp. xii + 84. By Mrs Cowley. BL: 11777. f. 17.

1(*c*)   *Albina, Countess Raimond; a Tragedy* . . . *as It is Performed at the Theatre-Royal in the Hay-market.* London: for L. Davis, T. Longman, J. Dodsley, T. Cadell, W. Owen, S. Crowder, T. Davies, T. Beckett, G. Kearsley, C. Dilly, T. Evans, Richardson and Urquhart, and R. Faulder, 1780. 3rd edn. 11 × 19.5 cm. Pp. [vi] + 84. By Mrs Cowley. LC: PR 1241. D7 v. 38 Rare Bk Coll.

1(*d*)   *Albina, Countess Raimond; a Tragedy* . . . *As It is Performed at the Theatre-Royal in the Hay-market.* London: L. Davis, T. Longman, J. Dodsley, T. Cadell, W. Owen, S. Crowder, T. Davies, T. Becket, G. Kearsley, C. Dilly, T. Evans, Richardson and Urquhart, and R. Faulder, 1780. 4th edn. 15.5 × 21 cm. Pp. [vi] + 84. By Mrs Cowley. LC: PR 1241. L6 vol. 93 Office.

1(*e*)   *Albina, Countess Raimond. A Tragedy* . . . London: George Cawthorn, 1797. 12 × 19.5 cm. 81 pp. By Mrs Cowley. [Included in *Bell's British Theatre,* vol. xxix.] BL: 2304. c.

1(*f*)   *Albina. A Tragedy.* London: Wilkie and Robinson, 1812. 2nd edn. 12.5 × 22 cm. 84 pp. By Mrs Cowley. BL: 642. i. 30(10).

2   *The Maid of Arragon; a Tale.* Part I [remainder first published in *Works* (1813)]. London: L. Davis, T. Longman,

J. Dodsley, T. Cadell, W. Owen, S. Crowder, T. Davies, T. Becket, G. Kearsley, C. Dilly, T. Evans, Richardson and Urquhart, R. Faulder, 1780. 20 × 24.5 cm. Pp. [iv] + 49. 2/6. By Mrs Cowley. *MR* 62: 378–81; BL: 11630. d. 7(8).

3(*a*)   *The Scottish Village: Or, Pitcairne Green. A Poem.* London: G. G. J. and J. Robinson, 1786. 21 × 26.5 cm. Pp. viii + 23. 2/-. By Mrs Cowley. BL: 11611. k. 8(11).

3(*b*)   *The Scottish Village: Or, Pitcairne Green. A Poem.* London: G. G. J. and J. Robinson, 1787. 20 × 25.5 cm. Pp. viii + 23. By Mrs Cowley. BL: 162. m. 38.

4(*a*)   *The Fate of Sparta; or, the Rival Kings. A Tragedy. As It is Acted at the Theatre-Royal, in Drury Lane.* London: G. G. J. and J. Robinson, 1788. 12 × 20.5 cm. Pp. viii + 87. 1/6. By Mrs Cowley. BL: 643. e. 17(1).

4(*b*)   *The Fate of Sparta; or, the Rival Kings. A Tragedy. As It is Acted at the Theatre-Royal, in Drury Lane.* London: G. G. J. and J. Robinson, 1788. 2nd edn. 12.5 × 20.5 cm. Pp. viii + 87. 1/6. By Mrs Cowley. BL: 643. h. 15(4).

4(*c*)   *The Fate of Sparta; or, the Rival Kings. A Tragedy. As It is Acted at the Theatre-Royal, in Drury Lane.* Dublin: Wilkinson, Burnet, Chamberlaine, Moncrieffe, Gilbert, Wilson, Wogan, Colles, Byrne, McDonnel, W. Porter, McKenzie, Colbert, Parker, Halpin, Jones, Lewis, Dornin, and Butler, 1788. 9 × 16.5 cm. Pp. x + 54. By Mrs Cowley. BL: 640. h. 35(2).

5   *The Poetry . . . To Which are Added Recollections . . .* London: J. Bell, 1788. 9.5 × 15 cm. Pp. [iv] + 139. 3/6 sewed. By Anna Matilda [Hannah Cowley] and General Sir William Waller. BL: C. 45. a. 6.

6   *The History of the County of Cumberland, and Some Places Adjacent, from the Earliest Accounts to the Present Time . . .* Carlisle/London: printed by F. Jollie/B. Law and Son, W. Clark, and T. Taylor [J. Taylor in vol. ii], 1794. 21.5 × 28.5 cm. 2 vols. [Mrs Cowley's 'Edwina' occupies pp. 5–16 of vol. ii]. By William Hutchinson and [Hannah Cowley]. BL: 190. b. 13.

7(a)   *The Siege of Acre. An Epic Poem. In Six Books.* London: J. Debrett, 1801. 21.5 × 26.5 cm. 156 pp. 9/- sewed. By Mrs Cowley. *MR* 35: 175–9; *CR* 32: 176–81; BL: 11641. h. 2.

7(b)   *The Siege of Acre. A Poem. In Four Books.* London: G. Wilkie and J. Robinson, 1810. 9.5 × 16 cm. Pp. xiv + 143. By Mrs Cowley. BL: 994. f. 6.

8   *The Works . . . Dramas and Poems.* London: Wilkie and Robinson, 1813. 13 × 21.5 cm. 3 vols. [Prose and verse.] By Mrs Cowley. BL: 840. g. 29.

COWPER, Maria Frances Cecilia, Mrs William (1726–97)

Daughter of Colonel Martin Madan and Judith Cowper, and cousin of the poet William Cowper, who assisted in the revision of her religious verse. She married another cousin, also called William Cowper, by whom she had seven children. (Lonsdale, Russell)

1(a)   *Original Poems, on Various Occasions.* Ed. William Cowper. London: J. Deighton, J. Mathews, and R. Faulder, 1792. 9.5 × 15.5 cm. Pp. viii + 115. 3/-. By a Lady. *CR* 6: 470–1; BL: 11687. a. 33.

1(b)   *Original Poems, on Various Occasions.* Ed. William Cowper. Philadelphia: printed by William Young, 1793. 9 × 14.5 cm. 111 pp. By a Lady. LC: PR 3379. C7 1793 copy 2 Office.

1(c)   *Original Poems, on Various Occasions.* Ed. William Cowper. London/Cambridge: Mathews and Leigh, and R. Faulder/ J. Deighton, 1807. 2nd edn. 9.5 × 16.5 cm. Pp. viii + 115. By a Lady. NYPL: 9-NASY.

1(d)   *Original Poems, on Various Occasions.* Ed. William Cowper. Newark[, NJ]: printed by E. B. Gould, 1808. 8 × 13.5 cm. 122 pp. By a Lady. Houghton: *EC75. C8397. A7920c.

1(e)   *Original Poems, on Various Occasions.* Ed. William Cowper. London: Mathews and Leigh, Crosby and Co., 1810. 3rd edn. 9.5 × 15 cm. Pp. xii + 115. By a Lady. BL: 11632. aa. 16.

1(f)   *Original Poems, on Various Occasions.* Ed. William Cowper. London: Sherwood, Neely, and Jones, [1810]. 3rd edn. 8.5 × 14 cm. Pp. xii + 115. By Mrs Cowper. BL: 11644. aa. 18.

Cox, Elizabeth

She lived in Philadelphia. HEHL L. Cat. attributes these volumes to Sarah Wharton.

1   *The Cottage Minstrel; or, Verses on Various Subjects.* Philadelphia: printed for the authoress by Joseph Rakestraw, 1827. 10.5 × 17.5 cm. 120 pp. By a Female of this City. HEHL: 431439.

2   *The Flowers of Autumn . . . To Which is Added, a Few Pieces . . .* Philadelphia: printed for the authoress by J. Richards, 1828. 8.5 × 14 cm. 108 pp. By the Authoress of the *Cottage Minstrel* [Elizabeth Cox] and a Young Female, Late of this City, Dec'd. [E. North]. Library Co. of Philadelphia: Am 1828 Cox/Vt/99 v. 2.

CRAWLEY, Eliza

She later became Mrs Murden. (Widener L. Cat.)

1   *Poems.* Charleston[, SC]: printed by J. Hoff, 1808. 11 × 18.5 cm. Pp. 18 + 5–112 [subscription edition]. By a Young Lady of Charleston. Houghton: *AC8. M9403. 808p.

2(*a*)   *Miscellaneous Poems.* Charleston[, SC]: for the author by Philip Hoff, 1826. 11 × 19 cm. 217 pp. [subscription edition]. By a Lady, of Charleston, South-Carolina. Widener: AL2493. 5. 14.

2(*b*)   *Miscellaneous Poems.* New York: printed for the author by Samuel Wood and Sons, 1827. 2nd edn. 11 × 18.5 cm. 179 pp. [subscription edition]. Widener: AL2493. 5. 15.

CRISTALL, Ann Batten (born *c.*1768)

Daughter of Joseph Alexander Cristall, a mariner, and his wife Anne, the daughter of a Penzance merchant. A younger brother was the painter Joshua Cristall. She seems to have become a schoolteacher. She knew Mary Wollstonecraft and the poet George Dyer. Southey met her in 1797 when he was 23. She is listed in the *Biographical Dictionary of Living Authors* (1816). (Lonsdale)

1   *Poetical Sketches.* London: J. Johnson, 1795. 11.5 × 19 cm. Pp. [xii] + 187 [subscription edition]. 5/- boards. By Ann Batten Cristall. *CR* 13: 286–92; BL: 11645. bb. 25.

CROKER, Margaret Sarah (born 1773)

Born at Holbeton, Devon. Her parents were Capt. Richard Croker and his wife Mary. Her novel *The Question, Who is Anna?* appeared in 1818. (Blain)

1   *A Monody on the Lamented Death of Her Royal Highness the Princess Charlotte-Augusta of Wales and of Saxe Cobourg Saalfield.* London: Edmund Lloyd and J. Booth, 1817. 18 × 23 cm. 24 pp. 3/-. By M. S. Croker. BL: 11641. f. 67(3).

2(*a*)   *Nugae Canorae.* London: for the author by J. Souter, 1818. 14.5 × 24 cm. Pp. xvi + 94 [subscription edition]. By Miss M. S. Croker, Author of *The Question.* BL: 11641. dd. 1.

2(*b*)   *Nugae Canorae.* London: for the author by Sherwood, Neely, and Jones, 1819. 14 × 23 cm. Pp. xvi + 94 [subscription edition]. By Miss M. S. Croker. BL: 11643. d. 5.

3   *A Tribute to the Memory of Sir Samuel Romilly.* London: John Souter, 1818. 13 × 21 cm. 14 pp. By Miss M. S. Croker. BL: 11644. d. 40(1).

4   *Monody on His Late Royal Highness the Duke of Kent.* London: Francis Westley, 1820. 13 × 21 cm. 14 pp. By Miss M. S. Croker. BL: 11644. d. 40(2).

CROSFIELD, Anne (1723–65)

She probably lived in Yorkshire. The name is an unusual one and a Francis Crosfield was living in Middleham, Yorks., whose son was born there in 1759; she was perhaps a member of the same family. (*Athenae Cantabrigienses, NUC*)

1(*a*)   *A Description of the Castle-hills, near Northallerton, a Poem. Written in the Year 1746 . . . To Which is Added, the Hermit, a Poem.* [1777?]. 10.5 × 18 cm. 16 pp. By Miss Crosfield and Dr Beattie. Houghton: *EC75. C8836. 777d.

1(*b*)   *The History of North-Allerton, in the County of York. To Which is Added a Description of the Castle-hills.* Northallerton/York: J. Langdale/Wilson, Spence, and Mawman, 1791. 12.5 × 20.5 cm. 88 pp. [Verse occupies pp. 71–88, Miss Crosfield's being found on pp. 71–80.] By Miss A. Crosfield [and another]. BL: 1303. b. 2.

1(*c*)   *The History and Antiquities of Northallerton, in the County of York.* Northallerton/London/York/Ripon: J. Langdale/

Longman, Hurst, Rees, Orme, and Brown/Wilson and
Sons, J. and G. Todd, and W. Wolstenholme/T. Langdale,
1813. 2nd edn. 9 × 15.5 cm. 78 pp. BL: 10358. aa. 53.

CROWTHER, Mrs

1   *Moral Tales and Poetic Essays.* Huddersfield: printed 'for the
subscribers' by Brook and Lancashire, 1802. 10 × 17 cm.
Pp. [viii] + 122 [verse confined to pp. 57–122; no list of
subscribers]. By Mrs Crowther. BL: 10347. de. 45.

CURLING, Mary Anne (born *c.*1796)

She was the daughter of a London tailor who died in 1809. Her mother
was a lace-cleaner. She won a suit for breach of promise of marriage
in 1819, the defendant being Pastor of the Baptist church in Oxford
Street. (*Report of the Trial Curling against Buck* (1820))

1(*a*)   *Poetical Pieces.* Dover: printed by W. Batcheller, 1831. 9 ×
14.5 cm. 52 pp. By M. A. Curling. BL: T. 1330(5).

1(*b*)   *Poetical Pieces . . . With Some Additional Pieces.* London:
Whittaker, Treacher, and Arnot, 1831. 8.5 × 14 cm. 54 pp.
By M. A. Curling. BL: 11644. a. 26.

CURRIE, Helen

According to the copyright information in *Poems*, she was a resident of
Pennsylvania.

1   *Poems.* Philadelphia: printed by Thomas H. Palmer, 1818.
[9 × 14 cm.—dimensions from p. [iii]]. Pp. viii + 6–150.
By Helen Currie. LC: PS 1474. C75 Rare Bk Coll.

CURSHAM, Mary Anne (died 1881)

She lived at Sutton, Notts. She was a contributor to the annuals, to *The
Amulet* in 1828, and to *The Forget-me-not* in 1830 and 1831. (Boase,
Boyle)

1(*a*)   *Martin Luther, a Poem.* London: for the authoress by
Longman, Hurst, Rees, Orme, Brown, and Green, 1825.
13 × 22 cm. Pp. [iv] + 82. BL: 993. i. 33.

1(*b*)   *Martin Luther, a Poem.* London: Geo. B. Whittaker, 1828.
12.5 × 20.5 cm. Pp. [iv] + 82. By Mary Anne Cursham.
BL: 11644. d. 27.

2   *Emmanuel Swedenborg, and Other Poems.* London: Fred.
        Pitman, [1832?]. 12 × 18.5 cm. Pp. [ii] + 80. By M. A. C.,
        Authoress of *Martin Luther, Norman Abbey*, etc. etc. Yale
        (Mudd): WA/27557.

3   *Poems, Sacred, Dramatic, and Lyric.* London/Nottingham:
        Hamilton, Adams, and Co./S. Bennett, 1833. 10 × 18 cm.
        289 pp. [subscription edition]. By Mary Ann Cursham.
        BL: 11644. cc. 6.

CURTIES, Marianne

A school-mistress, of Abbey House, Reading, Berks. (Shoberl)

1   *Classical Pastime, in a Set of Poetical Enigmas, on the Planets and
        Zodiacal Signs.* Reading/London: printed by Snare and Man/J.
        Richardson, 1813. 11.5 × 18.5 cm. 103 pp. 5/- boards. By
        Marianne Curties. *MR* 76: 213–14; BL: 11645. bb. 35.

CURTIS, Ann, Mrs C. (1764–1838)

Born in Worcester, Worcs., the seventh child of John Kemble, the
provincial theatrical manager, and of Sarah Wood, an actress. Sarah
Siddons and John Philip Kemble were older siblings. She was eccentric and physically awkward as a child and was apprenticed to a
mantua-maker, but she nevertheless became an actress. Her first husband, the actor C. Curtis, whom she married in 1783, proved to be a
bigamist. In 1792 she married William Hatton. She went to New York
City with him in 1793 and an opera with her libretto, *Tammany; or the
Indian Chief*, was performed there in 1794. The Hattons moved to
Swansea, Glamorganshire, where they kept a hotel. Between 1810 and
1831 she published fourteen novels. (Highfill)

1   *Poems on Miscellaneous Subjects.* London: for the author by
        Millan and Rae and J. Bowen, 1783. 10.5 × 17.5 cm. Pp.
        [vi] + x + 56 [subscription edition]. By Ann Curtis, Sister
        of Mrs Siddons. Houghton: 17446. 42. 76.

2   *Poetic Trifles.* Waterford: printed for the authoress by John
        Bull, 1811. 10.5 × 17.5 cm. Pp. xii + 387. By Anne of
        Swansea. HL; BL: 11645. aaa. 56(1).

CUTTS, Mrs

An unmarried woman. She knew the novelists Sarah Scott and Laurence
Sterne. (Blain)

1 (*a*) *Almeria: Or, Parental Advice: A Didactic Poem. Addressed to the Daughters of Great Britain and Ireland.* London/Doncaster: E. and J. Rodwell, H. Gardner, Mrs Denoyer/Smith, 1775. 19.5 × 26 cm. Pp. [ii] + 4 + 47 [subscription edition]. 3/-. By a Friend to the Sex. BL: 11632. g. 1.

1 (*b*) *Almeria: Or, Parental Advice: A Didactic Poem. Addressed to the Daughters of Great Britain and Ireland.* London/Doncaster: E. and J. Rodwell, H. Gardner, Mrs Denoyer/Smith, 1775. 2nd edn. 19.5 × 24.5 cm. Pp. [ii] + 47. By a Friend to the Sex. BL: 11630. e. 2(14).

D——, Emily

1 *The Muse and Poetess, a Lesson from Nature, and Other Poems.* London: J. Hatchard and Son, 1835. 10 × 16 cm. Pp. viii + 179. By Emily D****. BL: 992. g. 12.

DACRE, Lady, *see* WILMOT, Barbarina

DACRE, Charlotte (born 1782)

She was a daughter of John King (also known as Jacob Rey), a money-lender and blackmailer, and of his first wife Debora Lara, and Sophia Fortnum (q.v.) was a sister. She later became Mrs Byrne. Between 1805 and 1811 she published four novels, using the pseudonym Rosa Matilda. (Allibone, Blain, *NUC*)

1 *Trifles of Helicon.* London: James Ridgway, 1798. 12.5 × 21 cm. Pp. [ii] + 54. 3/-. By Charlotte and Sophia King. *CR* 22: 353–4; BL: 11642. bbb. 23.

2 *Hours of Solitude. A Collection of Original Poems, now First Published.* London: Hughes, and Ridgeway, 1805. 11.5 × 18.5 cm. 2 vols. By Charlotte Dacre, better known by the name of Rosa Matilda. BL: 11645. bb. 5.

3 *George the Fourth, a Poem: Dedicated to the Right Honourable the Marquis of Londonderry . . . To Which are Added Lyrics, Designed for Various Melodies.* London: Hatchard and Son, Mayhew and Co., 1822. 10 × 15.5 cm. 64 pp. By the Author of *Hours of Solitude.* BL: 11644. aaa. 17.

DALLOR, Frances, Mrs

1   *The Duel, an Original Poem*. London: W. Harding, 1832. 10.5 × 18 cm. 17 pp. BL: 11646. bb. 25.

DARK, Mariann

1   *Sonnets and Other Poems*. London: for the author by Sherwood, Neely and Jones, 1818. 9.5 × 15 cm. Pp. xl + 120 [subscription edition]. By Mariann Dark. BL: 11641. b. 58(1).

DARLING, Jessy Rolland, *see* DARLING, Patricia Rolland
She seems to have been a daughter of Patricia Rolland Darling (q.v.).

DARLING, Patricia Rolland, Mrs (died 1814)
A memorial poem by her son Peter in *Poetical Pieces* gives the date of her death.

1   *Poetical Pieces*. Edinburgh: printed for the author's family by Oliver and Boyd, 1817. 10 × 16.5 cm. 84 pp. By Patricia Rolland Darling, Jessy Rolland Darling, Mrs Home [and others]. BL: 1346. b. 43.

DARWALL, Elizabeth
Daughter of the poet Mary Whately and of the Revd John Darwall, Vicar of Walsall. (Lonsdale)

1   *The Storm, with Other Poems*. London/Birmingham: J. Ridgway/Knott and Lloyd, 1810. 9.5 × 15.5 cm. Pp. x + 159. By Elizabeth Darwall. BL: 1467. c. 30.

DASH, Mary
She probably lived in Brighton.

1   *Sacred and Moral Pieces*. Brighton: [printed by Elliott and Co.], 1827. 10.5 × 18.5 cm. Pp. xviii + 102 [subscription edition]. By Mary Dash. BL: 11644. cc. 31.

THE DAUGHTER OF A CLERGYMAN, *see* CHETWYND, Mary Anne

DAVIDSON, Lucretia Maria (1808–25)
Born in Plattsburg, NY. She was the daughter of Oliver Davidson, a physician, and of Margaret Miller. She was sent to Miss Willard's school

in Troy, NY, but she died of consumption. Several memoirs were written of her. (*DAB*)

1   *Amir Khan, and Other Poems: The Remains* . . . Ed. Samuel
     F. B. Morse. New York: G. and C. and H. Carvill, 1829.
     10.5 × 17.5 cm. Pp. xxxii + 174. By Lucretia Maria
     Davidson. BL: 11687. ccc. 21.

DAVIDSON, Margaret (died *c.*1781)

According to the autobiographical account in *The Extraordinary Life*, she
was the child of poor and uneducated parents in the parish of Killinchy
in the townland of Ballybreda. She was blinded by smallpox at the age
of 2 and received no formal education. As a child she became an
enthusiastic Christian and eventually, in spite of the opposition of her
family, a devout Methodist. She supported herself by spinning flax.

1   *The Extraordinary Life and Christian Experience of Margaret
     Davidson, (as Dictated by Herself) Who was a Poor, Blind
     Woman among the People Called Methodists, but Rich towards
     God, and Illuminated with the Light of Life. To Which are
     Added, Some of her Letters and Hymns.* Dublin: printed for
     the editor by Bennett Dugdale, 1782. 10 × 16.5 cm. Pp.
     viii + 164 [subscription copy; the verse being confined to
     pp. 154–64]. By the Revd Edward Smyth and Margaret
     Davidson. BL: 4902. b. 28.

DAVIES, Miss, *see* COLLECTIONS 2, 3

DAVIES, Blanche

1   *Octavia; or the Bride of St. Agnes. A Tragedy, in Five Acts.*
     Doncaster/York/Leeds/Hull: Brooke and Co. and C.
     White/Bellerby, Deighton/Hernaman and Perring/Wilson,
     and Peck and Smith, 1832. 13.5 × 21 cm. Pp. [ii] + 62. By
     Blanche Davies. BL: 11779. f. 23.

DAVIS, Miss, *see* DAVIES, Miss

DAVIS, Martha Ann, Mrs

In her book she addresses the 'Virginian public'. She seems, from
poems about and to them, to have had at least four children, at least
two of whom were daughters.

1   *Poems of Laura; an Original American Work.* Petersburg
     [: printed by Whitworth and Yancey], 1818. 11 × 19 cm.
     Pp. [ii] + 106 + iv. By Martha Ann Davis. Boston Public:
     A. 2133.

DAVIS, Mary Ann

1   *The Wild Flower Wreath. A Collection of Miscellaneous Poems.*
     With Reflections, &c. in Poetic Prose. Birmingham: printed by
     J. Moore, 1835. 9.5 × 16 cm. Pp. viii + 150. By Mary Ann
     Davis. BL: 11642. aa. 45.

DAVIS, Mary Anne

1(*a*) *Fables in Verse: From Aesop, La Fontaine, and Others.*
     London: J. Harris, 1813. 10 × 18 cm. Pp. xii + 190. By
     Mary Anne Davis. BL: 12305. cc. 32.

1(*b*) *Fables in Verse: From Aesop, La Fontaine, and Others.*
     London: G. and W. B. Whittaker, 1819. 2nd edn. 10.5 ×
     17.5 cm. Pp. xii + 192. By Mary Anne Davis. CUL: 8720.
     d. 485.

1(*c*) *Fables in Verse: From Aesop, La Fontaine, and Others.*
     London: A. K. Newman and Co., 1821. 2nd edn. 9.5 × 17
     cm. Pp. xii + 192. By Mary Anne Davis. Bodley: Montagu
     154.

1(*d*) *Fables in Verse: From Aesop, La Fontaine, and Others.*
     London: A. K. Newman and Co., 1822. 2nd edn. 9.5 ×
     16.5 cm. Pp. xii + 192. By Mary Anne Davis. BL: 12305.
     bb. 13.

[*See also*: 'Tributary Stanzas, to the Memory of . . . Frances
Augusta Bell (2 pp.) in Johnson Grant, *A Memoir of Miss Frances
Augusta Bell* . . . (1827).]

DAWSON, M. A.

1(*a*) *A Poem, Occasioned by the Partial Burning of York Cathedral:*
     Most Respectfully Inscribed to the Citizens of York. London/
     York/Dublin/Edinburgh: Hatchard and Son/Barclay/
     Tims/Oliphant, 1829. 10 × 16 cm. 24 pp. By Miss M. A.
     Dawson. Yale (Sterling): Ib55/T1/D326.

1(*b*) *A Poem Occasioned by the Partial Burning of York Cathedral: Most Respectfully Inscribed to the Citizens of York.* London/York/Dublin/Edinburgh: Hatchard and Son/ Barclay/Tims/Oliphant, 1829. 2nd edn. 9.5 × 16 cm. 24 pp. By Miss M. A. Dawson. BL: 11646. aaa. 33.

DAY, Eliza, Mrs Thomas (1734–1814?)

Her father was a farmer in Huntingdonshire, probably surnamed Nichols; one grandfather was Maximilian Crosland. She underwent a religious conversion in 1757 and became a Quaker. Her husband, Thomas Day, died in 1807, and at the time of his death they were living in Stockwell, Surrey. (*Friends' Books, Poems on Various Subjects*)

1 *Thoughts Occasioned by the Death of Maria: Who Departed this Life, August 8, 1788. Also on a Beloved Friend: Likewise on Visiting Eusebia's Tomb.* London: for the author by T. Scollick, T. Hunt, and J. Parsons, 1789. 12.5 × 21 cm. 16 pp. BL: 11644. d. 41(1).

2 *Serious Reflections on the Death of Johannes, Who was Shot by his Friend, July 12, 1789. Likewise on the Triumphant Death of Josephus, Aged Eighteen Years.* London: for the author by Trap, Riedel and Scollick, 1789. 12 × 18 cm. 31 pp. 6*d*. BL: 11644. cc. 28.

3 *A Poem on the Proclamation of Peace, Which Took Place the Twentieth of the Sixth Month . . . the Fifty-fourth Year of the Reign of King George the Third.* Tottenham: printed for the author by G. S. Coventry, 1814. 12.5 × 21 cm. 8 pp. 6*d*. BL: 11644. d. 41(2).

4 *Poems on Various Subjects, with Several Pieces, on the Death of Relatives and Friends, Written during the Last Fifty-seven Years of the Author's Life.* Tottenham: printed for the author by G. S. Coventry, 1814. 11.5 × 19.5 cm. 160 pp. BL: 11644. cc. 5.

DAY, Esther, Mrs Thomas (*c.*1752–92), *see also* SMITH, Jane 2

Her maiden name was Milnes and she attended Mrs Dennis's Female Boarding School in Queen Square, London, where much of her verse is said to have been composed. In 1778 she married the highly eccentric author of *Sandford and Merton.*

1 *Select Miscellaneous Productions . . . in Verse and Prose: Also, Some Detached Pieces of Poetry . . .* Ed. Thomas Lowndes.

London: Cadell and Davies, 1805. 11.5 × 19.5 cm. Pp. xiv + 52 + [12] + 204 [her poetry occupying pp. 37–71]. By Mrs Day, and others. BL: 11642. bbb. 26.

DAY, Martha (1813–33)

Born in New Haven, Conn. Her father, Jeremiah Day, was president of Yale University. She was educated at Claudius Herrick's school in New Haven and then at a boarding school at Greenfield, Mass., where she was first a pupil and eventually an assistant. (May)

1   *The Literary Remains . . . with Rev. Dr Fitch's Address at her Funeral; and Sketches of her Character.* Ed. [Prof. Kingsley]. New Haven[, Conn.]: Hezekiah Howe and Co., 1834. 12 × 19.5 cm. Pp. viii + 121 [verse occupies pp. 1–54]. By Martha Day. HEHL: 44420.

DAYE, Eliza

She seems, from her book, to have lived in Lancaster, Lancs.

1   *Poems, on Various Subjects.* Lancaster/Liverpool/London: the author and Walmsley and Holt/Jones, Gore, Wright and Ormandy/Johnson, 1798. 13 × 20.5 cm. Pp. xiv + 258 [subscription edition]. 7/- in boards, 7/6 hot-pressed. By Eliza Daye. BL: 11642. cc. 19.

DE CRESPIGNY, Lady Mary Champion (1748?–1812)

The only child of Joseph Clarke of Yorkshire. When she was 16 she married Claude Champion de Crespigny (who was created baronet in 1805). She also wrote *Letters of Advice from a Mother to a Son* (1803) and *The Pavilion* (1796), a novel. (Todd 1)

1   *A Monody to the Memory of the Right Honourable the Lord Collingwood.* London: Cadell and Davis, 1810. 19.5 × 25.5 cm. 23 pp. By Lady Champion de Crespigny. BL: 11645. h. 7.

DE CRESPIGNY, Caroline, Mrs Heaton Champion

The youngest daughter of Henry Bathurst, Bishop of Norwich. She married in 1820. (Boase)

1   *Remembrances of Friendship.* Cheltenham/London: G. A. Williams/Longman and Co., 1830. 10.5 × 15.5 cm. 44 pp. HL; BL: 11646. aaa. 25.

DE FLEURY, Maria

She was a Protestant polemicist of French origin and she lived in London. (Blain)

1   *Poems, Occasioned by the Confinement and Acquittal of the Right Honourable Lord George Gordon, President of the Protestant Association.* London: for the author, by Margram, Mrs Dee, Tillcock, 1781. 11 × 17.5 cm. 24 pp. By Maria de Fleury. BL: 1075. h. 16(1).

2(*a*)   *Unrighteous Abuse Detected . . .* Inference.

2(*b*)   *Unrighteous Abuse Detected and Chastised, or, a Vindication of Innocence and Integrity, being an Answer to a Virulent Poem Intituled, the Protestant Association.* London: printed for the author by R. Denham, 1781. 2nd edn. 10 × 17.5 cm. 23 pp. 3*d.* By Maria de Fleury. BL: 1163. b. 14(3).

3(*a*)   *Henry, or the Triumph of Grace. A Sacred Poem . . .* London: printed for the author by R. Denham, 1782. 12.5 × 20.5 cm. 40 pp. 1/-. By Maria de Fleury. BL: 11632. cc. 7.

3(*b*)   *Henry: Or, the Wanderer Reclaimed. A Sacred Poem. Humbly Addressed to British Youth.* London: printed for the author by W. Justins, 1786. 12.5 × 21.5 cm. 40 pp. 1/-. By Maria de Fleury. *MR* 81: 181; Bodley: Vet. A5 e. 4060.

4   *Hymns for Believer's Baptism.* London: Kirkham's Meeting-house, 1786. 8 × 13 cm. 23 pp. By Maria de Fleury. BL: 3435. aaa. 54(1).

5   *British Liberty Established, and Gallic Liberty Restored; or, the Triumph of Freedom. A Poem. Occasioned by the Grand Revolution in France . . .* London: for the author by J. Matthews, H. D. Symmonds, J. Nott, Ash, Thompson, Mrs Hancock, 1790. 12 × 18.5 cm. 38 pp. By Maria de Fleury. BL: 11632. bb. 19.

6(*a*)   *Divine Poems and Essays on Various Subjects . . .* London: for the author by T. Wilkins, Bellamy and Roberts, M. Trapp, M. Gurney, 1791. 13 × 21 cm. Pp. xii + 214 [verse and prose]. 3/- sewed. By Maria de Fleury. BL: 11632. e. 20.

6(*b*)   *Divine Poems and Essays, on Various Subjects . . .* Philadelphia: J. W. Scott, 1803. 17 cm. Pp. 252 + 10 [verse and prose]. By Maria De Fleury. *NUC* [Library Company of Philadelphia]. Not found.

6(*c*)   *Divine Poems and Essays, on Various Subjects. In Two Parts.*
New York: Deare and Andrews, 1804. 10 × 16.5 cm. 288
pp. [verse and prose]. By Maria De Fleury. NYPL: NDH.

[*See also*: 'An Ode Occasioned by the Death of Mrs . . .
Dowland' (1783, 7 pp.).]

DE KATZLEBEN, *see* BOWLES, Caroline

DE KRAFFT, Mary

1   *Poems, Chiefly Amatory.* Washington[, DC]: printed for the
publisher, 1809. 9.5 × 16 cm. 112 pp. By a Lady. LC: PS
1525. D75 1809 Office.

DELIA, *see* COLLECTIONS 14

DENNING, Elizabeth (died *c.*1820?)
She lived at Grassy-point, NY. She had sisters called Caroline, Rosette,
Jane Louise, and Elmina. Her father edited her book after her death.
(*Poems*)

1   *Poems . . . Presented by her Father to . . . in Remembrance.* Ed.
[Mr Denning]. New York: printed by [Abraham Paul],
1821. 12 × 19.5 cm. 123 pp. By Elizabeth Denning. BL:
11642. de. 41.

DERENZY, Margaret, Mrs (died 1829)
Her maiden name was Graves. (*NUC*)

1   *Poems Appropriate for a Sick or a Melancholy Hour.* Wellington,
Salop./London: F. Houlston and Son/Scatcherd and Co.,
[1824]. 9.5 × 16 cm. 203 pp. BL: 11646. bb. 14.

2   *A Whisper to a Newly-married Pair, from a Widowed Wife.*
Philadelphia: E. L. Carey and A. Hart, 1833. 5th edn. 8.5
× 14 cm. 103 pp. [verse confined to pp. 93–103, lacking in
previous editions]. BL: 8404. aa. 31.

3   *Parnassian Geography; or, the Little Ideal Wanderer.* Wellington,
Salop./London: F. Houlston and Son/Scatcherd and Co.,
[1824]. 8.5 × 14 cm. 148 pp. By the Author of *A Whisper
to a Newly-married Pair*, etc. BL: 10003. aa. 38.

4 *The Flowers of the Forest.* Wellington, Salop.: Houlston and Son, 1828. 8.5 × 14 cm. 142 pp. By the Author of *The Juvenile Wreath* and *A Gift from the Mountains.* BL: 994. c. 9.

5(a) *The Juvenile Wreath.* Wellington, Salop.: Houlston and Son, 1828. 8.5 × 14 cm. 86 pp. By the Author of *The Flowers of the Forest* and *A Gift from the Mountains.* BL: 994. c. 39.

5(b) *The Juvenile Wreath.* 1829. 2nd edn. Stainforth.

DEVERELL, Mary, Mrs (born 1737)

She was the daughter of a clothier in Gloucestershire, and was self-educated. She moved to London, but her title-pages continued to locate her in Gloucestershire. (Blain, *NUC*)

1 *Miscellanies in Prose and Verse, Mostly Written in the Epistolary Style: Chiefly upon Moral Subjects, and Particularly Calculated for the Improvement of Younger Minds.* London/Bristol/Bath/Oxford/Hereford/Tunbridge-Wells: for the author by Dodsley, Robson and Michell, Cadell, Rivingtons, Wilkie, Crowder, Mrs Davenhill/Cadell/Pratt and Clinch, Meyler/Fletcher/Pugh/Sprange, 1781. 10.5 × 17.5 cm. 2 vols. 7/-. By Mrs M. Deverell, Gloucestershire. BL: 722. c. 16, 17.

2(a) *Theodora & Didymus, or, the Exemplification of Pure Love and Vital Religion. An Heroic Poem, in Three Cantos.* London/Bath/Bristol: the author and Dodsley, Wilkie, Shepherdson and Co./Bull and Meyler/Lloyd, 1784. 13.5 × 22 cm. Pp. xxiv + 80 [subscription edition]. 5/- boards. By Mrs Mary Deverell, Gloucestershire. CUL: 7720. c. 130.

2(b) *Theodora and Didymus, or, the Exemplification of Pure Love and Vital Religion. An Heroic Poem, in Three Cantos. With an Appendix, Consisting of a Pindaric Ode, for the Queen's Birthday, 1786; and Poetical Epistles, on Various Moral and Entertaining Subjects.* London/Bath: for the author by Dodsley, Miss Davis, Robson, Cadell, Wilkie/Bull and Meyler, 1786. 2nd edn. 13 × 20.5 cm. Pp. xxviii + 80 + 32 [subscription edition]. 6/- boards. By Mrs Mary Deverell, Gloucestershire. BL: 11642. bbb. 37.

3 *Mary, Queen of Scots; an Historical Tragedy, or, Dramatic Poem.* London/Gloucester: for the author by Stockdale, Long, Richardson/Washbourn, 1792. 12.5 × 21 cm. Pp. [ii] +

116. 3/-. By Mrs M. Deverell, Gloucestershire. BL: 11778. f. 13.

DEVONSHIRE, the Duchess of, *see* CAVENDISH, Georgiana

DE WITT, Susan, Mrs Simeon (1778–1824)
Her father was the Revd William Lynn of New York City. In 1810 she married Simeon de Witt, a widower with six children. He was a surveyor and a scientist. (Blain, *NUC*)

1(*a*)   *The Pleasures of Religion: A Poem.* New-york: Wiley and Halsted, 1820. 9 × 14 cm. 72 pp. LC: PS 1537. D4 Office.

1(*b*)   *The Pleasures of Religion: A Poem.* New York: T. Harries, 1832. 8 × 12.5 cm. 72 pp. NEDL: KC19623.

DICKINSON, Eleanor, Mrs Robert
A Quaker. She was married to Robert Dickinson of Springfield Academy, Liverpool. Before her marriage her surname was Blakey. (*Friends' Books*)

1   *The Pleasures of Piety, with Other Poems.* London/Liverpool: Sherwood, Jones and Co./the authoress, 1824. 10 × 16.5 cm. Pp. viii + 84. By Eleanor Dickinson. BL: 994. f. 7.

2   *The Mamluk. A Poem.* London: Effingham Wilson, 1830. 11.5 × 18.5 cm. Pp. [iv] + 224. By Eleanor Dickinson. BL: 994. g. 13.

DIXON, Charlotte Eliza, Mrs, *see also* COLLECTIONS 32

1(*a*)   *The Mount of Olives, or the Resurrection and Ascension; a Poem. In Continuation of Calvary.* London: for the author by B. Crosby and Co., 1814. 9.5 × 15.5 cm. Pp. viii + 126. By Mrs Dixon. BL: 11645. aa. 40.

1(*b*)   *The Mount of Olives, or the Resurrection and Ascension; a Poem. In Continuation of Calvary.* London: for the author by J. Souter, 1815. 2nd edn. 9.5 × 16 cm. Pp. vi + 126. By Mrs Dixon. BL: 11645. aa. 39.

2   *'Bread Cast upon the Waters'.* London: Sea-book Depository and 1, Warwick Square, 1830. 10.5 × 17 cm. Pp. viii + 88. By Mrs Dixon, Author of the *Mount of Olives*, a Poem. BL: 11646. cc. 21.

DIXON, Sophie

Her preface is written from Dartmoor.

1   *Castalian Hours. Poems.* London: Longman, Rees, Orme, Brown, and Green, 1829. 13.5 × 21.5 cm. Pp. x + 220 [subscription edition]. By Sophie Dixon. BL: 994. i. 10.

DODS, Mary Diana

The illegitimate daughter of George Douglas, 15th Earl of Morton. She lived on the Continent in male disguise with Isabel Robinson Douglas and used the name Walter Sholto Douglas. She also wrote translations and fiction. (*Letters of Mary Wollstonecraft Shelley*, ed. Betty T. Bennett (1980–3))

1   *Dramas of the Ancient World.* Edinburgh/London: William Blackwood/T. Cadell, 1822. 13.5 × 22 cm. Pp. viii + 278. 10/6 boards. By David Lyndsay. *MR* 99: 370–7; BL: C. 126. h. 10.

DODSWORTH, Anna, Mrs Frank (*c.*1740–1801)

Daughter of Francis Burrell. Her mother died when Anna was young. She was married to Frank Dodsworth, Vicar of Dodington, Kent, for forty-three years. (*GM, Fugitive Pieces*)

1   *Fugitive Pieces.* Ed. [Mr Dodsworth]. Canterbury: printed [for private distribution] by Simmons and Kirby, 1802. 10.5 × 18.5 cm. Pp. iv + 107. By Mrs Dodsworth. BL: 11641. e. 10.

DORSET, Catherine Ann, Mrs Michael (1750?–1817?), *see also* SMITH, Charlotte 4(*a–b*)

The younger daughter of Nicholas Turner and Ann Towers, and a sister of Charlotte Smith (q.v.). She married Michael Dorset, a captain in the army, in 1770. She was widowed in 1805; they had at least one son. (*DNB*)

1(*a*)   *The Lion's Masquerade. A Sequel to the Peacock at Home.* London: J. Harris and B. Tabart, 1807. 9.5 × 11.5 cm. 16 pp. By a Lady. BL: C. 40. a. 57(4).

1(*b*)   *The Lion's Masquerade, a Sequel to the Peacock at Home.* London: J. Harris and B. Tabart, 1808. 10 × 13 cm. 16 pp. By a Lady. BL: 012806. de. 8(8).

2(*a*) *The Peacock 'At Home': A Sequel to the Butterfly's Ball.*
London: J. Harris, 1807. 9.5 × 11.5 cm. 16 pp. 1/- plain,
1/6 coloured. By a Lady. *MR* 54: 446–7; BL: C. 40. a.
57(2).

2(*b*) *The Peacock 'At Home': A Sequel to the Butterfly's Ball.*
London: J. Harris, 1808. 10 × 12 cm. 16 pp. By a Lady.
NLS: Mas. 47.

2(*c*) *The Peacock 'at Home': A Sequel to the Butterfly's Ball.* New
York: David Longworth, 1808. 9 × 14 cm. 20 pp. By a
Lady [Mrs Dorset] and [Mr Roscoe]. AAS: DATED PAMS.

2(*d*) *The Peacock at Home; and Other Poems.* London/Edinburgh:
John Murray, J. Harris/Manners and Miller, 1809. 10 ×
15.5 cm. Pp. vi + 126. By Mrs Dorset. Edinburgh: LL. 38.
17. 33.

2(*e*) *The Peacock 'At Home' . . . To Which is Added the Butterfly's
Ball; an Original Poem.* London: John Harris, [1810?]. 10.5 ×
18 cm. 24 pp. By a Lady [Mrs Dorset] and Mr Roscoe.
BL: 012806. f. 14.

2(*f*) *The Peacock 'At Home' . . .* 5th edn. Inference.

2(*g*) *The Peacock 'At Home' . . .* 6th edn. Inference.

2(*h*) *The Peacock 'At Home' . . .* 7th edn. Inference.

2(*i*) *The Peacock 'At Home' . . .* 8th edn. Inference.

2(*j*) *The Peacock 'At Home' . . .* 9th edn. Inference.

2(*k*) *The Peacock 'At Home' . . .* 10th edn. Inference.

2(*l*) *The Peacock 'At Home' . . .* 11th edn. Inference.

2(*m*) *The Peacock 'At Home' . . .* 12th edn. Inference.

2(*n*) *The Peacock 'At Home' . . .* 13th edn. Inference.

2(*o*) *The Peacock 'At Home' . . .* 14th edn. Inference.

2(*p*) *The Peacock 'At Home' . . .* 15th edn. Inference.

2(*q*) *The Peacock 'At Home' . . .* 16th edn. Inference.

2(*r*) *The Peacock 'At Home' . . .* 17th edn. Inference.

2(*s*) *The Peacock 'At Home' . . .* 18th edn. Inference.

2(*t*) *The Peacock 'At Home' . . .* 19th edn. Inference.

2(*u*) *The Peacock 'At Home' . . .* 20th edn. Inference.

2(*v*) *The Peacock 'At Home' . . .* 21st edn. Inference.

2(*w*)   *The Peacock 'At Home'* . . . 22nd edn. Inference.

2(*x*)   *The Peacock 'At Home'* . . . 23rd edn. Inference.

2(*y*)   *The Peacock 'At Home'* . . . 24th edn. Inference.

2(*z*)   *The Peacock 'At Home'* . . . 25th edn. Inference.

2(*aa*)   *The Peacock 'At Home': A Sequel to the Butterfly's Ball.* London: J. Harris, 1812. 26th edn. 10 × 13 cm. 16 pp. By a Lady. BL: 012806. i. 27(4).

2(*bb*)   *The Peacock 'At Home': Or Grand Assemblage of Birds* . . . *Illustrated with Elegant Engravings.* Philadelphia: Wm. Charles, 1814. 10.5 × 13.5 cm. 16 pp. 25 cents coloured, 18 cents plain. By Roscoe [Mrs Dorset]. NYPL: *KVD.

2(*cc*)   *The Peacock 'At Home': A Sequel to the Butterfly's Ball.* London: J. Harris, 1815. 27th edn. 9.5 × 12 cm. 11 pp. UCLA: Percival D73p.

2(*dd*)   *The Peacock 'At Home': A Sequel to the Butterfly's Ball.* London: J. Harris, 1817. 28th edn. 10 × 12.5 cm. 16 pp. By a Lady. UBC: SP PZ6 1817 D67. [Photocopy seen only.]

2(*ee*)   *The Peacock 'At Home,'* . . . *To Which is Added the Butterfly's Ball; an Original Poem* . . . London: J. Harris and Son, 1822. 10.5 × 17.5 cm. 24 pp. By a Lady [C. A. Dorset] and by Mr Roscoe. CUL: Lib. 7. 82. 28(1).

2(*ff*)   *The Peacock 'At Home',* . . . *to Which is Added the Butterfly's Ball; an Original Poem* . . . London: John Harris, 1824. 10.5 × 18 cm. 24 pp. By a Lady [C. A. Dorset] and Mr Roscoe. National Library of Ireland: 827. d. 8.

2(*gg*)   *The Peacock 'At Home'* . . . *And Butterfly's Ball; an Original Poem.* London: John Harris, 1831. 10.5 × 18 cm. 24 pp. [this copy lacks pp. 9–10]. By a Lady [C. A. Dorset] and Mr Roscoe. Bodley: 280 e. 3517.

2(*hh*)   *The Peacock 'At Home'* . . .; *and, Butterfly's Ball, an Original Poem* . . . London: J. Harris, 1834. 24 pp. By a Lady and by Mr Roscoe. *NUC.* Not found.

3   *The Lioness's Rout; being a Sequel to the Butterfly's Ball, the Grasshopper's Feast, and the Peacock 'At Home'.* London: B. Tabart, [1808]. 10 × 13 cm. 32 pp. By a Lady. BL: 11645. de. 51.

4(*a*)   *Think before You Speak: Or, the Three Wishes. A Tale.*
London: M. J. Godwin, 1809. 9.5 × 11.5 cm. 32 pp. By
the Author of *The Peacock at Home.* BL: C. 40. a. 57(3).

4(*b*)   *Think before You Speak.* London. 2nd edn. Inference.

4(*c*)   *Think before You Speak: Or the Three Wishes, a Poetic Tale.*
Philadelphia: Wm. Charles, 1810. First American from the
2nd London edn. 10 × 12.5 cm. 30 pp. Free Library of
Philadelphia: CB/1810/D738t.

4(*d*)   *Think before You Speak: Or, the Three Wishes. A Tale.*
Philadelphia: Johnson and Warner, 1810. 10.5 × 12.5 cm.
32 pp. By the Author of *The Peacock at Home.* NYPL:
*KVD.

4(*e*)   *Think before You Speak: Or, the Three Wishes. A Tale.*
Philadelphia: Johnson and Warner, 1811. 12mo. 32 pp. By
the Author of *The Peacock at Home.* Rosenbach No. 438.
Not located.

4(*f*)   *Think before You Speak; or the Three Wishes; a Poetic Tale.*
Philadelphia: Morgan and Sons, 1832. 1st American from
2nd London edn. 10.5 × 12.5 cm. 32 pp. Plain 18¾ cents,
coloured 25 cents. NYPL: *KVD.

5   *The Peacock Abroad; or Visits Returned.* Greenwich:
W. Richardson, 1812. 10 × 13 cm. 22 pp. BL: 12809. df. 9.

6   *The Peacock and Parrot, on their Tour to Discover the Author of
'The Peacock at Home'.* London: J. Harris, 1816. 10.5 × 13
cm. 31 pp. 1/- coloured. BL: 012806. de. 7(5).

DOWNING, Harriet, Mrs

She probably grew up in Dorset. She married a freemason and they
had children. She contributed to annuals, particularly to *The Forget-me-not*
in 1828 and 1829. The title-page of her *Remembrances of a Monthly Nurse*
(1852) describes her as 'the late Mrs H. Downing'. (Blain, Boyle)

1(*a*)   *Mary; or, Female Friendship; a Poem, in Twelve Books.* [Book I
only.] London: printed for the author by J. Croft, 1816.
18.5 × 23.5 cm. 8 pp. By a Lady. BL: 11641. h. 9(10).

1(*b*)   *Mary; or, Female Friendship: A Poem, in Twelve Books.* London:
for the author by James Harper, J. M. Richardson, T. and
J. Allman, 1816. 21 × 27 cm. Pp. viii + 182 [subscription
edition]. By Harriet Downing. BL: 642. 1. 23.

2   *The Child of the Tempest; and Other Poems*. London: J. Harwood, 1821. 12.5 × 21 cm. Pp. [x] + 76 [subscription edition]. By Harriet Downing. BL: 11644. d. 26.

3   *The Bride of Sicily, a Dramatic Poem*. London: Hurst, Chance, and Co., and John Sams, 1830. 13 × 21 cm. Pp. [iv] + 167. By Harriet Downing. BL: 1344. i. 49.

D——s [DAVIS?, DAVIES?], Miss, *see* COLLECTIONS 1(*a–c*)

DUDLEY, M. E.

Daughter of George Dudley, of Tipperary, and of Sarah Cove. On her father's death the family moved to Eastbourne, near Midhurst, Sussex. She supplied the poetry for the book she co-authored with her brother Howard, he being 15 at the time. (*DNB* (under Howard Dudley))

1(*a*)   *Juvenile Researches, or a Description of Some of the Principal Towns in the Western Part of Sussex, and the Borders of Hants. Interspersed with Various Pieces of Poetry, by a Sister* . . . Eastbourne: privately printed, 1835. 9 × 10.5 cm. Pp. viii + 123. By [Howard Dudley and M. E. Dudley]. BL: C. 44. a. 13.

1(*b*)   *Juvenile Researches, or a Description of Some of the Principal Towns in the West of Sussex, and the Borders of Hants. The Whole being Interspersed with Various Pieces of Poetry by a Sister*. Eastbourne: printed by Howard Dudley, 1835. 2nd edn. 8.5 × 11.5 cm. Pp. vii + 126 + v. By [Howard Dudley and M. E. Dudley]. BL: C. 44. a. 14.

DUDLEY, Mary, Lady

Daughter of James White, of Berrow, Som., and of his wife Eleanor, and sister of the popular actress Elizabeth Hartley. She married Sir Henry Bate Dudley, the famous 'fighting parson', in 1780. Her 'Passages Selected' first appeared in her husband's newspaper, the *Morning Herald*. (Highfill)

1(*a*)   *Passages Selected by Distinguished Personages . . . a Comi-tragedy* . . . Vol. i [of 4]. [London]: Ridgway, 1795. 8vo [prose and verse]. 2/6. By [Lady Dudley and another]. *CR* 17: 235. Not located.

1(*b*)   *Passages*. 2nd edn. Inference.

1(*c*) *Passages Selected by Distinguished Personages, on the Great Literary Trial of Vortigern and Rowena! A Comi-tragedy.* London: J. Ridgway, [n.d.]. Vol. i [of 4]. 3rd edn. 10 × 16 cm. Pp. viii + 101 [prose and verse]. By [Lady Dudley and another]. HEHL: 88232.

1(*d*) *Passages.* 4th edn. Inference.

1(*e*) *Passages Selected by Distinguished Personages, on the Great Literary Trial of Vortigern and Rowena; a Comi-tragedy.* Vol. i [of 4]. London: J. Ridgway, [1796?]. 5th edn. 9.5 × 16.5 cm. Pp. viii + 101 [prose and verse]. By [Lady Dudley and another]. BL: 1344. d. 9.

1(*f*) *Passages Selected by Distinguished Personages, on the Great Literary Trial of Vortigern and Rowena; a Comi-tragedy.* Vol. i [of 4]. London: J. Ridgway, [n.d.]. 6th edn. 9.5 × 16 cm. Pp. viii + 101 [prose and verse]. By [Lady Dudley and another]. Trinity: 91. q. 56. No. 1.

1(*g*) *Passages Selected by Distinguished Personages, on the Great Literary Trial of Vortigern and Rowena; a Comi-tragedy.* Vol. i [of 4]. London: J. Ridgway, [1795]. 7th edn. 10 × 16.5 cm. Pp. viii + 101 [prose and verse]. By [Lady Dudley and another]. BL: 11762. b. 18.

1(*h*) *Passages Selected by Distinguished Personages, on the Great Literary Trial of Vortigern and Rowena; a Comi-tragedy.* London: J. Ridgway, [n.d.]. Vol. i [of 4]. 8th edn. 10 × 15.5 cm. Pp. viii + 101 [prose and verse]. By [Lady Dudley and another]. HEHL: 260818.

2(*a*) *Passages Selected by Distinguished Personages, on the Great Literary Trial of Vortigern and Rowena; a Comi-tragedy.* Vol. ii [of 4]. London: J. Ridgway, [1796]. 9.5 × 16 cm. Pp. [2] + ii + 104 [prose and verse]. By [Lady Dudley and another]. BL: 993. a. 48.

2(*b*) *Passages Selected by Distinguished Personages on the Great Literary Trial of Vortigern and Rowena; a Comi-tragedy.* Vol. ii [of 4]. London: J. Ridgway, [1796?]. 2nd edn. 9 × 15.5 cm. Pp. [ii] + ii + 72 [prose and verse]. By [Lady Dudley and another]. BL: 1607/6044(2).

2(*c*) *Passages Selected by Distinguished Personages, on the Great Literary Trial of Vortigern and Rowena; a Comi-tragedy.* Vol. ii [of 4]. London: J. Ridgway, [n.d.]. 3rd edn. 9.5 × 15.5 cm. Pp. 2 + ii + 104 [prose and verse]. By [Lady Dudley and another]. HEHL: 482203.

2(*d*) *Passages Selected* . . . Vol. ii [of 4]. London: Ridgway, [1796?]. 4th edn. By [Lady Dudley and another]. *NUC*. Not found.

2(*e*) *Passages Selected by Distinguished Personages, on the Great Literary Trial of Vortigern and Rowena; a Tragi-comedy.* Vol. ii [of 4]. London: J. Ridgway, [n.d.]. 5th edn. 9 × 16 cm. Pp. 2 + ii + 104 [prose and verse]. By [Lady Dudley and another]. UCLA: PR 2950 D86p 1795b(2).

2(*f*) *Passages Selected by Distinguished Personages, on the Great Literary Trial of Vortigern and Rowena; a Comi-tragedy.* Vol. ii [of 4]. London: J. Ridgway, [n.d.]. 6th edn. 10 × 15.5 cm. Pp. ii + 104 [prose and verse]. By [Lady Dudley and another]. HEHL: 260818.

2(*g*) *Passages Selected by Distinguished Personages, on the Great Literary Trial of Vortigern and Rowena; a Comi-tragedy.* Vol. ii [of 4]. London: J. Ridgway, 1807. 7th edn. 10 × 16.5 cm. Pp. viii + 104 [prose and verse]. By [Lady Dudley and another]. BL: 11762. b. 18.

3(*a*) *Passages Selected by Distinguished Personages, on the Great Literary Trial of Vortigern and Rowena; a Comi-tragedy.* Vol. iii [of 4]. London: J. Ridgway, [n.d.]. 9.5 × 15.5 cm. Pp. 2 + ii + 96 [prose and verse]. By [Lady Dudley and another]. HEHL: 482203.

3(*b*) *Passages Selected by Distinguished Personages, on the Great Literary Trial of Vortigern and Rowena; a Comi-tragedy.* Vol. iii [of 4]. London: J. Ridgway, [n.d.]. 2nd edn. 9 × 16 cm. Pp. ii + 91 [prose and verse]. By [Lady Dudley and another]. UCLA: PR 2950 D86p 1795b(3).

3(*c*) *Passages Selected by Distinguished Personages, on the Great Literary Trial of Vortigern and Rowena; a Comi-tragedy.* Vol. iii [of 4]. London: J. Ridgway, [n.d.]. 3rd edn. 10 × 15.5 cm. Pp. ii + 96 [prose and verse]. By [Lady Dudley and another]. HEHL: 260818.

3(*d*) *Passages Selected by Distinguished Personages, on the Great Literary Trial of Vortigern and Rowena; a Comi-tragedy.* Vol. iii [of 4]. London: J. Ridgway, [n.d.]. 4th edn. 9.5 × 16.5 cm. Pp. [2] + ii + 96 [prose and verse]. By [Lady Dudley and another]. BL: 1344. d. 9.

3(*e*) *Passages Selected by Distinguished Personages, on the Great Literary Trial of Vortigern and Rowena; a Comi-tragedy.* Vol. iii [of 4]. London: J. Ridgway, [n.d.]. 5th edn. 10 × 16.5 cm. Pp. ii + 95 [prose and verse]. By [Lady Dudley and another]. BL: 11762. b. 18.

4(*a*) *Passages Selected by Distinguished Personages, on the Great Literary Trial of Vortigern and Rowena; a Comi-tragedy.* Vol. iv [of 4]. London: J. Ridgway, [1807]. 9.5 × 16.5 cm. Pp. viii + 128 [prose and verse]. By [Lady Dudley and another]. BL: 1344. d. 9.

4(*b*) *Passages.* Vol. iv. 2nd edn. Inference.

4(*c*) *Passages Selected by Distinguished Personages, on the Great Literary Trial of Vortigern and Rowena; a Comi-tragedy.* Vol. iv [of 4]. London: J. Ridgway, [n.d.]. 3rd edn. 10 × 16.5 cm. Pp. viii + 128 [prose and verse]. By [Lady Dudley and another]. BL: 11762. b. 18.

DUNCH, M. E.

1 *Leisure Moments, or Letters and Poems, &c. on Miscellaneous Subjects.* Greenwich: printed by Richardson, 1826. 11.5 × 19 cm. 118 pp. [subscription edition; prose and verse]. By a Lady. BL: 12354. aaa. 3.

DUNLAP, Jane, Mrs

From Boston, Mass. After her husband's death she lived in an 'obscure station of life'. (Todd 1)

1 *Poems, upon Several Sermons, Preached by the Rev'd, and Renowned, George Whitefield, while in Boston.* Boston[, Mass.]: next to the Writing School in Queen Street, 1771. 11 × 18 cm. 22 pp. LC: PS 737. D75 1771 Office.

DUNLOP, Frances Elizabeth, Mrs

Her book reveals that she was the daughter of a soldier and the wife of another. She lived in York.

1   *Edmond of Ryedale Vale; or the Widowed Bride, a Poem in Six Cantos.* York/London: for the author by T. Bolland/W. Sams, 1822. 12 × 20 cm. 251 pp. 7/- boards. By Frances Elizabeth Dunlop. *MR* 100: 217–18; BL: 11641. e. 12.

DUNNETT, Jane

1   *Poems on Various Subjects.* Edinburgh: printed by John Moir, 1818. 10 × 17 cm. 152 pp. By Jane Dunnett. BL: 11646. ccc. 30.

DUNSTERVILLE, Ann

1   *Poems.* Exeter: printed for the author by Trewman and Son, 1807. 9.5 × 15.5 cm. 76 pp. [subscription edition, the missing list of subscribers being promised for a subsequent volume]. By Ann Dunsterville, of Plymouth. BL: 11645. aa. 50.

D–V–S [DAVIS?, DAVIES?], Miss, *see* COLLECTIONS 3

EARLE, Miss

1   *Corinth, and Other Poems. Dedicated (by Permission) to the Right Hon. Viscountess Anson.* London: printed by Ellerton and Henderson, 1821. 13 × 21.5 cm. 111 pp. [subscription edition]. BL: 11642. cc. 20.

EDGAR, Miss

She seems to have lived in Edinburgh. Walter Scott subscribed for two copies of *Tranquillity*.

1(*a*)   *Tranquillity; a Poem. To Which are Added, Other Original Poems, and Translations from the Italian.* Dundee/Edinburgh/Glasgow/Aberdeen/Montrose: James Chalmers/Archibald Constable and Co., and John Ballantyne and Co./Brash and Reid/A. Brown/G. Murray, 1810. 13.5 × 21.5 cm. Pp. [iv] + 136. BL: 11641. f. 63.

1(*b*)   *Tranquillity, a Poem. To Which are Added Other Original Poems, and Translations from the Italian and Spanish.* Edinburgh/London: John Anderson, Jr./Simpkin and Marshall, 1824. 2nd edn. 13 × 21.5 cm. Pp. [vi] + 258 + 4 [subscription edition]. By Miss Edgar. BL: 11646. h. 3.

EDGWORTH, Temple, *pseudonym of* TEMPLEMAN, James

EDRIDGE, Rebecca, Mrs

1   *The Lapse of Time, a Poem, for the New Year.* Ux-
     bridge/London: printed by T. Lake/J. Robson, Rivingtons,
     1803. 18.5 × 22.5 cm. 14 pp. 1/-. By Rebecca Edridge. BL:
     11647. f. 13.

2   *The Scrinium.* London: G. and W. B. Whittaker, 1822. 10 ×
     17.5 cm. 2 vols. [Prose and, in vol. ii, about 30 pp. of
     verse.] By Rebecca Edridge. BL: N. 114.

EDWARDS, Miss

She also wrote *Otho and Rutha* (1780). *(BLC)*

1   *Miscellanies in Prose and Verse.* Edinburgh: for the author by
     C. Elliot, 1776. 9.5 × 16 cm. Pp. iv + 205 [subscription
     edition]. By Miss Edwards. BL: 1459. b. 18.

EDWARDS, Anna Maria

Her musical entertainment, *The Enchantress*, was performed at the Opera
House, Capel St., Dublin.

1   *Poems on Various Subjects.* Dublin: printed for the author by
     H. Colbert, 1787. 10 × 16 cm. [2 vols.] [subscription edi-
     tion; prose and verse]. By the Author of *The Enchantress*.
     BL: 11633. aa. 13.

ELEANOR, Aunt, *pseudonym?*

1   *Aunt Eleanor's Rhymes for the Nursery.* London: John
     Marshall, 1822. 10 × 15.5 cm. 30 pp. [interleaved with
     unpaginated engravings]. 1/-. BL: 012806. ee. 35(11).

ELFE, Anne

1   *The Lays of Caruth, Bard of Dinham; and Other Poems.*
     London: for the author by Lynott's Library and
     Woodham's, 1808. 8.5 × 14 cm. 48 pp. [pp. 31–43 are in
     verse]. By Anne Elfe. BL: 11645. a. 37.

2   *Original Poems.* Chepstow/Monmouth/Abergavenny/New-
     port/Cardiff/Gloucester/Hereford/Bristol/Bath: M. Willett/
     Tudor   and   Farror/Watkins/Lewis/Bird/Roberts/Davis/

Sheppard/Barrett, 1809. 10 × 17 cm. 115 pp. [subscription edition; prose and verse]. By Anne Elfe, Author of *The Lays of Caruth*, etc. BL: 11645. aaa. 32.

ELIZA (born *c*.1787), *see also* BROUGHTON, Eliza, DAY, Eliza, *and* GARRINGTON, Eliza

1   *Adversity; or, the Tears of Britannia. A Poem.* London: James Kirby, Shepperson and Reynolds, White and Son, 1789. 18 × 24.5 cm. Pp. ii + 36. 2/-. By a Lady. BL: T. 20(1).

ELIZABETH, *see also* VINCE, Elizabeth

1   *Elizabeth's Poems; or, Original Pieces for Children.* London: John Marshall, [1820?]. 8.5 × 14 cm. 65 pp. BL: T. 964*(1).

2   *Poetry and Prose . . . Including Some Original Correspondence with Distinguished Literary Characters.* Doncaster: printed by C. and J. White, 1821. 11.5 × 18.5 cm. Pp. xxviii + 137 [subscription edition]. By Elizabeth. BL: 12270. bbb. 14.

[*See also*: 'Mar Lodge. Written by Elizabeth, August 16, 1792' (1792, broadsheet).]

ELIZABETH I, Queen of England (1533–1603), *see* COLLECTIONS 21

ELIZABETH, Charlotte, *see* PHELAN, Charlotte Elizabeth

EL–K–R, Miss, *see* COLLECTIONS 1(*a–c*)

ELLET, Elizabeth Fries, Mrs William Henry (*c*.1812–77)

Born at Sodus Point, NY, to Dr William Nixon Lummis and his second wife Sarah Maxwell. She was educated at the Female Seminary at Aurora, NY. In about 1835 she married Dr William Henry Ellet, Professor of Chemistry at Columbia College, New York City. She was interested in foreign literatures (she read French, German, and Italian) and in history, including the history of American women. (*DAB*, Mainiero)

1   *Poems, Translated and Original.* Philadelphia: Key and Biddle, 1835. 11 × 17 cm. 229 pp. By Mrs E. F. Ellet. HEHL: 48941.

ELLIOT, Miss

1   *Fancy's Wreath; being a Collection of Original Fables and Allegorical Tales, in Prose and Verse, for the Instruction and Amusement of Youth.* London: White, Cochrane, and Co., 1812. 9.5 × 17 cm. Pp. xii + 159. By Miss Elliot. BL: 12304. bb. 21.

ELLIOTT, Julia Ann, Mrs Henry Venn (died 1841)

Daughter of John Marshall of Hallsteads, Ullswater. She married Henry Venn Elliott, a clergyman and schoolteacher, in 1833. They had five children. She died of scarlet fever. (*DNB* (under Henry Venn Elliott))

1   *Poems on Sacred Subjects.* London: private, 1832. 12mo. HL; not located.

ELLIOTT, Mary, Mrs (1794?–1870)

Her maiden name was Belson. Individual poems from her *Grateful Tributes* were often published anonymously and some poems with the same titles, e.g. 'My Sister', are often ascribed to her erroneously in library catalogues. (*OCCL*)

1(*a*)   *The Mice, and their Pic Nic. A Good Moral Tale.* London: printed for the author by W. and T. Darton, 1810. 10 × 12.5 cm. 30 pp. By a Looking-glass Maker. BL: 11658. de. 9.

1(*b*)   *The Mice, and their Pic Nic. A Good Moral Tale, &c.* London: printed for the author by W. and T. Darton, 1811. 9.5 × 12.5 cm. 30 pp. By a Looking-glass Maker. BL: 12809. aa. 3.

1(*c*)   *The Mice, and their Pic Nic. A Good Moral Tale.* London: printed by William Darton, 1813. 10 × 13 cm. 30 pp. 6*d.* plain, 1/- coloured. By a Looking-glass Maker. BL: 012806. i. 27(8).

2   *The Baby's Holiday; to Which is Added the White Lily.* London: printed by W. Darton, Jun., 1812. 9.5 × 12.5 cm. 32 pp. 1/-. By Mary Belson, Author of *Industry and Idleness, The Mice and their Pic Nic, Innocent Poetry, Precept and Example, Grateful Tributes,* and the *Orphan Boy.* Osborne: ii. 635.

3(*a*)   *Grateful Tributes; or, Recollections of Infancy.* London: printed by W. Darton, Jun., 1818. 10 × 12.5 cm. 32 pp. 1/6. By

M. Belson, Author of *Industry and Idleness, Innocent Poetry, Baby's Holiday, Precept and Example, The Mice and their Pic Nic*, etc. Osborne: ii. 635.

3(*b*)   *Grateful Tributes; or Recollections of Infancy*. New York: Samuel Wood and Sons, [n.d.]. 10.5 × 13.5 cm. 46 pp. By M. Belson, Author of *Industry and Idleness, Innocent Poetry, Baby's Holiday, Precept and Example*, etc. etc. NYPL: *KVD Elliott.

3(*c*)   *Grateful Tributes; or, Recollections of Infancy. Containing the Poems of My Father, My Mother, My Brother, My Sister, My Uncle, My Aunty, My Mammy, My Bible, My Grandfather, My Grandmother, My Childhood*. London: William Darton, 1822. 8.5 × 13 cm. 36 pp. 6*d*. By Mary Belson [and others—the last four poems]. NYPL: *KVD p. v. 32.

3(*d*)   *Grateful Tributes; or, Recollections of Infancy*. London: William Darton and Son, [1830?]. 9 × 14 cm. 35 pp. By M. Belson. BL: 11644. aa. 40.

4(*a*)   *Simple Truths in Verse, for the Amusement, and Instruction of Children, at an Early Age*. London: W. Darton, Jun., 1812. 8.5 × 13.5 cm. 104 pp. By Mary Belson, Author of *Innocent Poetry, Grateful Tributes, The Orphan Boy, Precept and Example, Industry and Idleness*, etc. etc. NYPL: *KL.

4(*b*)   *Simple Truths, in Verse; for the Amusement and Instruction of Children, at an Early Age*. London: W. Darton, 1816. 8.5 × 13.5 cm. Pp. iv + 140. By Mary Belson. BL: 11646. aa. 40.

4(*c*)   *Simple Truths . . .* 3rd edn. Inference.

4(*d*)   *Simple Truths . . .* 4th edn. Inference.

4(*e*)   *Simple Truths, in Verse; for Children at an Early Age*. London: William Darton and Son, [1830?]. 5th edn. 8.5 × 14 cm. 120 pp. By Mary Elliott. BL: 11646. a. 59.

4(*f*)   *Simple Truths in Verse, for the Amusement and Instruction of Children at an Early Age*. New York/Baltimore: Samuel Wood and Sons/Samuel S. Wood and Co., [183?]. 8.5 × 14 cm. 108 pp. By Mary Belson, Author of *Innocent Poetry, Grateful Tributes*, etc., etc. NEDL: Juv. 1830. 16.

5(*a*)   *Flowers of Instruction: Or, Familiar Subjects in Verse*. London: William Darton, 1820. 10 × 16 cm. 62 pp. 1/-. By Mary Elliott, (late Belson). Osborne: uncatalogued.

5(*b*)   *Flowers of Instruction: Or, Familiar Subjects in Verse.* London: William Darton, Harvey and Darton, and John Harris, [1820]. 10 × 16 cm. 64 pp. 1/-. By Mary Elliott. BL: 11644. aaa. 42.

6(*a*)   *The Sunflower; or, Poetical Truths, for Young Minds, Religious, Moral, Miscellaneous, and Historical; Forming a Collection of Original Poems, and Intended as a Continuation of 'Simple Truths in Verse'.* London: William Darton, 1822. 8.5 × 13.5 cm. 108 pp. 1/6 half-bound. By Mary Elliott, (late Belson) Author of *Simple Truths. MR* 100: 97; Bodley: 280 f. 1026.

6(*b*)   *The Sunflower; or, Poetical Truths, for Young Minds; Religious, Moral, Miscellaneous, and Historical; Forming a Collection of Original Poems, and Intended as a Continuation of 'Simple Truths in Verse'.* London: William Darton, [n.d.]. 8.5 × 13.5 cm. 108 pp. By Mary Elliott (late Belson). BL: 1210. i. 13.

7(*a*)   *Gems in the Mine; or, Traits and Habits of Childhood, in Verse.* London: William Darton, [1824]. 8.5 × 13.5 cm. 104 pp. By Mary Elliott. BL: 11645. de. 59.

7(*b*)   *Gems in the Mine; or Traits and Habits of Childhood, in Verse.* Salem/Lancaster: James R. Buffum/H. and G. Carter, and F. and J. Andrews, 1828. 9 × 14 cm. 104 pp. By Mary Elliot. NEDL: Juv. 828. 2.

8(*a*)   *The Rose, Containing Original Poems for Young People.* London: William Darton, [1824]. 10 × 16.5 cm. 36 pp. 1/- plain, 1/6 coloured. By their Friend, Mary Elliott. BL: 012806. ee. 34(7).

8(*b*)   *The Rose, Containing Original Poems for Young People.* London: William Darton, [1825?]. New edn. 10.5 × 17.5 cm. 36 pp. 1/- with plain plates, 1/6 with coloured plates. By Mary Elliott. BL: 11644. cc. 34.

9   *Innocent Poetry; Containing Moral and Religious Truths for Infant Minds.* London: William Darton, Harvey and Darton, John Harris, [1825?]. 8.5 × 13.5 cm. 72 pp. By Mary Elliott. BL: 11644. aa. 48.

10   *My Sister. A Poem.* New York: Baker, Crane and Day, [1830?]. 4.5 × 7.5 cm. 8 pp. By [Mary Elliott]. HEHL: 319502.

11   *Poetic Gift: Containing Mrs Barbauld's Hymns, in Verse.* New
      Haven: S. Babcock, [18?]. 9.5 × 15 cm. 24 pp. 6 cents. By
      Mary Belson, Author of *Innocent Poetry, Grateful Tributes, The
      Orphan Boy*, etc. LC: 18— Juvenile Coll.

[*See also*: 'Early Seeds, to Produce Spring Flowers' ([n.d.], about 6
pp. of verse interspersed with prose); 'The Progress of the
Quartern-loaf. A Poem' ([1820], 6 pp.).]

ELWES, Adelaide, Mrs Alfred W. (1786–1825)
Her maiden name was Brent. (*NUC*)

1   *The Potomac Muse.* Richmond[, Va.]: printed by T. W.
      White, 1825. 10 × 17 cm. 172 pp. By a Lady, a Native of
      Virginia [Mrs Alfred Elwes?]. HL; BL: 11686. aaa. 18.

EMBURY, Emma Catherine, Mrs Daniel (1806–63), *see also* COL-
LECTIONS 42, 43
Born in New York City. She was the daughter of Dr James Manley and
Elizabeth Post. She wrote for the *New York Mirror*. She married Daniel
Embury, president of the Atlantic Bank of Brooklyn, and lived in
Brooklyn for the rest of her life. She was a regular contributor to peri-
odicals and was on the editorial staffs of *Godey's Lady's Book, Graham's*,
and the *Ladies' Companion*. Collections of her short stories appeared in
the 1830s and 1840s. She became an invalid in 1848 and stopped writ-
ing. Her address, 'Female Education', became an anthology piece.
(*DAB*, Mainiero)

1   *Guido, a Tale; Sketches from History, and Other Poems.* New
      York: G. and C. Carvill, 1828. 11.5 × 19 cm. Pp. iv + 200.
      By Ianthe. HEHL: 389051.

EMMERSON, Mrs, *see* COLLECTIONS 39

EMRA, Lucy (*c*.1806–*c*.1835?)
Her anonymous book of poems, *The Types* (1836), is said to be by a
lady 'recently and suddenly deceased'. Other internal evidence points to
her having been 29 at the time of her death.

1(*a*) *Scenes in the Life & Death of a Missionary, and Other Original
        Poems.* London/Bristol: Hamilton, Adams, and Co./J.
        Chilcott, 1831. 8.5 × 14 cm. Pp. xii + 206. By L. Emra.
        BL: 11646. aa. 30.

1(*b*)   *Heavenly   Themes,   a   Selection   of   Original   Poetry.*
London/Bristol: Hamilton, Adams and Co./J. Chilcott,
1832. 8 × 13.5 cm. Pp. xii + 206. By Lucy Emra. BL:
11646. aa. 44.

ERSKINE, Eliza Bland, the Hon. Mrs Esme Steuart (born *c.*1795)
Her maiden name was Norton.

1   *Isabel, a Tale, in Two Cantos; and Other Poems.* London:
James Ridgway, 1814. 10.5 × 18.5 cm. Pp. [iv] + 148. By
the Honorable Mrs Esme Steuart Erskine. BL: 11645. bb.
15.

2   *Alcon Malanzore a Moorish Tale.* Brussels: printed by
Auguste Wahlen, 1815. 12.5 × 21 cm. Pp. [vi] + 193. By
the Honorable Mrs Esme Steuart Erskine. BL: 11641. f.
21.

ESPENER, Isabella, Mrs Charles
In addition to the information provided on her title-page, the text of
her book reveals that she published to relieve distress, that she was
writing from Barton (presumably in Westmorland), and that she had a
niece, a sister's child, called Mary Ann Adams.

1   *Sentimental Poetry, Acrostics, &c.* Hull: printed by J.
Hutchinson, 1826. 10.5 × 17 cm. 59 pp. [subscription edi-
tion]. By Mrs Espener, Widow of the Late Mr Charles
Espener, Woollen-draper, of Kingston-upon-Hull, 1826.
BL: 11652. f. 41.

EVANCE, S., *afterwards* Mrs B. HOOPER, *see also* COLLECTIONS
23(*a–b*)
According to her *Poems* she had a brother in the navy and she had sisters. She was a friend of the author Maria Barton. One of the printers
of *A Poem* was also named Evance.

1   *Poems . . . Selected from her Earliest Productions, to Those of the
Present Year.* Ed. [James Clarke]. London: Longman, Hurst,
Rees and Orme, 1808. 9.5 × 16 cm. Pp. xii + 131. 5/-
boards. By Miss S. Evance. *MR* 60: 216; BL: 11644. bb. 33.

2   *A Poem Occasioned by the Cessation of Public Mourning for Her
Royal Highness the Princess Charlotte; together with Sonnets and
Other Productions.* London: for the author by Suttaby,

Evance, and Fox, 1818. 10 × 16.5 cm. Pp. xii + 143. By Mrs B. Hooper. Bodley: 8°. X. 357. BS.

EVANS, Ann

She appears to have lived in Andover, Mass.

1(*a*)   *Africa, a Poem.* [Andover, Mass.: printed by Flagg and Gould, 1826]. 12.5 × 20 cm. 20 pp. Brown (Harris): E 92 a 76.

1(*b*)   *Africa, a Poem.* [Andover, Mass.: printed by Flagg and Gould, 1826]. 2nd edn. 12.5 × 19.5 cm. 20 pp. Brown (Harris): E 92 a 1.

EVANS, Margaret, Mrs George

From Portrane, near Dublin. Her book is dedicated to her daughter, a Mrs Putland. She mentions a Mrs Tindal who was a friend of her youth. She evidently travelled in Germany and France.

1   *Poems.* Paris: [printed by Davies and Robertson], 1834. 10.5 × 18 cm. 64 pp. By Mrs Evans. BL: 11649. e. 59.

EVATT, Anne

1   *An Address from Ireland to England; a Poem, on the Lamented Death of Her Royal Highness the Late Lovely Princess Charlotte of Wales.* Dublin: printed by John Jones, 1818. 13 × 18 cm. 24 pp. [subscription edition]. NYPL: CK p. v. 242.

EWING, Harriet

She writes from 'King's End' and dedicates her book to Lady Denny as if to a friend.

1   *Dunrie; a Poem.* Bath/London: printed by Richard Cruttwell/John Robinson, 1819. 12 × 19.5 cm. Pp. iv + 202. 7/- boards. By Harriet Ewing. *MR* 91: 439–40; BL: 11645. bb. 3.

F., B., *see* FINCH, Mrs B.

F., S. C., *see* FORD, Sarah Caroline

FAIRBROTHER, Mary Ann, Mrs

From her book one learns that her husband is dead and that she has four children and a fifth who is lost at sea.

1   *Poems; Chiefly Moral and Pastoral.* London: for the author by Vernor, Hood and Sharpe, and J. Hatchard, 1808. 9.5 × 16.5 cm. Pp. [ii] + 112 [subscription edition]. By Mary Ann Fairbrother. BL: 11632. aa. 21.

FAIRFAX, Lavinia

Daughter of Mary Fairfax of Gilling Castle near York. The British Library copy of *Rime* contains tipped-in correspondence from her mother with the poet Francis Wrangham who was evidently a family friend; his English verse translations of the poems are also written into the copy.

1   *Rime Italiane.* Londra [London]: G. Schulze, 1825. 11 × 18 cm. 24 pp. [the text on one side only of the 24 leaves]. By Una Signora Inglese. BL: C. 28. g. 10(1).

FAIRWEATHER, Mary, Mrs

The book is a posthumous one, an illustration of the author's tomb in Delhi being included. She appears to have lived in a military environment in India and to have had at least two children, one of whom died there in infancy.

1   *Hymns and Religious Poems, of a Practical Nature.* [Agra]: printed at the Agra Press, 1833. 10 × 15 cm. Pp. 116 + 4. 2 rupees. By Mrs Mary Fairweather. BL: 11632. aa. 22.

FALCONAR, Harriet

She was a daughter of William Falconar, the Scottish poet, and of Jane Hicks. She first contributed, with her sister Maria (q.v.), to the *European Magazine* in 1787. The Stainforth Album in the British Library contains an engraving of the two sisters by R. Cosway. The subscription list to *Poems* suggests family connections in the north of Scotland. (Blain, Lonsdale, Stainforth Album)

1(*a*) *Poems.* London: J. Johnson, Egertons, 1788. 10 × 15 cm. Pp. xliv + 124. 3/6 sewed. By Maria and Harriet Falconar. *MR* 78: 245; BL: 11632. aa. 23.

1(*b*) *Poems.* London: J. Johnson and Egertons, 1788. 2nd edn. 11 × 19 cm. Pp. xliv + 124 [subscription edition]. By Maria and Harriet Falconar. BL: 11644. eeee. 33.

2 *Poems on Slavery*. London: Egertons, Murray, J. Johnson, 1788. 10.5 × 17.5 cm. Pp. viii + 25. 1/6. By Maria Falconar, aged 17, and Harriet Falconar, aged 14. *MR* 79: 554–5; BL: 1164. e. 23.

3 *Poetic Laurels for Characters of Distinguished Merit; Interspersed with Poems, Moral and Entertaining: Dedicated to His Royal Highness George Prince of Wales*. London: J. Walter, 1791. 21 × 26.5 cm. Pp. xvi + 88 [subscription edition]. 5/-. By Maria and Harriet Falconar. BL: 1346. i. 29.

FALCONAR, Maria, *see* FALCONAR, Harriet

She was a daughter of William Falconar, the Scottish poet, and of Jane Hicks, and a sister of Harriet Falconar (q.v.). She began contributing poems to the *European Magazine* in 1786. (Blain, Lonsdale)

FALLOWS, Elizabeth, Mrs Thomas Mount (*c.*1803–33)

At her death her husband, who was Curate of All Souls, Marylebone, in London, edited the collection. (Allibone, *GM*)

1 *Poetical Remains of a Clergyman's Wife*. Ed. [T. M. F.] London: C. and J. Rivington, K. J. Ford and J. K. Starling, 1833. 11 × 18.5 cm. 124 pp. BL: 11644. ccc. 26.

FARLEY, Mrs

1(*a*) *Hymns and Reflections*. Inference.

1(*b*) *Hymns and Reflections*. Birmingham, [1835?]. 2nd edn. 12mo. *BLC*: 3425 aa. Not found.

FARRELL, Sarah, Mrs

Her maiden name was Fielding. She claims in her book to have been unhappy in her youth. She had children.

1 *Charlotte, or, a Sequel to the Sorrows of Werter: A Struggle between Religion and Love, in an Epistle from Abelard to Eloisa: Vision, or Evening Walk; and Other Poems*. Bath/London/Bristol/York/Gainsborough/Birmingham/Edinburgh/Dublin: for the author by Campbell and Gainsborough/Robinsons, Vernor, Hookham, Cadell/Bulgin and Brown/Wilson and Co./Mozely and Co./Pearson/Creech/Dugdale, 1792. 21 × 28 cm. Pp. vi + x

+ 80 [subscription edition]. 6/- sewed. By Mrs Farrell. *MR* 9: 442–3; BL: 11642. h. 17.

FAUGERES, Margaretta Van Wyck (1771–1801), *see also* BLEECKER, Ann Eliza

Born in New York City. She was the daughter of John J. Bleecker and Ann Eliza Schuyler (q.v.). She spent her childhood in Tomhanick, a village north of Albany, NY. Their family life was disrupted by the revolutionary war in 1777; they fled, several of them died, and her father was captured. In 1792, against her father's wishes, she married Peter Faugeres, a French Jacobin physician, who squandered the family fortune and died in 1798. She became a teacher in order to support herself and their daughter. (*DAB*, Mainiero)

1　*Belisarius: A Tragedy.* New York: printed by T. and J. Swords, 1795. 11.5 × 19.5 cm. 53 pp. By Margaretta V. Faugeres. BL: 11737. bb. 30.

FELL, Miss

The second daughter of Ralph Fell, of Newcastle, and of Sarah Carey. (BL copy of *A Poem* contains a family genealogy in MS)

1　*A Poem on the Times.* London: J. Wilkie and W. Goldsmith, 1774. 19 × 25 cm. 17 pp. 1/-. By Miss Fell, of Newcastle. BL: 11632. g. 65.

FELL, Elizabeth, Mrs (died 1780)

A Quaker from Saffron Waldon, Essex. (*Friends' Books, NUC*)

1　*Fables, Odes, and Miscellanious Poems.* London: J. Robson, 1771. 11 × 17.5 cm. Pp. vi + 166. 3/- bound. By Elizabeth Fell, of Saffron-Walden. *GM* 41: 560; *MR* 45: 412; CUL: 7720. d. 1446.

2　*Poems.* London: J. Robson, 1777. 20 × 25.5 cm. 93 pp. 4/- sewed. By Mrs Elizabeth Fell. *MR* 57: 490; BL: 79. b. 1.

A FEMALE

1　*Serious Reflections, Humbly Addressed to the Inhabitants of Great Britain, by a Female.* [London]: Scollick, [1791]. 4to. 28 pp. 1/6. *MR* 5: 104. Not located.

2   *Sacred Meditations, or, Serious Musings. In Rhyme.* London:
     printed by Jaques and Wright, 1824. 10.5 × 18 cm. 72 pp.
     By a Female. BL: T. 855(5).

A FEMALE CHRISTIAN

1   *Marriage and its Vows Defended . . . A Poem, Inscribed to the
     R******d Mr M*d*n.* London: J. Rozea, Richmond,
     Robinson, and W. Thomas, 1781. 20 × 26 cm. 15 pp. 1/-.
     By a Female Christian, but no Methodist. Bodley: 2799 d.
     78.

A FEMALE OF THIS CITY [Philadelphia], *see* Cox, Elizabeth

A FEMALE REFUGEE
According to the preface to her book, the author belonged to an aris-
tocratic family and was 18 when she wrote her tragedy.

1   *The Carthusian Friar; or, the Age of Chivalry. A Tragedy, in
     Five Acts, Founded on Real Events.* London: J. Owen and
     H. D. Symonds, 1793. 12 × 20 cm. Pp. viii + 78. 1/6. By a
     Female Refugee. *MR* 11: 269–71; BL: 163. k. 41.

FENN, Lady Eleanor (1743–1813), *see also* COLLECTIONS 10(*a–c*),
11(*a–b*)
The daughter of Sheppard Frere of Roydon, Suffolk. In 1766 she married Sir John Fenn, the antiquary who edited the 'Paston Letters'. They
had no children. She used the pseudonyms Mrs Lovechild and Mrs
Teachwell. She was active in the Sunday School movement and as a
philanthropist in Norfolk. (*DNB, OCCL*)

1   *The Blackberry Girl, a Pretty Story in Verse for Good Children.*
     Stanstead, L.C.: Walton and Gaylord, 1834. 8 × 12 cm. 8
     pp. By Mrs Lovechild. LC: Juv. Coll. 1834.

FENNO, Jenny
She seems to have been a member of the Second Baptist Church in
Boston, Mass. (Mainiero, Todd 1)

1(*a*) *Original Compositions, in Prose and Verse. On Subjects Moral
       and Religious.* Boston[, Mass.]: printed by Joseph Bumstead,
       1791. 8.5 × 14 cm. Pp. iii + 125. By Miss J. Fenno, of
       Boston. BL: 12274. a. 19.

1(*b*) *Original Compositions, in Prose and Verse. On Subjects Moral and Religious.* Wrentham[, Mass.]: printed by Nathaniel Heaton, Jr., 1803. 8.5 × 14 cm. 116 pp. [verse occupies pp. 5–71]. By Miss J. Fenno, of Boston. LC: PS 744. F307 1803 copy 2 Office.

FENTIMAN, Catherine, Mrs

The book is a twenty-seventh anniversary present to her husband. They lived at Claylands, Kennington.

1 *Scraps.* London: printed by Redford and Robins, 1824. 11 × 14 cm. 70 pp. BL: 11612. aa. 18.

FINCH, Mrs B.

From her book one learns that she was born in the country and was fond of botany. She wrote from 'Duncroft Cottage' and dedicated the book to her son.

1 *Sonnets, and Other Poems: To Which are Added Tales in Prose.* London: Blacks and Parry, 1805. 9 × 15.5 cm. Pp. xiv + 126. 4/- boards or 4/6. By [B. F.]. *MR* 48: 218–19; *CR* 6: 327–8; BL: 11632. aa. 20.

FITZOSNABURGH, Frances A.

1 *The Youth's New Monitor, Written and Most Respectfully Inscribed to the Marquis of Beaumont, Infant Son & Heir of the Noble House of Roxburghe.* London: W. Sams and Harvey and Darton, [1820?]. 11.5 × 18 cm. Pp. viii + 192 [prose and verse]. By Frances A. Fitzosnaburgh. BL: 8404. bb. 18.

FLETCHER, Bridget, Mrs Timothy (1726–70)

Born in Chelmsford, Essex. She was the daughter of Captain Zachariah Richardson. *Hymns* was edited by her son.

1 *Hymns and Spiritual Songs.* Ed. [Elijah Fletcher]. Boston[, Mass.]: printed by I. Thomas, 1773. 8.5 × 14.5 cm. 70 pp. By Bridget Fletcher, the Wife of Timothy Fletcher, Late, of Wesford, Deceased. AAS: DATED PAMS.

FLETCHER, Eliza, Mrs Archibald (1770–1858)

Born at Oxton, near Tadcaster, Yorks. She was the only daughter of a land surveyor named Dawson and his wife, a Miss Hill. Her mother died a few days after Eliza was born. She attended Manor School in York where, although 'four volumes of *The Spectator* constituted the whole school library', she became a great reader. In 1791 she married Archibald Fletcher, a Scottish advocate, and she lived in Edinburgh thereafter. They had at least four children. She was widowed in 1828. Her autobiography was published in 1874. (Blain, Boase, *DNB*)

1   *Elidure and Edward. Two Historical Sketches.* London: printed by Thomas Davison, 1825. 12.5 × 20 cm. Pp. xii + 125. BL: 11781. cc. 6.

FLORA, *pseudonym*

1   *Flora's Alphabet, for the Amusement and Instruction of Juvenile Naturalists.* London: E. Wallis, [c.1825]. 10 × 17 cm. 24 pp. [printed on one side only]. Osborne: ii. 679.

FLOWERDEW, Alice, Mrs (1759–1830)

She came from Lowestoft, Suffolk. When very young she became the second wife of Daniel Flowerdew, a Baptist, and went with him to Jamaica, where he held a government post. After his death in 1801 she returned to England. She opened a ladies' boarding school in Islington and moved it to Bury St Edmonds at some point between 1806 and 1811. (Blain, *NUC*)

1(*a*) *Poems, on Moral and Religious Subjects.* London/Oxford/ Norwich: H. D. Symonds, Mrs Gurney, E. Vidler/ Hanwell and Parker/Bacon, 1803. 10.5 × 17 cm. Pp. [vi] + 158 [subscription edition]. 3/6 boards. By A. Flowerdew. BL: 1467. c. 25.

1(*b*) *Poems, on Moral and Religious Subjects* . . . London/Oxford/ Norwich: H. D. Symonds, Mrs Gurney and E. Vidler/Hanwell and Parker/Bacon, 1804. 2nd edn. 10 × 17 cm. Pp. xvi + 119. By A. Flowerdew. BL: 11646. ccc. 29.

1(*c*) *Poems on Moral and Religious Subjects: To Which are Prefixed, Introductory Remarks on a Course of Female Education.* London: Sherwood, Neely, and Jones, 1811. 3rd edn. 10 × 16 cm. Pp. xii + 135. 5/-. By A. Flowerdew. *CR* 24: 106–7; BL: 11644. b. 26.

FOLLEN, Eliza Lee, Mrs Charles (1787–1860)

Born in Boston, Mass., the fifth of the thirteen children of Samuel Cabot, a merchant, and of Sarah Barrett. She was well educated. In

1828 she married Charles Follen, a German refugee, he being nine
years her junior. They were both members of Dr Channing's circle,
active in promoting Sunday Schools and opposing the slave trade, and
prominent in Boston literary and religious circles. Her husband was
Professor of German at Harvard from 1830 to 1835. They had one
son. (*DAB*, Mainiero)

1(*a*)   *Hymns, Songs and Fables, for Children*. Boston[, Mass.]:
         Carter, Hendee, and Babcock, 1831. 9 × 15 cm. Pp. [ii] +
         50. By the Author of *The Well-spent Hour*. LC: PS 1683. F4
         H8 1831 Office.

1(*b*)   *Hymns, Songs and Fables, for Children*. Boston[, Mass.]:
         Leonard C. Bowles, 1833. 2nd edn. 9 × 15 cm. 51 pp. By
         the Author of *The Well-spent Hour*. BL: 11687. a. 3.

2   *Little Songs, for Little Boys and Girls*. Boston[, Mass.]:
         Leonard C. Bowles, 1833. 8.5 × 11 cm. 66 pp. By the
         Author of *The Well Spent Hour*, etc. LC: PZ 83 F721 L.

FORD, Sarah Caroline

Her initials are identified in Stainforth.

1   *Miscellaneous Poems*. London: Page and Son, 1831. 10 × 16
         cm. 165 pp. By S. C. F. BL: 994. d. 16.

FORDYCE, Lady Margaret Lindsay, *see* LINDSAY, Lady Margaret *and*
COLLECTIONS 37

FORTNUM, Sophia, Mrs Charles (born 1782), *see also* DACRE,
Charlotte

She was a daughter of John King (also known as Jacob Rey), a money-
lender and blackmailer, and of his first wife Debora Lara, and was the
sister of Charlotte Dacre (q.v.). She married Charles Fortnum in 1801.
Between 1798 and 1805 she wrote five novels for the Minerva Press,
and she contributed verse to the newspapers, using the name 'Sappho'.
(Blain, Todd 1)

1   *Poems, Legendary, Pathetic, and Descriptive*. London: for the
         author by S. Burchett, 1804. 14 × 24 cm. Pp. xii + 75
         [subscription edition]. By Mrs Fortnum, Late Sophia King.
         BL: 1406. k. 6.

FRANCIS, Miss

1   *Santa Maura: Marion; and Other Poems.* London: John Warren, 1821. 9.5 × 16 cm. Pp. [iv] + 112. By Miss Francis. BL: 11644. aa. 67.

FRANCIS, Anne, Mrs Robert Bransby (1738–1800)

Daughter of the Revd Daniel Gittins, Rector of South Stoke, near Arundel, Sussex, and of Jane Sapp. She was educated by her father in classics and Hebrew. She married the Revd Robert Bransby Francis, Rector of Edgefield, near Holt, Norfolk. (*DNB, NUC,* Todd 1)

1   *A Poetical Translation of the Song of Solomon, from the Original Hebrew; with a Preliminary Discourse, and Notes, Historical, Critical, and Explanatory.* London: J. Dodsley, 1781. 20.5 × 26.5 cm. Pp. [vi] + xx + 102. 7/6 sewed. By Ann Francis. *MR* 66: 258–60; *CR* 53: 32–9; BL: 1215. g. 7.

2   *The Obsequies of Demetrius Poliorcetes: A Poem.* London/ Norwich/Holt: J. Dodsley/J. and C. Berry and W. Chase and Co./W. Page, 1785. 21 × 26.5 cm. 22 pp. 1/6. By Anne Francis, Author of *A Poetical Translation of the Song of Solomon.* Houghton: *EC75. F8470. 7850.

3   *Charlotte to Werter. A Poetical Epistle.* London: T. Becket, 1787. 21 × 26.5 cm. 24 pp. 1/6. By Anne Francis. *MR* 78: 351; Houghton: *EC75. F8470. 787c.

4(*a*)   *Miscellaneous Poems.* Norwich: for the author by the booksellers, 1790. 9.5 × 16 cm. 275 pp. 3/-. By a Lady. *CR* 70: 215; BL: 11633. aaa. 25.

4(*b*)   *Miscellaneous Poems.* London/Norwich/Holt: for the author by T. Becket and R. Baldwin/Yarington and Bacon/W. Page, 1790. 9.5 × 17 cm. Pp. [ii] + 275. By Anne Francis. BL: 11633. aaa. 20.

[*See also*: 'A Plain Address to My Neighbours' (1798, broadside).]

FRANCIS, Eliza S.

1   *The Rival Roses; or Wars of York and Lancaster. A Metrical Tale . . .* London: for the author by J. J. Stockdale, 1813. 13 × 21 cm. 163 pp. [subscription edition]. By [Eliza S. Francis]. BL: 11642. e. 30.

2   *Sir Wilibert de Waverley; or, the Bridal Eve. A Poem*. London:
       Samuel Leigh, 1815. 9.5 × 16 cm. Pp. vi + 87. 5/- boards.
       By Eliza S. Francis, Author of *The Rival Roses*, etc. *MR* 78:
       432–4; BL: 11645. aa. 43.

FRANCIS, Sophia L.
Author of four four-volume Gothic novels for the Minerva Press from
1804 to 1809.

1   *An Elegy, on Colonel R. Montgomery, Written on the Fatal Spot,
       Where the Lamentable Duel Transpired; and Most Humbly
       Dedicated to His Royal Highness the Prince of Wales*. London:
       for the author by W. Elkin, and E. Lawrence, [1803]. 18 ×
       23 cm. 14 pp. By S. L. Francis. BL: 840. k. 13(2).

FRANK, Mary
A Quaker, from Bristol. (*Friends' Books*)

1   *Miscellaneous Poems, and Paraphrases of Select Passages of the
       Hebrew Scriptures*. London: Harvey and Darton, and
       Edmund Fry, 1833. 10.5 × 16.5 cm. Pp. viii + 119. By
       Mary Frank. BL: 994. g. 15.

FRASER, Susan, Mrs
Material in the second edition of *Camilla* suggests that she had visited
Gibraltar and that she returned to England from Egypt in 1802 with
the 42nd regiment.

1(*a*)   *Camilla de Florian, and Other Poems*. London: for the author
       by J. Dick, 1809. 10 × 16.5 cm. Pp. 159 + [8] [subscription
       edition]. 4/6 boards. By an Officer's Wife. *MR* 60: 432–3;
       BL: 11642. b. 32.

1(*b*)   *Camilla de Florian, and Other Poems*. London: for the author
       by J. Dick, 1809. 2nd edn. 9.5 × 16.5 cm. Pp. 159 + [10]
       [subscription edition]. By an Officer's Wife. BL: 11646.
       bbb. 40.

1(*c*)   *Poems*. London: Lackington, Allen and Co., 1811. New
       edn. 9.5 × 16 cm. 159 pp. By Mrs Fraser. BL: 11644. bb.
       34.

FRENCH, Mrs M. G. G.

1   *The Contrast: Or the Natural and Spiritual Man Compared. 1788.*
London: printed by H. C. Hodson, 1824. 13 × 21 cm. 42
pp. [prose and verse; 'Poems' occupy pp. 21–42]. BL:
1570/2360.

A FRIEND TO YOUTH, *see* HOARE, Sarah

FRY, Caroline (1787–1846), *see also* COLLECTIONS 40(*a–d*), 44

Born in Tunbridge Wells, Kent. She was the ninth child of John Fry, a
prosperous farmer. According to *DNB* and *EC* he published a few
hundred copies of her *History of England in Verse* in 1802, but this
report remains unconfirmed. She was taught by her elder sisters. She
edited a successful periodical called the *Assistant of Education*, and contributed to such annuals as *The Amulet* and *The New Year's Gift*. Her
most popular book was *The Listener* (1830) which passed through thirteen editions in the next twenty-three years. She visited Paris in 1831
and married a Mr Wilson in the same year. There is a portrait of her
by Lawrence. (*DNB*)

1(*a*)   *A Poetical Catechism . . .* Inference.

1(*b*)   *A Poetical Catechism; or, Sacred Poetry: For the Use of Young
Persons.* London: for the author by Ogle, Duncan, and
Co., 1822. 2nd edn. 8.5 × 13 cm. 35 pp. By Caroline Fry.
BL: 11649. cc. 17(1).

1(*c*)   *A Poetical Catechism . . .* 3rd edn. Inference.

1(*d*)   *A Poetical Catechism; or, Sacred Poetry: For the Use of Young
Persons.* London: Baker and Fletcher, 1826. 4th edn. 8.5 ×
13.5 cm. 35 pp. 6*d.* By Caroline Fry. BL: 11649. cc. 19(1).

2(*a*)   *Serious Poetry.* London: Ogle, Duncan and Co., 1822. 9.5 ×
16.5 cm. Pp. viii + 116. By Caroline Fry. BL: 994. b. 12.

2(*b*)   *Serious Poetry.* London: Ogle, Duncan, and Co., 1823. 2nd
edn. 10 × 17 cm. Pp. viii + 116. By Caroline Fry, Author
of *Death, and Other Poems, The Poetical Catechism for the Use
of Young Persons,* etc. Bodley: Vet. A6 f. 132(1).

3   *Death, and Other Poems.* London: for the author by Ogle,
Duncan, and Co., 1823. 9.5 × 17 cm. Pp. vi + 110. By
Caroline Fry, Author of *Serious Poetry* and *A Poetical
Catechism for Young Persons.* Bodley: Vet. A6 f. 132(2).

FURLONG, W. Marianne, Mrs

The printed advertisement attached to the BL copy of *The Spectre Poverty* presents her as an English lady living in Edinburgh who is offering instruction in chalk drawing, flower painting, pencil drawing, and other decorative techniques, and in elocution and composition. She claims the patronage of the Duchess of Buccleuch.

1   *The Spectre Poverty; or the Realities of Life, Displayed under an Allegory.* Edinburgh: printed for the authoress at the University Press, 1834. 12.5 × 20 cm. 10 pp. BL: 11642. e. 25.

G., Mrs A., *see* GIBBS, Mrs A.

G., C. C. V., *see* WETHERELL, Mrs Dawson Bruce

G. E., *see* GARRAWAY, Ellen

G., P., *see* GURNEY, Priscilla

GARNETT, Catharine Grace, *see* GODWIN, Catharine Grace

GARRARD, Eliza

The title-page locates her in Bath.

1   *Miscellanies in Verse and Prose.* Bath/Reading/London: printed for the author by William Meyler/Smart and Cowslade/Robinsons, and Rivingtons, 1799. 12 × 20.5 cm. Pp. v + 235 [subscription edition; the verse occupying pp. 209–35]. 4/-. By Eliza Garrard, of Bath. *CR* 32: 354–5; BL: 12273. bbb. 7.

GARRAWAY, Ellen

Most of the subscribers are from the London area.

1   *Rhymes without Reason, with Reasons for Rhyming: To Which are Added, Two Prose Essays.* London: Rodwell and Martin, 1823. 17.5 × 23 cm. Pp. xxiv + 77 [subscription edition; the prose occupies pp. 69–77 only]. By the Author of No Other Publication!!! [E. G.]. Avero; BL: 11641. g. 20.

GARRINGTON, Eliza Sarah (born *c.*1787)

She was a teacher in a village school for girls in Essex. At the age of 19 she retired because of ill health. Her father had died in 1815. (*Spiritual Recreations*)

1   *Spiritual Recreations in the Chamber of Affliction: Or Pious Meditations in Verse; Written during a Protracted Illness of Thirteen Years.* Ed. [W. H. C.]. London/Burnham, Essex: Francis Westley, Hatchard and Son, Hamilton and Lawson/J. Garrington, 1821. 11 × 18.5 cm. Pp. xvi + 209 [subscription edition]. By Eliza. HL; BL: 11642. bbb. 12.

GAZUL, Clara, *pseudonym* of MERIMÉE, Prosper

GEARY, Elizabeth

1   *Juvenile Effusions; Moral and Religious.* London: printed for the author by J. Grainge, 1822. 11 × 18 cm. Pp. iv + 91. By Elizabeth Geary. BL: 11646. cc. 49.

GIBBS, Mrs A., *see* COLLECTIONS 17

The title-page of her *Selection, in Prose and Verse* describes her as being from Lamberhurst, Kent.

GIBSON, Charlotte Mary

She claims to have written most of her poems in early childhood and to be publishing them in aid of charity. She writes from Dalton Square.

1   *Original Poetry.* Lancaster: printed by W. Barwick, [1835]. 8 × 12.5 cm. 31 pp. By Charlotte Mary. BL: 1606/1059.

GILBERT, Ann, Mrs Joseph, *see* TAYLOR, Ann

GILDING, Elizabeth

She lived in Woolwich, Kent, and claims to be an orphan without formal schooling. Her book contains several poems to or about the Revd Daniel Turner, AM, of Woolwich, whom she seems subsequently to have married. (*The Breathings*, Stainforth)

1   *The Breathings of Genius. Being a Collection of Poems; to Which are Added, Essays, Moral and Philosophical.* London: J. Wilkie, J. Walter, W. Domville, [1776]. 13 × 21.5 cm. Pp. [vi] + 152. [Verse and prose.] 2/6. By Elizabeth Gilding, Woolwich, Kent. BL: 80. i. 4.

GODWIN, Catharine Grace (1798–1845)

The younger daughter of Thomas Garnett, MD. Her father died in 1802 and her mother shortly after Catharine was born. She and her sister were brought up by a Miss Worboys, a friend of their mother's. They lived at Barbon, near Kirkby-Lonsdale, Yorks. In 1834 she married Thomas Godwin, formerly of the East India Company. She contributed to several different annuals. Wordsworth knew her and wrote an analysis of her poetical strengths and weaknesses, in a private letter of 1829. (Boyle, *DNB*)

1   *The Night before the Bridal, a Spanish Tale. Sappho, a Dramatic Sketch, and Other Poems.* London: Longman, Hurst, Rees, Orme, Brown, and Green, 1824. 13 × 21.5 cm. Pp. xii + 220. 9/- boards. By Catharine Grace Garnett. *MR* 105: 92–8; BL: 994. h. 10.

2   *The Wanderer's Legacy; a Collection of Poems, on Various Subjects.* London: Samuel Maunder, 1829. 11 × 19.5 cm. Pp. [iv] + 277. By Catharine Grace Godwin (late Catharine Grace Garnett). BL: 994. h. 11.

3   *The Reproving Angel a Vision.* London: Sampson Low, 1835. 10.5 × 17.5 cm. 27 pp. By Catharine Grace Godwin. BL: T. 1897(16).

GOLDIE, Emma Mary

1   *Poems.* London: printed by A. J. Valpy, 1835. 11.5 × 19 cm. Pp. iv + 242. By Miss Emma Mary Goldie. BL: 994. h. 12.

GOLDRING, Mrs C. B.

1   *Lines on the Death of the Right Hon. Geo. Canning.* Cheltenham: printed by E. Matthews, 1828. 10 × 16 cm. 15 pp. By Mrs C. B. Goldring. BL: 11641. a. 25.

GOMERSALL, A., Mrs (born *c.*1750)

She lived in Leeds and was the author of three novels between 1789 and 1796. The preface to *Creation*, which is written from Newport, Shropshire, explains that she has been widowed after thirty-three years of marriage, that she is in her seventy-fourth year, and that a stroke has made it impossible for her to work. 500 copies of her book were sold. (Blain, Watt)

1   *Creation, a Poem.* Newport/London: for the author by J. Rowden/Black, Young, and Young, 1824. 10.5 × 18 cm. Pp. [ix] + vi + 89 [subscription edition]. By A. Gomersall. BL: 11633. b. 27.

GOOCH, Elizabeth Sarah, Mrs William (born 1756?)

Born in Edwinstow, Notts. She was the daughter of William Villa-Real, whose death in 1759 left her an heiress. She spent three years at Miss Latouche's boarding school, Little Chelsea. She married William Gooch in 1775 and they had two sons, but the marriage broke down and she was taken to France and abandoned there. She lived on a diminishing income in France and in England until in 1787 she was imprisoned for debt. Her autobiography, *The Life of Miss Gooch* (1792), adds many vivid details of her misfortunes, but may contain an element of fiction. (*Life*, Todd 1)

1   *Poems on Various Subjects.* London: printed by J. Bell, 1793. 19 × 24 cm. 36 pp. By Mrs Gooch. BL: 11632. g. 22.

2   *Monody to the Memory of His Grace the Duke of Bedford.* London: for the author and sold also by William Miller, H. D. Symonds, and W. Treppas, 1802. 20 × 25 cm. 12 pp. By Mrs Villa-Real Gooch. Houghton: *EC75. G5904. 802m.

GOOCH, Rebecca

The preface to *Original Poems* is written from Brandeston, Suffolk, and two of its booksellers, from Southwold and from Bungay, share the author's surname. A niece surnamed Pasley is mentioned.

1(*a*)   *Original Poems, on Various Subjects.* Southwold/London/Yarmouth/Bungay/Harleston/Halesworth: T. Gooch/W. Baynes/B. Gooch/P. Mitchell/C. Sewell/T. Tippell, 1821. 10.5 × 17 cm. 144 pp. [subscription edition, lacking a subscription list]. By Rebecca Gooch. Bodley: 280 f. 2551.

1(*b*)   *Original Poems, on Various Subjects.* London/Norwich/Yarmouth/Bungay/Harleston/Halesworth: Longman, Rees, Orme, Brown, and Green, Baldwin and Cradock, and G. B. Whittaker/Jarrold and Son, and R. Gooch/B. Gooch/T. Marston/C. Sewell/T. Tippell, 1828. 2nd edn. 10 × 16.5 cm. 144 pp. [subscription edition, lacking a subscription list]. By Rebecca Gooch. BL: 11646. bb. 29.

GOODALL, Harriott Anabella, Mrs Joseph

Daughter of J. Prior, assistant master at Eton. In 1788 she married Joseph Goodall, who was then an assistant master at Eton also. He went on to become Provost of Eton in 1801; after 1827 he was Rector of West Ilsley, Berks. (*Athenae Cantabrigienses*, *DNB* (under Joseph Goodall))

1   *The Emigrants; a Tale of Truth.* Eton: printed by E. Williams and Son, [1835]. 10 × 17.5 cm. Pp. viii + 49. By the Rector's Wife [H—— G——]. BL: 11646. eee. 3.

GORDON, Harriet Maria, *see* SMYTHIES, Harriet Maria

GORDON, Jamima (*c.*1806–18)

Her book was published after her death at the age of 12 from 'water in the head'. The introduction dwells on her good nature and piety.

1   *Juvenile Poems.* Ed. [J. S.]. Edinburgh: printed by J. Ruthven and Sons, 1819. 9 × 15.5 cm. 36 pp. By Jamima Gordon. NLS: NG 1170. e. 12. [Only photocopy seen.]

GORE, Catherine Grace Frances, Mrs Charles (1799–1861), *see also* COLLECTIONS 42

Born in East Retford, Notts. Her father was C. Moody, a wine merchant. In 1823 she married Captain Charles Arthur Gore of the 1st Life Guards. They had ten children. She wrote novels and plays and composed music, eventually producing about seventy works in almost two hundred volumes. She contributed to the annuals from 1828 onwards. In the 1830s she spent some years in Paris where she maintained a literary salon. The bankruptcy of her publishers in 1856 is said to have cost her £20,000. (Boase, Boyle, *CB*, *DNB*, Schlueter)

1   *The Two Broken Hearts: A Tale.* London: J. Andrews, 1823. 13 × 22.5 cm. Pp. [iv] + 100. *NUC*; BL: 11642. eee. 26.

2   *The Bond, a Dramatic Poem.* London: John Murray, 1824. 12 × 21 cm. 95 pp. By Mrs Charles Gore. BL: T. 1064(1).

GOULD, Hannah Flagg (1789–1865)

Born in Lancaster, Mass. She was the fifth child of Benjamin Apthorp Gould and Griselda Flagg. She moved with her parents to Newburyport in 1808. She began by contributing verse to periodicals. Her *Poems* went through several editions, being expanded to two volumes in 1836 and to three in 1841. Eight more books appeared from 1843 to 1863. (*DAB*)

1(*a*)　*Poems.* Boston[, Mass.]: Hilliard, Gray, Little, and Wilkins, 1832. 9 × 15 cm. Pp. viii + 174. By Miss H. F. Gould. HEHL: 42681.

1(*b*)　*Poems.* Boston[, Mass.]: Hilliard, Gray, and Co., 1833. 2nd edn. 9 × 15 cm. Pp. viii + 224. By Miss H. F. Gould. HEHL: 300858.

1(*c*)　*Poems.* Boston: Hilliard, Gray and Co., 1835. 3rd edn. 10.5 × 16.5 cm. Pp. viii + 239. By Miss H. F. Gould. NEDL.

[*See also*: 'Esther: A Scripture Narrative . . . Together with an Original Poem' (1835, 77 pp. (the verse being confined to pp. 71–7)).]

GRANDMAMMA

1(*a*)　*Grandmamma's Book of Rhymes, for the Nursery.* London: John Harris, 1831. 10.5 × 13 cm. Pp. vi + 76. Osborne: ii. 641.

1(*b*)　*Grandmamma's Book of Rhymes.* Boston[, Mass.]: Allen and Ticknor, 1833. Widener L. Cat. Not found.

GRANT, Anne, Mrs (1755–1838), *see also* COLLECTIONS 32, 41

Born in Glasgow. Her father, Duncan Macvicar, travelled to America with a commission in the 77th Foot in 1757, to be followed by his wife and child in 1758. He was involved in the unsuccessful Ticonderoga expedition, leaving his family at Albany, NY, in close association with the Schuyler family. In 1768 they returned to Scotland. In 1779 Anne married a clergyman named Grant who was garrison-chaplain at Fort Augustus and minister of the parish of Laggan in Inverness-shire. They had eight children. Her husband's death in 1801 left her almost penniless, but her first volume of poems had about 3,000 subscribers. She moved to Stirling and then to Edinburgh where she belonged to literary society. A privately funded pension of £100 was arranged for her in 1826. (*CB, DNB, GM*)

1(*a*)　*Poems on Various Subjects.* Edinburgh/London/Glasgow/ Perth/Aberdeen/Elgin/Inverness: for the author by Mundell and Son, Manners and Miller, Arch. Constable/ Longman and Rees, J. Hatchard/Brash and Reid/D. Peat/A. Brown/Isaac Forsyth/Young and Imray, 1803. 13

× 21.5 cm. 447 pp. [subscription edition]. 10/6 boards. By Mrs Grant, Laggan. BL: 993. k. 9.

1(*b*)   *The Highlanders, and Other Poems.* London: Longman, Hurst, Rees, and Orme, 1808. 2nd edn. 9.5 × 15.5 cm. Pp. xii + 300. By Mrs Grant, Laggan. BL: 11645. aa. 9.

1(*c*)   *The Highlanders, and Other Poems.* Edinburgh/London: printed by James Ballantyne/Longman, Hurst, Rees, and Orme, 1810. 3rd edn. 9.5 × 15.5 cm. Pp. viii + 356. By Mrs Grant, Laggan. BL: 11641. aa. 20.

1(*d*)   *The Highlanders, and Other Poems.* Philadelphia: M. Carey, 1813. From 2nd London edn. 9 × 14.5 cm. 144 pp. By Mrs Grant, of Laggan. NEDL: KC3812.

2   *Eighteen Hundred and Thirteen: A Poem, in Two Parts.* Edinburgh/London: printed by James Ballantyne and Co./Longman, Hurst, Rees, Orme, and Brown, 1814. 12.5 × 21 cm. Pp. [iv] + 146. By Mrs Grant, Laggan. BL: 11642. f. 12.

GRAVES, Louisa Carolina, Mrs Richard

1   *Desultory Thoughts on Various Subjects.* Brussels: printed at the British Press, 1819. 9.5 × 15.5 cm. Pp. viii + 104 [prose and verse]. By Louisa Carolina, Daughter of Sir John Colleton, Bart. Wife of Rear-Admiral Richard Graves, of Hembury-Fort, Devonshire. BL: 10825. aa. 30(2).

GRAY, Miss, of the City of Bristol, *see* COLLECTIONS 7

GRAY, Christian (born 1772)

She was the daughter of George Gray and Janet McDonald. Her title-pages describe her as having been blind from her infancy and as living first in Mundie and then in Milton, in the parish of Aberdalgie, Perthshire. Her farming family was ruined in the drought years of 1816–26. (Blain)

1   *Tales, Letters, and Other Pieces, in Verse.* Edinburgh: printed for the author by Oliver and Boyd, 1808. 9 × 15 cm. Pp. xii + 226. By Christian Gray, Blind from Her Infancy, in Mundie, Parish of Aberdalgie, Perthshire. BL: 1164. e. 1.

2   *A New Selection of Miscellaneous Pieces, in Verse*. Perth: printed
     for the author by R. Morison, 1821. 9 × 15 cm. 144 pp.
     By Christian Gray, Blind from Her Infancy, in Milton,
     Parish of Aberdalgie, Perthshire. BL: 11640. de. 3.

GREENSTED, Frances

At the time of publication she was living in Maidstone, Kent,
and had been a servant with the same family there for twenty
years. She was attempting to support an aged mother and mentions
that a second edition is to appear, but it has not been located. (*Fugitive
Pieces*)

1   *Fugitive Pieces*. Maidstone/London/Bath/Marlborough/Faver-
     sham/Chatham/Canterbury: printed for the author by D.
     Chalmers/Wilkie and H. D. Symonds/Hazard/Harold/
     Coveney/Etherington/Bristow, 1796. 12.5 × 21.5 cm. Pp.
     viii + 48 + 25 [subscription edition]. 3/-. By Frances
     Greensted. *MR* 23: 460; BL: 994. i. 13.

GREVILLE, Frances, Mrs Fulke (*c*.1726–89), *see* COLLECTIONS
1(*b–c*), 3, 13

She was the third daughter of James and Catherine Coote Macartney of
Longford in Ireland. She was a celebrated beauty and a wit and in
1748 she eloped with Fulke Greville, a man of fashion. They had at
least six children. Her 'Ode to Indifference' (or 'Prayer for
Indifference') was widely anthologized. She was a well-known literary
figure and Sheridan dedicated *The Critic* to her. (Blain, Lonsdale,
Todd 1)

GRIFFITH, Maria, *see* COLLECTIONS 55

She contributed to *Winter's Wreath* in 1828.

GRIFFITHS, J.

She seems to have lived in or near Birmingham. (*A Collection*)

1   *A Collection, of Juvenile Poems, on Various Subjects . . . Written
     Originally for her Own Amusement, and now Published at the
     Solicitations of her Acquaintance*. Warwick: printed for the
     author by J. Sharp, 1784. 15.5 × 20.5 cm. 40 pp. 1/-. By
     J. Griffiths. BL: 11633. e. 16.

GRIMSTONE, Mary Leman, Mrs

Both HL and *BLC* identify Mrs Grimstone with 'Oscar'. She was the author of the novel *Cleone, a Tale of Married Life* (1834) and it seems possible that it has been confused with Oscar's *Cleone* of 1821; the only similarity resides in the titles.

1   *Zayda, a Spanish Tale, in Three Cantos; and Other Poems, Stanzas, and Canzonets.* London: G. and W. B. Whittaker, 1820. 10 × 17 cm. Pp. xii + 163. 5/- boards. By Oscar. *MR* 93: 215–16; Trinity: O. m. 60. No. 4.

2   *Cleone, Summer's Sunset Vision, the Confession, with Other Poems and Stanzas.* London: G. and W. B. Whittaker, 1821. 10 × 16.5 cm. Pp. xii + 132. By Oscar, Author of *Zayda*, etc. HL; BL: 993. f. 35.

GUINNESS, Mrs John G.

Her book is dedicated to the Rt. Hon. the Viscountess de Vesci, and its profits are to aid a respectable family in reduced circumstances.

1   *Sacred Portraiture and Illustrations, with Other Poems.* Dublin: Richard Moore Tims and W. Curry, Jr., 1834. 13 × 22 cm. Pp. viii + 168. By Mrs John G. Guinness. BL: 11641. e. 15.

GUNNING, Susannah (1740?–1800)

She was the daughter of James Minifie, DD, and is chiefly remembered for the thirteen novels she produced between 1763 and 1800. She married John Gunning, a soldier who became a lieutenant-general but who led a 'dissolute life'. In 1791 the family became involved in a scandal over their only daughter's simultaneous flirtation with the Marquis of Lorne and the Marquis of Blandford, and it broke up. (*CB, DNB, GM*, Todd 1 and 2)

1   *Virginius and Virginia; a Poem, in Six Parts. From the Roman History . . . Dedicated to Supreme Fashion; but not by Permission.* London/Bath: for the author by Hookham and Carpenter, William Richardson/Meyler, [1792]. 21 × 26.5 cm. Pp. ix + 65. 5/-. By Mrs Gunning. BL: 644. k. 23(8).

GUPPY, Sarah, Mrs

1   *Essays on Various Subjects: In Which Some Characters of the Present Age are Introduced . . . To Which is Added Some Poetical*

Pieces . . . Bristol/London: printed by R. Edwards/T. Hurst, 1800. 2nd edn. 9 × 14.5 cm. 103 pp. [verse by Mrs Guppy is confined to pp. 43–4, 52, 60–1, 66–7, 82, and 101–3; it was not included in the first edition]. By Charles de la Garde and Mrs Guppy. BL: 12331. aa. 26.

GURNEY, Maria, Mrs (1802–68)
Her maiden name was Rowe. (Avero)

1   *Rhymes for my Children*. London: Smith, Elder and Co., 1835. 10 × 15.5 cm. Pp. viii + 100. By a Mother. BL: 994. g. 25.

G—v—L, Mrs, *see* GREVILLE, Frances

G—v–LLE, Hon. Mrs, *see* GREVILLE, Frances

H., Mrs, of Anne-Arundel County[, Md.], *see* COLLECTIONS 20

H., A. C., *see* HOWLAND, Avis C.

H——, Miss R——, *see* HORT, Miss R——

HALE, Martha, Mrs Bernard (died 1803)
She was the daughter of Richard Rigby of Mistley Hall, Essex. In 1750 she married Bernard Hale, an army officer. From 1773 she lived at the Chelsea Hospital, where her husband was Lieutenant-Governor. In *Poetical Attempts*, she mentions her children, one of whom died young. She includes one poem that was written in 1749. The book was published as a charitable contribution to a family in financial distress and the subscribers include many members of the nobility. (Blain)

1   *Poetical Attempts*. London: printed by T. Davison, 1800. 13.5 × 22.5 cm. Pp. xii + 156 [subscription edition]. £1/1/- boards. By Mrs Hale. *MR* 32: 194–7; BL: 11642. ee. 10.

HALE, Sarah Josepha, Mrs David (1788–1879)
Born in Newport, NH. She was the daughter of Captain Gordon Buell and Martha Whittlesy. She was well educated by her motherand, in classics, by her elder brother. In 1813 she married David Hale, a lawyer, and they had five children. After his death in 1822 she turned to writing. She edited the *Ladies' Magazine* (Boston, Mass.) and

then, until 1877, *Godey's Lady's Book* (Philadelphia). Her *Woman's Record: Or Sketches of Distinguished Women, from the Creation to A.D. 1854* appeared in 1855. (*DAB, Dictionary of Literary Biography*)

1   *The Genius of Oblivion; and Other Original Poems.* Concord: Jacob B. Moore, 1823. 10.5 × 17 cm. 147 pp. By a Lady of New-Hampshire. HEHL: 42557.

2   *Poems for our Children: Designed for Families, Sabbath Schools, and Infant Schools. Written to Inculcate Moral Truths and Virtuous Sentiments.* Part First. Boston[, Mass.]: Marsh, Capen and Lyon, 1830. 11.5 × 18 cm. 24 pp. By Mrs Sarah J. Hale. HEHL: 50802.

3   *The School Song Book. Adapted to the Scenes of the School Room. Written for American Children and Youth.* Boston[, Mass.]: Allen and Ticknor, 1834. 9 × 15 cm. 71 pp. By Mrs Sarah J. Hale, Editor of the *Ladies' Magazine*, and Author of *Flora's Interpreter*, etc. LC: PS 1774. H233 Office.

HALL, Anna Maria, Mrs Samuel Carter (1800–81),   *see* COLLECTIONS 46

Born in Dublin. She was a novelist and miscellaneous writer. Her mother was Sarah Elizabeth Fielding and her stepfather was George Carr. In 1824 she married Samuel Carter Hall with whom she collaborated as an editor and anthologist. She was actively interested in women's rights and she received a civil list pension in 1868. (*DNB*)

HALL, Clara, *see* COLLECTIONS 45, 46, 47, 48, 54

HAM, Elizabeth (1783–after 1852)

Born in North Perrott, near the Somerset–Dorset border. She was one of seven children of 'respectable parents'. She was sent away to school at an early age and became a governess, eventually to the Eltons in Clifton. She was a Unitarian. She was the author of *Infant's Grammar* and in 1845 of an anonymous novel. An abridged version of a journal by her has been published. (*Elizabeth Ham by Herself 1783–1820*, ed. Eric Gillett (1945))

1   *Elgiva, or the Monks. An Historical Poem. With Some Minor Pieces.* London: Baldwin, Cradock, and Joy, 1824. 13 × 21.5 cm. Pp. vii + 204. By [E. H.]. BL: 11646. h. 20.

HAMILTON, Lady Anne (1766–1846)

She was the eldest daughter of Archibald, 9th Duke of Hamilton, and of Lady Harriet Stewart. She was lady-in-waiting to Caroline, Princess of Wales, until 1813. In 1810 she received a legacy of £10,000 which she gave to her brother, Lord Archibald Hamilton, the political reformer. She appeared as the Queen's companion during the divorce proceedings in 1820. *Epics of the Ton* seems to have been one of the models for Byron's *English Bards and Scotch Reviewers*. (*DNB*)

1(a)   *The Epics of the Ton; or, the Glories of the Great World: A Poem, in Two Books, with Notes and Illustrations*. London: C. and R. Baldwin, 1807. 11.5 × 19.5 cm. Pp. [viii] + 269. 7/6 boards. *MR* 53: 203–7; *CR* 11: 357–65; *NUC*; HEHL: 298233.

1(b)   *The Epics of the Ton; or, the Glories of the Great World: A Poem, in Two Books, with Notes and Illustrations*. London: C. and R. Baldwin, 1807. 2nd edn. 11.5 × 20 cm. Pp. vi + 280. BL: 1162. l. 25.

1(c)   *The Epics of the Ton; or, the Glories of the Great World: A Poem, in Two Books, with Notes and Illustrations*. London: C. and R. Baldwin, 1807. 3rd edn. 11 × 18 cm. Pp. vi + 280. BL: 11642. c. 49.

HAMILTON, Sarah (*c.*1769–1843)

The youngest daughter of Robert Hamilton, MD, of Lynn, Norfolk. She died at Leamington. (*GM*)

1   *Sonnets, Tour to Matlock, Recollections of Scotland, and Other Poems*. London: J. Mawman, 1825. 12 × 19 cm. Pp. [iv] + 260. By a Resident of Sherwood Forest. BL: 993. a. 37.

2   *The Art of War; a Poem, in Six Books* . . . Trans. Miss Hamilton. London: J. Mawman, 1826. 12 × 20 cm. 131 pp. By Frederick III, King of Prussia. BL: 1065. l. 38.

3   *The Liberation of Joseph; a Sacred Dramatic Poem, in Two Parts: The Beauties of Vegetation, with Digressive Sketches of Norwich, &c. in Four Cantos: And Other Poems*. London: J. Mawman, 1827. 12 × 19 cm. Pp. xii + 178. By Miss Hamilton, Author of *Sonnets*, etc. BL: 994. i. 14.

4   *Alfred the Great, a Drama, in Five Acts*. London: Longman, Rees, Orme, Brown, and Green, 1829. 12.5 × 21 cm. 71 pp. BL: T. 1273(2).

HANDS, Elizabeth, Mrs

A servant in the Huddesford family of Allesley, near Coventry. By 1785 she had married a blacksmith who lived at Bourton, near Rugby. They had a daughter. Mrs Hands published verse under the pseudonym 'Daphne' in the *Coventry Mercury* and her book attracted 1,200 subscribers. (Landry, Lonsdale, Todd 1)

1   *The Death of Amnon. A Poem. With an Appendix:: Containing Pastorals, and Other Pieces.* Coventry: printed for the author by N. Rollason, 1789. 12.5 × 20.5 cm. Pp. [xxviii] + 127 [subscription edition]. 3/- sewed. By Elizabeth Hands. *MR* 3: 345–6; BL: 1466. h. 18.

HANSON, Martha

Sonnets is written from Belle-vue House. The author evidently spent her early years near Hurstpierpoint, Sussex.

1   *Sonnets and Other Poems.* London: J. Mawman and T. Lake, 1809. 9.5 × 16 cm. 2 vols. [subscription edition; vol. i of this copy lacks pp. 71–4]. By Martha Hanson. BL: 11642. bb. 28.

HARDCASTLE, Eliza Mary (1810–33)

According to Mrs Hardcastle's *Memoir*, Eliza Mary's father was a bookseller and stationer in Leeds. As a child she was delicate but pious. She became a schoolteacher and then, on her father's death, a teacher of music, drawing, 'etc.', in a school opened by her mother in 'a small market-town'.

1   *Memoir of a Beloved Daughter. By a Mother* . . . Leeds/London/Bradford/Keighley/Otley: for the author by M. Robinson, Baines and Newsome, Somerscale, Knight, and Cross/T. Hurst, and Hamilton, Adams, and Co./Inkersley and Co./Aked/Hodgson, 1834. 9.3 × 15 cm. 144 pp. [verse ('Hymns and Miscellaneous Pieces') occupies pp. 67–108]. BL: 4902. aaa. 1.

HARDWICKE, Countess of, Elizabeth Scott YORKE (1763–1858), *see also* COLLECTIONS 37

The third daughter of James Lindsay, 5th Earl of Balcarres, and of Ann Dalrymple. In 1782 she married the politician Philip Yorke, 3rd Earl of Hardwicke. They had a daughter or daughters. (*DNB*)

1   *The Court of Oberon, or the Three Wishes. A Drama in Three
     Acts.* London: printed at Shakspeare Press, 1831. 21.5 × 28
     cm. Pp. [vi] + 55. BL: 11779. l. 6.

HARPER, Catherine

1   *A Collection of Prayers for Household Use, with a Few Hymns
     and Other Poems.* Oxford/London: J. Parker/C. and J.
     Rivington, 1828. 10.5 × 17.5 cm. Pp. xxviii + 147 [verse
     occupying pp. 57–147]. HL; Bodley: 28. 871.

HARRIES, Margaret, *see* BARON WILSON, Mrs Cornwell

HARRIS, Henrietta, Mrs

She lived in Worcester for many years and had at least two children
who died young. Some of the poems in her book appeared earlier in
the *Worcester Journal.* (*Poems*)

1   *Poems, on Various Subjects: Dedicated, by Permission, to the Right
     Hon. Countess of Essex.* Worcester/London/Glocester and
     Hereford: for the author by J. Tymbs/J. Walker/the book-
     sellers, 1805. 9.5 × 16 cm. Pp. x + 158 [subscription edi-
     tion]. 5/-. By Henrietta Harris. BL: 11645. aa. 23.

HARRISON, Susanna (1752–84)

She was probably born in Ipswich to poor parents. She entered domestic service when she was 16 and taught herself to read and write afterwards. She became a permanent invalid in 1772. She gave her poems to
John Conder, a Congregationalist minister, for posthumous publication.
(*DNB*, Todd 1)

1(*a*) *Songs in the Night.* Ed. [John Conder]. London: T. Vallance
        and Alexander Hogg, 1780. 9 × 15.5 cm. Pp. iv + 153. 1/6.
        By a Young Woman under Deep Afflictions. Houghton:
        *EC75. H2483. 780s.

1(*b*) *Songs in the Night.* Ed. [John Conder]. London: T. Valance
        and Alexander Hogg, 1781. 2nd edn. 9.5 × 16.5 cm. Pp.
        xii + 164. 1/6. By a Young Woman under Heavy
        Afflictions. BL: 3437. e. 34.

1(*c*) *Songs in the Night.* Ed. [John Conder]. London/Bury/
        Ipswich: Vallance and Conder, R. Hawes/E. Rogers/C.
        Punchard, 1783. 3rd edn. 10 × 17 cm. Pp. xii + 164. 1/6.

By a Young Woman under Heavy Afflictions. BL: 11631. aaa. 16.

1(*d*)　*Songs in the Night.* Ed. [John Conder]. Ipswich/London/Braintree/Bury/Woodbridge: Punchard and Jermyn/Vallance and Conder, Buckland/Smitheman/Rogers/Loder, 1788. 4th edn. 10 × 16.5 cm. Pp. xiv + 202. 2/6 bound. By a Young Woman under Heavy Afflictions. BL: 3435. e. 24.

1(*e*)　*Songs in the Night.* 5th edn. Inference.

1(*f*)　*Songs in the Night.* Ed. [John Conder]. London: S. Conder and T. Conder, 1799. 6th edn. 10 × 17 cm. Pp. xiv + 202. 2/6 bound. By a Young Woman under Heavy Afflictions. BL: 11631. aaa. 41.

1(*g*)　*Songs in the Night.* Ed. [John Conder]. Edinburgh/Glasgow/London: J. Ogle/M. Ogle/R. Ogle, 1799. 6th edn. 8.5 × 14 cm. Pp. xvii + 226. By Susanna Harrison, a Young Woman, under Heavy Afflictions. Yale (Sterling): Im/H248/780f.

1(*h*)　*Songs in the Night.* 7th edn. Inference.

1(*i*)　*Songs in the Night . . .* Ed. [John Conder]. Exeter[, NH]: Angier March, 1802. 1st American from 4th London edn. 10 × 16.5 cm. Pp. xii + 202. By a Young Woman, under Heavy Afflictions. Houghton: *EC75. H2483. 780se.

1(*j*)　*Songs in the Night.* Ed. [John Conder]. London: W. Baynes, 1803. 8th edn. 8.5 × 14 cm. Pp. xx + 227. By Susanna Harrison, a Young Woman under Heavy Afflictions. BL: 11642. aa. 36.

1(*k*)　*Songs in the Night.* Ed. [John Conder]. London: W. Baynes, 1805. 8th edn. 9 × 13.5 cm. Pp. xx + 227. By Susanna Harrison, a Young Woman under Heavy Afflictions. BL: 11644. e. 73.

1(*l*)　*Songs in the Night . . . With a Supplement.* Ed. [John Conder]. Burlington[, NJ]: Stephen C. Ustick, 1807. 2nd American edn. 9 × 14 cm. Pp. xiv + 196. By a Young Woman under Heavy Afflictions. LC: PR 3506. H482 S6 Office.

1(*m*)　*Songs in the Night.* 9th edn. Inference.

1(*n*)　*Songs in the Night.* Ed. [John Conder]. London: W. Baynes, 1810. 10th edn. 9.5 × 15 cm. Pp. xx + 227. By Susanna

Harrison, a Young Woman under Heavy Afflictions. BL: 11645. aa. 58.

1 (*o*)   *Songs in the Night.* Ed. [John Conder]. London/ Glasgow/Edinburgh: T. Hamilton, R. Ogle/M. Ogle/J. Ogle, 1812. 11th edn. 8.5 × 13.5 cm. Pp. xx + 226. By Susanna Harrison, a Young Woman, under Heavy Affliction. Clark: BZ H322s 1812.

1 (*p*)   *Songs in the Night.* New Brunswick[, NJ]: printed by Lewis Deare, 1813. 7 × 12.5 cm. 215 pp. By a Young Woman under Heavy Afflictions. HEHL: 184857.

1 (*q*)   *Songs in the Night; by a Young Woman under Heavy Afflictions. With a Supplement.* Ed. John Conder. Lexington[, Ky.]: Thomas T. Skillman, 1814. 4th American edn. 213 pp. By Susanna Harrison. LC: PR 3506. H482 S6 1814 Rare Bk Coll.

1 (*r*)   *Songs in the Night.* 12th edn. Inference.

1 (*s*)   *Songs in the Night.* Ed. [John Conder]. London: W. Baynes, 1820. 13th edn. 8.5 × 13.5 cm. Pp. xx + 226. By Susanna Harrison, a Young Woman under Heavy Afflictions. BL: 11647. aa. 1.

1 (*t*)   *Songs in the Night.* 14th edn. Inference.

1 (*u*)   *Songs in the Night; with the Supplement . . . To Which is Added, a Remarkable Scene in the Author's Life.* Ed. [John Conder]. Philadelphia: W. W. Woodward, 1821. 6th American edn. 6.5 × 12.5 cm. 215 pp. By a Young Woman, under Heavy Afflictions for Twelve Years. Yale (Sterling): Im/H248/780j.

1 (*v*)   *Songs in the Night.* Ed. [John Conder]. London/Glasgow/ Aberdeen and Elgin: R. Baynes, and J. Bumpus/ T. Lochhead/J. Maitland, 1823. 15th edn. 9.5 × 15 cm. Pp. xx + 227. By Susanna Harrison, a Young Woman, under Heavy Afflictions. BL: 11644. aaa. 57.

HART, Mary Kerr, Mrs

In *Enigmettes* she acknowledges the patronage of James Reed of Ipswich.

1 (*a*)   *Heath Blossoms: Or Poems Written in Obscurity and Seclusion . . . With a Memoir of the Author.* Ballingdon/London/

Ipswich/Bury/Hadleigh/Woodbridge/Edinburgh: printed by W. Hill/Baldwin and Cradock/Deck, Shalders, Hunt, and Piper/Deck/Hardacre/Loder/Smith, [1830?]. 13 × 20.5 cm. 144 pp. [subscription edition]. By Mary Kerr Hart. BL: 11646. h. 17.

1(*b*)   *Heath Blossoms; or, Poems, Written in Seclusion and Reverse of Fortune.* Southampton/London: William Smart/T. Hurst, [1835?]. 2nd edn. 10 × 15.5 cm. Pp. xii + 100. By Mary Kerr Hart. BL: 11642. de. 21.

2   *Enigmettes, or Flora's Offering to the Young.* London: printed for the author by James Robins and Co., [1832]. 8.5 × 14.5 cm. Pp. xii + 95 [subscription edition]. By Mary Kerr Hart, Author of *Heath Blossoms*. BL: 994. d. 22.

HARVEY, Jane (born 1776)

She was the daughter of Lawrance and Elizabeth Harvey of Barnard Castle, Durham Co. Her book on Newcastle, *A Sentimental Tour*, appeared in 1794. She published a number of novels between 1802 and 1814, mostly with the Minerva Press. (Blain, Watt)

1   *Poems on Various Subjects.* Newcastle upon Tyne: printed by D. Akenhead and Sons, 1797. 13 × 22 cm. 44 pp. [subscription edition]. By Jane Harvey. BL: 11642. f. 24(2).

2(*a*)   *Poems, Original and Moral.* Inference.

2(*b*)   *Poems, Original and Moral.* 2nd edn. Inference.

2(*c*)   *Poems, Original and Moral, for the Use of Children.* [Title-page is the paper cover of the volume.] Derby: H. Mozley, [1820?]. 3rd edn. 6.5 × 10.5 cm. 31 pp. 2*d.* By Jane Harvey. BL: T. 962*(1).

3(*a*)   *Sacred Hymns, for the Use of Children; being Particularly Adapted for Sunday Schools.* Derby: Henry Mozley, [1818]. 7.5 × 13.5 cm. 47 pp. By Jane Harvey, Author of *Poems, Original and Moral, for the Use of Children.* BL: 3441. e. 78.

3(*b*)   *Sacred Hymns, for the Use of Children; being Particularly Adapted for Sunday Schools.* [Title-page is the paper cover of the volume.] Derby: H. Mozley, [1820?]. 2nd edn. 6.5 × 10.5 cm. 31 pp. 2*d.* By a Lady, Author of *Poems, Original and Moral, for the Use of Children.* BL: T. 962*(2).

HARVEY, Margaret (1768–1858)

She was the daughter of John Harvey, a surgeon, in Sunderland, Durham Co. She spent her early years at Newcastle-on-Tyne. In or about 1818 she moved to Bishop Wearmouth, Co. Durham, where she taught in a ladies' school. Her *Raymond de Percy: A Romantic Melodrama* was performed in Sunderland in 1822. (Boase, *DNB*)

1   *The Lay of the Minstrel's Daughter. A Poem, in Six Cantos . . . Dedicated, by Permission, to His Grace the Duke of Northumberland.* Newcastle upon Tyne: printed for the author by J. Marshall, 1814. 13 × 20.5 cm. 246 pp. [subscription edition]. 10/6 boards. By Margaret Harvey. BL: 11642. e. 17.

HASTINGS, Sally *or* Sarah (1773–1812)

Born in Lancaster, Pa. Her father, Robert Anderson, died when she was a child and her mother remarried. She herself made an unhappy marriage that ended in separation, with Enoch Hastings, a carpenter. Their only daughter died young. Hastings became housekeeper to her widowed brother, was the centre of a literary circle, and contributed to the local newspaper. (Leon Howard, 'Literature and the Frontier: The Case of Sally Hastings', *ELH* 7 (1940), 68–82)

1   *Poems, on Different Subjects. To Which is Added, a Descriptive Account of a Family Tour to the West; in the Year, 1800. In a Letter to a Lady.* Lancaster[, Pa.?]: for the author by William Dickson, 1808. 10 × 17 cm. 220 pp. [subscription edition]. By Sally Hastings. BL: 11633. bbb. 22.

HATFIELD, Sibella Elizabeth (1800–82)

Born in Falmouth, Cornwall. Her parents were John Westby Hatfield, an auctioneer, and his wife Sibella. She kept a girls' boarding school in Penzance. In 1833 she married Alfred Miles, a commander in the Royal Navy. They had two children. She was widowed in 1851. (*DNB* (under Alfred Miles))

1   *The Wanderer of Scandinavia, or, Sweden Delivered, in Five Cantos, and Other Poems.* London/Truro: Longman and Co./Carthew, 1826. 11 × 19 cm. 2 vols. [subscription edition]. 14/-. By Sibella Elizabeth Hatfield. *MR* 6: 413–14; BL: 994. i. 15.

2   *Moments of Loneliness, or, Prose and Poetic Efforts, on Various Subjects and Occasions.* London/Falmouth: Simpkin and Marshall/James Philp, 1829. 9.5 × 15.5 cm. Pp. viii + 5–204. By Sibella Elizabeth Hatfield. BL: 994. f. 9.

3   *Fruits of Solitude, or, Prose and Poetic Compositions; Consisting of Sketches of Natural and Moral Scenery; Tales, Essays, Meditations, &c. &c.* London/Plymouth: Longman, Rees, Orme and Brown, Whittaker, Treacher, and Arnott/ Edward Nettleton, 1831. 10 × 16 cm. Pp. viii + 212. By Sibella Elizabeth Hatfield. BL: 11644. aa. 1.

HATTON, Ann Julia, Mrs William, *see* CURTIS, Ann

HAWKE, Hon. Annabella Eliza Cassandra (1787–1818)

The youngest child of Martin Bladen, 2nd Baron Hawke, and Cassandra Turner. Her mother was the author of the anonymous novel *Julia de Gramont* (1788) and her brother also wrote verse. In 1811 she was living in Gloucester Place, Portman Square, in London. *The Jackdaw 'At Home'* is included in *Babylon, and Other Poems.* (*Burke's Peerage*)

1   *The Jackdaw 'At Home'.* London: Didier and Tebbett, 1808. 9.5 × 11.5 cm. 16 pp. By a Young Lady of Rank. BL: C. 40. a. 57(8).

2(*a*)   *Babylon; a Poem.* London, 1810. 4to. *CR* 20: 89–91. Not located.

2(*b*)   *Babylon, and Other Poems.* London: William Miller, 1811. 9.5 × 15.5 cm. Pp. viii + 144. 6/- boards. By the Hon. Annabella Hawke. *MR* 65: 442–4; BL: 11645. aa. 14.

HAWKINS, Miss L. M., *see* COLLECTIONS 41

HAWKINS, Susannah (1787–1868)

She was the daughter of a blacksmith who lived near Ecclefechan, Dumfriesshire. She worked as a herder of cattle and as a dairymaid. The proprietor of the *Dumfries Courier* printed her little volumes free and she sold them door to door for fifty years, travelling as far as Manchester to do so. (Boase, *DNB*)

1   *The Poetical Works.* Dumfries: printed for the author by [John M'Diarmid and Co.], 1829. 10 × 17 cm. 56 pp. By Susannah Hawkins. Davis: Kohler I 83–534.

HAY, Mrs. M. H.

1 *The Rural Enthusiast, and Other Poems.* London: Longman, Hurst, Rees, and Orme, 1808. 9.5 × 15.5 cm. Pp. [iv] + 168. 10/6 boards. By Mrs M. H. Hay. *MR* 57: 96–7; BL: 11644. b. 36.

HEAD, Catharine, Mrs

Her *Sketches in Prose and Poetry* (1837) is written from Kirkdale, Liverpool. In it she claims to be a sailor's wife. She was the author of an anonymous novel, *Rybrent de Cruce* (1829). (*BLC*)

1 *The Seven First Cantos of the Messiah: A Poem.* Trans. [Catharine Head]. London: Longman, Hurst, Rees, Orme, Brown, and Green, 1826. 13.5 × 21 cm. 2 vols. By F. T. Klopstock. BL: 1064. h. 15.

HEASELL, Anne

1(*a*) *The Morning Repast.* Inference.

1(*b*) *The Morning Repast; Consisting of Original Meditations & Hymns, with a Collection of Texts, Arranged for Daily Use in Private Devotion; also Four Songs for Zion's Pilgrims.* London/ Norwich/Derby/Edinburgh: Hamilton, Adams, and Co., Seeley and Sons, Westley and Davis/Jarrold and Son/ H. Mozley/Oliphant, 1832. 2nd edn. 6.5 × 10 cm. Pp. [ii] + 209 [prose and verse]. By Anne Heasell. BL: 3434. a. 41.

HEDGE, Mary Ann

1 *Original Poems.* London, 1820. 12mo. By [Mary Ann Hedge?]. HL. Not located.

2(*a*) *Juvenile Poems* . . . Inference.

2(*b*) *Juvenile Poems* . . . 2nd edn. Inference.

2(*c*) *Juvenile Poems: A Sequel to 'Original Poems'.* London/ Colchester: Baldwin, Cradock, and Joy, John Poole and Son/Swinborne and Walter, 1823. 3rd edn. 9 × 14 cm. Pp. vi + 97. By the author of *Affection's Gift*, etc. BL: 11645. cc. 43.

HEDGELAND, Isabella, Mrs, *see* KELLY, Isabella

HEMANS, Felicia Dorothea, Mrs Alfred (1795–1835), *see also* COLLECTIONS 32, 36, 38(*a–b*), 39, 40(*a–d*), 41, 42, 43, 44, 45, 46, 48, 49(*a–b*), 50(*a–c*), 52, 53, 54, 55, 56

The daughter of George Browne, a Liverpool merchant, and of Felicity Wagner. She was brought up at Gwrych, near Abergele, N. Wales. In 1812 she married Captain Alfred Hemans, an Irishman who had served in the army with her brothers. They had five children, but separated amicably in 1818. Her *Dartmoor* won the Royal Society of Literature prize in 1821. *The Vespers of Palermo* failed on the London stage. She moved to Dublin in 1831. (*DNB*, Todd 2)

1   *England and Spain; or, Valour and Patriotism.* London: T. Cadell and W. Davies, 1808. 20.5 × 26.5 cm. Pp. [ii] + 28. By Felicia Dorothea Browne. BL: 11602. gg. 22(4).

2   *Poems.* Liverpool/London: printed by G. F. Harris/T. Cadell and W. Davies, 1808. 21 × 27 cm. Pp. xxviii + 111 [subscription edition]. 15/- boards. By Felicia Dorothea Browne. *MR* 60: 323; BL: 841. k. 26.

3   *The Domestic Affections.* London: T. Cadell and W. Davies, 1812. 9.5 × 16.5 cm. Pp. [iv] + 172. By Felicia Dorothea Browne. BL: 11644. aaa. 27.

4(*a*)   *The Restoration of the Works of Art to Italy: A Poem.* Oxford/London: R. Pearson/J. Ebers, 1816. 13 × 21 cm. 23 pp. By a Lady. BL: 11642. cc. 32(3).

4(*b*)   *The Restoration of the Works of Art to Italy: A Poem.* Oxford/London: printed by W. Baxter/J. Murray, 1816. 2nd edn. 13.5 × 22 cm. Pp. [iv] + 37. 4/6. By Felicia Hemans. *MR* 82: 325–6; BL: 994. h. 13.

5(*a*)   *Modern Greece. A Poem.* London: John Murray, 1817. 12.5 × 20 cm. 67 pp. 5/6 sewed. By [Mrs Hemans]. *MR* 84: 31–4; BL: 992. i. 16(7).

5(*b*)   *Modern Greece. A Poem.* London: John Murray, 1821. New edn. 13.5 × 21 cm. 67 pp. BL: 11649. f. 15(3).

6   *Translations from Camoens, and Other Poets, with Original Poetry.* Oxford/London: J. Parker/J. Murray, 1818. 12.5 × 21 cm. 95 pp. By the Author of *Modern Greece*, and the *Restoration of the Works of Art to Italy*. BL: 992. i. 22(3).

7(*a*)   *Tales, and Historic Scenes, in Verse.* London: John Murray, 1819. 9.5 × 16 cm. Pp. [ii] + 255. 9/6 boards. By Felicia Hemans. *MR* 90: 408–12; BL: 994. f. 10.

7(*b*)   *Tales and Historic Scenes.* London: John Murray, 1824. 2nd edn. 12.5 × 21 cm. Pp. [ii] + 227. By Mrs F. Hemans. BL: 840. d. 27(3).

8   *Wallace's Invocation to Bruce. A Poem.* Edinburgh/London: William Blackwood/T. Cadell and W. Davies, 1819. 15.5 × 21 cm. 26 pp. By Mrs Hemans, Author of *The Restoration of the Works of Art to Italy, Modern Greece, Tales and Historic Scenes*, and Other Poems. NLS: NG. 1168. e. 30.

9(*a*)   *The Sceptic; a Poem.* London: John Murray, 1820. 13 × 22 cm. 38 pp. By Mrs Hemans. BL: 994. h. 14.

9(*b*)   *The Sceptic, a Poem. Stanzas to the Memory of the Late King.* London: John Murray, 1821. 2nd edn. 13 × 22 cm. 50 pp. By Mrs Hemans. BL: 994. h. 15.

10   *Stanzas to the Memory of the Late King.* London: John Murray, 1820. 13 × 21 cm. 16 pp. By Mrs Hemans. BL: T. 1063(1).

11   *Dartmoor; a Poem: Which Obtained the Prize of Fifty Guineas Proposed by the Royal Society of Literature.* London: printed for the Royal Society of Literature by J. Brettell, 1821. 17 × 23 cm. Pp. [ii] + 22. By Felicia D. Hemans. BL: 1346. g. 17.

12   *The Siege of Valencia; a Dramatic Poem. The Last Constantine: With Other Poems.* London: John Murray, 1823. 13 × 22 cm. Pp. iv + 319. By Mrs Hemans. BL: 994. h. 16.

13   *The Vespers of Palermo; a Tragedy, in Five Acts.* London: John Murray, 1823. 12.5 × 21 cm. Pp. [ii] + 116. 3/-. HL; BL: 1344. l. 43.

14(*a*) *The Forest Sanctuary; and Other Poems.* London: John Murray, 1825. 13 × 21.5 cm. Pp. vi + 205. 7/6. By Mrs Hemans. *MR* 2: 139–46; BL: 994. i. 16.

14(*b*) *The Forest Sanctuary; and Other Poems.* Boston[, Mass.]: Hilliard, Gray, Little, and Wilkins, 1827. 14 × 23 cm. Pp. ii + 232. By Mrs Felicia Hemans. NYPL: NCM.

14(*c*)   *The Forest Sanctuary: With Other Poems*. Edinburgh/London: William Blackwood/T. Cadell, 1829. 2nd edn. 10 × 17 cm. Pp. viii + 324. By Felicia Hemans. BL: 994. f. 11.

14(*d*)   *The Forest Sanctuary: With Other Poems*. Edinburgh/London: William Blackwood and Sons/T. Cadell, 1835. 3rd edn. 10.5 × 16.5 cm. Pp. viii + 324. By Felicia Hemans. NYPL: NCM.

15   *The League of the Alps, the Siege of Valencia, the Vespers of Palermo, and Other Poems*. [Half-title: *Poems*, vol. i.] Boston[, Mass.]: Hilliard, Gray, Little, and Wilkins, 1826. 13.5 × 22.5 cm. Pp. ii + 480. By Mrs Felicia Hemans. Widener: 18423. 9A.

16   *The Forest Sanctuary; and Other Poems*. [Half-title: *Poems*, vol. ii.] Boston[, Mass.]: Hilliard, Gray, Little, and Wilkins, 1827. 13.5 × 22.5 cm. Pp. ii + 231. By Mrs Felicia Hemans. Widener: 18423. 9. 2A.

17(*a*)   *Hymns on the Works of Nature, for the Use of Children*. Boston[, Mass.]: Hilliard, Gray, Little, and Wilkins, 1827. 11 × 16.5 cm. 35 pp. $1.25 a dozen, 35.5 cents for 3, 12.5 cents single. By Mrs Felicia Hemans. Houghton: *EC8. H3708. 827ha.

17(*b*)   *Hymns on the Works of Nature. For the Use of Children*. London: John Mardon, 1833 [reprinted from the American edn.]. 9 × 14.5 cm. Pp. [ii] + 49. By Mrs Felicia Hemans. BL: T. 1471(2).

17(*c*)   *Hymns for Childhood*. Dublin/London: William Curry, Jr., and Co./Simpkin and Marshall, 1834. 8 × 13.5 cm. 65 pp. By Felicia Hemans. BL: 844. c. 16.

18(*a*)   *Poems*. Boston[, Mass.]: Hilliard, Gray, Little, and Wilkins, 1827. Reprinted from the American octavo edn. [*i.e.* items 15 and 16]. 9.5 × 15.5 cm. 2 vols. By Mrs Felicia Hemans. NEDL: KC6008.

18(*b*)   *Poems*. Hartford[, Conn.]: Edward Hopkins, 1827. 3rd American edn. 9 × 14.5 cm. 348 pp. By Mrs Felicia Hemans. NYPL: NCM.

18(*c*)   *Poems*. Boston[, Mass.]: Hilliard, Gray, Little, and Wilkins, 1828. A new collection. 9 × 15 cm. 2 vols. By Mrs Felicia Hemans. Houghton: Nor 3828.

18(*d*) *The Poetical Works.* New York: Evert Duykinck, 1828. 4th American edn. 9 × 14 cm. 2 vols. By Mrs Felicia Hemans. BL: 12295. aa. 3.

18(*e*) *The Poetical Works . . . To Which is Added Many Pieces not Contained in Any Former Edition.* New Haven[, Conn.]: Nathan Whiting, 1828. 5th American edn. 9 × 15.5 cm. 2 vols. By Mrs Felicia Hemans. Yale (Sterling): In/H370/828k.

18(*f*) *The Poetical Works.* Philadelphia: Thos. T. Ash, 1832. 6 × 10 cm. 2 vols. By Mrs Hemans. BL: 11646. a. 1.

18(*g*) *Poems.* Boston[, Mass.]/New York/Philadelphia/Baltimore: Perkins and Marvin, and Russell, Odiorne and Co./ Jonathan Leavitt/French and Perkins/Armstrong and Plaskitt, 1833. 9.5 × 16 cm. 2 vols. By Mrs Felicia Hemans. Widener: 18424. 8.

19(*a*) *Records of Woman: With Other Poems.* Edinburgh/London: William Blackwood/T. Cadell, 1828. 10.5 × 17 cm. Pp. viii + 320. By Felicia Hemans. BL: 11646. bb. 2.

19(*b*) *Records of Woman: With Other Poems.* New York: William B. Gilley, 1828. 11 × 17.5 cm. 324 pp. By Felicia Hemans. NEDL: KPD534.

19(*c*) *Records of Woman: With Other Poems.* Edinburgh/London: William Blackwood/T. Cadell, 1828. 2nd edn. 10 × 17 cm. Pp. viii + 323. By Felicia Hemans. BL: 11646. bb. 5.

19(*d*) *Records of Woman: With Other Poems.* Edinburgh/London: William Blackwood/T. Cadell, 1830. 3rd edn. 10 × 17 cm. Pp. viii + 323. By Felicia Hemans. BL: 11646. bb. 6.

19(*e*) *Records of Woman; with Other Poems.* Edinburgh/London: William Blackwood/T. Cadell, 1834. 4th edn. 10 × 17 cm. Pp. viii + 325. By Felicia Hemans. BL: 11646. bb. 4.

20(*a*) *Songs of the Affections, with Other Poems.* Edinburgh/London: William Blackwood/T. Cadell, 1830. 10 × 17 cm. Pp. iv + 259. By Felicia Hemans. BL: 994. f. 12.

20(*b*) *Songs of the Affections, with Other Poems.* Philadelphia: Carey and Lea, 1831. 11 × 17.5 cm. 267 pp. By Felicia Hemans. AAS: G850. H487. S831.

20(*c*)   *Songs of the Affections.* New York/Philadelphia: D. Appleton and Co./Geo. S. Appleton, [n.d.]. 6.5 × 10 cm. 124 pp. By Mrs Hemans. NYPL: NCM.

20(*d*)   *Songs of the Affections, with Other Poems.* Edinburgh/London: William Blackwood and Sons/T. Cadell, 1835. 2nd edn. 10 × 17 cm. Pp. x + 259. By Felicia Hemans. BL: 11657. e. 43.

21(*a*)   *The Poetical Works of Hemans, Heber and Pollok. Complete in One Volume.* Philadelphia: John Grigg, 1831. 14 × 21.5 cm. Pp. xviii + 44 + 80 + vi + 348 [Mrs Hemans's poetry occupies the last 354 pp.]. NYPL: NCM.

21(*b*)   *The Poetical Works of Hemans, Heber and Pollok.* Philadelphia: John Grigg, 1833. 13.5 × 21.5 cm. Pp. xviii + 43 + 79 + vi + 348 [Mrs Hemans's poems occupying the third section]. Widener: 18424. 6. 13.

22   *National Lyrics, and Songs for Music.* Dublin/London: William Curry, Jr./Simpkin and Marshall, 1834. 10 × 16.5 cm. Pp. xiv + 341. By Felicia Hemans. BL: 994. f. 14.

23   *Scenes and Hymns of Life, with Other Religious Poems.* Edinburgh/London: William Blackwood/T. Cadell, 1834. 10 × 16 cm. Pp. xii + 247. By Felicia Hemans. BL: 994. f. 13.

24   *A Short Sketch of the Life of Mrs Hemans: With Remarks on her Poetry; and Extracts.* London/Lewisham: James Paul/Richard Ruegg, 1835. 6.5 × 10.5 cm. Pp. x + 82 [verse occupies pp. 33–82]. BL: 1164. a. 5.

HENNETT, Mrs

1   *Miscellaneous Poems, on Various Subjects, Designed for the Instruction and Entertainment of Youth.* Spilsby: printed for the author by R. Plant, 1820. 10.5 × 17 cm. Pp. viii + 172 [subscription edition]. 5/-. By Mrs Hennett. U. of Pennsylvania: Pn 821/H389.

HENRIETTA, *see* VALPY, Henrietta F.

HERON, Mary

She lived in Durham. Her *The Conflict; or, Sentimental Tales, in a Series of Letters* seems to have been first published in 1790. (Blain, *BLC*)

1   *Miscellaneous Poems.* Newcastle: for the author by T. Saint, 1786. 17.5 × 24 cm. 88 pp. [subscription edition]. By Mary Heron. BL: 11642. g. 24(1).

2   *Sketches of Poetry.* Newcastle: for the author by T. Saint, 1786. 18 × 24 cm. 28 pp. By Mary Heron, of Durham. BL: 11642. g. 24(2).

3   *Odes, &c. on Various Occasions.* Newcastle: printed by Hall and Elliot, 1792. 15.5 × 19.5 cm. 55 pp. By Mary Heron, Authoress of *The Conflict*, etc. BL: 11633. e. 18.

HEWITT, Elizabeth Catherine, Mrs

1   *Meditations, on Some of the Names and Covenant Characters of Christ. In Eighteen Poems.* London: for the author by Ebenezer Palmer, 1830. 8.5 × 14.5 cm. Pp. iv + 206. By Mrs Hewitt. Bodley: 30. 120.

HEWLETT, Elizabeth, Mrs William

Her book is dated from 'Magdalen Parish', Oxford.

1   *The Valley of Elah, or Faith Triumphant. A Poem.* Oxford: Haldon and Lowndes, 1822. 12 × 20 cm. Pp. viii + 41 [subscription edition]. By Mrs William Hewlett. BL: 11645. bbb. 43.

HILES, Mary

She writes from Kidderminster, Worcs. One poem, 'To my Pupils', suggests that she taught children.

1   *The Deluge and Other Poems.* Kidderminster/London: printed by Thomas Pennell/Wholesale Booksellers, 1828. 9.5 × 16.5 cm. Pp. xii + 146. By Mary Hiles. BL: 994. f. 16.

HILL, Elizabeth, *see* COLLECTIONS 12(*a–k*), 23(*a–b*)

HILL, Isabel (1800–42)

She was born in Bristol, Glos. Her parents and an older brother encouraged her to write. She describes herself as belonging to the ranks of 'scribbling spinsters'. Some of her poems appeared in such periodicals as the *Pocket Magazine* and the *Literary Museum*, and she contributed regularly to the annuals. She also wrote plays and translations from French. (Blain, Boyle, *Holiday Dreams*)

1(*a*)   *The Poet's Child: A Tragedy, in Five Acts.* London: John Warren, 1820. 12.5 × 21.5 cm. Pp. [vi] + 64. By Isabel Hill. BL: 841. f. 66.

1(*b*)   *The Poet's Child.* 1821. 2nd edn. Stainforth.

2   *Zaphna; or, the Amulet: A Poem.* London: W. Sams, 1823. 11 × 18.5 cm. Pp. iv + 93. 5/- boards. By Isabel Hill, Author of *The Poet's Child* and *Constance. MR* 100: 97–8; CUL: 1823 7 30.

3   *Holiday Dreams; or, Light Reading, in Poetry and Prose.* London/Edinburgh: Thomas Cadell/W. Blackwood, 1829. 11.5 × 19 cm. Pp. viii + 184. By Isabel Hill. BL: 994. h. 17.

HILL, Philippina Patience, Mrs Robert

Her maiden name was Burton. She began acting professionally at the Haymarket in London in 1770 and also took a part in the performance of her own unpublished play, *Fashion Displayed*. A report of her bankruptcy in 1772 records that she was known as Patience Yandall, milliner. About 1778 she married the actor, Robert Hill, but she was a widow by 1785. (Blain, Bodley LC, *The Diadem*, Highfill, *Portraits*, Todd 1)

1   *A Novel and Genuine Display on the Leading Disposition of the Human Mind. With a Sketch of Modern Life. In Which the Following Passions and Effects are Characterized: Ambition—Disappointment—Revenge—Madness—Suicide—Suspense—Hope—Love—Matrimony. With an Exordium and Epilogue. Dedicated (by Permission) to Her Grace the Duchess of Devonshire.* [*c.*1780]. 20.5 × 26.5 cm. 32 pp. [verse and prose]. By Mrs P. Hill. Bodley: G. Pamphl. 1817(14).

2   *The Diadem; or, King David, a Sacred Poem, Dedicated to Her Majesty.* [Number 1, of 3]. [No place, publisher, or date.] 12 × 20 cm. Pp. viii + 21 [subscription edition]. By Mrs Robert Hill. Bodley: Harding C 2065(8).

3   *The Diadem.* Number 2, of 3. Inference.

4   *Number the Third of the Diadem.* London: for the author by
     Southern, [n.d.]. 12 × 20 cm. Pp. vi + 3–25 [subscription
     edition]. By Mrs Robert Hill. Bodley: Harding C 2065(9).

5   *A Poem, Sacred to Freedom: And a Poem, Intitled, Beneficence.*
     [Dublin/London: for the author by Byrne/Southern,
     1780?] 12 × 19.5 cm. Pp. [iv] + 28 [subscription edition].
     By Mrs Robert Hill. Bodley: Godw-Pamphl. 1267(14).

6(a) *Portraits, Characters, Pursuits, and Amusements of the Present
     Fashionable World, Interspersed with Poetic Flights of Fancy.*
     Printed for subscribers only, [c.1785]. 11 × 17 cm. Pp. xii
     + 84 [subscription edition]. By Mrs P. Hill. Bodley: G.
     Pamph. 1601(7).

6(b) *Portraits, Characters, Pursuits, and Amusements of the Present
     Fashionable World, Interspersed with Poetic Flights of Fancy.*
     [London, 1795?] 9.5 × 15.5 cm. Pp. xii + 84 [subscription
     edition]. By Mrs P. Hill. BL: 11633. aa. 7.

7   *A Poem, to the Memory of the Truly-right-honourable William
     Burton Conyngham, Lately Deceased; Written, and Most
     Respectfully Addressed to the Right Honourable Lord Conyngham.*
     Dublin, 1796. 12 × 20.5 cm. 15 pp. By His Lordship's
     Most Obedient, Most Obliged, Humble Servant, Mrs
     Robert Hill. Bodley: Harding C 2065(7).

HILLS, Elise
She dedicated her book to the Duchess of Kent. She probably lived in
Portsmouth.

1   *Kebir, and Other Poems.* Portsmouth/London: printed by W.
     Harrison/Longman and Co., 1835. 9.5 × 14.5 cm. Pp. [vi]
     + 109 [subscription edition]. 5/-. By Elise Hills. BL:
     11646. aa. 49.

HINDMARSH, Isabella (c.1798–1823)
An obituary from the *Newheath Chronicle*, 6 December 1823, pasted
to the fly-leaf of the BL copy of her book, reports that she died on
1 December, aged 25. Her preface is signed 'Isabella Hindmarsh'.

1   *The Cave of Hoonga, a Tongaen Tradition, in Two Cantos. And
     Other Poems.* Alnwick: printed for the author by W.

Davison, 1818. 10 × 16.5 cm. 254 pp. By Miss Hindmarsh.
BL: 11645. aa. 22.

HITCHENER, Elizabeth (1782?–1822)

She was a schoolteacher in Cuckfield in Sussex. Shelley invited her to
live with him and Harriet Westbrook in 1812 and she instead
gave up her job to do so. After five months they fell out and she was
instead granted a pension of £100 a year. (*Letters of Elizabeth Hitchener to
Percy Bysshe Shelley*, ed. Walter Edwin Peck (1926), *Shelley Circle*)

1   *The Fire-side Bagatelle: Containing Enigmas on the Chief Towns
     of England and Wales.* London: J. Wallis, Harris, Darton
     and Harvey, 1818. 10 × 16.5 cm. Pp. viii + 39. By
     Elizabeth Hitchener. BL: 992. g. 27(5).

2   *The Weald of Sussex, a Poem.* London: Black, Young, and
     Young, 1822. 10.5 × 17 cm. Pp. xii + 149. By Miss E.
     Hitchener. BL: 11643. c. 20.

3   *Enigmas, Historical and Geographical.* London: Darton and
     Harvey, 1834. 11 × 19 cm. Pp. [ii] + 91. By a Clergyman's
     Daughter. HL; BL: 992. i. 29.

HOARE, Sarah (1777–1856)

She was the daughter of Samuel Hoare, the banker, and of his
first wife, Sarah Gurney. Both parents were Quakers. (*Friends' Books,
Memoirs of Samuel Gurney . . .* , ed. F. R. Pryor (1911))

1   *A Poem on the Pleasures and Advantages of Botanical Pursuits,
     with Notes; and Other Poems.* Bristol: printed by Philip Rose,
     [1825?]. 10 × 16.5 cm. Pp. x + 134. By a Friend to Youth.
     BL: 11645. aaa. 8.

2   *Poems on Conchology and Botany, with Plates and Notes.*
     London/Bristol: Simpkin and Marshall/Wright and
     Bagnall, 1831. 10 × 17.5 cm. Pp. iv + 106. By Sarah
     Hoare. BL: 11644. cc. 37.

[*See also*: 'The Pleasures of Botanical Pursuits. A Poem' (7 pp.) in
Priscilla Wakefield, *An Introduction to Botany . . .* (1818 and 1819).]

HODSON, Mrs Septimus, *see* HOLFORD, Margaret

HOFLAND, Barbara, Mrs Thomas Christopher, *see* HOOLE, Barbara

HOLCROFT, Miss, *see* COLLECTIONS 35

HOLDERNESS, Mary

1   *A Manual of Devotion; being Meditations and Hymns for Every Day in the Month.* London/Edinburgh/Glasgow/Dublin: James Duncan/Waugh and Innes/M. Ogle/R. M. Tims, 1825. 10.5 × 18 cm. Pp. xx + 152 [subscription edition; prose and about 33 pp. of verse]. By Mary Holderness, Author of *New Russia*, and *Manners and Customs of the Crim Tatars*. BL: 1018. e. 28.

HOLE, Mrs, of Sheffield, *see* COLLECTIONS 20

HOLFORD, Margaret (1778–1852), *see also* COLLECTIONS 32, 49(*a–b*)

She was the eldest daughter of Allen Holford and Margaret Wrench (*see* Holford, below). She became the second wife of the Revd Septimus Hodson in 1826. She was acquainted with Southey, Coleridge, and Landor, was a regular contributor to the annuals, and wrote translations of Italian works. (Blain, Boyle, *DNB* (under Hodson))

1(*a*)   *Elegiac Ode, to the Memory of Lieut.-Colonel Vassall.* Bristol: printed by Kemp and Co., 1808. 17.5 × 23 cm. 11 pp. BL: 1600/869.

1(*b*)   *Memoir of the Life of Lieutenant-Colonel Vassall.* Bristol: printed by Barry and Son, 1819. 11 × 18.5 cm. 59 pp. [pp. 49–59 are devoted to 'Elegiac Ode, to the Memory of Lieut.-Colonel Vassall' by 'Miss Holford'; the remainder is prose]. BL: 1202. a. 6.

2(*a*)   *Wallace; or, the Fight of Falkirk; a Metrical Romance.* London: T. Cadell and W. Davies, 1809. 20.5 × 27 cm. Pp. viii + 248. £1/5/- boards. *CR* 19: 130–49; *MR* 62: 26–39; BL: 1346. m. 8.

2(*b*)   *Wallace; or, the Fight of Falkirk; a Metrical Romance.* London: Longman, Hurst, Rees, Orme, and Brown, 1810. 2nd edn. 13 × 21 cm. Pp. viii + 252. By Miss Holford. BL: 11641. f. 33.

2(*c*)   *Wallace; or, the Fight of Falkirk; a Metrical Romance.* Philadelphia: J. and A. Y. Humphreys, 1810. 9.5 × 15.5

cm. 256 pp. By Miss Holford. Houghton: *EC8. H6696. 809wc.

3   *Poems.* London: Longman, Hurst, Rees, Orme, and Brown, 1811. 13.5 × 21.5 cm. Pp. [ii] + 117. By Miss Holford. BL: 11645. bbb. 25.

4(*a*)   *Margaret of Anjou: A Poem. In Ten Cantos.* London: John Murray, 1816. 21.5 × 28 cm. Pp. [ii] + 474. £2/2/- boards. By Miss Holford. *MR* 81: 354–62; BL: 11642. h. 41.

4(*b*)   *Margaret of Anjou. A Poem.* Philadelphia/Boston[, Mass.]: M. Carey/Wells and Lilly, 1816. 9 × 14.5 cm. 292 pp. By Miss Holford. Widener: 18426. 25v.

5   *The Past, etc.* London/Bath: Longman, Hurst, Rees, Orme, and Browne/John Upham, 1819. 12.5 × 21 cm. Pp. iv + 46. By Miss Holford, the Authoress of *Wallace.* BL: 992. i. 24(5).

[*See also* 'Lines to the Memory of Ensign George Holford Walker . . .' ([1832?], 2 pp.).]

HOLFORD, Margaret, Mrs Allen (*c.*1761–1834)
She was the daughter of William Wrench of Chester. She married Allen Holford of Davenham, Cheshire. She also wrote novels and comedies. She was the mother of Margaret Holford (q.v.). (Blain)

1   *Gresford Vale, and Other Poems.* London: Hookham and Carpenter, 1798. 20.5 × 26 cm. 44 pp. By M. Holford, BL: 644. k. 25(8).

HOLMES, Ann

1   *An Epic Poem on Adam and Eve. With Poetry, on Two Ladies in Disguise. A Short Pastoral: Also the Soliloquy of a Young Lady; together with a Poem, an Elegy, and a Vindication of Fate in Marriage: To Which is Added, Rules for Polite Behaviour.* Bedale: printed by Joseph Todd, 1800. 10 × 17 cm. 28 pp. 1/6. By Ann Holmes, Redmire, Wensleydale. BL: 11633. aa. 25.

HOME, Mrs, *see* DARLING, Patricia Rolland
The title-page of Darling's book in 1817 describes her as the late Mrs Home of Whitfield.

HOME, Anne, *see* HUNTER, Anne

HONORA, Lady, *pseudonym of* M'GIBBON, Alexander

HOOD, Catharine

1   *Remonstrance: With Other Poems.* London: for the author by
     R. Roe, T. N. Longman and O. Rees, J. Wright, and
     W. Phillips, 1801. 10.5 × 17.5 cm. Pp. [iv] + 112. 2/6. By
     Catharine Hood [and another]. *MR* 39: 328; *CR* 36:
     113–14; BL: 11633. aaa. 24.

HOOK, Harriet Horncastle, Mrs James (died 1808)
She was the daughter of a military officer named Madden and was
married by 1776 to the composer James Hook. They had at least two
sons. She also painted portrait miniatures. She died in South Lambeth,
London. (Highfill)

1   *Sacred Hours, Religious Poems.* 1806. O'D; Stainforth. Not
     located.

HOOLE, Barbara, Mrs T. Bradshawe (1770–1844)
Born in Sheffield, Yorks. Her father, Robert Wreaks, was a manufacturer. In 1796 she married T. Bradshawe Hoole, a merchant, whose
death two years later left her temporarily well off. The failure of the
firm in which her funds were invested made her turn to writing and
teaching. *The Clergyman's Widow* (1812) sold 17,000 copies, and by 1820
she had written more than twenty novels. She married Thomas
Christopher Hofland, an artist, in 1808. They had one son. Her *Poems*
sold nearly 2,000 copies and enabled her to open a school in
Harrogate. She wrote altogether about seventy works, of which nearly
300,000 copies were sold. (Allibone, *DNB* (under Hofland))

1   *Poems.* Sheffield/London: J. Montgomery/Vernor and
     Hood, [1805]. 9 × 15 cm. Pp. lii + 256 [subscription
     edition]. By Barbara Hoole. BL: 1346. c. 10.

2(*a*) *La Fête de la Rose.* Inference.

2(*b*) *La Fête de la Rose.* 2nd edn. Inference.

2(*c*) *La Fête de la Rose: Or, the Dramatic Flowers. A Holiday
        Present, for Young People.* London/Knaresborough/
        Harrogate/York: Longman, Hurst, Rees, and Orme, and
        Tabart and Co./Hargrove and Sons/Hargrove and Sons/
        Wilson and Son, and Todd and Sons, 1810. 3rd edn. 12 ×
        13.5 cm. 24 pp. By Mrs B. Hoole. Osborne: ii. 643.

3(*a*)   *A Season at Harrogate; in a Series of Poetical Epistles, from Benjamin Blunderhead, Esquire, to his Mother, in Derbyshire: With Useful and Copious Notes, Descriptive of the Objects Most Worthy of Attention in the Vicinity of Harrogate.* Knaresborough and Harrogate/London/Leeds/York/Doncaster/Rippon/Halifax/Sheffield/Liverpool: R. Wilson/Long-man, Hurst, Rees, Orme, and Brown/Robinson, Heaton, I. and I. Nicholls, and Baines/Wolstenholme, and Todd/Hunsley and Thomas/Langdale/Edwards/Miss Gales/Wright, 1812. 12.5 × 21.5 cm. 103 pp. BL: 11642. f. 2.

3(*b*)   *A Week at Harrogate. A Poem: In a Series of Letters, Addressed from Benjamin Blunderhead, Esq., to his Friend, Simon: Describing Whatever Principally Attracted his Attention, on his Journey (through York,) to, and during his Stay at that Celebrated Watering-Place.* Knaresbrough and Harrogate/London/York/Leeds and Ripon: for the author by Hargrove and Sons/Longman, Hurst, Rees, Orme, and Brown/Wilson and Son, and other booksellers/other booksellers, 1813. 2nd edn. 10 × 17 cm. 99 pp. CUL: S721. d. 81. 55.

HOOPER, Mrs B., *see* EVANCE, S.

HOPWOOD, D. Caroline, Mrs

Her father was a Lieutenant Skene, in the army, and her mother a Miss Law, the well-educated daughter of a physician in Carlisle, Cumb. She was one of three children. She was employed for a time as a housekeeper. She married and had two children. In 1768 she became a Methodist. For a while she kept a school, but was obliged to give it up because she had become a Quaker. (*An Account, Friends' Books*)

1   *An Account of the Life and Religious Experiences, of D. Caroline Hopwood, of Leeds, Deceased. Published at the Request of her Relations. To Which is Added, a Collection of Pieces in Prose and Poetry, on Various Subjects, Written by the Same Author.* Leeds: printed by E. Baines, 1801. 10 × 16.5 cm. 64 pp. [the verse occupying pp. 55–64]. BL: 4920. cc. 44(1).

HORT, Miss R——

1   *Poems on Miscellaneous Subjects.* London: Gale and Curtis,
     1811. 10 × 16.5 cm. 121 pp. 5/- boards. By Miss R——
     H——. BL: 11633. de. 29.

HORTON, Mary Lambert *or* Louisa (*c.*1804–*c.*1832)

Many of the poems in her posthumous book were previously published
in the Marblehead, Mass., and Salem *Registers*, signed M. L. H. or
M. Louisa. The preface gives her name as Mary Lambert. (*Poetical and
Prose Compositions*)

1   *Poetical and Prose Compositions.* Salem[, Mass.]: W. and S. B.
     Ives, 1832. 8.5 × 14 cm. Pp. iv + 88. By Mary L. Horton.
     BL: 11644. a. 54.

HORWOOD, Caroline

She later became Mrs Baker.

1(*a*)   *Original Poetry for Young Minds.* Inference.

1(*b*)   *Original Poetry for Young Minds.* London: Dean and Munday,
          1818. 2nd edn. 9 × 14 cm. 128 pp. By Miss Horwood. BL:
          11645. aa. 57.

1(*c*)   *Original Poetry for Young Minds.* London: A. K. Newman
          and Co., 1819. 2nd edn. 8.5 × 14 cm. 128 pp. By Miss
          Horwood, Author of *Moral Tales, Trifles for Children*, etc.,
          etc. Osborne: ii. 620.

1(*d*)   *Original Poetry for Young Minds.* London: Dean and Munday,
          1822. 3rd edn. 8.5 × 14.5 cm. 135 pp. By Miss Horwood.
          BL: 11645. aa. 45.

1(*e*)   *Original Poetry for Young Minds.* London: Dean and Munday,
          [1825]. 4th edn. 8 × 13.5 cm. 145 pp. By Miss Horwood.
          BL: 11645. aa. 37.

1(*f*)   *Original Poetry for Young Minds.* 5th edn. Inference.

1(*g*)   *Original Poetry for Young Minds.* London: A. K. Newman
          and Co., [1835]. 6th edn. 9 × 14 cm. 145 pp. 2/-. By Miss
          Horwood. BL: 11645. de. 6.

2(*a*)   *The Deserted Boy; or, Cruel Parents. A Tale of Truth. Calculated
          to Promote Benevolence in Children.* Philadelphia: Wm. Charles,
          1817. 10 × 13.5 cm. 12 pp. 12½ cents plain, 18¾ cents
          coloured. By Miss Horwood. LC: 1817 Juv. Coll.

2(*b*)   *The Deserted Boy; or, Cruel Parents. A Tale of Truth. Calculated to Promote Benevolence in Children.* Philadelphia: Morgan and Yeager, [1825?]. 10.5 × 12 cm. 12 pp. Plain 12.5 cents, coloured 18¾ cents. By Miss Horwood. NYPL: *KVD.

3(*a*)   *Little Emma and her Father. A Lesson for Proud Children.* Philadelphia: Morgan and Yeager, [1820]. 10 × 13 cm. 15 pp. By Miss Horwood. LC: Juv. Coll. 1820, copy 2.

3(*b*)   *Little Emma and her Father. A Lesson for Proud Children.* Philadelphia: Morgan and Yeager, [1825?]. 10 × 13 cm. 15 pp. NYPL: *KVD.

4(*a*)   *Blue Beard; or, the Effects of Female Curiosity. In Easy Verse.* London: Dean and Munday, 1821. 10 × 11.5 cm. 16 pp. By Miss Horwood. Osborne: i. 32.

4(*b*)   *Blue Beard; or, the Effects of Female Curiosity. In Easy Verse.* London: Dean and Munday, 1823. 10.5 × 12.5 cm. 16 pp. 6*d.* By Miss Horwood. Bodley: 25210 f. 419(1).

5   *The Brother & Sister; or, the Advantages of Good Behaviour. A Companion to Little Emma and her Father.* Philadelphia: W. Charles, [1825?]. 10.5 × 13 cm. 15 pp. By Miss Horwood. NYPL: *KVD.

[*See also*: 'Trifles for Children' (1801–2, 4 pp.).]

HORWOOD, E.

1   *Instructive Amusement for Young Minds, in Original Poetry.* London: A. Newman and Co., 1815. 14 cm. 120 pp. By E. Horwood. *NUC.* Not seen.

2   *Original Poetry for Little People.* London: Dean and Son, [1835]. 8.5 × 14 cm. 72 pp. By Miss E. Horwood. BL: 11645. aa. 46.

HOUGHTON, Jane (born *c.*1786)
She was a pupil at Mrs Melville's School in Liverpool.

1   *Blossoms of Genius.* Liverpool: printed by Robinson and Lang, [1798?]. 9.5 × 15.5 cm. Pp. [ii] + 107 [pp. 53–106 are prose]. By Jane Houghton, Aged Twelve Years. BL: 11644. b. 28.

HOUGHTON, Mary Arnald

Emilia is dated from Hereford.

1(*a*)   *Emilia of Lindenau; or, the Field of Leipsic. A Poem, in Four Cantos.* London: Whittingham and Arliss, 1815. 9 × 16 cm. Pp. viii + 201. By Mary Arnald Houghton. BL: 11644. aaa. 4.

1(*b*)   *Emilia of Lindinau; or, the Field of Leipsic. A Poem, in Four Cantos.* London: Whittingham and Arliss, 1815. 2nd edn. 9 × 16 cm. Pp. xii + 201. By Mary Arnald Houghton. BL: 11642. aaa. 18.

1(*c*)   *Emilia of Lindinau; or the Field of Leipsic. A Poem, in Four Cantos.* Philadelphia: Mathew Carey, 1816. 9 × 14.5 cm. Pp. xii + 200. By Mary Arnald Houghton. LC: PR 4806. H6 E5.

HOWITT, Mary, Mrs William (1799–1888), *see also* COLLECTIONS 43, 46, 48, 52, 54 *and* TURNER, Elizabeth, 3(b)

Born at Coleford, Glos. She was the daughter of Samuel Botham, a Quaker, and of Anne Wood. She was educated at home. In 1821 she married William Howitt, and they worked as joint authors thereafter. *DNB* lists forty-two titles written by her independently between 1834 and 1881. She was best known as a writer of tales for children; she translated from Swedish and Danish, including a number of Andersen's tales. She contributed to many of the annuals. In 1879 she received a civil list pension of £100. (Boyle, *CB*, *DNB*)

1   *The Forest Minstrel, and Other Poems.* London: Baldwin, Cradock, and Joy, 1823. 9.5 × 16 cm. Pp. xii + 197. By William and Mary Howitt. BL: 994. f. 17.

2(*a*)   *The Desolation of Eyam: The Emigrant, a Tale of the American Woods: And Other Poems.* London/Edinburgh/Dublin: Wightman and Cramp/Oliver and Boyd/W. Curry, Jr., 1827. 9.5 × 16 cm. Pp. xiv + 323. By William and Mary Howitt. BL: 994. f. 18.

2(*b*)   *The Desolation of Eyam: The Emigrant, a Tale of the American Woods: And Other Poems.* London/Edinburgh/Dublin: Wightman and Cramp/Oliver and Boyd/W. Curry, Jr., 1828. 2nd edn. [Date and edition added to engraved title-page.] 10 × 16.5 cm. Pp. xiv + 323. By William and Mary Howitt. BL: 11660. e. 35.

3   *The Seven Temptations.* London: Richard Bentley, 1834. 10 ×
         16 cm. Pp. x + 373. By Mary Howitt. BL: 1344. b. 18.

4(*a*)   *Sketches of Natural History.* London: Effingham Wilson,
         1834. 10 × 13 cm. Pp. vi + 167. By Mary Howitt. BL: 727.
         b. 7.

4(*b*)   *Sketches of Natural History.* Philadelphia: Conrad and
         Parsons, 1834. 10 × 13 cm. 180 pp. By Mary Howitt. LC:
         PZ 6. H842 SK.

HOWLAND, Avis C., Mrs

1(*a*)   *Tales for Thomas, Containing, The Soldier, The Present, The
         Return, The Mouse, The Dog, Little Harry, The Garden,*
         Strawberries, The Kite, The Black Man. New York: Mahlon
         Day, 1828. 6.5 × 10.5 cm. 17 pp. By A. C. M. of Newport,
         R.I. NYPL: *KVD.

1(*b*)   *Tales for Thomas, Containing The Soldier, The Present, The
         Return, The Mouse, The Dog, Little Harry, The Garden,*
         Strawberries, The Kite, The Black Man. New York: Mahlon
         Day, 1829. 6.5 × 11 cm. 18 pp. By A. C. H. of Newport,
         R.I. Princeton: Hamilton 1442s.

1(*c*)   *Tales for Thomas, Containing The Soldier, The Present, The
         Return, The Mouse, The Dog, Little Harry, The Garden,*
         Strawberries, The Kite, The Black Man. New York: Mahlon
         Day, 1833. 6.5 × 10.5 cm. 17 pp. By A. C. H. of Newport,
         R.I. Brown (Harris): 76/H864t.

2(*a*)   *Rhode-Island Tales.* New York: Mahlon Day, 1829. 9 × 14.5
         cm. 53 pp. By a Friend to Youth. LC: Juv. Coll. 1829.

2(*b*)   *Rhode-Island Tales.* New York: Mahlon Day, 1833. 9 × 13.5
         cm. 66 pp. By a Friend of Youth, of Newport R.I. Brown
         (Harris): 76/H864r/1833.

3   *Tales of Old Times.* New York: Mahlon Day, 1832. 8 × 14
         cm. 60 pp. By the Author of *Rhode Island Tales.* Yale
         (Beinecke): Za/H853/832t.

HOWORTH, Mrs J.

1   *The Poems.* Trans. Mrs Howorth. London: J. Bell, 1794.
         10.5 × 17.5 cm. Pp. xii + 155 [verse occupies pp. 1–16
         only]. By Baron Haller. BL: 11525. d. 13.

HUGHES, Anne, Mrs

She wrote four novels between 1786 and 1788. (Blain, *BLC*)

1   *Poems.* London: J. Dodsley, 1784. 13 × 21.5 cm. Pp. iv +
       131. 3/-. By Mrs Hughes. BL: 11632. f. 28.

2   *Moral Drama's Intended for Private Representation.* London:
       William Lane, 1790. 11 × 17.5 cm. Pp. [ii] + 244. By Mrs
       Hughes. BL: 11778. aaa. 28.

HUNT, Eliza

Judging from *Poems* she seems to have been needy. She laments the
death of a 4-year-old niece. Some of her verse was set to music by
I. Carter of Canterbury; the score is tipped into the book.

1   *Poems on Various Subjects.* North-Green: printed for the
       author by W. Stevens, 1808. 9.5 × 15.5 cm. Pp. 90 + 8
       [subscription edition]. By Eliza Hunt. BL: 11645. aa. 32.

HUNTER, Anne, Mrs John (1742–1821), *see also* COLLECTIONS 19,
21, 23(*a–b*), 32, 35

She was the eldest daughter of Robert Home, surgeon of Burgoyne's
Light Horse, and of Mary Hutchinson. She married the famous
London surgeon, John Hunter. They had four children; she was an
active bluestocking. (Lonsdale)

1(*a*)   *Poems.* London: T. Payne, 1802. 10.5 × 17.5 cm. Pp. viii +
         122. By Mrs John Hunter. BL: 11650. cc. 21(3).

1(*b*)   *Poems.* London: T. Payne, 1803. 2nd edn. 10 × 17.5 cm.
         120 pp. By Mrs John Hunter. BL: 11646. bbb. 10.

2(*a*)   *The Sports of the Genii.* London: T. Payne, 1804. 17 × 23.5
         cm. Pp. [iv] + 16 [interleaved with unpaginated en-
         gravings]. 10/6 sewed. By Mrs John Hunter. *MR* 48: 323;
         BL: 11642. f. 37.

2(*b*)   *The Sports.* 1816. 2nd edn. Stainforth. Not located.

[*See also*: 'A New Ballad Entitled . . . the Times' (1804, broadsheet).]

HUNTLEY, Lydia Howard, *see* SIGOURNEY, Lydia Howard

HUTCHINSON, the Misses, *see* COLLECTIONS 27

They were daughters of the antiquarian and topographer William Hutchinson of Barnard Castle, Co. Durham. (*DNB* (under William Hutchinson), *NUC*)

HUTTON, Mary, Mrs

She lived in Sheffield, Yorks., and was the second wife of a penknife cutler. She mentions a daughter who is ill and also a step-son and step-daughter. She writes from Butcher's Buildings, Norris-field. The book is published by private subscription and the list of subscribers is deliberately withheld. (*Sheffield Manor*)

1   *Sheffield Manor, and Other Poems.* Ed. [John Holland]. Sheffield: J. Blackwell, 1831. 10.5 × 17.5 cm. 96 pp. By Mary Hutton. BL: 11644. bbb. 7.

HYDE, Nancy Maria (1792–1816)

Born in Norwich, Conn. She was the youngest child of Elisha Hyde and Ann Hallam. She was a precocious and dedicated pupil who left school at 14. The family fortunes declined and she went to Hartford in 1811 to prepare herself as a teacher. Her journal and letters describe her experiences. She became a teacher but died of a fever following a severe cold. (*The Writings*)

1   *The Writings.* Ed. [Mrs Lydia Sigourney]. Norwich[, Conn.]: printed by Russell Hubbard, 1816. 12 × 19 cm. 252 pp. [subscription edition; about 26 pages of verse are distributed through the volume]. By Nancy Maria Hyde. HEHL: 301148.

IANTHE, *see* EMBURY, Emma Catherine

ILIFF, Maria, Mrs Edward Henry

An actress and singer. Her mother, Mrs Palmer, was housekeeper to the famous actress Mrs Spranger Barry, and Mrs Barry supervised her introduction to the stage. Her first professional performances in England took place in 1767 and she may have appeared previously in Ireland. She married, probably in 1785, but was separated from her husband by 1802. They had at least two children. (Highfill)

1(*a*)   *Poems, upon Several Subjects.* London: for the author by Vernor, Hood, and Sharpe, 1808. 10 × 16 cm. Pp. xxviii + 147 [subscription edition]. By Mrs Iliff. BL: 11633. aa. 28.

1(*b*)   *Poems, upon Several Subjects*. Malta: printed for the author at the Government Printing House, 1818. 2nd edn. 9.5 × 15.5 cm. Pp. xvi + 144 [subscription edition]. By Mrs Iliff. BL: 1164. e. 2.

INGLIS, Mrs Richmond
She lived in Edinburgh and, as the title-page explains, her father was Colonel James Gardiner.

1   *Anna and Edgar: Or, Love and Ambition. A Tale*. Edinburgh: for the author by William Creech, 1781. 17 × 22.5 cm. 53 pp. 2/6. By Mrs Richmond Inglis, Daughter of Colonel James Gardiner, Who Fell at the Battle of Preston, 1745. BL: 11657. g. 56(3).

INMAN, Miss, *see* COLLECTIONS 35

INSTONE, Sarah

1   *Poems on Several Occasions. Humbly Inscribed to the Honourable Miss Leigh*. Bridgnorth/London: G. Gitton/Robinsons, 1797. 11.5 × 18.5 cm. Pp. xxiv + 67 [subscription edition]. By Sarah Instone. BL: 11641. bb. 34.

IRELAND, [Stella?], Mrs Samuel
Information about the Ireland family is notoriously difficult to come by. *DNB* is sceptical about the existence of a wife, reporting the opinion that the Shakespearean forger, William Henry Ireland, was in fact the son of Samuel Ireland's housekeeper. Stella Ireland may be a 'ghost'. (*DNB*, Leeds University L. Cat.)

1   *The Doctor Dissected: Or, Willy Cadogan in the Kitchen. Addressed to All Invalids, and Readers of a Late Dissertation on the Gout, &c. &c. &c.* London: T. Davies and S. Leacroft, 1771. 17 × 23.5 cm. 21 pp. 1/-. By a Lady [Stella]. Leeds: Brotherton Collection.

2   *Modest Exceptions, from the Court of Parnassus, to Mrs Macaulay's Modest Plea*. London: J. Bew, 1774. 19.5 × 24.5 cm. 16 pp. 1/-. By the Author of *The Doctor Dissected* [Stella]. Yale (Beinecke): Miscellaneous Poems 78.

THE IRISH COTTAGER, *see* TAYLOR, Ellen

ISAACS, Mrs

She wrote six novels between 1801 and 1820. (*CB*)

1   *The Wanderings of Fancy; Consisting of Miscellaneous Pieces, in Prose and Verse.* London: C. Chapple, 1812. 13 × 22 cm. Pp. viii + 286 [about 36 pp. of verse; subscription edition]. By Mrs Isaacs, Authoress of *Ella St. Lawrence, Wood Nymph*, etc. BL: 1457. f. 2.

IVISON, Ursula

The Retired Penitent is a paraphrase of Edward Young's *The Centaur Not Fabulous.*

1   *The Retired Penitent, a Poem.* London: Mathews, Rivington, Meredith, 1794. 13 × 20.5 cm. 30 pp. 1/-. By Ursula Ivison. BL: 992. h. 20(2).

J., A. M., *see* JONES, Anna Maria

J. [JEVONS?], M. A., *see* COLLECTIONS 52

JACKSON, Miss, *see* SPENCER, Mrs Walter

JACKSON, Adelaide

1   *Fragments.* London: printed for the author by J. C. Kelly and Son, 1826. 12.5 × 20.5 cm. 88 pp. By a Lady. BL: 1466. h. 51(1).

JACOB, Catharine, Mrs

Her maiden name was Kunnison. *Poems* is dated from 4 Bugle Street, Southampton, Hants, and signed Catharine Jacob. She laments the death of an infant daughter and mentions a deceased husband and a son, William, who has gone to sea.

1   *Poems.* Southampton: printed for the author by E. Skelton and Co., 1821. 10 × 16 cm. Pp. viii + 78 [subscription edition—no list of subscribers]. By Mrs Jacob, (Late Miss C. Kunnison, of Southampton.) Author of *The Monk and the Vine-dresser, Feeling,* and *Old Times and New.* BL: 11644. bb. 4.

JAMES, Eliza, Mrs

She signs her full name to the dedication. She was evidently an actress at the theatre in Durham.

1   *Hours of Leisure. Poems.* Durham: printed for the author by
    G. Walker, [1807]. 10.5 × 17.5 cm. Pp. xx + 107 [subscrip-
    tion edition]. By Mrs James. BL: 11645. aaa. 24.

JAMIESON, Frances, Mrs

Her maiden name was Thurtle.

1   *Cadijah: The Black Prince. A Tragedy, in Five Acts.* London:
    G. B. Whittaker, 1825. 12.5 × 21 cm. Pp. [iv] + 104. By
    Mrs Jamieson. BL: 11779. f. 67.

JENKS, Jacquetta Agneta Mariana, *pseudonym of* BECKFORD, William

JERVICE, Sophia

1   *Ines, and Other Poems.* London: Thomas and Joseph
    Allman, and J. F. Dove, 1816. 12.5 × 20.5 cm. 208 pp.
    Avero; BL: 992. i. 19(1).

JEVONS, Mary Anne, Mrs Thomas (1795–1845), *see also*
COLLECTIONS 52

Born in Liverpool. She was the eldest daughter of William Roscoe, the historian, and of Jane Griffies, the daughter of a Liverpool trades-man. Her youth was spent in the constant companionship of her father. She was a Unitarian. In 1825 she married Thomas Jevons, a Liverpool iron merchant. The economist and logician William Stanley Jevons was their son. She contributed to many annuals and was editor of *The Sacred Offering* from 1831 to 1838. (Blain, Boyle, *DNB*)

1(*a*)   *Poems for Youth.* Liverpool/London: Robinson and
        Sons/Longman, Hurst, Rees, Orme, and Brown, Baldwin,
        Cradock and Co., George Cowie and Co., Hayward and
        Roscoe, 1820. 9.5 × 16.5 cm. Pp. iv + 106. By a Family
        Circle [M. A. Jevons, J. E. Roscoe and others]. Osborne:
        ii. 645.

1(*b*)   *Poems for Youth.* Part I [of 2]. London: Baldwin, Cradock
        and Co., 1821. 2nd edn. 9.5 × 16 cm. Pp. iv + 104. 3/6

boards. By a Family Circle [M. A. Jevons, J. E. Roscoe, and others]. BL: 11644. aaa. 9.

2   *Poems for Youth*. Part II [of 2]. London: Baldwin, Cradock, and Co., 1821. 9.5 × 16 cm. Pp. [ii] + 78. By a Family Circle [M. A. Jevons, J. E. Roscoe, and others]. BL: 11644. aaa. 9.

JEWSBURY, Maria Jane (1800–33), *see also* COLLECTIONS 42, 49(*a–b*), 53

Born at Measham, Derbyshire. She was the eldest daughter of Thomas Jewsbury. She was educated at a school in Shenstone kept by a Mrs Adams, but was removed from it at 14 because of delicate health. In or about 1818 the family moved to Manchester. When her mother died soon after, she was left to take care of a sister and three brothers. She first published a poem in *Aston's Manchester Herald*. Alaric Watts, the editor of the *Manchester Courier*, is said to have persuaded her to write professionally, and she contributed substantially to the annuals from 1825 on. In 1832 she married the Revd William Kew Fletcher, a chaplain in the service of the East India Company, and she accompanied him to India. She died of cholera in Poona. Wordsworth's poem 'Liberty' (1829) is addressed to her. (Boyle, *DNB*)

1   *Phantasmagoria; or, Sketches of Life and Literature*. London/ Edinburgh: Hurst, Robinson, and Co./Archibald Constable and Co., 1825. 11 × 19 cm. 2 vols. [Prose and verse.] BL: 838. g. 8.

2   *Lays of Leisure Hours*. London: J. Hatchard and Son, 1829. 10 × 17 cm. Pp. xii + 189. 5/-. By Maria Jane Jewsbury. *EC*; BL: 994. f. 20.

JOHNS, Mrs

She was perhaps the wife of the painter Ambrose Bowden Johns or of the painter Charles Alexander Johns, both of whom lived in Plymouth. Her *Poems* is a posthumous book that refers to a son who died in infancy and it exhibits an informed interest in theatre-going.

1   *Poems*. Plymouth: Clarence Press, [1800?]. 13 × 22 cm. 92 pp. [Mrs Johns's poems occupy pp. 75–91]. By Mr and Mrs Johns of Plymouth. BL: 11632. f. 31.

JOHNSON, Elizabeth, *see* APPENDIX 4

JOHNSON, Lucinda, *see* APPENDIX 4

JOHNSON, Mary F.

Original Sonnets is written from Wroxhall Farm, in the Isle of Wight.

1   *Original Sonnets, and Other Poems.* London: Longman, Hurst, Rees and Orme, 1810. 10 × 16 cm. Pp. [xvi] + 160. 4/- boards. By Mary F. Johnson. *MR* 65: 329–32; BL: 11644. aaa. 5.

JONES, Anna Maria, Lady

She was the eldest daughter of Jonathan Shipley, DD, the Bishop of St Asaph. She married the great orientalist, Sir William Jones, in 1783 and travelled with him to India. She returned to England in 1793 because of ill health; her husband died in India in the following year. (Allibone, *DNB*)

1   *The Poems.* Calcutta: printed [for the author?] by Thomson and Ferris, 1793. 13.5 × 21 cm. 68 pp. [subscription edition]. 1 gold mohur. By Anna Maria. BL: 992. h. 22(4).

JONES, Elizabeth C., Mrs

1   *Poems on Different Subjects, Original and Selected.* Providence [, RI]: printed by H. H. Brown, 1819. 10.5 × 17.5 cm. 48 pp. By Elizabeth C. Jones. LC: PS 2150. J75 P6 1819 Rare Bk. Coll.

2   *Original Poems, on Different Subjects* . . . Part 2 [of 2]. Providence[, RI], 1821. 18 cm. 47 pp. By Elizabeth C. Jones. *NUC.* Not found.

3   *Fugitive Poems.* Providence[, RI]: printed by Smith and Parmenter, 1828. 10.5 × 17 cm. 59 pp. By Mrs Elizabeth C. Jones. Widener: AL2171. 5. 75.

4   *Infantine Ditties.* Providence[, RI]: Cory, Marshall, and Hammond, 1830. 10 × 15.5 cm. 24 pp. By Mrs Elizabeth C. Jones, Author of *Fugitive Poems*, etc., etc. LC: Juv. Coll. 1830.

JONES, Mary Elizabeth, Mrs (died 1834)

She was the daughter of Henry James Pye, the poet laureate, and of his first wife, Mary Hook, who was also a writer. She married Captain Jones of the 35th Regiment. (*DNB* (under H. J. Pye))

1   *Poems on Several Occasions.* Stoke Park, 1802. 13 × 21 cm. Pp. iv + 40. LC: PR 5193. P7 P6 Office.

2   *Poems.* London: for the author by C. Chapple, 1826. 10.5 × 17.5 cm. 51 pp. [subscription edition]. By Mary Jones, Daughter of the Late H. J. Pye . . . Poet Laureat to His Majesty George the Third. BL: 11645. aaa. 25.

JONES, Sophia

She writes from Villiers Street in London. She evidently spent some of her childhood with the Duberlys at Stanmore Priory, Middx. (*Poetical Sketches*)

1   *Poetical Sketches.* Inscribed to Her Royal Highness the Princess Charlotte of Wales. London: printed for the authoress by C. Lowndes, 1808. 9.5 × 15.5 cm. 80 pp. By Sophia Jones. BL: 11645. aa. 48.

JORDAN, Judith, Mrs Jeremiah

As her title-page mentions, she had lived at Hucks Barn Farm, near Ludlow, Shrops.

1   *The Religious Breathings, and Exercises of a Mind, Spiritualized by, and Devoted to Jesus of Nazareth; being Some Poetical Essays and Plain Versifications on Various Subjects, Doctrinal, Experimental, and Humourous.* Ed. [James Ingram and John Palmer]. Shrewsbury: T. Wood, 1809. 8.5 × 14 cm. 125 pp. By Judith, Wife of Jeremiah Jordan, Late of Hucks Barn Farm, near Ludlow, Shropshire. BL: 11642. a. 21.

JOYNES, Lucy (died 1851)

She writes from Nottingham, Notts., and displays an interest in Home Missionaries and Sunday Schools. (*Occasional and Miscellaneous Poems*, Osborne)

1(*a*)   *Original Poetry for Infant and Juvenile Minds. In Two Parts.* [1817.] By Lucy Loynes [Joynes] of Nottingham. *ER* 29: 256. Not located.

1(*b*)   *Original Poetry for Infant and Juvenile Minds.* 2nd edn. Inference.

1(*c*)   *Original Poetry for Infant and Juvenile Minds.* 3rd edn. Inference.

1(*d*)   *Original Poetry for Infant and Juvenile Minds.* 4th edn. Inference.

1(*e*)   *Original Poetry, for Infant and Juvenile Minds. In Two Parts.* London/Wellington: Houlston and Son/Houlston and Son, 1833. 5th edn. 8.5 × 14 cm. 104 pp. By Lucy Joynes. Widener: 18427. 65.

2   *Occasional and Miscellaneous Poems.* Nottingham/London: printed for the author by Sutton and Son/Simpkin and Marshall, Baldwin, Cradock and Joy, 1820. 10 × 18 cm. 107 pp. 3/- boards. By Lucy Joynes. *MR* 94: 103; BL: 11645. aaa. 16.

3   *Mental Pictures, in Verse, for Infants.* London/Nottingham: Houlston and Co./W. Dearden, 1832. 8.5 × 13.5 cm. 62 pp. By Lucy Joynes. BL: 11645. a. 31.

4   *History and Rhyme, for Young Readers. The Four English Kings William. With Notes.* London/Nottingham: Hamilton and Adams, Houlston and Son/S. Bennett, 1834. 11.5 × 14 cm. 46 pp. 1/-. By Lucy Joynes, Author of *Original Poetry for Infant and Juvenile Minds, The Sabbath: A Discourse to Children, Mental Pictures, in Verse, for Infants.* Bodley: 22809. f. 6.

JUVENAL, Horace, *see* ROBINSON, Mary

K., A., *see* KNIGHT, Ann

KELLY, Isabella, Mrs Robert (*c.*1758–1857)
She was born in the Scottish highlands, and was the daughter of William Fordyce and Elizabeth Fraser. In 1789 she married Robert Kelly, a cavalry officer, but he and an infant child of theirs were both dead by 1794. She was left with three surviving children. She wrote ten romances for the Minerva Press and by 1819 had married a Mr Hedgeland. (Blain, *A Collection*)

1   *A Collection of Poems and Fables.* London/Edinburgh: W. Richardson, J. Debrett/J. Balfour, 1794. 13 × 21 cm. Pp. viii + 72 [subscription edition]. By Mrs Isabella Kelly. BL: 11633. e. 21.

2(*a*)   *Poems.* 1802. *CB.* Not located.

2(*b*)   *Poems and Fables on Several Occasions.* Chelsea/London: for the author by T. Faulkner/C. Chapple, 1807. 2nd edn. 9.5

× 17 cm. Pp. iv + 71. By Isabella Kelly. BL: 11646. bbb. 14.

KEMBLE, Frances Ann (1809–93)

She was generally known as Fanny Kemble. She was the daughter of Charles Kemble, the actor and producer, and of Maria Theresa (or Marie Thérèse) De Camp, the dancer and actress. She was educated mainly in France. In 1833 she accompanied her father to the United States and in 1834 she married Pierce Butler, a southern planter, and they had two children. They were divorced in 1848. She returned to the stage, appearing both in England and the USA. In 1849 she resumed her maiden name and retired to Lennox, Mass. Her *Journal of a Residence on a Georgian Plantation in 1838–1839* (1863) was praised by Henry James as 'one of the most animated autobiographies in the language'. (*CB*, *DNB*, Schlueter)

1(*a*)   *Francis the First. An Historical Drama.* London: John Murray, 1832. 13 × 21.5 cm. Pp. [iv] + 142. 5/6. By Frances Ann Kemble. Widener: 23498. 5. 6. 15.

1(*b*)   *Francis the First. An Historical Drama.* London: John Murray, 1832. 2nd edn. 12.5 × 20.5 cm. Pp. [ii] + 142. By Frances Ann Kemble. BL: 1509/219.

1(*c*)   *Francis the First. An Historical Drama.* London: John Murray, 1832. 3rd edn. 11.5 × 21.5 cm. 142 pp. 5/6. By Frances Ann Kemble. Indiana. [Photocopy seen only.]

1(*d*)   *Francis the First. An Historical Drama.* London: John Murray, 1832. 4th edn. 13.5 × 21 cm. Pp. [ii] + 142. 5/6. By Frances Ann Kemble. Widener: 23498. 5. 6. 19.

1(*e*)   *Francis the First. An Historical Drama.* London: John Murray, 1832. 5th edn. 13 × 20.5 cm. Pp. [iv] + 142. By Frances Ann Kemble. BL: 1344. l. 21(3).

1(*f*)   *Francis the First. A Tragedy, in Five Acts: As Performed at the Theatre Royal, Covent Garden.* New York: Peabody and Co., 1832. 12 × 19.5 cm. 63 pp. By Frances Ann Kemble. Princeton: Ex 3593. 999 v. 5(3).

1(*g*)   *Francis the First. A Tragedy, in Five Acts: As Performed at the Theatre Royal, Covent Garden.* Philadelphia: W. Turner, 1832. 9.5 × 15.5 cm. 79 pp. By Frances Ann Kemble. Pusey: TS Promptbook.

1(*h*)   *Francis the First. An Historical Drama.* 6th edn. Inference.

1(*i*)   *Francis the First. An Historical Drama.* London: John Murray, 1832. 7th edn. 12.5 × 21 cm. Pp. [iv] + 142. By Frances Ann Kemble. BL: T. 1273(9).

1(*j*)   *Francis the First. An Historical Drama.* London: John Murray, 1832. 8th edn. 13 × 21 cm. Pp. [iv] + 142. By Frances Ann Kemble. NYPL: NCR Kemble.

1(*k*)   *Francis the First. An Historical Drama.* 9th edn. Inference.

1(*l*)   *Francis the First. An Historical Drama.* London: John Murray, 1833. 10th edn. 13.5 × 21.5 cm. Pp. [iv] + 141. 5/6. By Frances Ann Kemble. U. of Pennsylvania: Furness C47/K31F.

1(*m*)   *Francis the First. A Tragedy in Five Acts: With Other Poetical Pieces.* New York: Peabody and Co., 1833. 6th American edn. 13 × 20.5 cm. Pp. 16 + 15–79. By Frances Ann Kemble. NYPL: NCO p. v. 750.

KENNEDY, Mrs, *see* COLLECTIONS 49(*a–b*)

KENNEY, Martha *or* Mary
The Bodley LC renders her given name as Mary.

1   *Charity: A Poem.* Bath/London: printed by Richard Cruttwell/T. Cadell, 1823. 13 × 21 cm. 15 pp. By the Author of *Letters on Prejudice, Sermons on Christian Responsibility*, etc. BL: T. 1063(13).

KENTISH, Mary, Mrs
Her book is dedicated to her two sons. She is not to be confused with Mrs John Kentish.

1(*a*)   *Poems on Various Subjects.* [London]: Longman, 1819. Crown 8vo. 6/- boards. By Mrs Kentish. *MR* 91: 214. Not located.

1(*b*)   *Poems on Various Subjects.* Liverpool/London/Edinburgh: George Cruickshank/Longman, Hurst, Rees and Co./A. Constable and Co., 1821. 2nd edn. 11 × 18.5 cm. Pp. viii + 136. By Mrs Kentish, Resident at St Salvador, Brazils. BL: 11642. bbb. 17.

KIDD, Jane, Mrs Thornhill

Her book was published in aid of the Missionary Schools of the Moravian Brethren. Her husband was a clergyman and they seem to have lived in Clapton, London. (*Poems and Hymns*)

1   *Poems and Hymns.* Sheffield/Huddersfield, Halifax and Leeds/London: for the author by J. Blackwell, and Miss Gales/the Booksellers/Hamilton, Adams, and Co., 1827. 11 × 18 cm. 216 pp. By Jane Kidd. BL: 11646. bb. 20.

KILNER, Dorothy (1755–1836)

She lived in Maryland Point, Essex, just outside London, with her sister-in-law Mary Ann (q.v.). She used the pseudonyms M. Pelham and M. P. She wrote in all eighteen books for children. (*CB*, Todd 1)

1   *Poems on Various Subjects, for the Amusement of Youth.* London: John Marshall and Co., [*c.*1785]. 9.5 × 15 cm. 102 pp. By [Dorothy Kilner and ? Mrs Mary Ann Kilner]. Osborne: ii. 646.

2   *Jingles; or, Original Rhymes for Children.* London: Richard Phillips, 1811. 10 × 12.5 cm. 60 pp. 6*d.* without plates, 1/6 with plain plates, 2/6 with coloured plates. By M. Pelham. BL: 12804. de. 54(2).

KILNER, Mary Ann, Mrs (1753–1831), *see* KILNER, Dorothy

Her maiden name was Maze. She lived with her sister-in-law Dorothy (q.v.). (*CB* (as Mary Jane Kilner), Todd 1)

KING, Charlotte, *see* DACRE, Charlotte

KING, E.

She lived in Croydon, Surrey.

1   *Poems and Reflections.* London: John Booth, 1815. 9.5 × 17 cm. Pp. lxvi + 143 [subscription edition]. By a Young Lady. BL: 11646. bb. 12.

KING, Harriet Rebecca

Poems reveals that she had suffered for many years from deafness; most of her verse is religious or elegiac.

1   *Poems.* Salisbury/London: Brodie and Dowding/Baldwin, Cradock, and Joy, 1823. 9.5 × 16 cm. Pp. xii + 62 [sub-

cription edition]. By Harriet Rebecca King. Davis: Kohler I 83–688.

2(*a*)   *Metrical Exercises upon Scripture Texts, and Miscellaneous Poems.* London: John Turrill, 1834. 9.5 × 16 cm. Pp. xx + 168. By Harriet Rebecca King. BL: 11644. bb. 29.

2(*b*)   *Metrical Exercises upon Scriptural Texts, and Miscellaneous Poems.* London: Smith, Elder and Co., 1834. 2nd edn. 10 × 17 cm. Pp. xxiv + 168 [subscription edition]. By Harriet Rebecca King. BL: 11644. bb. 30.

KING, Sophia, *see* FORTNUM, Sophia

KNIGHT, Ann, Mrs, *see* COLLECTIONS 38(*a–b*)
She was a Quaker whose maiden name was Waspe. She and her sisters helped to manage a school in Woodbridge, Suffolk. Bernard Barton, the 'corn law rhymer', lived in her house after his wife's death in 1808. (Osborne L. Cat.)

KNIGHT, Ann Cuthbert (died 1860)
She later married James Fleming. (Watters)

1   *Home: A Poem.* Edinburgh/London: Archd. Constable and Co./Longman, Hurst, Rees, Orme, and Brown, 1815. 10 × 17 cm. Pp. x + 98. By Ann Cuthbert Knight. NLS: T. 14. i.

2   *A Year in Canada, and Other Poems.* Edinburgh/London: Doig and Stirling/Baldwin, Cradock and Joy, 1816. 9.5 × 16 cm. Pp. [iv] + 126. 5/- boards. By Ann Cuthbert Knight. *MR* 79: 433; BL: 994. g. 20.

KNIGHT, Ellis Cornelia (1758–1837), *see also* COLLECTIONS 24
She was the only child of the second marriage of Sir Joseph Knight, Rear Admiral of the White, and of Philippina Deane. She was acquainted as a child with Sir Joshua Reynolds and Samuel Johnson. She was educated in London at a school kept by a Swiss pastor and was introduced to Continental literature there. After her father's death in 1776 she and her mother moved to Italy. When her mother died in 1799 she returned to England. She became companion to Queen Charlotte in 1805 and to Princess Charlotte in 1813. Her autobiography is an important source of information about the court. After 1816 she

spent most of her time on the Continent; she died in Paris. (*CB*, *DNB*, Barbara Luttrell, *The Prim Romantic* . . . (1965), Todd 1)

1 *The Battle of the Nile. A Pindarick Ode. To His Excellency the Rt. Honble. Sir William Hamilton, K.B. His Britannick Majesty's Minister Plenipotentiary and Envoy Extraordinary at the Court of the Two Sicilies Etc. Etc. Etc.* Vienna: printed by Widow Alberti, 1800. 20 × 24 cm. 13 pp. Houghton: *EC8. K7441. 800b.

2(*a*) *Translations from the German in Prose and Verse.* [Title-page on verso.] Trans. [Ellis Cornelia Knight]. Windsor: printed by E. Harding, 1812. 10 × 16.5 cm. Pp. [iv] + 111. BL: 3455. CC. 11.

2(*b*) *Prayers and Hymns, Translated from the German.* Trans. [Miss Ellis Cornelia Knight]. London: printed by W. Nicol, 1832. 10.5 × 17.5 cm. Pp. xii + 118 [prose and verse]. BL: 3455. CC. 19.

[*See also*: 'Lines Addressed to Victory in Consequence of the Success of Lord Cornwallis' (1793, 9 pp. of which pp. 5–9 are a translation into Italian); 'Presented to the Rt. Honble. the Lady Bruce. At her Visit to the Bodoni Press' (1793, 1 p.).]

KNIGHT, Henrietta, *see* LUXBOROUGH, Lady

KNIPE, Eliza, *see* COBBOLD, Elizabeth

L——, Mrs, *see* COLLECTIONS 31

L——, Mrs C——, *see* COLLECTIONS 31

L., E. S., *see* LAW, Elizabeth Susan

L., L. E., *see* LANDON, Letitia Elizabeth

A LADY, *see also* AUTHOR OF *Cato*, BALLANTYNE, Mrs John, BATTIER, Henrietta, BONHOTE, Mrs E., BURY, Catherine Maria, CARSTAIRS, Mrs Christian, CELESIA, Dorothea, COCKLE, Mrs, COLLECTIONS 10(*b*), 14, 16(*a–b*), 29(*a–b*), 53, CRAWLEY, Eliza, DE KRAFFT, Mary, DORSET, Mrs, DOWNING, Harriet, DUNCH, M. E., FENN, Lady Eleanor, FRANCIS, Ann, HARVEY, Jane, IRELAND, Mrs

Samuel, JACKSON, Adelaide, LARD, Mrs Rebecca Hammond, LAWRENCE, Mrs ROSE, LETCHES, Mrs, LUCAN, Margaret Bingham, Lady, MARTINEAU, Harriet, O'BRIEN, Mary, PERKINS, Mrs E. S., POGSON, Sarah, POTTS, Mrs Ethelinda Margaretta, PYE, Jael Henrietta, REID, Mrs, RICHINGS, Rebecca, RITSON, Mrs Anne, ROWSE, Mrs Elizabeth, SERRES, Mrs J. T., STRINGER, Mrs, TOMLINS, E. S., WILKINSON, Rebecca, *and pseudonym of* STEVENSON, John Hall

1   *The Conquest of Corsica by the French. A Tragedy.* London: for the author, 1771. 9.5 × 15.5 cm. 43 pp. By a Lady. HEHL: K-D 13.

2   *Original Poems, Translations, and Imitations, from the French, &c.* London: for the author by G. Robinson, 1773. 12 × 20 cm. 123 pp. By a Lady. BL: 11646. ff. 15.

3   *The Fine Gentleman's Etiquette; or, Lord Chesterfield's Advice to his Son, Versified.* London: T. Davies, 1776. 19 × 24 cm. 26 pp. 1/-. By a Lady. *MR* 55: 71; BL: 11633. f. 31.

4   *Poems for Ladies, Never before Published . . .* Ed. a Lady. London: for the editor by John Donaldson, 1777. 11 × 18.5 cm. Pp. vi + 180. BL: 992. b. 37(2).

5   *G**y's-Inn Gardens. A Visionary Satire.* London: for the authoress by J. Bew, 1778. 19 × 24.5 cm. 20 pp. By a Lady. Bodley: G. Pamph. 1720(15).

6   *Poems.* London: Henry Payne, 1781. 21.5 × 28.5 cm. Pp. [iv] + 204. By a Lady. BL: 11632. h. 10.

7   *The Family Picture. A Play. Taken from the French of Mons. Diderot's Père de Famille. With Verses on Different Subjects.* London: J. Donaldson and R. Faulder, 1781. 13 × 20 cm. Pp. x + 76 [subscription edition; the verse is confined to pp. 63–76]. By a Lady. BL: 11735. e. 19.

8   *The Tears of Britannia; Occasioned by the Late Indisposition of His Royal Highness the Prince of Wales. A Poem, Humbly Inscribed to His Royal Highness.* London: T. Becket, 1787. 20.5 × 26.5 cm. 16 pp. By a Lady. Houghton: *EC75. A100. 787t.

9   *An Elegy, on the Death of Mr Andrew Gifford Gwennap.* [1790: copy lacks title-page; the conjectural date is that of

Gwennap's death.] 14 × 18 cm. 8 pp. By a Lady. BL: 4903. cc. 14(2).

10   *Flights of Fancy, or Poetical Effusions.* London: printed by J. Long, 1791. 12.5 × 21 cm. 46 pp. [subscription edition]. By a Lady, Late of Mitcham, in the County of Surry. BL: 11632. c. 32.

11   *Poems, &c. Written by a Lady, in the Year 1783 or 1784. An Address to the People Called Quakers. An Address to Those in Power, in Behalf of Insolvent Debtors. Friendship: An Allegory. An Enigma, in French and English.* London: J. Parsons, 1791. 13 × 16.5 cm. 12 pp. CUL: Ddd. 25. 261[17].

12   *Reflections at the Tomb of Columbus.* London: C. and G. Kearsley, 1791. 21 × 26.5 cm. Pp. [iv] + 26. By a Lady. NYPL: *KL.

13   *Sonnets. By a Lady.* [London]: Debrett, 1793. 4to. 2/6. *CR* 10: 114–15. Not located.

14   *The Trap: A Poem. By a Lady.* [London]: Richardson, 1797. 4to. 2/6. *MR* 24: 87. Not located.

15   *Mary the Osier-peeler, a Simple but True Story: A Poem.* [London]: Rivingtons, 1798. 4to. 1/-. By a Lady. *MR* 26: 460. Not located.

16   *Poems.* London: printed by T. Baylis, 1798. 13 × 20.5 cm. 20 pp. By a Lady. BL: 11642. e. 16.

17   *Poems on Various Subjects.* London: printed for the author by A. Neil, 1798. 11.5 × 18.5 cm. 78 pp. By a Lady. BL: 11641. bb. 35.

18   *Love's Repository, or a New Collection of Valentines; Selected from the Best British Poets; with Considerable Alterations and Additions.* Ed. a Lady. London: Champante and Whitrow, 1800. 10.5 × 17 cm. 36 pp. By a Lady [and others]. BL: 11621. b. 23(1).

19   *Mary Queen of Scots, an Historical Ballad; with Other Poems.* London: John Stockdale, 1800. 10 × 17 cm. Pp. iv + 89. By a Lady. BL: 11641. b. 20.

20   *Almeda; or, the Neapolitan Revenge: A Tragic Drama.* London: H. D. Symonds, 1801. 13 × 21.5 cm. 71 pp. By a Lady. BL: 11779. f. 36.

21 *Lectures to Young Ladies. To Which are Added, Short Hymns, Suited to the Subjects.* Hartford: printed by John Babcock, 1801. 7 × 13.5 cm. 96 pp. [prose and verse, about 24 pp. of verse]. By a Lady. AAS: DATED PAMS.

22 *The Siege of Mansoul, a Drama, in Five Acts. The Diction of Which Consists Altogether in an Accommodation of Words from Shakespeare and Other Poets.* Bristol/London/Bath: W. Bulgin/Mathews, Longman and Rees, West and Hughes/S. Hazard, 1801. 12.5 × 21.5 cm. Pp. vi + 82. By a Lady. BL: 11781. f. 15.

23 *Variety: A Collection of Original Poems.* London/Stockton: James Wallis/Christopher and Jennet, 1802. 10 × 15.5 cm. Pp. viii + 167. By a Lady. BL: 11644. aa. 3.

24 *A Poetical Address from the Jerusalem to the Commanders and Officers, in the Service of the Honourable East India Company; Occasioned by Having Read Two Letters on East India Shipping* . . . London: printed by James Swan, 1803. 9.5 × 15 cm. 12 pp. By a Lady. BL: 992. g. 17(3).

25 *An Evening Walk in the Forest: A Poem Descriptive of Forest Trees.* London/Edinburgh: Jordan and Maxwell, Fremont/Manners and Miller, 1807. 10.5 × 18 cm. Pp. vi + 3–36. 1/6. By a Lady. University of Texas, at Austin: 821 Ev23 PCL.

26 *Grand-mamma: Or, the Christening 'Not at Home'.* London: J. Harris, [1808]. 9.5 × 12 cm. 31 pp. By a Lady, May, 1808. Osborne: ii. 640.

27 *Poems, Moral & Entertaining.* Doncaster: printed by W. Sheardown, 1808. 13 × 21.5 cm. Pp. xvi + 153 [subscription edition]. By a Lady. BL: 11642. f. 7.

28 *The Amusing Moralist, Containing a Collection of Fables from Aesop. Transposed into Easy Verse.* Doncaster: W. Sheardown, 1810. 10 × 17 cm. Pp. [ii] + 64. 1/6. By a Lady. Leeds: Brotherton Collection/Yorks, H-Don-8.

29 *Friendly Visits from the Muse; or, the Consolations of Solitude.* London: R. Dutton, 1810. 9.5 × 16.5 cm. Pp. x + 150. By a Lady. BL: 11642. b. 17.

30(a) *Original Fables . . . Dedicated to Her Royal Highness the Princess Charlotte of Wales.* London: B. Crosby and Co.,

1810. 9 × 16 cm. Pp. [xiv] + 236. By a Lady. BL: 12305. bb. 36.

30(*b*)   *Original Fables.* London: William Baynes, 1812. 8.5 × 15 cm. Pp. viii + 150. By a Lady. BL: 12304. aa. 21.

30(*c*)   *Original Fables.* London: James Wallis, 1815. 8.5 × 13.5 cm. Pp. viii + 150. By a Lady. BL: 12304. aa. 22.

31   *Original Poetry; Consisting of Fugitive Pieces . . . and Miscellaneous Poems . . .* Bath/London/Bristol: the Booksellers/Crosby and Co./the Booksellers, 1811. 11.5 × 19.5 cm. 115 pp. By a Lady Lately Deceased and Several Authors. BL: 11641. d. 60.

32(*a*)   *The Nursery Companion . . . Rules of English Grammar, in Verse.* Ludlow, 1813. By a Lady. Stainforth. Not located.

32(*b*)   *The Nursery Companion.* 2nd edn. Stainforth. Not located.

33   *Epistle to Bonaparte.* Philadelphia: C. Neal, 1814. 10.5 × 19 cm. 11 pp. By a Lady. BL: 11645. bb. 26.

34   *The Power of Christianity, or Abdallah and Sabat, a Poem.* Charleston, S.C.: Ladies' Benevolent and Protestant Episcopal Societies, 1814. 9.5 × 15.5 cm. 50 pp. [subscription edition]. By a Lady. AAS: DATED PAMS.

35   *Farewell for Ever! A Tale of the Last Century. Dedicated to Her Royal Highness the Princess Mary.* London: James Black, 1816. 12 × 20 cm. 42 pp. By a Lady. BL: 11633. cc. 3(4).

36   *Poems and Hymns.* Dublin: printed by A. O'Neil, 1816. 10 × 17 cm. 106 pp. By a Lady. BL: 11645. aaa. 29.

37   *The Crucifixion; a Poem, Written for Good-Friday: To Which is Added, an Ode for Easter-Day.* London: T. Cadell and W. Davies, 1817. 10.5 × 17.5 cm. Pp. x + 35. By a Lady. BL: 994. a. 1(3).

38   *Joseph and his Brethren, a Poem, in Four Books.* Ed. Joseph Kerby. Lewes/Brighton/London: for the editor by J. Baxter/the Booksellers/Burton and Smith, Williams and Co., Hamilton and Button, Baynes, Kent, Nisbet, Darton and Co., 1818. 10 × 16 cm. 106 pp. [subscription edition]. By a Lady. BL: 993. e. 34(2).

39   *Poems.* London: printed by B. R. Howlett, 1818. 10 × 16.5 cm. 54 pp. By a Lady. BL: 11646. bbb. 24.

40   *Detached Pieces, on Religious and Moral Subjects, in Prose and Verse.* London: printed by J. B. and John Courthope, 1819. 11 × 17.5 cm. Pp. viii + 88 [subscription edition]. By a Lady. BL: 11644. bbb. 15.

41   *Old John's Tale; or Half an Hour's Amusement to the Not Too Difficult to Please. An Irregular Poem . . . Cheerfully Dedicated to the Good-natured.* London/Doncaster: printed for the author by S. McDowall/E. Bisby and M. Simpson, 1819. 9.5 × 16 cm. Pp. [xvi] + 50 [subscription edition]. By a Lady. BL: 11646. bbb. 15.

42(*a*)   *The Snowdrop.* New York: Samuel Wood and Sons, [181?]. 7 × 13 cm. 20 pp. HEHL: 237912.

42(*b*)   *The Snowdrop . . .* 2nd edn. Inference.

42(*c*)   *The Snowdrop, or Poetry for Henry and Emily's Library.* London: J. Harris and Son, 1823. 3rd edn. 10 × 16.5 cm. 36 pp. By a Lady. BL: 11631. f. 45(4).

42(*d*)   *The Snowdrop; or, Poetry for Henry and Emily's Library.* London: John Harris, [*c*.1835]. 4th edn. 11 × 17.5 cm. 36 pp. By a Lady. Osborne: i. 78.

43   *The Mother's Gift.* York: printed by J. Kendrew, [1820?]. 6.5 × 9.5 cm. 15 pp. By a Lady. BL: 12803. a. 56(9).

44   *An Original Collection of Genteel and Fashionable Valentines. Containing Pleasing and Elegant Letters on Love & Courtship, with a Number of Valentines in Verse and Prose, None of Which have ever been Published.* London: printed by J. H. Cox, [1820?]. 10 × 17.5 cm. 28 pp. 6*d*. By a Lady. BL: 10920. bb. 16.

45   *Saul, a Tragedy; Translated from the Italian of Count Victorio Alfieri: And Jephtha's Daughter, a Scriptural Drama.* London: T. Cadell, 1821. 13 × 21.5 cm. 152 pp. By a Lady. HEHL: K-D522.

46   *Poems: Upon Various Subjects.* London: Sherwood, Neely, and Jones, 1822. 11 × 17.5 cm. 32 pp. By a Lady. BL: T. 854(5).

47   *Flowers of Fancy. Poems, on Various Subjects.* Norwich: T. Craske, 1823. 11.5 × 19.5 cm. 78 pp. By a Lady. BL: 11643. b. 46.

48   *The Rich Old Bachelor: A Domestic Tale. In the Style of Dr Syntax.* Canterbury: printed by Ward, 1824. 12.5 × 21.5 cm. 312 pp. By a Lady. BL: 1164. l. 16.

49(*a*)   *A Peep at the Esquimaux; or, Scenes on the Ice. To Which is Annexed, a Polar Pastoral.* London/Dublin: H. R. Thomas/ Westley and Tyrrell, 1825. 11 × 18 cm. Pp. viii + 58. By a Lady. BL: 11644. cc. 26.

49(*b*)   *A Peep at the Esquimaux; or, Scenes on the Ice. To Which is Annexed, a Polar Pastoral.* London/Dublin: H. R. Thomas/ Westley and Tyrrell, 1825. 2nd edn. 11 × 18.5 cm. Pp. viii + 58. By a Lady. BL: 994. e. 22.

49(*c*)   *A Peep at the Esquimaux; or, Scenes on the Ice. To Which is Annexed a Polar Pastoral.* London: T. and J. Allman, 1830. 11 × 18 cm. 64 pp. By a Lady. BL: 11644. cc. 27.

49(*d*)   *A Peep at the Esquimaux; or, Scenes on the Ice. To Which is Annexed, a Polar Pastoral.* London: T. Allman, 1833. 3rd edn. 10.5 × 17 cm. 64 pp. 3/- half bound. By a Lady. BL: 11644. bbb. 42.

50   *The Emblematical Garden, Illustrated by Coloured Engravings.* Dublin: printed by J. Jones, [n.d.]. 12 × 13 cm. [14 pp., printed on one side of the leaf only and interleaved with engraved pages]. By a Lady, Author of *The Indispensable Requisites for Dandies of Both Sexes.* Trinity: 26. y. 123.

51   *Poems.* Calcutta: Thacker and Co., 1828. 11.5 × 20.5 cm. 86 pp. 7 rupees. By a Lady. BL: 11642. e. 12.

52   *Two Poems, Founded on Texts of Scripture. With Lines on my Cottage, and a Poetical Epistle, to a Young Friend.* Newburyport: printed by W. and J. Gilman, 1829. 9.5 × 16 cm. 16 pp. By a Lady. Brown (Harris): 76/L15786t.

53   *Faith's Telescope; or, Views of Time and Eternity: With Other Poems.* Edinburgh/London: Oliver and Boyd/Simpkin and Marshall, 1830. 10.5 × 17.5 cm. 184 pp. By [a Lady]. BL: 11644. bb. 8.

54(*a*)   *The Multiplication Table, in Rhyme.* Boston[, Mass.]: Carter and Hendee, 1830. 8.5 × 14 cm. 15 pp. By a Lady. Brown (Harris): M961m/76.

54(*b*)   *The Multiplication Table, in Rhyme.* Boston[, Mass.]: Carter and Hendee, 1830. 2nd edn. 9.5 × 15 cm. 16 pp. By a Lady. Brown (Harris): 76/M962ml.

55   *Original Juvenile Poems.* London: C. Penny and Sons, [1830?]. 8.5 × 13.5 cm. 108 pp. By a Lady. BL: 11644. aa. 23.

56(*a*)   *Catechism in Rhyme, for Little Children: Intended Chiefly for the Use of Dame Schools.* London/Wellington, Salop.: Houlston and Son, 1831. 6 × 9.5 cm. 30 pp. By a Lady. BL: 12835. a. 76.

56(*b*)   *Catechism in Rhyme, for Little Children; Intended Chiefly for the Use of Dame Schools.* London: Houlston and Stoneman, [1835?]. 6 × 10 cm. 30 pp. By a Lady. BL: 11646. a. 6.

57   *Metrical Remembrances.* London: printed by [S. Bagster, Jr.], 1832. 6.5 × 10 cm. 32 pp. By a Lady. BL: T. 1386(8).

58   *The Rev. Jabez Bunting, or Begging: With Other Poems.* Leeds: printed for friends of the authoress by William Illingworth, 1833. 10 × 17 cm. 14 pp. By a Lady. BL: T. 1457(7).

59   *Poems for Children.* London: Darton and Harvey, 1834. 8.5 × 14 cm. Pp. iv + 66. By a Lady. BL: T. 1529(9).

60(*a*)   *An Alphabet of Animals.* By a Lady. Inference.

60(*b*)   *An Alphabet of Animals.* London/Leicester: Simpkin, Marshall, and Co./Winks and Son, [*c.*1835]. Revised edn. 7.5 × 11.5 cm. 30 pp. 1*d*. By a Lady. Osborne: ii. 673.

61   *Letters and Poems on Several Occasions.* London: printed for the authoress by Thomas Curson Hansard, 1835. 11 × 19 cm. Pp. xx + 280 [subscription edition; prose and verse]. By a Lady. BL: 12357. g. 16.

[*See also*: 'Lines, Addressed to Prince Leopold of Saxe-Cobourg, on the Death of his Consort . . .' (1817, 7 pp.).]

A LADY OF BALTIMORE, *see* COLLECTIONS 31

A LADY OF BOSTON, *see* SPROAT, Nancy

A LADY OF MARYLAND, *see* CHASE, Elizabeth

A LADY OF NEWRY
1   *Poems on Several Occasions.* Newry, 1807. O'D.

A LADY OF NINETY

The poem has been traditionally ascribed to a Mrs Pearson who kept a toyshop in Fleet Street and to Richard Scrafton Sharpe, who is said to have revised it. (*OCCL*)

1(*a*)   *Dame Wiggins of Lee, and her Seven Wonderful Cats. A Humourous Tale.* London: A. K. Newman and Co., 1823. 10 × 17 cm. 16 pp. [printed on one side only]. 'Written Principally' by a Lady of Ninety. Osborne: ii. 631.

1(*b*)   *Dame Wiggins of Lee and her Seven Wonderful Cats: A Humourous Tale.* London: Dean and Munday, and A. K. Newman and Co., [n.d.]. 10.5 × 18 cm. 31 pp. [paginated on one side only]. 1/-. 'Written Principally' by a Lady of Ninety. LC: Juv. Coll. 1830.

A LADY OF PHILADELPHIA, *see* BOTSFORD, Margaret

A LADY OF QUALITY, *pseudonym of* PRESTON, William

LAMB, Lady Caroline (1785–1828)

She was the fourth child and only daughter of Frederick Ponsonby, 3rd Earl of Bessborough, and of his wife Lady Henrietta Frances Spencer. At the age of 3 she was sent to Italy for six years and looked after by a servant. She was then sent to Devonshire House to be educated with her cousins. In 1805 she married the Hon. William Lamb (later Lord Melbourne); they had one child. She became infatuated with Lord Byron, but did not separate from her husband until 1824. Her novel *Glenarvon* was published anonymously in 1816. (*CB, DNB*, Elizabeth Jenkins, *Lady Caroline Lamb* (1932), Kunitz 1)

1   *Verses from Glenarvon: To Which is Prefixed the Original Introduction, Not Published with the Early Editions of that Work.* London: Henry Colburn, 1819. 11 × 18 cm. 48 pp. Houghton: *58–547.

2   *A New Canto.* London: William Wright, 1819. 12 × 21 cm. 16 pp. 1/-. *MR* 94: 329; BL: 11644. d. 20.

3   *Fugitive Pieces and Reminiscences of Lord Byron: Containing an Entire New Edition of the Hebrew Melodies, with the Addition of Several never before Published . . . also Some Original Poetry, Letters and Recollections of Lady Caroline Lamb.* London: Whittaker, Treacher, and Co., 1829. 12 × 19 cm. Pp. xxxvi

+ 196 [Lamb's poems occupy pp. 156–96]. By I. Nathan, [Lord Byron and Lady Caroline Lamb]. Leeds: Special Collections/Roth Collection.

LAMB, Mary Anne (1764–1847)

The daughter of John Lamb, an employee of Samuel Salt, MP, and of Elizabeth Field, and the sister of the writer Charles Lamb. She received her elementary education at William Bird's Academy in the City of London. She worked as a mantua-maker, but had access to Samuel Salt's private library. She was mentally unstable and in 1796, in a fit of madness, she stabbed her mother to death. Thereafter she was confined from time to time to private madhouses and was looked after by her brother. She was greatly valued by his literary circle, which included writers such as Coleridge and Hazlitt. She is believed to have written fourteen of the twenty *Tales of Shakespeare*, all but three of the stories in *Mrs Leicester's School*, and about a third of *Poetry for Children*. (*CB, DNB, The Works of Charles and Mary Lamb*, ed. E. V. Lucas (1903–5))

1(*a*)   *Poetry for Children, Entirely Original.* London: M. J. Godwin, 1809. 9 × 14.5 cm. 2 vols. By the Author of *Mrs Leicester's School* [Mary Lamb and Charles Lamb]. Houghton: *EC8. L1654. 809p.

1(*b*)   *Poetry for Children, Entirely Original.* Boston[, Mass.]: West and Richardson, and Edward Cotton, 1812. 8.5 × 14.5 cm. 144 pp. By the Author of *Mrs Leicester's School* [Mary Lamb and Charles Lamb]. AAS: Reserve, copy 1.

LAMBERT, Eliza

1   *Poetic Strains; or, Thoughts in Leisure Hours.* Derby: printed by William Horsley, 1830. 9.5 × 16 cm. 108 pp. By Eliza Lambert. BL: 11644. aaa. 35.

LAMONT, Mrs Aeneas

1   *Poems, and Tales in Verse.* London: for the author by Ogles, Duncan, and Cochran, 1818. 9.5 × 16 cm. Pp. vi + 179. By Mrs Aeneas Lamont. BL: 11644. aaa. 22.

LANDON, Letitia Elizabeth (1802–38), *see also* COLLECTIONS 39, 40(*c*), 41, 42, 43, 48, 53

Born in Chelsea, London. She was the daughter of John Landon, a partner in Adair's army agency in Pall Mall, and of a Miss Bishop, whose ancestry was Welsh. She went to the same school in Chelsea as Mary Russell Mitford (q.v.). She first contributed to William Jerdan's *Literary Gazette* in 1820 and she wrote regularly for the annuals. Distress over a broken engagement is said to have led to her marriage to George Maclean, the Governor of Cape Coast Castle in 1838. Four months later she was found dead with a bottle of prussic acid in her hand. (Boyle, *CB*, *DNB*, Schlueter)

1   *The Fate of Adelaide, a Swiss Romantic Tale; and Other Poems.* London: John Warren, 1821. 10 × 16 cm. Pp. [iv] + 154. By Letitia Elizabeth Landon. BL: 994. f. 21.

2(*a*)   *The Improvisatrice; and Other Poems.* London/Edinburgh: Hurst, Robinson and Co./Archibald Constable and Co., 1824. 10 × 16 cm. Pp. viii + 327. By L. E. L. BL: 11644. bb. 31.

2(*b*)   *The Improvisatrice* . . . 2nd edn. Inference.

2(*c*)   *The Improvisatrice; and Other Poems.* London/Edinburgh: Hurst, Robinson and Co./Archibald Constable and Co., 1824. 3rd edn. 10 × 17 cm. Pp. viii + 326. By L. E. L. BL: 994. f. 23(1).

2(*d*)   *The Improvisatrice; and Other Poems.* London/Edinburgh: Hurst, Robinson and Co./Archibald Constable and Co., 1825. 4th edn. 9.5 × 16 cm. Pp. viii + 326. By L. E. L. BL: 11644. b. 19.

2(*e*)   *The Improvisatrice* . . . 5th edn. Inference.

2(*f*)   *The Improvisatrice; and Other Poems.* London/Edinburgh: Hurst, Robinson and Co./Archibald Constable and Co., 1825. 6th edn. 10 × 16 cm. Pp. x + 326. By L. E. L. BL: 11644. b. 20.

2(*g*)   *The Improvisatrice; and Other Poems.* Boston[, Mass.]: Munroe and Francis, 1825. 9 × 14.5 cm. 287 pp. By L. E. L. NYPL: NCM.

2(*h*)   *The Improvisatrice; and Other Poems.* London: Longman, Rees, Orme, Brown, and Green, 1827. New edn. 10 × 16 cm. Pp. viii + 326. By L. E. L., Author of *The Troubadour*, *The Golden Violet*, etc. Widener: 18434. 24.

2(*i*)   *The Improvisatrice; and Other Poems.* London: Longman, Rees, Orme, Brown, and Green, 1831. New edn. 10.5 × 17 cm. Pp. viii + 326. By L. E. L. BL: 11660. aa. 1.

3(*a*) *The Troubadour; Catalogue of Pictures, and Historical Sketches.*
London/Edinburgh: Hurst, Robinson and Co./A. Constable
and Co., 1825. 10 × 16.5 cm. Pp. [vi] + 326. 10/6 boards.
By L. E. L. *MR* 107: 229–40; BL: 11644. aaa. 11.

3(*b*) *The Troubadour; Catalogue of Pictures, and Historical Sketches.*
Philadelphia: H. C. Carey and I. Lea, R. H. Small, John
Grigg, and Towar and Hogan, 1825. 10.5 × 18 cm. Pp. [vi]
+ 200. By L. E. L., Author of *The Improvisatrice.* NEDL:
KD6503.

3(*c*) *The Troubadour; Catalogue of Pictures, and Historical Sketches.*
London/Edinburgh: Hurst, Robinson and Co./A.
Constable and Co., 1825. 2nd edn. 10 × 16.5 cm. Pp. [vi]
+ 326. By L. E. L. BL: 994. f. 22.

3(*d*) *The Troubadour; Catalogue of Pictures, and Historical Sketches.*
London/Edinburgh: Hurst, Robinson and Co./A. Con-
stable and Co., 1825. 3rd edn. 9.5 × 17 cm. Pp. [iv] + 326.
By L. E. L. BL: 11646. cc. 7.

3(*e*) *The Troubadour; Catalogue of Pictures, and Historical Sketches.*
London: Longman, Rees, Orme, Brown, and Green, 1827.
New edn. 10 × 16.5 cm. Pp. [vi] + 326. By L. E. L. BL:
11641. df. 62.

4(*a*) *The Golden Violet, with its Tales of Romance and Chivalry: And
Other Poems.* London: Longman, Rees, Orme, Brown,
and Green, 1827. 9.5 × 16.5 cm. Pp. [vi] + 310. 10/6. By
L. E. L. *MR* 4: 57–65; BL: 994. f. 24.

4(*b*) *The Golden Violet, with its Tales of Romance and Chivalry: And
Other Poems.* Philadelphia: H. C. Carey and I. Lea, 1827.
10.5 × 17.5 cm. 244 pp. By L. E. L., Author of *The
Improvisatrice, The Troubadour,* etc. NYPL: NCM.

5(*a*) *The Poetical Works.* London: Longman, Rees, Orme, Brown
and Green, 1827. 9.5 × 16 cm. [3 vols.—no volume
numbers indicated]. By L. E. L. BL: 11613. a. 6.

5(*b*) *The Poetical Works.* London: Longman, Rees, Orme, Brown
and Green, [1830?]. New edn. 9.5 × 16 cm. Pp. x + 307.
By L. E. L. BL: 11659. a. 42.

6(*a*) *The Venetian Bracelet, the Lost Pleiad, a History of the Lyre, and
Other Poems.* London: Longman, Rees, Orme, Brown, and

Green, 1829. 10 × 17 cm. Pp. x + 307. By L. E. L. BL: 994. f. 23(2).

6(*b*) *The Venetian Bracelet, the Lost Pleiad, a History of the Lyre, and Other Poems.* Boston[, Mass.]: Cottons and Barnard, 1830. 10 × 16 cm. 236 pp. By L. E. L., Author of *The Improvisatrice, The Troubadour,* and *The Golden Violet.* NEDL: KC2048.

7 *Corinne; or, Italy . . . With Metrical Versions of the Odes by L. E. Landon.* Trans. Isabel Hill. London/Edinburgh/Dublin/Paris: Richard Bentley/Bell and Bradfute/Cumming/Galignani, 1833. 10 × 16.5 cm. Pp. lvi + 392 [three vols. in one]. By Madame de Staël. BL: 1153. a. 23.

8(*a*) *The Easter Gift, a Religious Offering.* London: Fisher, Son, and Co., 1832. 12 × 19 cm. 47 pp. By L. E. L. Bodley: 32. 869.

8(*b*) *The Easter Gift, a Religious Offering.* London: Fisher, Son, and Co., 1833. 12 × 19 cm. 47 pp. By L. E. L. HEHL: 443842.

9 *The Miscellaneous Poetical Works.* London: Saunders and Otley, 1835. 10 × 16 cm. Pp. viii + 352. By L. E. L. BL: 11611. aaa. 5.

10 *The Vow of the Peacock, and Other Poems.* London: Saunders and Otley, 1835. 10.5 × 16.5 cm. Pp. viii + 352. By L. E. L. BL: 993. d. 44.

LARD, Rebecca, Mrs (1772–1855)

Born in New Bedford, Mass., but she moved to Woodstock, Vt., at the age of 7. Her father was Jabez Hammond. She began school-teaching when she was 14. She married and had four children. After 1820 she lived in Indiana. (*The Bibliography of Vermont* . . . , ed. M. D. Gilman (Burlington, Vt., 1897))

1 *Miscellaneous Poems on Moral and Religious Subjects.* Woodstock[, Vt.]: printed by David Watson, 1820. 9.5 × 15.5 cm. 143 pp. [pp. 121–43 being prose letters]. By a Lady. Yale (Beinecke): Za/L3218/820.

2(*a*) *The Banks of the Ohio. A Poem.* Albany: printed by John C. Johnson, 1823. 12 × 20.5 cm. 16 pp. By Mrs Lard. NYPL: *KL Lard.

2(*b*)   *The Banks of the Ohio. A Poem.* Windsor, Vermont: printed by Simeon Ide, 1823. 11 × 19 cm. 12 pp. By Mrs Lard. Brown (Harris): 76 L321b.

LAURA, *see* MILLER, Anne, ROBINSON, Mary, *and* TRENCH, Melesina

LAURA MARIA, *see* ROBINSON, Mary

LAW, Hon. Elizabeth Susan (1799–1883)
She was the second daughter of Edward Law, 1st Baron Ellenborough, Lord Chief Justice, and of Anne Towry, a famous beauty. She married Charles, 2nd Baron Colchester, in 1836. (*DNB* (under Edward Law))

1(*a*)   *Il villaggio abbandonato* . . . Trans. [into Italian] E. S. L. London: Rodwell and Martin, 1825. 10 × 16 cm. 36 pp. By Oliver Goldsmith. Bodley: 2799 f. 437.

1(*b*)   *Il villagio abbandonato* . . . Trans. [into Italian] E. S. L. London: J. Rodwell, 1832. 9.5 × 17 cm. 36 pp. By Oliver Goldsmith. BL: 11645. aaa. 55(3).

2   *Il viaggiatore* . . . Trans. [into Italian] E. S. L. London: printed for J. Rodwell, 1832. 10 × 17 cm. Pp. [ii] + 59. By O. Goldsmith. BL: 1608/3070.

3   *Miscellaneous Poems. Dedicated to Joseph Jekyll, Esq.* [London: printed by Ibotson and Palmer] not published, 1832. 9.5 × 17 cm. Pp. vi + 104. By E. S. L. BL: 11645. aaa. 55(1).

4   *Giustina: A Spanish Tale of Real Life. A Poem in Three Cantos.* [London: printed by Ibotson and Palmer], but not published, 1833. 12 × 18.5 cm. Pp. [ii] + 63. By E. S. L. BL: 11642. bb. 5.

5   *Poems by Lady Colchester: Unpublished.* [The title taken from the cloth binding. The volume consists of *The Lady 'Arabella Stuart.' A Poem.*] [London: printed by G. Barclay, (1833?)]. 12 × 18.5 cm. Pp. [ii] + 126. By E. S. L. HRC Texas: PR. 4464. C5. L34.

6   *Views in London . . . Sketched from a Window in the 'Palais de la Verité.' And Extracts from an Album. Dedicated to Sophia, Countess of Darlington.* [Chiswick: printed by Charles

Whittingham], but not published, 1833. 12.5 × 19.5 cm. Pp. viii + 66. By an Amateur. BL: 11646. cc. 57.

LAWRENCE, ROSE, Mrs

She was the daughter of Joseph D'Aguilar, an army officer. She edited anthologies of verse for children and was the author of a prose translation of Goethe's *Götz von Berlichingen* in 1799. (Blain)

1(*a*)   *The Last Autumn at a Favourite Residence. With Other Poems.* London: N. Hailes, 1828. 10 × 16.5 cm. 104 pp. By a Lady. HL; NLS: Br. 1. 21.

1(*b*)   *The Last Autumn at a Favourite Residence. With Other Poems.* Liverpool/London: printed for G. and J. Robinson/ Longman, Rees, Orme, Brown and Green, 1829. 2nd edn. 10 × 18 cm. Pp. [x] + 160. By Mrs Lawrence. BL: 994. g. 22.

LEADBEATER, Mary, Mrs William (1758–1826)

Born in Baltimore in Ireland. She was the daughter of Richard Shackleton and his second wife Elizabeth Carleton. They were Quakers. She received a thorough education and when she went to London in 1784 she was received into Edmund Burke's circle (she was related to his former schoolmaster). In 1791 she married William Leadbeater, a small farmer and landowner, and they had several children. She kept the village post office in Baltimore. She corresponded with Burke, George Crabbe, Maria Edgeworth, and Melesina Trench (q.v.). (*CB, DNB, Friends' Books*)

1   *Poems . . . to Which is Prefixed her Translation of the Thirteenth Book of the Aeneid; with the Latin Original, Written in the Fifteenth Century, by Maffaeus.* Dublin/London: for the author by Martin Keene/Longman, Hurst, Rees and Orme, 1808. 12.5 × 21.5 cm. Pp. viii + 419. 8/- boards. By Mary Leadbeater (Late Shackleton). *MR* 57: 372–4; BL: 11641. e. 21.

LEE, Miss, of Maryland, *see* COLLECTIONS 20, 31

LEE, Harriet (1757–1851)

Born in London. Her father was the actor and manager John Lee; her mother was an actress. After her father's death in 1781 she kept a private school with her sister Sophia (q.v.) at Belvidere House, Bath. In

1786 her epistolary novel *The Errors of Innocence* appeared, and in 1787 her comedy *The New Peerage* was performed at Drury Lane. She and her sister are best known for *The Canterbury Tales* (5 vols., 1797–1805), from which Byron drew the plot of his *Werner*. She refused William Godwin's proposal of marriage in 1798. (*CB*, *DNB*, Todd 1)

1(*a*)   *The Mysterious Marriage, or the Heirship of Roselva. A Play, in Three Acts.* London: G. G. and J. Robinson, 1798. 12.5 × 21 cm. Pp. [iv] + 88 [verse and prose]. 2/-. By Harriet Lee. *CR* 22: 475–6; Houghton: *EC8. L5126. 798m.

1(*b*)   *The Mysterious Marriage, or the Heirship of Roselva. A Play, in Three Acts.* Dublin: P. Wogan, P. Byrne, W. Jones, J. Rice, N. Kelly, and G. Folingsby, 1798. 9.5 × 16.5 cm. 59 pp. [verse and prose]. By Harriet Lee. BL: 640. h. 14(7).

LEE, Sophia (1750–1824), *see also* SEWARD, Anna 2(*g–h*)

She was the older sister of Harriet Lee (q.v.) and at their mother's death took care of the family. The profits from her comedy, *The Chapter of Accidents*, at the Haymarket in London, enabled her to found the school in Bath where she made a home for her sisters. Her historical novel *The Recess* (1785) was well received. *Almeyda* was performed at Drury Lane with Mrs Siddons and John Philip Kemble in the cast, but it was unsuccessful. Her contribution to *The Canterbury Tales*, on which she collaborated with her sister, amounted to about a volume and a half of the five volumes. She gave up her school in 1803, having achieved financial independence. Her six-volume epistolary novel *The Life of a Lover* appeared in 1804; her comedy *The Assignation* was performed at Drury Lane in 1807 but was judged to be a failure. (*CB*, *DNB*, Schlueter, Todd 1)

1(*a*)   *A Hermit's Tale: Recorded by his Own Hand, and Found in his Cell.* London: T. Cadell, 1787. 20 × 26.5 cm. Pp. [ii] + 40. 2/-. CUL: 7720. b. 187.

1(*b*)   *A Hermit's Tale: Recorded by his Own Hand, and Found in his Cell.* Dublin: printed by J. Moore, 1787. 9 × 16 cm. 46 pp. 2/-. *MR* 77: 158; BL: 12330. aaa. 6(2).

1(*c*)   *A Hermit's Tale: Recorded by his Own Hand, and Found in his Cell.* London: T. Cadell, 1787. 2nd edn. 21 × 26 cm. 40 pp. 2/-. BL: 643. k. 4(8).

2(*a*)   *Almeyda; Queen of Granada. A Tragedy. In Five Acts . . . As Performed at the Theatre Royal, Drury-Lane.* London: Cadell and Davies, 1796. 13 × 20.5 cm. Pp. [iv] + 123. 2/-. By Sophia Lee. BL: 643. f. 4(5).

2(*b*)   *Almeyda, Queen of Granada. A Tragedy, in Five Acts . . . As Performed at the Theatre Royal, Drury-Lane.* Dublin: P. Wogan, P. Byrne, C. Brown, and G. Folingsby, 1796. 10 × 16.5 cm. 70 pp. By Sophia Lee. BL: 640. h. 34(2).

2(*c*)   *Almeyda: Queen of Granada. A Tragedy. In Five Acts . . . As Performed at the Theatre Royal, Drury Lane.* London: Cadell and Davis, 1796. 2nd edn. 12.5 × 20.5 cm. Pp. [vi] + 123. 2/-. By Sophia Lee. Yale (Beinecke): Plays 541.

2(*d*)   *Almeyda; Queen of Granada. A Tragedy. In Five Acts . . . As Performed at the Theatre Royal, Drury-Lane.* London: Cadell and Davis, 1796. 3rd edn. 12.5 × 20.5 cm. Pp. [vi] + 123. 2/-. By Sophia Lee. Yale (Beinecke): Plays 200.

Leech, Margaret

1   *Poems on Various Subjects.* London: printed by Whittingham and Rowland, 1816. 21 × 26.5 cm. Pp. [vi] + 195. By Miss Leech. BL: 11642. h. 12.

Leech, Sarah

An Irish writer. (O'D)

1   *Poems on Various Subjects.* 1828. O'D.

Le Fanu, Alicia, *the younger*

She was the daughter of Henry Le Fanu, a captain in the 56th Regiment, and of Anne Elizabeth Sheridan. Richard Brinsley Sheridan was her uncle, and Alicia Le Fanu the elder, whose writings are sometimes catalogued with hers, was an aunt.

1   *The Flowers; or, the Sylphid Queen: A Fairy Tale. In Verse . . .* London: J. Harris, 1809. 10 × 17 cm. 52 pp. By Miss Alicia Lefanu, Grand-daughter of the Late Thomas Sheridan, A.M. BL: 11633. aaa. 27.

2(*a*)   *Rosara's Chain: Or, the Choice of Life. A Poem.* London: M. J. Godwin, 1812. 9.5 × 15 cm. Pp. [ii] + 108. 6/- boards or 5/-. By Alicia Lefanu, Niece to the Right Honourable Richard Brinsley Sheridan. *MR* 68: 107; *CR* 1: 101–3; BL: 11644. b. 33.

2(*b*) *Rosara's Chain* . . . 2nd edn. Inference.

2(*c*) *Rosara's Chain: Or, the Choice of Life. A Poem.* London: M. J. Godwin and Co., 1815. 3rd edn. 10 × 17.5 cm. Pp. [ii] + 108. By Alicia Lefanu, Niece to the Right Honourable Richard Brinsley Sheridan. BL: 11644. f. 22.

2(*d*) *Rosara's Chain: Or, the Choice of Life. A Poem.* London: M. J. Godwin and Co., 1823. 9.5 × 16 cm. Pp. [ii] + 108. By Alicia Lefanu, Niece to the Right Honourable Richard Brinsley Sheridan. BL: 11644. b. 34.

LEFROY, Anne, Mrs John (*c.*1748–1804)
She was the eldest daughter of Edward Brydges and Jemima Egerton. In or about 1778 she married John Lefroy, Rector of Ashe, Hants. They had four children. She was a vigorous philanthropist, maintaining a school for poor children in her house and inoculating eight hundred of the poor with her own hands. She died as the consequence of a fall from a horse. (*Annual Register, GM*)

1 *Carmina Domestica; or Poems on Several Occasions. (The Majority Written in the Early Part of Life.)* Ed. [Christopher Edward Lefroy]. London: printed for the editor by Law and Gilbert, 1812. 12 × 18.5 cm. 184 pp. By Mrs Lefroy. BL: 11646. e. 5.

LEICESTER, Mrs, *see* COLLECTIONS 52

LEIGH, Helen, Mrs George
Her unmarried name may have been Baxter. She was the wife of George Leigh, a country curate in Middlewich, Cheshire, and the mother of seven. She seems to have been dead by 1795. (Blain, *Miscellaneous Poems*)

1 *Miscellaneous Poems.* Manchester: Clarkes, 1788. 18.5 × 23.5 cm. Pp. [ii] + 8 + 101 [subscription edition]. By Helen Leigh of Middlewich. BL: 11630. d. 14(7).

LE NOIR, Elizabeth Anne, Mrs Jean Baptiste (1754–1841)
She was the daughter of the poet Christopher Smart and of Anna Maria Carnan. She was educated in a convent in Boulogne. Her stepfather, the publisher John Newbury, after Smart's death in 1770

employed the widow and her two daughters in the office of the *Reading Mercury*. The sisters ultimately inherited the newspaper. In 1795 Elizabeth married Jean Baptiste Le Noir de la Brosse, one of the refugee French aristocrats who had settled in Reading; he was a teacher of French. (Blain, *CB*, *DNB*)

1(*a*) *Village Anecdotes; or, the Journal of a Year, from Sophia to Edward. With Original Poems.* London: Vernor and Hood, 1804. 10 × 16 cm. 3 vols. [prose with about 51 pp. of verse distributed through it]. By Mrs Le Noir. BL: 12611. b. 25.

1(*b*) *Village Anecdotes: Or, the Journal of a Year, from Sophia to Edward.* Reading/London: printed for the author by Smart and Co./Rivingtons and Vernor and Hood, [n.d.]. 2nd edn. 9.5 × 17.5 cm. 3 vols. [subscription edition; prose, with about 67 pp. of verse distributed through it]. By Mrs Le Noir. BL: 12613. cc. 14.

2(*a*) *Clara de Montfier, a Moral Tale. With Original Poems . . . Respectfully Inscribed to the Right Hon. Lady Charlotte Greville.* Reading/London: printed for the author by A. M. Smart and Co./Rivington's, 1808. 10.5 × 18 cm. 3 vols. [about 56 pp. of verse scattered through the volumes]. By Elizabeth Anne Le Noir, Author of *Village Anecdotes*. BL: 1153. i. 11.

2(*b*) *The Maid of La Vendée, being a Second Edition of Clara de Montfier . . . With Critical Remarks.* Ed. Dr Burney and the Revd C. Munter. Reading: printed for the author by M. Cowslade and Co., 1819. 10.5 × 17 cm. 3 vols. [prose with about 52 pp. of verse distributed through it]. By Mrs Le Noir. BL: 12612. e. 13.

3 *Miscellaneous Poems, Respectfully Inscribed to the Right Honourable Viscountess Sidmouth.* Vol. i [of 2]. Reading: for the author by M. Cowslade and Co., 1825. 10.5 × 17 cm. Pp. [6] + iv + 307. By Elizth. Anne Smart Le Noir. Bodley: 280 e. 1343.

4 *Miscellaneous Poems, Respectfully Inscribed to the Right Honourable Viscountess Sidmouth.* Vol. ii [of 2]. Reading: for the author by M. Cowslade and Co., 1826. 10.5 × 17 cm. Pp. iv + 246 + 94. By Elizth. Anne Smart Le Noir. Bodley: 280 e. 1344.

LENOX-CONYNGHAM, Elizabeth Emmet, Mrs George William

She was the daughter of the Irish lawyer, Robert Holmes. She contributed to such annuals as *The Keepsake, The Literary Souvenir,* and *The New Year's Gift* in 1831–4. (Boyle)

1   *The Dream, and Other Poems.* London: Edward Moxon, 1833. 12.5 × 21 cm. Pp. [vi] + 166. By Mrs George Lenox-Conyngham. BL: T. 1496. (16).

LEONARD, Eliza Lucy

1(*a*) *The Ruby Ring; or, Transformations.* London: John Sharpe, 1815. 10 × 12.5 cm. 50 pp. by Eliza Lucy Leonard. Osborne: ii. 649.

1(*b*) *The Ruby Ring; or, the Transformations.* London: N. Hailes, 1816. 10 × 13 cm. 64 pp. 4/- boards. By Eliza Lucy Leonard. *MR* 83: 97; BL: 11642. aa. 53.

2(*a*) *The Miller and his Golden Dream.* Wellington, Salop./London: F. Houlston and Son/Scatcherd and Letterman, 1822. 10.5 × 13 cm. 30 pp. 2/-. By Eliza Lucy Leonard. BL: 11642. aa. 59.

2(*b*) *The Miller and his Golden Dream.* Wellington, Salop.: F. Houlston and Son, 1827. 10.5 × 13 cm. 30 pp. 2/-. By the Author of *The Ruby Ring,* etc. Yale (Sterling): In/L552/822b.

LETCHES, Mrs

From *Poems on Several Occasions* one learns that she had four children and that she seems to have lived in Bristol. In one poem she calls herself 'Helena'.

1   *Poems on Several Occasions.* Bristol: W. Bulgin, 1792. 20.5 × 26.5 cm. 27 pp. By a Lady. BL: 1346. k. 34.

LEWIS, Sylvia, *see* CLARK, Sylvia

LICKBARROW, Isabella, *see also* COLLECTIONS 35

She lived in Kendal, Westmorland, and published to support 'herself and her orphan sisters'. Southey and Wordsworth were subscribers. (*A Lament, Poetical Effusions*)

1   *Poetical Effusions.* Kendal/London: printed for the authoress by M. Branthwaite and Co./J. Richardson, 1814.

13 × 19.5 cm. Pp. xii + 131 [subscription edition]. By Isabella Lickbarrow. BL: 11642. e. 2.

2 *A Lament upon the Death of Her Royal Highness the Princess Charlotte. And Alfred, a Vision.* Liverpool: printed by Mrs G. F. Harris and Bros., 1818. 11.5 × 19 cm. 34 pp. By Isabella Lickbarrow. BL: 11641. e. 22.

LIDDIARD, I. S. Anna, Mrs William

She was the daughter of Sir Henry Wilkinson. She married William Liddiard, a miscellaneous writer, who was first a soldier and then was ordained and became Rector of Knockmark, Co. Meath. They had one son. (*DNB* (under William Liddiard))

1 *Poems.* Dublin: printed at the Hibernia-Press Office, 1810. 10.5 × 17.5 cm. Pp. [viii] + 100. By J. S. Anna Liddiard. BL: 11646. bbb. 11.

2 *The Sgelaighe; or, a Tale of Old; with a Second Edition of Poems, Published in Dublin; and Additions.* Bath/London: printed Meyler and Son/G. Robinson and J. Harding, 1811. 10 × 16 cm. Pp. viii + 184. By Mrs Liddiard. BL: 11645. aa. 25.

3 (*a*) *Kenilworth and Farley Castle; with Other Poems.* Dublin: printed at the Hibernia-Press Office, 1813. 10.5 × 18 cm. Pp. xviii + viii + 144. By I. S. Anna Liddiard. BL: 11644. g. 41.

3 (*b*) *Kenilworth: A Mask.* Dublin/London: John Cumming/ Longman, Hurst, Rees, Orme, and Brown, 1815. 12.5 × 20 cm. Pp. viii + 112. By I. S. Anna Liddiard. BL: 992. i. 15(2).

4 *Mont St. Jean, a Poem, by William Liddiard . . . Theodore & Laura, a Tale, by I. S. Anna Liddiard, Author of Kenilworth, and Other Poems.* London/Dublin: Longman, Hurst, Rees, Orme, and Browne/John Cumming, 1816. 13 × 21 cm. Pp. viii + 72 [Anna Liddiard's contribution begins at p. 41]. BL: 992. i. 14.

LIGHTFOOT, Catherine Anne

1 *The Battle of Trafalgar; a Poem, in Six Cantos.* Sevenoaks/London: printed C. Payne/Whittaker, Treacher, and Co., [1833: Preface dated Feb. 1833]. 12 × 20 cm. Pp. [ii] + 148. BL: 11643. bb. 26.

LINDSAY, Lady Elizabeth Scott, *see* HARDWICKE, Countess of

LINDSAY, Lady Margaret (born *c.*1752), *see* COLLECTIONS 37

She was the second daughter of James Lindsay, 5th Earl of Balcarres, and of Anne Dalrymple, and she was the younger sister of Lady Anne Barnard (q.v.). In 1770 she married the wealthy banker Alexander Fordyce, who was spectacularly bankrupted in 1772 and who died in 1789. With her sister Lady Anne she maintained a literary salon in London. In 1812 she became the third wife of Sir James Bland Burges with whom she had had a romantic attachment when they were young.

LINWOOD, Mary (1755–1845)

Born in Birmingham. She moved to Leicester in the late 1700s. She was a musical composer and an artist in needlework. She specialized in the imitation of pictures in worsted embroidery, and an exhibition of a hundred of her copies of old masters and modern paintings was exhibited in London, Edinburgh, Dublin, and the chief provincial towns. She also wrote *Leicestershire Tales* (4 vols., 1808). (*DNB*)

1   *The Anglo-Cambrian; a Poem in Four Cantos.* London: Longman, Hurst, Rees, Orme, and Brown, 1818. 13 × 21 cm. Pp. [iv] + 94. By M. Linwood. BL: 992. i. 17(5).

LITTLE, Cynthia

1   *A Review of the First Masquerade at the Royal Gardens, Brighton; under the Patronage of the Tenth Royal Hussars.* London: printed for the authoress by Cunningham and Salmon, 1829. 9 × 14 cm. 72 pp. [the verse confined to pp. 55–72]. 1/6 boards. By Cynthia Little, Authoress of *Lara Cupid*, etc., etc. BL: 12331. aa. 34.

2   *The Mess-room; or, Cupid Fra Diavolo: A Humorous Poem.* London: the authoress, 1831. 10 × 17 cm. 23 pp. By Cynthia Little. BL: 11644. aaa. 52.

LITTLE, Janet (1759–1813)

She was the daughter of George Little of Nether Bogside, Ecclefechan, Dumfriesshire. She was a servant, patronized by Mrs Dunlop, Robert Burns's friend, who organized her subscription edition, which is said to have earned £50. She married John Richmond, a widowed labourer twenty years her senior with five children. (Lonsdale, Todd 1)

1   *The Poetical Works of Janet Little, the Scotch Milkmaid.* Air: printed by John and Peter Wilson, 1792. 12.5 × 20.5 cm. 206 pp. [subscription edition]. By Janet Little. BL: 11646. h. 10.

LIVINGSTON, Ann (Nancy) Hume, Mrs Henry Beekman (1763–1841)

Born in Philadelphia. She was the daughter of Dr William Shippen III and Alice Lee. She married Henry Beekman Livingston in 1781. They had one daughter, but the marriage was unhappy. She is best known for her journal, which was published in 1835. *Sacred Records* was written during confinement for a long illness. (*Dictionary of Literary Biography*)

1   *Sacred Records Abridged in Verse. Consisting of Some of the Parables and Miracles, the Life, Death, Resurrection and Ascension of the Blessed Saviour.* Philadelphia: for the author by T. S. Manning, 1817. 10.5 × 18 cm. 124 pp. By Ann Hume Shippen Livingston. AAS: DATED BOOKS.

LLOYD, Mary

1   *Brighton. A Poem. Descriptive of the Place and Parts Adjacent. And Other Poems.* London/Brighton, Worthing and Eastborne: J. Harding/all the booksellers, 1809. 11 × 18.5 cm. Pp. iv + 88 [subscription edition]. By Mary Lloyd. BL: 994. h. 18.

LLOYD, Mary Ann

1   *A Manual, Consisting of a Defence of the Bible, in an Original Manner, with an Appendix, in Prose and Verse, on Many Interesting Subjects.* London: for the authoress, 1820. 13.5 × 22 cm. Pp. viii + 188 [verse, pp. 160–81]. 7/6 boards. By Mrs M. A. Lloyd. BL: 1114. d. 14.

2   *Lines on the Passions. Addressed to a Young Gentleman Who Had Received an Anonymous Letter on the Ruling Passion of the Mind. To Which is Added a Sonnet to a Star.* London: for the author by W. Crawford, 1823. 13 × 21 cm. 20 pp. 1/- stitched [given on the fly-leaf of her *Think of Jesus* (1823)]. By Mary Ann Lloyd. BL: T. 1063(21).

3   *'Think of Jesus': A Poem Written for Good Friday, in the Year of Our Lord 1823.* London: for the author by Crawford, Plank

and Holloway, [1823]. 13 × 21 cm. 12 pp. By Mary Ann Lloyd. BL: T. 1063(15).

4   *The Funds and More Companies, with Technical Phrases on Stock, or, Flippancies of the Times. In Rhyme.* London: printed by J. Wilkins for the authoress, [1825]. 3rd edn. [for previous editions, see endnote]. 10 × 16 cm. 39 pp. By Mary Ann Lloyd. BL: T. 903(5).

[*See also*: 'Lines on being Present at the White Fast . . .' (1823, 2 pp.); 'Lines on Seeing the Constellation of the Eye of Providence . . .' (1823, 2 pp.); 'Lines on the Funds' (1823, 2 editions, 2 pp. each); 'Poems' (a collection of broadsheets: BL: 1346. i. 41); 'A Poetical Prayer . . .' (1823, 3 pp.); 'To the Gentlemen of the Stock Exchange' (1823, 2 editions, 2 pp. each); 'A Letter and Two Songs, Respectfully Inscribed to the Stock Exchange' ([1830], 8 pp. (prose and verse)); 'A Second Letter, and Two Poems' ([1831], 8 pp. (prose and verse)).]

LLOYD, Sarah Maria, Mrs Charles

She was the second wife of Dr Lloyd, a dissenting clergyman and schoolmaster. They had one son. (*DNB* (under Charles Lloyd))

1   *Majesty. The Lay of the New Year. A Tribute to the Memory of the Beloved Princess Charlotte of Saxe Cobourg.* Lowestoft/ Norwich/Yarmouth/Southwold: S. Gowing, and Stevenson, Matchett and Stevenson/Wilkin and Youngman/Alexander/Gooch, 1819. 13.5 × 22 cm. 16 pp. By Sarah Maria Lloyd, Wife of Dr Lloyd, of Keppell St., Russell Square, London. BL: 1480. dd. 4.

LOCKE, Mary

She was an orphan, brought up by her uncle, Edward Taylor, a man of literary tastes. She contributed verses to *GM* from 1791 to 1796. Her uncle's death in 1797 left her substantial property. By 1808 she had married William Mister, and she wrote a series of children's books under the name Mary Mister. (Lonsdale)

1   *Eugenius; or, Virtue in Retirement. A Poem.* London: T. Hookham, 1791. 18.5 × 25 cm. Pp. [ii] + 19. 1/6. By Mary Locke. *MR* 7: 229; Houghton: *EC75. L7941. 791e.

LOGAN, Maria

Her book suggests that she had been an invalid for seven years.

1(*a*)   *Poems on Several Occasions.* York: for the author by Wilson, Spence and Mawman, 1793. 18.5 × 23.5 cm. Pp. 14 + 7–64 [subscription edition]. By Maria Logan. BL: 11632. g. 63(3).

1(*b*)   *Poems on Several Occasions.* London/York/Leeds: T. Cadell/ J. Todd and Wilson and Co./J. Binns and J. Robinson, 1793. 2nd edn. 17.5 × 22.5 cm. 64 pp. By Maria Logan. BL: 1466. i. 4.

A LOOKING-GLASS MAKER, *see* ELLIOTT, Mary

LOUDON, Jane, Mrs John Claudius, *see* WEBB, Jane

LOVECHILD, Mrs, *see* FENN, Lady Eleanor

LOVECHILD, Goody, *see* SPROAT, Nancy

LOVEJOY, Miss, of the City of York, *see* COLLECTIONS 7

LOVEJOY, Lucretia, *see* APPENDIX 5

L–r–che, Mrs, *see* COLLECTIONS 1(*b–c*)

LUBY, Catherine

1   *The Spirit of the Lakes; or, Mucruss Abbey. A Poem, in Three Cantos. With Explanatory Notes from the Best and Most Approved Authorities.* London: Longman, Hurst, Rees, Orme, and Brown, and J. Ebers, 1822. 13 × 21.5 cm. Pp. xiv + 208 [subscription edition]. By Miss Luby. BL: 993. i. 32.

LUCAN, Lady, Margaret BINGHAM (died 1814)

She was the daughter of James and Grace Smith. In 1760 she married Sir Charles Bingham (later Baron Lucan). They had five children. She was an amateur artist whose illustrations for a five-volume Shakespeare have been admired. She knew Horace Walpole, Mary Delaney, and Samuel Johnson. She seems to have been the 'lady' on whose verses on Ireland Johnson objected to having to give an opinion in company. (Boswell, *Life of Johnson, Complete Peerage, DNB*, Todd 1)

1 *Verses on the Present State of Ireland.* London: P. Elmsly, 1778. 20.5 × 24.5 cm. Pp. ii + 20. 1/6. By a Lady. Houghton: *EC75. W1654. Zz797p16.

LUTTON, Anne (1791–1881)

She was the eleventh child of Ralph Lutton, a proprietor of estates around Moira, Co. Down, and of his cousin Anne Lutton. She wrote an epitaph for a mouse when she was 5 and was precociously bookish. She taught herself to read both ancient and modern languages, and she became a devout Methodist. After 1837 she lived in Bristol. 1,000 copies of her book were published, at a price of 4/-. (Anne Lutton, *Memorials of a Consecrated Life* . . . (1882))

1 *Poems on Moral and Religious Subjects.* Dublin/Belfast/London/Liverpool/Manchester: J. O. Bonsall and Co., T. W. Doolittle, R. M. Tims, William Curry, Jr. and Co./M. Jellett/J. Mason/Kaye/J. Everett, 1829. 14 × 22.5 cm. 208 pp. By Anne Lutton. BL: 11632. cc. 11.

LUXBOROUGH, Lady, Henrietta KNIGHT (1699–1756), *see* COLLECTIONS 15(*a–o*)

She was the only daughter of Henry, Viscount St John, and of his second wife, Angelica Magdalene Pillesoy, and she was half-sister to Henry St John, Viscount Bolingbroke. In 1727 she married Robert Knight. They had a son and two daughters. In 1736 she was accused of adultery and separated from her husband. Four of her poems appeared anonymously in Dodsley's *Collection of Poems.* (*CB, DNB*, Lonsdale)

LYNDSAY, David, *see* DODS, Mary Diana

LYON, Emma

She was the daughter of the Revd S. Lyon, a Hebrew teacher. She dedicates her book to the Princess of Wales, and her subscribers include members of the aristocracy and many academic people from Oxford, Cambridge, Eton, etc.

1 *Miscellaneous Poems.* Oxford/Cambridge/London: for the author by J. Parker, J. Cooke and R. Bliss/J. Deighton and Nicholson and Son/J. Hatchard and Wilson, 1812. 11 × 19 cm. Pp. xxiv + 152. 10/6 boards [subscription edition]. By

Miss Emma Lyon, Daughter of the Revd S. Lyon, Hebrew Teacher. BL: 994. f. 29.

M******, Lady, *see* MANNERS, Lady

M., Eleanor, *see* MONTAGU, Eleanora Louisa

M., I. A., *see* MERRYWEATHER, I. A.

M., J. E.

1   *The Crocus, Containing Original Poems for Young People.* London: William Darton, Harvey and Darton, and John Harris, [1824]. 10.5 × 17.5 cm. 36 pp. By J. E. M. BL: 11644. eeee. 43.

M., M., *see* MORPETH, Mary

MAB, Queen, *see* QUEEN MAB

MACAULEY, Elizabeth Wright (1785?–1837), *see also* COLLECTIONS 21

She was an actress until about 1817; then she became a preacher in London, and finally returned to acting. She died at York while on a lecture tour. Her *Pamphlet on the Dangers of a Theatrical Life* (1810) complains of the hazards endured by actresses. (*GM*)

1(*a*)   *Effusions of Fancy; Consisting of the Birth of Friendship, the Birth of Affection, and the Birth of Sensibility.* London: for the author by Longman, Hurst, Rees, Orme, and Brown, and T. Sotheran, 1812. 11 × 19.5 cm. Pp. xx + 140. By Miss Macauley. Bodley: 270 e. 1792.

1(*b*)   *Poetical Effusions; Consisting of the Birth of Friendship, the Birth of Affection, and the Birth of Sensibility.* London: Sotheran, 1812. 11.5 × 19 cm. Pp. xx + 140. By Miss Macauley. BL: 11632. aaa. 35.

2(*a*)   *Mary Stuart.* London/Edinburgh: for the author by Sherwood, Jones and Co., Andrews, Lloyd and Son/ Constable and Co., 1823. 13 × 21.5 cm. Pp. xiv + 138. 7/-. By Miss Macauley. BL: 1465. f. 12.

2(*b*)   *Mary Stuart.* London/Edinburgh: Sherwood, Jones and Co., Andrews, Lloyd and Son/Constable and Co., 1823. 2nd edn. 13 × 21 cm. Pp. xiv + 138. 7/-. By Miss Macauley. BL: 11646. h. 13.

2(*c*)   *Mary Stuart.* London/Edinburgh: for the author by Sherwood, Jones and Co., Andrews, Lloyd and Son/Constable and Co., 1823. 3rd edn. 12.5 × 20.5 cm. Pp. xiv + 138. 7/-. By Miss Macauley. BL: 11646. h. 14.

McCoy, Mary

1   *A Poem, in Answer to an Anonymous Pamphlet; in Three Letters, Called Friendly Hints to Catholic Emancipation.* Belfast: printed by Simms and McIntyre, 1813. 9.5 × 17 cm. 12 pp. By Mary M'Coy. BL: 4136. a. 65.

McDermott, Mary

1   *My Early Dreams.* Belfast: printed by F. D. Finlay, 1832. 10.5 × 17.5 cm. 228 pp. [subscription edition]. By M. McD. BL: 11644. bb. 26.

Mackey, Mary, Mrs

1   *The Scraps of Nature. A Poem. In One Volume.* London: printed for the authoress, 1810. 10 × 17 cm. Pp. viii + 372 + x. By Mrs Mary Mackey. BL: 11642. b. 50.

Maclaurin, Mary

She was the daughter of Colin Maclaurin and of Anne Stewart, the daughter of the Solicitor-general for Scotland. (*DNB* (under Colin Maclaurin))

1   *Poems.* Haddington: printed by George Miller and Son, 1812. 12.5 × 21 cm. Pp. [ii] + 40. By the Late Miss Mary Maclaurin, Daughter of the Late Mr Colin Maclaurin, Professor of Mathematics in the University of Edinburgh. BL: 11641. e. 28.

McMorine, Mary

1   *Poems, Chiefly on Religious Subjects. In Two Parts.* Edinburgh: printed for the author by J. Pillans and Sons, 1799. 10 ×

16.5 cm. 300 pp. By Mary McMorine, a Servant-maid. BL: 11646. bbb. 3.

McMULLAN, Maryanne *or* Mary Anne, Mrs W., *see also* COL-LECTIONS 29(*a–b*)

1   *The Crescent, a National Poem. To Commemorate the Glorious Victory at Algiers.* London: Longman, Hurst, Rees and Co., T. Egerton and E. Lloyd, 1816. 13.5 × 21 cm. Pp. [iv] + 61. By Mrs M'Mullan, Relict of W. M'Mullan, Esq. M.D. Royal Navy. BL: 11646. h. 9.

2   *The Naiad's Wreath.* London: Longman, Hurst, Rees and Co., T. Egerton and E. Lloyd, 1816. 12.5 × 20 cm. Pp. [iv] + 87. By Mrs M'Mullan. BL: 11645. bb. 32.

3   *Britain; or, Fragments of Poetical Aberration.* London: Longman, Hurst, Rees, Orme, and Brown, J. Hatchard and T. Egerton, 1818. 13 × 21 cm. Pp. [iv] + 109. 7/-. By Mrs M'Mullan. BL: 992. i. 22(5).

McTAGGART, Ann, Mrs (*c.*1753–1834)
She was the daughter of a naval officer named Hamilton. When she was 10 her mother died and she was sent to live with an uncle and aunt. In her *Memoirs of a Gentlewoman* (1830) she claims to be in her seventy-seventh year. (Blain, *NUC*)

1   *Constantia, a Tragedy, in Five Acts; and Valville; or, the Prejudices of Past Times; a Drama, in Five Acts.* London: M. A. Nattali, 1824. 9.5 × 16.5 cm. Pp. xxiv + 201 [subscription edition]. By Mrs A. M'Taggart, of Bristol. BL: 11779. aa. 64.

2(*a*)   *The New British Theatre; a Selection of Original Dramas, Not Yet Acted; Some of Which have been Offered for Representation, but Not Accepted* . . . London/Edinburgh/Dublin: Henry Colburn/G. Goldie/J. Cumming, 1814–15. 13.5 × 21 cm. 4 vols. 10/6 boards. [Includes 'Theodora; a Tragedy' (i. 277–338), 'Villario; a Play' (ii. 137–90), and 'Hortensia, a Tragedy' (iv. 147–98), all unattributed.] BL: 642. i. 1–4.

2(*b*)   *Plays: Theodora; Hortensia; Villario; and a Search after Perfection.* London: A. J. Valpy, 1832. 2nd edn. 10.5 × 16.5 cm. 2 vols. By Mrs A. M'Taggart, Author of *Memoirs of a Gentlewoman*. BL: 642. i. 1–4.

3   *Plays: Valville, or, the Prejudices of Past Times; Theodora; Hortensia; Villario; a Search after Perfection; and Constantia.* London: printed by A. J. Valpy, 1832. 10.5 × 16.5 cm. 2 vols. [verse and prose]. By Mrs A. M'Taggart, Author of *Memoirs of a Gentlewoman.* LC: PR 4971. M8 A19 1832.

MCWATTY, Alicia

1   *Poems on Various Subjects.* Newry, 1815. O'D.

MADDOCKS, Mrs

In *Scripture Female Portraits* she is said to be a widow, 'adopting this means for the purpose of obtaining a morsel of bread, to save her from perishing with hunger'. She belonged to a church under the pastoral care of the Revd T. James of the City Chapel in London.

1   *Scripture Female Portraits, in Verse, for the Instruction of Youth.* London: E. Wallis, 1820. 9 × 13.5 cm. 79 pp. Free Library of Philadelphia: ASSU/SC/M179S.

2(*a*)   *The Female Missionary Advocate. A Poem.* London: for the author by B. J. Holdsworth, 1827. 7 × 13 cm. 96 pp. HL; BL: 1121. a. 46.

2(*b*)   *The Female Missionary Advocate. A Poem.* London: Holdsworth and Ball, 1830. 2nd edn. 8 × 12.5 cm. Pp. viii + 93. By Mrs Maddocks, Author of *Scripture Portraits, Cottage Similes,* etc. BL: 11644. a. 24.

3   *Cottage Similes, or, Poems on Domestic Occurrences, Designed for Those in Humble Life.* Ed. [E. Henderson]. London: Holdsworth and Ball, 1829. 9 × 14 cm. Pp. viii + 79. By the Author of *The Female Missionary Advocate.* BL: 11644. aa. 49.

MAGRATH, Anne Jane (born *c.*1821)

An Irish writer. (O'D)

1   *Blossoms of Genius; Poems on Various Subjects.* Dublin: G. Tyrrell, 1834. 10 × 17 cm. Pp. [2] + 198 [subscription edition]. By Anne Jane Magrath. BL: 11644. bbb. 33.

MAHONY, Agnes (died *c.*1840)

An Irish writer who later married a Mr Hickson. (O'D)

1   *A Minstrel's Hours of Song; or Poems.* London: William
       Pickering, 1825. 10 × 16.5 cm. Pp. vi + 174. By Agnes
       Mahony. BL: 994. g. 24.

MAID, OLD, *pseudonym of* M'GIBBON, Alexander

MALLET, Mrs

1   *The Maid of the Isle, and Other Poems.* London: printed for
       the author by J. Phair, 1834. 10.5 × 17.5 cm. 61 pp. BL:
       11644. bbb. 25.

MAMMA

1   *Mamma's Verses; or, Lines for Little Londoners.* Brentford/
       London/Richmond: P. Norbury/Baldwin, Cradock, and
       Joy, and Sherwood, Jones and Co., and Hailes/Hughes,
       1824. 10 × 12.5 cm. 76 pp. BL: Ch. 810/205(4).

MANGNALL, Richmal (1769–1820)

She was the daughter of James Mangnall and Mary Kay. She was
adopted, on the death of her parents, by her uncle, John Kay, and educated at Mrs Wilson's school at Crofton Hall, near Wakefield, Yorks.
She became a schoolteacher and eventually succeeded Mrs Wilson. Her
Miscellaneous Questions for the Use of Young People appeared anonymously in
1800 and was often reissued; her *Compendium of Geography* had three editions between 1815 and 1829. (*GM, DNB*)

1   *Half an Hour's Lounge; or, Poems.* London: Longman, Hurst,
       Rees, and Orme, 1805. 10.5 × 17.5 cm. 80 pp. By Richmal
       Mangnall. BL: 11633. aaa. 30.

MANNERS, Catherine Rebecca, Lady (1766–1852)

She was the daughter of Francis Grey, and came from Lehena, Co.
Cork. In 1790 she married William Manners (later Talmash, Lord
Huntingtower of Leicester). They had at least one child. (*Complete
Peerage*, Todd 1)

1(*a*) *Poems.* London: printed by John Bell, 1793. 16 × 23.5 cm.
        Pp. [ii] + 126. £1/1/- boards. By Lady Manners. CUL:
        XIV. 5. 48.

1(*b*) *Poems.* London: John Booth, G. G. and J. Robinson,
        B. and J. White, 1794. 11.5 × 18 cm. Pp. [ii] + 152. 3/-. By
        Lady Manners. BL: 11646. cc. 36.

2   *Review of Poetry, Ancient and Modern. A Poem.* London:
     J. Booth, 1799. 20.5 × 26.5 cm. 30 pp. 2/6. By Lady
     M******. *MR* 30: 390–3; BL: 11631. g. 9.

MANT, Alicia Catherine (died 1869)
She was the daughter of Richard Mant, the Master of King Edward's
Grammar School, Southampton, Hants, and of a Miss Bingham.
(Allibone, *NUC*)

1   *Rhymes for Ellen.* 1825. *EC.* Not located.

MANT, Elizabeth, Mrs Richard (died 1846), *see* COLLECTIONS
25(*a–c*)
She was an orphan, from a Sussex family named Wood. In 1804 she
married Richard Mant (who in 1820 became Bishop of Down, Connor,
and Dromore) and they had two children. (*DNB* (under Richard Mant))

MANWARING, Miss
1   *The Slaves of Zanguebar; and Other Poems.* Birmingham/
     London: R. Wrightson/Baldwin, Cradock, and Joy, 1826.
     10 × 18 cm. Pp. viii + 128. By Miss Manwaring. BL:
     11633. aaa. 31.

MARIA, *see* BROOKS, Maria

MARIA, Laura, *see* ROBINSON, Mary

MARIA DE OCCIDENTE, *see* BROOKS, Maria

MARIA SOPHIA
1   *The Grave of the Suicide; the Parting Kiss; and Other Poems.*
     London: William Charlton Wright, 1824. 9.5 × 16 cm. Pp.
     viii + 126. By Maria Sophia. BL: 11644. bb. 12.

MARLEY, Mrs, *see* COLLECTIONS 41

MARSHALL, Julia Ann, *see* ELLIOTT, Julia Ann

MARTIN, Sarah Catherine (1768–1826)
The attribution is traditional but uncertain. (*OCCL*)

1(*a*)   *The Comic Adventures of Old Mother Hubbard and her Dog* [engraved title-page]. London: J. Harris, 1805. 9 × 11.5 cm. [14] pp. [printed on one side only]. By S. M. C. Osborne: ii. 683.

1(*b*)   *The Comic Adventures of Old Mother Hubbard, and her Dog.* London: J. Harris, 1806. 2nd edn. 9 × 11.5 cm. 14 pp. BL: 12806. aa. 38(4).

1(*c*)   *Old Mother Hubbard and her Dog.* London: printed by John Evans, [1810?]. 6 × 9 cm. 16 pp. BL: 11622. a. 1(16).

1(*d*)   *The Comic Adventures of Old Mother Hubbard and her Dog. Part II. With the Tale of the Cat and a Fish.* York: printed by J. Kendrew, [181?]. 6 × 9 cm. 22 pp. Cornell: Wordsworth PR 974. Y62. v. 1. No. 14. [Photocopy seen only.]

1(*e*)   *The Comic Adventures of Old Mother Hubbard and her Dog* [cover serves as title-page]. New York: printed at Porcupine Office, 1810. 9.5 × 12 cm. 14 pp. [printed on one side only]. 2/- plain, 3/- coloured. AAS: DATED PAMS.

1(*f*)   *Mother Hubbard and her Dog.* Edinburgh: G. Ross, 1813. 6 × 10 cm. 18 pp. 1*d.* BL: 12804. de. 64(1).

1(*g*)   *The Diverting History of Old Mother Hubbard and her Dog.* Otley: William Walker, [1815?]. 5.5 × 8.5 cm. 15 pp. ½*d.* BL: 12804. a. 3(1).

1(*h*)   *The Adventures of Mother Hubbard and her Dog.* [Title-page is the paper cover.] Cork: West and Coldwells, [1820?]. New edn. 6.5 × 10 cm. 19 pp. 1*d.* BL: 012806. de. 16(8).

1(*i*)   *Old Mother Hubbard and her Dog.* [Derby: printed by Thomas Richardson, 182?.] 9 cm. 11 pp. *NUC.* Not found.

1(*j*)   *Mother Hubbard and her Dog.* Devonport: printed by S. and J. Keys, [1820?]. 11 cm. 12 pp. *NUC.* Not seen.

1(*k*)   *The Comic Adventures of Old Mother Hubbard and her Dog. Part I.* York: James Kendrew, [1820?]. 6.5 × 9.5 cm. 16 pp. BL: 12803. a. 56(7).

1(*l*)   *Old Mother Hubbard and her Dog.* Banbury: printed J. G. Rusher, [1820?]. 6 × 9 cm. 15 pp. BL: 12805. a. 5(8).

1(*m*)   *Mother Hubbard.* Philadelphia/New York/Boston[, Mass.]/ Baltimore: Turner and Fisher/169 Broadway/James

Fisher/J. Keller, [182?]. 12 × 15.5 cm. [8] pp. [printed on one side only]. Boston Public: **H. 99. c 213.

1(*n*)   *The Comic Adventures of Old Mother Hubbard, and her Dog: In Which are Shewn the Wonderful Powers that Good Old Lady Possessed in the Education of her Favourite Animal.* London: J. Harris and Son, 1821. 10.5 × 17.5 cm. 16 pp. [printed on one side only]. CUL: Lib. 7. 82. 28(2).

1(*o*)   *The Comic Adventures of Old Mother Hubbard, and her Dog: In Which are Shewn the Wonderful Powers that Good Old Lady Possessed in the Education of her Favourite Animal.* London: J. Harris and Son, 1824. 10.5 × 16.5 cm. 15 pp. [printed on one side only]. Bodley: 2522 f. 8(5).

1(*p*)   *Old Mother Hubbard, and her Wonderful Dog.* Cooperstown[, NY]: H. and E. Phinney, 1829. 6.5 × 10 cm. 31 pp. HEHL: 443164.

1(*q*)   *The Adventures of Old Mother Hubbard and her Dog* [title taken from cover]. London: D. Carvalho, [*c*.1830]. 6th edn. 10.5 × 17.5 cm. [8] pp. [printed on one side only]. 6*d*. coloured. Osborne: ii. 684.

2(*a*)   *A Continuation of the Comic Adventures of Old Mother Hubbard, and her Dog* [engraved title-page]. London: J. Harris, 1806. 9.5 × 11.5 cm. [14] pp. [printed on one side only]. By S. C. M. Osborne: ii. 684.

2(*b*)   *A Continuation of the Comic Adventures of Old Mother Hubbard, and her Dog.* London: J. Harris, 1807. 9.5 × 12.5 cm. [12] pp. [printed on one side only]. By S. C. M. NEDL: KC138/Juv807.8.

2(*c*)   *A Continuation of the Comic Adventures of Old Mother Hubbard, and her Dog.* Boston[, Mass.]: printed by N. Coverley, Jr., 1813. 6 × 10 cm. [12] pp. LC: Juv. Coll. 1813.

[*See also*: 'The Comical Adventures of Mother Hubbard and Her Dog' (1826, 7 pp.).]

MARTINEAU, Harriet (1802–76)
Born in Norwich, Norfolk. She was the third daughter of Thomas Martineau, a fabric manufacturer, and of Elizabeth Rankin. Her parents were Unitarians and members of William Taylor's literary circle. She

was educated mainly at home, but spent two years at school in Norwich. She suffered from deafness. Her *Illustrations of Political Economy* (9 vols., 1832–4) sold about 10,000 copies and made her a literary celebrity. She wrote more than fifty books and was deeply involved in social reform. (*CB*, *DNB*, Todd 2, V. Wheatley, *The Life and Work* . . . (1957))

1   *Addresses; with Prayers and Original Hymns, for the Use of Families and Schools.* London/Norwich: Rowland Hunter/ S. Wilkin, 1826. 10.5 × 18 cm. Pp. viii + 152 [verse on pp. 10, 21, 32–3, 44–5, 59–60, 74–5, 86–7, 97–8, 110–11, 121–2, 135–6, 151–2]. By a Lady, Authoress of *Devotional Exercises for the Use of Young Persons.* BL: 1115. b. 12(1).

MARY, *see also* ST JOHN, Mary

1   *Mary's Book of Hymns.* 2nd Series. Concord: Hoag and Atwood, 1831. 6 × 10 cm. 16 pp. LC: Juv. Coll. 1831.

MARY, Queen of Scots (1542–87), *see* COLLECTIONS 39, ROBERTS, Mary, *and pseudonym of* SHILLITO, Charles

MARY SOPHIA

1   *Poems, on Various Subjects.* London: Sherwood, Neely, and Jones, 1810. 10.5 × 17.5 cm. Pp. viii + 126. By Mary Sophia. Bodley: Harding C 1937.

MASON, Mrs

An American writer. Her poems record the deaths of various children surnamed Clark. Only the last three pages of her book are by Blodget.

1   *Ellegiac Poems, Sacred to Friendship.* [?Greenwich, Mass.: John Howe, 1803 (lacks a title-page)]. 10.5 × 17 cm. [12] pp. By Mrs Mason and [Joseph Blodget]. Houghton: *AC8. M3810. 803e.

MASTERS, Mary, Mrs (1694?–1771), *see* COLLECTIONS 12(*a–k*)

She was the daughter of a Norwich schoolmaster and the author of *Poems on Several Occasions* (1733). She was a friend of Elizabeth Carter (q.v.), Catherine Macaulay, and Samuel Johnson. (Blain)

MATHEWS, Elizabeth Kirkham, Mrs Charles (died 1802)

She was the daughter of Dr George Strong and his wife Mary. At the time of her marriage to the comic actor Charles Mathews in 1797 she was a schoolteacher in Swansea, Glamorganshire. Between 1789 and 1793 she wrote five unsuccessful novels. She died of consumption. (Blain, *DNB* (under Charles Mathews), Todd 1)

1(*a*) *Poems.* Exeter/London: G. Dyer/W. Richardson, [1796]. 12 × 18.5 cm. Pp. [ii] + x + 66 [subscription edition]. 2/-. By Elizabeth Kirkham Strong. *CR* 16: 464; Houghton: *EC75. D7596. 781pb(B).

1(*b*) *Poems.* Doncaster/York/London: W. Sheardown/for C. Mathews and the booksellers/Rivingtons, Miller, Lane, Mathews, 1802. 10 × 16.5 cm. Pp. xvi + 115 [subscription edition]. By the Late Mrs Charles Mathews. HEHL: 104471.

MATILDA, Anna, *see* COWLEY, Hannah

MATTHEWS, Elizabeth

She was the proprietor of a school for young ladies in Barnsbury Park, Islington, London. In 1828 she contributed to the annual *The Pledge of Friendship.* (Boyle)

1(*a*) *Original Hymns and Moral Poems.* Inference.

1(*b*) *Original Hymns and Moral Poems, for Children and Young Persons.* London/Islington: Hamilton, Adams, and Co./ J. K. Starling, 1835. 2nd edn. 8.5 × 13.5 cm. Pp. xii + 96. By Elizabeth Matthews and R. BL: 3434. aa. 59.

MAXWELL, Georgiana Caroline

1 *Feudal Tales, Being a Collection of Romantic Narratives, and Other Poems, Humbly Dedicated by Permission to His Royal Highness the Prince Regent.* London: T. Hookham, Jr. and E. T. Hookham, [1810?]. 13.5 × 21.5 cm. Pp. iv + 116. By Caroline Maxwell. BL: 11642. f. 16.

MEDLEY, Sarah

She seems to have been the daughter of Samuel Medley, a prominent Baptist minister and hymn writer, and of Mary Gill. She lived in Liverpool and published in Liverpool periodicals. (*DNB* (under Samuel Medley))

1   *Original Poems, Sacred and Miscellaneous.* Liverpool/London: W. Robinson, the booksellers/J. Johnson, 1807. 10 × 16 cm. Pp. [vi] + 228. By Sarah Medley. BL: 11633. aa. 33.

MERRYWEATHER, Mrs. I. A.
She lived in Whitby, Yorks., and had at least one son. (*The Hermit*)

1(*a*)   *The Hermit.* Inference.

1(*b*)   *The Hermit of Eskdaleside, with Other Poems.* Whitby/ London: R. Kirby/Simpkin and Marshall, 1833. [2nd edn.] 10 × 17 cm. Pp. [vi] + 138 [subscription edition]. By I. A. M. BL: 11646. bbb. 38.

MEYNELL, Anna, *see* COLLECTIONS 1(*a–b*)

MEZIERE, Harriet, Mrs, *see* CHILCOT, Harriet

MILLER, Ann

1   *Tributary Lines; on the Death of the Late Mr Henry Longden, of Sheffield.* Sheffield: J. Montgomery, 1812. 11.5 × 19.5 cm. 8 pp. By Ann Miller. BL: 1465. h. 13(7).

MILLER, Anne, 'Lady' (1741–81), *see also* COLLECTIONS 1(*a–c*)
Her father, Edward Riggs, was a commissioner of customs in London; Margaret Piggott was her mother. She was an heiress. In 1765 she married Captain John Miller (he was made an Irish baronet in 1778 and combined her name with his after 1780 as Riggs-Miller). Her title was a courtesy one only. She held a literary salon at Batheaston near Bath and her *Letters from Italy* (3 vols.) appeared in 1776. (*CB, DNB*, Ruth Avaline Hesselgrave, *Lady Miller and the Batheaston Literary Circle* (1972), Todd 1)

1   *On Novelty: And on Trifles, and Triflers. Poetical Amusements at a Villa near Bath.* Bath: R. Cruttwell and all the booksellers, 1778. 19.5 × 25 cm. Pp. [ii] + 17. BL: 11632. h. 3.

MILLS, Elizabeth Willesford
She later became Mrs Borron. She contributed to the annuals *Friendship's Offering* and *The Pledge of Friendship* in 1827–8. (Boyle)

1   *Sibyl's Leaves: Poems and Sketches.* London: Longman, Rees, Orme, and Co., and G. B. Whittaker, 1826. 11 × 17.5 cm.

Pp. viii + 260 [pp. 183–210 are in prose]. By Elizabeth Willesford Mills. LC: PR 4149. B96.

MILNE, Christian *or* Charlotte, Mrs Peter (1773–after 1816)

Born in Aberdeen. She was the daughter of Thomas Ross, a cabinet-maker, and Mary Gordon. She was discouraged from writing as a child and suffered from consumption. In 1796 she married Peter Milne, a journeyman ship-carpenter in Footdee, Aberdeen. They had at least eight children. The subscription to *Simple Poems* earned her £100. (Blain, and *Sketches of Obscure Poets, with Specimens of their Writings* (1833))

1   *Simple Poems, on Simple Subjects.* Aberdeen: printed for the author by J. Chalmers and Co., 1805. 11 × 19 cm. 183 pp. [subscription edition]. By Christian Milne, Wife of a Journeyman Ship-carpenter, in Footdee, Aberdeen. BL: 11645. bbb. 42.

MILNES, Esther, *see* DAY, Esther

MINIFIE, Susannah, *see* GUNNING, Susannah

MITFORD, Mary Russell (1787–1855), *see also* COLLECTIONS 41, 42, 43, 49(*a–b*), 56

Born in Alresford, Hants. She was the daughter of Dr George Mitford and Mary Russell. She was a precocious child. The family moved to London and then to Reading in increasingly straitened circumstances, but in 1797 she won a lottery prize of £20,000. She attended a ladies' school in London. By 1820 the family was again in difficulties. Her *Julian*, *Foscari*, and *Rienzi* were all produced in London and she was a major contributor to the annuals. She is best known for *Our Village* (5 vols., 1824–32). (*CB*, *DNB*, Schlueter, Todd 2, V. Watson, *Mary Russell Mitford* (1949))

1(*a*)   *Poems.* London: Longman, Hurst, Rees, and Orme, 1810. 9.5 × 15.5 cm. Pp. vi + 156. By Mary Russell Mitford. BL: 11644. ee. 18.

1(*b*)   *Poems.* London: F. C. and J. Rivington, 1811. 2nd edn. 12.5 × 21 cm. Pp. viii + 278. By Mary Russell Mitford. BL: 11646. h. 4.

2   *Christina, the Maid of the South Seas; a Poem.* London: F. C. and J. Rivington and J. Hatchard, 1811. 13 × 21 cm. Pp. xii + 333. By Mary Russell Mitford. BL: 11646. h. 5.

3   *Watlington Hill; a Poem.* London: printed by A. J. Valpy,
        1812. 11 × 18 cm. 48 pp. By Mary Russell Mitford. BL: T.
        1897(4).

4(*a*) *Narrative Poems on the Female Character, in the Various*
        Relations of Life. Vol. i [no more published?]. London:
        F. C. and J. Rivington, 1813. 13.5 × 21 cm. Pp. xii + 331.
        By Mary Russell Mitford, Author of *Christina* and a
        Volume of *Miscellaneous Poems.* BL: 11646. h. 6.

4(*b*) *Narrative Poems on the Female Character, in the Various*
        Relations of Life. Vol. i [no more published?]. New York:
        Eastburn, Kirk and Co., 1813. 8.5 × 13.5 cm. 206 pp. By
        Mary Russell Mitford, Author of *Christina* and a Volume
        of *Miscellaneous Poems.* Houghton: *EC8. M6967. 813nb.

5(*a*) *Julian, a Tragedy in Five Acts.* London: G. and W. B.
        Whittaker, 1823. 13 × 21 cm. Pp. xii + 84. By Mary
        Russell Mitford. BL: 11779. f. 50.

5(*b*) *Julian, a Tragedy in Five Acts.* New-York: William B. Gilley,
        1823. 9.5 × 15 cm. 93 pp. By Mary Russell Mitford. LC:
        PR 5022. J8 1823.

5(*c*) *Julian, a Tragedy in Five Acts.* London: G. and W. B.
        Whittaker, 1823. 2nd edn. 13.5 × 22 cm. Pp. xii + 83. 4/-.
        By Mary Russell Mitford. BL: 11779. d. 24.

5(*d*) *Julian, a Tragedy in Five Acts.* London: G. and W. B.
        Whittaker, 1823. 3rd edn. 13 × 21 cm. Pp. xii + 83. 4/-. By
        Mary Russell Mitford. BL: 643. f. 24(2).

5(*e*) *Julian: A Tragedy, in Five Acts . . . From the Acting Copy . . .*
        Ed. D——g. London: John Cumberland, [1829]. 8.5 ×
        14.5 cm. [In vol. xxxii of *Cumberland's British Theatre.*] 58
        pp. By Mary Russell Mitford. BL: 642. a. 16.

5(*f*) *Julian: A Tragedy. In Five Acts.* Philadelphia: Carey and Lea,
        1831. 12 × 21 cm. 87 pp. Michigan: 822. 8 M683j Buhr.
        [Photocopy seen only.]

6(*a*) *Foscari: A Tragedy.* London: G. B. Whittaker, 1826. 13 × 21
        cm. Pp. iv + 78. By Mary Russell Mitford. BL: T. 1180(6).

6(*b*) *Foscari. A Tragedy, in Five Acts.* London: John Cumberland,
        [1828]. 9 × 14.5 cm. 59 pp. By Mary Russell Mitford. [In
        vol. xxxviii of *Cumberland's British Theatre.*] BL: 642. a. 19.

7　　*Dramatic Scenes, Sonnets, and Other Poems*. London: Geo. B. Whittaker, 1827. 12 × 19 cm. Pp. [iv] + 392. 10/6. By Mary Russell Mitford. *MR* 5: 203–9; HEHL: 232165.

8　　*Foscari & Julian: Tragedies*. London: Geo. B. Whittaker, 1827. 11.5 × 19 cm. Pp. viii + 251. By Mary Russell Mitford. BL: 11779. bb. 54.

9(*a*)　*Rienzi: A Tragedy, in Five Acts*. London: John Cumberland, 1828. 10 × 16.5 cm. 48 pp. By Miss Mitford. BL: 11644. bbb. 40(1).

9(*b*)　*Rienzi. A Tragedy* . . . 2nd edn. Inference.

9(*c*)　*Rienzi: A Tragedy, in Five Acts . . . First Performed at the Theatre Royal, Drury Lane, October 9, 1828*. London: John Cumberland, 1828. 3rd edn. 10 × 17 cm. 66 pp. By Miss Mitford. BL: 11779. aa. 65.

9(*d*)　*Rienzi: A Tragedy, in Five Acts*. London: John Cumberland, 1828. 4th edn. 10.5 × 18 cm. 66 pp. By Miss Mitford. BL: T. 1209(6).

9(*e*)　*Rienzi: A Tragedy, in Five Acts*. London: John Cumberland, [1828]. 9 × 14.5 cm. 66 pp. By Mary Russell Mitford. [In vol. xxiv of *Cumberland's British Theatre*.] BL: 642. a. 12.

9(*f*)　*Rienzi: A Tragedy . . . In Five Acts . . . With Introductory Remarks*. Boston[, Mass.]: Press of the Boston Daily Advertiser, 1829. 1st American from 3rd London edn. 10.5 × 15.5 cm. 71 pp. By Miss Mitford. Pusey: TS Promptbook.

9(*g*)　*Rienzi: A Tragedy, in Five Acts . . . First Performed at the Theatre Royal, Drury Lane, October 9, 1828*. New York: Elton and Perkins, 1829. 10 × 15.5 cm. 69 pp. By Miss Mitford. Pusey: TS Promptbook.

10(*a*)　*Charles the First, an Historical Tragedy, in Five Acts*. London: John Duncombe and Co., 1834. 13.5 × 20.5 cm. Pp. viii + 80. By Mary Russell Mitford. BL: T. 1604(7).

10(*b*)　*Alexander's Modern Acting Drama: Consisting of the Most Popular Plays, Produced at the Philadelphia Theatres, and Elsewhere*. Philadelphia: Carey and Hart, Hogan and Thompson, and W. Marshall and Co., 1835. 8.5 × 12.5 cm. 2 vols. ['Charles the First, an Historical Tragedy' by Mary

Russell Mitford occupies pp. 1–79 of vol. i]. NYPL: NCO.

M–LL–R, Mrs, *see* MILLER, Anne

M—N–LL, Miss, *see* MEYNELL, Anna

MONCKTON, Hon. Charlotte Penelope (died *c*.1805)

She was the daughter of Robert Monckton-Arundell, 4th Viscount Galway, and of Elizabeth Mathew. (*Complete Peerage, Lines*)

1   *Lines. Written on Several Occasions.* [N.p., n. publisher], 1806. 10 × 7 cm. 59 pp. By the Late Honble Charlotte Penelope Monckton. Princeton: (Ex) 3862. 202. 358s.

MONTAGU, Eleanora Louisa (1811–1903)

She was the daughter of George Conway Montagu of Lackham, Wilts. In 1843 she married Thomas Kibble Hervey, poet and editor. She contributed regularly to annuals from 1835 on, and especially to *The Literary Souvenir.* (Boyle, *DNB* (under Thomas Kibble Hervey))

1   *Edith of Graystock. A Poem.* London: Henry Lindsell, 1833. 13 × 20 cm. 100 pp. By Eleanor M. BL: T. 1422(13).

2(*a*)   *The Bard of the Sea-kings a Legend of Kingley-Vale with Other Poems.* Chichester: William Mason, 1833. 11.5 × 19 cm. 80 pp. By Eleanora Louisa Montagu. BL: T. 1457(11).

2(*b*)   *The Bard of the Sea-kings a Legend of Kingley-Vale with Other Poems.* London: Longman, Rees, Orme, Brown, Green, and Longman, 1833. 10.5 × 17 cm. 80 pp. By Eleanora Louisa Montagu. BL: 11644. eeee. 39.

MONTAGU, Lady Mary Wortley (1689–1762)

Born in London. She was the daughter of Evelyn Pierrepoint and Lady Mary Fielding. She married Edward Wortley Montagu in 1712 and they travelled widely. Her husband was ambassador to Turkey. They had two children. She did not publish under her own name but she contributed to the *Spectator* and collaborated with Pope and Gay. She is best known for her posthumous letters from Turkey and for championing the smallpox inoculation. (*CB, DNB*, Robert Halsband, *The Life* . . . (1957))

1(*a*)   *The Works . . . Including her Correspondence, Poems and Essays. Published by Permission from her Genuine Papers.* Ed.

[J. Dallaway]. London: Richard Phillips, 1803. 11 × 18.5 cm. 5 vols. [verse occupies pp. 97–254 of vol. v only]. £2 boards. By the Right Honourable Lady Mary Wortley Montagu. BL: 94. c. 18–22.

1(*b*) *The Works . . . Including her Correspondence, Poems, and Essays. Published by Permission from her Genuine Papers.* London: Richard Phillips, 1803. 10 × 17 cm. 5 vols. [the verse occupying pp. 105–262 of vol. v]. By the Right Honorable Lady Mary Wortley Montagu. BL: 1086. b. 19, 20.

1(*c*) *The Works.* 3rd edn. Inference.

1(*d*) *The Works . . . Including her Correspondence, Poems, and Essays. Published, by Permission, from her Genuine Papers.* London: Richard Phillips, 1805. 9.5 × 15.5 cm. 5 vols. By the Right Honourable Lady Mary Wortley Montagu. NEDL: KC12621.

1(*e*) *The Works . . . Including her Correspondence, Poems, and Essays. Published, by Permission, from her Genuine Papers.* London: Richard Phillips, 1805. 5th edn. 9.5 × 15.5 cm. 5 vols. [the verse occupying pp. 99–211 of vol. v]. By the Right Honourable Lady Mary Wortley Montagu. BL: 12295. bb. 1.

1(*f*) *The Works . . . Including her Correspondence, Poems, and Essays. Published, by Permission, from her Genuine Papers.* London: Richard Phillips, 1811. 6th edn. 7 × 13 cm. 2 vols. [the poetry being in vol. ii]. By the Right Honourable Lady Mary Wortley Montagu. Widener: 15494. 9.

1(*g*) *The Works . . . Including her Correspondence, Poems, and Essays. Published, by Permission, from her Genuine Papers.* London: Longman, Hurst, Rees, Orme, and Brown, John Murray, and Baldwin, Cradock, and Joy, 1817. 6th edn. 11.5 × 18.5 cm. 5 vols. [the poems being found in vol. v]. By the Right Honourable Lady Mary Wortley Montagu. Hilles: 824. M1. 1. 1.

1(*h*) *The Works . . . Including her Correspondence, Poems, and Essays. From her Genuine Papers.* London: printed for the proprietors by J. F. Dove, 1825. 7 × 12.5 cm. 560 pp. [the verse occupying pp. 462–529]. By the Right Honourable Lady Mary Wortley Montagu. Bodley: 2699 f. 330.

MONTAGUE, Lady Mary Seymour

1   *An Original Essay on Woman, in Four Epistles.* London: John
     Swan, 1771. 19.5 × 25 cm. Pp. xii + 55. 2/6. By a Lady.
     BL: 11602. gg. 29(10).

MONTOLIEU, Maria Henrietta, Mrs

1(*a*)   *The Gardens, a Poem.* Trans. [Mrs Montolieu]. London:
         printed by T. Bensley, 1798. 20.5 × 27 cm. Pp. [iv] + 120.
         By Abbé de Lille. BL: 83. g. 9.

1(*b*)   *The Gardens, a Poem.* Trans. Mrs Montolieu. London:
         Robson, White, Evans, and Kerby, 1805. 2nd edn. 13.5 ×
         22.5 cm. 147 pp. By the Abbé De Lille. BL: 11474. h. 18.

2(*a*)   *The Enchanted Plants, Fables in Verse. Inscribed to Miss
         Montolieu, and Miss Julia Montolieu.* London: printed by
         Thomas Bensley, 1800. 13.5 × 21.5 cm. Pp. [iv] + 93. 5/-
         boards. *MR* 33: 311–12; BL: 11642. f. 17.

2(*b*)   *The Enchanted Plants, Fables in Verse.* London: printed by
         Thomas Bensley, 1801. 2nd edn. 9.5 × 15.5 cm. Pp. viii +
         95. BL: 11644. aaa. 43.

2(*c*)   *The Enchanted Plants; Fables in Verse. Inscribed to Miss
         Montolieu, and Miss Julia Montolieu.* London: E. and S.
         Harding, 1803. 10.5 × 17 cm. 117 pp. Boston Public: XJ.
         803. M76E.

2(*d*)   *The Enchanted Plants; Fables in Verse. Inscribed to Miss
         Montolieu, and Miss Julia Montolieu.* New York: David
         Longworth, 1803. 10 × 16.5 cm. 117 pp. LC: PR 5036. M8
         E6 Office.

3   *The Festival of the Rose, with Other Poems.* London: printed
     by T. Bensley, 1802. 18.5 × 23.5 cm. Pp. vi + 77. By Mrs
     Montolieu. BL: 11632. g. 32.

4(*a*)   *The Enchanted Plants and Festival of the Rose, with Other Poems.*
         London: printed by Thomas Bensley, 1812. 11 × 18.5 cm.
         Pp. viii + 168. By Mrs Montolieu. BL: 1164. e. 13.

4(*b*)   *The Enchanted Plants, and Festival of the Rose, with Other
         Poems.* London: John Murray, 1822. 12 × 20 cm. Pp. viii +
         167. By Mrs Montolieu. BL: 11644. ccc. 31.

5   *Gethsemane, a Poem; Founded on the Messiah of Klopstock.*
London: R. H. Evans and J. Eedes, 1823. 11 × 16.5 cm. 2
vols. By Mrs Montolieu, Authoress of *The Enchanted
Plants*, &c. &c. BL: 994. a. 17.

MOODIE, Susanna, Mrs John Wedderburn, *see* STRICKLAND,
Susanna

MOODY, Elizabeth, Mrs Christopher Lake (died 1814), *see also*
COLLECTIONS 23(*a–b*)
Her unmarried name was Greenly. Her husband was a clergyman.
Some of her poems were included in the posthumous edition of
Edward Lovibond's poems in 1785. She reviewed for *MR* from 1789 to
1808. (Blain)

1   *Poetic Trifles.* London: T. Cadell, Jr., and W. Davies, 1798.
10 × 17.5 cm. Pp. xvi + 186. By Elizabeth Moody. BL:
11633. aaa. 32.

[*See also*: 'Anna's Complaint; or, the Miseries of War . . .' (in
Humanitas [George Miller], *War a System of Madness and Irreligion*
[1796], pp. 63–4).]

MOORE, Jane Elizabeth, Mrs (born 1738)
Her parents were French. Her father, M. Gobeil, was a leather manufacturer. She was sent away to school at the age of 3 following the
death of her mother. In 1761 she married Moore, a tradesman who
died in 1781, leaving her in financial difficulties. They had a daughter who
died in infancy. In 1785 her name appears in a list of bankrupts and she
is termed a 'leather dresser'; by that time she was living in Bermondsey,
London. (*GM, Genuine Memoirs of Jane Elizabeth Moore* (1785))

1   *Miscellaneous Poems, on Various Subjects.* Dublin: printed for
the author, 1796. 12.5 × 21.5 cm. Pp. [vi] + 158 [subscrip-
tion edition]. By Jane Elizabeth Moore. BL: 1164. i. 1.

[*See also*: 'Index' (6 pp.) in her *Genuine Memoirs . . .* (1785).]

MORE, Hannah (1745–1833), *see also* COLLECTIONS 10(*b*), 11(*b*),
12(*a–k*), 15(*a–o*), 17, 23(*a–b*), 25(*a–c*), 34(*a–b*), 44, 50(*a–c*), 52, *and*
FENN, Lady Eleanor
Born at Stapleton, near Bristol. She was the fourth of five daughters of
Jacob More, a schoolmaster, and of Mary Grace, a farmer's daughter.

Her parents made a point of preparing their daughters to be capable of making a useful independent living, and Hannah, because of her unusual promise, had Latin and mathematics included in her education. She was in turn a schoolteacher with her sisters in Bristol, a successful playwright in London, and a social reformer who took an active part in the campaigns to abolish the slave trade. She wrote numerous moral tracts for the labouring poor in association with the Clapham sect and organized practical experiments in the education of workers' families in the rural south-west. Her novel *Coeleb's in Search of a Wife* (1808) went through eleven editions in nine months, earning a profit of £2,000. Her popular poem *The Search for Happiness* appeared with her name in 1773 but was first published, anonymously, in 1768 and is therefore omitted from the list that follows. (*CB, DNB*, M. G. Jones, *Hannah More* (1952))

1(*a*) *The Inflexible Captive: A Tragedy.* Bristol/London/Bath: S. Farley and T. Cadell/T. Cadell, Carnan and Newbery, and J. Wilkie/Frederic and Bull, 1774. 13 × 21 cm. Pp. [vi] + 83. 1/6. By Miss Hannah More. *MR* 50: 243–51; BL: 162. k. 22.

1(*b*) *The Inflexible Captive: A Tragedy.* Bristol/London/Bath: S. Farley and T. Cadell/T. Cadell, Carnan and Newbery, and J. Wilkie/Frederic and Bull, 1774. 2nd edn. 10.5 × 17.5 cm. Pp. [vi] + 83. 1/6. By Miss Hannah More. BL: 11777. f. 53.

1(*c*) *The Inflexible Captive. A Tragedy.* Philadelphia: John Sparhawk, 1774. 3rd edn. 9.5 × 15.5 cm. Pp. [vi] + 70. By Miss Hannah Moore. LC: PR 3605. M6 A64 1774 copy 2.

1(*d*) *The Inflexible Captive: A Tragedy.* Bristol/London/Bath: S. Farley and T. Cadell/T. Cadell, Carnan and Newbery, and J. Wilkie/Frederic and Bull, 1774. 3rd edn. 12.5 × 19.5 cm. Pp. vi + 83. 1/6. By Miss Hannah More. BL: 11778. e. 22.

1(*e*) *The Inflexible Captive. A Tragedy.* Dublin: J. Williams, 1775. 9.5 × 16.5 cm. Pp. [vi] + 52. By Miss Hannah More. BL: 640. h. 35(8).

2(*a*) *Sir Eldred of the Bower, and the Bleeding Rock: Two Legendary Tales.* London: T. Cadell, 1776. 21.5 × 26.5 cm. Pp. [iv] + 49. 2/6. By Miss Hannah More. *MR* 54: 89–99; BL: 643. k. 12(7).

2(*b*) *Sir Eldred of the Bower, and the Bleeding Rock: Two Legendary Tales.* Dublin: W. Sleater, S. Price, W. Whitestone, J. Potts,

R. Cross, J. Williams, W. Colles, T. Walker, W. Wilson, W. Watson, S. Watson, T. Wilkinson, J. Hoey, R. Moncrieffe, J. Sheppard, W. Halhead, W. Spotswood, R. Stewart, T. Stewart, E. Cross, C. Jenkin, J. Hillary, T. Armitage, W. Gilbert, H. Burrowes, M. Mills, P. Higly, 1776. 11 × 17.5 cm. 32 pp. By Miss Hannah More. BL: 11630. bb. 3(3).

2(*c*)   *Sir Eldred of the Bower, and the Bleeding Rock: Two Legendary Tales.* London: T. Cadell, 1778. 2nd edn. 13 × 21 cm. Pp. [ii] + 49. By Miss Hannah More. CUL: 7720. c. 222.

2(*d*)   *Sir Eldred of the Bower, and the Bleeding Rock . . . The Splendid Shilling . . . Scenes of my Youth and Damon and Alfreda . . .* London: J. Roach, 1794 [No. VII of *Roach's Beauties of the Poets*]. 9 × 15.5 cm. 60 pp. 6*d*. By Miss Hannah More and others. BL: 11601. e. 20.

2(*e*)   *Sir Eldred of the Bower; a Legendary Tale, in Two Parts . . . and Edwin and Emma.* Manchester/London: G. Bancks/Lee and Hurst, [1800?]. 9 × 15 cm. 24 pp. By Hannah More and Mr Mallet. BL: 012611. de. 1(3).

3   *Ode to Dragon, Mr Garrick's House-dog, at Hampton.* London: T. Cadell, 1777. 17 × 22 cm. 14 pp. 6*d*. MR 56: 314; BL: 163. l. 67.

4(*a*)   *Percy, a Tragedy. As It is Acted at the Theatre-Royal in Covent-Garden.* London: T. Cadell, 1778. 13 × 20.5 cm. Pp. [vi] + 87. 1/6. BL: 11778. g. 29(3).

4(*b*)   *Percy, a Tragedy. As It is Acted at the Theatre-Royal in Covent-Garden.* Dublin: the Company of Booksellers, [n.d.]. 9.5 × 14.5 cm. Pp. [vi] + 62. Widener: 20427. 13. 77.

4(*c*)   *Percy, a Tragedy. As It is Acted at the Theatre-Royal in Covent-Garden.* Belfast: printed by James Magee, 1778. 9.5 × 16.5 cm. Pp. [vi] + 62. Bodley: Vet. A5. f. 1758.

4(*d*)   *Percy, a Tragedy. As It is Acted at the Theatre-Royal in Covent-Garden.* London: T. Cadell, 1778. 2nd edn. 12 × 19.5 cm. Pp. [vi] + 87. 1/6. Leeds: Special Collections/English K-O.033.

4(*e*)   *Percy, a Tragedy. As It is Acted at the Theatre-Royal in Covent-Garden.* London: T. Cadell, 1780. 3rd edn. 12.5 × 21 cm. Pp. [vi] + 87. 1/6. BL: 11778. g. 28(1).

4(*f*)   *Percy, a Tragedy. As It is Acted at the Theatre-Royal in Covent-Garden.* London: T. Cadell, 1784. 3rd edn. 12.5 × 20.5 cm. Pp. [vi] + 87. 1/6. Yale (Sterling): Im/813/778Pc.

4(*g*)   *Percy, a Tragedy. As It is Acted at the Theatre-Royal in Covent-Garden.* Dublin: R. Marchbank, 1785. 9.5 × 16.5 cm. Pp. [vi] + 62. BL: 11775. bb. 2.

4(*h*)   *Percy, a Tragedy. As It is Acted at the Theatre-Royal in Covent-Garden.* London: T. Cadell, 1788. 4th edn. 12 × 20 cm. Pp. [vi] + 87. 1/6. BL: 643. g. 18(7).

4(*i*)   *Percy: A Tragedy. . . . as Performed at the Theatres Royal Drury-Lane and Covent-Garden, Printed, under the Authority of the Managers, from the Prompt-book.* London: John Fairburn, [n.d.]. 8.5 × 14 cm. 48 pp. 6*d.* By Miss Hannah More. Widener: 20427. 13. 79.

4(*j*)   *Percy: A Tragedy . . . Adapted for Theatrical Representation, as Performed at the Theatres-Royal, London.* [*Deans' Edition of the British Theatre.*] Manchester/London/York: R. and W. Dean/Champante and Whitrow, B. Crosby and Co., Longman, Hurst, Rees, and Orme/Wilson and Spence, 1807. 8.5 × 15.5. 50 pp. 8*d.* By Hannah More. Leeds: Brotherton Collection.

4(*k*)   *The Modern Theatre; a Collection of Successful Modern Plays, as Acted at the Theatres Royal, London . . .* Vol. vii [of 10]. Ed. Mrs Inchbald. London: Longman, Hurst, Rees, Orme, and Brown, 1811. 8.5 × 15.5 cm. ['Percy, a Tragedy, in Five Acts. As Performed at the Theatre Royal, Covent-Garden' occupies pp. 181–236.] BL: 1345. b. 5.

4(*l*)   *Percy, a Tragedy. As It is Acted at the Theatre Royal in Covent-Garden.* London: T. Cadell and W. Davies, 1812. 5th edn. 13.5 × 22 cm. Pp. [vi] + 55. BL: 11777. f. 57.

4(*m*)   *Percy. A Tragedy, in Five Acts . . . Correctly Given, as Performed at the Theatres Royal.* [In *The English Theatre* (13 vols.), 'Tragedies', vol. iv.] London/Dublin/Edinburgh: D. S. Maurice, T. Hughes, J. Bysh/J. Cumming/J. Sutherland, [1815?]. 7.5 × 11.5 cm. 58 pp. By Mrs Hannah More. Leeds: Brotherton Collection.

4(*n*)   *Percy. A Tragedy, in Five Acts.* [Vol. x of *The English Theatre.*] London/Dublin/Edinburgh: D. S. Maurice, T. Hughes,

J. Bysh/J. Cumming/J. Sutherland, [1819]. 7 × 12 cm. 58
pp. By Mrs Hannah More. Houghton: *AC85. Al191.
Zz820e. v. 10.

4(*o*)   *The British Drama. A Collection of the Most Approved Tragedies,*
Comedies, Operas, & Farces. London: Jones and Co., 1824.
13.5 × 21 cm. 2 vols. ['Percy: A Tragedy, in Five Acts' by
Hannah More occupies pp. 517–31 of vol. i.] NYPL:
NCO.

5(*a*)   *The Works . . . in Prose and Verse.* Cork: printed by Thomas
White, 1778. 10 × 17 cm. Pp. [vi] + 415. [Verse occupies
pp. 135–415.] BL: 12271. aaa. 13.

5(*b*)   *The Works . . . in Prose and Verse.* Cork/Dublin: Thomas
White/P. Byrne, 1789. 10 × 17 cm. Pp. [vi] + 309. By Miss
Hannah More. Yale (Beinecke): 1974/3353.

5(*c*)   *The Works . . . In Eight Volumes: Including Some Pieces never*
before Published. London: T. Cadell, Jr., and W. Davies,
1801. 12 × 19 cm. 8 vols. [The verse is contained in vols.
i–iii.] By Hannah More. BL: 12269. bbb. 18.

5(*d*)   *The Works . . . Including Several Pieces never before Published.*
Dublin: D. Graisberry, 1803. 12.5 × 20.5 cm. 4 vols. [sub-
scription edition; the verse occupying vol. i and part of
vol. ii]. By Hannah More. Yale (Sterling): Im/M813/
C801b/1–4.

5(*e*)   *The Works . . . Including Several Pieces never before Published.*
Philadelphia/New York: Edward Earle/Eastburn, Kirk
and Co., 1813–14. 8.5 × 14 cm. 8 vols. [Verse confined to
vols. i and ii.] By Hannah More. Widener: 20426. 5.

5(*f*)   *The Works . . . Including Several Pieces never before Published.*
Philadelphia: Edward Earle, 1818. 10.5 × 17.5 cm. 8 vols.
[the verse is confined to vol. i]. By Hannah More. Yale
(Beinecke): 1974/3337.

5(*g*)   *The Works.* London: T. Cadell and W. Davies, 1818–19.
New edn. 12 × 19.5 cm. 18 vols. [actually 19]. [Verse in
vols. i–iii and in vol. vi, pp. 443–64.] By Hannah More.
BL: 12271. cc.

5(*h*)   *The Works.* London: T. Cadell, 1830. New edn. 11.5 × 19.5
cm. 11 vols. [Verse in vols. i and ii only.] By Hannah
More. BL: 494. a. 9.

5(*i*)　*The Works of Hannah More*. London: H. Fisher, R. Fisher and P. Jackson, 1834. 10 × 16.5 cm. 6 vols. [The verse is contained in vols. v and vi.] BL: 493. a. 25.

5(*j*)　*The Works*. New York/Boston[, Mass.]: Harper and Brothers/Munroe and Francis, 1835. 12 × 20 cm. 7 vols. [Verse confined to vols. i and v–vii.] By Hannah More. Widener: 20426. 8. 5.

6(*a*)　*The Fatal Falsehood: A Tragedy. As It is Acted at the Theatre-Royal, in Covent Garden*. London: T. Cadell, 1779. 8vo. Pp. viii + 83. 1/6. By the Author of *Percy*. BL: 11778. f. 18.

6(*b*)　*The Fatal Falsehood: A Tragedy. As It is Acted at the Theatre-Royal, in Covent-Garden*. London: T. Cadell, 1780. 2nd edn. 12 × 21 cm. Pp. viii + 83. 1/6. By the Author of *Percy*. BL: 11778. g. 28(2).

6(*c*)　*The Fatal Falsehood: A Tragedy. As It is Acted at the Theatre-Royal, in Covent-Garden*. London: T. Cadell, 1789. 3rd edn. 12 × 20.5 cm. Pp. viii + 83. 1/6. By the Author of *Percy*. Yale (Beinecke): Plays 596.

7(*a*)　*Sacred Dramas: Chiefly Intended for Young Persons: The Subjects Taken from the Bible. To Which is Added, Sensibility, a Poem*. London: T. Cadell, 1782. 11 × 18 cm. Pp. xii + 290. BL: 82. c. 24.

7(*b*)　*Sacred Dramas; Chiefly Intended for Young Persons: The Subjects Taken from the Bible. To Which is Added, Sensibility, a Poem*. London: T. Cadell, 1782. 2nd edn. 10.5 × 17.5 cm. Pp. xii + 290. Library Co. of Philadelphia: O Eng More/687.D.

7(*c*)　*Sacred Dramas; Chiefly Intended for Young Persons: The Subjects Taken from the Bible. To Which is Added, Sensibility, a Poem*. London: T. Cadell, 1783. 3rd edn. 11 × 18.5 cm. Pp. xii + 290. BL: 11778. aaa. 1.

7(*d*)　*Sacred Dramas; Chiefly Intended for Young Persons: The Subjects Taken from the Bible. To Which is Added, Sensibility, a Poem*. Dublin: printed by P. Byrne, 1784. 10.5 × 17.5 cm. Pp. xiv + 269. By Miss Hannah More. CUL: Hib. 7. 784. 76.

7(*e*)　*Sacred Dramas; Chiefly Intended for Young Persons: The Subjects Taken from the Bible. To Which is Added, Sensibility, a Poem*. London: T. Cadell, 1785. 4th edn. 11 × 18 cm. Pp. xii + 290. BL: 641. c. 29.

7(*f*) *Sacred Dramas; Chiefly Intended for Young Persons: The Subjects Taken from the Bible. To Which is Added, Sensibility, a Poem.* London: T. Cadell, 1787. 5th edn. 11 × 18 cm. Pp. xii + 290. Bodley: M. Adds. 108. e. 59.

7(*g*) *Sacred Dramas, Chiefly Intended for Young Persons: The Subjects Taken from the Bible. To Which are Added: Reflections of King Hezekiah, Sensibility, a Poem. And Essays on Various Subjects, Principally Designed for Young Ladies.* Philadelphia: Thomas Dobson, 1787. 9 × 15 cm. 191 pp. By Hannah More. HEHL: 386906.

7(*h*) *Sacred Dramas, Chiefly Intended for Young Persons: The Subjects Taken from the Bible. To Which are Added: Reflections of King Hezekiah, and Sensibility, a Poem.* Philadelphia: Thomas Dobson, 1787. 9 × 15 cm. 191 pp. By Hannah More. Houghton: *EC75. M8134. 782sf.

7(*i*) *Sacred Dramas: Chiefly Intended for Young Persons: The Subjects Taken from the Bible. To Which is Added, Sensibility, a Poem.* London: T. Cadell, 1789. 6th edn. 11 × 18 cm. Pp. xii + 290. BL: 11778. aaa. 29.

7(*j*) *Sacred Dramas: Chiefly Intended for Young Persons: The Subjects Taken from the Bible. To Which is Added, Sensibility, a Poem.* London: T. Cadell, 1791. 7th edn. 11.5 × 18 cm. Pp. xii + 290. HEHL: 66861.

7(*k*) *Sacred Dramas: Chiefly Intended for Young Persons. The Subjects Taken from the Bible. To Which is Added, Sensibility, a Poem.* London: T. Cadell, 1793. 8th edn. 11.5 × 18 cm. Pp. xii + 290 [the final page is misnumbered 260]. BL: 11784. aaa. 40.

7(*l*) *Sacred Dramas, Chiefly Intended for Young Persons; the Subjects Taken from the Bible. To Which is Added, Sensibility, a Poem.* London: T. Cadell and W. Davies, 1796. 9th edn. Pp. 10 + 260. *NUC.* Not seen.

7(*m*) *Sacred Dramas: Chiefly Intended for Young Persons. The Subjects Taken from the Bible. To Which is Added, Sensibility, a Poem.* London: T. Cadell, Jr., and W. Davies, 1798. 10th edn. 11.5 × 18 cm. Pp. xii + 290. Union: VT 29/M83/1798.

7(*n*) *Sacred Dramas: Chiefly Intended for Young Persons. The Subjects Taken from the Bible. To Which is Added, Sensibility, a Poem.*

London: T. Cadell, Jr., and W. Davies, 1799. 11th edn. 12 × 18.5 cm. Pp. xii + 290. CUL: 7100. d. 761.

7(*o*) *Sacred Dramas: Chiefly Intended for Young Persons. The Subjects Taken from the Bible.* London: T. Cadell, Jr., and W. Davies, 1800. 12th edn. 11 × 17.5 cm. 272 pp. BL: 11785. c. 6.

7(*p*) *Sacred Dramas, Chiefly Intended for Young Persons: The Subjects Taken from the Bible. To Which are Added, Reflections of King Hezekiah; Sensibility, a Poem; and Search after Happiness.* Boston[, Mass.]: Manning and Loring, 1801. 10 × 16 cm. 190 pp. By Hannah More. UCLA: CBC M81s 1801.

7(*q*) *Sacred Dramas: Chiefly Intended for Young Persons. The Subjects Taken from the Bible.* London: T. Cadell, Jr., and W. Davies, 1802. 13th edn. 11.5 × 18 cm. 271 pp. By Hannah More. BL: 1342. m. 32.

7(*r*) *Sacred Dramas: Chiefly Intended for Young Persons. The Subjects Taken from the Bible.* London: T. Cadell and W. Davies, 1805. 14th edn. 11.5 × 18 cm. 271 pp. By Hannah More. NEDL: KD61472.

7(*s*) *Sacred Dramas, Chiefly Intended for Young Persons: Subjects Taken from the Bible. To Which are Added, Reflections of King Hezekiah; Sensibility, a Poem; and Search after Happiness.* Newark[, NJ]: printed by W. Tuttle, 1806. 10 × 17 cm. 192 pp. By Hannah More. HEHL: 186129.

7(*t*) *Sacred Dramas: Chiefly Intended for Young Persons. The Subjects Taken from the Bible. To Which is Added Sensibility: An Epistle.* London: T. Cadell and W. Davies, 1809. 15th edn. 12 × 18 cm. 294 pp. By Hannah More. Leeds: Special Collections/English L-60 MOR.

7(*u*) *Sacred Dramas: Chiefly Intended for Young Persons. The Subjects Taken from the Bible. To Which is Added Sensibility: An Epistle.* London: T. Cadell, and W. Davies, 1810. 16th edn. 11.5 × 18 cm. By Hannah More. Yale (Sterling): Im/M813/182J.

7(*v*) *Sacred Dramas, Chiefly Intended for Young Persons: The Subjects Taken from the Bible. To Which are Added, Reflections of King Hezekiah; Sensibility, a Poem; and Search after Happiness.* Boston[, Mass.]: John West and Co., 1811. 10.5 × 17 cm. 191 pp. By Hannah More. LC: Juv. Coll. 1811.

7(*w*) *Sacred Dramas: Chiefly Intended for Young Persons. The Subjects Taken from the Bible. To Which is Added Sensibility: An Epistle.* London: T. Cadell and W. Davies, 1812. 17th edn. 11.5 × 19 cm. Pp. xii + 275. By Hannah More. BL: 1344. g. 9.

7(*x*) *Sacred Dramas: Chiefly Intended for Young Persons. The Subjects Taken from the Bible. To Which is Added Sensibility: An Epistle.* London: T. Cadell and W. Davies, 1815. 18th edn. 11.5 × 20 cm. Pp. xii + 287. By Hannah More. BL: 994. h. 19.

7(*y*) *Sacred Dramas: Chiefly Intended for Young Persons. The Subjects Taken from the Bible. To Which is Added, Sensibility: An Epistle.* London: T. Cadell and W. Davies, 1815. 19th edn. 7.5 × 12 cm. 200 pp. By Hannah More. Bodley: M. Adds. 108 f. 32.

7(*z*) *Sacred Dramas: Chiefly Intended for Young Persons. The Subjects being Taken from the Bible. To Which is Added, Sensibility: An Epistle.* London: T. Cadell and W. Davies, 1815. 20th edn. 7 × 12 cm. 200 pp. By Hannah More. Bodley: M. Adds. 108 f. 204.

7(*aa*) *Sacred Dramas. Chiefly Intended for Young Persons. The Subjects Taken from the Bible.* London/Birmingham: Whittingham and Arliss/Beilby and Knotts, 1816. New edn. 7.5 × 11.5 cm. Pp. 10 + 176. By Hannah More. BL: 11646. ppp. 18.

7(*bb*) *Sacred Dramas. Chiefly Intended for Young Persons. The Subjects Taken from the Bible.* London: C. Whittingham and R. Jennings, 1818. 8 × 12.5 cm. 184 pp. By Hannah More. Illinois: 821 Q 2E. 1818. [Photocopy seen only.]

7(*cc*) *Sacred Dramas: Chiefly Intended for Young Persons. The Subjects Taken from the Bible. To Which is Added, Sensibility: An Epistle.* London: T. Cadell and W. Davies, 1820. 22nd edn. 6.5 × 12 cm. 200 pp. By Hannah More. NLS: NG. 1586. g. 31.

7(*dd*) *Sacred Dramas. Chiefly Intended for Young Persons. The Subjects Taken from the Bible . . . With a Memoir of the Author.* Ed. [Anon.]. London/Edinburgh/Glasgow: R. Jennings, T. Tegg, A. K. Newman and Co./J. Sutherland/Richard Griffin and Co., 1823. 8 × 12.5 cm. 176 pp. By Hannah More. Bodley: Mal. K. 76.

7(*ee*) *Sacred Dramas; Chiefly Intended for Young Persons. The Subjects Taken from the Bible.* Edinburgh: Oliver and Boyd, [1825?]. New edn. 8 × 14 cm. 168 pp. By Hannah More. BL: 11783. a. 66.

7(*ff*) *Sacred Dramas, to Which are Added Reflections of King Hezekiah; Sensibility, a Poem; and Search after Happiness.* [Princeton, NJ?]: D. A. Borrenstein, 1826. 8 × 13 cm. 209 pp. By Hannah More. HEHL: 314822.

7(*gg*) *Sacred Dramas. Chiefly Intended for Young Persons. The Subjects Taken from the Bible . . .* London/Glasgow: Thomas Tegg, N. Hailes, Bowdery and Kerby/Richard Griffin and Co., 1827. 8 × 13 cm. 176 pp. By Hannah More. BL: 11658. de. 23.

7(*hh*) *Sacred Dramas: Chiefly Intended for Young Persons. The Subjects Taken from the Bible. To Which is Added, Sensibility: An Epistle.* London: T. Cadell, 1829. 24th edn. 12 × 20 cm. Pp. x + 178. By Hannah More. Houghton: *EC75. M8134. 782st.

7(*ii*) *Sacred Dramas: Chiefly Intended for Young Persons: The Subjects Taken from the Bible. To Which are Added Reflections of King Hezekiah, Parley the Porter, etc.* New York: Daniel Cooledge, 1834. 7 × 10.5 cm. 192 pp. By Hannah More. Boston Public: 7459a. 48.

8 *Sensibility: A Poetical Epistle to the Hon. Mrs Boscawen.* New Haven[, Conn.]: printed by Meigs, Bowen and Dana, [1785?]. 9 × 15 cm. 16 pp. By Miss More. Yale (Beinecke): Im/M813/785.

9 *Poems . . . to Wit, Sensibility; and Reflections of King Hezekiah.* Philadelphia: printed by Young, Stewart, and M'Culloch, 1785. 8 × 13.5 cm. 24 pp. By Miss Hannah More. Library Co. of Philadelphia: Api 785/y44.

10(*a*) *Florio: A Tale, for Fine Gentlemen and Fine Ladies: And, the Bas Bleu; or, Conversation: Two Poems.* London: T. Cadell, 1786. 18.5 × 24 cm. Pp. viii + 89. 3/-. BL: 11630. d. 4(1).

10(*b*) *Florio: A Tale, for Fine Gentlemen and Fine Ladies: And, the Bas Bleu; or, Conversation: Two Poems.* Dublin: Colles, White, Byrne, Cash, Heery, M'Kenzie and Moore, 1786. 11 × 18 cm. 95 pp. BL: 12699. a. 9(3).

10(*c*) *Florio: A Tale, for Fine Gentlemen and Fine Ladies: And, the Bas Bleu; or, Conversation. Two Poems.* London: T. Cadell, 1787. 2nd edn. 20.5 × 25.5 cm. Pp. viii + 89. 3/-. BL: 11641. g. 27.

11(*a*) *Slavery, a Poem.* London: T. Cadell, 1788. 20.5 × 25.5 cm. 20 pp. 1/6. By Hannah More. *MR* 78: 246–7; BL: 840. l. 14(8).

11(*b*) *Slavery, a Poem.* Philadelphia: printed by Joseph James, 1788. 8.5 × 13 cm. 12 pp. By Hannah More. Boston Athenaeum: Tr. D 71.

12 *The Shopkeeper Turned Sailor; or, the Folly of Going out of Our Element . . .* Part I [of 4]. London/Bath: J. Marshall and R. White/S. Hazard, [1796]. 12mo. 8 pp. ½*d.*, 2/3 a 100, 1/6 for 50, 9*d.* for 25. BL: 4418. e. 94(21).

13* *John the Shopkeeper Turned Sailor; or, the Folly of Going out of our Element. In Which a Particular Account is Given of the Several Branches of This Worthy Family.* Part II [of 4]. London/Bath: J. Marshall and R. White/S. Hazard, [n.d.]. 12 × 17.5 cm. 8 pp. ½*d.*, or 2/3 for 100, 1/6 for 50, 9*d.* for 25. HEHL: 195169.

14 *John the Shopkeeper Turned Sailor . . . Shewing How John and his Family actually Took Boat, and How They Had for a While a Most Delightful Sail on the Wide Ocean.* Part III [of 4]. London/Bath: J. Marshall and R. White/S. Hazard, [n.d.]. 12 × 17.5 cm. 8 pp. ½*d.*, or 2/3 a 100, 1/6 for 50, 9*d.* for 25. HEHL: 195169.

15 *John the Shopkeeper, Turned Sailor . . . In Which a Description is Given of John Himself Taking Charge of the Boat, and of his not Knowing How to Manage It, and of the Dreadful Event Which soon Happened in Consequence . . .* Part IV [of 4]. London/Bath: J. Evans and J. Hatchard/S. Hazard, [n.d.]. 12 × 17.5 cm. 8 pp. ½*d.*, or 2/3 a 100, 1/6 for 50, 9*d.* for 25. HEHL: 195169.

16 *John the Shopkeeper Turned Sailor; or, the Folly of Going out of our Element. In Four Parts.* London/Bath: J. Evans and Son, and J. Hatchard/J. Binns, [1800?]. 11.5 × 18 cm. 16 pp. 1*d.* By [Z]. BL: 4417. bb. 44(24).

17(*a*)   *The Story of Sinful Sally. Told by Herself* . . . London/Bath: J. Marshall and R. White/S. Hazard, [1796]. 11 × 16.5 cm. 8 pp. ½*d*. By [Z.]. BL: 4418. e. 94(20).

17(*b*)   *The Story of Sinful Sally. The Hampshire Tragedy. The Bad Bargain. And Robert and Richard.* London/Bath: J. Evans and Son and J. Hatchard/J. Binns, [n.d.]. 11.5 × 18 cm. 16 pp. 1*d*. or 6/6 a hundred. By [Z. and others?]. Bodley: 1419 e. 5974(70).

17(*c*)   *The Story of Sinful Sally; the Hampshire Tragedy; the Bad Bargain; and Robert and Richard.* London/Bath: J. Evans and Co., J. Hatchard/S. Hazard, [1805?]. 13 × 19 cm. 16 pp. 1*d*., or 4/6 a 100, 2/6 for 50, 1/6 for 25. By [Z. and others?]. Bodley: Johnson d. 134(51).

17(*d*)   *The Story of Sinful Sally, the Hampshire Tragedy, the Bad Bargain, and Robert & Richard.* London/Bath: Howard and Evans, and J. Hatchard/J. Binns, [*c*.1810]. 11 × 17.5 cm. 16 pp. 1*d*. By [Z. and others?]. BL: 3130. m. 11(15).

18   *The Carpenter; or, the Danger of Evil Company.* [1795]. 8.5 × 15 cm. 24 pp. [Included in *Cheap Repository Tracts, Published During the Year 1795*. London/Bath, [1796]. Vol. i.] By [Z. and others?]. Bodley: Vet. A5 f. 2874(29).

19   *The Sorrows of Yamba; or, the Negro Woman's Lamentation.* [1795]. 8.5 × 15 cm. 12 pp. [Included in *Cheap Repository Tracts, Published During the Year 1795*. London/Bath, [1796]. vol. i.] ½*d*. each, 2/3 a 100, 1/3 for 50, 6*d*. for 25. Bodley: Vet. A5 f. 2874(30).

20   *A Hymn of Praise for the Abundant Harvest of 1796.* London/Bath: J. Marshall and R. White/S. Hazard, [1796]. 10.5 × 17.5 cm. 8 pp. ½*d*., or 2/3 a 100, 1/6 for 50, 9*d*. for 25. By [Z]. Bodley: Vet. A5 e. 3944.

21   *The Lancashire Collier Girl, a True Story. To Which is Added Patient Joe, or the Newcastle Collier, and Dan and Jane; or Faith and Works: A Tale.* Dublin: William Watson and Son, [1800?]. 10.5 × 16.5 cm. 23 pp. [prose and verse, pp. 16–23 being in verse]. 1*d*. By [Z. and another?]. Bodley: Vet. A5 e. 3619(3).

22   *Turn the Carpet: A New Christian Hymn: The Noble Army of Martyrs: And, the Plow-boy's Dream.* London/Bath: Howard

and Evans, and J. Hatchard/Hazard and Binns, [n.d.]. 11.5 × 18 cm. 14 pp. 1*d*. By [Z. and M.]. BL: 3130. m. 11(22).

23   *Cheap Repository Tracts; Entertaining, Moral, and Religious.* London/Bath: F. and C. Rivington, J. Evans, J. Hatchard/S. Hazard, 1798. 10.5 × 17 cm. 2 vols. [Verse is confined to i. 422–60 and ii. 370–468.] Houghton: *EC75. M8134C. 1798.

24(*a*)   *Patient Joe. Wild Robert. Dan and Jane. And the Gin-Shop.* London/Bath: J. Evans and Son, J. Hatchard/J. Binns, [1800?]. 12 × 18 cm. 16 pp. 1*d*. By [Z. and others]. BL: 4417. bb. 44(16).

24(*b*)   *Patient Joe: Wild Robert: Dan and Jane: And the Gin-shop.* London/Bath: Howard and Evans and J. Hatchard/ Hazard and Binns, [*c*.1805?]. 12 × 17.5 cm. 16 pp. 1*d*., or 6/- a 100. By [Z. and others]. Bodley: Johnson d. 134(43).

24(*c*)   *Patient Joe: Wild Robert Dan and Jane: And the Gin-shop.* London/Bath: Howard and Evans, and J. Hatchard/J. Binns, [*c*.1810]. 11 × 18 cm. 16 pp. 1*d*. By [Z. and others]. BL: 3130. m. 11(27).

25   *The Riot; or, Half a Loaf is Better than No Bread. The Good Militia Man; or, the Man that is Worth a Host. The Loyal Sailor; or, No Mutineering.* London/Bath: J. Evans and Son and J. Hatchard/J. Binns, [1815]. 12 × 18.5 cm. 16 pp. 1*d*. or 6/6 a 100. By [Z]. Bodley: Johnson d. 134(47).

26(*a*)   *Poems.* London: T. Cadell and W. Davies, 1816. 11.5 × 20 cm. Pp. xii + 405. By Hannah More. BL: 994. h. 20.

26(*b*)   *Poems.* London: T. Cadell, 1829. New edn. 11.5 × 19 cm. 313 pp. By Hannah More. BL: 11643. e. 35.

27   *Tragedies.* London: T. Cadell and W. Davies, 1818. 12 × 20.5 cm. Pp. [ii] + 464. By Hannah More. CUL: S721. c. 81. 70.

28(*a*)   *The Twelfth of August; or the Feast of Freedom.* London: J. and T. Clarke, 1819. 12 × 19 cm. 8 pp. BL: 11662. bb. 2.

28(*b*)   *The Feast of Freedom, or, the Abolition of Domestic Slavery in Ceylon; the Vocal Parts Adapted to Music by Charles Wesley, Esq. Organist in Ordinary to His Majesty. To Which are Added,*

Several Unpublished Little Pieces. London: T. Cadell, 1827. 13 × 20.5 cm. 39 pp. By Hannah More. Bodley: G. Pamph. 2929(2).

29(*a*)　*Bible Rhymes, on the Names of All the Books of the Old and New Testament: With Allusions to Some of the Principal Incidents and Characters.* London: T. Cadell and Hatchard and Son, 1821. 12 × 20.5 cm. 94 pp. By Hannah More. BL: T. 1058(11).

29(*b*)　*Bible Rhymes, on the Names of All the Books of the Old and New Testament: With Allusions to Some of the Principal Incidents and Characters.* Boston[, Mass.]: West and Lilly, 1821. 9.5 × 16.5 cm. 72 pp. By Hannah More. Andover-Harvard: 824.5 More.

29(*c*)　*Bible Rhymes, on the Names of All the Books of the Old and New Testament: With Allusions to Some of the Principal Incidents and Characters.* London: T. Cadell and Hatchard and Son, 1822. 2nd edn. 8 × 12.5 cm. 111 pp. By Hannah More. BL: 11642. a. 50.

30(*a*)　*Sacred Dramas; the Search after Happiness; and Other Poems.* London: J. F. Dove, 1827. 7.5 × 13 cm. Pp. xx + 268. By Hannah More. Widener: 20427. 20.

30(*b*)　*Sacred Dramas; the Search after Happiness; and Other Poems.* London: Jones and Co., 1829. 5.5 × 8.5 cm. Pp. xvi + 255. By Hannah More. Bodley: 14770 g. 109.

30(*c*)　*Sacred Dramas; the Search after Happiness; and Other Poems.* London: Jones and Co., 1832. 5 × 8.5 cm. Pp. xvi + 255. By Hannah More. Yale (Beinecke): Zm/M81.

31(*a*)　*The Works . . . with a Sketch of her Life.* Boston[, Mass.]: S. G. Goodrich, 1827. 13.5 × 21.5 cm. 2 vols. By Hannah More. Schlesinger: 825. M83. 1. 1.

31(*b*)　*The Works . . . with a Sketch of her Life.* Philadelphia: J. J. Woodward, 1830. 13.5 × 22 cm. 2 vols. By Hannah More. NEDL: KF13451.

31(*c*)　*The Works . . . with a Sketch of her Life.* Philadelphia: J. J. Woodward, 1832. 13.5 × 22 cm. 2 vols. By Hannah More. AAS: G526. M835. W832.

31(d)   *The Works.* New York: Harper and Brothers, 1835. First complete American edn. 17.5 × 26.5 cm. 2 vols. [prose and verse, the verse being in vol. i]. By Hannah More. Bodley: Vet. K6 d. 27(1 and 2).

32   *Search after Happiness; and Other Poems: Sacred Dramas; and Essays on Various Subjects.* London: T. Allman and Son, [n.d.]. 7.5 × 11.5 cm. 285 pp. [verse and prose]. By Hannah More. Bodley: 270 g. 1065.

33   *The Poetical Works . . . With a Memoir of the Author.* London: Scott, Webster, and Geary, 1835. 8 × 14 cm. Pp. xxiv + 504. By Hannah More. Yale (Sterling): Im/M813/C835.

[*See also*: 'Bishop Bonner's Ghost' (1789, pp. [ii] + 4); 'The Hackney Coachman; or, the Way to Get a Good Fare' ([1796], 6 pp.); 'The Riot; or, Half a Loaf is Better than No Bread. In a Dialogue between Jack Anvil and Tom Hod . . .' (*c.*1796, broadsheet); 'Turn the Carpet; or, the Two Weavers' (1796, 7 pp.), by Z.; 'The Divine Model: or, Christian's Exemplar. To Which is Added, the Dram Shop' (*c.*1800, prose with 5 pp. of verse); 'The Ship-wreck. To Which is Added, the Execution of Wild Robert' (1800, prose with 4 pp. of verse); 'The Happy Waterman, to Which is Added a Hymn of Praise for an Abundant Harvest' (1815, 3 pp. of verse); 'Lines' (1827, 1 p.).]

MORGAN, Lady, *see* OWENSON, Sydney

MORISON, Hannah, Mrs?
'On the Death of a Beloved Infant' in her *Poems* suggests that she was a mother.

1   *Poems on Various Subjects.* Newry: printed by Alexander Wilkinson, 1817. 9.5 × 17 cm. Pp. x + 5–210 [subscription edition]. By Hannah Morison. Bodley: Harding C 3457.

MORLEY, Countess of, *see* PARKER, Frances

MORPETH, Mary, *or* OXLIE *or* OXLEY, Mary
A seventeenth-century Scottish writer who was a friend of William Drummond of Hawthornden. She lived in Morpeth, Northumberland. (Blain, *Various Pieces*)

1   *Various Pieces of Fugitive Scotish Poetry; Principally of the Seventeenth Century.* Ed. [David Laing]. Edinburgh: W. and D. Laing, [1825]. 11.5 × 18.5 cm. Pp. xxxvi + [214] [8 pp. devoted to verse by M. M., *i.e.* Mary Morpeth?]. BL: 1077. h. 31.

MORTON, Sarah Wentworth, Mrs Perez (1759–1846)

Born in Boston, Mass. She was the daughter of James Apthorp and Sarah Wentworth. The family was a wealthy and distinguished one and she was given an unusual education. In 1781 she married the lawyer Perez Morton. They had five children. She began contributing to the *Massachusetts Magazine* in 1789 under the name 'Philenia'. Her poetry was widely praised in the 1790s, in England as well as in the United States. (*DAB*, Emily Pendleton and Milton Ellis, *Philenia, the Life and Works* . . . (1931))

1   *Ouâbi: Or the Virtues of Nature. An Indian Tale. In Four Cantos.* Boston[, Mass.]: printed by I. Thomas and E. T. Andrews, 1790. 13.5 × 21 cm. 52 pp. By Philenia, a Lady of Boston. HEHL: 7686.

2(*a*)   *Beacon Hill. A Local Poem, Historic and Descriptive.* Book I. Boston[, Mass.]: for the author by Manning and Loring, 1797. 22 × 27.5 cm. 56 pp. By [S. M.]. HEHL: 137574.

2(*b*)   *The Virtues of Society. A Tale, Founded on Fact.* Boston[, Mass.]: printed for the author by Manning and Loring, 1799. 22 × 27.5 cm. 46 pp. By the Author of *The Virtues of Nature.* Houghton: *fAC7. M8468. 799v.

3   *My Mind and its Thoughts, in Sketches, Fragments, and Essays.* Boston[, Mass.]: Wells and Lilly, 1823. 13.5 × 22.5 cm. Pp. xx + 195 [prose and verse]. By Sarah Wentworth Morton, of Dorchester, Mass. Houghton: *AC7. M8468. 823m.

A MOTHER, *see also* COLLECTIONS 20, 48, 54 *and* GURNEY, Maria

1   *The Remembrance: A Small Collection of Tales, Essays, Dialogues, with Some Original Poems. Written by a Mother for her Absent Child.* London: John Marshall, 1806. 9.5 × 15 cm. Pp. [ii] + 140 [about 13 pp. of verse]. BL: 012807. de. 49.

2   *Detached Pieces of Poetry. Written by a Mother, and Dedicated to her Daughters.* Canterbury: printed [for the author?] by

Rouse, Kirkby, and Lawrence, 1808. 9.5 × 16 cm. Pp. viii + 95 [subscription edition]. BL: 11631. aa. 21.

3   *Letters in Rhyme, from a Mother at Home to her Children at School.* London: Francis Westley, 1824. 8.5 × 15 cm. 88 pp. By [a Mother]. BL: 11642. aaa. 58.

MOTT, Mrs Isaac Henry Robert

1   *Sacred Melodies, Preceded by an Admonitory Appeal to the Right Honourable Lord Byron, with Other Small Poems.* London: for the author by Francis Westley, 1824. 11.5 × 19 cm. Pp. xvi + 110. By Mrs I. H. R. Mott. BL: 994. h. 21.

M'TAGGART, Ann, *see* McTAGGART, Ann

MURDEN, Eliza, Mrs, *see* CRAWLEY, Eliza

MURPHY, Anna

1   *A Short Account of a Few of the Most Remarkable Trees and Plants; to Which are Added, Miscellaneous Poems.* London: printed for the author by T. Gillet, 1808. 10 × 16.5 cm. Pp. vi + 140 [subscription edition; verse occupies pp. 109–35]. By Anna Murphy. BL: 7030. bb. 34.

MURRY, Ann (born *c.*1755)

Born in London. She was the daughter of a wine merchant. She became a private tutor and was attached to the royal nursery. She is best known for her *Mentoria: Or, the Young Lady's Instructor, in Familiar Conversations* (1788). She was still alive in 1816. (Blain, Lonsdale)

1(*a*)   *Poems on Various Subjects.* London: for the author by Edward and Charles Dilly, J. Robson and J. Walter, 1779. 19.5 × 24.5 cm. Pp. [x] + 147 [subscription edition]. 5/- sewed. By Ann Murry, Author of *Mentoria*. BL: 1346. k. 51.

1(*b*)   *Poems on Various Subjects.* London: for the author by Edward and Charles Dilly, J. Robson, and J. Walter, 1779. 2nd edn. 18 × 21 cm. Pp. [x] + 147 [subscription edition]. 5/- sewed. By Ann Murry, Author of *Mentoria*. BL: 11632. f. 43.

MUZZY, Harriet, Mrs

She was an American writer, widowed and impoverished after a long illness. She had one daughter, aged 11 in 1821. She contributed verse to periodicals and her dialogue of poems with the editor of her volume had previously appeared in newspapers. (*Poems*)

1   *Poems, Moral and Sentimental.* Ed. Caroline Matilda Thayer. New York: printed by F. W. Ritter, 1821. 11 × 18.5 cm. 200 pp. By Harriet Muzzy. BL: 11686. e. 23.

NEALDS, Adeline Martha, Mrs Charles

She had five children. Her husband, who was a priest at Wicklewood, Norfolk, died in 1829. (*GM, Athenae Cantabrigienses*)

1   *Poems.* London: C. J. G. and F. Rivington, 1829. 13 × 20 cm. Pp. xxii + 140 [subscription edition]. By Mrs Charles Nealds. BL: 991. h. 39.

NEWCASTLE, Duchess of, *see* CAVENDISH, Margaret

NEWMAN, Sarah (born *c.*1752)

Born in Odiham, Hants. She was an orphan and her only formal education was 'occasional lessons from a schoolmaster'. She was employed as a domestic servant, but by 1811 was reduced to taking in sewing and raking hay in the fields. She lived in the village of Sutton. Her income from her savings was £3 a year. She had more than 500 subscribers. (*Friends' Books, Poems*)

1   *Poems, on Subjects Connected with Scripture.* Ed. [Elijah Waring]. Alton/London/Sherborne: W. Pinnock/Hatchard, Setchell and Son, I. and A. Arch, Darton and Harvey/E. Penny, 1811. 12 × 20.5 cm. Pp. viii + 60 [subscription edition]. By Sarah Newman. BL: 11633. e. 27.

NICHOLS, Anne Susanna

1   *Journal of a Very Young Lady's Tour from Canonbury to Aldborough, through Harwich, Colchester, etc., Sept. 13–21, 1804. Written Hastily on the Road, as Circumstances Arose.* London, 1804. 12 × 19.5 cm. 16 pp. HL; BL: T. 1057(14).

NICHOLSON, Margaret, *pseudonym of* SHELLEY, Percy Bysshe

N—M—R—D, Her Gr–ce the D—ss of, *see* NORTHUMBERLAND, Duchess of

NOOTH, Charlotte
She was the daughter of a London surgeon. She was the author of a novel, *Eglantine, or the Family of Fortescue* (1808). (Blain)

1   *Original Poems, and a Play.* London: Longman, Hurst, Rees, Orme, and Brown, 1815. 14 × 22 cm. Pp. [ii] + 156 + [15] [subscription edition]. By Charlotte Nooth. BL: 11623. k. 9.

NORNA, *see* BROOKS, Mary E.

NORTH, E., *see* COX, Elizabeth

NORTHAMPTON, Lady, *see* COMPTON, Margaret Maclean

NORTHUMBERLAND, Elizabeth Smithson, Duchess of (1716–76), *see* COLLECTIONS 1(*c*)
She was the only daughter of Algernon Seymour, Baron Percy. In 1740 she married Hugh Smithson, who in 1750 succeeded to the title by virtue of his wife and changed his surname to Percy. She was a member of the Batheaston circle, remembered for having chosen a buttered muffin as the subject of *bouts rimés*. Goldsmith is said to have written 'Edwin and Angelina' for her amusement. (*Complete Peerage, DNB*)

NORTON, Caroline Elizabeth Sarah, the Hon. Mrs George Chapple (1808–77), *see also* COLLECTIONS 42, 50(*a–c*), 52, 55, 56
Born in London. She was the second daughter of Thomas Sheridan and Caroline Henrietta Callander. Her mother was a minor novelist and her father, who was colonial treasurer at the Cape of Good Hope, also wrote verse. She was educated at home. In 1827 she married the Hon. George Chapple Norton, but the marriage ended in separation and she was deprived of their three children. She wrote much for the annuals and published four novels after 1835. In 1857, after the death of her first husband, she married Sir William Stirling-Maxwell. (Boyle, *CB, DNB*, Todd 2)

1(*a*)   *The Sorrows of Rosalie. A Tale. With Other Poems.* London: John Ebers, 1829. 10.5 × 17 cm. Pp. xii + 136. BL: 993. d. 50.

1(*b*) *The Sorrows of Rosalie.* 2nd edn. Inference.

1(*c*) *The Sorrows of Rosalie.* 3rd edn. Inference.

1(*d*) *The Sorrows of Rosalie. A Tale. With Other Poems.* London: John Ebers and Co., 1829. 4th edn. 12 × 19 cm. Pp. xiv + 217. BL: 991. f. 30.

2(*a*) *The Undying One, and Other Poems.* London: Henry Colburn and Richard Bentley, 1830. 12.5 × 21 cm. Pp. viii + 272. By the Honble Mrs Norton. BL: C. 57. l. 16.

2(*b*) *The Undying One, and Other Poems.* London: Henry Colburn and Richard Bentley, 1830. 2nd edn. 13 × 21 cm. Pp. viii + 272. By the Honble Mrs Norton. BL: 994. h. 23.

3 *Poems.* Boston[, Mass.]: Allen and Ticknor, 1833. 11 × 17.5 cm. 148 pp. By the Honble Mrs Norton. BL: 994. h. 23.

4 *The Coquette, and Other Tales and Sketches, in Prose and Verse.* London: Edward Churton, 1835. 11 × 18 cm. 2 vols. [about 135 pp. of verse]. By the Hon. Mrs Norton. Illinois: 823 N82C. [Photocopy seen only.]

5 *Kate Bouverie, and Other Tales and Sketches, in Prose and Verse* [the title-page, preliminaries, and Chapter 1 are missing from this copy; the title-page has been transcribed from vol. ii and the measurements taken from it. A complete copy of vol. i only is at LC: PR 5112. N5 A67]. Philadelphia/Boston[, Mass.]: E. L. Carey and A. Hart/ W. D. Ticknor, 1835. 11 × 17.5 cm. 2 vols. [about 53 pp. of verse]. By the Hon. Mrs Norton, Author of *The Wife, Woman's Reward,* etc., etc. NEDL: KPD335.

NORTON, Eliza Bland, *see* ERSKINE, the Hon. Mrs Esme Steuart

O., S., *see* OWENSON, Sydney

O'BRIEN, Mary, Mrs Patrick

1 *The Pious Incendiaries; or, Fanaticism Display'd. A Poem.* London: for the author by S. Hooper, Stockdale, Edgertons, and Richardson, 1785. 15.5 × 23.5 cm. Pp. [iv] + 100. By a Lady. BL: 78. i. 6.

2 *The Political Monitor; or Regent's Friend. Being a Collection of Poems Published in England during the Agitation of the Regency:*

Consisting of Curious, Interesting, Satyrical and Political Effusions of Poetry. Dublin: for the author by William Gilbert, 1790. 12.5 × 20 cm. 51 pp. By Mrs Mary O'Brien, Wife of Patrick O'Brien, Esq., and Author of *Charles Henley.* BL: 11641. bb. 43.

O'CALLAGHAN, Matilda Sophia

1   *The Glories of Jesus; or Considerations Calculated to Excite and Preserve Divine Love in our Hearts* . . . Trans. Matilda Sophia O'Callaghan. Dublin: printed for the translator by John Coyne, 1835. 6.5 × 10 cm. Pp. viii + 188 [verse on pp. 168–82 only]. 1/-. By Vincent Huby. BL: 11646. a. 7.

AN OFFICER'S WIFE, *see* FRASER, Susan

OFFLEY, Mrs
She seems to have lived in Dorchester, Dorset. *(BLC)*

1(*a*)   *The Assize Ball: Or, Lucy of the Moor.* London: J. Hatchard and F. Westley, 1820. 12 × 20 cm. 16 pp. BL: 994. l. 1(6).

1(*b*)   *The Assize Ball: Or, Lucy of the Moor.* Dorchester/London: J. Criswick/J. Hatchard and F. Westley, 1820. 2nd edn. 12 × 19.5 cm. 16 pp. BL: 11644. cc. 59(2).

1(*c*)   *The Assize Ball: Or, Lucy of the Moor.* Dorchester/London: J. Criswick/J. Hatchard and F. Westley, 1820. 3rd edn. 12 × 19 cm. 16 pp. BL: 11602. f. 20(4).

OKE, Eliza, Mrs

1   *Sacred Poems, on Various Subjects.* London: printed by J. C. Bridgewater, 1834. 10 × 17 cm. 46 pp. [subscription edition—no list of subscribers]. By Mrs Oke. BL: 11644. bb. 16.

O'KEEFFE, Adelaide D. (1776–1855?)
Born in Dublin. She was the only daughter of John O'Keeffe, the playwright and song-writer. She looked after him in his old age (he had been blind since the end of the 1790s) and edited some of his work. She contributed poems to the Taylors' *Original Poems for Infant Minds.* Her *Patriarchal Times; or the Land of Canaan; a Figurative History* (1811) had two editions. She was living in Southampton shortly before her death. (Blain, Boase, *CB*, *DNB* (under John O'Keeffe))

1(*a*)   *Original Poems; Calculated to Improve the Mind of Youth, and Allure It to Virtue*. Part I [of 2]. London: J. Harris, 1808. 9 × 12 cm. 16 pp. By Adelaide. Osborne: ii. 654.

1(*b*)   *Original Poems; Calculated to Improve the Mind of Youth, and Allure It to Virtue*. Part I [of 2]. Philadelphia: Johnson and Warner, 1810. 10 × 13.5 cm. 14 pp. By Adelaide. LC: 1810 Juv. Coll.

2(*a*)   *Original Poems; Calculated to Improve the Mind of Youth, and Allure It to Virtue*. Part II [of 2]. London: J. Harris, 1808. 9 × 12 cm. 16 pp. By Adelaide. Osborne: ii. 654.

2(*b*)   *Original Poems; Calculated to Improve the Mind of Youth, and Allure It to Virtue*. [Part II of 2]. Philadelphia: Benjamin Warner, 1821. 9.5 × 12.5 cm. 16 pp. By Adelaide. LC: 1810 Juv. Coll.

3   *National Characters Exhibited in Forty Geographical Poems . . .* Lymington/London:/Darton, Harvey, and Darton, 1818. 8.5 × 13.5 cm. Pp. vi + 139. By Miss O'Keeffe. BL: 11645. de. 46.

4   *A Trip to the Coast; or, Poems Descriptive of Various Interesting Objects on the Sea-shore*. London: Darton, Harvey, and Darton, 1819. 8.5 × 13.5 cm. Pp. viii + 157. By Miss O'Keefe. BL: 1210. b. 20.

AN OLD MAID, *pseudonym of* M'GIBBON, Alexander

O'NEILL, Frances, Mrs, *see also* COLLECTIONS 16(*a*–*b*)

Her unmarried name was Carroll. She seems to have come to London from Dublin. (Blain)

1   *Poetical Essays; being a Collection of Satirical Poems, Songs and Acrostics*. London: for the author by A. Young, 1802. 10 × 18 cm. 60 pp. By Mrs Frances O'Neill. BL: 11633. aaa. 34.

OPIE, Amelia, Mrs John (1769–1853), *see also* COLLECTIONS 23(*a*–*b*), 30(*a*–*g*), 35, 38(*a*–*b*), 40(*a*–*d*), 41, 43, 48, 50(*a*–*c*), 52, 54

Born in Norwich, Norfolk. She was the only child of James Alderson, MD, and of Amelia Briggs. They were prosperous Unitarians. On her mother's death in 1784 she became her father's hostess. She had radical political sympathies. In 1798 she married the painter John Opie and went to London. On his death in 1807 she returned to Norwich, visiting London for a few weeks each year. She contributed much to the annuals and wrote novels until 1825 when she became a Quaker and gave them up. The poems in the first edition of *The Father and Daughter* (1, below) do not appear in subsequent editions, being issued as a separate volume (3, below). (Boyle, *CB*, *DNB*, *Friends' Books*)

1   *The Father and Daughter, a Tale in Prose: With an Epistle from the Maid of Corinth to her Lover; and Other Poetical Pieces.* London: Longman and Rees, 1801. 10 × 17.5 cm. Pp. vii + 244 [verse occupying pp. 209–44]. 4/6 boards. By Mrs Opie. *MR* 35: 163–6; Bodley: 249 s. 261.

2   *Elegy to the Memory of the Late Duke of Bedford; Written on the Evening of his Interment.* London: T. N. Longman and O. Rees, 1802. 20 × 26.5 cm. 16 pp. 1/-. By Mrs Opie. *MR* 38: 99; *CR* 36: 475–6; BL: 11642. h. 14.

3(*a*)   *Poems.* London: T. N. Longman and O. Rees, 1802. 9 × 16 cm. Pp. iv + 192. By Mrs Opie. BL: 11644. aaa. 31.

3(*b*)   *Poems.* London: T. N. Longman and O. Rees, 1803. 2nd edn. 9 × 15.5 cm. Pp. iv + 185. By Mrs Opie. BL: 11644. aaa. 34.

3(*c*)   *Poems.* London: Longman, Hurst, Rees, and Orme, 1804. 3rd edn. 9.5 × 16 cm. Pp. iv + 185. By Mrs Opie. BL: 11644. aaa. 32.

3(*d*)   *Poems.* London: Longman, Hurst, Rees, and Orme, 1806. 4th edn. 9 × 16 cm. Pp. iv + 185. By Mrs Opie. BL: 11644. aaa. 33.

3(*e*)   *Poems.* London: Longman, Hurst, Rees, and Orme, 1808. 5th edn. 9.5 × 15.5 cm. Pp. iv + 185. By Mrs Opie. BL: 11633. aa. 35.

3(*f*)   *Poems.* London: Longman, Hurst, Rees, Orme, and Brown, 1811. 6th edn. 10 × 17 cm. Pp. iv + 185. By Mrs Opie. BL: 11644. c. 23.

4(*a*)   *The Warrior's Return, and Other Poems.* London: Longman, Hurst, Rees, and Orme, 1808. 10 × 16.5 cm. Pp. vi + 185. By Mrs Opie. BL: 11633. aaa. 35.

4(*b*)   *The Warrior's Return, and Other Poems.* Philadelphia: Bradford and Inskeep, 1808. 10.5 × 18 cm. 191 pp. By Mrs Opie. Houghton: *EC8. Op331. 808wb.

4(*c*)   *The Warrior's Return, and Other Poems.* London: Longman, Hurst, Rees, and Orme, 1808. 2nd edn. 9.5 × 16 cm. Pp. vi + 185. By Mrs Opie. Bodley: 280 f. 2294.

4(*d*)   *The Warrior's Return, and Other Poems.* New York: Inskeep and Bradford, 1808. 10 × 17.5 cm. 191 pp. By Mrs Opie. HEHL: 188504.

5   *The Negro Boy's Tale, a Poem, Addressed to Children.* London: Harvey and Darton, and S. Wilkin, 1824. 10.5 × 18 cm. Pp. viii + 16. By Amelia Opie. Osborne: ii. 655.

6   *The Black Man's Lament; or, How to Make Sugar.* London: Harvey and Darton, 1826. 10.5 × 16.5 cm. 25 pp. By Amelia Opie. BL: T. 1271(2).

7   *Lays for the Dead.* London: Longman, Rees, Orme, Brown, Green, and Longman, 1834. 9.5 × 17 cm. Pp. viii + 144. By Amelia Opie. BL: 994. g. 27.

OSCAR, *see* GRIMSTONE, Mary Leman

OSGOOD, Frances Sargent, Mrs Samuel Stillman (1811–50)

Born in Boston, Mass., but she grew up in Hingham. She was the daughter of Joseph Locke and Mary Ingersoll Foster. In 1835 she married Samuel Stillman Osgood, a portrait painter. They had two daughters. She published substantially in the 1840s and was editor of the *Ladies' Companion* and she was known as a friend of Edgar Allan Poe. (Blain, *DAB*, Hale, May)

1   *Philosophical Enigmas; a Series of Poetical Enigmas.* London: Rock, [183?]. By Frances S. Osgood. *NUC.* Not found.

OWENSON, Sydney (1783–1859)

She was the eldest child of Robert Owenson, the Irish actor and composer, and of Jane Hill. Her life is confusingly recorded. She lived in Dublin and then worked briefly as a governess. In 1812 she married Sir Charles Morgan, a physician. She became a permanent member of the household of the Marquess of Abercorn and was a familiar figure in fashionable and literary circles in Dublin and London. She began to write novels in 1804 (*The Wild Irish Girl* (1806) went through seven editions in two years and made her famous), and her songs, set to Irish tunes, are said to have influenced Thomas Moore. *The Mohawks* (1822), a satirical poem, is sometimes attributed to her, but unconvincingly. (Boase, *DB*, *DNB*, *Lady Morgan's Memoirs* (1863))

1   *Poems, Dedicated by Permission, to the Right Honorable the Countess of Moira* . . . Dublin/London: Alex. Stewart/ Philips, 1801. 11 × 18 cm. 157 pp. [subscription edition]. By Sidney Owenson. Houghton: *EC8. M8236. 801p.

2(*a*)   *The Lay of an Irish Harp; or Metrical Fragments.* London: Richard Phillips, 1807. 11 × 18.5 cm. Pp. xvi + 199. By Miss Owenson. BL: 1164. k. 16.

2(*b*)   *The Lay of an Irish Harp; or Metrical Fragments.* New York: E. Sargeant, D. Longworth, George Jansen, Alsop, Brannon and Alsop, Matthias Ward, E. Duyckinck, J. Osborn, T. and J. Swords, Campbell and Mitchell, M. Harrisson, Saml. A. Burtus, and Benj. Crane, 1808. 9.5 × 15.5 cm. 152 pp. By Miss Owenson. BL: 11644. aa. 37.

2(*c*)   *The Lay of an Irish Harp; or Metrical Fragments.* [Philadelphia: T. S. Manning, 1810?]. 10.5 × 16.5 cm. 180 pp. By Miss Owenson. LC: PR 5059. M3 L3 1810 (Toner Coll.).

[*See also*: 'To Marianne Howard, July, 1818', paginated 3–11, without title-page or evidence of publication is attributed in BL copy (11652. aaa. 32) to S. O.; 'Fragments Found (after her Decease)' contains the same material printed on pp. 39–47, again without title-page or evidence of publication.]

OXLIE *or* OXLEY, Mary, *see* MORPETH, Mary

P., A. E., *see* POLGLASE, Ann Eaton

P., M., *see* KILNER, Dorothy

P., S. S., *see* PUGH, Sarah S.

PAGAN, Isabel (*c.*1742–1821)

She lived in Ayrshire where she carried on an unlicensed trade in whisky. She was lame from infancy, and she is reported as having been unsociable, but she used to sing and recite at drinking parties with friends. She is best known for two songs (not included in her collection), 'Ca' the yowes to the knowes' (later revised by Burns) and 'Crook and plaid'. (Blain, *DNB*)

1   *A Collection of Songs and Poems on Several Occasions.* Glasgow: printed by Niven, Napier and Khull, 1803. 10 × 16.5 cm. 76 pp. By Isabel Pagan. BL: 11641. b. 32.

PARDOE, Julia (1806–62)

Born in Beverley, Yorks. She was the second daughter of Major Thomas Pardoe. She was a novelist, travel writer, and popular historian, most of her publications appearing after 1835. She contributed regularly to the annuals from 1828 on. She received a civil list pension in 1860. (Boase, Boyle, *DNB*, Hale)

1   *The Nun, a Poetical Romance, and Two Others*. London: for the author by Longman, Hurst, Rees, Orme, Brown, and Green, 1824. 13 × 21.5 cm. 228 pp. HL; BL: 993. i. 37.

2   *The Plague a Poem* . . . [the facing page gives the title in Italian]. Trans. Miss Pardoe. London: for the author by Dulau and Co., Saunders and Otley, and Rolandi, 1834. 11 × 18.5 cm. Pp. xii + 153. By Guido Sorelli. BL: 1063. l. 25.

PARKER, Frances, Countess of Morley (1781–1857), *see also* COLLECTIONS 41

She was the daughter of Thomas Talbot of Wymondham, Norfolk. In 1809 she became the second wife of John Parker, Earl of Morley. She was a famous talker, a painter, and a novelist. (Boase, *DNB* (under John Parker))

1   *The Nose, a Poem, in Six Stanzas* . . . *Dedicated to All Unmarried Ladies Who May Profit by the Example, and Take Warning from the Fate of Dorothy Spriggins*. [London: printed by Howlett and Brimmer], 1831. 14 × 22.5 cm. 8 pp. [interleaved with illustrations]. By [Frances Parker?]. BL: 11633. cc. 4.

2   *The Flying Burgermaster[.] A Legend of the Black Forest*. 1832. 13.5 × 22 cm. 14 pp. [interleaved with illustrations]. BL: 11646. h. 12.

PARMINTER, Anne, Mrs

He is Risen is dedicated to the governors of Christ's Hospital, where her children have been accepted as pupils; the customary terms of acceptance make it likely that she was a widow of reduced means and that her husband had been a clergyman. An MS note in the Bodley copy gives her address as Bolton Street, Piccadilly, in London.

1   *He is Risen; an Easter-offering. Inscribed, by Permission, to the Governors and Masters of Christ's Hospital.* London:

Rivingtons, 1817. 20 × 27 cm. 12 pp. 1/6. By [A. P.]. Bodley: Vet. A6 d. 25.

2   *The Votive Wreath, and Other Poems.* London: for the authoress by J. Bulcock, Hatchard and Son, Bowdery and Kirby, and W. Marsh, 1826. 13.5 × 22 cm. Pp. xxiv + 176. 10/-. By Mrs Parminter. BL: 994. i. 21.

PARSONS, Eliza Dwight, Mrs (1790–1855)

An American writer whose maiden name was Willard.

1   *Poems, on Various Subjects.* Troy: printed by F. Adancourt, 1826. 9.5 × 15.5 cm. 255 pp. By Eliza Dwight Willard Parsons. BL: 11687. aa. 19.

PARSONS, Letitia, Mrs (1744–1806)

She became blind at about the age of 30 and claimed to have begun writing verse because of her blindness. She seems to have been a Baptist. 'On our Marriage Union' suggests that she had been married for more than forty years. She had a sister whose name was Mrs Coe and her husband may have been William Parsons, the co-publisher of the second edition of her book and the author of an elegy on her in it. (*Verses*)

1   *Verses, Hymns and Poems, on Various Subjects; Composed under a Long Series of Affliction and Deprivation of Sight.* Hawkhurst/Pembury: John Parsons/Dickins, 1806. 10 × 17 cm. 104 pp. By Mrs Letitia Parsons, of Hawkhurst. BL: 11641. aaa. 40.

2   *Verses Hymns and Poems, on Various Subjects. Composed under a Long Series of Affliction and Deprivation of Sight . . . Being the Second and Last Part of her Compositions . . .* Hawkhurst/Marden/Sandhurst/Pembury: John and William Parsons/Richard Parsons/Mrs Maskall/Thomas Coe, 1808. 10 × 17 cm. 54 pp. 1/-. By Mrs Letitia Parsons. BL: 11641. aaa. 40.

3   *Verses Hymns and Poems, on Various Subjects; Composed under a Long Series of Affliction and Deprivation of Sight.* Pembury/Tonbridge: Thomas Coe/T. Dakens, 1815. 10 × 18 cm. Pp. 88 + 42. By Mrs Letitia Parsons. Illinois: 821. P254v. [Photocopy seen only.]

Parsons, Mary

1   *Cries out of the Depths. Poems on Sacred Subjects.* London/
     Bristol/Birmingham/Liverpool/Wellington/York/Edin-
     burgh/Dublin: for the author by E. Wallis, Conder,
     Burton and Co., Hamilton, Westley/W. Bulgin, Hillyard
     and Morgan/Beilby and Co./Gregson/Houlston and Sons/
     Alexander/Whyte and Co./M. and T. Webb, 1819. 9 × 16
     cm. Pp. [x] + 310. By Mary Parsons. BL: 994. b. 23.

Pasty, Carolina Petty, *see* Cobbold, Elizabeth

Patrickson, Margaret (born *c.*1787)

She claims to be 19 years old and to have written most of the poems
five years earlier; she also professes 'total ignorance of the rules of
poetical composition'. One poem, 'Retrospection', suggests that she
comes from Kent, near the Medway, and that she is now obliged to
live in London. She addresses an aunt as Mrs B———n, perhaps Barton,
as there are four subscribers of that name.

1   *Miscellaneous Poems.* London: R. Faulder, 1806. 9.5 × 15.5
     cm. 2 vols. [subscription edition]. By Margaret Patrickson.
     BL: 11646. bbb. 17.

Patullo, Margaret (*c.*1775–1847)

Her dates are derived from the tombstone in the churchyard of St
John's Episcopal Church in Edinburgh.

1   *The Christian Psalter; a New Version of the Psalms of David,
     Calculated for All Denominations of Christians.* Edinburgh/
     Perth/Dundee/Glasgow/London: for the author by David
     Peat, David Morison, Jr., and Co., Oliver and Boyd/James
     Dewar/James Chalmers/Robertson and Atkinson/G. B.
     Whittaker and James Duncan, 1828. 10.5 × 18 cm. Pp. xii
     + 363. By Margaret Patullo, Perth. BL: 843. h. 3.

Pearson, Mrs, *see* A Lady of Ninety

Pearson, Ann, Mrs William Fenwick

As her first title-page reveals, her father was William Henderson of
Hoastman, Newcastle, and she lived in Hexham. She began to write
poetry in 1815. (*The Grateful Remembrance*)

1   *The Grateful Remembrance; in Letters of Advice to an Absent Niece, on Different Subjects.* Hexham: printed by I. Dickenson and Son, 1816. 13 × 22 cm. 72 pp. [subscription edition; prose and verse]. By Ann Pearson, Wife of William Fenwick Pearson, Hexham, and Daughter of the Late William Henderson, Hoastman, Newcastle. Bodley: 260 e. 30.

2   *Miscellaneous Pieces.* Hexham: printed for the author by M. Armstrong, 1834. 12.5 × 21 cm. 36 pp. 1/-. By Ann Pearson. BL: 11633. c. 57(1).

PEARSON, Susanna (1779–1827), Mrs George, *see also* COLLECTIONS 25 (*a–c*)

Born in Donington, Lincs. She was one of six children of a surgeon and apothecary named Flinders. Her mother died when Susanna was young. She was employed as a domestic servant. She became a Baptist and shortly after married George Pearson. The 1800 volume is so much simpler in style and contents than the 1790 one as to make one wonder whether both are by the same hand, but the Fitzwilliams subscribed to both and her religious conversion may be the cause of the disparity. (George Pearson, *Memoirs of the Life and Character . . .* (1829))

1   *Poems, Dedicated by Permission, to the Right Honourable the Countess Fitzwilliam.* Sheffield/London: printed by J. Gales/G. G. J. and J. Robinson, T. Cadell, and C. Forster, 1790. 18 × 23.5 cm. 68 pp. [subscription edition]. 4/-. By S. Pearson. *CR* 70: 533–6; *MR* 4: 579; BL: 11630. d. 14(8).

2   *Poems on Various Subjects.* London: J. Rivington, T. Hurst, and Chapell, 1800. 9.5 × 15.5 cm. Pp. xii + 82 [subscription edition]. By S. Pearson. BL: 1507/71(1).

PELHAM, Mary, *see* KILNER, Dorothy

PENNY, Anne, Mrs Peter (1731–84)

She was the daughter of the Revd Owen Hughes of Bangor, Carnarvon. In 1746 she married Captain Thomas Christian, a retired but wealthy naval officer. Their son became an admiral. She published volumes of verse in the 1750s and 1760s. Her second marriage was to Peter Penny (or Penné); she was left in financial difficulties in 1779. (Blain, *CB*, Lonsdale)

1   *Poems, with a Dramatic Entertainment*. London: for the author by J. Dodsley, P. Elmsly, T. Davis and F. Newbery, [1771]. 18.5 × 23.5 cm. Pp. [xvi] + 220 [subscription edition]. By **** *****. Bodley: 2799 d. 169.

2   *An Invocation to the Genius of Britain*. London: for the author by J. Dodsley, 1778. 20 × 25 cm. 15 pp. 1/-. *MR* 58: 470; *NUC*; BL: 11662. d. 4.

3   *Poems*. London: for the author by J. Dodsley and P. Elmsly, 1780. 17.5 × 22.5 cm. Pp. [viii] + 244 [subscription edition]. BL: 11642. g. 11.

[*See also*: 'Pastoral Elegy' (1773, 2 pp.).]

PERKINS, Elizabeth Steele, Mrs

1(*a*)   *The Botanical and Horticultural Meeting, or Flora's and Pomona's Fête. A Poem, in Humble Imitation of the Butterfly's Ball, &c. &c. and Respectfully Dedicated to the Members of the Various Botanical and Horticultural Societies*. Birmingham: Beilby, Knott, and Beilby, 1834. 12.5 × 19.5 cm. 27 pp. 2/6 [charity edition]. By a Lady, from Notes by John Quill. Yale (Sterling): In/P419/834.

1(*b*)   *The Botanical and Horticultural Meeting, or Flora's and Pomona's Fête. A Poem, in Humble Imitation of the Butterfly's Ball* . . . Birmingham: Beilby, Knott, and Beilby, 1834. 2nd edn. 12 × 19 cm. 27 pp. 2/6. By a Lady. BL: 11641. e. 20.

1(*c*)   *The Botanical and Horticultural Meeting* . . . 3rd edn. Inference.

1(*d*)   *The Botanical and Horticultural Meeting, or Flora and Pomona's Fête. A Poem, in Humble Imitation of the Butterfly's Ball* . . . London: James Cochrane and Co., 1835. 4th edn. 11.5 × 18 cm. 27 pp. By a Lady. BL: 11643. bb. 38.

PETERS, Phillis, Mrs John, *see* WHEATLEY, Phillis

PHELAN, Charlotte Elizabeth, Mrs (1790–1846), *see also* COLLECTIONS 48

Born in Norwich, Norfolk. She was the daughter of the Revd Michael Browne. When she was young she married Captain Phelan of the 60th Regiment and spent two years with him in Nova Scotia. They returned to Kilkenny where Phelan had an estate. They separated in 1824 and she moved to Clifton and then to London. She remarried in 1841 Lewis Hyppolytus Joseph Tonna. She wrote particularly for Protestant religious societies, and composed songs and poems for the Orange cause. (*CB, DNB*)

1   *The Shepherd Boy, and the Deluge.* London: Francis Westley, 1823. 8.5 × 13.5 cm. 36 pp. By Charlotte Elizabeth. Bodley: 14770 f. 284(3).

2(*a*)   *Osric: A Missionary Tale; with the Garden, and Other Poems.* Dublin/London/Edinburgh/Glasgow/Bristol: W. Curry, Jr., and Co./Hatchard and Son, Francis Westley, C. B. Whitaker/Waugh and Innes, and W. Oliphant/Chalmers and Collins/W. Bulgin, [1825?]. 13 × 22 cm. Pp. 134 + 53. By Charlotte Elizabeth. BL: 11642. f. 19.

2(*b*)   *Osric, a Missionary Tale; with the Garden, and Other Poems.* London: James Nisbet, 1826. 2nd edn. 10.5 × 18 cm. Pp. viii + 230. By Charlotte Elizabeth. BL: 11642. c. 50.

3   *Izram, a Mexican Tale; and Other Poems.* London: James Nisbet, 1826. 10.5 × 18 cm. Pp. [ii] + 230. By Charlotte Elizabeth. BL: 994. h. 7.

[*See also*: 'A Visit to St. George's Chapel, Windsor . . .' (n.d. [lacks a title-page], 7 pp.).]

PHELPS, Mrs

'Suttee' was the topic chosen for the Oxford Prize Poem of 1831. She was not eligible to compete and her poem was written before the results of the competition were known. She had a son named Henry and presumably was connected in some way to the Oxford community. (*CB, The Suttee*)

1   *The Suttee, and Other Poems.* Thame: H. Bradford, [1831?]. 10.5 × 18 cm. Pp. [ii] + 76. By Mrs Phelps. BL: 11644. cc. 32.

PHILENIA, *see* MORTON, Sarah Wentworth

PHILIPPART, C., Mrs John

Her husband was a writer on military matters. (Allibone, *DNB* (under John Philippart), Shoberl)

1(*a*)   *Muscovy; a Poem, in Four Cantos: With Notes, Historical &*
         Military: Also Several Detached Pieces. London/Edinburgh:
         Patrick Martin and Co./John Ballantyne and Co., 1813.
         19.5 × 22 cm. 159 pp. [subscription edition]. By Mrs John
         Philippart. NYPL: NCM.

1(*b*)   *Muscovy; a Poem, in Four Cantos: With Notes, Historical &*
         Military: Also Several Detached Pieces. London/Edinburgh/
         Dublin: C. J. Barrington and Henry Colburn/Ogles/C. P.
         Archer, 1814. 2nd edn. 14 × 22.5 cm. 159 pp. [subscrip-
         tion edition]. By Mrs Philippart. BL: 1465. e. 13.

[*See also*: 'Victoria' (1813, 7 pp.).]

PHILIPPS, Janetta
Shelley praised her poems, is believed to have offered to pay for their
publication, and was active in collecting subscribers. (*Shelley Circle*)

1   *Poems.* Oxford: printed by Collingwood and Co., 1811. 12
         × 18.5 cm. Pp. [x] + 68 [subscription edition]. By Janetta
         Philipps. BL: 11642. c. 42.

PHILLIPS, Catharine, Mrs William (1726/7–94), *see also* COLLEC-
TIONS 44
She was the daughter of Henry Payton of Dudley, Worcs., a Quaker
minister, and of Ann Fowler of Evesham, Worcs. She attended Rachel
Trafford's boarding school in London. As a Quaker minister herself,
she travelled in England, Scotland, and Ireland. From 1753 to 1756 she
was in America (where she travelled 8,750 miles). She also visited
Holland, using interpreters. In 1772 she married William Phillips, a
widower with two children, and she continued her itinerant ministry,
travelling sometimes with him. (*DNB, Friends' Books, Memoirs of the Life
of Catherine Phillips* (1797))

1   *The Happy King. A Sacred Poem: With Occasional Remarks.*
         Respectfully Addressed to George the Third. Printed for the
         author, 1794. 12.5 × 20.5 cm. Pp. x + 136. By Catharine
         Phillips. BL: 11645. bbb. 45.

PICKERING, Mrs I., *see* POINTON, Priscilla

PICKERING, Amelia
Her book had about 1,000 subscribers.

1(*a*)   *The Sorrows of Werter: A Poem*. London: T. Cadell, 1788. 21
        × 26.5 cm. Pp. xxii + 69 [subscription edition]. By Amelia
        Pickering. BL: 1346. m. 11.

1(*b*)   *The Sorrows of Werter: A Poem*. London: printed by J. Bailey,
        1812. 9 × 14 cm. 48 pp. Yale (Beinecke): Z/Jc4a/P5/812.

PICKERSGILL, Mrs Henry William

Her husband was a portrait painter. They had one son who became an
artist. (*CB, DNB* (under Henry William Pickersgill))

1   *Tales of the Harem*. London: Longman, Rees, Orme,
     Brown, and Green, 1827. 10.5 × 18 cm. Pp. [vi] + 191. By
     Mrs Pickersgill. BL: 11646. ccc. 16.

PIKE, Sarah Leigh, *see* PYKE, Sarah Leigh

PILKINGTON, Jane, Mrs, *see* PILKINGTON, Mary

PILKINGTON, Mary, Mrs (1766–1839), *see also* COLLECTIONS 20

Her father was a surgeon named Hopkins. At his death, when she was
15, she went to live with her grandfather, who was a clergyman. In
1786 she married Pilkington, her father's successor. They lived in Ely
for a time, and then he became a naval surgeon and she found employ-
ment as a governess. She became a prolific author of novels and other
works; *DNB* lists forty-five titles. *NUC* lists items 1(*a*) and 1(*b*) separately as by Jane Pilkington, while acknowledging that the dedication is
signed M. Pilkington. J. was perhaps her husband's initial. (Blain, *CB,
DNB, NUC,* Watt)

1(*a*)   *Miscellaneous Poems*. London/Cambridge: T. Cadell, Jr., and
        W. Davies/J. Deighton and W. Lunn, 1796. 9.5 × 16 cm. 2
        vols. 10/6 boards. By Mrs J. Pilkington. *MR* 21: 110; BL:
        994. g. 29.

1(*b*)   *Miscellaneous Poems*. London: Vernor and Hood, 1799. 2nd
        edn. 9.5 × 15.5 cm. 2 vols. By Mrs J. Pilkington. BL:
        11632. a. 29, 30.

2   *Original Poems*. London/Cambridge: for the author by
     Vernor, Hood, and Sharpe/J. Deighton, 1811. 9.5 × 16
     cm. Pp. [xiv] + 191 [subscription edition]. By Mrs
     Pilkington. BL: 11644. aaa. 29.

PINDAR, Patt., *see* BATTIER, Henrietta

PINDAR, Polly, *pseudonym*

1   *The Mousiad: An Heroic Poem.* Canto I. Dublin: printed by
     P. Byrne, 1787. 12.5 × 19.5 cm. 16 pp. 1/-. By Polly
     Pindar, Half-sister to Peter Pindar. *MR* 77: 159; Bodley:
     Vet. A5 e. 4290(6).

PIOZZI, Hester Lynch, Mrs Gabriel (1741–1821), *see* COLLECTIONS
6, 8, 25(*a–c*)
She was the daughter of John Salusbury and Hester Maria Cotton. In
1763 she married Henry Thrale, a rich brewer of Southwark. Samuel
Johnson was a close friend of both of them. They had twelve
children, most of whom died in infancy. After her husband's death she
married, in 1784, the Italian musician Gabriel Piozzi. She went to Italy
with him and was for a time in contact with the Della Cruscan group
in Florence. She wrote reminiscences of Johnson and *British Synonymy*
(1794). (James L. Clifford, *Hester Lynch Piozzi* (1941), *DNB*)

PIZEY, Susannah

1   *Poems.* London/Bury St. Edmunds: printed for the
     authoress/J. Rackham, 1817. 9.5 × 16 cm. Pp. viii + 85
     [subscription edition]. By Susannah Pizey. BL: 11646. aaa.
     32.

PLOMLEY, Mary Ann

1   *Rural Lays.* London/Cranbrook: Darton and Harvey/S.
     Dobell, 1826. 10.5 × 17.5 cm. Pp. xvi + 111 [subscription
     edition]. By Mary Ann Plomley. BL: 11646. cc. 41.

POGSON, Sarah
She seems later to have married a Mr Smith and to have lived in
Charleston, SC. (Frank Pierce Hill, *American Plays . . . a Bibliographical
Record* (1934), NYPL L. Cat., Sabin)

1   *The Female Enthusiast: A Tragedy, in Five Acts.* Charleston:
     printed for the author by J. Hoff, 1807. 11 × 19 cm. 51
     pp. By a Lady. LC: PS 991. A1 F4 Office.

2   *Daughters of Eve, . . . Published in Aid of the New York Female
     Association. For the Support and Instruction of the Indigent Deaf*

and Dumb; there being at this Time Seventy Applicants, Who can-
not be Received at the Institution from Inadequate Funds.
Schenectady: printed by G. Ritchie, Jr., 1826. 10.5 × 18
cm. 91 pp. [subscription edition]. By a Lady. NYPL;
Columbia: B812 D26/P5/1826.

POINTON, Priscilla, Mrs I. PICKERING (*c.*1754–1801)
Born in Lichfield, Staffs. She was blind from the age of 12. In 1788 she
married I. Pickering, a saddler in Chester, who had died by 1794. Her
Poems had more than 1,000 subscribers. (Lonsdale)

1   *Poems on Several Occasions.* Birmingham: printed for the
     author by T. Warren, 1770. 12.5 × 21 cm. Pp. lxiv + 108
     [subscription edition]. 5/-. By Miss Priscilla Pointon of
     Lichfield. BL: 11633. e. 31.

2   *Poems . . . To Which are Added Poetical Sketches.* Ed. [Joseph
     Weston]. Birmingham/London: printed by E. Piercy/J.
     Johnson, [1794]. 12.5 × 20 cm. Pp. iv + 80 + 36. 5/-. By
     Mrs Pickering and the Author and Translator of *Philotoxi*
     Ardenae [John Morfitt and John Weston]. BL: 11633.
     bb. 33.

POLGLASE, Ann Eaton, Mrs John
She seems to have been the wife of John Polglase of Bristol, Glos.
(*Friends' Books*)

1   *The Shipwreck; a Tale of Arabia: And Other Poems.* London:
     Hamilton and Adams, and E. Fry, 1827. 10.5 × 18.5 cm.
     Pp. [viii] + 252. By A. E. P. BL: 11645. bb. 31.

PORDEN, Eleanor Anne (1795?–1825)
She was the daughter of William Porden, an architect, and of his wife
Mary. In 1823 she married the Arctic explorer John (later Sir John)
Franklin. They had one daughter. (*DNB*)

1   *The Veils; or the Triumph of Constancy. A Poem, in Six Books.*
     London: John Murray, 1815. 13 × 21.5 cm. Pp. x + 290.
     10/6 boards. By Miss Porden. *MR* 85: 39–54; BL: 959. f.
     23.

2   *The Arctic Expeditions. A Poem.* London: John Murray,
     1818. 13 × 21 cm. 30 pp. 2/6. By Miss Porden. *MR* 87:
     324–5; BL: 992. i. 22(6).

3   *Ode Addressed to the Right Honourable Lord Viscount Belgrave,*
     on his Marriage with the Right Honourable Lady Elizabeth Mary
     Leveson Gower, September 16, 1819. London: printed for the
     author by Cox and Baylis, 1819. 12.5 × 20 cm. 16 pp. By
     Miss Porden. BL: B. 700(10).

4   *Ode on the Coronation of His Most Gracious Majesty George the*
     Fourth, July 19, 1821. London: printed for the author by
     Cox and Baylis, 1821. 11.5 × 18.5 cm. 16 pp. By Miss
     Porden. Bodley: 3967 e. 105(10).

5   *Cœur de Lion; or the Third Crusade. A Poem, in Sixteen Books.*
     London: G. and W. B. Whittaker, 1822. 12.5 × 21.5 cm. 2
     vols. By Eleanor Anne Porden, Author of *The Veils, The*
     Arctic Expeditions, and Other Poems. BL: 994. h. 25.

[*See also*: 'Charity. A Second Contribution in Aid of the Bedford
Free School, Argyll Rooms, May 5th, 1821' ([1821], 4 pp.).]

PORTER, Anna Maria (1780–1832), *see also* COLLECTIONS 19, 32,
41, 45, 48, 56

Born in Durham. She was the daughter of William Porter, an army surgeon, and of Jane Blenkinsop, and she was a younger sister of Jane
Porter, the historical novelist. She grew up in Edinburgh. Her first
collection of tales was published in 1795; her 'Fair Fugitives', with
music by Busby, was performed at Covent Garden in 1803 but was not
well received. She is best known for her novel *The Huguenot Brothers*
(1807). The catalogues of Bodley and NLS both ascribe *Original Poems*
on Various Subjects, by a Young Lady, Eighteen Years of Age (n.d.) to her,
but some of the poems in it pre-date her birth. (*CB, DNB* (also under
Robert Ker Porter))

1(*a*) *Ballad Romances, and Other Poems.* London: Longman,
       Hurst, Rees, Orme, and Brown, 1811. 10 × 16.5 cm. Pp.
       viii + 196. 7/- boards. By Miss Anna Maria Porter. *MR*
       67: 325–6; BL: 11641. aa. 35.

1(*b*) *Ballad Romances, and Other Poems.* Philadelphia/Boston[,
       Mass.]: M. Carey/Wells and Lilly, 1816. 8.5 × 14.5 cm. Pp.
       viii + 196. By Miss Anna Maria Porter, Author of *The*
       Hungarian Brothers, etc., etc. BL: 11646. aaa. 70

PORTER, Sarah Martyn, Mrs John (died 1831)

She married John Porter, a physician, in 1767. They had five children
and lived in Plymouth, NH. (Blain)

1(*a*)   *The Royal Penitent. In Three Parts. To Which is Added, David's Lamentation over Saul and Jonathan.* Concord[, Mass.]: George Hough, 1791. 9.5 × 16 cm. 19 pp. By Mrs Sarah Porter, of Plymouth in Newhampshire. LC: PS 824. P8 R6 1791 Office.

1(*b*)   *The Royal Penitent. In Three Parts. To Which is Added, David's Lamentation over Saul and Jonathan.* Newburyport: printed by G. J. Osborne, [1793]. 9 × 14.5 cm. 21 pp. By Mrs Sarah Porter, of Plymouth in New-Hampshire. AAS: DATED PAMS.

POTTS, Ethelinda Margaretta, Mrs Cuthbert

She was the daughter of John Thorpe and Catharina Holker, and the wife of Cuthbert Potts, a surgeon. She had at least one son. (*DNB* (under John Thorpe and Laurence Holker Potts))

1   *Moonshine.* London: Longman, Hurst, Rees, Orme, and Brown, 1814. 12 × 20.5 cm. 2 vols. £1/1/- boards. *MR* 75: 328; BL: 11642. dd. 1.

2   *A Visit to Bonaparte, in Plymouth-Sound. With Another Piece Descriptive of Stoke.* Dock/Plymouth/Stonehouse: G. Granville/S. Rowe/W. Gray, 1815. 11.5 × 20 cm. 14 pp. By a Lady [Mrs E. M. Potts? (MS attribution in BL copy)]. BL: 11645. bb. 26.

3(*a*)   *Moonshine . . . Containing Sketches in England and Wales.* London: printed by Davison, Simmons, and Co., 1832. 2nd edn. Pp. xvi + 170. BL: 994. i. 37.

3(*b*)   *Moonshine . . . Containing Sketches in England and Wales.* London: J. Rodwell and H. J. McClary, 1833. 2nd edn. 13.5 × 21 cm. Pp. xvi + 268. BL: 991. i. 22.

4(*a*)   *Moonshine . . . Containing Miscellaneous Trifles.* London: Davison, Simmons, and Co., 1832. 2nd edn. 13.5 × 22 cm. Pp. viii + 171–268 + 136. LC: PR 5189. P53 M7 1832.

4(*b*)   *Moonshine . . . Containing Miscellaneous Trifles.* London: J. Rodwell and H. J. McClary, 1833. 2nd edn. 13 × 21.5 cm. Pp. xii + 301 + 6. BL: 991. i. 22.

5   *Moonshine . . . Containing Unconnected Trifles, and Appendix.* London: printed by William Wilcockson, 1835. 13 × 21.5 cm. Pp. x + 135–369 + 65. BL: 994. i. 38.

POULTER, Louisa Frances

1   *Imagination; a Poem. In Two Parts.* London: J. Hatchard and Son, 1820. 13 × 21.5 cm. Pp. [iv] + 103. BL: 992. i. 25(1).

POWELL, Anne

Perhaps the Quaker of that name, from Wiltshire. (*Friends' Books*)

1   *Clifton, Caractacus, Boadicea, and Other Pieces.* Bristol: the Albion Press, 1821. 11 × 18.5 cm. 128 pp. By Anne Powell. BL: 11644. c. 19.

POWER, Marguerite (1789–1849)

Born at Kockbrit, Co. Tipperary. She was the fourth child of Edmund Power and Ellen Sheehy. Her tyrannical and widely detested father forced her into a marriage with Captain Maurice St Leger Farmer, another unstable man, when she was 14. She left her husband after three months and returned home. He died in 1817 and in 1818 she married the immensely wealthy Charles John Gardiner, 2nd Viscount Mountjoy and 1st Earl of Blessington, and took her place as one of the most fashionable hostesses of London. After her husband's death in 1829, financial circumstances led her to supplement her income by writing. She is said to have earned between £2,000 and £3,000 a year, but not enough to maintain the family's establishment. When bankruptcy occurred she and her son-in-law, the Count D'Orsay, fled to France, where she died within a month. (Boyle, *CB*, *DNB*)

1   *Rambles in Waltham Forest. A Stranger's Contribution to the Triennial Sale for the Benefit of the Wanstead Lying-in Charity.* London: printed by J. L. Cox, 1827. 18.5 × 22.5 cm. Pp. [i] + 33. BL: 11642. g. 23.

PRESCOTT, Rachel

Shoberl identifies her as the 'friend of Dr (John Boniot) de Mainauduc'. He was a notorious quack and she apparently acted as an assistant at his lectures on mesmerism and was his literary executor when he died in 1797. (*GM*, Shoberl)

1   *Poems.* London: for the author by Richardsons, 1799. 13.5 × 22 cm. 84 pp. 2/-. By Rachel Prescott. Newberry: Y 185. P 8945. [Photocopy seen only.]

2   *Poems.* London: Longman, 1812. 8vo. 84 pp. 2/6. By Miss Prescott. *CR* 4: 441–2; *MR* 73: 208–9. Not located.

PRIDEAUX, Mrs, *see* COLLECTIONS 4

PROWSE, Marianne, Mrs Isaac S.

She lived in Teignmouth in Devon. She was acquainted with Keats, who wrote letters to her and her mother and sisters in 1818. Her son, William Jeffery Prowse, wrote humorous verse. (*DNB* (under William Jeffery Prowse), *KL*)

1   *Poems.* London: Smith, Elder and Co., and Baldwin and Cradock, 1830. 11 × 19 cm. Pp. iv + 183 [subscription edition]. By I. S. Prowse. BL: 994. h. 26.

PUGH, Sarah S.

1   *Poems Addressed to Various Literary Characters.* Weymouth: printed for the author by G. Kay, 1827. 10 × 16 cm. Pp. viii + 112. By S. S. P. HL; BL: 11646. bbb. 5.

PYE, Jael Henrietta, Mrs Robert Hampden (1737?–82)

She was a Jewish convert to Christianity whose maiden name was Mendez. She married John Neil Campbell in 1762 and then Robert Hampden Pye, an officer in the guards and brother of the poet laureate, H. J. Pye, in 1766. Her *Peep into the Gardens at Twickenham* forced her upon Horace Walpole's reluctant attention. (Todd 1, *WL*)

1(*a*)   *Poems.* London: J. Walter, 1771. 10 × 16.5 cm. 82 pp. By a Lady. BL: 11632. aa. 32.

1(*b*)   *Poems.* London: J. Walter, 1772. 2nd edn. 10 × 16.5 cm. Pp. iv + 96. By Mrs Hampden Pye. HEHL: 344276.

PYE, Mary Elizabeth, *see* JONES, Mary Elizabeth

PYKE, Sarah Leigh

1   *Israel, a Juvenile Poem.* Bath/London/Taunton: printed for the author by R. Cruttwell/Scatcherd and Co./J. Poole, 1795. 13 × 20 cm. 2 vols. By Serena. BL: 11644. d. 28.

2   *The Triumph of the Messiah.* Exeter/London/Bristol/ Bath/Axminster/Plymouth: S. Woolmer/J. Conder/Gutch/ Upham/J. R. Small/P. Nettleton, 1812. 10 × 17.5 cm. Pp. [viii] + 216 [subscription edition]. By Sarah Leigh Pyke, Author of *Israel, a Poem*, by Serena. BL: 11644. bb. 38.

3   *Eighty Village Hymns.* Taunton: printed by W. Bragg, 1832. 7.5 × 12.5 cm. 84 pp. By Sarah Leigh Pyke. BL: 3435. aaa. 12.

QUEEN MAB, *pseudonym, see* APPENDIX 6

QUIGLEY, Catharine

1   *Poems.* Dublin: printed for the author by T. Courtney, 1813. 9.5 × 16.5 cm. Pp. [viii] + 192 [subscription edition]. By Catharine Quigley. BL: 11641. b. 36.

2   *The Microscope; or Village Flies, in Three Cantos; with Other Poems, never before Published.* Monaghan: printed for the author by Nathaniel Greacen, 1819. 9.5 × 17 cm. Pp. vi + 114. By Catharine Quigley. BL: 11632. aaa. 43.

R****, Mrs, *see* COLLECTIONS 16(*a–b*)

RADCLIFFE, Ann, Mrs William (1764–1823), *see also* COLLECTIONS 35, 36

Born in London. She was the only daughter of William Ward and Ann Oates, and through her mother's family was familiar with literary society when young. When she was 23, she married William Radcliffe, a student of law who became editor and owner of the *English Chronicle.* With her second book, *A Sicilian Romance,* she began a sequence of significant Gothic novels of which *The Mysteries of Udolpho* (1794) and *The Italian* (1797) are the most highly regarded. Her mother's death in 1797 made her financially independent and she stopped publishing. Poetry was regularly scattered through her novels and the collection from them in *Poems* was published without her knowledge and apparently in the belief that she had died. (*CB, DNB*)

1(*a*)   *The Poems.* London: J. Bounden, 1815. 10 × 16.5 cm. Pp. 9–114. By Mrs Ann Radcliffe, Author of *The Mysteries of Udolpho,* etc., etc., etc. BL: 11644. eee. 33.

1(*b*)   *The Poems.* London: J. Smith, 1816. 9.5 × 16 cm. 118 pp. By Mrs Ann Radcliffe, Author of *The Mysteries of Udolpho,* etc., etc., etc. BL: 1607/4641.

2(*a*)   *Gaston de Blondeville, or the Court of Henry III. Keeping Festival in Ardenne, a Romance. St. Alban's Abbey, a Metrical Tale; with Some Poetical Pieces.* London: Henry Colburn, 1826. 11 × 19 cm. 4 vols. [The verse occupies vol. iv, vol. iii, pp. 89–375, and vol. i, pp. 150–71.] By Anne Radcliffe. BL: N.378, 379.

2(*b*) *Gaston de Blondeville, or the Court of Henry III. Keeping Festival in Ardenne, a Romance. St. Alban's Abbey, a Metrical Tale; with Some Poetical Pieces . . . To Which is Prefixed a Memoir of the Author, with Extracts from her Journals.* Philadelphia: H. C. Carey and I. Lea, 1826. 10.5 × 18 cm. 4 vols. in 2 [prose and verse, the verse being mainly in vols. iii and iv]. By Anne Radcliffe, Author of *The Mysteries of Udolpho, Romance of the Forest,* etc. NEDL: KE19044.

2(*c*) *The Posthumous Works . . . Comprising Gaston de Blondeville, a Romance; St. Alban's Abbey, a Metrical Tale, with Various Poetical Pieces. To Which is Prefixed a Memoir of the Authoress, with Extracts from her Private Journals.* London: Henry Colburn, 1833. 11.5 × 18.5 cm. 4 vols. [most of the poetry being in vols. iii and iv]. By Anne Radcliffe, Authoress of *The Mysteries of Udolpho,* etc. Widener: 18497. 3.

3 *The Poetical Works . . . St. Alban's Abbey, a Metrical Romance; with Other Poems.* London: for Henry Colburn, 1834. 12 × 19 cm. 2 vols. By Anne Radcliffe, Authoress of *The Mysteries of Udolpho, Romance of the Forest,* etc. BL: 11609. f. 3, 4.

[*See also*: 'The Mysteries of Udolpho, a Romance; Interspersed with Some Pieces of Poetry' ([London], 1794, about 26 pp. of verse in 4 vols.; also [Dublin], 1794, 1795, [Boston, Mass.], 1795, 1799, 1800, 1803, 1806, 1810, 1823, 1824, [Philadelphia], 1828).]

THE RECTOR'S WIFE, *see* GOODALL, Harriott Anabella

REEVE, Sophia, Mrs
She came from Norwich and was also the author of *The Mysterious Wanderer* (1807), a novel. (Watt)

1 *The Flowers at Court.* London: for the author by C. and R. Baldwin, 1809. 10 × 16 cm. 30 pp. 2/6 boards. By Mrs Reeve. *MR* 59: 439–40; *CR* 16: 211; BL: 11641. b. 37.

2 *Holiday Annals, Interspersed with Tales & Poetical Pieces, for Young People.* Norwich/London/Gainsborough: Stevenson,

Matchett and Stevenson/Scatcherd and Letterman, Baldwin, Craddock and Joy/Darton, Harvey and Co., J. Harris, [1820?]. 9 × 15.5 cm. 156 pp. [of which 13 pp. are in verse]. By Mrs Reeve, of Norwich. BL: 12808. aa. 23.

3(*a*)   *Christmas Trifles; Consisting Principally of Geographical Charades, Valentines, and Poetical Pieces, for Young Persons.* Norwich/London/Derby: John Stacy/Longman, Hurst, Rees, Orme, Brown, and Green, Harvey and Darton/Henry Mozley, 1826. 10.5 × 16.5 cm. 64 pp. By Mrs Reeve. BL: 11644. bb. 32.

3(*b*)   *Christmas Trifles; Consisting Principally of Geographical Charades, Valentines, and Poetical Pieces, for Young Persons.* London/Norwich: Longman, Rees, Orme, Brown, and Green, Harvey and Darton/John Stacy, 1827. 9.5 × 16 cm. 61 pp. By Mrs Reeve. BL: 11644. aa. 14.

REEVES, Eliza

1   *Poems on Various Subjects.* London: for the author by C. Dilley, 1780. 19.5 × 25 cm. Pp. xviii + 224 [subscription edition]. By Eliza Reeves. BL: 11633. g. 31.

REID, Mrs M. A., *see also* COLLECTIONS 29(*a–b*)

1   *The Harp of Salem; a Collection of Historical Poems, from the Scriptures. Together with Some Reflective Pieces.* Edinburgh: James Taylor Smith and Co., 1827. 11.5 × 19.5 cm. Pp. vi + 224. By a Lady. BL: 11646. d. 46.

REMINGTON, Miss, *see* COLLECTIONS 21

RENNIE, Eliza, *see also* COLLECTIONS 42

1   *Poems.* London: B. E. Lloyd and Son, 1828. 9.5 × 16.5 cm. Pp. viii + 182. By Eliza Rennie. BL: 994. f. 33.

RENOU, Sarah

1(*a*)   *The Temple of Truth. A Poem, in Five Cantos.* London/Bristol: Baldwin, Cradock and Joy/Browne and Manchee, 1818. 12.5 × 20 cm. Pp. [iv] + 102. By Sarah Renou, Author of *Village Conversations, or the Vicar's Fire-side.* BL: 994. l. 1(2).

1(*b*)   *The Temple of Truth. A Poem, in Five Cantos.* Edinburgh/ London: James Taylor Smith and Co./Baldwin, Cradock, and Joy, 1821. 2nd edn. 12 × 19.5 cm. Pp. [iv] + 102. By Sarah Renou. BL: 11644. ccc. 27.

1(*c*)   *The Temple of Truth. A Poem.* London/Bristol: Baldwin, Cradock, and Joy/T. J. Manchee, 1822. 2nd edn. 13 × 21 cm. Pp. [iv] + 102. By Sarah Renou. BL: 11644. d. 36.

A RESIDENT OF SHERWOOD FOREST, *see* HAMILTON, Sarah

RHODES, Henrietta

1   *Poems and Miscellaneous Essays.* Brentford: printed [for the author?] by P. Norbury, 1814. 15 × 24.5 cm. Pp. xvi + 80 [subscription edition]. By Henrietta Rhodes. BL: 11641. f. 49.

RIBBANS, Rebecca (1794?–1821)
Her dates are derived from her *Lavenham Church.*

1   *Lavenham Church, a Poem.* Ed. [Frederick Ribbans]. Ipswich/ Hadleigh/Sudbury/Ballingdon/Bury/Thetford/ London/Lavenham: Cowell/Hardacre/Bickmore/Hill/Deck/ Rogers/Rodwell and Martin/Classical and Commercial Boarding School, 1822. 21.5 × 27.5 cm. 29 pp. [subscription edition]. 5/-. By Rebecca Ribbans. BL: 10350. g. 1(8).

2   *Effusions of Genius.* Ipswich/London/Bury/Cambridge/ Ballingdon/Hadleigh/Colchester/Chelmsford/Norwich/ Woodbridge: Ribbans, and Deck and Shalders/Longman and Co., Hamilton, Adams and Co., and G. B. Whittaker/Deck, Dingle and Ray/Hall/Hill/Hardacre/Swinborne and Co./Guy/Stacy/Loder, 1829. 10 × 17 cm. Pp. xx + 127 [subscription edition]. By Rebecca Ribbans. BL: 11633. b. 45.

RICHARDSON, Caroline E., Mrs George G. (1777–1853)
Born at Forge, Dumfriesshire. She was the wife of George Richardson, a servant of the East India Company. She was the author of *Adonia*, a novel, and was eventually proprietor of the *Berwick Advertiser*. (*DNB* (under Charlotte Caroline Richardson), *GM*)

1(*a*)   *Poems.* Edinburgh/London: Cadell and Co./Simpkin, Marshall and Co. and William Crofts, 1828. 10.5 × 18 cm. Pp. vi + 227. By Mrs G. G. Richardson, Dumfries. BL: 11644. cc. 25.

1(*b*)   *Poems.* Edinburgh/London: Cadell and Co./Simpkin, Marshall and Co. and William Crofts, 1828. 2nd edn. 10 × 17.5 cm. Pp. vi + 227. By Mrs G. G. Richardson, Dumfries. BL: 994. g. 31.

1(*c*)   *Poems.* Edinburgh/London/Dumfries: Cadell and Co./ Simpkin, Marshall, and Co., William Crofts/John Sinclair, 1829. 3rd edn. 11.5 × 19.5 cm. Pp. x + 239. By Mrs G. G. Richardson, Dumfries. BL: 11644. d. 14.

2   *Poems . . . Second Series.* London/Edinburgh: William Crofts/Cadell and Co., 1834. 12 × 20 cm. Pp. vi + 264. By Mrs G. G. Richardson. BL: 994. i. 24.

RICHARDSON, Charlotte Caroline, Mrs (1775–1850?)

Born in York. Her maiden name was Smith. She went into service at 16 and in 1802 married a shoemaker named Richardson. Her husband and their infant child both died of consumption. She opened a school that was successful for a while. Mrs Newcome Cappe appealed through *GM* for subscribers to her *Poems*, and 600 copies were sold in addition to the subscription copies. Library catalogues routinely confuse her with her namesake (below). (*DNB, GM*)

1(*a*)   *Poems Written on Different Occasions.* Ed. Catharine Cappe. York/London: Wilson and Spence, J. Todd, J. Wolstenholme/J. Johnson, J. Hatchard and J. Mawman, 1806. 11 × 18.5 cm. Pp. xxiv + 10–129 [subscription edition]. By Charlotte Richardson. BL: 1466. g. 6.

1(*b*)   *Poems Written on Different Occasions . . . To Which is Prefixed Some Account of the Author, together with the Reasons Which Have Led to their Publication.* Ed. Catharine Cappe. Philadelphia: Kimber, Conrad, and Co., 1806. 11 × 19 cm. 128 pp. By Charlotte Richardson. LC: PR 5226. R25 P6 Rare Bk Coll.

1(*c*)   *Poems Written on Different Occasions.* Ed. Catharine Cappe. York/London: Wilson and Spence, J. Todd and J. Wolstenholme/J. Johnson, J. Hatchard and J. Mawman, 1806.

2nd edn. 11 × 18 cm. Pp. xxiv + 9–129 [subscription edition]. By Charlotte Richardson. BL: 11642. bb. 33.

2   *Poems, Chiefly Composed during the Pressure of Severe Illness.* Vol. ii [of 2, the first being *Poems Written on Different Occasions* (1806)]. Ed. [Catharine Cappe]. York/London: Wilson and Son, W. and R. Spence, Todd and Sons, and J. Wolstenholme/J. Johnson, Longman, Hurst, Rees, and Orme, J. Mawman and J. Hatchard, 1809. 11 × 18 cm. 146 pp. [subscription edition]. By Charlotte Richardson. BL: 11642. bb. 33.

RICHARDSON, Charlotte Caroline, Mrs
She seems to have lived in Frosterly, Co. Durham. (*BLC*)

1   *Waterloo, a Poem, on the Late Victory . . . To Which is Added, Truth, a Vision.* London: printed by Theodore Page, [1815]. 10 × 17 cm. 16 pp. 6*d.* By Charlotte Caroline Richardson. BL: 11644. bb. 41.

2   *Isaac and Rebecca.* London: Darton, Harvey, and Darton, 1817. 10.5 × 12 cm. 24 pp. By Charlotte Caroline Richardson. BL: T. 965*(2).

3   *Harvest, a Poem, in Two Parts; with Other Poetical Pieces.* London/Whitby: for the author by Sherwood, Neely and Jones, Westley and Parish, Egerton, Hatchard, Asperne, Mrs Richardson/Clark and Medd, 1818. 13.5 × 21.5 cm. Pp. [vi] + 112 [subscription edition]. By Charlotte Caroline Richardson. BL: 1466. g. 11.

4   *Ludolph, or the Light of Nature, a Poem.* London/Whitby: Sherwood, Jones and Co., Hatchard and Son/Rogers and Kirby, 1823. 12.5 × 21 cm. Pp. [ii] + 127. By Charlotte Caroline Richardson, author of *Harvest*, the *Soldier's Child*, etc. BL: 11644. d. 19.

RICHARDSON, Mrs George G., *see* RICHARDSON, Caroline E.

RICHARDSON, Sarah, Mrs Joseph (died 1824)
Her maiden name was Fawcett. She was the wife of Joseph Richardson, who was a lawyer and an MP. They had four daughters. Her husband was also the author of satirical verse and comedy as well as

being one of the proprietors of Drury Lane Theatre in London; when he died in 1803, leaving her in financial distress, she edited his *Literary Relics* (1807) and embarked on a literary career of her own. (Blain, *DNB* (under Joseph Richardson), *GM*)

1   *Original Poems, Intended for the Use of Young Persons.* London: Vernor, Hood, and Sharpe, 1808. 9.5 × 15.5 cm. Pp. xii + 132. By Mrs Richardson. BL: 994. g. 30.

2(*a*)   *Ethelred, a Legendary Tragic Drama.* London: Lowndes and Hobbs, [1809?]. 12.5 × 20.5 cm. Pp. xvi + 92 [subscription edition]. By Mrs Richardson, One of the Patentees of the Late Theatre-Royal, Drury Lane, and Widow of the Late Joseph Richardson, Esq., M.P. BL: 1465. g. 1(2).

2(*b*)   *Ethelred, a Legendary Tragic Drama, in Five Acts.* London: C. Lowndes, [1810?]. 2nd edn. 13 × 20 cm. [title-page repaired]. Pp. xiv + 92 [subscription edition]. By Mrs Richardson. BL: 841. h. 2.

3   *Gertrude, a Tragic Drama, in Five Acts.* London: C. Lowndes, [1810?]. 13 × 21.5 cm. Pp. xvi + 66 [subscription edition]. By Mrs Richardson. BL: 11779. g. 4.

4   *Abridged History of the Bible, in Verse.* Parts I and II [of 16]. London: W. Davis, J. C. Bingham, Sherwood, Neeley and Jones, 1820. 22 × 27.5 cm. 68 pp. 5/- each Part. By Mrs Richardson. BL: 689. g. 6(1).

5   *Abridged History of the Bible, in Verse.* Parts III and IV [of 16; paper covers but no new title-page, pagination continuous from Parts I and II]. London: all the booksellers, 1821. 22 × 27.5 cm. Pp. 69–132. 5/- each Part. By Mrs Richardson. BL: 689. g. 6(2).

6   *Abridged History of the Bible, in Verse.* Part V [of 16; paper covers but no new title-page; paginated continuously with Parts I–IV]. London: all the booksellers, 1822. 22 × 27.5 cm. Pp. 133–64. 5/- the Part. By Mrs Richardson. BL: 689. g. 6(3).

RICHINGS, Rebecca

She was the daughter of Thomas Richings of Oxford and her book is dedicated to her brother, Benjamin, who was Vicar of Mancetter, War. (*Alumni Oxonienses*, MS note in BL copy of *Elijah*)

1   *Elijah: A Poem*. London: L. B. Seeley and J. Conder, 1818. 13 × 21 cm. Pp. viii + 47. By a Lady. BL: 11643. bbb. 25(2).

RIDDELL, Maria, Mrs Walter (1772?–1808), *see* COLLECTIONS 16(*a–b*)

She was the youngest of seven children of William Woodley and Frances Payne; he was the owner of an estate in Antigua and she was an heiress from St Kitts. Maria was born and educated in England but left for the Leeward Islands in 1788 and published a book about her voyage in 1792. In 1790 she became the second wife of Walter Riddell, a half-pay officer. They had two daughters. The family moved to Woodley Park and frequently entertained Burns there (he comments favourably on her poetical talents in a letter to his friend Smellie). Her husband died in 1802 and in 1808 she married Colonel Philipps Lloyd Fletcher. (*CB*, Hugh S. Gladstone, *Maria Riddell, the Friend of Burns* (1915))

RIMMERT, Jane

1   *Recollections and Poems*. London: for the author by C. S. Arnold, 1825. 11.5 × 18.5 cm. Pp. viii + 55. By Jane Rimmert. BL: 11644. cc. 9.

RING, Mrs Thomas

A Few Words of Advice and Consolation . . . (1812) contains letters from the Revd John Newton to Christiana, who writes a preface from Reading. She is identified in MS on the title-page of the Bodley copy as Mrs Ring of Reading. The letters are dated 1792.

1   *Divine Poems; together, with a Journal of Our Lord's Gracious Dealings with the Soul of the Authoress*. Ed. [T. Harrison]. St. Ives/London/Bristol/Shrewsbury/Sunderland/Newark upon Trent: printed by W. Davis/G. Terry and Walsh/W. Brown/W. Eddowes/W. Graham/D. Holt, [1792]. 11.5 × 19.5 cm. Pp. x + 85 [prose and verse]. By Christiana, Ramsay, Huntingdonshire. Bodley: 1419 e. 720.

RIPLEY, Dorothy (1767–1831)

Born in England. She was the daughter of William Ripley, a Methodist minister in Whitby, Yorks., and of Dorothy, his wife. She left for America in 1802 as a Quaker missionary to serve African and Indian congregations. She edited *Memoirs of William Ripley* (1827). (Blain, and *Letters Addressed to Dorothy Ripley* (2nd edn., n.d.), *NUC*)

1(*a*)　The Bank of Faith and Works United. Philadelphia: printed for the authoress by J. H. Cunningham, 1819. 10 × 17 cm. 204 pp. [prose and 12 pp. of verse]. By Dorothy Ripley. Newberry: Ayer 266 R5 1819. [Photocopy seen only.]

1(*b*)　The Bank of Faith and Works United. Whitby: printed for the authoress by G. Clark, 1822. 2nd edn. 18 cm. Pp. vi + 306. By Dorothy Ripley, Citizen of This World, but Going above to the New Jerusalem. *NUC*. Not seen.

2　[*An Address to All in Difficulties*. Bristol: printed by Rose, 1821?] [title-page lacking]. 9.5 × 17 cm. 20 pp. [prose and 10 pp. of verse]. By Dorothy Ripley. BL: 4405. bbb. 41(2).

RITSON, Anne, Mrs

1　A Poetical Picture of America, being Observations Made during a Residence of Several Years, at Alexandria, and Norfolk, in Virginia; Illustrative of the Manners and Customs of the Inhabitants: And Interspersed with Anecdotes, Arising from a General Intercourse with Society in that Country, from the Year 1799 to 1807. London: for the author by Vernor, Hood, and Sharpe, 1809. 10.5 × 17.5 cm. Pp. [xii] + 177 [subscription edition]. By a Lady. HEHL: 16292.

2(*a*)　Classical Enigmas, Adapted to Every Month in the Year . . . London: W. Darton, 1811. 11 × 13 cm. 30 pp. By a Lady. BL: 12305. aa. 22.

2(*b*)　Classical Enigmas, Adapted to Every Month in the Year . . . London: W. Darton, Jr., 1815. New edn. 10 × 12.5 cm. 62 pp. 6*d*. By Mrs Anne Ritson. BL: 12304. aa. 33.

3　The Poetical Chain, Consisting of Miscellaneous Poems, Moral, Sentimental, and Descriptive, on Familiar and Interesting Subjects. London: for the author by Ellerton and Henderson, Sherwood, Neely and Jones, J. Booth, W. Darton and W. Austen, 1811. 10 × 16.5 cm. Pp. [viii] + 227. 7/6 boards. By Mrs Ritson. *MR* 67: 323–4; BL: 11644. bbb. 18.

4(*a*)　Exercises for the Memory: An Entire New Set of Improving Enigmas, being the Forty English and Twelve Welch Counties, in

Verse . . . London: J. and E. Wallis, 1813. 8 × 14 cm. 107 pp. By Anne Ritson. UCLA: CBC R512e 1813.

4(*b*)   *Exercises for the Memory: An Entire New Set of Improving Enigmas, being the Forty English and Twelve Welch Counties, in Verse* . . . London: Wallis and Son, 1814. 2nd edn. 8 × 13.5 cm. 107 pp. By Anne Ritson. BL: 12305. aa. 21.

4(*c*)   *Exercises for the Memory: An Entire New Set of Improving Enigmas, being the Forty English, and Twelve Welch, Counties, in Verse* . . . London: E. Wallis, 1818. 2nd edn. 9.5 × 15 cm. 108 pp. By Anne Ritson. BL: 1210. i. 12.

ROBERTS, Emma (1794?–1841), *see also* COLLECTIONS 46, 48

Born at Methley, near Leeds. She was the posthumous daughter of Captain William Roberts, paymaster in an army regiment. She grew up in Bath with her mother, 'a lady of literary pretensions'. She became a close friend of Letitia Landon (q.v.), whom she met while reading in the British Museum. In 1828 she went to India with a sister who had married an officer in the Bengal infantry. On her sister's death she took up journalism in Calcutta, writing for the *Oriental Observer*. She returned to England in 1832 and then went back to India, where she died. She was a regular contributor to the annuals from 1826 to 1838, and she provided the text for White's *Views in India* (1838). (Blain, Boyle, *CB*, *DNB*, *GM*)

1   *Almegro, a Poem, in Five Cantos.* London: H. Hodson, Bohn, and Walker, 1819. 12.5 × 21 cm. Pp. [iv] + 151. HL; BL: 992. i. 24(1).

2(*a*)   *Oriental Scenes, Dramatic Sketches and Tales, with Other Poems.* Calcutta: for the author by Norman Grant, 1830. 11.5 × 18.5 cm. Pp. viii + 264 + xvii [subscription edition]. By Emma Roberts. BL: 11643. bb. 46.

2(*b*)   *Oriental Scenes, Sketches, and Tales.* London: Edward Bull, 1832. 12.5 × 19.5 cm. Pp. xii + 204. By Emma Roberts. BL: 993. g. 28.

ROBERTS, Mary (1763–1848)

She was the daughter of Samuel Roberts of Sheffield and of Elizabeth Wright. She is often confused with a cousin of the same name. (Blain, *DNB* (under Samuel Roberts))

1   *The Royal Exile; or, Poetical Epistles of Mary, Queen of Scots, During her Captivity in England: With Other Original Poems.* Ed. [Samuel Roberts]. London/Sheffield: Longman, Hurst, Rees, Orme, and Brown, Taylor and Hessey/Miss Gales and the other booksellers, 1822. 12.5 × 21.5 cm. 2 vols. 14/- boards [subscription copy]. By Mary, Queen of Scots and a Young Lady. *NUC*; *MR* 99: 210–11; BL: 11644. h. 40.

ROBERTS, Mary Ann

1   *Poems. The Sisters; a Scottish Legend. Mary; a Tale of the Highlands.* London: William Pickering, 1830. 10 × 16 cm. Pp. [iv] + 103. By M. A. Roberts. CUL: N. 27. 10⁴.

ROBERTS, R. (1730?–88)

The elder sister of Dr Roberts, high master of St Paul's School, London. She wrote sermons, translations from French, and possibly some fiction in periodicals. (Blain, *GM*, Todd 1)

1   *Malcolm, a Tragedy.* London: for the author, 1779. 13 × 21.5 cm. Pp. [ii] + 76. BL: 163. k. 64.

2   *Albert, Edward and Laura, and the Hermit of Priestland; Three Legendary Tales.* London: T. Cadell, 1783. 18 × 22 cm. 68 pp. 3/-. By R. Roberts. BL: 161. m. 29.

ROBERTSON, Eliza (*or* Elizabeth) Frances (1771–1805)

Her father was an 'oilman' of Horselydown, London, her mother, Eliza Earle, the daughter of a woollen-draper. According to her own account, she was neglected as a child. In 1787 she became a schoolteacher. She and her father became sunk in debt. She was for a time a governess, but she professed expectations of being an heiress and on being disappointed in these was imprisoned for debt. She died in the Fleet Prison. (*The Life and Memoirs of Mrs Robertson, of Blackheath* (1802), Todd 1)

1   *Consolatory Verses . . . with Some Account of the Life and Character of the Author. To Which are Added Observations, Moral, Juridical, and Elucidatory, on her Very Remarkable Case, and its Important Relation to the Public Safety.* Ed. Ματ Θυνεγνος. London: Jones and Bumford, 1808. 9 × 16 cm. 304 pp. [verse occupies pp. 107–73]. By the late Eliza F. Robertson. BL: 1414. a. 33.

ROBINSON, Mrs E.

She lived in Stapleford, Leics. She was dead by 1816. (*The Power, Wisdom*)

1 *The Power, Wisdom, and Goodness of God Displayed in the Works of Creation and Redemption; a Poem.* Liverpool: printed by T. Kaye, 1816. 11.5 × 19 cm. 24 pp. By the Late Mrs E. Robinson. BL: 1465. h. 13(8).

ROBINSON, Ellen, Mrs

She appears to have kept a bookshop in Liverpool. She explains in the introduction to *A Tribute* that despite her social station, 'facility of composition allows her to avoid neglecting her domestic claims'.

1(*a*) *Poem, Written on the Death of the Rev. Thos. Spencer, in Four Parts* . . . Liverpool: J. Mollison and Reston and Taylor, 1811. 13 × 21 cm. 31 pp. By Ellen Robinson. BL: 4906. cc. 25(1).

1(*b*) *Poem Written on the Death of* . . . *Spencer.* 1812. 2nd edn. Inference.

1(*c*) *Poem, Written on the Death of the Rev. Thos. Spencer, in Four Parts* . . . Liverpool: printed for the author and all the booksellers by A. Fleetwood, 1823. 3rd edn. 12.5 × 20 cm. 18 pp. By Ellen Robinson. Yale (Beinecke): College Pamphlets vol. 1250.

2 *Poems on Different Subjects.* Liverpool: printed for the authoress and other booksellers by G. Wood, 1814. 12.5 × 20 cm. 32 pp. By Ellen Robinson. Yale (Beinecke): College Pamphlets vol. 1250.

3(*a*) *A Tribute of Sorrow and Affection to the Memory of a Beloved Son, of Extraordinary Promise, Who was Accidentally Drowned* . . . *in the Sixteenth Year of his Age.* Liverpool: Robert Tilling, [1821?]. 12.5 × 20.5 cm. 16 pp. By Ellen Robinson, Authoress of a Poem on the Death of Spencer, etc. BL: 11642. e. 11.

3(*b*) *A Tribute of Sorrow and Affection to the Memory of a Beloved Son, of Extraordinary Promise, Who was Accidentally Drowned by Falling from the Prince's Dock Pier-head into the River Mersey, September 23, 1821, in the Sixteenth Year of his Age.* Liverpool: Robert Tilling and the authoress, [1821]. 2nd edn. 12.5 × 20 cm. 16 pp. By Ellen Robinson, Authoress of a *Poem on* the *Death of Spencer*, etc. Yale (Beinecke): College Pamphlets vol. 1250.

ROBINSON, Maria Elizabeth (died 1818), *see* COLLECTIONS 18

She was the daughter of Mary Robinson (below). She was the author of *The Shrine of Bertha* (1794), a novel, and editor of her mother's auto-biography. She lived in Englefield Green, Berks., in the cottage in which her mother died. (*Shelley Circle*, Watt)

ROBINSON, Mary, Mrs Thomas (1758–1800), *see also* COLLECTIONS 5(*d*), 19, 21, 35, 53

She was the daughter of John Darby, a merchant, and of Maria Seys. She attended the Bristol school run by Hannah More (q.v.) and her sisters. Her father absconded to Labrador and she and her mother moved to London, where she was a pupil of the gifted but alcoholic Meribah Lorington in Chelsea. In 1774 she married Thomas Robinson, an articled lawyer's clerk. They had two children, only one of whom survived infancy. She began writing verse when her husband was imprisoned for debt. 'Perdita', as she was called because of her success in *The Winter's Tale*, became famous as a comic actress at Drury Lane, temporarily captivating the Prince of Wales, with whom she fell in love. At the age of 24 she suffered a miscarriage that left her partly para-lysed. She became a popular novelist but died in penury. She was respected as a writer by such young Bristol romantics as Southey and Coleridge. (*CB*, *DNB*, Todd 2)

1   *Poems*. London: C. Parker, 1775. 9.5 × 15 cm. Pp. [iv] + 134. 2/6 sewed. By Mrs Robinson. *MR* 53: 262; BL: 11643. aa. 38.

2   *Captivity, a Poem. And Celadon and Lydia, a Tale. Dedicated, by Permission, to Her Grace the Duchess of Devonshire*. London: T. Becket, [1777]. 16.5 × 22 cm. Pp. [5] + 8–48. 2/-. By Mrs Robinson. *MR* 57: 328; BL: 161. m. 30.

3(*a*)   *Ainsi va le monde*. Inference.

3(*b*)   *Ainsi va le monde, a Poem. Inscribed to Robert Merry, Esq. A.M. Member of the Royal Academy of Florence; and, Author of the Laurel of Liberty and the Della Crusca Poems*. London: printed by John Bell, 1790. 2nd edn. 19.5 × 26.5 cm. Pp. [ii] + 16. 1/6. By Laura Maria. Widener: 18447. 21. 5. [Photocopy seen only.]

3(*c*) *Ainsi va le monde, a Poem. Inscribed to Robert Merry, Esq. A.M. Member of the Royal Academy of Florence; and, Author of the Laurel of Liberty and the Della Crusca Poems.* London: printed by John Bell, 1796. 18.5 × 23 cm. [13 pp.]. 1/6. By Laura Maria. Yale (Beinecke): Im/R564/790A.

4 *The Beauties of Mrs Robinson. Selected and Arranged from her Poetical Works.* Ed. [Anon.]. London: H. D. Symonds, 1791. 11 × 18 cm. Pp. vi + 50. 1/6. By Mrs Robinson. *MR* 7: 90–1. USC: Spec. Coll. 820 H 784 tM 1782(2).

5 *Poems.* London: printed by J. Bell, 1791. 12.5 × 19 cm. Pp. xxiv + 223 [subscription edition]. £1/1/- boards. By Mrs M. Robinson. BL: 11642. e. 37.

6 *Monody to the Memory of Sir Joshua Reynolds, Late President of the Royal Academy, &c. &c. &c.* London: printed by J. Bell, 1792. 20.5 × 26.5 cm. 16 pp. 1/6. By Mrs Mary Robinson. BL: 11630. f. 46.

7(*a*) *Poems.* Vol. ii [sequel to *Poems* (1791)]. London: J. Evans and T. Becket, 1793. 11 × 18.5 cm. Pp. viii + 226. 12/- in boards. By Mrs M. Robinson. BL: 11642. e. 37.

7(*b*) *Poems.* London: J. Evans and T. Becket, [n.d.]. New edn. 11 × 18.5 cm. Pp. viii + 226. 6/-. By Mrs Mary Robinson. Bodley: Harding C 2602.

8 *Modern Manners, a Poem. In Two Cantos.* London: for the author by James Evans, 1793. 21 × 26.5 cm. 32 pp. 4/-. By Horace Juvenal. *CB*; BL: 644. k. 23(12).

9 *Monody to the Memory of the Late Queen of France.* London: J. Evans and T. Becket, 1793. 21.5 × 26.5 cm. Pp. [ii] + 27. 4/6. By Mrs Mary Robinson. *MR* 13: 115–17; BL: 11631. h. 9.

10 *An Ode to the Harp of the Late Accomplished and Amiable Louisa Hanway.* London: printed by John Bell, 1793. 8vo. 8 pp. 6*d*. By Mary Robinson. *CR* 7: 353–4; *NUC*. Not seen.

11 *Sight, the Cavern of Woe, and Solitude. Poems.* London: J. Evans and T. Becket, 1793. 20.5 × 25.5 cm. Pp. iv + 32. 2/6. By Mrs Mary Robinson. BL: 11630. f. 47.

12(*a*) *Sappho and Phaon. In a Series of Legitimate Sonnets, with Thoughts on Poetical Subjects, and Anecdotes of the Grecian*

Poetess. London: for the author by Hookham and Carpenter, 1796. 9 × 16 cm. 82 pp. 7/- boards. By Mary Robinson. *MR* 24: 17–19; BL: 11643. a. 9.

12(*b*)   *Sappho and Phaon. In a Series of Legitimate Sonnets, with Thoughts on Poetical Subjects, and Anecdotes of the Grecian Poetess.* London: A. K. Newman and Co., 1813. New edn. 10 × 16.5 cm. 82 pp. By Mary Robinson. BL: 11641. b. 39.

13   *The Sicilian Lover. A Tragedy. In Five Acts.* London: printed for the author by Hookham and Carpenter, 1796. 13.5 × 21.5 cm. Pp. [ii] + 80. 5/-. By Mary Robinson, Author of *Poems, Angelina*, etc., etc. *MR* 19: 311–14; BL: 11777. g. 32.

14   *Lyrical Tales.* London/Bristol: T. N. Longman and O. Rees/Biggs and Co., 1800. 9.5 × 15.5 cm. Pp. [2] + [1] + 2–218. 5/- boards. By Mrs Mary Robinson. *MR* 36: 26–30; BL: 11646. aa. 38.

15(*a*)   *Memoirs . . . Written by Herself. With Some Posthumous Pieces.* London: R. Phillips, T. Hurst, and Carpenter, 1801. 4 vols. [vol. iv and part of vol. iii are devoted to verse]. 9 × 16 cm. £1/1/- boards. By the Late Mrs Robinson. *MR* 36: 344–50; BL: 10825. aa. 6.

15(*b*)   *Memoirs . . . Written by Herself. With Some Posthumous Pieces.* Ed. [Mary M. Robinson]. New York: T. and J. Swords, P. A. Mesier, and W. A. Davis, 1801. 10.5 × 17.5 cm. 2 vols. [verse by the author is confined to vol. ii with a concentration of it on pp. 144–68, where it is accompanied by contributions from others]. By the Late Mrs Robinson. LC: DA 538. A35 A17 (Toner Coll.).

15(*c*)   *Memoirs . . . Written by Herself. With a Number of Posthumous Pieces.* Philadelphia: printed by T. and William Bradford, 1802. 9.5 × 16.5 cm. 237 pp. By the Late Mrs Robinson. Library Co. of Philadelphia: Am 1802 Rob/63146.D.

15(*d*)   *Memoirs . . . Written by Herself.* London: Richard Phillips, 1803. 9 × 15.5 cm. 2 vols. [verse occupies pp. 187–256 of vol. ii]. By the Late Mrs Robinson. BL: G. 13972.

16(*a*)   *The Poetical Works.* Ed. [M. E. Robinson]. London: Richard Phillips, 1806. 11 × 18.5 cm. 3 vols. By the Late Mrs Mary Robinson. *CB*; BL: 11611. c. 22–4.

16(*b*)   *The Poetical Works . . . Including the Pieces Last Published.*
London: Jones and Co., 1824. 13.5 × 21.5 cm. 232 pp. By
the Late Mrs Mary Robinson. Widener: 18447. 20. 9.

[*See also*: 'The Mistletoe.—A Christmas Tale' by Laura Maria
(1800, broadsheet).]

RODGERS, Vincentia (*fl.* 1790–1842)
She was an Irish writer. (O'D)

1   *Cluthan and Malvina; an Ancient Legend. With Other Poems.*
Belfast: F. D. Finlay, 1823. 11 × 18.5 cm. 102 pp. [sub-
scription edition]. By Miss Vincentia Rodgers. BL: 11643.
f. 2.

ROGERS, Miss, of Staffordshire, *see* COLLECTIONS 4

ROLLS, Mary, Mrs Henry
Daughter of Richard Hillary and Hannah Wynne. She was the wife of
a clergyman who was Rector of Barnwell St Andrew in 1818, of All
Saints in 1819, and then of Aldwinkle All Saints, Northants., from 1820
until his death in 1838. She was a regular contributor to the annuals
from 1828 to 1836. (*Alumni Oxonienses*, Blain, Boyle)

1   *Sacred Sketches from Scripture History.* London: Law and
Whittaker, 1815. 11 × 18.5 cm. Pp. viii + 120. 6/- boards.
By Mrs Hen. Rolls. *MR* 78: 434; BL: 11642. bbb. 59.

2   *Moscow. A Poem.* London: Law and Whittaker, Sherwood,
Neely and Jones, and all other booksellers, 1816. 12.5 × 20
cm. 31 pp. By Mrs Hen. Rolls, Authoress of *Sacred Sketches
from Scripture History.* BL: 992. i. 15(5).

3   *A Poetical Address to Lord Byron.* London: W. Hone, 1816.
14 × 22.5 cm. 8 pp. 6*d.* By Mrs Henry Rolls, Authoress of
Sacred Sketches from Scripture History—Moscow—and Other
Poems. Houghton: 17495. 697. 18*.

4   *The Home of Love, a Poem. Dedicated, by Permission, to Her
Royal Highness the Princess Charlotte of Wales.* London/
Oxford/Cambridge/Liverpool/Coventry/Warwick: Lloyd,
Sherwood and Co./Parker/Deighton/Willan/Rollason and
Merridew and Co./Sharpe, 1817. 12 × 20 cm. 31 pp. 2/6.
By Mrs Henry Rolls. *MR* 83: 96; BL: 1465. e. 19.

5   *Legends of the North, or, the Feudal Christmas; a Poem.*
       London: W. Simpkin and R. Marshall, 1825. 13 × 22 cm.
       Pp. xii + 272. 9/- boards. By Mrs Henry Rolls. *MR* 108:
       44–7; BL: 1164. k. 21.

[*See also*: 'Lines Addressed to the Members of the Royal National
Institution for the Preservation of Life from Shipwreck . . .'
(1825, 3 pp.).]

ROSCOE, Jane Elizabeth (1797–1853), *see also* COLLECTIONS 45, 48
and JEVONS, Mary Anne 1(*a–b*), 2

Born in Liverpool. She was the daughter of William Roscoe, the histo-
rian, and of Jane Griffies. She married the Revd Francis Hornblower.
She contributed to the annuals from 1829 to 1832. (Boase, Boyle,
DNB)

1(*a*)   *Poems.* London: Baldwin, Cradock, and Joy, 1820. 10 ×
         16.5 cm. Pp. [ii] + 66. 3/6 boards. By One of the Authors
         of *Poems for Youth by a Family Circle. MR* 94: 211–13; BL:
         11644. cc. 35.

1(*b*)   *Poems.* London: Baldwin, Cradock, and Joy, 1821. 2nd edn.
         10 × 17 cm. Pp. [ii] + 66. By One of the Authors of *Poems
         for Youth, by a Family Circle.* BL: 11645. aaa. 48.

ROSE, Miss, of the City of Canterbury, *see* COLLECTIONS 7

ROSE, A., *see* COLLECTIONS 9

Ross, Anne

She is identified as 'Miss A. Ross, Millener' by an MS note on the title-
page of the BL copy of 1(*a*).

1(*a*)   *Poems on Several Occasions.* Glasgow: printed by A. Duncan
         and R. Chapman, 1791. 11 × 19 cm. 61 pp. By A. Ross.
         BL: 11645. bb. 39.

1(*b*)   *Poems on Several Occasions.* Glasgow: printed by A. Duncan
         and R. Chapman, 1791. 2nd edn. 13 × 22 cm. 64 pp. By
         A. Ross. NLS: I. 37. d. [Photocopy seen only.]

1(*c*)   *A Collection of Poems.* Glasgow: printed by R. Chapman,
         1798. 3rd edn. 12 × 19.5 cm. Pp. [ii] + 103 [subscription
         edition]. By Anne Ross. CUL: 7720. d. 613.

[*See also*: 'Robin Redbreast's Address to Certain Ladies. A Song' (2 pp. in *Poetry Original and Selected* [1796]).]

ROWDEN, Frances Arabella (died *c.*1840)

Her father was a clergyman; her mother ran a school at Henley-on-Thames, Oxon. She became a governess and then a schoolteacher in London. In 1820 she opened a school in Paris and she became the second wife of Mr St Quintin, the proprietor of her London school. Letitia Landon, Caroline Lamb, and Mary Russell Mitford (qq.v.) were among her pupils. (Blain)

1(*a*)   *A Poetical Introduction to the Study of Botany*. London: White and Hookham, 1801. 17.5 × 26.5 cm. Pp. [14] + lxxii + 167 [subscription edition]. 10/6 or, large paper £1/1/-. By Frances Arabella Rowden. *MR* 40: 30–2; BL: 11630. f. 50.

1(*b*)   *A Poetical Introduction to the Study of Botany*. London: Longman, Hurst, Rees, Orme, and Brown, J. White and Cochrane, J. Murray, J. Harris, 1812. 2nd edn. 10 × 16.5 cm. Pp. xxviii + 260. 10/6 boards. By Frances Arabella Rowden. *MR* 70: 98–9; BL: 7030. bb. 41.

1(*c*)   *A Poetical Introduction to the Study of Botany*. London: G. and W. B. Whittaker, 1818. 3rd edn. 10.5 × 17 cm. Pp. xxvi + 260. By Frances Arabella Rowden. BL: 7030. bb. 42.

2(*a*)   *The Pleasures of Friendship; a Poem, in Two Parts*. London: Longman, Hurst, Rees, and Orme, 1810. 10 × 16 cm. Pp. xii + 139. By Frances Arabella Rowden. BL: 11644. b. 30.

2(*b*)   *The Pleasures of Friendship; a Poem, in Two Parts*. London: Longman, Hurst, Rees, Orme, and Brown, J. White and Cochrane, J. Murray and J. Harris, 1811 [engraved title-page is dated 1812]. 2nd edn. 10 × 16 cm. Pp. xiv + 165. 8/- boards. By Frances Arabella Rowden. *MR* 67: 434; BL: 11641. b. 40.

2(*c*)   *The Pleasures of Friendship; a Poem, in Two Parts*. London: G. and W. B. Whittaker, 1818. 3rd edn. 9.5 × 15.5 cm. Pp. xvi + 165. By Frances Arabella Rowden. BL: 11644. b. 35.

ROWE, Hannah

1   *A Pindaric Poem. Consisting of Versified Selections, from the Revelation of St. John*. Rochester/London: printed by

W. Gillman/James Evans, 1789. 21.5 × 27.5 cm. 48 pp. By Hannah Rowe. BL: 11642. h. 44(3).

ROWLES, Charlotte

1   *Nadaber, a Tradition: With Other Poems.* London: for the authoresses by Samuel Bagster, 1829. 10.5 × 18.5 cm. Pp. [vi] + 267. By Charlotte and Martha Rowles. BL: 994. h. 27.

2   *Eastern Scenes in Early Ages.* London/Wrexham/Yeovil: Thomas Ward/T. Painter/W. Porter, 1835. 9 × 14 cm. 71 pp. By Charlotte Rowles. BL: 994. g. 33.

ROWLES, Martha, *see* ROWLES, Charlotte, 1

ROWSE, Elizabeth, Mrs

1   *A Grammatical Game, in Rhyme.* London/Bath/Cambridge: for the author by Darton and Harvey, Tabart, Conder, Gurney, Wilmott and Hill/Smith/Flower, 1802. 10.5 × 17 cm. 27 pp. [with a fold-out cloth board for players, in separate slip case]. 10/6 [the price given on the title-page of 2(*a*)]. By a Lady. Osborne: uncatalogued.

2(*a*)   *Outlines of English History, in Verse.* London: J. Burditt, Darton and Harvey, Harris, Peacock, Wilmott and Hill, Kent, 1808. 11 × 19 cm. Pp. [iv] + 115. 3/6 boards. By Elizabeth Rowse. *MR* 56: 209–10; BL: 994. e. 37.

2(*b*)   *Outlines of English History, in Verse.* London: Darton, Harvey, and Darton, 1811. 2nd edn. 8.5 × 13.5 cm. Pp. iv + 120. By Elizabeth Rowse. BL: 11633. a. 37.

2(*c*)   *Outlines of English History, in Verse; and an Additional Chapter of the Succession of Nations in Britain, and the Kings Who Have Reigned in England since William the Conqueror.* Clapham/London: H. N. Batten/S. Bagster, 1833. 3rd edn. 10.5 × 18 cm. Pp. viii + 135. 5/- in cloth. By Mrs Rowse. BL: 994. e. 38.

ROWSON, Susanna, Mrs William (1762–1824)

Born in Portsmouth, Hants. She was the only daughter of Lieutenant William Haswell, RN, and Susanna Musgrave. She lived in New

England from 1766 to 1788 and became a governess on her return to England. In 1786 she married William Rowson, a hardware merchant who was also a trumpeter in the Royal Horse Guards. She began to publish fiction in the same year. Her husband was declared bankrupt in 1790, but her novel *Charlotte Temple* (1791) is said to have sold 25,000 copies. She went on stage and then emigrated to the United States with her husband. Her play, *Slaves in Algiers, or a Struggle for Freedom* (1794), was a hit. On retiring from the stage in 1797 she opened a school for girls in Boston and became editor of the *Boston Weekly Magazine*. (*CB*, *DNB*, R. W. G. Vail, *S.H. Rowson: A Bibliographical Study* (1933))

1   *Poems on Various Subjects.* London: G. G. and J. Robinson, 1788. 8vo. 72 pp. 3/-. By Mrs Rowson, Author of *The Inquisitor*, etc. *MR* 81: 85. Not located.

2   *A Trip to Parnassus; or, the Judgment of Apollo on Dramatic Authors and Performers. A Poem.* London/'Town and Country': John Abraham/all other booksellers, 1788. 22.5 × 28 cm. Pp. iv + 26. 2/-. Houghton: fAC7. R7997. 788t.

3   *Miscellaneous Poems.* Boston[, Mass.]: for the author by Gilbert and Dean and W. P. and L. Blake, 1804. 11 × 17.5 cm. 227 pp. [subscription edition]. By Susanna Rowson, Preceptress of the Ladies' Academy, Newton, Mass. BL: 11686. d. 38.

R———s, Mrs, *see* COLLECTIONS 1 (*a–c*)

RUEFUL, Mrs, *pseudonym?*

1   *Prose and Poetry, on Religious, Moral, and Entertaining Subjects, with a Brief, but Authentic, & Affecting History of Orenzo and Sarah, from the Year 1793 to the Present Day.* Bristol: printed for the author by George Ruth, [1800?]. 10.5 × 18.5 cm. Pp. viii + 208 + 2. 3/6. By Mrs Rueful. Bodley: 280 e. 3561.

RUTHERFOORD, Eliza, Mrs
She had a brother who went to India, and she was presumably a mother. (*Maternal Sketches*)

1   *Maternal Sketches; with Other Poems.* London: Holdsworth and Ball, 1832. 11 × 19 cm. Pp. x + 176. By Eliza Rutherfoord. BL: 11646. e. 18.

RYAN, Eliza, Mrs Edward

If the autobiographical information in *Poems on Several Occasions* is to be relied upon, she lived at different times in Ireland and at Bath, her husband's name was Edward, and by 1816 they had been married for at least fifteen years.

1   *Poems on Several Occasions.* Dublin: printed for the author by John Jones, 1816. 10.5 × 18 cm. Pp. 120 + vii. By Mrs Ryan. BL: 11645. bb. 19.

RYVES, Elizabeth *or* Eliza (1750–97), *see also* COLLECTIONS 35

Her father was an Irish army officer. She lost her property through a lawsuit and eked out a precarious living as a miscellaneous writer in London. She wrote several translations of French works. Her novel *The Hermit of Snowdon* (1789) is said to have been partly autobiographical; Isaac Disraeli includes her in his *Calamities of Authors.* (*CB, DNB*)

1   *Poems on Several Occasions.* London: for the author by J. Dodsley, 1777. 13.5 × 21.5 cm. Pp. [xvi] + 6–176 [subscription edition]. 5/-. By Elizabeth Ryves. *MR* 58: 237; BL: 992. l. 35(2).

2   *Ode to the Rev. Mr Mason.* London: J. Dodsley, 1780. 21 × 25.5 cm. 15 pp. 1/-. By Eliza Ryves. Yale (Beinecke): Miscellaneous Poems 4.

3   *Dialogue in the Elysian Fields, between Caesar and Cato.* London: R. Faulder, 1784. 21.5 × 27.5 cm. Pp. [iv] + 12. 1/6. By Eliza Ryves, Author of *An Ode to Mr Mason* and *An Epistle to Lord John Cavendish. CR* 58: 306–8; BL: 11632. h. 19(3).

4   *An Epistle to the Right Honourable Lord John Cavendish, Late Chancellor of the Exchequer.* London: J. Dodsley, 1784. 21.5 × 27.5 cm. 17 pp. 1/-. By Miss Ryves, Author of *An Ode to Mr Mason.* BL: 11632. h. 19(2).

5   *The Hastiniad; an Heroic Poem. In Three Cantos.* London: J. Debrett, 1785. 21 × 27.5 cm. 21 pp. 1/6. By [Eliza Ryves?]. *MR* 72: 389; BL: 11630. f. 26.

6   *Ode to the Right Honourable Lord Melton, Infant Son of Earl Fitzwilliam.* London: for the author, 1787. 21.5 × 27.5 cm. 16 pp. 1/-. BL: 11632. h. 19(4).

RYVES, Mrs F.

She lived at Ryves Castle, and to judge from her subscription list was well connected, especially in Ireland and the West Indies. (*Cumbrian Legends*)

1   *Cumbrian Legends; or, Tales of Other Times: Dedicated to Her Royal Highness the Princess Charlotte of Wales* . . . Edinburgh: for the author, 1812. 10 × 16.5 cm. Pp. viii + 184 [subscription edition]. 10/6 boards. By Mrs Ryves, of Ryves Castle. *MR* 76: 211; BL: 11642. aaa. 29.

S——, Mrs

1   *The Force of Example: A Nursery Rhyme. From the Celebrated Lessons for Children by Mrs Barbauld.* London: M. J. Godwin and Co., 1822. 10.5 × 17.5 cm. 19 pp. By [Mrs S——]. Osborne: ii. 638.

S., Mrs D., *see* COLLECTIONS 16(*b*)

S., Elizabeth, *see* SMITH, Elizabeth

S., J., *see* STEWART, Jessie

SAFFERY, Maria Grace, Mrs John (1772–1858)

Born in Newbury, Berks. She was the daughter of William Andrews and of a mother who was a woman of literary tastes. They moved to Salisbury and in 1799 she became the second wife of John Saffery, a Baptist minister. They had six children. Subsequently she ran a school for girls in Salisbury. From 1835 to 1858 she lived at Bratton, Wilts. Her hymns appear in many collections. (Boase, *DNB*)

1   *Cheyt Sing. A Poem* . . . *Inscribed, by Permission, to the Right Hon. Charles James Fox, Esq.* [London]/Newbury/Salisbury: for the author by J. Woodhouse/Fuller/Collins and Johnson, 1790. 19.5 × 24.5 cm. 38 pp. 2/6. By a Young Lady of Fifteen. *MR* 2: 234–5; BL: 11632. g. 10.

2   *Poems on Sacred Subjects.* London/Edinburgh: Hamilton, Adams and Co., Darton and Harvey/Waugh and Innes, 1834. 11.5 × 19 cm. Pp. x + 218 [subscription edition]. By Maria Grace Saffery. BL: 994. l. 28.

ST JOHN, Mary (died *c.*1830)

She grew up in Queen's Co., Ireland, probably at Stradbally. Her book was published to raise money for missions in Sierra Leone. She contributed verse to the *Dublin Examiner.* (Blain)

1   *Ellauna: A Legend of the Thirteenth Century; in Four Cantos, with Notes . . . Dedicated, with Permission, to the House of Leix.* Dublin: William Henry Tyrrell, 1815. 12 × 21.5 cm. 128 pp. [subscription edition]. By Mary. O'D; BL: 11646. h. 19.

SANDERS, Charlotte Elizabeth

1   *Poems on Various Subjects.* London: Wilkie, [1787?]. 9.5 × 16 cm. Pp. [xiv] + 200 [subscription edition]. 3/- sewed. By Charlotte Eliz. Sanders. *MR* 79: 168; BL: 11633. aa. 41.

SANDERS, Maria Ruth

1   *Original Rhymes, on Various Subjects.* London: printed for the authoress by Roberts and Blatch, 1833. 9.5 × 17.5 cm. Pp. xii + 211 [subscription edition]. By Maria R. Sanders. BL: 11646. bb. 28.

SANDERSON, Mrs A.

Her maiden name was Stephenson. (*Poems*)

1   *Poems, on Various Subjects.* North Shields: printed for the author by W. Barnes, 1819. 9 × 16 cm. Pp. xvi + 112 [subscription edition]. By A. Sanderson. BL: 11645. aa. 31.

[*See also*: 'A Letter Addressed to the Officers . . . Also War in the West . . . a Poem' (1819, pp. 15–20 in verse); 'A Poem . . . Inscribed . . . to . . . the Queen' (1820, 7 pp.).]

SAPPHO, *pseudonym*

1   *Elephantasmagoria; or, the Covent Garden Elephant's Entrance into Elysium: Being a Letter from the Shade of Garrick, to John Philip Kemble, Esq.* London: Cradock and Joy, Collins, and Hookham, 1812. 14 × 22 cm. Pp. xvi + 47. 2/-. By Sappho. *MR* 69: 213–14; Pusey: Thr 481. 7. 15.

SARGANT, Jane Alice, Mrs

She also wrote plays and novels. (Allibone)

1(*a*)   *Sonnets and Other Poems.* London: for the author by Hatchard, 1817. 12.5 × 21 cm. Pp. xxiv + 120 [subscription edition]. By Jane Alice Sargant. BL: 11641. e. 37.

1(*b*)   *Sonnets and Other Poems.* London: for the author by Hatchard, 1818. 2nd edn. 12 × 20.5 cm. Pp. xii + 120. By Jane Alice Sargant. BL: 11644. d. 13.

2   *Extracts from the Pilgrimage of St. Caroline: With Notes, by an Englishwoman.* London: W. Wright, 1821. 13 × 21 cm. 87 pp. BL: 8135. ccc. 29(5).

SARGEANT, Anne Maria (1809?–52)

She contributed to *Chambers's Journal* and *La Belle Assemblée*, and she wrote fiction and books for children. (Bowes)

1   *The Isle of Wight, and Other Poems.* London/Bath/Bristol/ Southampton/Portsea/Ryde/Newbury: for the author by Seguin and Cope/Godwin/Bulgin/Drury/Horsey, Jr./ Rowden, Newport and Hellier/Newbury, 1832. 13.5 × 21 cm. Pp. [iv] + 103 [subscription edition]. By Anne Maria Sargeant. BL: 11644. d. 25.

SAUNDERS, Mary (born 1813)

She was the daughter of John Saunders, a bookseller and publisher in Exeter, Devon, and of Sarah Northcote. John Saunders, her co-author, was her older brother. She married John Bennett with whom she also collaborated as an author. She outlived her brother, who died in 1895. (Bowes, *DNB* (under John Saunders))

1   *Songs for the Many.* Lincoln, 1834. 8vo. By Two of the People [John Saunders and Mary Saunders]. HL. Not located.

SAVAGE, Mary, Mrs William

She was perhaps the mother of the George Savage who attended Eton from 1758 to 1769, and, if so, her husband was William Savage (one of her poems is addressed to her son at Eton). She contributed verse to *GM* in 1763. (Blain, Lonsdale)

1   *Poems on Various Subjects and Occasions; (from the Author's Manuscript, in the Hands of the Editor.)* London: C. Parker, 1777. 9.5 × 15.5 cm. 2 vols. 5/- sewed. By Mrs Savage. *CR* 44: 151–2; BL: 11633. aa. 42, 43.

SAVELL, Mrs, *see* COLLECTIONS 35

Savory, Martha (1781–1851)

She was the daughter of Joseph and Anna Savory. She was a Quaker missionary who travelled extensively on the Continent. In 1826 she became the second wife of J. Yeardley, also a missionary, who had accompanied her on a trip up the Rhine. She established a school for girls in Corfu. She turned against her *Poetical Tales* and had the unsold copies destroyed; some survived with the altered title *Pathetic Tales* and authorship attributed to Mrs Smith. (*DNB*, *Friends' Books*)

1   *Inspiration, a Poetical Essay*. London: John and Arthur Arch, 1805. 12.5 × 20 cm. 20 pp. By Martha Savory. BL: 11644. cc. 61(2).

2(*a*)   *Poetical Tales, Founded on Facts*. London: for the author by Darton and Harvey, 1808. 10 × 17 cm. Pp. [iv] + 148. 4/-boards. By M. Savory. *MR* 57: 92–4; BL: 11645. aa. 28.

2(*b*)   *Pathetic Tales, Founded on Facts*. London: James Goodwin, 1813. 10 × 16 cm. Pp. [iv] + 148. By Mrs Smith. BL: 11645. aa. 27.

3   *Life's Vicissitudes; or, Winter's Tears. Original Poems . . . Containing the Mausoleum, Sacred to the Memory of a Great Lady: And Various Fugitive Pieces*. London: for the author by G. Robinson, 1809. 11 × 17 cm. Pp. [vi] + 128. By Mrs Savory. BL: 11645. aaa. 17.

4   *An Original Wreath of Forget-me-not: Presented to Those Who Love to Reflect on Heavenly Things*. London/York: for the Infant School at Burton by Harvey and Darton, Edmund Fry/William Alexander and Son, 1829. 8.5 × 13 cm. Pp. [ii] + 66. By Martha Yeardley. BL: 11644. a. 79.

5   *True Tales from Foreign Lands. In Verse. Designed for the Young*. London/York: Darton and Clark, E. Fry and Son/W. Hipsley, [1835?]. 9 × 13.5 cm. 39 pp. 8*d*. By M. Yeardley. BL: 11647. aa. 74.

Sawyer, Anna, Mrs

1   *Poems on Various Subjects . . . With Notes, Historical and Explanatory*. Birmingham: printed for the author by Swinney and Hawkins, 1801. 13 × 21 cm. 92 pp. [subscription edition]. 5/-. By Anna Sawyer. BL: 11642. e. 8.

SCOT, Elizabeth, Mrs Walter (1729–89)

Born in Edinburgh. She was the daughter of David Rutherford and Alice Watson. She was educated in French and Latin and began writing verse at an early age. She married Walter Scot of Wauchope, near Jedburgh. (Blain)

1   *Alonzo and Cora, with Other Original Poems, Principally Elegiac* . . . London/Bath/York/Edinburgh: Bunney and Gold, Rivington, Robinsons, Cadell and Davies, Egerton, Faulder/Crutwell/Tessyman/Creech, 1801. 13 × 21 cm. Pp. [xvi] + 168 [subscription edition]. 10/6 boards. By Elizabeth Scot, a native of Edinburgh. *MR* 38: 436–7; BL: 11642. e. 20.

SCOTT, Elizabeth, *see* COLLECTIONS 35

SCOTT, Mary (1751–93)

She was the daughter of a linen manufacturer. She was a friend of Anna Seward and Anne Steele (qq.v.). In 1788 she married John Taylor, a Quaker. She was a Unitarian and lived in Milborne Port, Som. (Blain, and *The Female Advocate*)

1(*a*) *The Female Advocate; a Poem. Occasioned by Reading Mr Duncombe's Feminead.* London: Joseph Johnson, 1774. 17.5 × 23 cm. Pp. viii + 41. 2/-. By Miss Scott. *MR* 51: 387–90; BL: 11631. f. 34.

1(*b*) *The Female Advocate; a Poem. Occasioned by Reading Mr Duncombe's Feminead.* London: Joseph Johnson, 1775. 19.5 × 24.5 cm. Pp. viii + 41. By Miss Scott. BL: 11631. g. 18.

2   *Messiah: A Poem, in Two Parts, Published for the Benefit of the General Hospital at Bath.* Bath/London: all the booksellers/J. Johnson, 1788. 19.5 × 26 cm. 55 pp. 2/-. By Miss Scott, Author of *The Female Advocate*. *MR* 79: 277–8; BL: 11631. g. 19.

SEARCH, Sappho, *pseudonym of* BLACK, John

SELLON, Martha Ann

She was the daughter of the Revd William Sellon, of Clerkenwell, London, and of Sarah Littlehates. *The Caledonian Comet* was an answer to J. Taylor's *The Caledonian Comet* of 1810 (on Walter Scott). *CB* gives her name as Mary A. Sellon. (Blain, *CB*)

1   *The Caledonian Comet Elucidated.* London: F. C., and
        J. Rivington, 1811. 13 × 21 cm. 23 pp. BL: 1346. f. 42.

2   *Individuality; or the Causes of Reciprocal Misapprehension: In Six
        Books. Illustrated with Notes.* London: Robert Baldwin, 1814.
        13.5 × 21 cm. Pp. viii + 438. 12/- boards. By Martha Ann
        Sellon. *MR* 77: 350–6; BL: 11633. f. 27.

SERENA, *see* PYKE, Sarah Leigh

SERRES, Olivia, Mrs John Thomas, *self-styled* Princess Olive of
Cumberland (1772–1834)

She was the daughter of Robert Wilmot, a house-painter in Warwick,
and of his wife Anna Maria. She received lessons in drawing from the
marine painter John Thomas Serres and married him in 1791. They had
two daughters, but separated in 1804. She exhibited landscapes and in
1806 was appointed landscape painter to the Prince of Wales. From
1817 she claimed to be the daughter of the Duke of Cumberland, and
went to law over the claim, which was dismissed. (*DNB*)

1   *Flights of Fancy: Consisting of Miscellaneous Poems. With the
        Castle of Avola, an Opera, in Three Acts.* London: J. Ridgway,
        1805. 11.5 × 19 cm. Pp. viii + 190. 10/6 boards. By Mrs
        J. T. Serres. *MR* 50: 206–8; BL: 11641. e. 55.

SERRES, Mrs W., *see* COLLECTIONS 29(*a–b*)

SEWARD, Anna (1747–1809), *see also* COLLECTIONS 4, 17, 18, 46, 48

Born in Eyam, Derbyshire. She was the daughter of Thomas Seward
and Elizabeth Hunter, of Lichfield. Her father was headmaster of
Lichfield grammar school and had been Samuel Johnson's teacher. Her
father's death in 1790 left her with an income of £400 a year. She
became known as the 'swan of Lichfield'. Walter Scott was her literary
executor.

1(*a*) *Elegy on Captain Cook. To Which is Added, an Ode to the Sun.*
        London: J. Dodsley, 1780. 18.5 × 24.5 cm. 23 pp. 1/6. By
        Miss Seward. BL: 11632. g. 44.

1(*b*) *Elegy on Captain Cook. To Which is Added, an Ode to the Sun.*
        London: J. Dodsley, 1780. 2nd edn. 19.5 × 24.5 cm. 23
        pp. 1/6. By Miss Seward. BL: 11630. d. 8(12).

1(*c*)   *Elegy on Captain Cook. To Which is Added, an Ode to the Sun.* London: J. Dodsley, 1781. 3rd edn. 20 × 26.5 cm. 23 pp. 1/6. By Miss Seward. BL: 11632. h. 14.

1(*d*)   *Elegy on Captain Cook. To Which is Added an Ode to the Sun.* Lichfield/London: J. Jackson/J. Dodsley, 1784. 4th edn. 20 × 23.5 cm. 25 pp. 1/6. By Miss Seward. BL: 11632. g. 43.

2(*a*)   *Monody on Major Andrè. To Which are Added Letters Addressed to Her by Major Andrè, in the Year 1769.* Lichfield/ London/ Oxford/Cambridge/Bath: for the author by J. Jackson/ Robinson, Cadell and Evans/Prince/Merrill/Pratt and Clinch, 1781. 21 × 25.5 cm. Pp. iv + 47. 2/6. By Miss Seward (Author of the Elegy on Capt. Cook). BL: 162. m. 62.

2(*b*)   *Monody on Major Andrè. To Which are Added Letters Addressed to Her by Major Andrè, in the Year 1769.* Lichfield/London/ Oxford/Cambridge/Bath: for the author by J. Jackson/ Robinson, Cadell and Evans/Prince/Merrill/Pratt and Clinch, 1781. 2nd edn. 21.5 × 27.5 cm. Pp. vi + 47. 2/6. By Miss Seward (Author of the Elegy on Capt. Cook). BL: 11630. g. 44.

2(*c*)   *Monody on Major Andrè.* 3rd edn. Inference.

2(*d*)   *Monody on Major Andrè.* 4th edn. Inference.

2(*e*)   *Monody on Major Andre, (Who was Executed at Tappan, November — — 1780.) . . . To Which are Added, Major Andre's Letters, Addressed to Miss Seward, when in his 18 Year.* Philadelphia: Enoch Story, [178?]. 10.5 × 16.5 cm. 47 pp. [the letters occupy pp. 31–46]. By Miss Seward. LC: PR 3671. S7 M6 1780 Office.

2(*f*)   *Monody on Major Andre, (Who was Executed at Tappan, November — — 1780.) . . . To Which are Added Major Andre's Letters. Addressed to Miss Seward, when at his 18th Year.* New York: Thomas Allen, 1788. 10.5 × 17.5 cm. 48 pp. [pp. 19–41 being prose and pp. 43–8 being occupied by Sophia Lee's 'Edmund of the Vale']. By Miss Seward. LC: AC 901. H3 v. 102.

2(*g*)   *Monody on Major Andre, (Who was Executed at Tappan, November — — 1780.) . . . To Which are Added Major Andre's*

Letters, Addressed to Miss Seward, when at his 18 Year. Philadelphia: Enoch Story, [1790?]. 10 × 16 cm. 56 pp. [pp. 31–46 being prose, and pp. 49–56 being occupied by Sophia Lee's 'Edmund of the Vale']. By Miss Seward. LC: PR 3671. S7 M6 1790 Rare Bk Coll.

2(*h*)   *Monody on the Unfortunate Major Andre; Who was Executed at Tappan, November —, 1780 . . . To Which are Added, Major Andre's Letters. Addressed to Miss Seward, when at his 18th Year.* New York: T. Allen, 1792. 2nd New York edn. 9 × 15 cm. 48 pp. By Miss Seward. NYPL: *KD.

2(*i*)   *Monody on the Unfortunate Major Andre; Who was Executed at Tappan, Nov. —, 1780 . . . To Which are Added Major Andre's Letters Addressed to Miss Seward, when at his Eighteenth Year.* Hanover[, NH]: printed by Josiah Dunham, 1794. 11 × 17 cm. 48 pp. [pp. 19–20 and 25–32 are missing from this copy; the missing pages are present in a copy at NYPL which lacks a title-page: *KD 1794 Seward]. By Miss Seward. AAS: DATED BOOKS.

2(*j*)   *Monody on Major Andre.* Boston[, Mass.]: W. Spotswood and C. P. Wayne, 1798. 4th American edn. 10 × 17.5 cm. 22 pp. By Miss Seward. [Bound together with *Amelia; or, the Faithless Briton. An Original American Novel, Founded upon Recent Facts. To Which is Added, Amelia, or Malevolence Defeated, and, Miss Seward's Monody on Major Andre*, but separately paginated.] HEHL: 8058.

2(*k*)   *Monody on Major Andrè . . . To Which are Added, Letters Addressed to Her by Major Andrè, in the Year 1769.* Ed. E. C. G. Penzance: printed by T. Vigurs, 1806. 11 × 18 cm. Pp. [ii] + 58. By Miss Seward. NYPL: *KL Seward.

2(*l*)   *An Authentic Narrative of the Causes Which Led to the Death of Major Andrè . . . To Which is Added a Monody on the Death of Major Andrè.* London: Mathews and Leigh, 1808. 12 × 20.5 cm. Pp. viii + 357 [the Monody occupies pp. 307–35]. By Joshua Hett Smith and Miss Seward. BL: 279. g. 25.

2(*m*)   *Monody on Major Andre; and Elegy on Captain Cook. Also . . . Sympathy. A Poem.* London: Longman, Hurst, Rees, Orme, and Brown, J. Otridge, Taylor and Hessey, Rodwell and Martin, T. and G. Underwood, R. Jennings, Hailes, and

J. Harper, 1817. 10th edn. 9.5 × 16 cm. 178 pp. By Miss Seward and Mr Pratt. Yale (Sterling—Franklin Collection): 503 An3 1781j.

2(*n*)   *Monody on Major Andrè; and Elegy on Captain Cook . . . Also, Sympathy.—A Poem.* London: Otridge and Rackham, 1821. New edn. 9.5 × 15.5 cm. 178 pp. By Miss Seward and Mr Pratt. AAS: G850. S514. M821.

3   *Poems . . . To Which are Added, Letters Addressed to Her by Major Andrè, in the Year 1769.* Dublin: printed by P. Byrne and C. Jackson, 1781. 5th edn. 11 × 18 cm. 69 pp. By Miss Seward. CUL: Hib. 7. 772. 60(2).

4   *Poem to the Memory of Lady Miller.* London: G. Robinson, 1782. 20.5 × 25.5 cm. Pp. ii + 20. 1/6. By Miss Seward. *MR* 67: 46–9; BL: 11632. g. 41.

5(*a*)   *Louisa, a Poetical Novel, in Four Epistles.* Lichfield/London: J. Jackson/G. Robinson, 1784. 18 × 24 cm. Pp. vi + 95. 3/6. By Miss Seward. *MR* 71: 335–41; BL: 11632. g. 45.

5(*b*)   *Louisa, a Poetical Novel, in Four Epistles.* Dublin: Jenkin, White, Byrne, Burton, Cash, and Davis, 1784. 11.5 × 19 cm. Pp. viii + 85. By Miss Seward. Bodley: Don. e. 467.

5(*c*)   *Louisa, a Poetical Novel, in Four Epistles.* Lichfield/London: J. Jackson/G. Robinson, 1784. 2nd edn. 20.5 × 25.5 cm. Pp. vi + 95. By Miss Seward. BL: 11632. g. 42.

5(*d*)   *Louisa, a Poetical Novel, in Four Epistles.* Lichfield/London: J. Jackson/G. Robinson, 1784. 3rd edn. 21.5 × 28 cm. Pp. [ii] + 93. 3/6. By Miss Seward. BL: 11630. f. 58.

5(*e*)   *Louisa, a Poetical Novel, in Four Epistles.* Lichfield/London: J. Jackson/G. Robinson, 1784. 4th edn. 20.5 × 26.5 cm. Pp. [ii] + 93. By Miss Seward. BL: 11632. h. 15.

5(*f*)   *Louisa, a Poetical Novel, in Four Epistles.* New Haven[, Conn.]: Abel Morse, 1789. 5th edn. 11 × 18 cm. Pp. [iv] + 83. By Miss Seward. LC: PR 3671. S7 L7 1789 Office.

5(*g*)   *Louisa, a Poetical Novel, in Four Epistles.* London/Litchfield: T. Cadell/Morgan, 1792. 5th edn. 20.5 × 26 cm. Pp. [ii] + 93. By Miss Seward. BL: 840. i. 19.

6   *Ode on General Eliott's Return from Gibraltar.* London: T. Cadell, 1787. 19 × 25.5 cm. 11 pp. 1/-. By Anna Seward. BL: 11631. g. 21.

7(*a*)　*Llangollen Vale, with Other Poems.* London: G. Sael, 1796. 21 × 27 cm. Pp. [ii] + 48. 3/-. By Anna Seward. *MR* 20: 151–4; BL: 78. f. 65.

7(*b*)　*Llangollen Vale, with Other Poems.* London: G. Sael, 1796. 2nd edn. 20 × 25 cm. Pp. [ii] + 48. By Anna Seward. BL: 1491. b. 16.

7(*c*)　*Llangollen Vale, with Other Poems.* London: G. Sael, 1796. 3rd edn. 21 × 26.5 cm. Pp. [ii] + 179. By Anna Seward. Yale (Beinecke): 1973/783.

8(*a*)　*Original Sonnets on Various Subjects; and Odes Paraphrased from Horace.* London/Birmingham/Lichfield: G. Sael/Swinney/Morgan, 1799. 21 × 26.5 cm. Pp. x + 179. 6/6 sewed. By Anna Seward. *MR* 29: 361–9; *CR* 26: 33–8; Bodley: 2799 d. 110.

8(*b*)　*Original Sonnets on Various Subjects; and Odes Paraphrased from Horace.* London/Birmingham/Lichfield: G. Sael/Swinney/Morgan, 1799. 2nd edn. 18.5 × 23.5 cm. Pp. x + 179. By Anna Seward. BL: 11632. g. 63(1).

8(*c*)　*Original Sonnets on Various Subjects; and Odes Paraphrased from Horace.* London/Birmingham/Lichfield: G. Sael/Swinney/Morgan, 1799. 3rd edn. 21 × 27 cm. Pp. viii + 179. 6/6. By Anna Seward. Library Co. of Philadelphia: O Eng Sew/Log 878. Q.

9　*Blindness, a Poem . . . Written at the Request of an Artist, Who Lost his Sight by the Gutta Serena, in his Twenty-eighth Year, and Who was Therefore Obliged to Change his Profession for That of Music; Patronised by the Duchess of Leeds, to Whom this Poem is, by Permission, Dedicated.* Sheffield: printed for William Platt, 1806. 22 × 27.5 cm. 12 pp. By Anna Seward. BL: 11633. h. 12.

10　*The Poetical Works . . . with Extracts from her Literary Correspondence.* Ed. Walter Scott. Edinburgh/London: John Ballantyne and Co./Longman, Hurst, Rees, and Orme, 1810. 11 × 17.5 cm. 3 vols. £1/11/6 boards. By Anna Seward. *MR* 69: 20–34; BL: 1340. c. 10–12.

11(*a*)　*The Beauties . . ., Carefully Selected and Alphabetically Arranged, under Appropriate Heads.* Ed. W. C. Oulton. London: C.

Chapple, 1813. 10 × 18 cm. Pp. xxiii + 263 [prose and verse]. By Anna Seward. BL: 12270. bbb. 26.

11(*b*) *The Beauties . . ., Carefully Selected, and Alphabetically Arranged under Appropriate Heads.* Ed. W. C. Oulton. London: A. K. Newman and Co., 1822. 11 × 18 cm. Pp. xxiv + 263 [prose and verse]. By Anna Seward. BL: 12270. bbb. 17.

SEWELL, Mrs, *see* YOUNG, Mary

SEWELL, Mary, Mrs George
She lived in Chertsey, Surrey. (*Poems*, Shoberl)

1(*a*) *Poems.* Egham and Chertsey/London/Bath/Canterbury/Uxbridge: R. Wetton/Robson, H. D. Symonds, Longman and Rees, Marsh and Dunsford/Hazard/Claris and Marrable/Lake, 1803. 9.5 × 15.5 cm. Pp. viii + xxxii + 265 [subscription edition]. 7/- boards. By Mrs G. Sewell. *MR* 44: 101–2; BL: 11641. b. 43.

1(*b*) *Poems.* Egham and Chertsey/London/Bath/Canterbury/Uxbridge: R. Wetton and Sons/Robson, H. D. Symonds, Longman and Rees, Marsh and Dunsford/Hazard/Claris and Marrable/Lake, 1803. 2nd edn. 9.5 × 15 cm. Pp. xxxii + 265. By Mrs G. Sewell, Relict of the Late Revd Geo. Sewell, Rector of Byfleet, Surrey. Bodley: 280 n. 813.

2 *Poems.* Egham and Chertsey/London/Canterbury/Bath/Uxbridge: R. Wetton and Sons/Longman, Hurst, Rees, and Orme, H. D. Symonds, Marsh and Dunsford, Nornaville and Fell/Claris and Marrable/Crutwell and Hazard/Lake, 1805. 9.5 × 16 cm. 2 vols. [The title-page of vol. ii bears the subtitle '(To Which are Added Essays, Moral and Religious)'.] By Mrs G. Sewell. BL: 11641. aa. 37, 38.

3 *Trafalgar: A Poem, to the Memory of Lord Nelson, Who Received a Mortal Wound in the Late Naval Engagement off Trafalgar, in the Hour of Victory. October 21, 1805.* Chertsey/London: R. Wetton and Son/Nornaville and Fell, 1806. 18.5 × 22.5 cm. 11 pp. By Mrs Sewell. HEHL: 334538.

4 *Poems and Essays.* Vol. iii [of 3, sequel to *Poems* (1805)]. Chertsey/London/Canterbury/Bath/Uxbridge/Egham: R.

Wetton/Longman, Hurst, Rees and Orme, Nornaville and Fell/Claris and Marrable/Crutwell and Hazard/Lake/C. C. Wetton, 1809. 9.5 × 16 cm. Pp. iv + x + ii + 224 [subscription edition; verse occupies pp. 1–153]. By Mrs G. Sewell. BL: 11641. aa. 39.

SEYMOUR, Charlotte

1   *The Powers of Imagination, a Poem. In Three Parts. Written at the Age of Sixteen.* London: T. N. Longman and O. Rees, T. Cadell and W. Davies, 1803. 18 × 23 cm. Pp. viii + 130. £1/1/- boards. By Miss Charlotte Seymour. *MR* 43: 183–5; HEHL: 476196.

SHELLEY, Elizabeth (1794–1831)

She was the daughter of Sir Timothy Shelley and Elizabeth Pilfold, and the younger sister of Percy Bysshe Shelley. There is some doubt as to how many of the poems in their book were hers, Richard Garnett in the 1898 facsimile suggesting that about five were. The book was withdrawn and suppressed when it turned out that some of Elizabeth's poems were derived from poems by Matthew Lewis; surviving copies are exceedingly rare. (*CB, Shelley Circle*)

1   *Original Poetry; by Victor and Cazire.* Worthing/London: printed for the authors by C. and W. Phillips/J. J. Stockdale, 1810. 15 × 25 cm. 64 pp. By [Elizabeth Shelley and another]. BL: Ashley 4030.

SHEPHERD, Mrs

1   *Poems.* London: for the author by J. Harris, 1807. 10 × 17.5 cm. Pp. xii + 201 [subscription edition]. By Mrs Shepherd. BL: 11642. aa. 28.

SHERIDAN, Miss [Mrs?], *see* COLLECTIONS 42

SHERIDAN, Mrs Brinsley, *see* COLLECTIONS 53

SHERIDAN, Frances, Mrs Thomas (1724–66), *see* COLLECTIONS 25(*a–c*)

Born in Dublin. She was the second daughter of the Revd Dr Michael Chamberlaine, Archdeacon of Glendalough, and of Anastasia Whyte. In

1747 she married Thomas Sheridan. They had four children, Richard Brinsley Sheridan being one of them. Her anonymous novel, *Memoirs of Miss Sydney Biddulph* (1761), was well received, was translated into French, and prompted Samuel Johnson's remark, 'I know not, Madam, that you have a right, upon moral principles, to make your readers suffer so much'. Her comedy *The Discovery* was successfully produced by Garrick at Drury Lane in 1763. (James Boswell, *Life of Johnson*, CB, *DNB*, Alicia Lefanu, *Memoirs of the Life and Writings* (1824))

SIGOURNEY, Lydia Howard, Mrs Charles (1791–1865), *see also* COLLECTIONS 40(*c*)

Born in Norwich, Conn. She was the daughter of Ezekiel Huntley, the general manager of an estate, and of Zerviah Wentworth. She became a schoolteacher in Norwich and then in Hartford. In 1819 she married Charles Sigourney, a widower with three children. She was a prodigious contributor to periodicals, annuals, and gift books, publishing more than sixty-five books in all. She visited Europe in 1840 and was celebrated as the 'American Hemans'. (*DAB*, Gordon S. Haight, *Mrs Sigourney: The Sweet Singer of Hartford* (1930))

1   *Moral Pieces, in Prose and Verse.* Hartford[, Conn.?]: printed by Sheldon and Goodwin, 1815. 10 × 17.5 cm. Pp. xii + 276 [subscription edition]. By Lydia Huntley. HEHL: 5721.

2   *Traits of the Aborigines of America. A Poem.* Cambridge[, Mass.]/Boston[, Mass.]: the University Press/Cummings and Hilliard, 1822. 12 × 19.5 cm. 285 pp. HEHL: 108590.

3(*a*)   *Poems.* Boston[, Mass.]/Hartford[, Conn.]/New York: S. G. Goodrich, and Bowles and Dearborn/H. and F. J. Huntington/G. and C. Carvill, 1827. 10.5 × 18 cm. 228 pp. By the Author of *Moral Pieces in Prose and Verse.* HEHL: 46145.

3(*b*)   *Poems.* Philadelphia: Key and Biddle, 1834. 10.5 × 16.5 cm. 288 pp. By Mrs L. H. Sigourney. HEHL: 81522.

4   *Lays from the West: Poems.* Ed. Joseph Belcher. London: Thomas Ward and Co., 1834. 6.5 × 10.5 cm. Pp. viii + 102. By Mrs L. H. Sigourney. BL: 11646. a. 4.

5   *Poetry for Children.* Hartford[, Conn.]: Robinson and Pratt, 1834. 10.5 × 14 cm. 102 pp. By the Author of *How to be Happy.* Yale (Beinecke): Za/Si26/834P.

6   *Lays of the Heart, with Oriska and Other Poems*. London: Knight and Son, [1835?]. 7.5 × 12 cm. Pp. x + 208. By Mrs Lydia H. Sigourney. BL: 11688. a. 24.

7   *Simple Tales for my Own Children, in Poetry and Prose*. London: Knight and Son, [1835?]. 9 × 14 cm. 172 pp. By Mrs L. H. Sigourney. BL: 12331. aa. 33.

8   *Zinzendorff, and Other Poems*. New-York/Boston[, Mass.]: Leavitt, Lord and Co./Crocker and Brewster, 1835. 10.5 × 18.5 cm. 300 pp. By Mrs L. H. Sigourney. LC: PS 2832. Z5 1835.

SIKES, Mrs S.

1   *Hymns and Poems, on Moral Subjects. Addressed to Youth.* London: Bowdery and Kerby, 1815. 10.5 × 17.5 cm. Pp. xv + 128 [pp. xiii–xv in this copy being bound in following p. 128; subscription edition]. By Mrs S. Sikes. BL: 12612. bbb. 5.

A SISTER, *see also* WALSH, Miss

1   *A Sister's Poems; for the Amusement and Instruction of Children.* London: William Darton, and Harvey and Darton, and John Harris, [c.1825]. 8.5 × 14 cm. Pp. vi + 174. Osborne: ii. 661.

2   *United Efforts. A Collection of Poems, the Mutual Offspring of a Brother and Sister.* London/Dover: Sherwood, Gilbert and Piper/W. Batcheller, 1831. 10 × 16 cm. Pp. [vi] + 100. BL: 11644. aa. 5.

SKETCH, Sally, *pseudonym*

1   *An Alphabetical Arrangement of Animals for Little Naturalists.* [London]: Harris and Son, 1821. 12.5 × 10.5 cm. 28 pp. [printed on one side only]. By Sally Sketch. Osborne: i. 105.

SLEIGH, Isabella, Mrs William (*c.*1791–1818)

Born in London. She was the daughter of Peter Michael Morrell, a French Roman Catholic who died when she was young, and of a Miss Butcher, a Methodist. She herself was brought up as a Methodist. She married the Revd William Sleigh and they had at least one son. They seemed to have lived in Barnstaple, Devon. (*Poems*)

1   *Poems, Moral and Religious . . . to Which is Prefixed a Prefatory Address to the Reader; Including a Few Sketches of her History and Character . . .* Ed. [William Sleigh]. Barnstaple: J. Avery, 1819. 9 × 16 cm. Pp. xiv + 120. By Mrs Sleigh. BL: 994. g. 34.

SMALLPIECE, Anna Maria

She evidently grew up in Woburn, Beds. (*Original Sonnets*)

1   *Original Sonnets, and Other Small Poems.* London: J. Johnson, 1805. 9.5 × 15.5 cm. Pp. vi + 182. By Anna Maria Smallpiece. BL: 11644. aaa. 19.

SMITH, Mrs, *see* SAVORY, Martha

SMITH, Charlotte, Mrs Benjamin (1749–1806), *see also* COLLECTIONS 10(*b*), 11(*b*), 15(*l–o*), 20, 23(*a–b*), 25(*a–c*), 52 *and* FENN, Lady Eleanor

She was the eldest daughter of Nicholas Turner and Anna Towers. In 1765 she married Benjamin Smith; they had twelve children. In 1782 her husband was imprisoned for debt and she spent seven months in prison with him. In the hope of earning some money, and with the help of William Hayley, she published her sonnets. She separated from her husband. Between 1788 and 1793 she published four novels of which *The Old Manor House* (1793) is usually thought to be the best. Opie painted her portrait. (*CB, DNB*)

1(*a*)   *Elegiac Sonnets, and Other Essays.* London: J. Dodsley, 1784. 19.5 × 23.5 cm. Pp. viii + 26. 2/-. By Charlotte Smith, of Bignor Park, in Sussex. BL: 11632. g. 46.

1(*b*)   *Elegiac Sonnets, and Other Essays.* Chichester/London: printed by Dennett Jaques/Dodsley, Gardner, Baldwin and Bew, 1784. 2nd edn. 19 × 25.5 cm. Pp. viii + 26. 2/-. By Charlotte Smith. BL: 11631. g. 23.

1(*c*)   *Elegiac Sonnets . . . With Twenty Additional Sonnets.* London: J. Dodsley, H. Gardner, J. Bew, [1786]. 3rd edn. 21 × 26 cm. Pp. viii + 44. 3/-. By Charlotte Smith. BL: 1346. i. 34.

1(*d*)   *Elegiac Sonnets.* London: J. Dodsley, H. Gardner, and J. Bew, 1786. 4th edn. 16.5 × 24 cm. Pp. viii + 44. By Charlotte Smith. BL: 11633. dd. 4.

1(*e*)   *Elegiac Sonnets . . . With Twenty Additional Sonnets.* Philadelphia: Thomas Dobson, 1787. New edn. 10.5 × 16.5 cm. 36 pp. By Charlotte Smith. LC: PR 3688. S4 E5 1787 Office.

1(*f*)   *Elegiac Sonnets . . . With Additional Sonnets and Other Poems.* London: T. Cadell, 1789. 5th edn. 10 × 15.5 cm. Pp. xxvi + 83 [subscription edition]. 10/6. By Charlotte Smith. BL: 993. c. 43(2).

1(*g*)   *Elegiac Sonnets . . . With Additional Sonnets and Other Poems.* Dublin: printed by Bernard Dornin, 1790. 6th edn. 10.5 × 17 cm. Pp. xii + 81. By Charlotte Smith. BL: 11631. aa. 30.

1(*h*)   *Elegiac Sonnets . . . With Additional Sonnets and Other Poems.* London: T. Cadell, 1792. 6th edn. 10 × 15.5 cm. Pp. xvi + 106. By Charlotte Smith. HEHL: 434679.

1(*i*)   *Elegiac Sonnets . . . With Additional Sonnets and Other Poems.* London: T. Cadell, Jr. and W. Davies, 1795. 7th edn. 9.5 × 15.5 cm. Pp. xvi + 106. By Charlotte Smith. BL: 11633. a. 40.

1(*j*)   *Elegiac Sonnets, and Other Poems.* Worcester[, Mass.]/Boston[, Mass.]: Isaiah Thomas/Thomas and Andrews, 1795. 1st Worcester from 6th London edn. 9 × 15.5 cm. 126 pp. By Charlotte Smith. LC: PR 3688. S4 E5 1795 Rare Bk Coll.

1(*k*)   *Elegiac Sonnets . . . With Additional Sonnets and Other Poems.* Boston[, Mass.]: William Spotswood, 1795. 7th edn. 8 × 13.5 cm. Pp. [vi] + 64. By Charlotte Smith. BL: 11686. a. 20.

1(*l*)   *Elegiac Sonnets, and Other Poems.* Vol. i [of 2]. London: T. Cadell, Jr. and W. Davies, 1797. 8th edn. 9.5 × 15.5 cm. Pp. xvi + 106. By Charlotte Smith. BL: 11646. a. 76.

1(*m*)   *Elegiac Sonnets, and Other Poems.* Vol. i [of 2; uniform with the 2nd edn. of vol. ii]. London: T. Cadell, Jr., and W. Davies, 1800. 9th edn. 9.5 × 15 cm. Pp. xvi + 106. By Charlotte Smith. BL: 11633. aaa. 40.

1(*n*)   *Elegiac Sonnets, and Other Poems.* Vol. i [of 2; uniform with the 4th edn. of vol. ii]. London: T. Cadell and W. Davies, 1811. 10th edn. 10 × 16 cm. Pp. xvi + 106. By Charlotte Smith. BL: 11641. b. 45.

2(*a*)   *The Emigrants, a Poem, in Two Books.* London: T. Cadell, 1793. 18.5 × 23 cm. Pp. xii + 68. 3/- boards. By Charlotte Smith. *MR* 12: 375–6; BL: 11632. g. 47.

2(*b*)   *The Emigrants, a Poem, in Two Books.* Dublin: John Rice, 1793. 12.5 × 19.5 cm. 36 pp. By Charlotte Smith, Author of *Elegiac Sonnets, Ethelinda, Celestina,* etc. etc. Library Co. of Philadelphia: O Eng Smit/51619. O. 7.

3(*a*)   *Elegiac Sonnets, and Other Poems.* Vol. ii [of 2, a sequel to the 5th edn. of 1789]. London: T. Cadell, Jr., and W. Davies, 1797. 10 × 15.5 cm. Pp. [xiv] + xx + 117 [subscription edition]. 6/- boards. By Charlotte Smith. *MR* 24: 458–9; BL: 1346. a. 39.

3(*b*)   *Elegiac Sonnets, and Other Poems.* Vol. ii [of 2; uniform with the 8th edn. of vol. i]. London: T. Cadell, Jr. and W. Davies, 1797. 9.5 × 15.5 cm. Pp. [xiv] + xx + 117 [subscription edition]. By Charlotte Smith. BL: 11646. a. 76.

3(*c*)   *Elegiac Sonnets, and Other Poems.* Vol. ii [of 2; uniform with the 9th edn. of vol. i]. London: T. Cadell, Jr., and W. Davies, R. Noble, 1800. 2nd edn. 9.5 × 15 cm. Pp. [vi] + 141. By Charlotte Smith. BL: 11633. aaa. 40, 41.

3(*d*)   *Elegiac Sonnets, and Other Poems.* Vol. ii [of 2; uniform with the 9th edn. of vol. i]. London: T. Cadell and W. Davies, 1806. 3rd edn. 10 × 16 cm. Pp. [vi] + 141. By Charlotte Smith. BL: 11633. aaa. 42.

3(*e*)   *Elegiac Sonnets, and Other Poems.* Vol. ii [of 2; uniform with the 10th edn. of vol. i]. London: T. Cadell and W. Davies, 1811. 4th edn. 10 × 16 cm. Pp. [viii] + 141. By Charlotte Smith. BL: 11641. b. 45.

4(*a*)   *Conversations Introducing Poetry: Chiefly on Subjects of Natural History. For the Use of Children and Young Persons.* London: J. Johnson, 1804. 10 × 16.5 cm. 2 vols. [Prose with verse examples distributed throughout.] 7/- boards. By Charlotte Smith. *MR* 49: 79–82; BL: 11805. bbb. 20.

4(*b*)   *Conversations Introducing Poetry, Chiefly on Subjects of Natural History, for the Use of Young Persons.* London: Whittingham and Arliss, and I. Bumpus and Sharpe and Son, 1819. 8.5 × 14 cm. 2 vols. [prose with verse examples distributed throughout]. BL: 7206. a. 29.

5   *Beachy Head: With Other Poems . . . Now First Published.*
     London: for the author by J. Johnson, 1807. 10 × 16 cm.
     Pp. x + 219. 6/- boards. By Charlotte Smith. *MR* 56:
     99–101; BL: 11641. b. 44.

6   *Elegiac Sonnets, and Other Poems . . . Comprised in One
     Volume.* London: Jones and Co., 1827. 5.5 × 9 cm. Pp.
     xxviii + 107. By Charlotte Smith. BL: 11631. a. 41.

SMITH, Elizabeth

Although *BLC* identifies her as being 'of Birmingham', 'of Truro'
seems more suitable. The subscription list in 1780 contains more than
2,000 names and is recommended as a useful directory of Cornish resi-
dents of the period. (*BLC*, Boase and Courtney)

1(*a*)   *Life Review'd: A Poem; Founded on Reflections upon the Silent
          Inhabitants of the Church-yard of Truro, in the County of
          Cornwall. To Which is Added, an Elogy on the Late Rev. Mr
          Samuel Walker, Who was Many Years Curate of that Borough.*
          Exeter: printed for the author by B. Thorn, 1780. 14 × 18
          cm. Pp. ii + xxviii + 132 [subscription edition]. By
          E. Smith. BL: 11633. bbb. 35.

1(*b*)   *Life Review'd: A Poem; Founded on Reflections upon the Silent
          Inhabitants of the Church-yard of Truro, in the County of
          Cornwall. With An Elogy on the Late Rev. Mr Samuel Walker,
          Who was Many Years Curate of that Parish. To Which are
          Added, the Lord's Prayer, Creed, and Ten Commandments;
          Paraphrased; &c.* Ilminster: printed for the authoress by A.
          Crocker, 1781. 11.5 × 18 cm. Pp. ii + 132. By Eliz. Smith.
          BL: 11631. bb. 79.

1(*c*)   *Life Review'd: A Poem; Founded on Reflections upon the Silent
          Inhabitants of the Church-yard of Truro, in the County of
          Cornwall. With an Elogy on the Late Rev. Mr Samuel Walker,
          Who was Many Years Curate of that Borough. To Which are
          Added, the Lord's Prayer, Creed, and Ten Commandments,
          Paraphrased; &c.* Exeter: printed for the author by
          B. Thorn and Son, 1781. 13.5 × 17.5 cm. Pp. ii + 132. By
          E. Smith. BL: 11632. e. 68.

1(*d*)   *Life Review'd: A Poem; Founded on Reflections upon the Silent
          Inhabitants of the Church Yard of Truro, in the County of
          Cornwall, with an Elogy on the Late Rev. Mr Samuel Walker,*

Who was Many Years Curate of that Borough. To Which are Added, the Lord's Prayer, Creed, and Ten Commandments. Paraphrased, &c. Birmingham: printed for the author by Pearson and Rollason, 1782. 12.5 × 21 cm. Pp. ii + [xii] + 132 [subscription edition]. By E. Smith. BL: 11633. cc. 1(1).

1(*e*)   *Life Review'd: A Poem; Founded on Reflections upon the Silent Inhabitants of the Church Yard of Truro, in the County of Cornwall, with an Elogy on the Late Rev. Mr Samuel Walker, Who was Many Years Curate of that Borough. To Which are Added, the Lord's Prayer, Creed, and Ten Commandments, Paraphrased, &c.* Birmingham: for the author by Pearson and Rollason, 1783. 6th edn. 12.5 × 21 cm. Pp. ii + xviii + 132 [subscription edition]. By Elizabeth Smith. BL: 11633. e. 35.

1(*f*)   *Life Review'd: A Poem; Founded on Reflections upon the Silent Inhabitants of the Church Yard of Truro, in the County of Cornwall, with an Elegy on the Late Rev. Mr Samuel Walker, Who was Many Years Curate of that Borough. To Which are Added, the Lord's Prayer, Creed, and Ten Commandments. Paraphrased, &c.* Glo[u]cester: printed for the author by R. Raikes, 1783. 13 × 20.5 cm. Pp. viii + 132 [subscription edition]. By Elizabeth Smith. BL: 11633. e. 34.

2   *The Brethren; a Poem: In Four Books. Paraphrased from Part of the History of Israel and his Family, in Holy Writ . . .* Birmingham: printed for the author by Pearson and Rollason, 1787. 11.5 × 19 cm. Pp. iv + 158 + [vi] [subscription edition]. By Elizabeth Smith. BL: 11632. d. 35.

3   *Israel, a Poem: In Four Books . . .* Birmingham: for the authoress by Brown and Bentley, 1789. 11 × 17.5 cm. Pp. iv + 118 + [6] [subscription edition]. 2/6. By Elizabeth Smith. BL: 11631. aa. 31.

SMITH, Elizabeth (1776–1806), *see also* COLLECTIONS 23(*a–b*), 29(*a–b*), 44

She was the daughter of George and Juliet Smith. Her father was a banker; her mother was Juliet Mott. She had little formal education but developed an early gift for languages in her father's library. She became a formidable linguist and her translation, *The Book of Job* (1810), and her *Vocabulary, Hebrew, Arabic, and Persian* (1814) were both respectfully received. Her father's bank failed in 1793, leaving the family destitute. (*Biographies of Good Women*, Blain, *DNB*, memoir in 1(*d*))

1(*a*)   *Fragments, in Prose and Verse: By a Young Lady, Lately Deceased. With Some Account of her Life and Character.* Ed. the author of *Sermons on the Doctrines and Duties of Christianity* [H. M. Bowdler]. Bath/London/Edinburgh: printed by Richard Cruttwell/Cadell and Davies, Hatchard/S. Cheyne, 1808. 10.5 × 19 cm. Pp. viii + 219 [approx. 23 pp. of verse]. BL: 12273. c. 13.

1(*b*)   *Fragments, in Prose and Verse: By a Young Lady, Lately Deceased. With Some Account of her Life and Character.* Ed. the author of *Sermons on the Doctrines and Duties of Christianity* [H. M. Bowdler]. Bath/London/Edinburgh: printed by Richard Cruttwell/Cadell and Davies, Hatchard/S. Cheyne, 1808. 2nd edn. 11.5 × 18.5 cm. Pp. viii + 219. BL: 12273. c. 13.

1(*c*)   *Fragments, in Prose and Verse: By a Young Lady, Lately Deceased. With Some Account of her Life and Character.* Ed. the author of *Sermons on the Doctrines and Duties of Christianity* [H. M. Bowdler]. Bath/London/Edinburgh: printed by Richard Cruttwell/Cadell and Davies, Hatchard/S. Cheyne, 1808. 3rd edn. 11.5 × 18.5 cm. Pp. viii + 219. BL: 12273. c. 14.

1(*d*)   *Fragments, in Prose and Verse: By a Young Lady, Lately Deceased. With Some Account of her Life and Character.* Ed. the author of *Sermons on the Doctrines and Duties of Christianity* [H. M. Bowdler]. Bath/London/Edinburgh: printed by Richard Cruttwell/Cadell and Davies, Hatchard/S. Cheyne, 1808. 4th edn. 11.5 × 18 cm. Pp. viii + 219. BL: 12273. c. 15.

1(*e*)   *Fragments, in Prose and Verse: By a Young Lady, Lately Deceased. With Some Account of her Life and Character.* Ed. the author of *Sermons on the Doctrines and Duties of Christianity* [H. M. Bowdler]. Bath/London/Edinburgh: printed by Richard Cruttwell/Cadell and Davies, Hatchard/S. Cheyne, 1808. 5th edn. 11 × 18 cm. Pp. viii + 219. BL: 12273. c. 16.

1(*f*)   *Fragments, in Prose and Verse: By a Young Lady, Lately Deceased. With Some Account of her Life and Character.* Ed. the author of *Sermons on the Doctrines and Duties of Christianity* [H. M. Bowdler]. Dublin: W. Watson, 1808. 10 × 17.5 cm. Pp. viii + 232. BL: 12270. bb. 23.

1(*g*) *Fragments, in Prose and Verse: By a Young Lady, Lately Deceased. With Some Account of her Life and Character.* Ed. the author of *Sermons on the Doctrines and Duties of Christianity* [H. M. Bowdler]. Bath/London/Edinburgh: printed by Richard Cruttwell/Cadell and Davies, Hatchard/S. Cheyne, 1809. 6th edn. 11.5 × 18.5 cm. Pp. viii + 219. BL: 1162. k. 20.

1(*h*) *Fragments, in Prose and Verse: By a Young Lady, Lately Deceased. With Some Account of her Life and Character.* Ed. the author of *Sermons on the Doctrines and Duties of Christianity* [H. M. Bowdler]. Bath/London/Edinburgh: printed by Richard Cruttwell/Cadell and Davies, Hatchard/S. Cheyne, 1809. 7th edn. 12 × 18 cm. Pp. viii + 219. BL: 12273. c. 17.

1(*i*) *Fragments in Prose and Verse . . . With Some Account of her Life and Character.* Ed. H. M. Bowdler. Bath/London/ Edinburgh: printed by Richard Cruttwell/Cadell and Davies, Hatchard/S. Cheyne, 1809. 12 × 20.5 cm. 2 vols. [Title-page of vol. ii reads *Memoirs of Frederick and Margaret Klopstock. Translated from the German.*] By Miss Elizabeth Smith, Lately Deceased. BL: 12270. ee. 8.

1(*j*) *Fragments, in Prose and Verse . . . With Some Account of her Life and Character.* Vol. i [of 2, uniform with vol. ii of 1810]. Ed. H. M. Bowdler. Bath/London/Edinburgh: printed by Richard Cruttwell/Cadell and Davies, Hatchard/S. Cheyne, 1810. New edn. 13 × 20.5 cm. Pp. xii + 274. By Miss Elizabeth Smith. BL: 1341. k. 18.

1(*k*) *Fragments in Prose and Verse . . . With Some Account of her Life and Character.* [According to i. 240.] Ed. H. M. Bowdler. Boston[, Mass.]: Munroe and Francis, Samuel H. Parker, 1810. 11 × 18.5 cm. 240 pp. By Miss Elizabeth Smith. BL: 4968. d. 11.

1(*l*) *Fragments, in Prose and Verse . . . With Some Account of her Life and Character.* Vol. i [of 2, vol. ii dated 1812]. Ed. H. M. Bowdler. Bath/London/Edinburgh: printed by

Richard Cruttwell/Cadell and Davies, Hatchard/S. Cheyne, 1811. New edn. 13.5 × 21.5 cm. Pp. xii + 274. By Miss Elizabeth Smith. BL: 1341. k. 2.

1(*m*) *Fragments, in Prose and Verse . . . With Some Account of her Life and Character*. Ed. H. M. Bowdler. Burlington, NJ: D. Allinson and Co., 1811. 10.5 × 17 cm. 261 pp. By Miss Elizabeth Smith. BL: 12270. bbb. 20.

1(*n*) *Fragments, in Prose and Verse . . . With Some Account of her Life and Character*. [Vol. i of 2, uniform with vol. ii of 1812.] Ed. [H. M. Bowdler]. London: T. Cadell and W. Davies, 1814. New edn. 14 × 22 cm. Pp. xii + 174. By Miss Elizabeth Smith. BL: 12270. ee. 9.

1(*o*) *Fragments, in Prose and Verse . . . With Some Account of her Life and Character*. Vol. i [of 2, uniform with vol. ii of 1818]. Ed. H. M. Bowdler. London: T. Cadell and W. Davies, 1818. New edn. 13 × 21 cm. Pp. xii + 274. By Miss Elizabeth Smith. BL: 12272. f. 12.

1(*p*) *Fragments, in Prose and Verse . . . With Some Account of her Life and Character*. Vol. i [of 2, uniform with vol. ii of 1826]. Ed. H. M. Bowdler. London: T. Cadell, 1824. New edn. 13 × 21 cm. Pp. xii + 274. By Miss Elizabeth Smith. BL: 12270. ee. 10.

2(*a*) *Fragments, in Prose and Verse . . . With Some Account of her Life and Character*. Ed. H. M. Bowdler. Bath/London/ Edinburgh: printed by Richard Cruttwell/Cadell and Davies, Hatchard/S. Cheyne, 1809. 12.5 × 20.5 cm. Vol. ii [of 2]. [The title-page of vol. ii is *Memoirs of Frederick and Margaret Klopstock*, the half-title being *Fragments, in Prose and Verse*. Vol. ii adds approx. 16 pp. of verse, much of it translation.] By Miss Elizabeth Smith. BL: 12270. ee. 8.

2(*b*) [*Fragments, in Prose and Verse*. Vol. ii (of 2, uniform with vol. i of 1810).] *Memoirs of Frederick and Margaret Klopstock*. Trans. [Elizabeth Smith]. Bath/London/Edinburgh: Richard Cruttwell/Cadell and Davies, Hatchard/S. Cheyne, 1810. 13 × 20.5 cm. Pp. xiv + 242. BL: 1341. k. 18.

2(*c*) [*Fragments, in Prose and Verse*. Vol. ii (of 2, vol. i dated 1811).] *Memoirs of Frederick and Margaret Klopstock*. Trans. [Elizabeth Smith]. Bath/London/Edinburgh: printed by

Richard Cruttwell/Cadell and Davies, Hatchard/S. Cheyne, 1812. 13 × 21.5 cm. Pp. xiv + 242. BL: 1341. k. 2.

2(*d*) [*Fragments, in Prose and Verse.* Vol. ii (of 2, uniform with vol. i of 1818).] *Memoirs of Frederick and Margaret Klopstock.* Trans. [Elizabeth Smith]. London: T. Cadell and W. Davies, 1818. 13 × 21 cm. Pp. xiv + 242. BL: 12272. f. 12.

2(*e*) [*Fragments, in Prose and Verse.* Vol. ii (of 2, uniform with vol. i of 1824).] *Memoirs of Frederick and Margaret Klopstock.* Trans. [Elizabeth Smith]. London: T. Cadell, 1826. 13 × 21 cm. Pp. xiv + 242. BL: 12270. ee. 10.

SMITH, Elizabeth

She seems to have lived in Malvern, Worcs. (*Poems on Malvern*)

1(*a*) *Poems on Malvern, and Other Subjects.* Worcester/London: T. Eaton/Longman, Rees, Orme, Brown, and Green, 1829. 10 × 16 cm. 112 pp. [subscription edition]. By Elizabeth Smith. BL: 11644. aa. 57.

1(*b*) *Poems on Malvern, and Other Subjects.* Worcester/London: T. Eaton and Son/Longman, Rees, Orme, Brown, and Green, 1834. 2nd edn. 10.5 × 16.5 cm. 116 pp. [subscription edition]. By Elizabeth Smith. BL: 11644. aaa. 48.

SMITH, Jane

She was a governess in the family of William Ker of Birmingham. *Admonitory Epistles* also had an 1842 edition. (*Admonitory Epistles*)

1 *Admonitory Epistles, from a Governess to her Late Pupils; Comprising a Brief View of those Duties, the Performance of Which is Most Likely to Promote their Happiness in this Life, and Ensure to Them the Joys of Eternity.* Birmingham: printed by Richard Peart, 1824. 10.5 × 17.5 cm. 120 pp. [subscription edition; prose and verse, 9 pp. of verse]. By Jane Smith [and Esther Milnes]. Yale (Mudd): WA/19135.

SMITH, Jane, Mrs

According to the *MR* review, she was a shopkeeper and a fortune-teller.

1 *Select Poems on Various Subjects, with an Introduction, wherein is Briefly Stated Some Observations on the Progress of Astronomy among the Ancients.* London: printed for Mrs Smith, [1790].

12mo. 71 pp. 2/6. By Jane Smith. *MR* 3: 220–2. Not located.

SMITH, Sarah Louisa P., Mrs Samuel Jenks (1811–32)
She was born in Detroit, Mich., but grew up in Newton, Mass. Her father's name was Hickman. She was carefully educated by her mother. When she was 16 she married Samuel Jenks Smith of Providence. (Griswold, May)

1   *Poems.* Providence[, RI]: A. S. Beckwith, 1829. 11 × 19 cm. 250 pp. By S. Louisa P. Smith. BL: 11686. aaa. 43.

SMITH, Sarah Pogson, *see* POGSON, Sarah

SMITH, Mrs T.
She seems to have been a friend of the poet Thomas Campbell. (*Poetic Flowers*)

1(*a*)   *Poetic Flowers.* Inference.
1(*b*)   *Poetic Flowers.* Geneva: printed by J. J. L. Sestié, 1824. 2nd edn. 12 × 19.5 cm. 26 pp. By Mrs T. Smith. BL: 1465. h. 13(3).

SMYTHIES, Harriet Maria, Mrs William Yorick (1813–83)
She was born in Margate, Kent, and was the daughter of Edward Lesmoin Gordon and Jane Halliday. She is best known as the author of a series of novels that were published between 1838 and 1862. She married the Revd William Yorick Smythies in 1842 and they had at least five children. (Blain)

1   *The Bride of Siena. A Poem.* London: Saunders and Otley, 1835. 12 × 19.5 cm. Pp. viii + 124. Yale (Sterling): In/Sm99/835B.

SNOWDEN, Eleanor

1(*a*)   *The Maid of Scio: A Tale of Modern Greece. In Six Cantos.* Dover: printed by G. Chapman, 1829. 8.5 × 14.5 cm. 128 pp. By Eleanor Snowden. BL: 994. f. 35.
1(*b*)   *The Maid of Scio: A Tale of Modern Greece. In Six Cantos.* London: C. Tilt, 1832. 2nd edn. 9 × 14.5 cm. 128 pp. By Eleanor Snowden. BL: 11646. aa. 29.

2   *The Moorish Queen; a Record of Pompeii; and Other Poems.*
London/Dover: Longman and Co., Whittaker and Co.,
W. Joy/W. Batcheller, 1831. 12 × 19 cm. 166 pp. [pp. 1
and 2 numbered v and vi]. By Eleanor Snowden, Author
of *The Maid of Scio.* BL: 994. i. 25.

SOTHEBY, Eliza

1   *Patient Griselda. A Tale. From the Italian of Bocaccio.*
Bristol/London: printed by Biggs and Cottle/T. N.
Longman, 1798. 16 × 20.5 cm. 33 pp. 2/6. By Miss
Sotheby. *MR* 30: 462–3; BL: 643. k. 4(15).

SOUTHCOTT, Joanna (1750–1814)

Born in Gittisham, Devon. She was the daughter of William and
Hannah Southcott. She worked as a shop girl and then as a domestic
servant, mainly in Exeter. At the age of 42 she became a Methodist,
but within a year, convinced of her own special religious inspiration,
broke from the Methodists and began to utter prophecies. In 1802 she
moved to London, where she had numerous followers. In 1813 her
announcement that she was about to give birth to a 'Shiloh' stimulated
public interest, but by the time of her death she was generally regarded
as being mentally unbalanced. (*DNB*)

1   *Letters and Communications . . . Lately Written to Jane Townley.*
Stourbridge: printed by J. Heming, 1804. 13 × 21 cm. 128
pp. [prose and verse, about 60 pp. of verse]. 2/3. By
Joanna Southcott, the Prophetess of Exeter. Chapin.

2   *Wisdom Excelleth the Weapons of War, and herein is shewn that
Judgments are the Strange Works of the Lord, but Mercy His
Darling Attribute.* Ed. [Ann Underwood]. [Southwark/
Exeter/Leeds/York/Stourbridge/Ilminster/Birmingham/
Gravesend/Greenwich: W. Tozer/W. Symonds, and
the Miss Eveleighs/S. Hirst/W. Wadman/James Light/
Edmund Baker/C. Bradley/R. Goldsmith/T. Turpin,
1814]. 11.5 × 19.5 cm. 48 pp. [prose and verse, about 15
pp. of verse]. 1/-. Chapin.

SPENCE, Sarah, Mrs George

Her maiden name was Crompton. She probably came from Yarmouth,
Norfolk. She married about 1790, her husband being a widower. They
had one child. (Blain)

1   *Poems and Miscellaneous Pieces.* Bury St. Edmund's/London: for the author by P. Gedge/J. Johnson, 1795. 10 × 15.5 cm. Pp. xxiv + 130 [subscription edition]. 4/6 boards. By Sarah Spence. *MR* 17: 358; BL: 994. g. 35(1).

2   *Poems and a Meditation.* Colchester/London: printed for the author by Swinborne and Walter/Baldwin, Cradock, and Joy, Hatchard and Son, Rodwell and Martin, 1821. 12.5 × 20.5 cm. Pp. viii + 23. By S. Spence. BL: 11644. d. 16.

SPENCER, Mrs Walter

1   *Poetical Trifles: Or, Miscellaneous Poems on Various Subjects.* London: for the author by herself and Shatwell, Sewell and Hookham, 1781. 9.5 × 15.5 cm. Pp. viii + 88. By Mrs Spencer, Late Miss Jackson, from Manchester. BL: 11644. aa. 26.

2   *Commemorative Feelings, or Miscellaneous Poems. Interspersed with Sketches in Prose on the Sources of Pensive Pleasure.* London: for the author by White, Cochrane and Co., and J. Carpenter, 1812. 10 × 16 cm. Pp. x + 163. BL: 11644. aaa. 8.

3   *Miscellaneous Poems.* Windsor: printed by E. Harding, 1812. 16 × 20 cm. Pp. vi + 90. Princeton: Ex 3938. 957. 1812.

SPROAT, Nancy, Mrs (1766–1827)

An American writer. Her maiden name was Dennis. (*NUC*)

1(*a*)   *Ditties for Children.* New York/Baltimore: Samuel Wood and Sons/Samuel S. Wood and Co., [1813]. 8.5 × 13 cm. 36 pp. By a Lady of Boston. Houghton: *EC8. T2153. D825s(4).

1(*b*)   *Ditties for Children.* Philadelphia: Johnson and Warner, 1813. 9.5 × 14 cm. 45 pp. By a Lady of Boston. AAS: DATED PAMS.

1(*c*)   *Ditties for Children.* Philadelphia: Benjamin Warner, 1818. 9 × 14.5 cm. 36 pp. By a Lady of Boston. Brown (Harris): S7715d/76.

2   *Poems, on Different Subjects.* Boston[, Mass.]: West and Richardson, 1813. 7.5 × 13 cm. 117 pp. By a Lady. AAS: DATED BOOKS.

3(*a*) *Poetic Tales, for Children.* New York: Samuel Wood, 1814. 9 × 14 cm. [title-page damaged; measurements of next leaf given]. 48 pp. By the Authoress of *Stories for Children,* by Goody Lovechild, and *Ditties for Children,* by a Lady of Boston. NYPL: *KVD Poetic.

3(*b*) *Poetic Tales for Children.* Northampton[, ?Mass.]: E. Turner, [n.d.]. 8.5 × 14 cm. 24 pp. Brown (Harris): S7715p/76.

3(*c*) *Poetic Tales, for Children.* New York: S. Wood, 1815. 14 cm. 48 pp. By the Authoress of *Stories for Children,* by Goody Lovechild, and *Ditties for Children,* by a Lady of Boston. *NUC.* Not seen.

3(*d*) *Poetic Tales, for Children.* New York: Samuel Wood and Sons, 1817. 8.5 × 14 cm. 48 pp. By the Authoress of *Stories for Children,* by Goody Lovechild, and *Ditties for Children,* by a Lady of Boston. AAS: DATED PAMS.

3(*e*) *Poetic Tales, for Children.* New York/Baltimore: Samuel Wood and Sons/Samuel S. Wood and Co., 1819. 8.5 × 13.5 cm. 48 pp. By the Authoress of *Stories for Children* by Goody Lovechild, and *Ditties for Children* by a Lady of Boston. Houghton: *EC8. T2153. D825s(5).

3(*f*) *Poetic Tales, for Children.* New York: Samuel Wood and Sons, [n.d.]. 10 × 17.5 cm. 36 pp. By the Authoress of *Stories for Children,* by Goody Lovechild, and *Ditties for Children,* by a Lady of Boston. Boston Public: **H. 99c. 435.

4(*a*) *Stories for Children; in Familiar Verse.* Boston[, Mass.]: West and Richardson, 1813. 9 × 14.5 cm. 35 pp. By Goody Lovechild. AAS: DATED PAMS.

4(*b*) *Stories for Children; in Familiar Verse.* Colchester[, Conn.]: Thomas M. Skinner and Co., 1814. 9 × 13 cm. 35 pp. By Goody Lovechild. AAS: DATED PAMS.

4(*c*) *Stories for Children; in Familiar Verse.* Boston[, Mass.]: Munroe and Francis, and David Francis, 1819. 8.5 × 14.5 cm. 35 pp. By the Author of *Poetic Tales.* NYPL: *KVD Stories.

4(*d*) *Stories for Children; in Familiar Verse.* Philadelphia: printed by Joseph Rakestraw, 1819. 9.5 × 14.5 cm. 36 pp. By

Goody Lovechild, Authoress of *Poetic Tales*, and *Ditties for Children*, by a Lady of Boston. AAS: DATED PAMS.

4(*e*) *Stories for Children; in Familiar Verse.* Montpelier[, Vt.]: E. P. Walton, 1821. 8.5 × 13.5 cm. 32 pp. By Goody Lovechild. Brown (Harris): 76/S7715s/1821.

4(*f*) *Stories for Children in Familiar Verse.* Boston[, Mass.]: Munroe and Francis, [n.d.]. 8 × 14 cm. 35 pp. By Mrs Nancy Sproat, Author of *Poetic Tales*, *Ditties for Children*, *Good Girl's Soliloquy*, etc. AAS: BIND COLL. B.

4(*g*) *Stories for Children in Familiar Verse* [title-page is the verso of the cover]. Boston[, Mass.]/New York: Munroe and Francis/C. S. Francis, 1829. 9 × 14.5 cm. 35 pp. By Mrs Nancy Sproat, Author of *Poetic Tales*, *Ditties for Children*, *Good Girl's Soliloquy*, etc. Columbia: Hist. Col. Children's Lit.

5(*a*) *Short Songs* [cover serves as title-page]. Boston[, Mass.]: printed by Munroe and Francis, [1815?]. 7.5 × 10 cm. 28 pp. By Mrs Sproat, of Taunton, (Mass.). Houghton: *EC75. B2323H. 1819.

5(*b*) *Short Songs* [cover serves as title-page]. Greenfield, Mass.: A. Phelps, 1825. 8.5 × 10 cm. 23 pp. By Mrs Sproat. AAS: CL-Pam. S771. S559. 1825.

6 *Lullabies for Children.* Taunton[, Mass.]: printed by A. Danforth, 1818. 8.5 × 13.5 cm. 12 pp. By Mrs N. Sproat, Authoress of *Ditties for Children*, *Poetic Tales*, etc., etc. Houghton: *EC8. T2153. D825s(6).

7(*a*) *A Present to Children.* New York/Baltimore: Samuel Wood and Sons/Samuel S. Wood and Co., 1820. 10 × 13 cm. 29 pp. [pp. 13–14 missing in this copy]. By the Author of *Ditties for Children*, *Poetic Tales*, *Good Girl's Soliloquy*, etc., etc. Rutgers. [Photocopy seen only.]

7(*b*) *A Present to Children.* New York/Baltimore: Samuel Wood and Sons/Samuel S. Wood and Co., [1830]. 10.5 × 13 cm. 29 pp. By the Author of *Ditties for Children*, *Poetic Tales*, *Good Girl's Soliloquy*, etc. etc. Princeton: Hamilton 1439(a).

8(*a*) *Little Ditties for Little Children.* New York/Baltimore: Samuel Wood and Sons/Samuel S. Wood and Co., 1821. 7 × 13 cm. 23 pp. By the Author of *Poetic Tales*, *Good Girl's*

Soliloquy, Present for Children, etc., etc. Brown (Harris): 76/S7715li.

8(*b*)   *Little Ditties for Little Children*. Northampton[, ?Mass.]: E. Turner, [n.d.]. 7.5 × 12 cm. 18 pp. Brown (Harris): 76/S7715li/181-?

8(*c*)   *Little Ditties for Little Children*. New York: Samuel Wood and Sons, [n.d.]. 7 × 13 cm. 23 pp. By the Author of *Poetic Tales, Good Girl's Soliloquy, Present for Children*, etc., etc. HEHL: 237910.

9   *Poems for Children*. Boston[, Mass.]: Samuel T. Armstrong, and Crocker and Brewster, 1823. 8.5 × 14 cm. 36 pp. By the Author of *Ditties for Children, Poetic Tales*, etc. Brown (Harris): 76/S7715pc.

10   *Village Poems*. New York: Samuel Wood and Sons, [1830?]. 9 × 14.5 cm. 67 pp. By Mrs N. Sproat. NYPL: NBHD.

SPROULE, Harriet Letitia

1   *The Following Poems were Composed during a Painful and Protracted Illness; and are Now Presented by her Affectionate Family, to Those Friends by Whom She was Known and Valued, as a Memorial* . . . [London?, 1820?] 12.5 × 21 cm. Pp. [iv] + 216. By Harriet Letitia Sproule. BL: 11643. i. 7.

SPURRELL, Mrs, *see* COLLECTIONS 12(*b–k*)

STANLEY, Mrs George (1796?–1861)

The identification is uncertain, but she was probably Mrs Stanley, the actress, whose maiden name was Fleming, and who married the comic actor George Smith. She was noted for playing the parts of old women. Her daughter Emma was a popular actress. (Boase, *DNB*)

1   *Tales and Poems*. London: J. Booth, 1818. 9 × 16.5 cm. Pp. xiv + 136 [subscription edition; prose and verse]. By Mrs Stanley. BL: 994. g. 36.

STARKE, Mariana (1762?–1838)

She was the daughter of Richard Starke, former Governor of Fort St George, Madras, where Mariana spent her early years, and of Mary Hughes. Her comedy *The Sword of Peace* (1789) was professionally performed, and like *The Widow of Malabar* it used Indian material. Seven years in Italy spent nursing an invalid relation led to her *Letters from Italy* (1800). In later life she became known for her reliable guidebooks for European travellers. (*CB, DNB*)

1(*a*)   *The Poor Soldier; an American Tale: Founded on a Recent Fact. Inscribed to Mrs Crespigny.* London: J. Walter, 1789. 18 × 23 cm. Pp. viii + 43. 2/6. *CR* 67: 470; HEHL: 139426.

1(*b*)   *The Poor Soldier; an American Tale: Founded on a Recent Fact. Inscribed to Mrs Crespigny.* London: J. Walker, 1789. 2nd edn. 21.5 × 26.5 cm. Pp. viii + 43. Houghton: *EC8. St286. 789pb.

2(*a*)   *The Widow of Malabar. A Tragedy, in Three Acts. As It is Performed at the Theatre-Royal, Covent-Garden.* London: William Lane, 1791. 12 × 19.5 cm. 47 pp. BL: 11777. f. 72.

2(*b*)   *The Widow of Malabar. A Tragedy, in Three Acts. As It is Performed at the Theatre-Royal, Covent-Garden.* Dublin: P. Wogan, P. Byrne, J. Moore, J. Jones, A. Grueber, W. Jones, G. Draper, R. White, J. Rice, P. Moore, 1791. 10 × 17 cm. 59 pp. BL: 11779. aa. 71.

2(*c*)   *The Widow of Malabar. A Tragedy. As It is Performed at the Theatre-Royal, Covent-Garden.* Philadelphia: E. Story, [1791?]. 9.5 × 16 cm. Pp. [vi] + 36. By Mariana Starke. LC: PR 1241. A5.

2(*d*)   *The Widow of Malabar. A Tragedy, in Three Acts. As It is Performed at the Theatre-Royal, Covent-Garden.* London: William Lane, 1791. 2nd edn. 12 × 20 cm. Pp. xvi + 47. 1/6. By Mariana Starke. Bodley: Vet. A5 e. 1408.

2(*e*)   *The Widow of Malabar. A Tragedy, in Three Acts. As It is Performed at the Theatre-Royal, Covent-Garden.* London: William Lane, 1791. 3rd edn. 13 × 21.5 cm. 47 pp. BL: 163. i. 45.

2(*f*)   *The Widow of Malabar, a Tragedy, as It is Performed at the Theatre-Royal, Covent-Garden. With Unive[r]sal Applause.* London: J. Barker, 1796. New edn. 12.5 × 21.5 cm. 47 pp. 1/6. By Mariana Starke. HEHL: K-D 317.

2(*g*)   *The Widow of Malabar. A Tragedy, as It is Performed at the Theatre-Royal, Covent-Garden.* London: J. Barker, 1799. New edn. 12.5 × 20.5 cm. 47 pp. 1/6. By Mariana Starke. BL: 1344. i. 12.

3(a) *The Tournament, a Tragedy; Imitated from the Celebrated German Drama, Entitled Agnes Bernauer, Which was Written by a Nobleman of High Rank, and Founded on a Fact that Occurred in Bavaria about the Year M,CCCC,XXXV.* London: R. Phillips, T. Hurst, Carpenter and Co., 1800. 12.5 × 20.5 cm. Pp. [ii] + 64. 2/-. By Mariana Starke. *MR* 33: 317; BL: 163. i. 43.

3(b) *The Tournament, a Tragedy: Imitated from the Celebrated German Drama, Entitled, Agnes Bernauer, Which was Written by a Nobleman of High Rank, and Founded on a Fact, that Occurred in Bavaria about the Year 1435 . . . As Performed at the New-York Theatre. From the Prompt-book. By Permission of the Manager.* New York: David Longworth, 1803. 9.5 × 15 cm. 60 pp. By Mariana Starke, Author of *The Widow of Malabar*, etc. Houghton: *EC8. St286. 800tb.

4 *The Beauties of Carlo-Maria Maggi, Paraphrased: To Which are Added, Sonnets . . .* Exeter/London/Bath: printed for the author by S. Woolmer/Longman, Hurst, Rees, and Orme/Upham, and Barratt, 1811. 11.5 × 18.5 cm. Pp. [iv] + 51. 3/-. By Mariana Starke, Author of *The Widow of Malabar, The Tournament, Letters from Italy*, etc. *MR* 66: 324–5; Union: VT/31/S79/1811.

STEEL, Mrs M.

1 *Pathetic and Religious Poems.* Saxmundham: printed for the authoress by L. Brightly, 1834. 9.5 × 15 cm. 40 pp. 1/-. By Mrs Steel. BL: 11644. a. 4.

STEELE, Anne (1716 or 1717–78), *see also* COLLECTIONS 10(b), 11(b), 12(a–k), 36, 44

Born in Broughton, Hants. She was the eldest daughter of William Steele, a timber merchant and Baptist lay preacher. Her fiancé was drowned a few hours before their wedding was to have taken place. She used the pen-name 'Theodosia' and some of her hymns have found a lasting place in Baptist hymnals. Her complete works were published in 1863. (*CB, DNB*, Ronald W. Thomson, 'Anne Steele, 1716–1778', *Baptist Quarterly*, 21 (1966))

1   *Danebury: Or the Power of Friendship, a Tale. With Two Odes.* Bristol/London: T. Cadell and T. Evans/J. Johnson, [1779]. 19 × 24 cm. 32 pp. 1/6. By a Young Lady. Stainforth; BL: 11630. d. 5(2).

2(*a*)   *Miscellaneous Pieces in Verse and Prose.* Ed. [Caleb Evans]. Bristol/London: printed by W. Pine/T. Cadell, T. Mills, and T. Evans, J. Buckland and J. Johnson, 1780. [Issued as vol. iii of a new edn. of *Poems on Subjects Chiefly Devotional* (1760).] 10.5 × 16.5 cm. Pp. xxiv + 224. 3/-. By Theodosia. BL: 11632. e. 59.

2(*b*)   *Poems on Subjects Chiefly Devotional.* Ed. [Caleb Evans]. London: J. C. Kelly, 1817. 6 × 10.5 cm. Pp. xxxii + 13–361. By Theodosia. BL: 11632. a. 53.

2(*c*)   *Poems on Subjects Chiefly Devotional.* Ed. [Caleb Evans]. London: J. C. Kelly, 1818. 6.5 × 10 cm. Pp. xxxii + 13–361. By Theodosia. BL: 11644. a. 19.

3   *The Works . . . Complete in Two Volumes. Comprehending Poems on Subjects Chiefly Devotional: And Miscellaneous Pieces in Prose and Verse: Heretofore Published under the Title of Theodosia.* Boston[, Mass.]: Munroe, Francis and Parker, 1808. 10.5 × 17.5 cm. 2 vols. By Mrs Anne Steele. BL: 12270. bbb. 22.

STEELE, Mary, Mrs

A Quaker from Croydon, Surrey. Her book was published posthumously, edited by her daughter. (*Friends' Books*)

1   *The Miscellany, Consisting of Extracts and Anecdotes, in Prose and Poetry, Instructive, Moral, and Religious.* Ed. [Anon.]. London: Harvey and Darton, 1828. 11 × 19 cm. Pp. iv + 66 [verse occupies pp. 49–66]. By Mary Steele. BL: 4413. cc. 35.

STEELE, Sarah, *see also* FENN, Lady Eleanor

She seems to have been an Irish writer. Her subscribers were mostly Irish, one of them being Laurence Steele of Drogheda, Co. Louth. The BL copy contains an MS letter from her to Southey, asking for advice.

1   *Eva, an Historical Poem, with Illustrative Notes, Accompanied by Some Lyric Poems.* Dublin/London/Edinburgh: for the author by John Jones/, 1816. 12 × 19.5 cm. Pp. xiv +

v–xxii + 101 [subscription edition]. By Sarah Steele. BL: 1466. g. 42.

STEWART, Jessie, *see also* COLLECTIONS 43

1   *Ode to Dr Thomas Percy, Lord Bishop of Dromore; Occasioned by Reading the Reliques of Ancient English Poetry.* Edinburgh/ London: Mundell and Son/Longman and Rees, 1804. 28 × 37.5 cm. 38 pp. By [J. S.]. HL; Houghton: *fEC8. St493. 804O.

STOCKDALE, Mary R. (born *c.*1769?)
Born in London. She was the daughter of the publisher John Stockdale and of Mary Ridgway, also a publisher's daughter. She was educated at home. Her *Mirror of the Mind* (1810) contains autobiographical material. She contributed to the *Morning Post* from 1811 to 1814 and to *The Juvenile Forget-me-not* in 1829 and 1830. (Blain, Boyle, *DNB* (under John Stockdale))

1(*a*)   *The Family Book; or, Children's Journal. Consisting of Moral and Entertaining Stories . . . From the French of M. Berquin. Interspersed with Poetical Pieces, Written by the Translator.* Trans. Miss Stockdale. London: John Stockdale, 1798. 10 × 17.5 cm. Pp. xii + 294 [approx. 16 pp. of verse]. BL: 1210. m. 38.

1(*b*)   *The Family Book; or, Children's Journal. Consisting of Moral and Entertaining Stories . . . From the French of M. Berquin. Interspersed with Poetical Pieces, Written by the Translator . . .* Trans. Miss Stockdale. London: John Stockdale, 1799. 2nd edn. 10 × 17.5 cm. Pp. xii + 294. BL: Ch. 790/100.

2   *The Effusions of the Heart: Poems . . . Dedicated, by Permission, to Her Majesty.* London: John Stockdale, 1798. 11 × 18.5 cm. 160 pp. 5/- boards. By Miss Stockdale. *CR* 22: 352; BL: 993. k. 28(1).

3   *The School for Children; or, Selection of Instructive and Entertaining Tales: Proper to Form the Heart of Infancy to the Hatred of Vice, and the Love of Virtue. From the French of Lombard de Langres. Interspersed with Poetical Pieces, Written by the Translator . . .* London: John Stockdale, 1800. 10 × 17 cm. Pp. xii + 220 [about 16 pp. of verse]. By Miss Stockdale, Author of *Effusions of the Heart, Poems,*

and Translator of *The Children's Journal*. Bodley: Vet. A5 e. 5870.

4(*a*)   *The Mirror of the Mind. Poems* . . . London: John Stockdale, 1810. 12.5 × 21 cm. 2 vols. By Miss Stockdale. BL: 80. b. 24.

4(*b*)   *The Mirror of the Mind, and Other Poems*. London: Thomas McLean, 1817. 12.5 × 20.5 cm. 2 vols. BL: 11646. ff. 11.

5   *The Christian Poet's Lament over the Christian Statesman. An Elegy on the Right Hon. Spencer Perceval*. London: John Stockdale, 1812. 13 × 21.5 cm. 21 pp. 1/6. By Miss Stockdale. Houghton: *EC8. St624. 812c.

6   *The Widow and her Orphan Family. An Elegy*. London: John Stockdale, 1812. 13.5 × 21.5 cm. 19 pp. 1/-. By Miss Stockdale. BL: 11646. ff. 20.

7   *The Mother and Child; a Poem*. London: Mary Stockdale, 1818. 13.5 × 21.5 cm. 28 pp. 2/-. By Miss Stockdale. Houghton: *EC8. St624. 818m.

8   *A Plume for Sir Samuel Romilly; or, the Offering of the Fatherless: An Elegy*. London: for Mary Stockdale, 1818. 13 × 20.5 cm. 20 pp. 1/6. By Miss Stockdale. Houghton: *EC8. St624. B826m.

9   *A Shroud for Sir Samuel Romilly: An Elegy*. London: for Mary Stockdale, 1818. 13 × 21.5 cm. 33 pp. By Miss Stockdale. BL: 11646. ff. 12.

10   *A Wreath for the Urn: An Elegy on Her Royal Highness Princess Charlotte of Wales and Saxe-Cobourg; with Other Poems*. London: for Mary Stockdale, 1818. 13 × 21.5 cm. 22 pp. 1/6. By Miss Stockdale. BL: 11641. f. 69(22).

[*See also*: 'The Wedding Ring. A Funereal Offering' (1821, 7 pp.).]

STOKES, Catharine

1   *Poems, on Subjects, Religious, Moral, &c. &c. &c.* Salisbury: printed by J. A. Gilmour, 1818. 10 × 16 cm. Pp. 78 + 2. By Catharine Stokes, of Damerham. BL: 11644. aaa. 25.

STOPFORD, Octavia

The book is dedicated from Brunswick Terrace, Scarborough, Yorks.

1   *Sketches in Verse, and Other Poems*. Hull: printed for the author by I. Wilson, 1826. 11 × 19 cm. Pp. xii + 142 [subscription edition]. By Octavia Stopford. BL: 11645. bb. 38.

STRATFORD, Agnes

She was the only sister of Thomas Stratford, Rector of Gallstown, Co. Westmeath. She had been left destitute by his death and published a subscription edition of his play *Lord Russell*, which was unsuccessfully produced at Drury Lane in London in 1794. (*The Labyrinth*)

1   *The Labyrinth; or, Fatal Embarrassment. A Tragedy*. London: for the author, [1795?]. 13 × 21.5 cm. Pp. 4 + vi + 72 [subscription edition]. By [Agnes Stratford, after Corneille]. BL: 11777. f. 16.

STRATTON, Jemima Maria

1   *The Maid of the Castle, a Legendary Tale*. [London]: Lane, 1794. 4to. 3/-. By Jemima Maria Stratton. *MR* 15: 215. Not located.

STRETTLE, Miss

1   *The Dorias; a Historical Drama. In Five Acts*. Edinburgh/London: William Blackwood and Sons/John Murray, 1835. 10.5 × 17 cm. Pp. [ii] + 95. BL: 11779. aa. 59.

STRICKLAND, Agnes (1796–1874)

Born in London. She was a daughter of Thomas Strickland and his second wife Elizabeth Homer. She was a sister of Susanna Strickland and Catherine Parr Traill (qq.v.). She was educated by her father, who believed that girls and boys should be educated in the same way. Her *Lives of the Queens of England* (12 vols., 1840–8) was written in collaboration with her sister Elizabeth. She was a major contributor to the annuals from 1827 on. (Boyle, *CB*, *DNB*, Una Pope-Hennessey, *Agnes Strickland . . .* (1940))

1   *Worcester Field; or, the Cavalier. A Poem in Four Cantos, with Historical Notes*. London: Longman, Rees, Orme, Brown, and Green, [1826]. 10 × 16 cm. Pp. [ii] + 163. By Agnes Strickland. BL: 994. g. 37.

2   *The Seven Ages of Woman, and Other Poems*. London: Hurst, Chance and Co., 1827. 10 × 17 cm. Pp. viii + 152. By Agnes Strickland. BL: 11642. aaa. 25.

3   *Demetrius: A Tale of Modern Greece: In Three Cantos. With Other Poems.* London: James Fraser, 1833. 10.5 × 16.5 cm. Pp. [ii] + 171. By Agnes Strickland. BL: 994. g. 38.

STRICKLAND, Lucinda

1   *Christmass in a Cottage.* London: T. Becket, 1790. 21 × 26.5 cm. 16 pp. 1/-. By Lucinda Strickland. Houghton: *EC75. St856. 790c.

STRICKLAND, Mrs M.

1   *Miscellaneous Poems, and Other Compositions.* Exeter: Trewman, 1790. By Mrs M. Strickland. *BC* 4: 671–2; *GM* 63: 1127. Not located.

STRICKLAND, Susanna (1803–85), Mrs John Wedderburn MOODIE, *see also* COLLECTIONS 47, 48

She was a daughter of Thomas Strickland and his second wife Elizabeth Homer, and a sister of Agnes Strickland and Catherine Parr Traill (qq.v.). She married John Wedderburn Moodie, a half-pay officer, with whom she went to Upper Canada in 1832. She is best known as the author of two accounts of her experiences there, *Roughing It in the Bush* (1852) and *Life in the Clearings* (1853). She contributed verse and prose to *La Belle Assemblée* from 1827 to 1830 and also to a number of annuals. (Boyle, *CB*, *DNB*, Susanna Moodie, *Letters of a Lifetime*, ed. Carl Ballstadt, Elizabeth Hopkins, and Michael Peterman (1985))

1   *Enthusiasm; and Other Poems.* London: Smith, Elder, and Co., 1831. 9.5 × 16 cm. Pp. viii + 214. By Susanna Strickland (now Mrs Moodie). BL: 994. f. 37.

STRINGER, Mrs

1   *The Chain of Affection; a Moral Poem: And Other Pieces.* Richmond: J. Darnill, [1830?]. 10 × 16.5 cm. 46 pp. By a Lady. BL: 11644. cc. 3.

STRONG, Elizabeth Kirkham, *see* MATHEWS, Elizabeth Kirkham

STUART-WORTLEY, Lady Emmeline Charlotte Elizabeth, *see* WORTLEY, Lady Emmeline Charlotte Elizabeth Stuart

SUDLEY, Viscountess, Mary Gore (*c.*1767–1832)
She was the daughter and heiress of Thomas Crispe of Parold Hall, Lancs. In 1787 she married Arthur Saunders Gore, Earl of Arran and Viscount Sudley. She was governess to Princess Charlotte. (*Complete Peerage*)

1   *The Following Lines were Spoken at a Fête, at Frogmore, Given by Her Majesty, on the Princess Amelia's, and Princess of Orange's Birth-day, August the Eighth, 1799.* Windsor: printed by C. Knight, [1799]. 11.5 × 18 cm. 8 pp. By [Mary Sudley—MS signature]. BL: 1608/5070.

2   *An Address to His Majesty, on his Late Providential Escape from the Horrid Attack of an Assassin, at Drury-Lane Theatre, May 15th, 1800.* Windsor: printed by C. Knight, 1800. 14.5 × 23.5 cm. 8 pp. BL: 1600/1282.

[*See also*: 'Come Royal George, and All Thy Court' (1800, broadsheet).]

SUSAN, *see* COLLECTIONS 18 *and* WINTER, Susan

SUSANNA, *pseudonym* (born *c.*1775)
She seems to have belonged to a family that was well to do; they had a 'summer residence in the country'. (*Poems*)

1   *Poems.* Ed. W. F., Jr. London: Charles Dilly, 1789. 17.5 × 24 cm. 31 pp. 1/6. By Susanna. BL: 11630. d. 10(2).

SUTCLIFF, Ann (1767–1800)
She was the daughter of John Hirst of Fairfield near Sheffield. She married Richard Sutcliff. They were Quakers. (*Friends' Books, Poems*)

1   *Poems.* Sheffield: *Iris* office, 1800. 11.5 × 19.5 cm. 32 pp. By Ann Sutcliff. BL: 1465. h. 13(6).

SWARBRECK, Delia Caroline, Mrs Samuel Dukinfield
She writes from Richmond, Yorks.

1(*a*)   *Valencia: A Tragedy, in Five Acts; and Who Could Believe It? A Comedy, in Five Acts.* Richmond[, Yorks.]: printed for the author by M. Bell, 1830. 13.5 × 21.5 cm. Pp. xx + 156 [subscription edition; verse and prose]. By Mrs Saml. Dukinfield Swarbreck. BL: 841. g. 2(3).

1(*b*)   *Valencia: A Tragedy, in Five Acts.* Richmond[, Yorks.]: printed for the author by M. Bell, 1830. [2nd edn.] 13 × 21.5 cm. 70 pp. By Mrs Saml. Dukinfield Swarbreck. BL: 11779. bb. 58.

SWINNEY, Jane

1   *A Collection of Poems.* Rochester/London/Chatham/ Brompton/Canterbury/Maidstone/Tonbridge/Sevenoaks/ Dover/Ramsgate/Margate/Chelmsford, Essex: printed by Gillman and Etherington/J. Evans/Townson/Tracy/ Simmons and Co. and Bristow/Blake and Walker/ Wise and Knight/Clout/Ledger/Burgess/Silver and Hall/ Clacker, 1792. 11 × 18 cm. Pp. xii + 200 [subscription edition]. 5/-. By a Young Lady. BL: 11643. e. 4.

SYKES, Mrs S., *see* SIKES, Mrs S.

SYMMONDS, Caroline, *see* SYMMONS, Caroline

SYMMONS, Caroline (1789–1803), *see also* COLLECTIONS 53

She was the daughter of the Revd Charles Symmons and Elizabeth Foley. She died in a flu epidemic, and Wrangham's memoir of her (1, below) stresses her precocity, her devoutness, and her active but anonymous philanthropy. (*CB*, *DNB* (under Charles Symmons), *Poems*)

1   *The Raising of Jairus' Daughter; a Poem . . . To Which is Annexed a Short Memoir, Interspersed with a Few Poetical Productions, of the Late Caroline Symmons.* London/ Cambridge/York: J. Mawman/Deighton/Todd, Wolsten-holme, Wilson and Spence, 1804. 11 × 17.5 cm. Pp. viii + 45 [about 10 pp. of verse by Symmons]. By Francis Wrangham. BL: 10347. e. 7(2).

2   *Poems.* London: J. Johnson, 1812. 12.5 × 20.5 cm. Pp. xvi + 412 [her poems occupy pp. 25–81]. 12/- boards. By Caroline Symmons and Charles Symmons. *MR* 82: 182–91; BL: 11641. f. 56.

A TABBY, *pseudonym*

1   *The Fishes' Feast, with a Mermaid's Song, Dedicated to the Author of the Peacock at Home, with a Poetical Address. To*

Which is Added the Ape's Concert. London: R. Spencer and
T. Hughes, 1808. 10.5 × 16.5 cm. 24 pp. By A. T——y
[Tabby?]. BL: T. 443(4).

TAGGART, Cynthia (1801–49)
Born in Rhode Island. She was the daughter of William Taggart, a revo-
lutionary soldier. She was a lifelong invalid and a Baptist. (Griswold,
May, *Poems* (1834 and 1848 editions))

1(*a*)   *Poems.* Providence[, RI]: Cranston and Hammond, 1834.
         Ed. [William Taggart]. 11.5 × 19 cm. Pp. xxiv + 98. By
         Cynthia Taggart. BL: 11686. c. 5.

1(*b*)   *Poems.* Cambridge[, Mass.]: printed by Charles Folsom,
         1834. 2nd edn. 10.5 × 17.5 cm. Pp. xl + 104. By Cynthia
         Taggart. BL: 11686. aaa. 14.

TALLANT, Anne
Her preface is dated from Lincoln.

1(*a*)   *Octavia Elphinstone, a Manx Story. And Lois, a Drama,*
         Founded on a Legend in the Noble Family of ——. London:
         J. Hatchard and Son, 1834. 12 × 19 cm. 2 vols. [the verse
         confined to pp. 217–316 of vol. ii]. By Anne Tallant. BL:
         N. 1585.

1(*b*)   *Octavia Elphinstone, a Manx Story. And Lois, a Drama.*
         London: Saunders and Otley, 1835. 12.5 × 20 cm. 2 vols.
         [the verse confined to ii. 217–316]. By Miss Anne Tallant.
         Houghton: 19462. 24. 19*.

TATLOCK, Eleanor
She was the daughter of Richard Tatlock, a naval surgeon, and of
Elizabeth Smith. She lived in the village of Great Marlow, Bucks., in
1811, and claims to have been contributing to the annuals for more
than twelve years. She seems to have been a Methodist. (Blain, and
Poems)

1   *Poems.* London/Sandwich: for the author by S. Burton,
         Williams, and Hamilton/Cocking, 1811. 10.5 × 17.5 cm.
         2 vols. By Eleanor Tatlock. BL: 11644. bbb. 5.

TATTERSHALL, S. E., *see* COLLECTIONS 29(*a–b*)

TAYLOR, Ann (1782–1866), *see also* COLLECTIONS 11(*b*), 26(*a–d*), 38(*a–b*)

She was the daughter of Isaac Taylor, the engraver, and she grew up in Lavenham, Suffolk, where her father was minister to a non-conformist congregation in Colchester. He educated his own children. She won a prize for the solution of puzzles in *Minor's Pocket Book* for 1798, became a contributor to the annual, and established a connection with the Quaker publishers Darton and Harvey. With her sister Jane (q.v.) she contributed to various children's books. In 1811 the family moved to Ongar, Essex. In 1813 she married the Revd Joseph Gilbert, as his second wife. (*CB, DNB*)

1(*a*)   *Original Poems, for Infant Minds*. London: Darton and Harvey, 1804. 8 × 13 cm. Pp. [vi] + 107. By [Ann and Jane Taylor, and others]. Osborne: Stewart A 1 a.

1(*b*)   *Original Poems, for Infant Minds*. London: Darton and Harvey, 1805. 8 × 13 cm. Pp. [vi] + 106. By Several Young Persons. BL: C. 117. a. 58.

1(*c*)   *Original Poems, for Infant Minds*. Vol. i [of 2]. London: Darton and Harvey, 1805. 3rd edn. 8.5 × 13.5 cm. Pp. viii + 100. By Several Young Persons. Osborne: ii. 664.

1(*d*)   *Original Poems, for Infant Minds*. Vol. i [of 2]. London/Bucklersbury: Darton and Harvey/T. Conder, 1806. 4th edn. 8.5 × 13.5 cm. Pp. viii + 100. By Several Young Persons. Osborne: ii. 664.

1(*e*)   *Original Poems, for Infant Minds*. Philadelphia: Kimber, Conrad, and Co., 1806. 8.5 × 14 cm. 112 pp. By Several Young Persons. UCLA: CBC T2140 1806a.

1(*f*)   *Original Poems, for Infant Minds*. Vol. i [of 2]. 5th edn. Inference.

1(*g*)   *Original Poems, for Infant Minds*. Vol. i [of 2]. 6th edn. Inference.

1(*h*)   *Original Poems, for Infant Minds*. Vol. i [of 2]. London/Bucklersbury: Darton and Harvey/T. Conder, 1808. 7th edn. 8.5 × 13.5 cm. Pp. viii + 100. By Several Young Persons. BL: 11645. de. 5.

1(*i*)   *Original Poems for Infant Minds*. Vol. i [of 2]. Newburyport: William Sawyer and Co., 1808. 8.5 × 14 cm. 108 pp. By Several Young Persons. Osborne: Stewart A 1 zz.

1(*j*)   *Original Poems for Infant Minds.* Vol. i [of 2]. 8th edn. Inference.

1(*k*)   *Original Poems for Infant Minds.* Vol. i [of 2]. 9th edn. Inference.

1(*l*)   *Original Poems for Infant Minds.* Vol. i [of 2]. 10th edn. Inference.

1(*m*)   *Original Poems, for Infant Minds.* Vol. i [of 2]. London/ Bucklersbury: Darton, Harvey, and Darton/ T. Conder, 1811. 11th edn. 8.5 × 13.5 cm. Pp. viii + 100. By Several Young Persons. Osborne: Stewart A 1 k.

1(*n*)   *Original Poems for Infant Minds . . .* Vol. i [of 2]. 12th edn. Inference.

1(*o*)   *Original Poems, for Infant Minds . . .* Vol. i [of 2]. London/ Bucklersbury: Darton, Harvey, and Darton/Josiah Conder, 1813. 13th edn. 8.5 × 14 cm. Pp. viii + 100. By Several Young Persons. Osborne: ii. 664.

1(*p*)   *Original Poems, for Infant Minds.* Vol. i [of 2]. London/ Bucklersbury: Darton, Harvey, and Darton/Josiah Conder, 1814. 14th edn. 8.5 × 14 cm. Pp. viii + 99. By Several Young Persons. Osborne: Stewart A 1 n.

1(*q*)   *Original Poems, for Infant Minds.* Vol. i [of 2]. London: Darton, Harvey, and Darton, and J. Conder, 1815. 15th edn. 9 × 14 cm. Pp. viii + 100. By Several Young Persons. Osborne: Stewart A 1 o.

1(*r*)   *Original Poems for Infant Minds . . .* Vol. i [of 2]. 16th edn. Inference.

1(*s*)   *Original Poems, for Infant Minds.* Vol. i [of 2]. London: Darton, Harvey, and Darton, and J. Conder, 1817. 17th edn. 8.5 × 13.5 cm. Pp. viii + 100. By Several Young Persons. Osborne: Stewart A 1 q.

1(*t*)   *Original Poems, for Infant Minds.* Vol. i [of 2]. London: Darton, Harvey and Darton, and J. Conder, 1818. 18th edn. 8.5 × 13.5 cm. Pp. viii + 100. By Several Young Persons [Jane Taylor, Ann Taylor, Adelaide O'Keeffe and others]. Osborne: i. 80.

1(*u*)   *Original Poems for Infant Minds . . .* Vol. i [of 2]. 19th edn. Inference.

1(*v*) *Original Poems for Infant Minds* . . . Vol. i [of 2]. 20th edn. Inference.

1(*w*) *Original Poems, for Infant Minds*. Vol. i [of 2]. 21st edn. Inference.

1(*x*) *Original Poems, for Infant Minds*. Vol. i [of 2]. 22nd edn. Inference.

1(*y*) *Original Poems, for Infant Minds*. Vol. i [of 2]. London: Harvey and Darton, 1825. 23rd edn. 9 × 13.5 cm. Pp. viii + 100. By Several Young Persons. Osborne: ii. 664.

1(*z*) *Original Poems, for Infant Minds*. Vol. i [of 2]. London: Harvey and Darton, 1826. 24th edn. 8.5 × 13.5 cm. Pp. viii + 100. By Several Young Persons. Bodley: 25210 f. 366.

1(*aa*) *Original Poems, for Infant Minds*. Vol. i [of 2]. 25th edn. Inference.

1(*bb*) *Original Poems, for Infant Minds*. Vol. i [of 2]. London: Harvey and Darton, 1828. 26th edn. 8.5 × 14 cm. Pp. viii + 100. By Several Young Persons. Bodley: 25210 f. 353.

1(*cc*) *Original Poems, for Infant Minds*. Vol. i [of 2]. 27th edn. Inference.

1(*dd*) *Original Poems, for Infant Minds*. Vol. i [of 2]. 28th edn. Inference.

1(*ee*) *Original Poems, for Infant Minds*. Vol. i [of 2]. London: Harvey and Darton, 1832. 29th edn. 8.5 × 14 cm. Pp. viii + 100. By Several Young Persons. Osborne: Stewart A 1 cc.

2(*a*) *[Original] Poems, for Infant Minds* [title-page damaged]. Vol. ii [of 2]. London/Bucklersbury: Darton and Harvey/ Thomas Conder, 1805. 8.5 × 13.5 cm. Pp. vi + 121. By Several Young Persons [Ann and Jane Taylor and others]. Osborne: ii. 664.

2(*b*) *Original Poems, for Infant Minds*. Vol. ii [of 2]. 2nd edn. Inference.

2(*c*) *Original Poems, for Infant Minds*. Vol. ii [of 2]. London/Bucklersbury: Darton and Harvey/T. Conder, 1806. 3rd edn. 8.5 × 13.5 cm. Pp. vi + 128. 1/6. By Several Young Persons. Osborne: Stewart A 1 c.

2(*d*) *Original Poems, for Infant Minds.* Vol. ii [of 2]. 4th edn. Inference.

2(*e*) *Original Poems, for Infant Minds.* Vol. ii [of 2]. 5th edn. Inference.

2(*f*) *Original Poems, for Infant Minds.* Vol. ii [of 2]. 6th edn. Inference.

2(*g*) *Original Poems, for Infant Minds.* Vol. ii [of 2]. Newburyport: William Sawyer and Co., 1808. 8.5 × 14 cm. 120 pp. By Several Young Persons. Osborne: Stewart A 1 zz.

2(*h*) *Original Poems, for Infant Minds.* Vol. ii [of 2]. London/Bucklersbury: Darton, Harvey, and Darton/T. Conder, 1811. 7th edn. 8 × 13.5 cm. Pp. vi + 118. By Several Young Persons. Osborne: Stewart A 1 g.

2(*i*) *Original Poems, for Infant Minds.* Vol. ii [of 2]. 8th edn. Inference.

2(*j*) *Original Poems, for Infant Minds.* Vol. ii [of 2]. 9th edn. Inference.

2(*k*) *Original Poems, for Infant Minds.* Vol. ii [of 2]. 10th edn. Inference.

2(*l*) *Original Poems, for Infant Minds.* Vol. ii [of 2]. London: Darton, Harvey, and Darton, and Josiah Conder, 1814. 11th edn. 8.5 × 14 cm. Pp. viii + 128. By Several Young Persons. BL: 11645. de. 5.

2(*m*) *Original Poems, for Infant Minds.* Vol. ii [of 2]. 12th edn. Inference.

2(*n*) *Original Poems, for Infant Minds.* Vol. ii [of 2]. 13th edn. Inference.

2(*o*) *Original Poems, for Infant Minds.* Vol. ii [of 2]. London: Darton, Harvey and Darton, and J. Conder, 1818. 14th edn. 8.5 × 14 cm. Pp. viii + 128. By Several Young Persons [Jane Taylor, Ann Gilbert, Adelaide O'Keeffe, and others]. Osborne: i. 80.

2(*p*) *Original Poems, for Infant Minds.* Vol. ii [of 2]. London: Darton, Harvey, and Darton, and J. Conder, 1819. 15th edn. 8 × 13.5 cm. Pp. viii + 128. By Several Young Persons. Osborne: ii. 664.

2(*q*)   *Original Poems, for Infant Minds.* Vol. ii [of 2]. 16th edn. Inference.

2(*r*)   *Original Poems, for Infant Minds.* Vol. ii [of 2]. 17th edn. Inference.

2(*s*)   *Original Poems, for Infant Minds.* Vol. ii [of 2]. 18th edn. Inference.

2(*t*)   *Original Poems, for Infant Minds.* Vol. ii [of 2]. 19th edn. Inference.

2(*u*)   *Original Poems, for Infant Minds.* Vol. ii [of 2]. 20th edn. Inference.

2(*v*)   *Original Poems, for Infant Minds.* Vol. ii [of 2]. 21st edn. Inference.

2(*w*)   *Original Poems, for Infant Minds.* Vol. ii [of 2]. London: Harvey and Darton, 1827. 22nd edn. 8.5 × 14 cm. Pp. viii + 130. By Several Young Persons. Bodley: 25210 f. 344(2).

2(*x*)   *Original Poems, for Infant Minds.* Vol. ii [of 2]. London: Harvey and Darton, 1828. 23rd edn. 8.5 × 14 cm. Pp. viii + 130. By Several Young Persons. Bodley: 25210 f. 384.

2(*y*)   *Original Poems, for Infant Minds.* Vol. ii [of 2]. 24th edn. Inference.

2(*z*)   *Original Poems, for Infant Minds.* Vol. ii [of 2]. London: Harvey and Darton, 1832. 25th edn. 8.5 × 14 cm. Pp. viii + 130. By Several Young Persons. Osborne: uncatalogued.

2(*aa*)   *Original Poems, for Infant Minds.* Vol. ii [of 2]. London: Darton and Harvey, 1833. 26th edn. 9 × 14 cm. Pp. viii + 130. By Several Young Persons. Osborne: Stewart A 1 z.

2(*bb*)   *Original Poems, for Infant Minds.* Vol. ii [of 2]. London: printed by Darton and Harvey, 1834. 27th edn. 8.5 × 14 cm. Pp. [ii] + 130. By Several Young Persons. NYPL: 9-NASY.

2(*cc*)   *Original Poems for Infant Minds.* Vol. ii [of 2]. London: Darton and Harvey, 1835. New edn. 9 × 14 cm. Pp. viii + 130. By Several Young Persons. BL: 942. a. 12.

3(*a*)   *Original Poems, for Infant Minds.* Philadelphia: Kimber, Conrad, and Co., 1806. 8.5 × 13.5 cm. 112 pp. By Several Young Persons [Ann and Jane Taylor and others]. LC: Juv. Coll. 1806.

3(*b*)   *Original Poems, for Infant Minds.* Newburyport[, Mass.]: William Sawyer and Co., 1808. 2 vols. 8.5 × 14.5 cm. By Several Young Persons. LC: Juv. Coll. 1808.

3(*c*)   *Original Poems, for Infant Minds.* Boston[, Mass.]: West and Richardson, 1813. 8.5 × 14.5 cm. 180 pp. By Several Young Persons. LC: Juv. Coll. 1813.

3(*d*)   *Original Poems, for Infant Minds.* Philadelphia: Solomon W. Conrad, 1816. 9 × 13.5 cm. 2 vols. By Several Young Persons. Yale (Beinecke): Is94/tl/v. 2.

3(*e*)   *Original Poems, for Infant Minds.* Philadelphia: L. B. Clarke, 1830. 9 × 14.5 cm. 144 pp. By Ann and Jane Taylor, and Others. NYPL: NAS.

3(*f*)   *Original Poems, for Infant Minds.* Philadelphia: Thos. T. Ash, 1834. 9 × 14 cm. 180 pp. By the Taylor Family [Ann and Jane Taylor and Others]. NYPL: NAS.

3(*g*)   *Original Poems, for Infant Minds.* Philadelphia: L. B. Clarke, 1835. 8.5 × 14.5 cm. 144 pp. By Ann and Jane Taylor, and others. LC: Juv. Coll. 1835.

4(*a*)   *Rural Scenes; or a Peep into the Country, for Good Children.* London: Darton and Harvey, 1805. [Contains two engravings dated 1806; another copy (Osborne: uncatalogued) has the engravings undated.] 9 × 15 cm. 62 pp. [prose and verse]. By [Ann and Jane Taylor]. Osborne: Stewart A 2 b.

4(*b*)   *Rural Scenes: Or, a Peep into the Country, for Good Children.* London: Darton and Harvey, 1806. 9 × 14.5 cm. 144 pp. [prose and verse]. 2/6. Osborne: Stewart A 2 c.

4(*c*)   *Rural Scenes or a Peep into the Country for Children.* London: Darton, Harvey and Darton, [1814]. 9.5 × 15 cm. 60 pp. [prose and verse]. 2/6. Osborne: ii. 814–15.

4(*d*)   *Rural Scenes or a Peep into the Country. For Children.* London: Darton, Harvey and Darton, [1818]. 9.5 × 15.5 cm. 60 pp. [prose and verse]. Osborne: uncatalogued.

4(*e*)   *Rural Scenes or a Peep into the Country. For Children.* London: Harvey and Darton, [1826]. 9.5 × 15 cm. 50 pp. [prose and verse]. Osborne: i. 191.

4(*f*) *Rural Scenes or a Peep into the Country for Good Children.* London: Darton, Harvey, and Darton, [1826]. 9.5 × 15 cm. 60 pp. [prose and verse]. 2/6. Osborne: i. 191.

4(*g*) *Rural Scenes, or, a Peep into the Country.* Black Rock: printed by Smith H. Salisbury, 1827. 7 × 11 cm. 64 pp. [prose and verse]. LC: Juv. Coll. 1827.

5(*a*) *Rhymes for the Nursery.* London: Darton and Harvey, 1806. 8 × 13.5 cm. Pp. viii + 95. By the Authors of *Original Poems* [Ann and Jane Taylor]. BL: Ch. 800/129.

5(*b*) *Rhymes for the Nursery.* London: Darton and Harvey, 1807. 2nd edn. 8.5 × 13 cm. Pp. viii + 95. By the Authors of *Original Poems.* Osborne: ii. 665.

5(*c*) *Rhymes for the Nursery* . . . 3rd edn. Inference.

5(*d*) *Rhymes for the Nursery.* London: Darton, Harvey, and Darton, 1810. 4th edn. 8 × 13 cm. Pp. viii + 95 [pp. 91–5 partly torn out in this copy]. Osborne: Stewart A 4 d.

5(*e*) *Rhymes for the Nursery* . . . 5th edn. Inference.

5(*f*) *Rhymes for the Nursery* . . . 6th edn. Inference.

5(*g*) *Rhymes for the Nursery.* London/Bucklersbury: Darton, Harvey, and Darton, 1813. 7th edn. 8.5 × 13.5 cm. Pp. viii + 94. By the Authors of *Original Poems.* Osborne: Stewart A 4 g.

5(*h*) *Rhymes for the Nursery.* London: Darton, Harvey and Darton, and J. Conder, 1814. 8th edn. 8.5 × 13.5 cm. Pp. viii + 94. Osborne: i. 80.

5(*i*) *Rhymes for the Nursery* . . . 9th edn. Inference.

5(*j*) *Rhymes for the Nursery.* Utica[, NY]: Camp, Merrell and Camp, 1815. 8.5 × 14 cm. 72 pp. By the Authors of *Original Poems.* Yale (Beinecke): Is94/tl/v. 2.

5(*k*) *Rhymes for the Nursery.* London: Darton, Harvey, and Darton, 1818. 10th edn. 8 × 13.5 cm. Pp. viii + 94. By the Authors of *Original Poems.* Osborne: uncatalogued.

5(*l*) *Rhymes for the Nursery.* London: Darton, Harvey, and Darton, and J. Conder, 1818. 11th edn. 8.5 × 14 cm. Pp. viii + 94. By the Authors of *Original Poems.* BL: 11645. aa. 13.

5(*m*) *Rhymes for the Nursery*. London: Harvey and Darton, and J. Conder, 1820. 12th edn. 8 × 13.5 cm. Pp. viii + 94. By the Authors of *Original Poems*. BL: 1506/160.

5(*n*) *Rhymes for the Nursery* . . . 13th edn. Inference.

5(*o*) *Rhymes for the Nursery*. London: Harvey and Darton, 1822. 14th edn. 8.5 × 13.5 cm. Pp. viii + 96. By the Authors of *Original Poems*. Osborne: Stewart A 4 n.

5(*p*) *Rhymes for the Nursery* . . . 15th edn. Inference.

5(*q*) *Rhymes for the Nursery*. London: Harvey and Darton, 1824. 16th edn. 8.5 × 13.5 cm. Pp. viii + 96. By the Authors of *Original Poems*. NEDL: Juv 824. 42.

5(*r*) *Rhymes for the Nursery* . . . 17th edn. Inference.

5(*s*) *Rhymes for the Nursery* . . . 18th edn. Inference.

5(*t*) *Rhymes for the Nursery*. London: Harvey and Darton, 1827. 19th edn. 8.5 × 14 cm. Pp. viii + 96. By the Authors of *Original Poems*. Osborne: ii. 665.

5(*u*) *Rhymes for the Nursery*. London: Harvey and Darton, 1828. 20th edn. 9 × 13.5 cm. Pp. viii + 96. By the Authors of *Original Poems*. BL: 11644. aa. 82.

5(*v*) *Rhymes for the Nursery*. London: Harvey and Darton, 1828. 21st edn. 9 × 14 cm. Pp. viii + 96. By the Authors of *Original Poems*. Osborne: Stewart A 4 u.

5(*w*) *Rhymes for the Nursery*. London: Harvey and Darton, 1829. 22nd edn. 9 × 14 cm. Pp. viii + 3–94. By the Authors of *Original Poems*. Bodley: 25210 f. 355.

5(*x*) *Rhymes for the Nursery*. London: Harvey and Darton, 1831. 23rd edn. 8.5 × 14.5 cm. Pp. viii + 96. By the Authors of *Original Poems*. Osborne: ii. 665.

5(*y*) *Rhymes for the Nursery*. 3 Parts [of 3]. [The title-page to Part I and the first 6 pages are missing in this copy; title-page information is taken from the title-page to Part II. The Parts seem to have been first offered as separate books; this set is bound together with a cover that reproduces the title-pages but alters the date to 1832 and was probably marketed as a collected set.] New York: Mahlon Day, 1831. 9.5 × 13 cm. Pp. 7–47 + 47 + 46. By the Authors of *Original Poems*. Yale (Beinecke): Is94/tl/v. 2.

5(*z*)   *Rhymes for the Nursery* . . . 24th edn. Inference.

5(*aa*)   *Rhymes for the Nursery* . . . 25th edn. Inference.

5(*bb*)   *Rhymes for the Nursery.* London: Darton and Harvey, 1834. 26th edn. 9 × 14 cm. Pp. viii + 96. By the Authors of *Original Poems.* Bodley: Johnson f. 406.

5(*cc*)   *Rhymes for the Nursery.* London: Darton and Harvey, 1835. 27th edn. 9 × 14 cm. Pp. viii + 96. By the Authors of *Original Poems.* BL: 11646. aa. 61.

6(*a*)   *Select Rhymes for the Nursery, with Copperplate Engravings.* London: Darton and Harvey, 1808. 9.5 × 15.5 cm. 48 pp. 1/-. By [Ann and Jane Taylor]. Osborne: i. 81.

6(*b*)   *Select Rhymes for the Nursery. Embellished with Thirty Engravings on Wood.* Boston[, Mass.]: Munroe and Francis, [n.d.]. 8.5 × 13.5 cm. 70 pp. Houghton: *EC8. T2153. D825s(2).

6(*c*)   *Select Rhymes for the Nursery.* Philadelphia: Johnson and Warner, 1810. 10 × 16.5 cm. 48 pp. LC: 1810 Juv. Coll.

6(*d*)   *Select Rhymes for the Nursery, with Copper-plate Engravings.* London: Harvey and Darton, 1822. 10.5 × 16 cm. 48 pp. 1/-. BL: 012806. ee. 35(3).

6(*e*)   *Select Rhymes for the Nursery. With Thirty-two Wood Engravings.* Boston[, Mass.]: Munroe and Francis, [*c.*1825?]. 9 × 14.5 cm. 70 pp. Houghton: Typ 870. 25. 8234.

6(*f*)   *Select Rhymes for the Nursery.* New York: Mahlon Day, 1832. 6.5 × 10.5 cm. 18 pp. [3 cents?] Free Library of Philadelphia: ROS 777.

7   *The Wedding among the Flowers.* London: Darton and Harvey, 1808. 9.5 × 12 cm. 16 pp. By One of the Authors of *Original Poems, Rhymes for the Nursery,* etc. [Ann Taylor]. BL: CH 800/31.

8(*a*)   *Hymns for Infant Minds.* By [Ann and Jane Taylor]. Inference.

8(*b*)   *Hymns for Infant Minds.* Boston[, Mass.]: Munroe, Francis and Parker, [n.d.]. 7.5 × 12.5 cm. 68 pp. By the Author of *Original Poems for Infant Minds, Rhymes for the Nursery,* etc. Boston Public: XJ. 810. G37H.

8(*c*)   *Hymns for Infant Minds.* Bucklersbury/London: T. Conder/Darton, Harvey and Co. and Conder and Jones,

1810. 2nd edn. 8.5 × 14 cm. Pp. viii + 100. By the Authors of *Original Poems, Rhymes for the Nursery*, etc. BL: 11644. e. 5.

8(*d*)   [*Hymns for Infant Minds*] [title-page missing]. [Boston, Mass.: S. T. Armstrong, 1810?]. [2nd edn.]. 7 × 13 cm. 91 pp. LC: PR 4712. G6 H8 1810.

8(*e*)   *Hymns for Infant Minds.* Hartford[, Conn.?]: Peter B. Gleason and Co., 1811. 8 × 14 cm. 72 pp. By the Author of *Original Poems, Rhymes for the Nursery*, etc. Yale (Beinecke): Is 94/tl/v. 2 (G).

8(*f*)   *Hymns for Infant Minds.* 3rd edn. Inference.

8(*g*)   *Hymns for Infant Minds.* 4th edn. Inference.

8(*h*)   *Hymns for Infant Minds.* London/Bucklersbury: Darton, Harvey and Co., and Conder and Jones/Josiah Conder, 1812. 5th edn. 8.5 × 13.5 cm. Pp. viii + 100. By the Authors of *Original Poems, Rhymes for the Nursery*, etc. Osborne: i. 79–80.

8(*i*)   *Hymns for Infant Minds.* Norwich: printed by Z. Webb, 1812. 9.5 × 15 cm. 72 pp. By the Author of *Original Poems, Rhymes for the Nursery*, etc. LC: 1812 Juv. Coll.

8(*j*)   *Hymns for Infant Minds.* Boston[, Mass.]: printed by Samuel T. Armstrong, 1813. 5th edn. 7 × 13.5 cm. 91 pp. $7.75 a hundred, $1.20 a dozen, 12 cents single. By the Author of *Original Poems, Rhymes for the Nursery*, etc. Boston Public: **H. 99c. 187.

8(*k*)   *Hymns for Infant Minds.* London/Bucklersbury: Darton, Harvey, and Darton, Taylor and Hessey, Conder and Jones/Josiah Conder, 1814. 6th edn. 8.5 × 13.5 cm. Pp. viii + 100. By the Authors of *Original Poems, Rhymes for the Nursery*, etc. UCLA: CBC G 37 1814a.

8(*l*)   *Hymns for Infant Minds . . . To Which are Added Lines on the Death of Mrs Harriet Newell and the Twins.* Boston[, Mass.]: Samuel T. Armstrong, 1814. 6th edn. 7 × 12 cm. 66 pp. $7.75 a hundred, $1.20 a dozen, 12 cents single. By the Author of *Original Poems, Rhymes for the Nursery*, etc. Boston Public: Acc. 66–450.

8(*m*) *Hymns for Infant Minds.* Newburyport[, Mass.]: W. B. Allen and Co., 1814. 8 × 14.5 cm. 71 pp. $8.00 a hundred, $1.12 a dozen, 12 cents single. By the Author of *Original Poems, Rhymes for the Nursery*, etc. Boston Public: XJ. 814. G37H.

8(*n*) *Hymns for Infant Minds.* London: Josiah Conder, and Darton, Harvey, and Darton, and Taylor and Hessey, and Conder and Jones, 1815. 7th edn. 8.5 × 13.5 cm. Pp. viii + 98. By the Authors of *Original Poems, Rhymes for the Nursery*, etc. Osborne: uncatalogued.

8(*o*) *Hymns for Infant Minds.* Boston[, Mass.]: Lincoln and Edmands, 1815. 4th edn. 8.5 × 14 cm. 71 pp. $8.00 a hundred, $1.12 a dozen, 12¢ each. By the Author of *Original Poems, Rhymes for the Nursery*, etc. LC: 1815 Juv. Coll.

8(*p*) *Hymns for Infant Minds.* London: Josiah Conder, and Darton, Harvey and Darton, and Taylor and Hessey, 1816. 8th edn. 9 × 14 cm. Pp. viii + 98. By the Authors of *Original Poems, Rhymes for the Nursery*, etc. Osborne: ii. 663.

8(*q*) *Hymns for Infant Minds.* Newburyport[, Mass.]: W. B. Allen and Co., 1816. 8.5 × 14.5 cm. 71 pp. By the Author of *Original Poems, Rhymes for the Nursery*, etc. UCLA: CBC 122032.

8(*r*) *Hymns for Infant Minds.* London: Josiah Conder, and Darton, Harvey, and Darton, and Taylor and Hessey, 1817. 9th edn. 9 × 14 cm. Pp. viii + 98. By the Authors of *Original Poems, Rhymes for the Nursery*, etc. BL: 3434. aaa. 42.

8(*s*) *Hymns for Infant Minds.* Greenfield, Mass.: Denio and Phelps, 1817. 7.5 × 13 cm. 72 pp. $8.00 a hundred, $1.12 a dozen, 12 cents single. By the Author of *Original Poems, Rhymes for the Nursery*, etc. Yale (Beinecke): Is 94/tl/v. 2 (G).

8(*t*) *Hymns for Infant Minds.* London: Josiah Conder, and Darton, Harvey, and Darton, and Taylor and Hessey, 1818. 10th edn. 8.5 × 13.5 cm. Pp. viii + 98. By the Authors of *Original Poems, Rhymes for the Nursery*, etc. BL: 3437. e. 11.

8(*u*) *Hymns for Infant Minds.* New Haven[, Conn.]: Sydney's Press, 1818. 8.5 × 14.5 cm. 64 pp. By the Author of *Original Poems, Rhymes for the Nursery*, etc. Minnesota: Y245/G372. [Photocopy seen only.]

8(*v*)   *Hymns for Infant Minds*. Boston[, Mass.]: Munroe and Francis, and David Francis, 1818. 7.5 × 13 cm. 70 pp. By the Authors of *Original Poems for Infant Minds, Rhymes for the Nursery*, etc. etc. LC: Juv. Coll. 1818.

8(*w*)   *Hymns for Infant Minds*. Boston[, Mass.]: Lincoln and Edmands, 1818. 8.5 × 14 cm. 70 pp. By the Author of *Original Poems, Rhymes for the Nursery*, etc. UCLA: CBC G37 1818.

8(*x*)   *Hymns for Infant Minds*. London: B. J. Holdsworth, and Darton, Harvey, and Darton, 1819. 11th edn. 9 × 14 cm. Pp. viii + 98. By the Authors of *Original Poems, Rhymes for the Nursery*, etc. BL: 3434. aaa. 43.

8(*y*)   *Hymns for Infant Minds*. Boston[, Mass.]: Benjamin Crocker, 1819. 8.5 × 13.5 cm. 71 pp. 12 cents single, $1.12 a dozen, $8.00 a hundred. By the Author of *Original Poems, Rhymes for the Nursery*, etc. LC: Juv. Coll. 1819.

8(*z*)   *Hymns for Infant Minds . . . To Which are Added Lines on the Death of Mrs Harriet Newell, and the Twins*. Boston[, Mass.]: Samuel T. Armstrong, 1819. 7th edn. 7 × 13 cm. 71 pp. $7.75 a 100, $1.20 a dozen, 12 cents single. By the Author of *Original Poems, Rhymes for the Nursery*, etc. LC: Juv. Coll. 1819.

8(*aa*)   *Hymns for Infant Minds*. London/Edinburgh/Glasgow: B. J. Holdsworth, Harvey and Darton/W. Oliphant/Chalmers and Collins, 1820. 12th edn. 8.5 × 14 cm. Pp. viii + 98. By the Authors of *Original Poems, Rhymes for the Nursery*, etc. Leeds: Special Collections/Education 375. 2 TAY.

8(*bb*)   *Hymns for Infant Minds*. Canandaigua: printed by J. D. Bemis and Co., 1820. 7 × 11.5 cm. 71 pp. By the Author of *Original Poems, Rhymes for the Nursery*, etc. Boston Public: 7443. 45.

8(*cc*)   *Hymns for Infant Minds*. Hartford[, Conn.]: printed by Geo. Goodwin and Sons, 1820. 7 × 13 cm. 71 pp. By the Author of *Original Poems, Rhymes for the Nursery*, etc. Boston Public: XJ. 820. G37Hd.

8(*dd*)   *Hymns for Infant Minds*. Newburgh[, NY]/Catskill: Uriah C. Lewis/Junius S. Lewis, 1820. 8.5 × 13.5 cm. 70 pp. By the

Author of *Original Poems, Rhymes for the Nursery*, etc. Yale (Beinecke): Pequot G 37.

8(*ee*)   *Hymns for Infant Minds*. Philadelphia: American Sunday School Union, [182?]. 9 × 14.5 cm. 85 pp. Chiefly by the Author of *Original Poems, Rhymes for the Nursery*, etc. LC: Juv. Coll. 182–.

8(*ff*)   *Hymns for Infant Minds*. Canandaigua: printed by J. D. Bemis and Co., 1820. 7 × 12 cm. 71 pp. By the Author of *Original Poems, Rhymes for the Nursery*, etc. LC: Juv. Coll. 1820.

8(*gg*)   *Hymns for Infant Minds*. London/Edinburgh/Glasgow: B. J. Holdsworth, and Harvey and Darton/W. Oliphant/Chalmers and Collins, 1821. 13th edn. 8.5 × 14 cm. Pp. viii + 98. By the Authors of *Original Poems, Rhymes for the Nursery*, etc. BL: 3440. g. 4.

8(*hh*)   *Hymns for Infant Minds*. New-Haven/Charleston: John Babcock and Son/S. and W. R. Babcock, 1821. 8.5 × 14 cm. 64 pp. By the Author of *Original Poems, Rhymes for the Nursery*, etc. Boston Public: XJ. 821. G37H.

8(*ii*)   *Hymns for Infant Minds*. London/Edinburgh/Glasgow/Dublin: B. J. Holdsworth, and Harvey and Darton/W. Oliphant/Chalmers and Collins/R. M. Tims, 1822. 14th edn. 8.5 × 14 cm. Pp. [iv] + 98. By the Authors of *Original Poems, Rhymes for the Nursery*, etc. BL: 3440. g. 8.

8(*jj*)   *Hymns for Infant Minds*. London/Edinburgh/Glasgow/Dublin: B. J. Holdsworth, and Harvey and Darton/W. Oliphant/Chalmers and Collins/R. M. Tims, 1823. 15th edn. 9 × 14 cm. Pp. [iv] + 98. By the Authors of *Original Poems, Rhymes for the Nursery*, etc. BL: 3434. aaa. 44.

8(*kk*)   [*Hymns for Infant Minds*. Andover[, Mass.]: American Tract Society, 1823. 4th edn.] [Title-page missing.] 11 × 17.5 cm. 28 pp. Brown (Rockefeller): PR 4712 G6 H8 1823.

8(*ll*)   *Hymns for Infant Minds*. Canandaigua: printed by J. D. Bemis and Co., 1824. 7.5 × 13 cm. 71 pp. By the Author of *Original Poems, Rhymes for the Nursery*, etc. UCLA: CBC G37 1824.

8(*mm*) *Hymns for Infant Minds*. London/Edinburgh/Glasgow/Dublin: B. J. Holdsworth/W. Oliphant/Chalmers and

Collins/R. M. Tims, 1825. 16th edn. 8.5 × 14 cm. Pp. [iv] + 98. By the Authors of *Original Poems, Rhymes for the Nursery*, etc. Osborne: ii. 663.

8(*nn*)   *Hymns for Infant Minds.* London/Edinburgh/Glasgow/ Dublin: J. Holdsworth/W. Oliphant/Chalmers and Collins/ R. M. Tims, 1825. 17th edn. 9 × 14 cm. Pp. [iv] + 98. By the Authors of *Original Poems, Rhymes for the Nursery*, etc. BL: 3434. aaa. 45.

8(*oo*)   *Hymns for Infant Minds* [cover serves as title-page]. Boston[, Mass.]: Lincoln and Edmands, 1825. 7.5 × 13 cm. 48 pp. LC: 1825 Juv. Coll.

8(*pp*)   *Hymns for Infant Minds.* London/Edinburgh/Glasgow/ Dublin: B. J. Holdsworth/W. Oliphant/Chalmers and Collins/R. M. Tims, 1826. 18th edn. 8.5 × 14 cm. Pp. [iv] + 98. By the Authors of *Original Poems, Rhymes for the Nursery*, etc. BL: 3434. aaa. 46.

8(*qq*)   *Hymns for Infant Minds.* New Haven[, Conn.]: Sidney's Press, 1826. 8 × 13.5 cm. 72 pp. By the Author of *Original Poems, Rhymes for the Nursery*, etc. Yale (Beinecke): Is 94/tl/1 (G–K).

8(*rr*)   *Hymns for Infant Minds.* [Boston, Mass.]: American Tract Society, 1826. 5th edn. 9.5 × 17 cm. 28 pp. Chicago: PZ 163. G46 H9 1826, EB Childrens. [Photocopy seen only.]

8(*ss*)   *Hymns for Infant Minds.* 19th edn. Inference.

8(*tt*)   *Hymns for Infant Minds.* New York: Mahlon Day, 1827. 11 × 18 cm. 23 pp. By the Author of *Original Poems, Rhymes for the Nursery*, etc. UCLA: CBC G37 1827.

8(*uu*)   *Hymns for Infant Minds.* Hallowell: Glazier and Co., 1827. 8 × 14.5 cm. 69 pp. By the Author of *Original Poems, Rhymes for the Nursery*, etc. Andover-Harvard.

8(*vv*)   *Hymns for Infant Minds.* London/Edinburgh/Glasgow/ Dublin: Holdsworth and Ball/W. Oliphant/W. Collins/ R. M. Tims, 1828. 20th edn. 8.5 × 14 cm. Pp. [iv] + 98. By the Authors of *Original Poems, Rhymes for the Nursery*, etc. BL: 1607/6075.

8(*ww*) *Hymns for Infant Minds.* Philadelphia: American Sunday School Union, 1828. 8.5 × 13.5 cm. 85 pp. By the Author of *Original Poems, Rhymes for the Nursery*, etc. BL: 864. b. 12.

8(*xx*) *Hymns for Infant Minds.* Hallowell: Glazier and Co., 1828. 2nd Hallowell edn. 6.5 × 11 cm. 64 pp. By the Author of *Original Poems, Rhymes for the Nursery*, etc. Osborne: Stewart A 10 1111.

8(*yy*) *Hymns for Infant Minds.* London/Edinburgh/Glasgow/Dublin: Holdsworth and Ball/W. Oliphant/W. Collins/R. M. Tims, 1829. 21st edn. 8.5 × 14 cm. Pp. [iv] + 98. By the Authors of *Original Poems, Rhymes for the Nursery*, etc. Bodley: 14722 f. 88.

8(*zz*) *Hymns for Infant Minds.* London/Edinburgh/Glasgow/Dublin: Holdsworth and Ball/W. Oliphant/W. Collins/R. M. Tims, 1830. 22nd edn. 8.5 × 14 cm. Pp. [iv] + 98. By the Authors of *Original Poems, Rhymes for the Nursery*, etc. UCLA: CBC G37 1830a.

8(*aaa*) *Hymns for Infant Minds.* New York: American Tract Society, [1830]. 7.5 × 11.5 cm. 104 pp. By [Ann and] Jane Taylor. UCLA: CBC G37 1830.

8(*bbb*) *Hymns for Infant Minds.* 23rd edn. Inference.

8(*ccc*) *Hymns for Infant Minds.* London/Edinburgh/Glasgow/Dublin: Holdsworth and Ball/W. Oliphant/W. Collins/R. M. Tims, 1832. 24th edn. 8.5 × 14 cm. Pp. [iv] + 98. By the Authors of *Original Poems, Rhymes for the Nursery*, etc. BL: 11644. a. 39.

8(*ddd*) *Hymns for Infant Minds.* London: Jackson and Walford, 1834. 25th edn. 9 × 14 cm. Pp. [iv] + 98. By the Authors of *Original Poems, Rhymes for the Nursery*, etc., etc. Osborne: uncatalogued.

8(*eee*) *Hymns for Infant Minds.* London: Jackson and Walford, 1834. 26th edn. 9 × 14 cm. Pp. [iv] + 98. By the Authors of *Original Poems, Rhymes for the Nursery*, etc., etc. HEHL: 289823.

8(*fff*) *Hymns for Infant Minds.* London: Jackson and Walford, 1835. 27th edn. 8.5 × 14 cm. Pp. [iv] + 98. By the Authors of *Original Poems, Rhymes for the Nursery*, etc., etc. UCLA: CBC G37 1835.

9(a) *My Mother a Poem Embellished with Designs* [engraved title-page only]. London: P. W. Tomkins, [1807]. 16.5 × 21.5 cm. 9 pp. [9 leaves with versos blank]. By a Lady [Ann Taylor]. BL: 1500/73.

9(b) *My Mother. A Poem* [cover serves as title-page]. Philadelphia: Wm. Charles, 1816. 11 × 13 cm. 6 pp. [printed on one side only]. 12½ cents plain, 18¾ cents coloured. By a Lady. LC: 1816 Juv. Coll.

9(c) *My Mother. A Poem.* New York: Mahlon Day, [183?]. 4.5 × 7.5 cm. 8 pp. NYPL: *KVM.

9(d) *My Mother, a Poem.* New York: Mahlon Day, 1831. 6 × 11 cm. 17 pp. NY State: N821. 79, G46m. [Photocopy seen only.]

9(e) *My Mother; a Poem for a Good Little Girl.* New Haven: S. Babcock, 1835. 6.5 × 10.5 cm. 16 pp. NYPL: *KVD.

10 *Signor Topsy-Turvy's Wonderful Magic Lantern; or, the World Turned upside down.* London: Tabart and Co., 1810. 10 × 13 cm. 71 pp. 3/6 bound. By the Author of *My Mother*, and Other Poems [Ann Taylor]. BL: Ch 810/10.

11 *The World Turn'd upside down, or the Wonderful Magic Lantern.* Part II. Philadelphia: Wm. Charles, 1814. 10.5 × 13.5 cm. 14 pp. By [Ann Taylor]. AAS: DATED PAMS.

12 *Hymns for Little Children.* New York: S. Wood and Sons, 1818. 6.5 × 10.5 cm. 26 pp. By [Ann and Jane Taylor]. LC: Juv. Coll. 1818.

13(a) *Original Hymns for Sunday Schools.* London/Bucklersbury: Josiah Conder/W. Kent, 1812. 8.5 × 13.5 cm. 54 pp. By the Authors of *Hymns for Infant Minds, Original Poems*, etc. [Ann and Jane Taylor]. Osborne: uncatalogued.

13(b) *Original Hymns for Sunday Schools.* 2nd edn. Inference.

13(c) *Original Hymns for Sunday Schools.* London: Josiah Conder and W. Kent, 1814. 3rd edn. 8.5 × 14 cm. 54 pp. Osborne: ii. 663.

13(d) *Original Hymns for Sunday Schools.* London: J. Conder and W. Kent, 1816. 4th edn. 8.5 × 13.5 cm. 54 pp. By the

Authors of *Hymns for Infant Minds*, *Original Poems*, etc. BL: 3437. aa. 29.

13(*e*) *Original Hymns for Sunday Schools*. London: for the authors by Jackson and Walford, [n.d.]. 6 × 9.5 cm. 46 pp. 2*d*. or 14/- per 100. By Ann and Jane Taylor. Trinity: 150. u. 93(5).

13(*f*) *Original Hymns for Sunday Schools*. London: for the authors by Jackson, Walford, and Hodder, [182?]. Stereotype edn. 7 × 10.5 cm. 46 pp. 2*d*. or 14/- per 100. By Ann and Jane Taylor, Authors of *Hymns for Infant Minds*, *Original Poems*, etc., etc. Union: VR 67/1812T/1822.

13(*g*) *Original Hymns for Sabbath Schools*. Hartford[, Conn.]: S. G. Goodrich, 1820. 7.5 × 13 cm. 24 pp. By the Authors of *Hymns for Infant Minds*, *Original Poems*, etc. Osborne: Stewart A 14 j.

13(*h*) *Original Hymns for Sunday Schools*. Philadelphia: American Sunday School Union, [182?]. 6.5 × 10 cm. 48 pp. 3¾ cents. By Ann and Jane Taylor. NYPL: *KVD Gilbert.

13(*i*) *Original Hymns for Sunday Schools*. London: for the authors by B. J. Holdsworth, [1823?]. Stereotype edn. 6.5 × 10.5 cm. 46 pp. 2*d*. or 14/- per 100. By Ann and Jane Taylor. Osborne: i. 80.

14(*a*) *City Scenes: Or, a Peep into London, for Good Children*. London: Darton and Harvey, 1809. 9 × 15.5 cm. 72 pp. [prose and verse]. [Revised] by the Author of *Rural Scenes* [Ann and Jane Taylor]. Osborne: uncatalogued.

14(*b*) *City Scenes; or a Peep into London, for Children*. London: Darton, Harvey and Darton, 1814. 9.5 × 15.5 cm. Pp. [ii] + 72 [prose and verse]. 2/6 half-bound. Osborne: ii. 814.

14(*c*) *City Scenes, or a Peep into London. For Children*. [Engraved title-page.] London: Darton, Harvey and Darton, 1818. 9 × 15 cm. Pp. 2 + 72 [prose and verse]. 2/6 half-bound. Osborne: i. 191.

14(*d*) *City Scenes, or a Peep into London. For Children*. London: Darton, Harvey and Darton, 1823. 9 × 15.5 cm. 72 pp. [prose and verse]. Bodley: Vet. A6 f. 2.

15(*a*) *Little Poems for Little Readers* [title-page has been bound into the back of this copy]. New York: Samuel Wood,

1813. 6.5 × 10 cm. 28 pp. By [Ann Taylor]. NYPL: *KVD Gilbert.

15(*b*) *Little Poems for Little Readers.* New York: Samuel Wood, 1814. 6.5 × 10 cm. 28 pp. [pp. 27 and 28 preceding the title-page in this copy]. LC: Juv. Coll. 1814.

15(*c*) *Little Poems for Little Readers.* New York: Samuel Wood, 1815. 6 × 10 cm. 29 pp. NYPL: *KVD Gilbert.

15(*d*) *Little Poems for Little Readers.* New York: S. Wood and Sons, 1816. 6 × 10 cm. 28 pp. LC: Juv. Coll. 1816.

15(*e*) *Little Poems for Little Readers.* New York: S. Wood and Sons, 1818. 6.5 × 10.5 cm. 28 pp. UCLA: CBC G37li 1818.

15(*f*) *Little Poems for Little Readers.* New York/Baltimore: Samuel Wood and Sons/Samuel S. Wood and Co., 1819. 6.5 × 10.5 cm. 28 pp. NYPL: *KVD.

15(*g*) *Little Poems for Little Readers.* Wendell, Mass.: J. Metcalf, 1826. 6.5 × 12.5 cm. 23 pp. UCLA: G37li 1826.

16 *The Linnet's Life. Twelve Poems with a Copper Plate Engraving to Each.* London: G. and W. B. Whittaker, and B. J. Holdsworth, 1822. 9.5 × 15.5 cm. 36 pp. By [Ann Gilbert and Jane Taylor]. Osborne: ii. 663.

17(*a*) *Hymns for Infant Schools, Partly Original, and Partly Selected, from 'Hymns for Infant Minds', and 'Original Hymns for Sunday Schools', by Ann and Jane Taylor.* London: B. J. Holdsworth, 1827. 10 × 16.5 cm. 36 pp. 4*d.* or 3/6 per dozen. By Mrs Gilbert (Late Ann Taylor). BL: T. 1217(3).

17(*b*) *Hymns for Infant Schools.* 2nd edn. Inference.

17(*c*) *Hymns for Infant Schools, Party Original, and Partly Selected, by Request, from 'Hymns for Infant Minds', and 'Original Hymns for Sunday Schools', by Ann and Jane Taylor.* London: Holdsworth and Ball, 1830. 3rd edn. 10 × 15.5 cm. 36 pp. 4*d.* or 3/6 per dozen. By Mrs Gilbert, (Late Ann Taylor). NYPL: *C p. v. 506 (11).

18 *Original Anniversary Hymns, Adapted to the Public Services of Sunday Schools and Sunday School Unions.* London: B. J. Holdsworth, 1827. 8 × 13.5 cm. 76 pp. 6*d.* or 5/- per dozen. By Mrs Gilbert (Late Ann Taylor). BL: T. 1217(1).

19   *Poetic Trifles, or Pretty Poems, for Young Folks, Selected from the Best Juvenile Writers.* Banbury: J. G. Rusher, [*c*.1830]. 7.5 × 11.5 cm. 16 pp. 1*d*. By [Ann Gilbert and Jane Taylor]. Osborne: ii. 665.

[*See also*: 'My Mother. A Poem' (n.d., 6 pp.).]

TAYLOR, Ellen

She was the daughter of an 'indigent cottager'. She had been a servant but by 1792 was running a small school. Some of her poems had previously appeared in the newspapers; the collection was published without her knowledge. (Lonsdale)

1   *Poems.* [London]: printed [for the author?] by G. Draper, 1792. 17.5 × 22 cm. Pp. [iv] + 14 [subscription edition]. By Ellen Taylor, the Irish Cottager. BL: 11632. f. 62.

TAYLOR, Emily (1795–1872), *see also* COLLECTIONS 40(*a–d*), 45, 47, 48, 51, 52, 54

Born at Banham, Norfolk. One of six children of Samuel Taylor, a farmer. Their mother died when Emily was an infant. She was musically gifted, but suffered from deafness caused by childhood scarlet fever. She ran a school for children in the village of New Buckenham where singing was stressed. She moved to London in 1842 and continued teaching. She wrote many books for children and edited collections of poetry. (*CB, DNB* (under Edgar Taylor), *Sketch of Emily Taylor, by a Friend* (1872))

1   *The Vision of Las Casas, and Other Poems.* London: Taylor and Hessey, 1825. 10 × 16.5 cm. Pp. viii + 122. By Emily Taylor. BL: 994. g. 40.

2   *Poetical Illustrations of Passages of Scripture.* Wellington, Salop./London: F. Houlston and Son/Taylor, and Hessey, 1826. 10 × 16.5 cm. Pp. viii + 78. By Emily Taylor. BL: 994. a. 30.

TAYLOR, Hannah, Mrs Henry (1774–1812)

An Irish writer and a Quaker. She was the eldest of the six children of William Harris, a seaman. She married Henry Taylor, a shipmaster, and they had one daughter who died young. (Blain, and *Friends' Books, Memoir*)

1   *Memoir of Hannah Taylor: Extracted from her Own Memorandums.* Ed. [her sister]. York/London/Bristol/ Dublin: W. Alexander/Harvey and Darton, W. Phillips, and W. Darton/M. M. and E. Webb/Christopher Bentham, 1820. 10.5 × 17.5 cm. 168 pp. [prose and verse, the verse occupying pp. 133–68]. By Hannah Taylor. BL: 1112. d. 22.

TAYLOR, Jane (1783–1824), *see also* TAYLOR, Ann, COLLECTIONS 10(*b*), 11(*b*), 22(*a–b*), 26(*a–d*), 40(*a–d*), 43, 44, 53, *and* FENN, Lady Eleanor

The younger sister of Ann Taylor (q.v.). She began by contributing to *Minor's Pocket Book* in 1804. Until 1812 she collaborated with her sister on children's books. Her *Display, a Tale for Young People* (1815) went through several editions. She was a regular contributor to *Youth's Magazine*. (*CB, DNB*)

1(*a*)   *Essays in Rhyme, on Morals and Manners.* London: Taylor and Hessey, and Josiah Conder, 1816. 10 × 16.5 cm. Pp. [ii] + 174. 6/- boards. By Jane Taylor, Author of *Display: A Tale*, and One of the Authors of *Original Poems for Infant Minds, Hymns for Infants*, etc. MR 82: 432–3; Widener: 20435. 15. 5.

1(*b*)   *Essays in Rhyme, on Morals and Manners.* Boston[, Mass.]/ New York/Philadelphia: Wells and Lilly/Van Winkle and Wiley/M. Carey, 1816. 9 × 14.5 cm. Pp. [ii] + 117. By Jane Taylor, Author of *Display: A Tale*, and One of the Authors of *Original Poems for Infant Minds, Hymns for Infant Minds*, etc. Widener: 20435. 15.

1(*c*)   *Essays in Rhyme, on Morals and Manners.* London: Taylor and Hessey, and Josiah Conder, 1816. 2nd edn. 10 × 16.5 cm. Pp. [ii] + 174. By Jane Taylor. Osborne: ii. 663.

1(*d*)   *Essays in Rhyme, on Morals and Manners.* London: Taylor and Hessey, and Josiah Conder, 1817. 3rd edn. 9.5 × 16 cm. Pp. [ii] + 174. By Jane Taylor, Author of *Display: A Tale*, and One of the Authors of *Original Poems for Infant Minds, Hymns for Infant Minds*, etc. BL: 11646. ccc. 32.

1(*e*)   *Essays in Rhyme, on Morals and Manners.* London: Taylor and Hessey, 1820. 4th edn. 10 × 16 cm. Pp. [ii] + 174. By Jane Taylor, Author of *Display: A Tale*, and One of the

Authors of *Original Poems for Infant Minds*, *Hymns for Infant Minds*, etc. BL: 11646. cc. 17.

1(*f*) *Essays in Rhyme, on Morals and Manners.* London: Taylor and Hessey, 1825. 5th edn. 11 × 17 cm. Pp. [ii] + 175. By Jane Taylor, Author of *Display: A Tale*, and One of the Authors of *Original Poems for Infant Minds*, *Hymns for Infant Minds*, etc. BL: 11647. ccc. 15.

1(*g*) *Essays in Rhyme on Morals and Manners.* London: John Taylor and Houlston and Son, 1830. 4th edn. 10 × 16.5 cm. Pp. [ii] + 175. By Jane Taylor, Author of *Display, a Tale*, and One of the Authors of *Original Poems for Infant Minds*, *Hymns for Infant Minds*, etc. Osborne: uncatalogued.

1(*h*) *Essays in Rhyme, on Morals and Manners.* Boston[, Mass.]: Perkins and Marvin, 1831. From 4th London edn. 9 × 15.5 cm. 108 pp. By the Late Jane Taylor. U. of Pennsylvania: 823/T214D.

1(*i*) *Essays in Rhyme, on Morals and Manners.* Boston[, Mass.]: Perkins and Marvin, 1832. From 4th London edn. 10 × 18 cm. 108 pp. By the Late Jane Taylor. NYPL: NCM.

2(*a*) *The Contributions of Q. Q. to a Periodical Work: With Some Pieces not before Published.* London: B. J. Holdsworth, 1824. 11 × 18 cm. 2 vols. [Prose with about 35 pp. of verse interspersed.] By the Late Jane Taylor. BL: 1115. a. 27.

2(*b*) *The Contributions of Q. Q. to a Periodical Work: With Some Pieces not before Published.* Ed. [I. Taylor, Jr.]. London: B. J. Holdsworth, 1826. 2nd edn. 10.5 × 17.5 cm. 2 vols. By the Late Jane Taylor. BL: 012642. n. 229.

2(*c*) *The Contributions of Q. Q. to a Periodical Work: With Some Pieces not before Published.* New York: E. Bliss and E. White, John P. Haven, Collins and Hannay, G. and C. Carvill, and Collins and Co., 1826. 11.5 × 19.5 cm. 2 vols. By the Late Jane Taylor. Yale (Sterling): In/T213/826/1–2.

2(*d*) *The Contributions of Q. Q. to a Periodical Work: With Some Pieces not before Published.* Ed. [I. T. [Isaac Taylor], Jr.]. New York: G. and C. Carvill, E. Bliss, and John P. Haven, 1827. 11 × 18 cm. 2 vols. By the Late Jane Taylor. HEHL: 138923.

2(*e*)   *The Contributions of Q. Q. to a Periodical Work: With Some Pieces not before Published.* London: B. J. Holdsworth, 1828. 3rd edn. 10 × 17.5 cm. 2 vols. By the Late Jane Taylor. Berkeley: 952 T243c 1828. [Photocopy seen only.]

2(*f*)   *The Contributions of Q. Q. to a Periodical Work: With Some Pieces not before Published.* London: Holdsworth and Ball, 1829. 4th edn. 18 cm. 2 vols. By Jane Taylor. Newberry. [Photocopies of title-pages seen only.]

2(*g*)   *The Contributions of Q. Q. to a Periodical Work: With Some Pieces not before Published.* London: Holdsworth and Ball, 1830. 5th edn. 10.5 × 18 cm. 2 vols. By the Late Jane Taylor. Osborne: Stewart A 43 e.

2(*h*)   *The Contributions of Q. Q. to a Periodical Work: With Some Pieces not before Published.* Philadelphia: Thomas Kite, 1830. 8.5 × 14.5 cm. 264 pp. By the Late Jane Taylor. Widener: Phil 8894. 2.

2(*i*)   *The Contributions of Q. Q. to a Periodical Work, with Some Pieces not before Published.* London: Jackson and Walford, 1834. 7th edn. 11 × 19 cm. 2 vols. By the Late Jane Taylor. Osborne: Stewart A 43 g.

3(*a*)   *Memoirs and Poetical Remains . . . with Extracts from her Correspondence.* Ed. Isaac Taylor. London: B. J. Holdsworth, 1825. 12 × 19.5 cm. 2 vols. [the verse occupies ii. 3–137]. By the Late Jane Taylor. NLS: Bm. 7. 13–14.

3(*b*)   *Memoirs and Poetical Remains . . . with Extracts from her Correspondence.* Ed. Isaac Taylor. London: B. J. Holdsworth, 1826. 2nd edn. 10.5 × 17 cm. 2 vols. By the Late Jane Taylor. BL: 11644. eee. 22.

3(*c*)   *Memoirs and Poetical Remains . . . with Extracts from her Correspondence . . .* Boston[, Mass.]/Newburyport[, Mass.]/ New York/Philadelphia/Baltimore: Crocker and Brewster/ Samuel N. Tenney/John P. Haven, G. and C. Carvill/ W. W. Woodward/Cushing and Jewett, 1826. 12.5 × 19 cm. 316 pp. [verse occupies pp. 147–214]. By Isaac Taylor and Jane Taylor. Widener: 20435. 18.

3(*d*)   *Memoirs and Poetical Remains . . . with Extracts from her Correspondence.* Philadelphia: J. J. Woodward, 1827. 8.5 × 14 cm. 330 pp. [prose and verse]. By Isaac Taylor and Jane Taylor. NEDL: KC14511.

3(*e*)   *Memoirs and Poetical Remains* . . . New York, 1827. *NUC.* Not seen.

3(*f*)   *Memoirs, Correspondence, and Poetical Remains.* [London]: Holdsworth and Ball, 1831. 10.5 × 17.5 cm. Pp. xii + 369 [prose and verse]. By [Isaac Taylor and] Jane Taylor. Widener: 20435. 18. 5.

4(*a*)   *Poetical Remains . . . with Extracts from her Correspondence.* Ed. Isaac Taylor. Philadelphia: William Stavely, 1828. 8.5 × 14 cm. 144 pp. [prose and verse]. By the Late Jane Taylor. AAS: G850. T241. P828.

4(*b*)   *Poetical Remains . . . with Extracts from her Correspondence.* Ed. Isaac Taylor. Lowell[, Mass.]: Thomas Billings, 1829. 8 × 14 cm. 144 pp. By the Late Jane Taylor. LC: PR 5549. T2 1829.

4(*c*)   *Poetical Remains and Correspondence* . . . Ed. Isaac Taylor. Boston[, Mass.]: C. D. Strong, 1832. New edn. 9 × 15 cm. 144 pp. By the Late Jane Taylor. Boston Public: 4579. a. 25.

4(*d*)   *Poetical Remains and Correspondence.* Ed. Isaac Taylor. Boston[, Mass.]: Water Street Bookstore, 1833. New edn. 10 × 16.5 cm. 144 pp. By the Late Jane Taylor. HEHL: X 66149.

5(*a*)   *The Writings.* Boston[, Mass.]/Philadelphia: Perkins and Marvin/French and Perkins, 1832. 9 × 15.5 cm. 5 vols. [prose and verse, the poetry occupies i. 275–346, ii. 265–7, 285–7, iii. 80–2, 91–3, 117–20, 205–12, 237–8, 248–52, iv. 115–16 and—new pagination—1–108, v. 127–296]. By Jane Taylor. Osborne: Stewart B 13 a.

5(*b*)   *The Writings* . . . New York/Boston[, Mass.]: Saxton and Miles/Saxton and Peirce, [1835]. 11 × 18 cm. 3 vols. [the poetry occupies i. 275–346 and—new pagination—1–108, iii. 127–296]. By Jane Taylor. NYPL: NCG.

TEMPLE, Laura Sophia (1763–after 1820), *see also* COLLECTIONS 23(*a–b*)?

She was the daughter of Lieutenant-Colonel Richard Temple and his wife Frances. She married Samuel B. Sweetman who went bankrupt about 1817. (Allibone, Blain, *GM*, Shoberl)

1   *Poems.* London: R. Phillips, 1805. 10 × 16.5 cm. Pp. vi + 192. 5/- boards. By Laura Sophia Temple. *MR* 51: 102–3; BL: 11641. b. 49.

2   *Lyric and Other Poems.* London/Bristol: Longman, Hurst, Rees, and Orme/W. Sheppard, 1808. 9 × 16 cm. Pp. [xiv] + 145. 4/- boards. By Laura Sophia Temple. *MR* 57: 94–6; BL: 11644. aa. 2.

3   *The Siege of Zaragoza, and Other Poems.* London: William Miller and W. Bulmer and Co., 1812. 11.5 × 18.5 cm. Pp. [ii] + 150. 8/- boards. By Laura Sophia Temple, Author of *Lyric Poems*, etc. BL: 11644. cc. 23.

THAYER, Caroline Matilda (1787?–1844), *see* MUZZY, Harriet

An American writer. Her maiden name was Warren. She married and had three children. She was a Methodist and worked as a schoolteacher in Massachusetts and New York State. She was the editor of Muzzy's *Poems* and included some of her own compositions as part of a poetical dialogue between them. (Kunitz 2)

THEODOSIA, *see* STEELE, Anne

THOMAS, Ann, Mrs

Her title-page describes her as the widow of an officer in the Royal Navy and as resident in Millbrook, Cornwall. Her *Adolphus de Biron, a Novel* appeared in 1795. (*BLC*)

1   *Poems, on Various Subjects.* Plymouth/London/Sherborne/Exeter/Millbrook: M. Haydon and Son/B. Law/R. Goadby/R. Trewman/the author, 1784. 20 × 25 cm. Pp. [iv] + 44 + [8] [subscription edition]. 3/-. By Mrs Ann Thomas, of Millbrook, Cornwall, an Officer's Widow of the Royal Navy. *MR* 73: 389; *CR* 61: 72; Bodley: Vet. A5 d. 822.

THOMAS, Elizabeth, Mrs Thomas (born 1771)

Born at Berry, Devon. She was the wife of the Revd Thomas Thomas, the Vicar of Tidenham. They had children. She wrote eight novels, most of them for the Minerva Press. (Blain)

1   *The Confession; or, the Novice of St. Clare and Other Poems.* London: W. Simpkin and R. Marshall, 1818. 9.5 × 16 cm.

Pp. xvi + 88. 4/- boards. By the Author of *Purity of Heart*.
BL: 11644. b. 12.

2   *Serious Poems; Comprising the Churchyard; Village Sabbath;
Deluge, &c. &c.* London: Whittaker, Treacher, and Co.,
1831. 11 × 18 cm. Pp. viii + 276. By Mrs Thomas. BL:
994. h. 30.

THOMPSON, Eliza

A number of the poems in her first book had appeared previously in
the newspapers, signed 'Eliza'. 'The Christmas Frolic' was mocked by
the critics and it is reissued in *Retaliation*. (*Poems*)

1   *Poems on Various Subjects.* London: for the author, by W.
Richardson, 1787. 21 × 26 cm. 48 pp. [subscription edi-
tion]. 2/6. By Miss Eliza Thompson. *MR* 77: 493–4; BL:
643. k. 16(3).

2   *Retaliation; or, the Reviewers Review'd. A Satirical Poem.*
London: for the author by Boosy and Walker, 1791. 22 ×
28 cm. Pp. iv + 18. 1/6. By a Lady. BL: 1602/394.

THRALE, Hester Lynch, Mrs Henry, *see* PIOZZI, Hester

THURTLE, Frances, *see* JAMIESON, Frances

TIERNAN, Mary Anne

Her book is published with 'the special approbation of Prince Leopold',
a sign, perhaps, of a court connection.

1(*a*)   *Monody on the Death of Princess Charlotte* . . . Inference.

1(*b*)   *Monody on the Death of Her Royal Highness the Princess
Charlotte of Wales. To Which is Added, Desolation, a Dream,
Inscribed to the Princess of Wales.* London: for the author by
Sherwood, Neely, and Jones, 1818. 2nd edn. 13 × 20.5 cm.
23 pp. 2/-. By M. A. Tiernan. BL: 11644. ccc. 13.

TIGHE, Mary, Mrs Henry (1772–1810), *see also* COLLECTIONS 35,
38(*a–b*), 40(*a–d*), 43, 50(*a–c*), 52, 53

Born in Dublin. She was the daughter of the Revd William Blachford,
a well-to-do librarian, and of Theodosia Tighe. In 1793 she married her

cousin Henry Tighe, MP for Kilkenny. They had no children. She died of consumption. Only a few copies of *Mary* were printed for private distribution. (*CB, DNB*, MS annotations on Houghton copy of *Mary*)

1(*a*)   *Psyche; or, the Legend of Love.* London: [James Carpenter], 1805. 9.5 × 12 cm. Pp. viii + 214. BL: C. 95. b. 38.

1(*b*)   *Psyche, with Other Poems.* London: Longman, Hurst, Rees, Orme, and Brown, 1811. 20.5 × 25.5 cm. Pp. xii + 314. £1/11/6 boards. By the Late Mrs Henry Tighe. *MR* 66: 138–52; BL: 11642. h. 18.

1(*c*)   *Psyche, with Other Poems.* London: Longman, Hurst, Rees, Orme, and Brown, 1811. 3rd edn. 13 × 21 cm. Pp. xvi + 314. By the Late Mrs Henry Tighe. BL: 11641. e. 46.

1(*d*)   *Psyche, with Other Poems.* London: Longman, Hurst, Rees, Orme, and Brown, 1812. 4th edn. 13 × 20.5 cm. Pp. xvi + 311. By the Late Mrs Henry Tighe. BL: 11641. e. 47.

1(*e*)   *Psyche, with Other Poems.* Philadelphia: J. and A. Y. Humphreys, 1812. 9 × 15 cm. Pp. x + 230. By the Late Mrs Henry Tighe. Houghton: *EC8. T4484. 811pd.

1(*f*)   *Psyche, with Other Poems.* London: Longman, Hurst, Rees, Orme, and Brown, 1816. 5th edn. 13.5 × 21.5 cm. Pp. xvi + 311. By the Late Mrs Henry Tighe. BL: 994. h. 31.

2   *Mary, a Series of Reflections during Twenty Years.* [Dublin?], 1811. 8.5 × 13.5 cm. 35 pp. Houghton: *EC8. T4484. 811m.

TIMBURY, Jane (born *c.*1749)
She ran a small school in Westminster, London, from 1788 to 1803, maintaining her mother and sister. Author of *The Male Coquet; a Novel* (1788) and *The Philanthropic Rambler* (1790). (Blain, Watt)

1   *The History of Tobit; a Poem: With Other Poems, on Various Subjects.* London: for the author and by Egertons, and Jameson, 1787. 12 × 20.5 cm. Pp. x + 60 [subscription edition]. 2/6 sewed. By Jane Timbury. BL: 11632. c. 58.

2   *The Story of Le Fevre, from the Works of Mr Sterne. Put into Verse.* London: R. Jameson, 1787. 11.5 × 18.5 cm. 31 pp. By Jane Timbury. BL: 11633. bbb. 37.

3   *The Power of Music; a Poem*. London: R. Jameson, 1787. 10.5
       × 18.5 cm. 23 pp. 1/-. By the Author of *Tobit*. BL: 11633.
       bb. 1(1).

TOMLINS, Elizabeth Sophia (1763–1828)

She was the daughter of Thomas Tomlins, a solicitor. She educated his
other children after her mother died, and supervised his financial
concerns for some years before his death in 1815. She was a regular
contributor to periodicals from 1780 on. She died after falling from her
pony. (*DNB* (under Sir Thomas Edlyne Tomlins), *GM*)

1   *Tributes of Affection: With the Slaves; and Other Poems*.
       London: T. N. Longman and C. Dilly, 1797. 11 × 18 cm.
       143 pp. By a Lady and Her Brother [Elizabeth Sophia
       Tomlins and E. Tomlins]. BL: 11644. cc. 21.

TONGE, Eliza, Mrs

She writes from Cheltenham, Glos., giving her Christian name, and
mentioning six of her children by name. Some of her poems had been
published before in periodicals. (*Poetical Trifles*)

1   *Poetical Trifles*. Cheltenham: O. Watts, [1832]. 10.5 × 18 cm.
       Pp. vi + 110. By Mrs Tonge. BL: 11644. bbb. 34.

TONNA, Charlotte Elizabeth, *see* PHELAN, Charlotte Elizabeth

TRAILL, Catharine Parr, Mrs Thomas (1802–99)

Born in London. She was the fifth daughter of Thomas Strickland and
Elizabeth Homer, and the sister of Agnes Strickland (q.v.) and Susanna
Moodie (q.v.). In 1832 she married Thomas Traill, a second lieutenant
in the 21st Foot. She went with him to Canada and wrote much about
life in eastern Ontario. (Boase, *CB*)

1   *The Flower-basket; or Poetical Blossoms: Original Nursery Rhymes
       and Tales*. London: A. K. Newman and Co., [*c*.1825]. 10 ×
       17 cm. 32 pp. By the Author of *Adventures of a Field-mouse,
       Lessons for the Nursery Tell-tale*, etc. Osborne: ii. 666.

TREFUSIS, Elizabeth (1763?–1808)

She was the daughter of Robert Cotton Trefusis, of Trefusis, Cornwall,
and of Anne St John, and was the sister of Lord Clinton. She became
impoverished through rash generosity. In Beloe's *Sexagenarian* she
figures as the eccentric royalist poet Ella. (Blain, Rowton)

1   *Poems and Tales.* London: Samuel Tipper, 1808. 10 × 16
     cm. 2 vols. 10/- boards. By Miss Trefusis. *MR* 57: 206–9;
     BL: 11641. a. 57, 58.

TRENCH, Melesina, Mrs Richard (1768–1827)

Born in Dublin. She was the daughter of Philip Chenevix and Mary
Elizabeth Gervais. After her parents' deaths she was brought up by her
grandfather, Bishop Chenevix, and her kinswoman Lady Lifford and,
after 1779, by her maternal grandfather, Archdeacon Gervais, in whose
library she educated herself. In 1786 she married Colonel Richard St
George, who died two years later. In 1799 she began to travel on the
Continent, where she remained until 1807. In 1803 she married Richard
Trench. She had at least three children. She is best known for her
Remains (2 vols., 1862), an edition of her journals and letters. (*DNB*)

1   *Campaspe, an Historical Tale; and Other Poems.* Southampton:
     printed [for the author?] by T. Baker, 1815. 11.5 × 20.5
     cm. 46 pp. BL: 11644. cc. 59(1).

2   *Ellen: A Ballad: Founded on a Recent Fact. And Other Poems.
     Sold for the Benefit of the House of Protection.* Bath: printed by
     Richard Cruttwell for the booksellers, 1815. 12 × 19 cm.
     49 pp. BL: 11643. bb. 15(5).

3   *Laura's Dream; or, the Moonlanders.* London: J. Hatchard,
     1816. 12.5 × 20 cm. 47 pp. BL: 992. i. 12(9).

4   *Aubrey. In Five Cantos.* Southampton: printed [for
     I. Fletcher] by T. Baker, 1818. 12 × 20 cm. 78 pp. Yale
     (Sterling): In/T722/815C.

5   *A Monody on the Death of Mr Grattan.* London: James
     Ridgway, 1820. 13 × 20 cm. 8 pp. 1/-. CUL: Lib. 7. 81.
     22(5).

TROLLOPE, Frances, Mrs Thomas Anthony (1780–1863)

Born in Stapleton, near Bristol, Glos. She was the youngest daughter of
William Milton, a clergyman, and of Frances Gresley. In 1809 she married Thomas Anthony Trollope, a barrister who failed in various walks
of life. They had five children, one of whom was the novelist Anthony
Trollope. Her *Domestic Manners of the Americans* was well received in
1832. After her husband's death in 1835 she turned to novel writing
and produced a series of popular books in the 1840s and 1850s. Her
best known novels are *The Vicar of Wrexhill* (1837) and *The Widow
Barnaby* (1838). (Boase, *CB*, *DNB*, Todd 2)

I   *The Mothers' Manual; or, Illustrations of Matrimonial Economy.*
    An Essay in Verse. London: Treuttel and Würtz and
    Richter, 1833. 14.5 × 23.5 cm. Pp. [ii] + 82. BL: 11623.
    k. 13.

TUCK, Elizabeth

I   *The Juvenile Poetical Moralist.* Frome, 1821. 8vo. HL. Not
    located.

2   *Vallis Vale, and Other Poems.* London/Bath/Frome:
    Longman, Hurst, and Co., J. B. Holdsworth, C. Penny/T.
    Smith/M. and S. Tuck, 1823. 11.5 × 18.5 cm. Pp. viii +
    102. BL: 11644. ccc. 25.

TUITE, Elizabeth Dorothea, Lady (1764–1850)
She was a daughter of Thomas Cobbe, of Newbridge, Co. Dublin, and
of Elizabeth Dorothea Beresford. She married Sir Henry Tuite in 1784.
Her *Miscellaneous Poems* appeared in 1841. (Blain)

1(*a*)   *Poems.* London: T. Cadell, Jr. and W. Davies, 1796. 9.5 ×
        16 cm. Pp. [iv] + 199. 10/6 boards. By Lady Tuite. *MR*
        21: 110; BL: 1607/3322.

1(*b*)   *Poems.* London: the booksellers, 1799. 2nd edn. 10 × 15.5
        cm. Pp. [iv] + 199. By Lady Tuite. BL: 11644. bb. 25.

TURNER, Annette, Mrs Charles TINSLEY (1808–85)
Born in Preston, Lancs. Her father was Thomas Milner Turner and her
mother may have been a Miss Carruthers. She married Charles Tinsley,
a solicitor, in 1833. She wrote several novels and another volume of
her poems appeared in 1848, entitled *Lays for the Thoughtful and Solitary.*
(Blain)

I   *The Children of the Mist, the Conqueror, and Other Poems.*
    London: G. Lutz, and R. P. Moore, 1827. 11.5 × 18.5 cm.
    By Miss Annette Turner. BL: 11644. cc. 29.

TURNER, Elizabeth, Mrs (*c.*1774–1846)
She was active in the Bible Society and lived in Liverpool for the last
thirty years of her life. (*GM*)

1(*a*)   *The Daisy; or, Cautionary Stories in Verse. Adapted to the Ideas*
        of Children from Four to Eight Years Old. London: J. Harris
        and Crosby and Co., 1807. 9 × 13.5 cm. [30] pp. [with

illustrations on facing pages not included in the count].
1/-. *MR* 55: 440; Osborne: uncatalogued.

1(*b*)   *The Daisy; or Cautionary Stories in Verse. Adapted to the Ideas of Children from Four to Eight Years Old.* Part I. Philadelphia: Jacob Johnson, 1808. 9 × 14 cm. [32] pp. HEHL: 141737.

1(*c*)   *The Daisy, or Cautionary Stories in Verse. Adapted to the Ideas of Children from Four to Eight Years Old.* London: J. Harris, and Crosby and Co., 1810. 8.5 × 13.5 cm. 66 pp. BL: 11645. de. 53.

1(*d*)   *The Daisy* . . . 3rd edn. Inference.

1(*e*)   *The Daisy, or Cautionary Stories, in Verse. Adapted to the Ideas of Children from Four to Eight Years Old.* London: J. Harris and Crosby and Co., 1814. 4th edn. 8.5 × 13 cm. 66 pp. UCLA: CBC G755e 1818(3).

1(*f*)   *The Daisy* . . . 5th edn. Inference.

1(*g*)   *The Daisy, or Cautionary Stories, in Verse. Adapted to the Ideas of Children from Four to Eight Years Old.* London: J. Harris, and Baldwin, Cradock, and Joy, 1816. 6th edn. 8.5 × 13.5 cm. 66 pp. BL: 11641. de. 51(1).

1(*h*)   *The Daisy* . . . 7th edn. Inference.

1(*i*)   *The Daisy* . . . 8th edn. Inference.

1(*j*)   *The Daisy* . . . 9th edn. Inference.

1(*k*)   *The Daisy, or, Cautionary Stories, in Verse. Adapted to the Ideas of Children from Four to Eight Years Old.* London: J. Harris and Son, and Baldwin, Cradock, and Joy, 1823. 10th edn. 8.5 × 13.5 cm. 66 pp. Bodley: 25210 f. 390(7).

2(*a*)   *The Cowslip, or More Cautionary Stories in Verse.* [London]: J. Harris and B. Crosby, 1811. 9.5 × 12.5 cm. 68 pp. By the Author of that Much-admired Little Work, Entitled *The Daisy.* NEDL: Juv 811.2.

2(*b*)   *The Cowslip, or More Cautionary Stories, in Verse.* London: J. Harris and B. Crosby, 1812. 2nd edn. 8 × 12.5 cm. 68 pp. By the Author of that Much-admired Little Work, Entitled *The Daisy.* NLS: Mas. 48.

2(*c*)   *The Cowslip, or More Cautionary Stories in Verse.* Philadelphia, [etc.]: Johnson and Warner, 1813. 15 cm. 64 pp. By the Author of . . . *The Daisy. NUC.* Not seen.

2(*d*)   *The Cowslip, or More Cautionary Stories, in Verse.* London:
J. Harris and B. Crosby, 1814. 3rd edn. 8 × 12.5 cm. 68
pp. By the Author of that Much-admired Little Work
Entitled *The Daisy.* Osborne: i. 82.

2(*e*)   *The Cowslip, or More Cautionary Stories, in Verse.* London:
J. Harris, and Baldwin, Cradock, and Joy, 1815. 4th edn.
8.5 × 13.5 cm. 68 pp. By the Author of that Much-
admired Little Work Entitled *The Daisy.* BL: 11641. de.
51(2).

2(*f*)   *The Cowslip, or More Cautionary Stories in Verse.* London:
J. Harris and Baldwin, Cradock and Joy, 1817. 5th edn. 8
× 13 cm. 68 pp. By the Author of that Much-admired
Little Work Entitled *The Daisy.* BL: 11601. aa. 46(3).

2(*g*)   *The Cowslip* . . . 6th edn. Inference.

2(*h*)   *The Cowslip; or, More Cautionary Stories in Verse.* London:
J. Harris and Son, and Baldwin, Cradock, and Joy, 1820.
7th edn. 8.5 × 13 cm. 68 pp. By the Author of that Much-
admired Little Work Entitled *The Daisy.* UCLA: CBC
G755e 1818(4).

2(*i*)   *The Cowslip; or, More Cautionary Stories, in Verse.* London:
J. Harris and Son, and Baldwin, Cradock, and Joy, 1822.
8th edn. 8.5 × 13.5 cm. 68 pp. By the Author of that
Much-admired Little Work Entitled *The Daisy.* Bodley:
25210 f. 390(6).

2(*j*)   *The Cowslip; or, More Cautionary Stories in Verse.* London:
J. Harris and Son, Baldwin, Cradock, and Joy, 1824. 9th
edn. 8.5 × 13.5 cm. 68 pp. By the Author of that Much-
admired Little Work Entitled *The Daisy.* Boston Public:
6569[a]. 132.

2(*k*)   *The Cowslip; or, More Cautionary Stories, in Verse.* London:
John Harris, and Baldwin, Cradock, and Joy, 1825. 10th
edn. 8.5 × 13 cm. 68 pp. By the Author of that Much-
admired Little Work Entitled *The Daisy.* BL: 012806. i.
29(4).

3(*a*)   *The Pink: A Flower in the Juvenile Garland. Consisting of Short
Poems, Adapted to the Understanding of Young Children.*
London: Baldwin, Cradock, and Joy, and N. Hailes, 1823.
8.5 × 13 cm. 68 pp. BL: 012806. i. 29(3).

3(*b*) *The Pink or, Child's First Book of Poetry.* London: Darton and Co., [1835?]. New edn. 12 × 15 cm. 64 pp. By the Author of *The Daisy, The Cowslip,* etc. and Mary Howitt. BL: 11644. aa. 59.

4 *Cautionary Stories, Containing the Daisy and Cowslip, Adapted to the Ideas of Children from Four to Eight Years Old.* London: John Harris and Baldwin, Cradock and Joy, 1825. 10 × 13 cm. 66 pp. NLS: Mas. 51.

TURNER, Margaret

1 *The Gentle Shepherd, a Scotch Pastoral . . . Attempted in English.* Trans. Margaret Turner. London: for the author [translator] by G. Nicol, 1790. 13.5 × 21.5 cm. Pp. xiv + 104 + 6 [subscription edition]. 5/- or 6/- boards. By Allan Ramsay. *CR* 70: 453; *MR* 6: 170–2; BL: 11778. d. 3.

[*See also*: 'Syllabus of a Course of Botanical Lectures' (1818, 6 pp.).]

TWAMLEY, Louisa Anne (1812–95), *see also* COLLECTIONS 53

She was an accomplished artist who illustrated her own books on flowers. In 1844 she married Charles Meredith and went with him to Australia. She wrote *Notes and Sketches of New South Wales* (1846) and other books about Australia and New Zealand. (*CB*, Hale)

1 *Poems.* London: Charles Tilt, 1835. 12 × 19 cm. Pp. xii + 183. By Louisa Anne Twamley. BL: 991. h. 32.

TYRO, Theresa, *pseudonym?*

1 *The Feast of the Fishes; or, the Whale's Invitation to his Brethren of the Deep.* London: J. Harris, 1808. 10 × 12 cm. 14 pp. By [Theresa Tyro]. Osborne: ii. 667.

UNA SIGNORA INGLESE, *see* FAIRFAX, Lavinia

UPTON, Catherine, Mrs

From her anonymous book *The Siege of Gibraltar* (1781) one learns that she was married to a lieutenant in the army and had at least two children. She provides quite an interesting account of her experiences under fire. Her title-page mentions that she kept a school. Her father

lived in Nottingham and she seems to have come from there herself.
(*Miscellaneous Pieces*)

1   *Miscellaneous Pieces, in Prose and Verse*. London: the
     authoress, T. and G. Egerton, G. Robinson, 1784. 21 ×
     26.5 cm. Pp. viii + 51 [pp. 33–51 are in prose]. 2/-. By
     Mrs Upton, Authoress of *The Siege of Gibraltar* and
     Governess of the Ladies Academy, No. 43, Bartholomew
     Close. BL: 643. k. 16(1).

['An Address to Aeolus' (2 pp.) is included in her *The Siege of
Gibraltar* (1781).]

V., Charlotte T. S., *see* COLLECTIONS 35

V., Mary V., *pseudonym of* JEFFERSON, Thomas

VALPY, Henrietta F.
Possibly a daughter of Richard Valpy of Reading School. (*DNB*)

1   *Autumnal Leaves*. London: James Cochrane, 1834. 11 × 17
     cm. Pp. xii + 154. By Henrietta. BL: 994. c. 34.

VARDILL, Anna Jane (1781–1852)
She was the daughter of John Vardill, an American professor and
clergyman who moved to England in 1774. She lived variously in
Galloway, London, and Lincs. She began contributing verse to the
European Magazine in 1814. Between 1820 and 1826 she married a Mr
Niven. (Blain)

1(*a*)   *Poems and Translations, from the Minor Greek Poets and Others;
         Written Chiefly between the Ages of Ten and Sixteen*. London:
         Longman, Hurst, Rees, and Orme, and J. Asperne, and
         T. Becket, 1809. 9.5 × 15.5 cm. Pp. viii + 167. 7/- boards.
         By a Lady. *MR* 62: 284–7; BL: 11644. aaa. 7.

1(*b*)   *Poems and Translations, from the Minor Greek Poets and Others;
         Written Chiefly between the Ages of Ten and Sixteen*. London:
         Longman, Hurst, Rees, Orme, and Brown, and
         J. Asperne, and T. Becket, 1816. 2nd edn. 10 × 16 cm. Pp.
         viii + 198. By a Lady. BL: 11644. bbb. 17.

1(*c*)   *Poems and Translations, from the Minor Greek Poets and Others;
         Written Chiefly between the Ages of Ten & Sixteen*. London:
         Longman, Hurst, Rees, and Orme, and J. Asperne, and

T. Becket, 1809 [n.d.: this copy has an engraved title-page only, displaying the date of the first edition]. 3rd edn. 9.5 × 15.5 cm. Pp. viii + 222. By a Lady. BL: 11644. aaa. 6.

2   *The Pleasures of Human Life, a Poem.* London: Longman, Hurst, Rees, Orme, and Brown, 1812. 21.5 × 27 cm. Pp. [ii] + 100. 15/- boards. By Anna Jane Vardill. *MR* 69: 161–6; BL: 11642. h. 21.

VARIOUS FEMALE WRITERS, *see* COLLECTIONS 28(*a–b*)

VAUGHAN, Mrs

1   *The Grecians. A Tragedy. In Five Acts.* London: printed for the author by [J. Darling], 1824. 13.5 × 21 cm. 56 pp. By Mrs Vaughan. BL: 11778. f. 22.

VICTOR AND CAZIRE, *see* SHELLEY, Elizabeth

VINCE, Elizabeth

1   *The Mystic Wreath; or, Evening Pastime: Consisting of Enigmatical Poems, Charades, Anagrams, Conundrums, Rebuses, &c. &c.* London: sold for the authors by Sherwood, Gilbert, and Piper, 1829. 10.5 × 17 cm. Pp. xxiv + 276 [subscription edition]. By Susan and Elizabeth [Susan Winter and Elizabeth Vince]. BL: 1042. b. 10.

VINCE, Susan, *see* VINCE, Elizabeth
She later became Mrs Winter. (Stainforth)

VOKE, Mrs
She lived in Gosport, Hants. (*Poems*)

1   *Poems. Inscribed to the Missionary Society, by their Friend.* Southampton/London: T. Baker/T. Chapman, 1796. 12.5 × 20 cm. 56 pp. Bodley: 14770 e. 935(5).

WAIBLINGER, Catherine
She was a teacher at the Ladies' Boarding School, Bedford, Beds. (*Metrical Lessons*)

1   *Metrical Lessons and Fragments, in Remembrance of Days that are Gone.* London/Bedford: Baldwin, Cradock, and Joy, and C. B. Merry, 1823. 10 × 16.5 cm. 96 pp. BL: 11644. b. 16.

WALKER, Mary, *see* BAILEY, Mary

WALLIS, Hannah

She grew up in an Essex village. She was elderly by 1787. A review in *MR* refers to her as a 'poor Methodist'. (Lonsdale)

1   *The Female's Meditations; or, Common Occurrences Spiritualized, in Verse.* London: for the author by Matthews, Buckland, Murray, Sibly, and Boultwood, 1787. 15.5 × 20.5 cm. Pp. xii + 185. 3/6 sewed. By Hannah Wallis. BL: 994. i. 33(2).

WALSH, Miss

1   *Poems. By a Sister.* London/Bristol and Clifton: J. Walsh, J. Hatchard, E. Williams, and J. M. Richardson/the booksellers and libraries, 1812. 10.5 × 17.5 cm. Pp. xlviii + 119 [subscription edition]. BL: 11642. c. 33.

WARD, Catharine *or* Catherine George (born 1787)

Born in Scotland. She was the author of many novels; she also wrote for children and acted on the Edinburgh stage. Her first husband died in 1824 and her only child in 1816. She was gaoled for her husband's debts. She was married again, to James M. Mason. She was assisted by the Royal Literary Fund. (Blain)

1(*a*) *Poems.* Edinburgh: printed by John Moir, 1805. 12.5 × 20.5 cm. 43 pp. [subscription edition]. By Catharine George Ward, Late of the Theatre-Royal, Edinburgh. BL: 11644. ccc. 16.

1(*b*) *Poems.* Coventry/London: for the author by R. Pratt/ Longman and Co., 1812. 9.5 × 16 cm. Pp. viii + 60 [subscription edition]. By Catherine George Ward. HEHL: 288302.

2   *Tales of the Glen.* London/Windsor: for the author by Roach, and Hatchett/C. Knight, 1813. 10 × 16.5 cm. Pp. viii + 52 [subscription edition]. By C. G. Ward, Author of *The Daughter of St. Omar, My Native Land, Batchelor's Heiress, Corinna,* etc. BL: 11644. bb. 23.

3   *The Dandy Family, or the Pleasures of a Ball Night.* London: G. Martin, [1815]. 10 × 15.5 cm. [the cover serves as title-page and is handwritten]. 15 pp. [printed on one side only]. 1/- coloured. By Mrs Catherine Ward, Author of *The Gipsey's Wedding, Cottage Story's,* &[c.]. BL: 11644. bb. 28.

4   *Maid, Wife, and Mother; or, Woman! A Poem . . . Dedicated, by Permission, to Her Royal Highness the Princess of Wales.* London: Matthew Iley, 1819. 12 × 19.5 cm. 19 pp. By Mrs Catherine G. Ward. Bodley: G. Pamph. 1301(16).

5   *Miscellaneous Poems.* London: for the author by Gold and Northhouse, Taylor and Hessey, and Chapple, 1820. 10 × 16 cm. Pp. [viii] + 84. By Mrs Catherine G. Ward, Author of *Woman, a Poem, Tales of the Glen, Cottage Stories, The Primrose Girl,* etc. BL: 11644. aaa. 24.

[*See also*: 'A Tributary Poem, on the . . . Death of . . . Princess Charlotte' (1817, 7 pp.).]

WARD, Mary

She writes from Brixham, Devon, and dedicates her book to the Countess of Loudon and Moira. Her subscription list is a modest one, but she seems to have some link with Rathby Hall, the seat of Robert Carr Brackenbury.

1   *Original Poetry.* Bath: printed [for the author?] by Hazard and Binns, 1807. 11 × 18 cm. Pp. x + 192 [subscription edition]. By Mary Ward. BL: 11644. cc. 12.

WARDLE, Charlotte

1   *St Aelian's, or the Cursing Well. A Poem.* London: for the author by G. Cowie and Co., 1814. 13.5 × 21.5 cm. Pp. vi + 112. By Charlotte Wardle. BL: 992. k. 30.

2   *Norway: A Poem.* London: J. Ridgway, [1814]. 11 × 18 cm. 29 pp. By Charlotte Wardle. [The English title is on the verso; facing it is the Norwegian title: *Norge: En Poetisk Efterligning.* [Trans.] N. H. Jaeger. Christiania: N. J. Berg. The English and Norwegian are on facing pages throughout.] BL: 11644. c. 13.

WARE, Mary

Her maiden name was Tarrant. (Shoberl)

1   *Poems. Consisting of Translations, from the Greek, Latin, &*
    Italian. With Some Originals. London: T. Cadell and W.
    Davies, 1809. 10 × 17 cm. Pp. viii + 230. 7/- boards. By
    Mrs Ware, of Ware Hill, Herts. *MR* 60: 250–3; BL: 11641.
    b. 53.

WARING, S.

Minstrelsy is dated from Wyards and addressed to a brother's children in
Glamorgan. Bodley L. Cat. lists her as Susanna Boone.

1   *The Wild Garland; or, Prose and Poetry Connected with English*
    Wild Flowers. Intended as an Embellishment to the Study of
    Botany. London: Harvey and Darton, 1827. 10.5 × 17.5 cm.
    80 pp. [about 20 pp. of verse distributed through the vol-
    ume]. By the Author of *The Life of Linnaeus, in a Series of*
    Letters [S. Waring] and [with selections from Mrs Grant,
    Mrs Smith, and others]. BL: 724. a. 36.

2   *The Minstrelsy of the Woods; or, Sketches and Songs Connected*
    with the Natural History of Some of the Most Interesting British
    and Foreign Birds. London: Harvey and Darton, 1832. 10.5
    × 18.5 cm. Pp. xii + 227 [about 46 pp. of verse]. By the
    Author of *The Wild Garland.* Bodley: 32. 213.

WARREN, Mercy, Mrs James (1728–1814)

Born in Barnstaple, Mass. She was the third of the thirteen children of
James Otis and Mary Allyne. Her father was a merchant, farmer, and
lawyer. She had no formal education apart from attendance at her
brothers' lessons and access to her uncle's library. In 1754 she married
General James Warren, and she acted as hostess to George
Washington, John Adams, and Alexander Hamilton at the time of the
revolution. *The Adulateur*, a political satire, first appeared in instalments
in the *Massachusetts Spy*. She also wrote a *History of the American Revolution*
(3 vols., 1805). (Alice Brower, *Mercy Warren* (1896), Todd 1)

1   *The Adulateur. A Tragedy, as It is now Acted in Upper Servia.*
    Boston[, Mass.]: the New Printing Office, 1773. 11.5 ×
    18.5 cm. 30 pp. [incomplete copy]. LC: PS 858. W8 A63
    1773 Office.

2(*a*)   *The Group.* Boston[, Mass.]: Edes and Gill, 1775. 12.5 × 19
    cm. 22 pp. LC: PS 858. W8 A7 Office.

2(*b*)   *The Group, a Farce: As Lately Acted, and to be Re-acted, to the Wonder of All Superior Intelligences; nigh Head Quarters, at Amboyne. In Two Acts.* New-york: printed by John Anderson, [1775]. 12.5 × 19.5 cm. 15 pp. LC: PS 858. W8 A72 Office.

2(*c*)   *The Group, a Farce: As Lately Acted, and to be Re-acted, to the Wonder of All Superior Intelligences; nigh Head Quarters, at Amboyne. In Two Acts.* Philadelphia: printed by James Humphreys, Jr., 1775. 11 × 19 cm. 16 pp. Brown (Harris): 76/W2913g/1775.

3   *Poems, Dramatic and Miscellaneous.* Boston[, Mass.]: I. Thomas and E. T. Andrews, 1790. 10.5 × 17.5 cm. 252 pp. By Mrs M. Warren. BL: 1344. c. 40.

WASHBOURN, Mrs, *see* COLLECTIONS 47, 48

WASSELL, Mary Ann

1(*a*)   *The Rivals; or, the General Investigation.* London: for the author, 1815. 12 × 20.5 cm. 47 pp. 3/-. By Miss Wassell. BL: 11644. d. 8.

1(*b*)   *The Rivals; or, the General Investigation.* London: the author and, for her, Sherwood, Neely, and Jones, and C. Chapple, 1815. 2nd edn. 12.5 × 19.5 cm. 47 pp. 3/-. By Miss Wassell. BL: 11644. d. 9.

WATKINS, H.

According to her title-page, she and her sister were from Stoke Lane, Som.

1   *Poems, on a Variety of Subjects.* Bath/London: printed by Meyler and Son [for the authors?]/G. Robinson, 1812. 11.5 × 18.5 cm. Pp. xii + 7–136 [subscription edition]. 4/- boards. By the Miss Watkins of Stoke-Lane, Somersetshire [H. Watkins and J. P. Watkins]. *MR* 69: 329; BL: 11644. cc. 24.

WATKINS, J. P., *see* WATKINS, H.

WATKIS, Frances

Her book is dedicated to Lord Combermere. She seems to have had a brother who was military.

1   *The Earl of Warwick; or, The Rival Roses; in Eight Books. With Other Poems.* Liverpool/London: printed for the author by Thos. Kaye/Baldwin, Craddock and Joy, 1815. 14 × 22.5 cm. Pp. viii + 159 [subscription edition]. By Frances Watkis. BL: 11645. g. 43.

WATTS, Susanna *or* Susannah (1768–1842), *see also* COLLECTIONS 32

She was the daughter of John Watts and Mary Halley. She taught herself French and Italian. She was a prose writer, an artist, and an editor of anthologies for children. She was a Baptist. (Blain)

1   *Chinese Maxims. Translated from the Oeconomy of Human Life. Into Heroic Verse. In Seven Parts.* Leicester: printed [for the author?] by John Gregory, 1784. 9.5 × 16 cm. Pp. iv + 72. 2/6. *CR* 59: 393–4; BL: 11644. aaa. 41.

2   *Original Poems, and Translations; Particularly Ambra. From Lorenzo de' Medici.* London/Leicester: F. and C. Rivington/ all the booksellers, 1802. 13.5 × 21.5 cm. Pp. viii + 144. 4/- boards. Chiefly by Susanna Watts [also an anonymous gentleman]. *CR* 37: 434–9; BL: 11644. d. 24.

3   *Elegy on the Death of the Princess Charlotte Augusta of Wales.* Leicester: I. Cockshaw, Jr., [1817]. 12 × 18.5 cm. 24 pp. By Susanna Watts. Widener: Br 2103. 27. 12.

4(a)   *The Insects in Council, Addressed to Entomologists, with Other Poems.* London/Leicester: J. Hatchard and Son, Hurst, Chance, and Co., Simpkin and Marshall/A. Cockshaw, 1828. 10.5 × 17.5 cm. Pp. xii + 72. By Susanna Watts. BL: 11646. cc. 37.

4(b)   *The Insects in Council, Addressed to Entomologists, with Other Poems.* London: J. Hatchard and Son, Simpkin and Marshall, and Renshaw and Kirkman, 1835. 10.5 × 17.5 cm. Pp. xii + 72. By Susannah Watts. BL: 11642. aa. 16.

WEBB, Jane (1807–58), *see also* COLLECTIONS 46, 48

Born near Birmingham. Her father was Thomas Webb. Her *The Mummy, a Tale of the Twenty-second Century* (1827) drew her to the attention of John Claudius Loudon, the landscape gardener and horticultural writer, whom she married in 1830. They had one daughter. She contributed to such annuals as *The Literary Souvenir, The Amulet,* and *The Juvenile Forget-me-not.* Her most successful book was *The Ladies' Companion to the Flower Garden* (1841), of which it is reported that more than 20,000 copies were sold. After her husband's death in 1843 she received a civil list pension. (Boyle, *DNB*)

1   *Prose and Verse.* Birmingham/London: R. Wrightson/ Baldwin, Cradock, and Joy, 1824. 11 × 18 cm. Pp. [ii] + 125 [verse occupies pp. 87–125]. By Jane Webb. BL: 12270. bbb. 19.

WEBSTER, Miss (*c.*1785–1803)

1   *A Poem, on that Important Subject, Repentance. Wrote by Miss Webster, on her Death Bed, Who Died at Liverpool 30th of April, 1803, in the 18th Year of her Age. To Which is Added, the Lamentation of a Lost Soul by the Same Author.* Leeds: printed for the benefit of Thomas Hill by Edward Baines, [1803?]. 9.5 × 15.5 cm. 8 pp. 1*d.* By Miss Webster. BL: 10347. de. 2(14).

WEBSTER, Ann

1   *Solitary Musings.* London: for the author by J. Kershaw, 1825. 11 × 19.5 cm. 75 pp. By Ann Webster. BL: 11642. bb. 8.

WEDDERBURN, Margaretta

She seems to have lived in Edinburgh. A Miss Wedderburn of George Square subscribed, along with Walter Scott, to Edgar's *Tranquillity* (see above). If, as seems possible, she is the same person, she was the daughter of James Alexander Wedderburn, the Solicitor-General for Scotland.

1(*a*)   *Mary Queen of Scots, an Historical Poem, with Other Miscellaneous Pieces.* Edinburgh/London/Glasgow: for the author by all the booksellers, 1811. 9.5 × 15.5 cm. Pp. iv + 111 [pp. i–ii appear twice in this copy]. By Margaretta Wedderburn. BL: 11644. b. 38.

1(*b*)   *Mary Queen of Scots; an Historical Poem, with Other Miscellaneous Pieces.* [1818]. 12mo. By Margaretta Wedderburn. *ER* 29: 512. Not located.

WELLER, Mary-Ann R.

She writes from Birmingham.

I   *Pastoral and Descriptive Poems* . . . Birmingham: printed by
        Grafton and Reddell, 1802. 10 × 16.5 cm. 143 pp. By
        Mary-Ann R. Weller. BL: 11641. b. 54.

WELLS, Anna Maria, Mrs Thomas (1794 *or* 1795–1868)

Born in Gloucester, Mass. Her maiden name was Foster. She was educated in Boston and began to write verses when she was very young.
In 1829 she married Thomas Wells of the US revenue service. She
contributed to periodicals and after her husband's death she supported
herself and their five children by keeping a seminary for young ladies.
(Griswold, May)

I   *Poems and Juvenile Sketches*. Boston[, Mass.]: Carter, Hendee
        and Babcock, 1830. 12 × 18.5 cm. 104 pp. By Anna Maria
        Wells. BL: 11686. aaa. 7.

WELLS, Elizabeth

I   *Poems and Dialogues on Various Subjects*. London: F. C. and
        J. Rivington, and Law and Gilbert, 1812. 12 × 18 cm. Pp.
        viii + 146. By Elizabeth Wells. BL: 11644. c. 25.

WELSH, Mrs T., *see* COLLECTIONS 53

WEST, Harriett, Mrs John (1789–1839)

Born at Bolton-Percy. She was the daughter of the Revd Christopher
Atkinson, Rector of Wethersfield, Essex, and of a Miss Leycester. In
1807 she married John West. They had at least three children. She is
said to have been exceptionally devout. (John West, *A Memoir* (1840))

1(*a*) *Sacred Poems for Sundays and Holidays, throughout the Year*.
        London: John W. Parker, 1833. 9 × 13.5 cm. Pp. viii +
        173. By Mrs West. BL: 863. l. 27.
1(*b*) *Sacred Poems for Sundays and Holidays, throughout the Year*.
        London: John W. Parker, 1833. 2nd edn. 8 × 13 cm. Pp.
        viii + 171. By Mrs West. BL: 11646. aa. 43.

WEST, Jane, Mrs Thomas (1758–1852), *see also* COLLECTIONS 35, 41

Born in London and moved to Desborough, Northants, at the age of
11. She was the daughter of John and Jane Iliffe. She was self-educated

and she began to write verse at the age of 13. She married Thomas West, a yeoman farmer, and they had three children. She was a novelist as well as a poet; her *A Tale of the Time* (1799) is typical of her in its rejection of Jacobin ideals. She sometimes used the pseudonym 'Prudentia Homespun'. Benjamin West's *Miscellaneous Poems* (1780) are sometimes attributed to her by mistake. (*CB, DNB*, Todd 2)

1   *Miscellaneous Poetry . . . Written at an Early Period of Life.* London: W. T. Swift, 1786. 17.5 × 23.5 cm. Pp. [ii] + 44. 2/6. By Mrs West. *MR* 75: 69–70; BL: 11631. g. 25.

2   *The Humours of Brighthelmstone.* London/Brighthelmstone [Brighton]: for the author by Scatcherd and Whitaker, T. Hookham, J. Strahan, and W. Richardson/A. Crawford, 1788. 19.5 × 25 cm. 15 pp. 1/-. By J. West. *MR* 78: 351; BL: 643. k. 18(9).

3   *Miscellaneous Poems, and a Tragedy.* York/London/ Northampton/Harborough/Kettering: printed [for the author?] by W. Blanchard/R. Faulder/T. Burnham/ W. Harrod/N. Collis, 1791. 13 × 21.5 cm. Pp. [iii] + v + 222 [subscription edition]. 5/- sewed or 4/-. By Mrs West. *MR* 7: 259–64; *CR* 4: 203–6; BL: 992. k. 28(2).

4   *An Elegy on the Death of the Right Honourable Edmund Burke.* London: T. N. Longman, 1797. 20 × 25 cm. 19 pp. 1/-. By Mrs West, Author of *The Gossip's Story, Miscellaneous Poems, A Tragedy*, etc. BL: 11633. g. 40.

5   *Poems and Plays.* Vols. i and ii [of 4]. London: T. N. Longman and O. Rees, 1799. 10 × 16 cm. 10/- boards. By Mrs West. *MR* 30: 262–5; BL: 11644. b. 24.

6   *Poems and Plays.* Vols. iii–iv [of 4]. London: Longman, Hurst, Rees, and Orme, 1805. 10 × 16 cm. By Mrs West. BL: 11644. b. 24.

7(*a*)   *The Mother: A Poem, in Five Books.* London: Longman, Hurst, Rees, and Orme, 1809. 10 × 16 cm. Pp. [iv] + 242. By Mrs West, Author of *Letters to a Young Man*, etc. BL: 994. f. 38.

7(*b*)   *The Mother: A Poem, in Five Books.* London: Longman, Hurst, Rees, and Orme, 1810. 2nd edn. 11 × 17.5 cm. Pp. [iv] + 242. By Mrs West, Author of *Letters to a Young Man*, etc. BL: 11641. de. 11.

WETHERELL, Mrs Dawson Bruce

1   *Tales of Many Climes . . . Number One, Containing 'The Broken Vow', a Tale of Caledonia; and 'Rollania', a Turkish Tale.* Dublin: W. Curry, Jun. and Co., 1832. 11 × 18 cm. 82 pp. 3/6. By C. C. V. G., the Translator of *Les quatres âges de la vie.* BL: 993. e. 7.

WEYLAR, Maria, *see* BARRELL, Maria

WEYMOUTH, Sarah (*c.*1802–26)

She died of consumption. She had lived at Collaton, Devon. (*Rural Poems*)

1   *Rural Poems; with Other Fugitive Pieces.* London/Devonport: G. B. Whittaker/R. Williams, 1827. 10 × 16 cm. Pp. viii + 100 + [15] [subscription edition]. By the Late Sarah Weymouth, of Collaton, near Kingsbridge, Devon. BL: 11644. aa. 42.

WHEATLEY, Phillis, Mrs John PETERS (*c.*1753–84), *see also* COLLECTIONS 17

She was brought from Senegal to the USA at the age of about 7. She was purchased as a servant by Susanna Wheatley and her husband John, a Boston tailor, in 1761. They encouraged her precocity. She published first in the Newport *Mercury*, but became widely known for her elegy on George Whitefield. She visited London in 1771 and was manumitted in 1774. In 1778 she married John Peters and they had three children. By 1779 they were in financial difficulties and she attempted to publish a subscription edition of her poems without success. (Shirley Graham, *The Story of Phillis Wheatley* (1949))

1(*a*)   *An Elegiac Poem, on the Death of that Celebrated Divine, and Eminent Servant of Jesus Christ, the Reverend and Learned George Whitefield* . . . Boston[, Mass.]: Ezekiel Russell and John Boyles, [1770]. 15.5 × 19.5 cm. 8 pp. By Phillis, a Servant Girl, of 17 Years of Age. HEHL: 85362.

1(*b*)   *An Elegiac Poem, on the Death of that Celebrated Divine, and Eminent Servant of Jesus Christ, the Reverend and Learned George Whitefield* . . . Newport, RI: S. Southwick, [1770]. 13 × 18.5 cm. 8 pp. By Phillis, a Servant Girl, of 17 Years of Age, Belonging to Mr J. Wheatley, of Boston:—She has been but 9 years in this Country from Africa. NYPL (Schomburg): 811-W.

2(*a*)   *Poems on Various Subjects, Religious and Moral.* London/ Boston[, Mass.]: A. Bell/Cox and Berry, 1773. 12.5 × 19 cm. 127 pp. 2/-. By Phillis Wheatley, Negro Servant to Mr John Wheatley . . . *MR* 49: 457–9; HEHL: 123558.

2(*b*)   *Poems on Various Subjects, Religious and Moral.* Philadelphia: Joseph Crukshank, 1786. 9.5 × 15.5 cm. 68 pp. By Phillis Wheatley, Negro Servant to Mr John Wheatley, of Boston, in New-England. LC: PS 866. W5 1786 Office.

2(*c*)   *Poems on Various Subjects, Religious and Moral.* Philadelphia: printed by Joseph James, 1787. 9.5 × 16.5 cm. 58 pp. By Phillis Wheatley, Negro Servant to Mr John Wheatley, of Boston, in New England. LC: PS 866. W5 1787 Office.

2(*d*)   *Poems on Various Subjects, Religious and Moral.* Philadelphia: Joseph Crukshank, 1789. 10 × 16 cm. 68 pp. By Phillis Wheatley, Negro Servant to Mr John Wheatley, of Boston, in New England. LC: PS 866. W5 1789 Office.

2(*e*)   *Poems on Various Subjects, Religious and Moral.* Albany[, NY]: Thomas Spencer, 1793. 10 × 15 cm. 92 pp. By Phillis Wheatley, Negro Servant to Mr John Wheatley, of Boston, in New-England. LC: PS 866 W5 1793 Office.

2(*f*)   *Poems on Various Subjects, Religious and Moral.* Ed. John Wheatley. Philadelphia: William W. Woodward, 1801. 10 × 16.5 cm. Pp. 169–224 [the pagination begins at 169] [subscription edition]. By Phillis Wheatley, Negro Servant to Mr John Wheatley, of Boston, in New England. NYPL: *KL.

2(*g*)   *The Negro Equalled by Few Europeans. Translated from the French. To Which are Added, Poems on Various Subjects, Moral and Entertaining.* Philadelphia: William W. Woodward, 1801. 9.5 × 15.5 cm. 2 vols. [subscription edition; the verse occupies pp. 167–238 of vol. ii]. By [Joseph Lavallé] and Phillis Wheatley, Negro Servant to Mr John Wheatley, of Boston, in New England. Houghton: *AC7. W5602. A801l.

2(*h*)   *Poems on Various Subjects, Religious and Moral . . . Dedicated to the Countess of Huntington.* Walpole[, NH]: Thomas and

Thomas, 1802. 9 × 14 cm. 86 pp. By Phillis Wheatley, Negro Servant to Mr John Wheatley, of Boston, in New England. Houghton: *AC7. W5602. 773pg.

2(*i*)   *Poems on Various Subjects, Religious and Moral.* Hartford[, Conn.]: printed by Oliver Steele, 1804. 10.5 × 16.5 cm. 94 pp. By Phillis Wheatley, Negro Servant to the Late Mr John Wheatley, of Boston (Mass.). Houghton: *AC7. W5602. 773ph.

2(*j*)   *The Interesting Narrative of the Life of Olaudah Equiano, or Gustavus Vassa, the African. Written by Himself . . . To Which are Added, Poems on Various Subjects, by Phillis Wheatly, Negro Servant to Mr John Wheatly of Boston in New England.* Halifax: printed by J. Nicholson and Co., 1814. 9.5 × 16.5 cm. 516 pp. [the verse occupies pp. 441–514]. BL: 10605. aa. 32.

2(*k*)   *Poems, on Various Subjects, Religious and Moral.* 'London . . . printed. Reprinted in New England', 1816. 10 × 16.5 cm. 120 pp. By Phillis Wheatley, Negro Servant to Mr John Wheatley, of Boston, in New-England. Houghton: *AC7. W5607. 773pi.

3(*a*)   *Memoir and Poems.* Boston[, Mass.]: Geo. W. Light, 1834. 11.5 × 17 cm. 103 pp. By Phillis Wheatley, a Native African and a Slave. HEHL: 8057.

3(*b*)   *Memoir and Poems . . . Dedicated to the Friends of the Africans.* Boston[, Mass.]: Light and Horton, 1835. 2nd edn. 9.5 × 14.5 cm. 110 pp. By Phillis Wheatley, a Native African and a Slave. Yale (Beinecke): JWJ/Zan/W56/834b.

4   *An Elegy, Sacred to the Memory of that Great Divine, the Reverend and Learned Dr Samuel Cooper . . .* Boston[, Mass.]: E. Russell, 1784. 15 × 20 cm. 8 pp. By Phillis Peters. HEHL: 31766.

5(*a*)   *Poems.* Inference.

5(*b*)   *Poems on Comic, Serious, and Moral Subjects.* London: J. French, [1787?]. 2nd edn. 11 × 18.5 cm. 127 pp. By Phillis Wheatley, Negro Servant to Mr John Wheatley, of Boston in New England. NYPL (Schomburg): *811-W.

6   *A Beautiful Poem on Providence; Written by a Young Female Slave. To Which is Subjoined a Short Account of this*

Extraordinary Writer. Halifax: printed by E. Gay, 1805. 10.5 × 17 cm. 8 pp. LC: PS 866. W5 B4 1805 Rare Bk Coll.

[*See also*: 'An Elegiac Poem on the Death of . . . George Whitefield . . .' (3 pp., in Ebenezer Pemberton, *Heaven the Residence of the Saints* . . . 1771); 'To Mrs Leonard on the Death of her Husband' (1771, broadside); 'An Elegy, to Miss Mary Moorhead, on the Death of her Father, the Rev. Mr John Moorhead . . .' (1773, broadside); 'To the Honorable Thomas Hubbard, Esq., on the Death of Mrs Thankfull Leonard' (1773, broadside); 'Liberty and Peace, a Poem' (1784, 4 pp.).]

WHITMORE, Lucy Elizabeth Georgina, Lady

1(*a*)   *Family Prayers for Every Day in the Week, Selected from Various Portions of the Holy Bible, with References. To Which are Added, a Few Prayers for Persons in Private; and Fourteen Original Hymns*. London: J. Hatchard and Son, 1824. 13.5 × 21.5 cm. Pp. [iv] + 111 [verse occupies pp. 81–111]. BL: 844. l. 15.

1(*b*)   *Family Prayers for Every Day in the Week, Selected from Various Portions of the Holy Bible, with References. To Which are Added, a Few Prayers for Persons in Private; and Fourteen Original Hymns*. London: John Hatchard and Son, 1827. 2nd edn. 10.5 × 17.5 cm. Pp. [iv] + 111 [the verse occupies pp. 81–111]. BL: 1578/2357.

1(*c*)   *Family Prayers for Every Day in the Week, Selected from Various Portions of the Holy Bible, with References. To Which are Added, a Few Prayers for Persons in Private; and Fourteen Original Hymns*. London: John Hatchard and Son, 1832. 3rd edn. 11 × 18.5 cm. Pp. [iv] + 111. BL: 875. e. 17.

A WHORE OF QUALITY, *see* APPENDIX 7

THE WIFE OF AN OFFICER

Her book reveals only that both her husband and her brother served under Wellington in the Peninsula.

1   *Poems Founded on the Events of the War in the Peninsula*. [Hythe: printed by W. Tiffen], 1819. 13 × 20.5 cm. Pp. xiv + 136. By the Wife of an Officer. Davis: Kohler I, 83–1343.

A WILD IRISH WOMAN, *pseudonym*

1   *The House Queen Caroline Built. An Effusion.* London: for
     the author, 1820. 13 × 22 cm. 13 pp. By a Wild
     Irishwoman. Houghton: *EC8. C2212. B820p2.

2   *The Magic Lantern; or, Green Bag Plot Laid Open; a Poem* . . .
     London: S. W. Fores and R. Fores, 1820. 13 × 21.5 cm. 43
     pp. 2/-. By a Wild Irish Woman, Author of *The House that
     Queen Caroline Built*, and Other Fugitive Pieces. BL: 10807.
     ff. 5(4).

WILKES, Ann

1   *Poems, on Subjects Temporal and Divine.* Birmingham: printed
     by T. Chapman, 1808. 9 × 14.5 cm. 60 pp. 9*d*. By Ann
     Wilkes. BL: 11644. aa. 43.

WILKINSON, Rebecca, *see also* COLLECTIONS 11(*b*), 26(*a–d*)

Her *Sermons* were translated into the Delaware language in 1803, evidence, presumably, of the use being made of them by missionaries.

1(*a*)   *Sermons to Children: To Which are Added Short Hymns, Suited to
         the Subjects.* Philadelphia: printed by W. Young, 1795. 6.5 ×
         10 cm. 159 pp. [prose and verse]. By a Lady. AAS: DATED
         BOOKS.

1(*b*)   *Sermons to Children; to Which are Added, Short Hymns, Suited to
         the Subjects.* Boston[, Mass.]: Samuel Hall, 1797. 7 × 10.5
         cm. 105 pp. By a Lady. AAS: DATED BOOKS.

1(*c*)   *Sermons to Children; to Which are Added, Short Hymns, Suited to
         the Subjects.* Boston[, Mass.]: Hall and Hiller, 1804. 11 cm.
         123 pp. By a Lady. *NUC.* Not seen.

1(*d*)   *Sermons to Children. To Which are Added Short Hymns, Suited to
         the Subjects.* Philadelphia: Jacob Johnson, 1805. 8.5 × 10 cm.
         94 pp. By a Lady. AAS: DATED PAMS.

1(*e*)   *Sermons to Children; to Which are Added Short Hymns, Suited to
         the Subjects.* Springfield[, Mass.]: printed by Henry Brewer,
         1807. 7 × 12 cm. 107 pp. By a Lady. AAS: DATED BOOKS.

1(*f*)   *Sermons to Children. To Which are Added, Short Hymns, Suited
         to the Subjects.* Hartford[, Conn.]: printed by Lincoln and
         Gleason, 1808. 7.5 × 14 cm. 72 pp. By a Lady. NYPL:
         *KVD.

1(*g*) *Sermons to Children: To Which are Added, Short Hymns, Adapted to the Subjects.* Newburyport[, Mass.]: W. and J. Gilman, 1808. 8 × 13 cm. 62 pp. By a Lady. AAS: DATED BOOKS.

1(*h*) *Sermons to Children. To Which are Added, Short Hymns, Suited to the Subjects.* Boston[, Mass.]: T. B. Wait and Sons, 1814. 9 × 10.5 cm. 91 pp. By a Lady. HEHL: 327120.

1(*i*) *Sermons to Children. To Which are Added Short Hymns Suited to the Subjects . . . Composed for the New-York Widow's Society.* Morris-town[, NY]: printed by Henry P. Russell, 1815. 9 × 14 cm. 88 pp. By a Lady. Princeton: NJI/653. 815. 3.

1(*j*) *Sermons to Children to Which are Added Short Hymns, Adapted to the Subjects.* [Cover serves as title-page.] Nottingham/ London: Sutton and Son/W. Kent, and Simpkin and Marshall, 1816. 6.5 × 10 cm. 102 pp. By a Lady. Bodley: 100 g. 251.

1(*k*) *Sermons to Children to Which are Added Short Hymns Suited to the Subject.* London: the Philanthropic Society and Hatchard and Simpkin and Marshall, [n.d.]. 5th edn. 8.5 × 11 cm. Pp. iv + 3–85. By a Lady. NEDL: Juv 830. 28.

1(*l*) *Sermons to Young Children.* London: Religious Tract Society, [n.d.]. 128 pp. *NUC.* Not seen.

1(*m*) *Sermons to Children. To Which are Added Short Hymns, Suited to the Subjects.* Andover[, Mass.]: New England Tract Society, 1816. 3rd edn. 12 × 19.5 cm. 36 pp. By a Lady. Illinois: X252. W659S. RBX. [Photocopy seen only.]

1(*n*) *Sermons to Children: To Which are Added, Short Hymns, Suited to the Subjects.* Albany[, NY]: printed by Websters and Skinners, 1817. 8.5 × 10.5 cm. 93 pp. By a Lady. AAS: DATED PAMS.

1(*o*) *Fifteen Sermons for Children: To Which are Added, Select Hymns, Suited to the Subjects.* Edinburgh: W. Aitchison, 1819. 6 × 10 cm. 94 pp. By a Lady. NLS: Hall. 195. k.

1(*p*) *Sermons to Children.* 6th edn. Inference.

1(*q*) *Sermons to Children: To Which are Added, Short Hymns, Suited to the Subjects.* Calcutta: printed by the School Press, Dhurumtula, 1820. 7th edn. 7.5 × 10 cm. 87 pp. By a Lady. BL: 4474. a. 99.

1 (*r*) *Sermons to Children. To Which are Added Short Hymns, Suited to the Subjects.* Philadelphia: Benjamin Warner, 1821. 8.5 × 14 cm. 72 pp. By a Lady. LC: BV 4315. W45 Office.

1 (*s*) *Sermons to Children. To Which are Added, Short Hymns, Suited to the Subjects* [cover serves as title-page]. Canandaigua: J. D. Bemis and Co., 1821. 7.5 × 12.5 cm. 72 pp. By a Lady. Columbia: Hist. Col. Children's Lit.

WILKINSON, Sarah Scudgell (died after 1830)

She was a novelist, an author of abridgements, and a teacher. She contributed to periodicals. (Blain)

1 *The Turtle Dove; or Cupid's Artillery Levelled against Human Hearts, being a New and Original Valentine Writer. For the Present Year.* London: W. Perks, [*c.*1810?]. 11 × 19 cm. 28 pp. 6*d.* By Sarah Wilkinson. Bodley: Harding E 295.

2 *Love and Hymen; or the Gentleman's and Ladies Polite and Original Valentine Writer. For the Present Year.* London: W. Perks, [*c.*1815?]. 9.5 × 17.5 cm. 28 pp. 6*d.* By Sarah Wilkinson. Bodley: Johnson e. 1379.

3 *Hodgson's Universal Valentine Writer, for the Current Year, being a Choice Collection of Original Amatory Epistles, Addresses, Answers, &c. &c. . . .* London: Hodgson and Co., [1820?]. 11 × 18 cm. 24 pp. 6*d.* By Sarah Wilkinson. BL: T. 854(3*).

4 *Carvalho's Road to Hymen, or Cupid's Directory. Including Amatory Verses, Odes, Sentimental, Serious, and Comic, for Ladies and Gentlemen. For the Present Year.* London: S. Carvalho, [n.d.]. 3rd edn. 10 × 18 cm. 28 pp. 6*d.* By Sarah Scudgell Wilkinson. Bodley: Johnson e. 1380.

WILLARD, Emma, Mrs John (1787–1870)

Born in Berlin, Conn. She was the ninth child of Captain Samuel Hart and Lydia Hinsdale. Her father was active in political and civic life. She became a schoolteacher, and was in charge of the Female Academy in Middlebury, Vt. In 1809 she became the third wife of John Willard and resigned. They had one child. In 1814 she opened her own Middlebury Female Seminary where, unusually, mathematics and philosophy formed part of the curriculum. Her *Address to the Public . . . Proposing a Plan for*

Improving Female Education (1819) sets out her views. In 1821 she opened Emma Willard's Troy Female Seminary, in Troy, NY. She was widowed in 1825 and in 1838 she made an unhappy marriage with Dr Christopher Yates, from whom she was divorced in 1843. Her school was internationally famous. (*DAB*)

1   *The Fulfilment of a Promise; by Which Poems . . . are Published, and Affectionately Inscribed to her Past and Present Pupils.* New York: White, Gallaher and White, 1831. 8.5 × 14 cm. 124 pp. By Emma Willard. HEHL: 44529.

WILLIAMS, Miss

1   *Dependance, a Poem.* London: printed by Lowndes and Hobbs, [1815?]. 10 × 15.5 cm. Pp. [ii] + 34. By Miss Williams (Sister of Joseph Williams, Esq.) of Glanravon. BL: 992. g. 22(1).

2   *Fashion: A Poem.* London, 1816. 11.5 × 18 cm. 10 pp. By Miss Williams, Author of *Dependance, Invocation to Fortune,* etc. etc. etc. Bodley: G. Pamph. 1593(10).

WILLIAMS, A.

She was the postmistress of Gravesend, Kent. (*Original Poems*)

1   *Original Poems and Imitations.* London: for the author by W. Harris, 1773. 12.5 × 20.5 cm. Pp. [vi] + 191. By A. Williams. BL: 11642. e. 44.

WILLIAMS, Catharine R., Mrs Horatio N. (1787–1872)

Born in Providence, RI. She was the daughter of Captain Alfred and Amey R. Arnold. As a consequence of her mother's early death, she was brought up by two maiden aunts and given a religious education. In 1824 she married Horatio N. Williams of New York but she left him two years later, taking their daughter with her, and obtained a divorce. She opened a school in Providence, but her health broke down. She turned to writing and published popular religious, historical, and biographical works as well as poetry. (*DAB*)

1   *Original Songs, on Various Subjects.* Providence[, RI]: printed by H. H. Brown, 1828. 9 × 15.5 cm. 107 pp. By Mrs Williams. LC: PS 3319. W587.

WILLIAMS, Helen Maria (1762–1827), *see also* COLLECTIONS 13, 40(*c*), 52

Born in London but brought up in Scotland. She was the daughter of Charles Williams, an army officer, and of Helen Hay. Her first book was seen through the press by a family friend, the dissenting minister Andrew Kippis. She went to France in 1788 and became and remained an enthusiastic supporter of the revolution. She was imprisoned for a time. Her *Letters from France 1792–6* (4 vols., 1796) is still worth reading. She translated Humboldt's *Travels* (7 vols., 1814). Her *Perourou, the Bellows-mender* (1801) was adapted as a successful play, *The Lady of Lyons*, by Bulwer Lytton in 1838. (*CB, DNB*)

1   *Edwin and Eltruda. A Legendary Tale.* Ed. [And. Kippis]. London: T. Cadell, 1782. 20 × 26 cm. Pp. iv + 31. 2/-. By a Young Lady. *MR* 67: 26–30; *CR* 53: 213–18; BL: 163. m. 64.

2   *An Ode on the Peace.* London: T. Cadell, 1783. 20 × 26 cm. 20 pp. 1/-. By the Author of *Edwin and Eltruda.* BL: 11641. h. 4(3).

3   *Peru, a Poem. In Six Cantos.* London: T. Cadell, 1784. 21 × 27 cm. Pp. viii + 95. 4/- sewed. By Helen Maria Williams. BL: 1346. i. 21.

4(*a*)   *Poems.* London: Thomas Cadell, 1786. 10.5 × 17.5 cm. 2 vols. [subscription edition]. 6/- or 5/- sewed. By Helen Maria Williams. *MR* 75: 44–9; *CR* 62: 62–3; BL: 239. h. 3.

4(*b*)   *Poems.* London: T. Cadell, 1791. 2nd edn. 10.5 × 18 cm. 2 vols. By Helen Maria Williams. BL: 994. g. 44.

5   *A Poem on the Bill Lately Passed for Regulating the Slave Trade.* London: T. Cadell, 1788. 20 × 26 cm. 23 pp. 1/6 sewed. By Helen Maria Williams. BL: 11641. h. 4(1).

6(*a*)   *Julia, a Novel; Interspersed with Some Poetical Pieces.* London: T. Cadell, 1790. 10.5 × 17.5 cm. 2 vols. [about 30 pp. of verse]. By Helen Maria Williams. BL: N. 2320.

6(*b*)   *Julia: A Novel Interspersed with Some Poetical Pieces.* Dublin: Chamberlaine and Rice, [etc.], 1790. 16.9 cm. 2 vols. By Helen Maria Williams. *NUC.* Not seen.

7   *A Farewell, for Two Years, to England. A Poem.* London: T. Cadell, 1791. 20 × 26 cm. 15 pp. 1/6. By Helen Maria Williams. BL: 11641. h. 4(2).

8(*a*)   *Poems, Moral, Elegant and Pathetic . . . and Original Sonnets.*
Ed. [Helen Maria Williams]. London: E. Newbery, and
Vernor and Hood, 1796. 10.5 × 16.5 cm. Pp. [ii] + 220
[Williams's contribution on pp. 211–20]. 6/- boards. By
Helen Maria Williams [and others]. *MR* 22: 102; BL:
011604. ee. 65.

8(*b*)   *Poems, Moral, Elegant and Pathetic . . . and Original Sonnets.*
Ed. [Helen Maria Williams]. London: J. Harris, and
Vernor and Hood, 1803. 10 × 16 cm. Pp. [ii] + 220
[Williams's contribution on pp. 211–20]. By Helen Maria
Williams [and others]. BL: 11644. bb. 10.

8(*c*)   *Recueil de poésies, extraites des ouvrages . . .* Trans. [into
French] Stanislas de Boufflers and Mr Esménard. Paris:
Cocheris Fils, 1808. 13.5 × 21.5 cm. Pp. viii + 137. By
Helena-Maria Williams. BL: 1162. i. 4.

9   *The Charter, Lines Addressed . . . to her Nephew Athanase
C. L. Coquerel, on his Wedding Day.* Paris, 1819. 12 × 20.5
cm. 8 pp. By Helen Maria Williams. BL: 11641. e. 54.

10   *Poems on Various Subjects. With Introductory Remarks on the
Present State of Science and Literature in France.* London:
G. and W. B. Whittaker, 1823. 13.5 × 22.5 cm. Pp. xliv +
298. 12/- boards. By Helen Maria Williams. *MR* 102:
20–31; BL: 994. h. 33.

[*See also*: 'Ode to Peace' (1786?, 4 pp.); 'Verses Addressed . . . to
her Two Nephews' (1809, 7 pp.).]

WILLIAMS, Jane (1806–85)
Born in Chelsea, London. She was the daughter of David and Eleanor
Williams. She spent her early life in Talgarth, Brecon., where she
learned Welsh and acquired a taste for Welsh literature. She is best
known for her *History of Wales* (1869). Her *The Literary Women of England*
(1861) is also of interest.

1   *Miscellaneous Poems.* Brecknock: printed [for the author?] by
Priscilla Hughes, 1824. 10 × 17 cm. Pp. viii + 37 [subscrip-
tion edition]. By Jane Williams. BL: 11644. bb. 11.

WILLIAMS, Sarah Johanna
She writes from Nottingham.

1 *Sherwood Forest, a Poem.* Nottingham/Mansfield/Newark/
Retford: printed by George Stretton/R. Collinson/S. and
C. Ridge/T. Turvey, 1832. 11.5 × 19 cm. 38 pp. By Sarah
Johanna Williams. BL: 11644. ccc. 24.

WILMORE, Sarah

She writes from Elm-Hill, near Worcester. (*The Progress and Comforts*)

1 *The Progress and Comforts of Religion; an Essay, in Blank Verse.*
Stourport: printed for the author by G. Nicholson, [1820].
12.5 × 20.5 cm. Pp. x + 66 [subscription edition]. By Sarah
Wilmore. BL: 11644. d. 3.

WILMOT, Barbarina, Mrs Valentine Henry (1768–1854), *see also*
COLLECTIONS 32

She was the third daughter of Admiral Sir Chaloner Ogle, Bart., and of
Hester Thomas. She married Valentine Henry Wilmot, an officer in the
guards, and they had a daughter. In 1819, she married Thomas Brand,
20th Baron Dacre. Her *Ina* was performed at Drury Lane in 1815. She
is said to have been generally accomplished, particularly as an artist.
(*DNB*)

1(*a*) *Ina, a Tragedy; in Five Acts.* London: John Murray, 1815.
12.5 × 20.5 cm. Pp. [iv] + 71. 3/-. By Mrs Wilmot. BL:
11779. f. 73.

1(*b*) *Ina, a Tragedy; in Five Acts.* London: John Murray, 1815.
2nd edn. 12.5 × 21 cm. Pp. [iv] + 71. By Mrs Wilmot. BL:
643. f. 17(4).

1(*c*) *Ina, a Tragedy; in Five Acts.* London: John Murray, 1815.
3rd edn. 13 × 20.5 cm. Pp. [iv] + 71. 3/-. By Mrs Wilmot.
BL: 11779. f. 74.

2(*a*) *The Canzoni* . . . [also a title-page in Italian and facing
Italian text throughout]. Trans. Barbarina Wilmot.
[London: printed by W. Bulmer and Co., but not published, 1815?]. 11 × 18 cm. 23 pp. By Petrarch. BL: C. 28.
g. 10(2).

2(*b*) *Due canzoni* . . . Trans. [B. Wilmot]. [English and Italian
on facing pages.] Rome: privately printed, 1818. 13 × 19.5
cm. 17 pp. By Petrarch. BL: 1463. h. 16(3).

2(*c*) *Due canzoni* . . . Trans. [B. Wilmot]. [English and Italian on facing pages.] Naples: privately printed, 1819. 12.5 × 20 cm. 27 pp. By Petrarch. BL: 1062. i. 18(2).

2(*d*) *Essays on Petrarch*. London: John Murray, 1823. 13.5 × 21 cm. Pp. vi + 325. [Lady Dacre's translations of Petrarch's canzone and sonnets occupy pp. 279–325, the Italian text being given on the verso pages.] By Ugo Foscolo. BL: 1062. h. 27.

3 *Dramas Translations and Occasional Poems*. London: John Murray ['not published'], 1821. 14 × 22.5 cm. 2 vols. By Barbarina Lady Dacre. BL: 11771. ee. 9.

WILSON, Ann, Mrs

1 *Jephthah's Daughter. A Dramatic Poem*. London: W. Flexney, 1783. 12 × 19.5 cm. Pp. viii + 55. 1/6. By Mrs Ann Wilson. *MR* 69: 439; BL: 11777. f. 75.

WILSON, Anne

1 *Teisa: A Descriptive Poem of the River Teese, its Towns and Antiquities*. Newcastle upon Tyne: printed for the author, 1778. 20.5 × 25.5 cm. 68 pp. By Anne Wilson. BL: 11632. h. 17.

WILSON, Mrs C. B., *see* BARON WILSON, Margaret

WILSON, Margaret, *see* BARON WILSON, Margaret

WILSON, Susannah (born 1787)

Her date of birth appears in *Familiar Poems*.

1 *Familiar Poems, Moral and Religious*. Ed. [W. H.]. London: Darton, Harvey, and Co., 1814. 8.5 × 13.5 cm. 161 pp. 2/- boards. By Susannah Wilson. *MR* 76: 212; BL: 11644. aa. 24.

WILSON, Mary, Mrs William Carus

Her maiden name was Letablère. She was married to the Revd Carus Wilson who is believed to have been the model for Mr Brocklehurst in *Jane Eyre*. They lived near Kirkby Lonsdale at Cowan Bridge, where he presided over the Clergy Daughters' School. (*Blue Guide*)

1   *A Mother's Sermons for her Children. With Original Hymns and Prayers.* Kirkby Lonsdale/London: Arthur Foster/L. B. Seeley and Sons, 1829. 8 × 14 cm. Pp. vii + 242 [about 15 pp. of verse]. 2/6. By the Author of *A Mother's Stories for her Children, Scripture Questioning Cards*, etc. HL; BL: 4412. aaa. 35.

WINCHILSEA, Countess of, Anne FINCH (1661–1720), *see* COLLECTIONS 20

She was the daughter of Sir William Kingsmill and a maid of honour to Mary of Modena. She married Heneage Finch, who became 4th Earl of Winchilsea. She was a friend of Alexander Pope, Elizabeth Rowe, and other writers and is now remembered mainly for her poem *The Spleen* (1701). (Blain, *DNB*, Todd 2)

WINFORD, Miss, *see also* COLLECTIONS 4

1   *Hobby-horses; Read at Bath-Easton.* London: for the author by J. Dodsley, 1780. 20.5 × 26 cm. 16 pp. 1/-. BL: 163. m. 18.

WINGROVE, Ann

1   *Letters, Moral and Entertaining.* Bath/London: Bull and Hensleys and the other libraries/Wallis, 1795. 9 × 15.5 cm. Pp. xxxii + 150 [subscription edition; about 12 pp. of verse scattered through the volume]. 3/6. By Ann Wingrove. Bodley: 26520 f. 220.

WINSCOM, Jane, Mrs Thomas (*c.*1754–1813)

Her father was John Cave of Talgarth, Brecon., an exciseman and a glover. She married Thomas Winscom, an excise officer in Bristol in 1783. They had at least two sons. (Blain, *GM*, Lonsdale)

1(*a*)   *Poems on Various Subjects, Entertaining, Elegiac, and Religious.* Winchester: printed for the author by J. Sadler, 1783. 10 × 17 cm. Pp. [ii] + 28 + iv + 150 [subscription edition]. By Jane Cave. BL: 11632. aaa. 10.

1(*b*)   *Poems on Various Subjects, Entertaining, Elegiac, and Religious. With a Few Select Poems from Other Authors.* Bristol: for the author, 1786. 9.5 × 15.5 cm. Pp. [xviii] + 172 [subscription edition]. By Miss Cave, now Mrs W[inscom]. BL: 993. c. 43(1).

1(*c*)   *Poems on Various Subjects, Entertaining, Elegiac, and Religious. With a Few Select Poems, from Other Authors.* Shrewsbury: printed for the author by T. Wood, 1789. 2nd edn. 10.5 × 17.5 cm. Pp. [xiv] + 190 [subscription edition]. By Miss Cave. Now Mrs W———. BL: 11632. c. 6.

1(*d*)   *Poems on Various Subjects, Entertaining, Elegiac, and Religious.* Bristol: printed [for the author?] by N. Biggs, 1794. 4th edn. 10.5 × 17 cm. Pp. [x] + 204 [subscription edition]. By Miss Cave, now Mrs Winscom. BL: 11633. aaa. 7.

1(*e*)   *Poems on Various Subjects, Entertaining, Elegiac, and Religious.* Bristol: printed [for the author?] by N. Biggs, 1795. 4th edn. 10.5 × 17.5 cm. Pp. [x] + 192 [subscription edition]. By Miss Cave, now Mrs Winscom. BL: 11633. aaa. 8.

WINTER, Anna Maria

1   *The Fairies, and Other Poems.* Dublin: John Chambers, 1833. 11.5 × 18.5 cm. Pp. viii + 184. By Anna Maria Winter, Author of *Thoughts on the Moral Order of Nature.* BL: 11644. cc. 46.

WINTER, Susan, Mrs, *see* VINCE, Susan

WOLFERSTAN, Elizabeth, Mrs Samuel Pipe (1763–1845)

She was the daughter of Philip Jervis of Netherseal, Leics. Her husband was an antiquary and a landowner. She lived in Statfold, Staffs. (Blain, *GM*)

1(*a*)   *The Enchanted Flute, with Other Poems; and Fables from La Fontaine.* London: Longman, Hurst, Rees, Orme, and Brown, 1822. 13 × 21 cm. Pp. vi + 140. By E. P. Wolferstan. Davis: Kohler I, 83–1383.

1(*b*)   *The Enchanted Flute, with Other Poems; and Fables from La Fontaine.* London: Longman, Hurst, Rees, Orme, and Brown, 1823. 13 × 21.5 cm. Pp. xii + 440. By E. P. Wolferstan. BL: 992. k. 34.

2   *Eugenia: A Poem. In Four Cantos.* London: Longman, Hurst, Rees, Orme, Brown, and Green, 1824. 13 × 21 cm. 61 pp. By E. P. Wolferstan. BL: T. 1060(6).

3   *The Fable of Phaeton.* Trans. [E. P. Wolferstan]. London: printed [for the translator?] by John Bowyer Nichols,

1828. 13.5 × 22 cm. 59 pp. [English and Latin on facing pages]. By Ovid. BL: 1001. k. 19.

4(*a*)   *Fairy Tales, in Verse.* Lichfield: printed by T. G. Lomax, 1829. 13 × 21 cm. 32 pp. Bodley: Vet. A6 e. 1059.

4(*b*)   *Fairy Tales, in Verse.* London/Lichfield: Baldwin and Cradock/T. G. Lomax, 1830. 12.5 × 20.5 cm. 32 pp. BL: 11644. cc. 58(2).

4(*c*)   *Fairy Tales, in Verse.* London/Lichfield: Baldwin and Cradock/T. G. Lomax, 1833. 2nd edn. 12.5 × 20.5 cm. 32 pp. BL: 11644. cc. 58(1).

A WOMAN OF FASHION, *see* APPENDIX 8

WOOD, Agnes M. (died 1827)

Her family owned the shipbuilding firm, K. Wood and Sons, Maryport, near Liverpool. She was evidently ill in 1824, and died in 1827. The book, however, was precipitated by her brother Wilton's unexpected death in a carriage accident in 1832; his speeches, elegiac tributes to him, and her verses are combined in it. (*A Selection*)

1   *A Selection of Scraps, in Prose and Verse . . . Found after their Decease, and Printed as a Memorial, for the Gratification of their Parents and Near Relatives.* Liverpool: printed by George Groom, 1832. 9 × 15 cm. 54 pp. [about 37 pp. of verse]. By Agnes M. Wood and her Brother, Wilton Wood. Davis: Kohler I, 83–1384.

WOOD, Susan

1   *Literary Exercises; or, Short Essays on Various Subjects: Also, Thoughts on a One All-perfect Cause, from the Visible World, in Blank Verse. The Whole being a Miscellaneous Performance.* Bury St. Edmund's/London: G. Ingram/J. Sharpe, 1802. 12 × 19.5 cm. 78 pp. [of which pp. 34, 61–2, and 74–8 are occupied by verse]. By Susan Wood. BL: 1091. f. 23.

WOODCOCK, Mrs Henry

1   *Laura, a Tale.* London: John Murray, 1820. 13 × 21.5 cm. 47 pp. By Mrs Henry Woodcock, of Michelmersh, Hants. BL: 992. i. 25(4).

WORTH, Anne, Mrs William (1776–1813)

Her maiden name was Sadler. Her husband was a clergyman. She died in Burslem, Staffs. (*GM, Poems*)

1   *Poems, Moral and Sacred . . . To Which is Prefixed, an Account of her Life and Death.* Ed. Her Husband. Macclesfield/ London: for the editor/Baynes, 1813. 9.5 × 16.5 cm. Pp. [4] + xx + 40. By the Late Mrs Anne Worth. BL: 11644. bbb. 9.

WORTLEY, Lady Emmeline Charlotte Elizabeth Stuart (1806–55)

She was the second daughter of John Henry Manners, 5th Duke of Rutland, and of Lady Elizabeth Howard. In 1831 she married the Hon. Charles Stuart-Wortley. They had three children. In 1837 and 1840 she edited *The Keepsake*. She continued to publish verse until 1851, especially in the annuals. She died in Lebanon after being kicked by a mule near Jerusalem. (Boyle, *CB*, *DNB* (under Stuart-Wortley))

1   *Poems.* London: John Murray, 1833. 10 × 16.5 cm. Pp. viii + 278. By Lady Emmeline Stuart Wortley. BL: 993. d. 53.

2   *London at Night; and Other Poems.* London: Longman, Rees, Orme, Brown, Green, and Longman, 1834. 11 × 17.5 cm. Pp. [vi] + 100. By Lady Emmeline Stuart Wortley. BL: T. 1523(7).

3   *The Knight and the Enchantress; with Other Poems.* London: Longman, Rees, Orme, Brown, Green, and Longman, 1835. 12 × 19 cm. Pp. [iv] + 131. By Lady Emmeline Stuart Wortley. BL: 994. h. 35.

4   *Travelling Sketches in Rhyme.* London: Longman, Rees, Orme, Brown, Green, and Longman, 1835. 11.5 × 19 cm. Pp. [iv] + 116. By Lady E. S. Wortley. BL: T. 2035(3).

5   *The Village Churchyard; and Other Poems.* London: Longman, Rees, Orme, Brown, Green, and Longman, 1835. 11.5 × 19 cm. Pp. viii + 266. By Lady Emmeline Stuart Wortley. BL: 994. h. 34.

WRIGHT, Frances (1795–1852)

Born in Dundee, Perthshire. She was the daughter of James Wright and Camilla Campbell. She was brought up in England by an aunt. Her father, who died when she was 2½, held and promulgated radical opinions which she came to share. In 1818 she went to the USA with a younger sister for two years and wrote her *Views of Society and Manners in America* (1821). *Altorf* was produced in New York in 1819. From 1821 to 1824 she lived in Paris. In 1824 she bought land in Tennessee with the intention of liberating slaves, but the experiment was unsuccessful. From 1829 to 1836 she was a public lecturer on emancipation and female suffrage, the leader of the 'Fanny Wright societies'; according to Mrs Trollope (q.v.) she was a majestic and effective speaker. In 1838 she married M. Phiquepal-Darusmont. They had one daughter but subsequently separated. (Blain, *DNB*)

1(*a*) *Altorf, a Tragedy . . . First Represented in the Theatre of New-York, Feb. 19, 1819.* Philadelphia: M. Carey and Son, 1819. 11 × 18.5 cm. Pp. v + 2–83. By Frances Wright. BL: 11791. c. 53.

1(*b*) *Altorf; a Tragedy . . . As Represented in the Theatres of New York and Philadelphia.* London: Longman, Hurst, Rees, Orme, and Brown, 1822. 12.5 × 21 cm. Pp. viii + 93. By Frances Wright, Author of *Views of Society and Manners in America.* BL: T. 1068(11).

WRIGHT, Mary Bestwick

1 *The Cypress Wreath: A Collection of Poems.* London/Leicester/Loughborough/Nottingham/Boston/Derby/Southwell: printed for the author/W. Hextall/H. Buck/S. Bennett/J. Noble/H. Mozley/J. Simpson, 1828. 9.5 × 15 cm. Pp. xx + 256 [subscription edition]. By Mary Bestwick Wright. BL: 11644. aaa. 1.

WYATT, Gertrude

1 *Miscellaneous Poems.* London: Charles Frederick Cock, 1829. 9.5 × 16 cm. Pp. xx + 95 [subscription edition]. By a Young Lady. BL: 11644. b. 2.

WYKE, Anne

1 *Bertha, a Tale of the Waldenses; and Other Poems.* Shrewsbury/London: Charles Hulbert/Longman, Rees, Orme, Brown, and Green, 1830. 10.5 × 18.5 cm. Pp. x + 140. By Anne Wyke. BL: 11641. c. 61.

YARROW, Mrs

1 *Original Poems; Including a Tribute of Justice Addressed to the Right Honourable the Earl of Liverpool, to Charles Nicholas Pallmer, Esq. to the Rev. Samuel Whitelock Gandy. &c. &c.* London/Richmond[, Surrey]/Kingston-upon-Thames: Hatchard and Son, Sherwood and Co./R. Hughes/ J. Attfield, 1824. 12 × 19.5 cm. 124 pp. By Mrs Yarrow. BL: 11644. ccc. 33.

YEARDLEY, Martha, *see* SAVORY, Martha

YEARSLEY, Ann, Mrs John (1756–1806), *see also* COLLECTIONS 13, 17

She was the daughter of Ann Cromartie, a milkwoman of Clifton Hill, Bristol, Glos. She had little education. She married John Yearsley, a labourer, in 1774 and they had six children. Hannah More (q.v.) became interested in her and helped her to obtain more than 1,000 subscribers for *Poems on Several Occasions*; however, patron and protégée had a falling out. In 1793 she opened a circulating library at Bristol Hot Wells. Her *Earl Goodwin* was performed in Bath and in Bristol in 1789, and her historical novel *The Royal Captives* (4 vols.) appeared in 1795. (*CB, DNB*)

1(*a*) *Poems, on Several Occasions.* Ed. [Hannah More]. London: T. Cadell, 1785. 19 × 24 cm. Pp. xxx + 127. 6/- sewed [subscription edition]. By Ann Yearsley, a Milkwoman of Bristol. *MR* 73: 216–21; BL: T. 25(7).

1(*b*) *Poems, on Several Occasions.* London: T. Cadell, 1785. 2nd edn. 20.5 × 26 cm. Pp. xxxii + 127 [subscription edition]. By Ann Yearsley, a Milkwoman of Bristol. CUL: Syn. 4. 78. 13.

1(*c*) *Poems, on Several Occasions.* Ed. [Hannah More]. London: T. Cadell, 1785. 3rd edn. 13 × 21 cm. Pp. lvi + 100 [subscription edition]. By Ann Yearsley, a Milkwoman of Bristol. BL: 11644. d. 33.

1(*d*) *Poems, on Several Occasions.* Ed. [Hannah More]. London: G. G. J. and J. Robinson, 1786. 4th edn. 13 × 21 cm. Pp. xxxii + 103. By Ann Yearsley, a Milkwoman of Bristol. BL: 11644. d. 32.

2   *Poems on Various Subjects.* Ed. [Hannah More]. London: for
     the author by G. G. J. and J. Robinson, 1787. 21 × 26.5
     cm. Pp. xl + 168 [subscription edition]. By Ann Yearsley,
     a Milkwoman of Clifton. BL: 643. k. 16(4).

3   *A Poem on the Inhumanity of the Slave-trade. Humbly Inscribed to
     the Right Honourable and Right Reverend Frederick, Earl of
     Bristol, Bishop of Derry, &c. &c.* London: G. G. J. and
     J. Robinson, [1788?]. 20 × 24 cm. Pp. [ii] + 30. 2/-. By
     Ann Yearsley. *MR* 78: 246; BL: 11641. g. 47(3).

4   *Stanzas of Woe, Addressed from the Heart on a Bed of Illness, to
     Levi Eames, Esq. Late Mayor of the City of Bristol.* London:
     G. G. J. and J. Robinson, 1790. 21 × 26.5 cm. Pp. [iv] +
     30. 2/-. By Ann Yearsley, a Milk-woman of Clifton. *MR* 5:
     222–3; BL: 11641. h. 5(1).

5   *Earl Goodwin, an Historical Play . . . Performed with General
     Applause at the Theatre-Royal, Bristol.* London: G. G. J. and
     J. Robinson, 1791. 20.5 × 26.5 cm. Pp. [x] + 92. 3/6. By
     Ann Yearsley, Milk-woman, of Clifton. *MR* 6: 347–8; BL:
     11641. h. 6(4).

6(*a*) *Reflections on the Death of Louis XVI.* Bristol/Bath: for the
        author by the booksellers, 1793. 21 × 26.5 cm. 8 pp. By
        Ann Yearsley. BL: 11641. h. 5(2).

6(*b*) *Reflections on the Death of Louis XVI.* Bristol/Bath: the
        author and the booksellers for the author/the booksellers,
        1793. [New edn.—the 'finis' vignette removed from p. 8
        and the catchword 'Sequel' added, to allow the binding in
        of *Sequel to Reflections* (see 7 below).] 21 × 26.5 cm. 8 pp.
        By Ann Yearsley. BL: 11641. h. 6(2).

7   *Sequel to Reflections on the Death of Louis XVI.* Bristol/Bath:
     for the author by the booksellers, 1793. 21 × 26.5 cm. 8
     pp. By Ann Yearsley. BL: 11641. h. 5(2).

8   *An Elegy on Marie Antoinette of Austria, Ci-devant Queen of
     France: With a Poem on the Last Interview between the King of
     Poland and Loraski.* Bath/Bristol: for the author by the
     booksellers, [1795?]. 21 × 26.5 cm. 15 pp. 1/-. By Ann
     Yearsley. BL: 11641. h. 5(3).

9   *The Rural Lyre; a Volume of Poems: Dedicated to the Right
     Honourable the Earl of Bristol, Lord Bishop of Derry.* London:

G. G. and J. Robinson, 1796. 20 × 26 cm. Pp. xii + 142 [subscription edition]. 10/6 boards. By Ann Yearsley. *CR* 19: 462–3; BL: 11641. h. 6(1).

YORKE, Elizabeth, *see* HARDWICKE, Countess of

YOUNG, Hannah, Mrs C. G.

She was a Quaker from Milverton, Som. (*Friends' Books*)

1   *An Elegy on the Death of Richard Reynolds, with Other Poems.* London/Bristol: J. and A. Arch, Darton and Harvey, J. Booth/Barry and Son, and F. C. Cookworthy, 1818. 13.5 × 21.5 cm. Pp. [ii] + 44. HL; BL: 11643. bbb. 16(4).

YOUNG, Mary

Bodley L. Cat. identifies her with Mary Julia Young (below).

1(*a*)   *Horatio and Amanda, a Poem.* London: J. Robson, 1777. 16.5 × 21.5 cm. 20 pp. 1/-. By a Young Lady. *MR* 57: 77; BL: 164. n. 64.

1(*b*)   *Horatio and Amanda, a Poem.* London, 1788. 11.5 × 17.5 cm. 8 pp. By a Young Lady. NYPL: NCE p. v. 109(1).

2   *Innocence: An Allegorical Poem.* London/Uxbridge: T. Hookham/T. Lake, 1790. 18.5 × 24 cm. Pp. ii + 16. 1/6. By Miss Mary Young. *MR* 1: 450; BL: 11641. g. 46.

YOUNG, Mary Julia (died 1821)

She was the daughter of Sir William Young of Delaford, the Governor of Dominica and Tobago, and of Elizabeth Taylor. She married George Sewell, Rector of Byfleet. She died in Chertsey, Surrey. An MS note in the BL copy of her *Poems* identifies her, mistakenly, with Mary Young (above). (Blain, *CB*, *GM*, Shoberl)

1(*a*)   *Genius and Fancy; or, Dramatic Sketches.* London: H. D. Symonds, and J. Gray, [1792?]. 20 × 24.5 cm. 16 pp. By a Lady. BL: 11630. e. 13(9).

1(*b*)   *Genius and Fancy; or, Dramatic Sketches: With Other Poems on Various Subjects.* London: H. D. Symonds, and W. Lee, and J. Gray, 1795. 18.5 × 23.5 cm. 48 pp. By Mary Julia Young. BL: 11630. e. 18(4).

2   *Adelaide and Antonine: Or, the Emigrants: A Tale.* London:
        J. Debrett, Booker, Keating, Lewis, and Robinsons, 1793.
        20 × 24.5 cm. 14 pp. 1/-. By Mary Julia Young. BL:
        11641. g. 45.

3(*a*) *Poems.* London: William Lane, 1798. 10 × 17.5 cm. Pp. iv +
        172. By Mary Julia Young, Author of *Rose-mount Castle.*
        BL: 11644. bbb. 32.

3(*b*) *The Metrical Museum. Part I. Containing, Agnes, or the
        Wanderer, a Story Founded on the French Revolution. The Flood,
        an Irish Tale. Adelaide and Antonine, or the Emigrants. With
        Other Original Poems.* London: J. Fisher, [1801]. 10 × 18 cm.
        98 pp. By Mary Julia Young, Authour [*sic*] of *Rosemount
        Castle.* BL: 11644. bbb. 14.

A YOUNG FEMALE OF THIS CITY, *see* COX, Elizabeth

A YOUNG LADY, *see also* B., L. M., KING, E., PORTER, Anna
Maria, ROBERTS, Mary, SAFFERY, Maria Grace, SEWELL, Mrs G.,
STEELE, Anne, SWINNEY, Jane, WYATT, Gertrude, YOUNG, Mary
Julia, *and* APPENDIX 9

1   *Original Poems on Various Subjects.* London: T. Cadell,
        T. Longman, W. Nicoll and J. Ridley, [1772]. 18.5 × 25.5
        cm. Pp. viii + 91 [subscription edition]. By a Young Lady,
        Eighteen Years of Age. Bodley: G. Pamph. 1696(26).

2   *Effusions of Female Fancy . . . Consisting of Elegys, and Other
        Original Essays in Poetry.* New York/Baltimore/
        Philadelphia: for the author, 1784. 10.5 × 17.5 cm. 62 pp.
        By a Young Lady, Native of America. AAS: DATED BOOKS.

3   *The Deserter. A Poem, in Four Cantos: Describing the
        Premature Death of a Youth of Eighteen, Who Perished through
        Ill-timed Severity in Dover-Castle on the 5th of March, 1788 . . .*
        London: for the author by Faulder, Hookham, Davies,
        Debrett, Knight, Botyter, and Robinson, [1788?]. 21 × 27
        cm. 19 pp. 1/6. By a Young Lady. *MR* 80: 181; BL: 643.
        k. 18(5).

4   *Birth-day Reflections.* Bath: S. Hazard, 1801. 12.5 × 20.5 cm.
        8 pp. 2*d.* or 14/- per 100. 'Written by a Young Lady,
        Nov. 15, 1767'. BL: 11631. bbb. 55.

5   *Expostulation; a Poem . . . In Two Parts.* Bath/Bristol/
    London/Oxford: J. Bally/W. Sheppard/Longman, Hurst,
    Rees, and Orme/printed by N. Bliss, 1808. 13.5 × 21.5
    cm. 28 pp. 2/-. By a Young Lady. BL: 11646. h. 22.

6(*a*) *Verses for Little Children . . .* London: Darton, Harvey, and
    Darton, 1813. 9.5 × 11 cm. 24 pp. 6*d.* By a Young Lady,
    for the Amusement of Her Brothers and Sisters. Osborne:
    uncatalogued.

6(*b*) *Verses for Little Children . . .* London: Harvey and Darton,
    1821. 10 × 11.5 cm. 24 pp. 6*d.* By a Young Lady, for the
    Amusement of Her Junior Brothers and Sisters. BL: Ch.
    810/205(8).

7   *Stanzas, Occasioned by the Death of the Rev. Thomas Coke,
    LL.D. on his Voyage on a Mission to India.* London:
    T. Blanshard, and J. Bruce, and W. Kent, 1814. 10 × 16
    cm. 11 pp. By a Young Lady. BL: 11646. aaa. 7.

8   *Eloise, and Other Poems on Several Occasions.* Leith/
    Edinburgh/London: for the author by James Burney/
    Archibald Constable and Co., and Manners and Miller/
    Longman, Hurst, Rees, Orme, and Brown, 1815. 11 × 18
    cm. Pp. xii + 181 [subscription edition]. By a Young Lady.
    BL: 11645. bb. 24.

9   *Old Grand-papa, and Other Poems, for the Amusement of
    Children.* London: Darton, Harvey, and Darton, 1815. 9.5 ×
    15 cm. 48 pp. 1/-. By a Young Lady. BL: 11645. aa. 26.

10 *Calliope and Euterpe, a Poem.* Durham, 1817. By a Young
    Lady. Stainforth. Not located.

11 *Lines from the Pen of a Young Lady, Occasioned by Reading an
    Address to the Inhabitants of Ramsgate, Written by Nathaniel
    Gundry, Esq. on the Distribution of the Sacrament Money, Which
    Has Been Monthly Collected at the Episcopal Chapel, in
    Ramsgate, ever since its Consecration.* Ramsgate: printed by W.
    Goldsmith, 1819. 9 × 14.5 cm. 12 pp. BL: 1506/770(1).

12 *Poems on Various Subjects.* Margate/London:G. Wither-
    den/Sherwood, Neely, and Jones, and T. Blanshard,
    [1819]. 13.5 × 21 cm. 119 pp. By a Young Lady Who
    through Accident was entirely Deprived of Hearing when
    only Eight Years of Age and Who, since that

Period has Continued Impenetrably and Incurably Deaf [the author of 11, above]. BL: 11642. dd. 4.

13   *Original Poetry, on Various Important Subjects.* Leeds: printed by Henry Cullingworth, 1821. 8.5 × 14 cm. 24 pp. By a Young Lady. BL: 11644. a. 56.

14   *Ceres and Agenorica, a Poem.* Hull: printed by Isaac Wilson, 1822. 7.5 × 14 cm. 23 pp. By a Young Lady. BL: 11645. aa. 36.

15   *Alphabetical Garland. An Original Poem* [cover serves as title-page]. Providence[, RI]: J. S. Horton, 1823. 8 × 11.5 cm. 16 pp. [printed on one side only]. By a Young Lady. Brown (Harris): 76/AL924a.

16   *Poetical Effusions.* Bath: S. Bennett, and Binns, 1824. 11 × 18 cm. 116 pp. [subscription edition]. By a Young Lady, Author of *The Willow Branch.* BL: 11650. bbb. 20.

17   *Henry and Kate, a Poem.* London/Birmingham: George B. Whittaker/W. Hodgetts, 1825. 11 × 18 cm. 65 pp. By a Young Lady. BL: 11644. eeee. 47.

18   *Miscellaneous Poems, Moral and Religious.* Dublin: printed for the author by John Jones, 1826. 8.5 × 13 cm. 68 pp. By a Young Lady. BL: 1606/1529.

19   *Poetic Fugitives.* London: Lupton Relfe, 1827. 11 × 17 cm. Pp. xx + 148 [subscription edition]. By a Young Lady. BL: 11644. c. 61.

20   *Miscellaneous Poems.* Bath: printed by Richard Cruttwell, 1828. 12.5 × 21 cm. Pp. xii + 56 [subscription edition]. By a Young Lady. BL: 11632. f. 52.

21   *The Pensée.* London: J. Hatchard and Son, 1830. 10 × 15.5 cm. Pp. vi + 3–126. By a Young Lady. BL: T. 1310(3).

22   *Madam Tabby's Rout, or the Grimalkin Party's Frolics and Adventures.* London: H. Mockett, 1832. 10.5 × 17 cm. 12 pp. [printed on one side of the leaf only]. By a Young Lady. BL: 11644. c. 9.

23   *The Promise, a Poetic Trifle.* Liverpool: Thos. Kaye, 1834. 8 × 12.5 cm. Pp. viii + 106. By a Young Lady [and Mrs Barbauld and M. E. C.]. BL: 11645. de. 14.

A YOUNG LADY OF BALTIMORE, *see* COLLECTIONS 31

A YOUNG LADY OF CHARLESTON

1   *Poems.* Charleston, S.C.: printed by J. Hoff, 1808. 10.5 ×
     16.5 cm. Pp. 18 + 5–112 [subscription edition]. By a
     Young Lady of Charleston. HEHL: 377983.

A YOUNG LADY OF THIRTEEN, *see* COLLECTIONS 54

Z, *see* MORE, Hannah

Appendix: Female Pseudonyms

Books that seem to have been written by men who used female pseudonyms. Pseudonyms that have been identified appear as entries in the main text.

AIR-BRAIN, Harriet

1   *A Most Eloquent and Panegyrical Petition to the Prime Minister . . . Dedicated to Peter Pindar, Esq.* London, [1790]. By Harriet Air-Brain. [Internal evidence.]

BRITTLE, Emilly

2   *The India Guide; or, Journal of a Voyage, to the East Indies, in the Year MDCCLXXX, in a Poetical Epistle to her Mother.* Calcutta, 1785. By Miss Emilly Brittle. [Internal evidence.]

C——, Lady

3   *The Whim!!! Or, the Maid-stone Bath. A Kentish Poetic. Dedicated to Lady Worsley.* London, 1782. By [Lady C——?; the attribution, on p. v, seems to be ironical].

JOHNSON, Elizabeth, *see* JOHNSON, Lucinda, below

JOHNSON, Lucinda

4   *A Tribute to the Memory of Mrs Eliz^h. Johnson, Late of Chapel-Town, near Leeds. Respectfully Dedicated to Miss Wilson.* Huddersfield, 1819. By Lucinda Johnson. [A half-title precedes the title-page 'Poems, by Elizabeth and Lucinda Johnson—private'. The preface claims that the author is a man.]

LOVEJOY, Lucretia

5   *An Elegy on the Lamented Death of the Electrical Eel, or Gymnotus Electricus. With the Lapidary Inscription, as Placed on a Superb Erection, at the Expence of the Countess of H——, and*

Chevalier-Madame d'Eon de Beaumont. London, 1777. By Lucretia Lovejoy, Sister to Mr. Adam Strong, Author of *The Electrical Eel.* [Internal evidence.]

QUEEN MAB

6   *The Modern Minerva; or, the Bat's Seminary for Young Ladies. A Satire on Female Education.* London, 1810. By Queen Mab. [Internal evidence.]

A WHORE OF QUALITY

7   *The Whore: A Poem.* London, [1782?]. By a Whore of Quality. [Internal evidence.]

A WOMAN OF FASHION

8   *The Temple of Prostitution: A Poem. Dedicated to the Greatest ***** in Her Majesty's Dominions.* London, 1779. By a Woman of Fashion. [Internal evidence.]

A YOUNG LADY

9   *An Epistle from a Young Lady to an Ensign in the Guards, upon his being Ordered to America.* London, 1779. [The author speaks of himself in the preface as a man.]

Note on the Annual Rate of Publication

In preparing these statistics and the accompanying graph the following categories of works that are included in the bibliography have been omitted: undated works, works that are known only by inference, works that have not been located or that if located in catalogues have not been found when sought. In all, 258 such works have been omitted. The few instances of two-volume works that were published one volume a year for two successive years are included in the statistics as if each volume were an independent publication.

Year	First editions	All editions
1770	4	5
1771	8	10
1772	2	3
1773	6	8
1774	5	9
1775	6	13
1776	6	9
1777	9	11
1778	7	10
1779	5	7
1780	12	17
1781	12	19
1782	5	7
1783	7	12
1784	16	24
1785	9	13
1786	9	19
1787	16	30
1788	17	26
1789	11	21
1790	17	24
1791	22	31

Year	First editions	All editions
1792	18	24
1793	20	31
1794	9	14
1795	15	22
1796	24	35
1797	10	17
1798	19	25
1799	9	20
1800	22	28
1801	15	22
1802	20	27
1803	14	28
1804	12	16
1805	24	37
1806	14	28
1807	15	30
1808	46	77
1809	23	33
1810	30	61
1811	26	47
1812	36	57
1813	23	41
1814	28	50
1815	34	67
1816	29	58
1817	17	29
1818	45	76
1819	31	52
1820	42	69
1821	32	57
1822	26	48
1823	37	59
1824	38	55
1825	36	66
1826	38	65
1827	32	55
1828	30	57
1829	36	59

Year	First editions	All editions
1830	37	60
1831	26	38
1832	37	67
1833	34	59
1834	38	60
1835	45	72
TOTALS	1402	2325

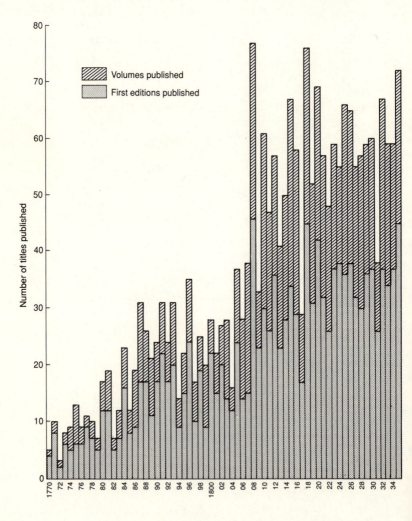

Index of Authors' Names

The entries in the body of the text are arranged alphabetically by author's names. The names used there are repeated in this index and other names (married names, unmarried names, pseudonyms, etc.) are added to them here with cross-reference to the names used for the entries.

EMMERSON, Mrs

EMRA, Lucy

ERKSINE, Eliza Bland, the Hon. Mrs Esme Steuart

ESPENER, Isabella, Mrs Charles

EVANCE, S., Mrs B. HOOPER

EVANS, Ann

EVANS, Margaret, Mrs George

EVATT, Anne

EWING, Harriet

F., B., *see* FINCH, Mrs B.

F., S. C., *see* FORD, Sarah Caroline

FAIRBROTHER, Mary Ann, Mrs

FAIRFAX, Lavinia

FAIRWEATHER, Mary, Mrs

FALCONAR, Harriet

FALCONAR, Maria

FALLOWS, Elizabeth, Mrs Thomas Mount

FARLEY, Mrs

FARMER, Marguerite, Mrs Maurice St Leger, *see* POWER, Marguerite

FARRELL, Sarah, Mrs

FAUGERES, Margaretta Van Wyck

FELL, Miss

FELL, Elizabeth, Mrs

FEMALE, A

FEMALE CHRISTIAN, A

FEMALE OF THIS CITY, A, *see* COX, Elizabeth

FEMALE REFUGEE, A

FEMALE WRITERS, *see* VARIOUS FEMALE WRITERS

FENN, Lady Eleanor

FENNO, Jenny

FENTIMAN, Catherine, Mrs

FIELDING, Anna Maria, *see* HALL, Anna Maria

FIELDING, Sarah, *see* FARRELL, Sarah

FINCH, Anne, Mrs Heneage, *see* WINCHILSEA, Countess of

FINCH, Mrs B.

FITZOSNABURGH, Frances A.

FLEMING, Ann Cuthbert, Mrs James, *see* KNIGHT, Ann Cuthbert

FLEMING, Henrietta, *see* BATTIER, Henrietta

FLETCHER, Bridget, Mrs Timothy

FLETCHER, Eliza, Mrs Archibald

FLINDERS, Susanna, *see* PEARSON, Susanna

FLORA, *pseudonym*

FLOWERDEW, Alice, Mrs

FOLLEN, Eliza Lee, Mrs Charles

FORD, Sarah Caroline

FORDYCE, Lady Margaret Lindsay, *see*

LINDSAY, Lady Margaret

FORTNUM, Sophia, Mrs Charles, *see also* DACRE, Charlotte

FOSTER, Anna Maria, *see* WELLS, Anna Maria

FOWLER, Eliza, *see* HAYWOOD, Eliza

FRANCIS, Miss

FRANCIS, Anne, Mrs Robert Bransby

FRANCIS, Eliza S.

FRANCIS, Lydia Maria, *see* CHILD, Lydia Maria

FRANCIS, Sophia L.

FRANK, Mary

FRANKLIN, Eleanor Anne, Mrs John, *see* PORDEN, Eleanor Anne

FRASER, Susan, Mrs

FRENCH, Mrs M. G. G.

FRERE, Eleanor, *see* FENN, Lady Eleanor

FRIEND TO THE SEX, A, *see* CUTTS, Mrs

FRIEND TO YOUTH, A, *see* HOARE, Sarah

FRY, Caroline

FURLONG, W. Marianne, Mrs

G., Mrs A., *see* GIBBS, Mrs A.

G., C. C. V., *see* WETHERELL, Mrs Dawson Bruce

G., E., *see* GARRAWAY, Ellen

G., P., *see* GURNEY, Priscilla

GARDINER, Miss, *see* INGLIS, Mrs Richmond

GARNETT, Catharine Grace, *see* GODWIN, Catharine Grace

GARRARD, Eliza

GARRAWAY, Ellen

GARRINGTON, Eliza Sarah

GAZUL, Clara, *pseudonym of* MERIMÉE, Prosper

GEARY, Elizabeth

GIBBS, Mrs A.

GIBSON, Charlotte Mary

GILBERT, Ann, Mrs Joseph, *see* TAYLOR, Ann

GILDING, Elizabeth

GITTINS, Anne, *see* FRANCIS, Anne

GOBEIL, Jane Elizabeth, *see* MOORE, Jane Elizabeth

GODWIN, Catharine Grace

GOLDIE, Emma Mary

GOLDRING, Mrs C. B.

GOMERSALL, A., Mrs

GOOCH, Elizabeth Sarah, Mrs William

GOOCH, Rebecca

GOODALL, Harriott Anabella, Mrs Joseph

GORDON, Harriet Maria, *see* SMYTHIES, Harriet Maria

McCoy, Mary
McDermott, Mary
Mackey, Mary, Mrs
Maclaurin, Mary
Maclean, Letitia Elizabeth, Mrs George, *see* Landon, Letitia Elizabeth
McMorine, Mary
McMullan, Maryanne *or* Mary Anne, Mrs W.
McTaggart, Ann, Mrs
Macvicar, Anne, *see* Grant, Anne
Mcwatty, Alicia
Madan, Maria Frances Cecilia, *see* Cowper, Maria Frances Cecilia
Madden, Harriet Horncastle, *see* Hook, Harriet Horncastle
Maddocks, Mrs
Magrath, Anne Jane
Mahony, Agnes
Maid, Old, *pseudonym of* M'Gibbon, Alexander
Mallet, Dorothea, *see* Celesia, Dorothea
Mallett, Mrs
Mamma
Mangnall, Richmal
Manley, Emma Catherine, *see* Embury, Emma Catherine
Manners, Catherine Rebecca, Lady
Manners, Lady Emmeline Charlotte Elizabeth Stuart, *see* Wortley, Lady Emmeline Charlotte Elizabeth Stuart
Mant, Alicia Catherine
Mant, Elizabeth, Mrs Richard
Manwaring, Miss
Mapes, Elizabeth, *see* Bonhote, Elizabeth
Maria, *see* Brooks, Maria
Maria, Laura, *see* Robinson, Mary
Maria de Occidente, *see* Brooks, Maria
Maria Sophia
Marley, Mrs
Marshall, Julia Ann, *see* Elliott, Julia Ann
Martin, Sarah Catherine
Martineau, Harriet
Mary, *see also* St John, Mary
Mary, Queen of Scots
Mary Sophia
Mason, Mrs
Masters, Mrs
Mathews, Elizabeth Kirkham, Mrs Charles
Matilda, Anna, *see* Cowley, Hannah
Matthews, Elizabeth
Maxwell, Georgiana Caroline

Maze, Mary Ann, *see* Kilner, Mary Ann
Mears, Sarah, *see* Cassan, Sarah
Medley, Sarah
Mendez, Jael Henrietta, *see* Pye, Jael Henrietta
Meredith, Louisa Anne, Mrs Charles, *see* Twamley, Louisa Anne
Merryweather, Mrs I. A.
Meynell, Anna
Meziere, Harriet, Mrs, *see* Chilcot, Harriet
Miles, Sibella Elizabeth, Mrs Alfred, *see* Hatfield, Sibella Elizabeth
Miller, Ann
Miller, Anne, 'Lady'
Mills, Elizabeth Willesford
Milne, Christian *or* Charlotte, Mrs Peter
Milnes, Esther, *see* Day, Esther
Milton, Frances, *see* Trollope, Frances
Minifie, Susannah, *see* Gunning, Susannah
Mister, Mary, *see* Locke, Mary
Mitford, Mary Russell
M—ll—r, Mrs, *see* Miller, Anne
M—n—ll, Miss, *see* Meynell, Anna
Monckton, Hon. Charlotte Penelope
Montagu, Eleanora Louisa
Montagu, Lady Mary Wortley
Montague, Lady Mary Seymour
Montolieu, Maria Henrietta, Mrs
Moodie, Susanna, Mrs John Wedderburn, *see* Strickland, Susanna
Moody, Catherine Grace Frances, *see* Gore, Catherine Grace Frances
Moody, Elizabeth, Mrs Christopher Lake
Moore, Frances, *see* Brooke, Frances
Moore, Jane Elizabeth, Mrs
More, Ann, *see* Candler, Ann
More, Hannah
Morgan, Lady, *see* Owenson, Sydney
Morison, Hannah, Mrs
Morley, Countess of, *see* Parker, Frances
Morpeth, Mary, *or* Oxlie *or* Oxley, Mary
Morrell, Isabella, *see* Sleigh, Isabella
Morton, Sarah Wentworth, Mrs Perez
Mother, A, *see also* Gurney, Maria
Mott, Mrs Isaac Henry Robert
M'Taggart, Ann, *see* McTaggart, Ann
Mulso, Hester, *see* Chapone, Hester
Murden, Eliza, Mrs, *see* Crawley, Eliza
Murphy, Anna
Murry, Ann
Muzzy, Harriet, Mrs

Index of Titles

Many of the titles in this index have been abbreviated. Titles given in quotation marks and without an entry number are of works less than 8 pages in length that are included in the endnote of the author named.

Index of Publishers

Publishers are grouped under the name of the place of publication, the names being given in alphabetical order. The names given in capitals are those of the authors. A single asterisk (*) preceding an item number indicates private publication on the author's behalf; a dagger (†) indicates that the name given is that of the printer rather than the publisher—often an indication of private publication. Congers are alphabetized according to the surname of the first member named; the other members are also individually alphabetized with cross-reference to the conger or congers to which they belonged. Books that do not record the name of publisher or printer are excluded from this index. The reversal of surname and given name of the first publisher of each conger is required by the alphabetization of the entries: when the second name to appear is a given name rather than a surname (e.g. Daniel Ruff, below) the given name is italicized (e.g. Ruff, *Daniel P.*). Cross-references are confined within the same place of publication; there is no necessary connection between publishers with the same name in different locations.

Aberdeen, Aberdeenshire

Brown, A.: EDGAR 1(*a*); GRANT 1(*a*)
Chalmers, J., and Co.: MILNE †1
Maitland, J.: HARRISON 1(*v*)

Abergavenny, Mon.

Watkins: BOWEN, M. 1; ELFE 2

Abingdon, Md.

Ruff, *Daniel P.*: ALLEN, Mrs B. 1

Agra, India

Agra Press: FAIRWEATHER †1

Air (Ayr), Ayrshire

Wilson, *John* and *Peter*: LITTLE †1
Wilson, *Peter*, see John Wilson

Albany, NY

Johnson, *John*: LARD †2(*a*)
Skinners, see Websters
Spencer, *Thomas*: WHEATLEY 2(*e*)
Websters and Skinners: WILKINSON †1(*n*)

Alnwick, Nthb.

Davison, W.: HINDMARSH †1

Alton, Hants

Pinnock, W.: NEWMAN 1

Andover, Mass.

American Tract Society: TAYLOR, A. 8(*kk*)
Flagg and Gould: COLLECTIONS †26(*a*),
 †26(*b*), †26(*c*), †26(*d*); EVANS, A. †1(*a*),
 †1(*b*)
Gould, see Flagg
New England Tract Society: WILKINSON
 1(*m*)

Angers, France

Pavie, L.: ATTERSOLL 1

Annapolis, Md.

Green, *Frederick*: COLLECTIONS †20

Appleby, Westm.

Chapelhow: COLLECTIONS 35

Bury (St. Edmund's), Suff.

Deck: ACTON 1(*a*), 1(*b*); COBBOLD 6; HART
   1(*a*); RIBBANS 1
Deck, Dingle and Ray: RIBBANS 2
Dingle, *see* Deck, Dingle
Gedge, P.: SPENCE *1
Ingram, G.: WOOD, S. 1
Rackham, J.: PIZEY †1
Ray, *see* Deck, Dingle

Calcutta, India

Ferris, *see* Thomson
Grant, *Norman*: ROBERTS, E. *2(*a*)
School Press, Dhurumtula: WILKINSON, R.
   †1(*q*)
Thacker and Co.: A LADY 51
Thomson and Ferris: JONES, A. †1

Cambridge, Cambs.

Deighton: ROLLS 4; SYMMONS 1
Deighton, J.: COWPER 1(*c*); PILKINGTON 2
Deighton, J., and W. Lunn: PILKINGTON
   1(*a*)
Deighton, J., and Nicholson and Son:
   LYON 1
Deightons: BENTLEY 1(*b*)
Flower: ROWSE 1
Hall: RIBBANS 2
Lunn, W., *see* J. Deighton, and W. Lunn
Merrill: SEWARD 2(*a*), 2(*b*)
Nicholson and Son, *see* J. Deighton, and
   Nicholson

Cambridge, Mass.

Folsom, *Charles*: TAGGART 1(*b*)
University Press: SIGOURNEY 2

Canandaigua, NY

Bemis, J. D., and Co.: TAYLOR, A. †8(*bb*),
   8(*ff*), 8(*ll*); WILKINSON 1(*s*)

Canterbury, Kent

Bristow: GREENSTED 1; *see also* Simmons
   and Co.
Claris and Marrable: SEWELL 1(*a*), 1(*b*), 2, 4
Kirby, *see* Simmons and Kirby
Kirkby, *see* Rouse
Lawrence, *see* Rouse
Marrable, *see* Claris
Rouse, Kirkby, and Lawrence: A MOTHER
   †2
Saffery, J.: BURGESS, E. *1(*a*)
Simmons and Co. and Bristow: SWINNEY 1

Simmons and Kirby: DODSWORTH †1
Ward: A LADY †48
Ward, *Henry*: BURGESS, E. 1(*b*)

Cardiff, Glamorgan

Bird: ELFE 2

Carlisle, Cumb.

Jollie: COLLECTIONS 35
Jollie, F.: COWLEY †6

Catskill, NY

Lewis, *Junius S.*: TAYLOR, A. 8(*dd*)

Charleston, SC

Babcock, S. and W. R.: TAYLOR, A. 8(*hh*)
Hoff, J.: CRAWLEY †1; POGSON 1; A
   YOUNG LADY OF CHARLESTON 1
Hoff, *Philip*: CRAWLEY *2(*a*)
Ladies' Benevolent and Protestant
   Episcopal Societies: A LADY 34

Chatham, Kent

Etherington: GREENSTED 1
Townson: SWINNEY 1

Chelmsford, Esx.

Clacker: SWINNEY 1
Guy: RIBBANS 2

Chelsea, Middx.

Faulkner, T.: KELLY *2(*b*)

Cheltenham, Glos.

Booksellers, the: COOPER, C. 1
Matthews, E.: GOLDRING †1
Watts, O.: TONGE 1
Williams, G. A.: DE CRESPIGNY, C. 1

Chepstow, Mon.

Rogers, S.: BOWEN, M. 1
Willett, M.: ELFE 2

Chertsey, Sur.

Wetton, R.: SEWELL 1(*a*), 4
Wetton, R., and Son: SEWELL 3
Wetton, R., and Sons: SEWELL 1(*b*), 2

Chichester, Susx.

Jaques, *Dennett*: SMITH, C. †1(*b*)

Harvey and Darton, and S. Wilkin: OPIE 5

Harwood, J.: DOWNING 2

Hatchard: SARGANT *1(*a*), *1(*b*); *see also* Cadell and Davies, Hatchard; Cadell, Longman; Philanthropic Society; C. J. G. and F. Rivington, Seeleys; John Robinson, and Hatchard; Sherwood, Neely, and Jones, Westley; Wilkie and Robinson, and Hatchard

Hatchard and Son: DAWSON 1(*a*), 1(*b*); *see also* Baldwin, Cradock, and Joy, Hatchard; Bulcock; T. Cadell and Hatchard; Longman and Co., Hatchard; Longman, Rees, Orme, Brown, and Green, Hatchard; Sherwood, Jones and Co., Hatchard; Francis Westley, Hatchard

Hatchard and Son, Mayhew and Co.: DACRE 3

Hatchard and Son and Seeley and Son: BAILEY *3

Hatchard and Son, Seeley, W. Benning: BROWNE, M. A. 1

Hatchard and Son, Sherwood and Co.: YARROW 1

Hatchard and Son, Francis Westley, C. B. Whitaker: PHELAN 2(*a*)

Hatchard, and Baldwin, Cradock and Joy: A LADY 37

Hatchard, Setchell and Son, I. and A. Arch, Darton and Harvey: NEWMAN 1

Hatchard, J.: BETHAM 2; BRISTOW 1; TRENCH 3; *see also* J. Evans and Co.; J. Evans, and Son; J. Evans and J. Hatchard; Howard; J. Johnson, J. Hatchard; J. Johnson, Longman; Longman and Rees, J. Hatchard; Longman, Hurst, Rees, Orme, and Brown, J. Hatchard; F. and C. Rivington, J. Evans; F. C. and J. Rivington, and J. Hatchard; Vernor, Hood and Sharpe, and J. Hatchard; J. Walsh

Hatchard, J., and Son: BURTON 1; CLARA, Cousin 1(*a*), 1(*b*); COPE 3; JEWSBURY 2; POULTER 1; TALLANT 1(*a*); WHITMORE 1(*a*); A YOUNG LADY 21

Hatchard, J., and Son, Hurst, Chance, and Co., Simpkin and Marshall: WATTS 4(*a*)

Hatchard, J., and Son, Simpkin and Marshall, and Renshaw and Kirkman: WATTS 4(*b*)

Hatchard, J., and F. Westley: OFFLEY 1(*a*), 1(*b*), 1(*c*)

Hatchard, J., and Wilson: LYON 1

Hatchard, *John*: BROWN, M. 1

Hatchard, *John*, and Son: WHITMORE 1(*b*), 1(*c*); *see also* Wm. Charlton Wright

Hatchett, *see* Roach

Hawes, Clarke, and Collins: COLLECTIONS 1(*a*)

Hawes, R., *see* Vallance and Conder, R. Hawes

Hayward, *see* Longman, Hurst, Rees, Orme, and Brown, Baldwin

Henderson, *see* Ellerton

Hessey, *see* Taylor

Hill, *see* J. Burditt; Darton and Harvey, Tabart

Hobbs, *see* Lowndes and Hobbs

Hodder, *see* Jackson, Walford

Hodgson and Co.: COLLECTIONS 33; WILKINSON, S. S. 3

Hodson, H., Bohn, and Walker: ROBERTS, E. 1

Hodson, H. C.: FRENCH †1

Hogg, *Alexander*, *see* T. Vallance

Holdsworth and Ball: COLLECTIONS 44; MADDOCKS 2(*b*), 3; RUTHERFOORD 1; TAYLOR, A. 8(*vv*), 8(*yy*), 8(*zz*), 8(*ccc*), 17(*c*); TAYLOR, J. 2(*f*), 2(*g*), 3(*f*)

Holdsworth, B. J.: MADDOCKS *2(*a*); TAYLOR, A. 8(*mm*), 8(*pp*), *13(*i*), 18; TAYLOR, J. 2(*a*), 2(*b*), 2(*e*), 3(*a*), 3(*b*); *see also* G. and W. B. Whittaker, and B. J. Holdsworth

Holdsworth, B. J., and Darton, Harvey, and Darton: TAYLOR, A. 8(*x*)

Holdsworth, B. J., (and) Harvey and Darton: TAYLOR, A. 8(*aa*), 8(*gg*), 8(*ii*), 8(*jj*)

Holdsworth, J.: TAYLOR, A. 8(*nn*)

Holdsworth, J. B., *see* Longman, Hurst, and Co.

Holloway, *see* Crawford, Plank

Hone, W.: ROLLS 3

Hood, *see* Vernor and Hood; Vernor, Hood

Hookham, *see* Cradock and Joy, Collins; Faulder, Hookham; Robinsons, Vernor; Spencer; White and Hookham

Hookham and Carpenter: HOLFORD, M., *formerly* WRENCH 1; ROBINSON, M. *12(*a*), †13

Hookham and Carpenter, William Richardson: GUNNING *1

Rochester, Kent

Etherington, *see* Gillman
Gillman and Etherington: SWINNEY †1
Gillman, W.: ROWE †1

Royston, Herts.

Warren, J.: COLLECTIONS 33
Warren, *John*: COLLECTIONS 39

Ryde, IOW

Hellier, *see* Rowden
Newport, *see* Rowden
Rowden, Newport and Hellier: SARGEANT 1

St. Ives, Corn.

Davis, W.: RING †1

Salem, Mass.

Buffum, *James R.*: ELLIOTT, M. 7(*b*)
Ives, S. B., *see* W. Ives
Ives, W. and S. B.: HORTON 1

Salisbury, Wilts.

Brodie and Dowding: KING, H. R. 1
Collins and Johnson: SAFFERY 1
Dowding, *see* Brodie
Gilmour, J. A.: STOKES †1
Johnson, *see* Collins

Sandhurst, Berks.

Maskall, Mrs: PARSONS, L. 2

Sandwich, Kent

Cocking: TATLOCK 1

Saxmundham, Suff.

Brightly, L.: STEEL †1

Schenectady, NY

Ritchie, G., Jr.: POGSON †2

Sevenoaks, Kent

Clout: SWINNEY 1
Payne, C.: LIGHTFOOT †1

Sheffield, Yorks.

Blackwell, J.: HUTTON 1
Blackwell, J., and Miss Gales: KIDD *1
Booksellers, the other, *see* Miss Gales, and
  the other booksellers
Gales, Miss: HOOLE 3(*a*); *see also* J.
  Blackwell and Miss Gales
Gales, Miss, and the other booksellers:

ROBERTS, M. 1
Gales, J.: PEARSON, S. †1
Iris office: SUTCLIFF 1
Montgomery, J.: HOOLE 1; MILLER, Ann 1
Platt, *William*: SEWARD 9

Sherborne, Dor.

Goadby, R.: THOMAS, A. 1
Penny, E.: NEWMAN 1

Shipston on Stour, War.

Bromley: CLARKE, Anne 1(*b*)

Shrewsbury, Salop.

Eddowes, W.: RING 1
Hulbert, *Charles*: Wyke 1
Wood, T.: JORDAN 1; WINSCOM †1(*c*)

Southampton, Hants

Baker, T.: TRENCH †1, †4; VOKE 1
Drury: SARGEANT 1
Skelton, E., and Co.: JACOB †1
Smart, *William*: HART 1(*b*)

Southwark, Sur.

Tozer, W.: SOUTHCOTT 2

Southwell, Notts.

Simpson, J.: WRIGHT, M. B. 1

Southwold, Suff.

Gooch: LLOYD, S. M. 1
Gooch, T.: GOOCH, R. 1(*a*)

Spilsby, Lincs.

Plant, R.: HENNETT †1

Springfield, Mass.

Brewer, *Henry*: WILKINSON †1(*e*)

Stamford, Lincs.

Booksellers, the: ADCOCK *1

Stanstead, Esx.

Gaylord, *see* Walton
Walton and Gaylord: FENN 1

Stockton, Durham Co.

Christopher and Jennet: A LADY 23
Jennet, *see* Christopher

Stonehouse, Devon

Gray, W.: POTTS 2

Index of the Locations of Individual
Publishers outside London

Names of countries or states are only recorded in this index if more than one place of publication shares the same name (for the full list see the Index of Publishers). With the exception of Boston, Lincs. (so designated to distinguish it from the much more frequently mentioned Boston, Mass., which is rendered simply as Boston), if US and UK places share the same name, the name of the US state is provided with the place name. When more than one US place shares the same name, the state is given for both; similarly, if more than one UK place share the same name, the county is provided.